Praise for *ABOUT TOWN*

"Equable, affectionate, and comprehensive. . . . Yagoda interviews some 50 writers, editors, and artists, burrows like a mad mole in 2,500 archival bins, and is blessed with a genius for apt quotation."

—*New York Times Book Review*

"A cultural history of the magazine itself rather than of the colorful personalities that most *New Yorker* memoirs have focused upon. . . . Yagoda ably treats both time and place—the years before television shouldered its way into the center of the cultural life of the city and the nation—and makes an excellent case that the *New Yorker* was, simply, the best magazine ever published in America."

—*Chicago Sun-Times*

"A lively history."

—*Newsweek*

"A fresh history [that] has something of the original *New Yorker* élan."

—*Entertainment Weekly*

"An incisive history of the magazine from its founding by its first editor, Harold Ross, to its present operation by media mogul Samuel I. Newhouse Jr. . . . Set in the trademark *New Yorker* font, illustrated further with photographs, cartoons, correspondence, and memos from Harold Ross, [*About Town*] is dressed for success."

—*Booklist*

"An awesomely comprehensive biography of an American institution."

—*Kirkus*

"Coming on the heels of insider accounts by Ved Mehta, Lillian Ross, and Renata Adler, Ben Yagoda's *About Town* provides some welcomed distance from their partisan bickering."

—*Austin-American Statesman*

"Yagoda achieves a far greater degree of accuracy than memoirists who rely predominantly on their own collections."

—*Brill's Content*

ABOUT TOWN

~~~~~

Also by Ben Yagoda

Will Rogers: A Biography

The Art of Fact: An Anthology of Literary Journalism

ABOUT TOWN

The *New Yorker* and the World It Made

BEN YAGODA

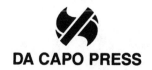

DA CAPO PRESS

Designed by Erich Hobbing
Set in Bembo

Cataloging in Publication data is available from the Library of Congress.

First Da Capo Press Edition 2001
ISBN 0-306-81023-9

Published by Da Capo Press
A Member of the Perseus Books Group
http://www.perseusbooksgroup.com

1 2 3 4 5 6 7 8 9—05 04 03 02 01

In memory of Harriet Yagoda,
New Yorker reader

CONTENTS

Our Far~Flung Correspondence

Toward the end of World War II, a young American woman named Hannah M. Turner was serving in a Red Cross Clubmobile unit in northern Italy. One evening she was asked to report to one of the medical aid stations, to help with the wounded who were waiting to be evacuated by truck and ambulance to a rear hospital. "Most of the men were not even conscious," Mrs. Turner recalled in a letter she wrote me in 1996,

> but I knelt down by one who was, looked at his dog tag to see his name and, holding his hand, I looked at him and said something. I don't remember what. Then he said, "If you could have anything right now, what would it be? I don't mean anything abstract . . . something physical, something you could put your hands on." And without a second thought, I said, "An issue of the *New Yorker* magazine." He looked stunned, then he started to laugh and his eyes lit up and I found out he had been a student (Dartmouth, I think) when he enlisted after his brother was killed in the Pacific. But what he really wanted to talk about was the *New Yorker*. So we reminisced about our favorite cartoons and writers and spent perhaps fifteen minutes in another world, one that was familiar and funny and far, far away from that one.

Hannah Turner was recounting her experience to me because of a one-sentence author's query I had placed in the *New York Times Book Review,* asking to hear from "longtime readers" of the *New Yorker* who would be willing to fill out a survey about their relationship with the magazine. I felt there would be a sizable response, but I certainly didn't expect nearly seven hundred cards and letters to come back, saying, as if in unison, "I thought you'd never ask!" Many of the people who replied—including Mrs. Turner—didn't want to wait for the survey and put their thoughts and experiences down right away. Seven clusters of questions, most of them open-ended, were sent out to all the respondents.* Remarkably, almost half of them took the time and effort to complete the survey, some going on for three or four single-spaced pages.

You couldn't imagine a survey about *Mademoiselle, Popular Mechanics,* or *U.S. News and World Report* eliciting this kind of response—but, then, the *New Yorker,* since its beginning in 1925, was never like any other magazine. In a review of Brendan Gill's book *Here at the New Yorker* in the *New York Times Book Review* in 1975, John Leonard called it "the weekly magazine most educated Americans grew up on." He went on: "Whether we read it or refused to read it—which depended, of course, on the sort of people we wanted to be—it was as much a part of our class conditioning as clean fingernails, college, a checking account, and good intentions. For better or worse, it probably created our sense of humor." More than that: the *New Yorker* did more than any other entity to create "our" sense of what was proper English prose and what was not, what was in good taste and what was not, what was the appropriate attitude to take, in print, toward personal and global happenings. "The *New Yorker* cartoon" and "the *New Yorker* short story," meanwhile, transcended mere genres and became cultural categories, the very names implying a specific kind of aesthetic lens on experience.

And more than *that:* the *New Yorker* resonates throughout the culture. To understand this, one need look no further than the press coverage given to the abrupt resignation of Tina Brown as editor of the magazine in the summer of 1998. The *New Yorker* at that point was a weekly magazine that had lost money for thirteen consecutive years, that had a modest circulation of eight-hundred-odd thousand, that (creatively) was awkwardly suspended between the Standards and Ideals of its classic version and the up-to-the-minute cocktail of glitz, hype, and topicality brought in by Brown when

---

*"1. When did you start reading the *New Yorker*? Why? How old were you? Where were you living? What was your occupation? Why do you think you have kept reading it over the years?

"2. What have been some of your favorite or most memorable stories, articles, drawings, or covers in your years of reading the magazine? List as many or as few as you care to.

"3. How do you read the magazine? That is, what do you and what don't you read, and in what order? Do you make a point of not opening up an issue until you've finished the last one? When the *New Yorker* had bylines at the ends of articles, did you make a point of not checking the byline until you had finished the article? Etc.

"4. What do you do with your old issues? Do you do anything special with covers (e.g., use them as wallpaper)?

"5. Do you recall patronizing any *New Yorker* advertisers? Which ones?

"6. Since Tina Brown became editor in 1993, do you feel that the quality of the *New Yorker* has been generally (a) better, (b) worse, or (c) about the same? (Elaborate, if you'd like to.) If (b), were you tempted to cancel your subscription, and did you?

"7. Please feel free to add anything significant about you and the *New Yorker*."

she arrived in 1992.Yet the *New York Times* put the story on the front page—above the fold; *Time* magazine devoted six pages to the departure of Brown and her replacement by *New Yorker* writer David Remnick.

Typography offers a more subtle—indeed, a by and large subliminal—sign.The *New Yorker's* first art director, Rea Irvin, designed a distinctive display type for the magazine that has since then been known by his name. With the widespread adoption of computer typesetting in the 1980s, Irvin type, with minuscule variations, became available to any designer who wanted to suggest, however improbably, a product's upscale urbanity. And so it can be seen, to name just a few examples, in the logos for the television show *Frasier*; for the department store Bergdorf Goodman; for the Atlantis Hotel in the Bahamas; for the cover of Alice Munro's book of short stories *The Moons of Jupiter*; and for a new model of Cadillac called the Catera. (The Catera went further, using in its ads in the *New Yorker* and elsewhere a *New Yorker* boldface body type in addition to the Irvin display type.)

The surveys I got back gave flesh and blood to the notion of the bond between the *New Yorker* and its readers. Every one of the respondents—most of whom lived outside the New York metropolitan area—described a deep connection to the magazine, usually pedagogical and always personal. As one wrote, "What I'm probably trying to say is that I've always felt sort of *nourished* by the *New Yorker*, finishing an issue feeling not only entertained (transported in some cases) but enlightened, learning something about a subject that was written by a master of his craft . . . Hersey, McPhee, Flanner, Angell. A glorious list!" Many made some variation of the statement that life without the *New Yorker* was unimaginable (and so most of them kept up their subscriptions despite the changes made by Tina Brown, which were disliked by a vast majority). Often, they reported making the symbolic link tangible, through physically holding on to their old *New Yorkers*, month after month, year after year, decade after decade. A surprising number (12 percent, to be exact) reported taking the further step of using the covers for various artistic or decorative purposes, as if it were important for the *New Yorker* to be permanently visible in their homes. One woman wrote, "I've framed covers, used as folders whole covers, papered walls and covered chests, boxes, tins, and frames with cut up covers." People said they used *New Yorker* covers to paper the walls of a bathroom; a stairway; a summer cottage; a utility room; a wall in the guest room; a closet wall; and a closet-turned-wetbar.

They told stories about the *New Yorker* and themselves, not as dramatic as Hannah Turner's bedside encounter in northern Italy, but vivid nonetheless:

~~~~~~

In 1927–28-ish I was a freshman at the University of Tennessee. It was a time when instructors, usually from up East, came through on one-year contracts.

I was in a class—history?—such a young man was teaching. After one class, he stopped me with a magazine he wanted me to read. I was the only person he'd come across in Knoxville who would like the *New Yorker*.

Each week I stopped with my quarter at I. Beiler's Smoke Shop for my copy ... we were a small group of elite but faithful customers.

In the early days of the New Deal, when the world was young, some of us who were with the Tennessee Valley Authority used to meet at lunch at the S & W cafeteria. At one table we always shared our favorite cartoons of the *New Yorker's* week.

~~~~

By the time I was nine (1938) it was my Saturday-night ritual. My sister and I had supper early and I saved the *New Yorker* to read Saturday nights while my parents had dinner and before I was sent to bed. If it came on Friday I waited until Saturday to open it. When I was ten I went to camp for the first time. There was a camp train out of Grand Central; you met by your camp banner and each camp had its own car or half car. People bought things to read in the station; a lot of the campers bought comic books but I bought the *New Yorker*.

~~~~

On what was the most difficult day of my life—in 1963—a just-off-the-stand *New Yorker* was my companion, on my ride home, by subway and bus from the college I was attending to my home and the saddest news that was to await me. While I didn't know how sad the news was actually to be—I knew that there were going to be rough times ahead of me—my *New Yorker* was my security blanket. What more is there to say?

~~~~

I was a high school student in Washington, D.C., at the time I started reading it, but my family is originally from New York City (I was born there) and having the *New Yorker* on hand seemed to reinforce my sense of being, at core, a New Yorker myself. Certainly at 16 I was attracted to the magazine's aura of sophistication and intellectual hipness. I would take my copy to the pool and while other teenage girls lounged around their copies of *Seventeen* propped up in front of them, absorbed by such articles as how to clear up your complexion or gloss your lips, I sat reading book-length treatises about the war in Vietnam, about the prospect of nuclear winter, about the world of the autistic and schizophrenic (and feeling very adult for doing so).

~~~~

I can hardly remember a time when I wasn't reading the *New Yorker*. As a 15-year-old school girl in the Bronx, riding the IRT to Hunter High School,

I was swept away by the seductive world it represented, all grace, charm, and sophistication, light-years away from life as I knew it on the Grand Concourse. At Barnard College I preferred the company of other *New Yorker* readers since their identification with the magazine mirrored mine. Of course, being young and arrogant, I think we missed much of the substance and absorbed only the surface.

~~~

I must have started reading the *New Yorker* when I was 18; I remember subscribing to the magazine in 1943, when I was 19. My uncle had given me $5.00 (a fairly large gift then) with instructions to "buy yourself something you want," and I decided to invest in a subscription. I became addicted and never looked back. I had arrived in this country in 1940 as a refugee from Nazi Germany, and was living in Forest Hills, New York. By day, I worked as a secretary in Manhattan; at night, I was a student at Hunter College. I did a lot of reading on the subway, and remember a half-admiring comment by a colleague or fellow-student who saw me with the *New Yorker* that it was a "pretty sophisticated magazine."

~~~

I was drafted in the Army of the United States on September 12, 1945, two months after graduating from high school and reaching the age of eighteen. A few weeks later I came across my first ever copy of the *New Yorker* in an Armed Services Edition and have read it ever since. I was attracted to the magazine by the wit of the comments that followed the bloopers in books, magazines, and newspapers, and the cartoons, especially those of George Price.

~~~

I had a ritual for attacking this ritualistic magazine. It had no table of contents then either—just the reverse snobbery of those little bylines preceded by diffident dashes—and I would plunge in backward, scanning first for the names under the long articles, canvassing the short story credits, and breathlessly surveying the poems.

I did all this in a cold sweat to the thumping accompaniment of my heart. What terrified me was the possibility of finding a story or poem by someone I *knew.* Someone who had been an idiot in college, or a known nose-picker, or who (in combination with one or both of these things) was *younger* than me. Even by one or two months.

It was not that I merely read the *New Yorker;* I lived it in a private way. I had created for myself a *New Yorker* world (located somewhere east of Westport and west of the Cotswolds) where Peter DeVries (punning softly) was forever lifting a glass of Piesporter, where Niccolo Tucci (in a plum velvet dinner jacket) flirted in Italian with Muriel Spark, where Nabokov sipped tawny port from a prismatic goblet (while a Red Admirable perched on his pinky), and where John Updike tripped over the master's Swiss shoes, excusing himself charmingly (repeating all the while that Nabokov was the best writer of English currently holding American citizenship). Meanwhile, the Indian writers clustered in a corner punjabbering away in Sellerian accents (and giving off a pervasive odor of curry) and the Irish memoirists (in fishermen's sweaters and whiskey breath) were busily snubbing the prissily tweedy English memoirists.

~~~~~

The last, I hasten to disclose, is not a survey response at all, but a passage from Erica Jong's novel *Fear of Flying,* narrated by the main character, Isadora Wing. Jong was writing in the early 1970s about the year 1960 or thereabouts. If an educated audience feels any such vicarious fellowship today, I suppose it would be with the disembodied voices of National Public Radio—Susan Stamberg and Bob Edwards and Daniel Schorr and Bailey White and all the rest. But in the flush times of post–World War II America, my respondents were telling me, the only cocktail party in town was the *New Yorker.*

In truth, I already knew this was the case. As I read page after page of this heartfelt testimony, I kept thinking back to my own connection to the magazine. My mother, coming to New York as a "career girl" in the 1940s, seized on the *New Yorker* as a kind of talisman for Manhattan sophistication. The magazine accompanied her to the suburbs and there grew in stature, into a paragon of English prose, critical acumen, and political judgment. There was no *New Yorker* wallpaper in our house, but there was my mother's elaborate system of putting check marks on the issues she had begun reading, double checks on the ones she had finished. (My father, a scattershot reader, often made a mess of the system.) She was overjoyed when Pauline Kael sent a signed note in response to a fan letter, and proudly pasted it in the front of one of Kael's books. Like many of the respondents, I couldn't recall a time when *New Yorkers* weren't around the house, and like them, I started with the cartoons before graduating to the funny little Newsbreaks at the bottom of the columns, the reviews (Kael and Whitney Balliett), the humor pieces (S. J. Perelman, Woody Allen, Ian Frazier), the articles (John McPhee on Bill Bradley, Calvin Trillin on Fats Goldberg, Roger Angell on baseball), and finally the short stories of John Updike, Ann Beattie, and Bobbie Ann Mason. For my birthday one year, my mother gave me two shares of *New Yorker* stock. But being a part-owner gave me no edge in cracking the magazine. Like some of the people who filled out the surveys,

I began collecting my own sheaf of *New Yorker* rejection notes before concluding that, just as I would never be able to dunk a basketball, I was not destined to sip anything at Isadora's imaginary soirée.

Time passed. In 1985, the privately held Advance Communications (in the person of S. I. Newhouse) took control of the magazine, and I was forced to relinquish my stock. What I recall as a return on investment of about 800 percent helped ease the pain. Two years later, I read the exhaustive news coverage of the awkward dismissal of William Shawn, the editor since 1952, and the arrival of Robert Gottlieb. In 1992, Gottlieb was in turn replaced by Tina Brown, accompanied by more headlines.

One less momentous article appeared in the *Times* in 1991. It said that the magazine, then moving from one side of West Forty-third Street to the other, was donating its editorial files to the New York Public Library. I clipped that article, and a subsequent one announcing that the *New Yorker* Records, having been duly classified, cataloged, and dispersed into some twenty-five hundred archival boxes, would be opened to researchers in the spring of 1994. One day that June, I showed up at the Manuscript Division on the third floor, yellow researcher's card in hand.

I began ordering boxes from a descriptive list in a black loose-leaf notebook and read until the library closed at 6 P.M. I returned another day, and then another, and ultimately spent a good part of that summer dipping my big toe into the collection. The most striking of many striking things about it was its richness. The files covered the years 1925, when the *New Yorker* began, to the early eighties. For most of that time people actually communicated by writing letters back and forth—and they kept the carbon copies! I read thousands of pieces of correspondence between *New Yorker* editors and such contributors as James Thurber, E. B. White, Edmund Wilson, John Updike, John Cheever, Vladimir Nabokov, Mary McCarthy, J. D. Salinger, John Hersey, Irwin Shaw, John O'Hara, Peter Taylor, Jean Stafford, Woody Allen, Donald Barthelme, Ann Beattie, Bobbie Ann Mason, and many, many others. Some of the letters were historical curiosities. In 1928, the future playwright Clifford Odets, then a touring actor who was trying to break into the magazine as a writer (he never succeeded), wrote, from Philadelphia, to the editor Katharine Angell: "Chalk one up for the *New Yorker*. Lou Powers, our character woman, fell off her dressing room stool when she came to that 'cow is not content' (drawing by Frueh) business in last week's issue. The actors on stage had to 'ad lib' frantically while she gained her composure."

Then there was the carbon of a 1929 letter from Harold Ross, who founded the magazine and remained editor until his death in 1951, trying to recruit his friend Groucho Marx as a contributor: "If you would listen to me, you would write a lot and get a big reputation as a writer and plenty of publicity for the Marx Brothers which, God knows, they need."

Hidden away in one file was a 1949 letter written by a seventeen-year-old from Shillington, Pennsylvania:

> I would like some information on those little filler drawings you publish and, I presume, buy. What size should they be? Mounted or not? Are there any preferences as to subject matter, weight of cardboard, and technique?
>
> I will appreciate any information you give me, for I would like to try my hand at it.

There was no response in the file, nor was John Updike ever successful in placing any kind of artwork in the magazine. Four and a half years later, however, just after graduating from Harvard, Updike sold the first of (many) stories and the first of (many) poems to the *New Yorker*. On his way to England, where he had a one-year postgraduate fellowship, he stopped in to see fiction editor William Maxwell, who described the meeting in a memo to his colleague Katharine White. (This was the same person as Katharine Angell; she changed her name following her marriage in 1929 to E. B. White, whose nickname was Andy.)

> Just a note to tell you that Updike turned up and I took him to lunch. Had you met him? Very modest, shy, intelligent humorous youngster, slightly gawky in his manner and already beginning, being an artist, to turn it into a kind of style, by way of self-defense. Andy and Thurber are his gods. Our buying a story seems to have momentarily floored him, but I don't expect it will outlast the publication of the story. He hopes also to be a comic artist. Is married. Distrusts adventure and is, in short, true to type. I liked him very much, and Shawn told me to tell him that when he came back to this country, if he wanted to work here, we'd find something.

Needless to say, not every prospective contributor met with as much success as Updike. The *New Yorker* Records held carbons of enough rejection notes—some of them quite detailed—to make a grim anthology. They were written to the likes of Gertrude Stein, Flannery O'Connor, Thomas Pynchon, Jack Kerouac, Nelson Algren, Joseph Heller, Lillian Hellman, Kurt Vonnegut Jr., William Gass, and just about every other American writer practicing in the final two-thirds of the twentieth century. Rejectees usually took their medicine quietly, but someone who did not was Cynthia Ozick. "Gentlemen," she wrote on January 5, 1962:

> For a number of years now I have been sending you poems, and until very recently I have always found you entirely reliable. Exactly seven days after each new poem has been dropped into the mail, it has come punctually home, accompanied by that little rejection slip of yours marked with the number 1 in the left-hand bottom corner. (*You* know the one.) You have, as I

say, been altogether faithful and dependable. For example, it is never six days, it is certainly never eight or nine days. It is always seven days to the minute, and your conscientious devotion to precision all these years has been matched, to my knowledge, only by the butcher's deliver-boy, whose appearance is also predicated on a seven-day cycle.

This time, however, you have failed me. A poem of mine, entitled "An Urgent Exhortation to His Admirers and Dignifiers: Being the Transcript of an Address Before the Mark Twain Association by Samuel Clemens, Shade," reached you on December 18, 1961, and, though eighteen days have already passed, a daily inspection of my letterbox yields nothing. I have enough confidence in your hitherto clean record of never considering anything I have submitted not to be tempted into the unworthy suspicion that the delay is actually caused by your *liking* this poem. What *has* been shattered, I must admit, is my sense of serenity, of certitude, nay, of *security*—not to mention my sense of rhythm. Does this mean you can no longer be relied on to conform to the seven-day schedule you have consistently adhered to in the past? In short, is the Age of Doubt truly upon us? O tempora!

Or (but I venture this with a cheery hopefulness I do not dare to feel) is it only that you have finally gone and lost my manuscript? I realize I am probably being too sanguine in putting forth this rosy possibility, but I guess I am just basically an optimistic sort. Please reassure me that this, rather than some flaw in your clockworks (even to contemplate which disillusions me hideously), is the real nature of the difficulty.

I expect your answer in seven days.

There was no answer in the file, nor was the poem ever published in the *New Yorker*—although, some twenty years later, Ozick became a regular contributor to the magazine.

From my reading of past books about the *New Yorker*, I had known Harold Ross was an inveterate letter- and memo-writer. There in the library were a plentiful supply of his famous "query sheets," with numbered questions (most famously, "Who he?") corresponding to points in the story where the author had committed ambiguity, illogic, or confusion. And there were hundreds of wonderful stream-of-consciousness outpourings, typed (badly) by himself. One—undated, but from the 1930s—was in response to E. B. White, his most valued contributor, who had objected to a *New Yorker* ad containing the phrase "Satin Tissue." (The first page of Ross's typescript is reproduced on page 20.)

The files also shed light on the most celebrated art form to come out of the *New Yorker*—the cartoon. There were minutes of the famous "art meeting," where Ross would accept, reject, or give orders for improving the cartoons submitted that week. On March 28, 1933, a Carl Rose cartoon with the cap-

Mr. White: copy $2-7$ 7

Reference yours of   May 3rd, regarding mention of toilet paper. I appreciated ~~the~~ your sincerity and the legitimateness of ~~intent~~ your and am, I think,
among the first always to distinguish between a Ballyhoo joke about toilet
paper and a "would be serious, or reasonable comment on an abstract idea."
Nevertheless, the word toilet paper in print ~~~~ inevitably presents
a picture to me that is distasteful ~~and~~, frequently, sickening. It would, for
instance, ruin my meal if ~~~~ read ~~such~~ it ~~~~ while eating. It
~~might~~ ~~~~ easily cause vomiting. Things like that have caused
vomiting. The fact that we allow ~~it~~ toilet paper to be advertised, under the name
"Satin Tissue" has nothing to do with this matter. I have never been
nauseated by a Satin Tissue ad, possibly because I have never read ~~~~ it.
~~it~~ I have, however, reflected often on the ~~~~ problem of accepting
the advertising of certain ~~~~ products ~~~~ which affect the squeamish ~~~~
~~~~ and have realized that we have a certain responsibility toward a
manufacturer of a legitimate, if, upon occasion, distasteful product. I think
we much allow toilet paper companies to advertise and to allow them to use
euphemism even if it sounds like Nice ~~~~ Nellyism. Admittedly there
are certain words that I cannot be used; admittedly we all (and that means you)
avoid them in conversation, ~~~~ using/synonyms ~~~~ weak or
~~~~ euphemisms ~~~~ or circumlocutions ~~~~. Moreover, I
would point out that all I do is express my opinion when asked, or set down a

Insert A I was against "Zip" which pulled out ~~~~ the hair on ~~~~
women's legs (by applying like a mustard plaster). This seemed to me to ~~~~
be over the line, although I had to admit that the manufacturers were probably
honest, legitimate, and well-intiontioned, and that they were benefactors to
women, who are probably better with out ~~the~~ hair ~~on~~ their legs.

my instinctive response. Neither, I have long been aware, may be worth much while
~~~~ I have a sensitive and easily-upset stomach, ~~~~
~~depraved in most~~ ~~~~ ~~~~ ~~~~ ~~~~
~~~~ ~~~~ ~~~~ ~~~~

E. B. White had objected, on the grounds of euphemism, to an advertisement in the
New Yorker for "Satin Tissue." Editor Harold Ross's response (his first-draft typescript is shown) is revealing, as to both the editor's profound squeamishness and the
seriousness with which he took matters large and small.

tion "Speak, Mr. Pennywhistle, speak to me" came up for discussion. Ross's curt suggestion: "Reduce Mr. Pennywhistle and make him concave." A 1929 memo to Ross from Katharine Angell described the *seventeen* cartoon genres that had already, just four years into the magazine's existence, become clichés.

But the files offered more than fascinating footnotes to literary and journalistic history. I gradually sensed that the correspondence they held told, en masse, a story. The story was how a tiny weekly humor magazine, founded in the jazz age on champagne vapor, became, within about ten years, a major literary enterprise, publishing the fiction of John O'Hara, Irwin Shaw, and Kay Boyle; the journalism of Alva Johnston, Joseph Mitchell, and A. J. Liebling; the comic art of Charles Addams, Helen Hokinson, and Peter Arno; and the humor and essays of E. B. White, James Thurber, and S. J. Perelman—and then how *that* magazine changed over the decades to adapt to new artists and new times.

On the one hand, it was possible to see the taste and vision of the editors broadening to accept this work. But what was even more fascinating, I could also see an artist or writer latching onto what had already been published in the magazine and extrapolating from it something wonderful and new. In time, this process begat whole new graphic and literary genres, and enduring work—a Charles Addams or Saul Steinberg cartoon, a humor piece by Thurber, a John Cheever short story, a piece of reportage by Joseph Mitchell or A. J. Liebling—that simply would not have existed in the absence of the *New Yorker*. The aesthetic that eventually came to inform the *New Yorker* had its shortcomings. It was rarely receptive to elliptical, experimental, gritty, or subversive artists, or to work that came from the margins of society. And it did provide a home to writing that was precious, smug, tiresomely literal, too long, or just plain dull. Yet the *New Yorker* at its best—and it was quite often at its best—had a unique quality in our literary culture. It was mindful of readers, aiming to amuse them, delight them, instruct them, or transport them; it always respected their intelligence and never pandered.

As an example of how one of the magazine's genres evolved, consider the case of Irwin Shaw. In 1935, a barely published twenty-two-year-old, Shaw began peppering the *New Yorker* with submissions. One short story, "Second Mortgage," elicited a sympathetic rejection from editor John Mosher: "We have a feeling in general that a story so ambitious, so sad, of such generally dismal setting, hardly has a place in a more or less cheerful or humorous magazine. We think, however, that you write with considerable distinction and we want you to do more at once and send them all to us."

Mosher obviously paused before writing the next paragraph: "I did not mean to indicate above that we do not publish stories of tragedy, but that we are perhaps more demanding and critical in such cases than we are in our lighter moments. After all, I suppose that it is perfectly justifiable, and that the grimmer aspects of life require more delicate handling than the more comic."

Reading between the lines of Mosher's letter, one could sense the *New Yorker* poised on the precipice of change, ready to expand its own definition of suitable fiction. Shaw seized the moment, continued submitting, and eventually published such ambitious, sad stories as "Sailor off the *Bremen,*" "The Girls in Their Summer Dresses," and "The City Was in Total Darkness," which stretched the *New Yorker* story, figuratively and literally. (Shaw kept breaking his own record for the longest piece of fiction in the magazine.) But that did not mean author and magazine henceforth were in perfect harmony, and in fact in the mid-1950s they had a painful, acrimonious divorce. Until that point, editors such as Gus Lobrano continually tried to rein in Shaw's melodramatic and expressionistic urges, while Shaw continually tried to get the magazine to be less bound by various kinds of propriety. Upset over the rejection of a story called "Africa Without Germans," he wrote Lobrano in 1943 that he was infuriated by

> the patronizing sniffing of critics when they call my stories "*New Yorker* stories," meaning thereby something pallid and cold that is inexplicably used to pad out the space between cartoons and the Talk of the Town. . . . The trouble is, I think, that you're overworking your famous urbanity and objectivity to a point where too much of your stuff has a high, even gloss, whether it's on the subject of death, disaster, love, anything. . . .
>
> There is no reason for losing urbanity, but there is place for emotion, place for personal writing, too. It is not as though the *New Yorker* has remained unchanged from beginning to now. It has changed and changed, all for the better . . . and it will undoubtedly keep on changing, it if wants to keep its place. What I'm trying to do is accelerate the change, make it operate for my own advantage, naturally. [Ellipses Shaw's.]

Jumping ahead thirty years, one could chart the process of the magazine and another vitally important contributor adapting to each other. One of the several hundred fiction manuscripts that arrived at the *New Yorker* one week in 1972 was a short story called "Blue Eggs," written by a young college English instructor named Ann Beattie. It found its way from the slush pile to the desk of fiction editor Roger Angell, and he wrote to Beattie: "These little slices and moments are often surprisingly effective, but the story itself seems to get away from you as it goes along. It seems possible that there is more form than substance here, but perhaps that is unfair. What I most admire is your wit and quickness and self-assurance. I hope you will let us see more of your work, and that you will address your future submissions directly to me." Angell rejected thirteen of Beattie's stories over the next twenty-two months. He was usually patient and encouraging, but sometimes a bit of exasperation showed through. At one point, he wrote: "I wish you would try a very quiet and modest story—one that relies on no devices and is content merely to bring us to its discoveries. But whatever you do write, please continue to send it to us."

Beattie tried to balance her own artistic needs with the requirements expressed by Angell. Finally, in November 1973, she submitted a story called "A Platonic Relationship," along with a cover note indicating she had tried to meet the magazine more than halfway: "In this story I have taken pains to do something you have said might work several times before: to write a simple story. No times shifts, characters named, backgrounds understandable, and hopefully not entirely depressing."

Sitting in the Rare Books and Manuscript Room, reading Angell's reply, I found myself getting a little choked up. He wrote:

> Oh, joy ...
>
> Yes, we are taking A PLATONIC RELATIONSHIP, and I think this is just about the best news of the year. Maybe it isn't the best news for you, but there is nothing that gives me more pleasure (well, *almost* nothing) than at last sending an enthusiastic yes to a writer who has persisted through as many rejections and rebuffs as you have. It's a fine story, I think—original, strong, and true.

At the end of the summer, I knew I would write a book about the *New Yorker*. I was aware that mine would hardly be the first; I had pleasurably read the two most famous, Gill's *Here at the New Yorker* and Thurber's *The Years with Ross*. But neither Gill nor Thurber nor any other author had had access to the *New Yorker* Records. What's more, theirs and every other book ever written about the magazine had been biographical, autobiographical, or anecdotal in emphasis. (Thomas Kunkel's fine biography of Harold Ross, *Genius in Disguise,* came out the following year; it was followed by memoirs from *New Yorker* writers Ved Mehta, Lillian Ross, and Renata Adler.) What I had in mind was a critical and cultural history. It would consider, first, the *content* of the magazine—how its original form came to be, and how and why it evolved over the years. Second, I would look at the role the *New Yorker* has played in American cultural life—among the literati and among people like my mother and Isadora Wing—for the seventy-five years of its existence.

In writing this book, my main resource has been the *New Yorker* Records. But I also sat down and read the entire run of the *New Yorker* from 1925 to 1935, when the magazine underwent its most revolutionary change, and as many of the more than three thousand subsequent issues as time allowed. I canvassed the voluminous secondary literature on the magazine and its contributors. I interviewed more than five dozen *New Yorker* artists, writers, and editors, from William Steig and the late Emily Hahn, who first appeared in its pages in 1929; to Philip Hamburger, William Maxwell, and the late Joseph Mitchell and Brendan Gill, who came in the thirties; to Gardner Botsford and Eleanor Gould Packard, from the forties; to Whitney Balliett and Roger Angell, from the fifties; to Calvin Trillin and Jonathan Schell, from the sixties; to Ian Frazier and Daniel Menaker, from the seventies; to eighties arrivals Bill McKibben and Robert Gottlieb; all the way up to David Remnick, who grew up in a house where the New Yorker was reverently read. I corresponded on paper with John Updike and via E-mail with Garrison Keillor. And, of course, I surveyed more than three hundred "longtime readers."

What this additional research revealed was a story that amplified and paralleled the one in the files: the story of the New Yorker as an institution. It had to do with the effect of the New Yorker on the creative artists linked to it, people such as Updike and Shaw and Beattie and Cheever and Steinberg and dozens of others, and also with what it meant (for themselves and the magazine) that such figures as Ernest Hemingway, Norman Mailer, Wallace Stevens, Robert Lowell, Jules Feiffer, Grace Paley, and Tom Wolfe were so resolutely not of the New Yorker. The additional story was about the way the New Yorker—modestly under Harold Ross, to a much greater extent under William Shawn—became more than a magazine. It became a totem for the educated American middle and upper-middle classes. It became the repository for increasingly high standards of English prose, taste, conscience, and civility. And gradually, all that weight proved to be too much for a weekly magazine to bear.

A word about perimeters. I have chosen to end the book proper in 1987, when Shawn was dismissed by Si Newhouse; an epilogue takes the story up to the present. That is not to imply that the magazine as it exists today doesn't have loyal readers or publish significant work. However, its story as a unique and influential institution in our culture, as I see it, is a two-act drama; when Shawn made his exit, the curtain came down.

We begin with a prologue, commencing with Harold Ross's arrival in Manhattan in 1919. Before joining him there, let's return for a moment to Hannah Turner and her Dartmouth man at the medical aid station in Italy. "They came to carry his stretcher away," she wrote to me, "and I leaned over and kissed his cheek (most of his head was bandaged) and told him how much those minutes had meant to me. He didn't need to tell me what they meant to him . . . his eyes and the grip on my hand told me everything.

"When I was able to check on him at the hospital a few days later, they said he had not survived the trip back."

CHAPTER ONE

METROPOLITAN LIFE

1919~25

Harold Ross, who was born in Aspen, Colorado, and grew up in Salt Lake City, first saw New York City in 1913, when he was twenty-one years old and had already worked as a newspaper reporter in Sacramento, Panama, New Orleans, and Atlanta. Even years later, when Ross was the editor of a magazine universally deemed the embodiment of urban sophistication, people thought of him as if he wore overalls and had a blade of grass permanently protruding from his mouth. Janet Flanner, who like many of his writers was devoted to him, described him as "a big-boned westerner . . . who talked in windy gusts that gave a sense of fresh weather to his conversation. His face was homely, with a pendant lower lip; his teeth were far apart, and when I first knew him, after the First World War, he wore his butternut-colored thick hair in a high, stiff pompadour, like some wild gamecock's crest, and he also wore anachronistic, old-fashioned, high laced shoes, because he thought Manhattan men dressed like what he called dudes." On that first New York stop, Ross had even rougher edges than when Flanner met him and, not surprisingly, made little impression on the metropolis. He did secure temporary jobs at papers in northern New Jersey and in Brooklyn, but was unable to get hired in Manhattan and concluded that New York was not for him. He went (back) West until he was stopped by the Pacific Ocean and, in San Francisco, embarked on what would be his longest reporting stint, on the *Call*. It ended in 1917, soon after the United States entered World War I, when Ross volunteered for the Eighteenth Engineering Regiment. He was sent to France and eventually found his way to an editor's position at *Stars and Stripes,* the soldier's weekly magazine.

While he was overseas, his *Stars and Stripes* colleague Alexander Woollcott, formerly the *New York Times* drama critic, introduced him to Jane Grant, a

Times reporter and a classically trained singer, who had taken a leave during the war to entertain the troops in Europe. Ross was smitten, and as their relationship grew more serious, they talked about where they might live after the armistice. Ross at first wanted "no part" of New York—"a terrible place"; his thought was to return to the West Coast and eventually charter a boat and sail to the South Seas. But Grant, a New York enthusiast as only a migrant can be (she was born in Missouri, raised in Kansas), wore him down, and when Ross was offered a job as editor of a new, New York–based weekly aimed at returning veterans, *The Home Sector,* he accepted.

The New York in which Ross took up residence in 1919 was a far different place from the one he had glimpsed six years earlier. For one thing, it was bigger. Between 1910 and 1920, the population of the metropolitan area increased from 7.5 million to 9 million, a 20 percent gain. (This was the culmination of an even more dramatic 300 percent population gain between 1880 and 1920.) Most of the increase was a result of the last stage of the biggest immigration wave in the country's history, but a significant portion came from within the United States. Between 1910 and 1930 the number of native-born New York City residents from states other than New York doubled, to a total of 722,837. When one bears in mind the significant number who would have died or moved away in that period, and the many migrants who came from upstate New York—as momentous a journey as from Ohio or Alabama—it follows that the total inflow was significantly greater than the net increase of some 358,000.

A small subset of this group, of which Harold Ross was a member, had an influence on the character of the city far beyond their number. In the realms of activity and creation collectively known as "culture," New York had rather suddenly become a national magnet for talent and ambition. In her book *Terrible Honesty,* the historian Ann Douglas lists some of the other men and women who arrived in the city from the hinterlands in the teens and twenties: Sinclair Lewis, Elinor Wylie, Hart Crane, Sara Teasdale, Katherine Anne Porter, Thomas Wolfe, Edna St. Vincent Millay, Marianne Moore, Louise Bogan, Robert Sherwood, Edna Ferber, John Dos Passos, George S. Kaufman, Ludwig Lewisohn, Gilbert Seldes, Van Wyck Brooks, Katharine Cornell, Laurette Taylor, Charles Gilpin, Paul Robeson, Zora Neale Hurston, Noble Sissle, Eubie Blake, Langston Hughes, Duke Ellington, Ethel Waters, Bix Beiderbecke, Cole Porter, Jean Toomer, Damon Runyon, Robert Benchley, James Thurber, Louise Brooks, Al Jolson, and Raymond Hood.*

---

*Among the names Douglas could also have included on the list were Harold Ross, Jane Grant, Katharine White, James M. Cain, Donald Ogden Stewart, John O'Hara, Frank Sullivan, Marc Connelly, Ring Lardner, Helen Hokinson, S. N. Behrman, John Held Jr., Fannie Hurst, Kenneth Burke, Sally Benson, George Abbott, Robert Coates, Malcolm Cowley,

Of course, young people of talent and ambition had journeyed from provinces to city for centuries, but something was different about the pull of New York in the postwar period. Another immigrant from the West, a Minnesotan who settled in the city the year after Ross, recalled the metropolitan excitement years later. New York, F. Scott Fitzgerald wrote, "had all the iridescence of the beginning of the world. The returning troops marched up Fifth Avenue and girls were instinctively drawn East and North toward them—this was the greatest nation and there was gala in the air." The presiding tropes, as Ann Douglas has observed, were ascendance and transcendence: aviators, flagpole sitters, Babe Ruth's home runs, jazz musicians' improvised arpeggios, hemlines, and the stock market all kept going up, as if the laws of gravity had temporarily been suspended. Prohibition (enacted in 1919 but virtually unenforced), far from bringing people down, propelled them above the law as they gave the password at speakeasies and made their own bathtub gin. The objective correlative was the skyscraper. A 1916 zoning law required that upper stories be stepped back, so that the arching tower of the building could rise over only 25 percent of the site. This not only saved Manhattan from becoming dark and claustrophobic, it led to streamlined buildings that seemed to effortlessly reach ever new heights; over the 1920s, the average height of the skyline increased by one hundred feet.

In all, the sense of New York as being at the very center of things, spreading since the consolidation of the five boroughs in 1897, reached its zenith in the 1920s. As the decade neared its end, the *Nation* wrote, "All over the country the ambitious and the eager, the want-to-be-wealthy and the would-be smart, have their eyes on Manhattan Island. It is a recognized truth that people must be judged by what they want to be as well as by what they are, and on this basis at least half of the residents of the United States are New Yorkers."

Not only people but institutions were coming to New York. In the eighteenth and nineteenth centuries, the book and magazine publishing industries had been somewhat decentralized, with the highest concentration of outposts in New York, Philadelphia, and Boston, but with significant enterprises in such far-flung cities as Chicago or Indianapolis. In the years straddling the turn of the century, however, New York became the literary center of the country, and in the late teens and the twenties that process accelerated. Joining such venerable firms as Doubleday, Harper and Brothers, and Charles Scribner's Sons, a host of publishers began operations in the late teens and the

---

Christopher Morley, Thyra Samter Winslow, Philip Barry, Ben Hecht, Floyd Dell, Allen Tate, Joseph Wood Krutch, Burton Rascoe, Harold Stearns, William Rose Benét, Stephen Vincent Benét, Maxwell Bodenheim, and Will Rogers.

twenties: Alfred A. Knopf (1915), Boni and Liveright (1917), Harcourt, Brace (1919), Delacorte Press (1921), W. W. Norton (1923), Simon and Schuster (1924), William Morrow (1926), Viking Press (1926), John Day (1926), Vanguard Press (1926), Random House (1927), and Farrar and Rinehart (1929). Following this near-frenzy of activity came ancillary enterprises—"book clubs" such as the Book-of-the-Month Club and the Literary Guild, both started in 1926, and two book-review forums begun in 1924, the *Saturday Review of Literature* and the Sunday Books section of the *New York Herald Tribune*.

New York had long been the nation's theatrical capital. In the first two decades of the century, that status was solidified by the Theater District's move up from Union Square to Times Square, its subsequent illumination as the Great White Way, and the concurrent diminution of that nineteenth-century fixture, the touring stock company. The city had twenty theaters in 1903 and eighty in 1927; with this building boom, naturally, came more productions—157 in the 1920–21 season, an all-time peak of 280 in 1927–28. Meanwhile, a series of new media, cultural delivery systems, and technologies that formed the basis of twentieth-century mass culture were all based in the city: the vertically integrated music industry known collectively as Tin Pan Alley, vaudeville, advertising, motion pictures (although beginning around 1915 they began their migration to California), wire services and newspaper syndicates, and later, radio and television.

At first Ross took a small apartment in Greenwich Village, venturing from it now and then to tour the different parts of the city with Jane Grant. Roughly simultaneously, he sold her on himself and she sold him on New York, and they married early in 1920. Two years later (by that time *The Home Sector* had folded and Ross was editing the American Legion's house organ), they bought two side-by-side buildings on West Forty-seventh Street, in the chancy, aptly named Hell's Kitchen neighborhood, with the odd idea of turning the property into a sort of commune. Even odder, the idea worked. They sold a quarter share each to Woollcott and to a college classmate of his, a New York lawyer named Hawley Truax. Even after living quarters were carved out for the four, enough room was left over to rent out two additional apartments. There were several shared spaces, notably a twenty-five-foot-square living room with two fireplaces and a badly out-of-tune piano; once the residents were settled, they carried out Woollcott's resolution, acceded to by the rest, to conduct a permanent "open house." In her memoir, *Ross, the New Yorker and Me*, Grant described the night George Gershwin tried out a "new composition" called "Rhapsody in Blue," and went on to list some other notable moments and guests: "a poem read by Edna St. Vincent Millay; Scott Fitzgerald telling the plot of his new book; a monologue by Robert

Benchley or Marc Connelly; . . . a scene from a play Ethel Barrymore was rehearsing; a new song from Irving Berlin."

Ross and Grant's New York was a city of social circles—some intersecting, some concentric, some discrete—and a remarkable number of them found their way to the house on Forty-seventh Street. Given the profession of Ross, Grant, and Woollcott, it wasn't surprising that they would have fallen in with the journalistic set—and a large set it was, with a dozen daily newspapers and a thriving collection of magazines that covered some combination of literary, artistic, theatrical, political, and cultural matters. Woollcott, a capaciously eccentric, famously difficult yet witty, magnetic, and obsessively social figure, brought in people from the theater and from his wide circle of general acquaintance. Some significant subcultures had only one or two representatives. Thus the glamorous Millay was something like a celebrity poster girl, standing in for the entire venerable Greenwich Village world of poetry, radical politics, and bohemianism—the world of Mabel Dodge, Floyd Dell, Hart Crane, Djuna Barnes, Malcolm Cowley, and John Reed, of the *Nation* and the *New Republic* and the little literary magazines.* The visual arts were represented only by commercial illustrators such as Ralph Barton, Rea Irvin, and Neysa McMein (also glamorous, and the person responsible for introducing Ross and Grant to an expatriate friend of hers named Janet Flanner). The upper-class New York of "The 400," the most important circle of all just twenty years before, was rapidly losing its relevance, but it was not yet out for the count and was extremely attractive to Woollcott, well-known for his social climbing. A key connection of his was with Alice Duer Miller, a novelist and poet (most famous for "The White Cliffs," written on the eve of World War II), who came from a prominent and wealthy New York family and was active in high society.

A signal feature of all this social intercourse is that it did not go on in a vacuum. The term *public relations* was coined in May 1920 by Edward Bernays, who needed to describe his profession in a wedding announcement, but for a decade or more, it had been understood that publicity, as much as verses or wheat, was a valuable commodity, and practitioners responsible for securing it had been multiplying. In fact, it was as a direct result of press

---

*In truth, the vitality and influence of Village life had been ebbing since its peak in the midteens. Dismayed by the superficiality and acquisitiveness of American life in the twenties, numerous Villagers had already expatriated to Europe, while others had moved to universities or rural areas. The case against American culture was classically made in the 1922 symposium *Civilization in the United States: An Inquiry by Thirty Americans* and the process classically documented by Cowley in his memoir *Exile's Return*. At the end of the decade, many in this group would move back to New York and contribute to the *New Yorker*. Of course, it would never have occurred to Ross or Woollcott and their set to object to superficiality or acquisitiveness, or for that matter to go abroad again.

agents that the decade's most famous circle—a circle at which Ross and Woollcott were at the center—came into being. In the summer of 1919, one of John Peter Toohey's clients was Eugene O'Neill, a thirty-year-old playwright who had never had a production on Broadway. Toohey concocted an item about O'Neill that he thought would be good for Woollcott's Sunday column and so phoned a mutual friend and fellow press agent, Murdock Pemberton, to arrange a lunch. The three met at the Algonquin Hotel, a popular literary and theatrical spot. Not only did Woollcott refuse to run the item, but he pompously monopolized the conversation with disquisitions about his wartime experiences. To get back at him, Pemberton and Toohey invited several dozen of Woollcott's friends and colleagues to the Algonquin the following week, to conduct what would in later years be called a roast. The guests included Ross and Grant; three staffers at *Vanity Fair* magazine, Dorothy Parker, Robert Benchley, and Robert Sherwood; Franklin P. Adams, who had been on *Stars and Stripes* with Ross and Woollcott and who, as "FPA," wrote the popular "Conning Tower" column in the *New York Tribune*; and another prominent *Tribune* columnist, Heywood Broun. It was so much fun that the group decided to make it a daily lunchtime powwow. Initially, the group sat at a long side table in the Pergola Room (now the Oak Room), but in 1920 the Algonquin's manager, Frank Case, moved them to a circular table in the middle of the Rose Room. And thus the Round Table was born.

In retrospect, the consensus seems to be that the Round Table's reputation exceeded its virtues. Ross later said (to H. L. Mencken) of the Round Table, "I never heard any literary discussion or any discussion of any other art—just the usual personalities of some people getting together, and a lot of wisecracks and quoting of further wisecracks." Edmund Wilson, characteristically, was more cutting. He wrote in his journal that he "did not find them particularly interesting. They all came from the suburbs and 'provinces,' and a sort of tone was set—mainly by Benchley, I think—deriving from a provincial upbringing of people who had been taught a certain kind of gentility, who had played the same games and who had read the same children's books—all of which they were now able to mock from a level of New York sophistication. I found this rather tiresome, since they never seemed to be able to get above it." Nevertheless, the table quickly attracted additional regulars—among them the second-string *Times* critic under Woollcott, George S. Kaufman; his future collaborator, Marc Connelly; vaudeville and Broadway performer Harpo Marx; and music critic Deems Taylor—and slightly more gradually developed an aura of wit and sophistication that has not dimmed to this day. It is not hard to see why the group and their remarks became famous. It would only have been surprising if these ambitious writers, most of whom conducted columns or whole magazines, had *not* used the opportunity to promote their friends and themselves. In the event, they did it so strenuously that the Algonquin group became as famous for its literary logrolling as for its wit. Nor was it a closed circle, as far as publicity went. Pemberton and Toohey would feed the members' quips to columnists who *didn't* sit at the table, either because the utterers paid them (not likely), or Frank Case paid them (probable), or they just enjoyed placing an item (almost certain). The remarkable result was that this group of several dozen friends and colleagues, none of them at this point outstandingly accomplished, became intimately known to the hundreds of thousands and eventually millions of readers of the public prints.

The key logroller was Adams, who was only thirty-eight years old in 1919 but was still the elder statesman of the group. His column (which would move from the *Tribune* to the *World* in 1922) was a mix of Adams's own comments and witticisms and light verse submitted by the world at large (George S. Kaufman, Ira Gershwin, James Thurber, and E. B. White all found the first prominent platform for their work in "The Conning Tower"). Plugs for FPA's friends were especially oppressive in his regular feature "The Diary of Our Own Samuel Pepys," a chronicle of his comings and goings written in mock-seventeenth-century style. People named in it were not identified or described, and their first names were generally represented by an initial rather than a name, so implicit was the assumption that the reader knew who they were and cared what they did. Between 1919 and 1925, Ross appeared in "The Diary" thirty-five times. (The first entry was dated June 2, 1919: "A. Woollcott to dinner, and H. Ross, and Mistress Caroline Mundell, and H. Broun and Miss R. Hale, nee Hale, and thenafter I to the playhouse and saw "The Scandals of 1919," a pretentious harlequinade with much good dancing, but nothing I took for humour.")* Although this was twelve fewer mentions than McMein, for whom Adams carried a torch, and fourteen fewer than the estimable Woollcott, it was more than Broun, Parker, Benchley, or Millay—rather impressive since for most of the period Ross was editing an obscure house organ for a veterans' organization and was commonly viewed as a hayseed.

Part of the unreal frivolity of the twenties was that intelligent people should have occupied themselves with card, board, and parlor games to a degree not seen before or since, and these pursuits created slightly varied offshoots of existing social circles. In "The Diary of Our Own Samuel Pepys," there are accounts of competitions at cribbage, backgammon, obscure word

---

*Caroline Mundell was a writer. Ruth Hale, another press agent, was married to Heywood Broun. Adams's joke stemmed from Hale's ardent belief that women should keep their names after marriage. Jane Grant thought so, too, and the two of them later founded the Lucy Stone League to promote the idea.

games, pachisi, casino, hearts, and numerous others. The most important game was poker, which Ross, Woollcott, and Adams had started playing together during the war, in the back room of a Monmartre *boîte*, joined by their *Stars and Stripes* colleague Grantland Rice, and occasionally Ring Lardner and Heywood Broun when their journalistic duties took them to Paris. After the armistice the game migrated to Manhattan, and Adams dubbed it the Thanatopsis Pleasure and Inside Straight Club, named after the club frequented by the people of Gopher Prairie, Minnesota, in Sinclair Lewis's *Main Street*. Eventually it found its way to West Forty-seventh Street and began to attract some high-stakes players—including Henry "Harry" Miller, husband of Alice; Herbert Bayard Swope, the editor of the *World*; and Raoul Fleischmann, an heir to the General Baking Company (he was related to the owners of Fleischmann Yeast Company), who for some years had been resisting a life of business but had maintained it out of a sense of family responsibility. For a time Fleischmann had courted Neysa McMein, and through her, in 1921, met FPA, who brought him into the charmed world of "The Conning Tower."

In an unpublished, undated reminiscence that gives some of the carefree feel of the social and historical moment, Fleischmann described his entry and the momentous business connection it led to:

> Frank [Adams] asked me to play poker later that week at the apartment of George Kaufman, and it was there that I met some of the personnel of "Thanatopsis." The players at that time were Frank, George, Marc Connelly, Henry Miller, Harold Ross, John Peter Toohey, and occasionally Woollcott, Irving Berlin, Broun, and one or two others. Without formality or initiational fanfares, I became a "member," and for ten years I had more fun than I can say. Harry Miller and I were then the only businessmen in the outfit, and the gambling phase was secondary to the great fun and gaiety of the meetings. Ross was an enthusiastic, wild sort of player, and with his unparalleled pompadour and Mongolian features he was something to see in action. From 1921, my wife and I began to associate more and more with the vaguely defined group of the Algonquin Round Table set and the Thanatopsis crowd. . . . We saw a lot of these amusing and interesting people, and had a happy and quite carefree life.
>
> The General Baking Company was going great guns, and the goose honked high. My deep feeling of responsibility to my mother and sisters was rapidly being removed through the remarkable improvement in their financial condition, and the need for me to remain with the baking company in order to watch their interests (as well as mine) seemed clearly no longer necessary. During the evenings, I often spoke about my growing boredom with baking—it doubtless became quite boring to hear about it. At any rate, one day early in 1924, Ross asked me to lunch and suggested we start a new

comic paper. What I knew about publishing was zero, but I got some figures on paper and printing costs from a friend. They looked sour, so Ross and I agreed to forget it.

A couple of months later, Ross called me again; this time the idea was that the magazine was to be built around New York, with humor as merely an adjunct of the publication, rather than its basis. We again got figures, and why they now looked better, God knows, but they did. At any rate, we agreed to embark in the coming autumn.

According to Jane Grant, Ross had been talking for some time about starting a publishing enterprise of his own. He had several ideas: a daily newspaper covering shipping news, a line of paperback books, and the project that began to dominate his and Grant's discussions, the one he eventually asked Fleischmann to bankroll—the "comic paper." As Ross doubtless realized, it was a good time to start a magazine. Thanks to a booming economy, favorable postage rates, the consolidation of a national advertising market, and technological advances that allowed speedy photo reproduction, printing, and binding, periodicals boomed in the period as they had never done before. (Also significant was that with radio in its infancy and television not yet conceived, no *other* medium existed that allowed advertisers to reach a national audience.) Between 1915 and 1925, gross national advertising in general magazines increased more than fivefold, from $25.3 million to $143.2 million. Among the bright young people who had seized the day were DeWitt Wallace, who started his *Reader's Digest* in 1922, and Briton Hadden and Henry Luce, who put out the first issue of *Time* the following year.

But what would Ross's big idea be? He did not and would never think of himself as a humor writer, but he had already served as a humor *editor:* during the War, as an offshoot to *Stars and Stripes,* he had profitably put out a pamphlet of soldiers' jokes called *Yank Talk.* Now, after his years of drudgery on the American Legion weekly, Ross understandably wanted his own venture to be enjoyable. "I started this magazine because I thought it would be so much fun to run a humorous magazine, you'd just sit and laugh at funny contributions all the time," he wrote to his friend Frank Sullivan in 1931. What was more significant, he had joined a New York realm in which humor was the coin—the jokes and comical conceits with which its members filled their essays, columns, and plays, and the wisecracks and puns that filled their conversation. It was a rare moment in literary history when funny writers were respected—not only by the Algonquin set but in the culture at large—as much as or more than any other kind. With the occasional exception of a Sinclair Lewis, Scott Fitzgerald, or a few years later, Ernest Hemingway, novelists were seen by Ross and his friends as sentimental, provincial, solemn, boring, or, like Edith Wharton, a curious remnant of the past century. (One reason Fitzgerald's and Lewis's first books, *This Side of Paradise* and *Main Street,* got so much attention when they were published in 1920 was the thrilling rarity of novelists who spoke to the new class taking hold of literature and the media.) Serious poets were considered either homely or obscure. Both classes of writers were just too heavy, weighing readers down with their metaphors, "difficult" meanings, and ponderous social significance. Theodore Dreiser, to pick a particularly humorless example, though he was forty-nine at the dawn of the twenties, seemed a dark and immovable antique to the New York set; he was, as Dorothy Parker would put it in a *New Yorker* review a half dozen years hence, "a dull, pompous, dated, and darned near ridiculous writer."

But humorists could float above the sentimental and mundane, and so they did in remarkable number. At or near the peak of their powers in the early twenties were Parker, Sullivan, Benchley, Kaufman, Donald Ogden Stewart, Don Marquis, George Ade, Will Rogers, Milt Gross, George S. Chappell, Clarence Day, Will Cuppy, Irvin S. Cobb, Rube Goldberg, Stephen Leacock, and the man Ross believed to be the best writer of his generation, Ring Lardner. Of course, heartland comedians such as Rogers or Cobb were sometimes condescended to by the Algonquin set, but their enterprise was more significant than their particular merits. Everyone could agree that the notion of earning one's keep as a writer of humorous prose, barely thinkable today, was not only admirable but possible. (Humor was also thriving in the silent films of Chaplin, Keaton, and their colleagues, on the Broadway and vaudeville stages, and in the funny papers.) It was bedrock faith for scores of talented young men and women just starting out, people such as White, Thurber, Corey Ford, and S. J. Perelman. As Ford wrote years later, "The early Twenties marked the peak of comic writing in this country, a flowering of satire and parody and sheer nonsense that has never been equalled before or since, a galaxy of our greatest funnymen gathered together at one transcendent moment like a configuration of planets which would not occur again in a lifetime."

Of course, there already were humorous magazines on America's newsstands. The two most prominent comic papers were *Life* and *Judge,* national weeklies that had been around since the 1880s. (A third similar magazine, *Puck,* had folded in 1917.) Although *Judge* had originally had a strong political slant, and *Life*—the home of Charles Dana Gibson's girls—was better known for its art and was marginally more upscale (it had ads for Cadillacs and high-class tailors, compared to *Judge*'s ones for patent medicines and correspondence courses), by the early twenties it was hard to tell them apart. Both were filled with humorous drawings and brief pieces or gags that, while occasionally pointed and funny (*Life* published Robert Benchley, Corey Ford,

Gluyas Williams, Dorothy Parker, and other future *New Yorker* stalwarts), tended to be short on subtlety or what was coming to be called sophistication.

From the issue of *Life* that came out the week of the *New Yorker's* premiere issue:

NATURAL QUERY

CUSTOMER: What is your price per gross on engagement rings?

WHOLESALE JEWELER: Are you going to open a store or are you a movie actor?

From the issue of *Judge* that came out the same week:

Lady Driver (at garage)—Do you charge batteries here?

Proprietor—Sure we do.

Lady Driver—Then put a new one in this car and charge it to my husband.

Such gags were weak enough in print, but even worse in graphic form: the cartoons in these magazines too often consisted of captions precisely like the above, beneath illustrations of the scene in question. *Life* and especially *Judge* were suffused with an old-fashioned, heavy strain that stood out in the airy twenties like a mahogany secretary in an art deco penthouse. E. B. White, who was also finding himself bemused by the prevailing sensibility of the national magazines, later put the problem in a nutshell: "Jokes were mostly he-and-she, essays were tweedy, feature writing was at a low ebb, humor was barber shop." Ross, seeking to find a distinctive and potentially profitable niche for his new venture, naturally gravitated to the kind of sharper-edged humor that he and his friends would actually find funny. For several years, he studied the magazines from which he would need to differentiate his. Jane Grant recalled, "Our apartment was filled with copies of *Punch, Simplicimus,* and other foreign magazines which we studied for layout; we culled the old files of *Leslie's, Gleason's, Harper's Weekly,* and of course old and new copies of *Life, Judge, The Smart Set,* and *American Mercury.*"

It is an interesting list, showing, if nothing else, that Ross and Grant were hardly flying into the venture on the seat of their pants. *Punch,* founded in London in 1841 and the editorial home of George du Maurier and Charles Keene, was the model for all subsequent humorous magazines. *Simplicimus* was its German counterpart. Frank Leslie's *Popular Monthly,* which published from 1876 to 1906, was influential in its use of timely illustrations; *Gleason's Pictorial Drawing-Room Companion* was a Boston weekly that ran only from 1851 to 1859; and *Harper's Weekly* (1857–1916) was renowned for its engravings and woodcuts by Thomas Nast and others. The *Smart Set* and *American Mercury* were more to the point. The former, published since 1890 and subtitled "A Magazine of Cleverness," was a trailblazer in bringing a measure of sophistication to the magazine world. Always placing an emphasis on fiction, it had published the first works of O. Henry and James Branch Cabell, as well as stories by D. H. Lawrence, James Joyce, and Ford Madox Ford. Since 1914, the *Smart Set* had been coedited by H. L. Mencken and George Jean Nathan, who continued to print literary fiction (including works by Dreiser, Willa Cather, Sherwood Anderson, and Somerset Maugham, and F. Scott Fitzgerald's first published short story, "Babes in the Woods"), were open to young writers such as S. N. Behrman and Thyra Samter Winslow, and also made the magazine a personal forum for their own wide-ranging commentaries on and critiques of American life and letters. But the *Smart Set*'s profitability had never approached its influence. In 1923, its circulation was less than twenty-five thousand; with revenues too low to make the move from uncoated stock, the magazine could not accomodate for either advertising or graphic art, both of which required glossy paper. That year, Nathan and Mencken left to start a new magazine, *American Mercury,* which had much the same flavor and limitations. (Significant, for Ross's purposes, was a common feature of both magazines, the "Americana" section, which began in the *Smart Set* in 1923 and continued on in *American Mercury.* It featured verbatim quotations from publications around the country, with deadpan or subtly sardonic introductions. The formula, slightly altered, would show up in the *New Yorker* as a bottom-of-the-column feature called Newsbreaks.)

Grant's list of magazines has one significant omission, left out, perhaps, because it was just too obvious to mention—*Vanity Fair.* This monthly had been launched in 1913 by Condé Nast, publisher of the highly successful fashion magazine *Vogue,* as a bid to reach a wider public. Edited from the outset by Frank Crowninshield, *Vanity Fair* unabashedly told its readers that, merely by virtue of *being* its readers, they belonged to a privileged group. "That we are trying to appeal to Americans of some little sophistication, we not only admit but boast of," Crowninshield wrote in an early issue, "but not that pseudo-sophistication bred of money alone, but rather the sophistication which is the natural and happy result of wide travel, some little knowledge of the world, and a pleasing familiarity with the five arts and the four languages." Crowninshield was a connoisseur of the visual arts, and he used the magazine, which was printed on heavy coated stock, not only to chronicle and promote avant-garde artists as Picasso, van Gogh, and Matisse, but to print the work of the period's best illustrators, caricaturists, and photographers, notably Edward Steichen. The formula was immensely successful: in 1915, *Vanity Fair* published the most advertising inches of any American magazine, and it continued to thrive into the twenties. (In a way the *New Yorker* of subsequent years would echo, the magazine's literary-artistic emphasis presented an intriguing contrast with the products being advertised—high-end men's fashion, jewelry, automobiles.) *Vanity Fair* also published top-drawer humor and for a brief moment was the employer of three members of the Algonquin set—Parker, Benchley, and Sherwood. (Parker resigned in 1920 over a principle of editorial independence; Benchley and Sherwood followed her in protest.) And a list of some of the writers and artists who appeared in its pages reads like a roster of future *New Yorker* contributors: Heywood Broun, Donald Ogden Stewart, Ralph Barton, Woollcott, and others.

But Ross would never have thought of starting a publication in any significant way modeled on *Vanity Fair*. He had been changed by New York, to be sure, but not enough to willingly print the works of Aldous Huxley, T. S. Eliot, Ferenc Molnár, Gertrude Stein, or Djuna Barnes, to name some *Vanity Fair* contributors from a single issue (July 1923). While Ross's intelligence and taste have been unfairly maligned for seven and a half decades, sometimes grossly so, he never developed the slightest interest in or appreciation of music, fine art, or highbrow literature, and *Vanity Fair* was steeped in all three. In 1923, its book critic was an exceedingly bright young man whose byline was still "Edmund Wilson, Jr."; the *New Yorker* would not be ready for Wilson's intellectual sensibility until it was nearly twenty years old. Nor had Ross lost his newsman's sense of the world. He had no interest in producing a "newsmagazine," as Luce and Hadden were doing with *Time,* but he did want his journal to be on top of current events the way no monthly could.

Vanity Fair differed in yet another way from the magazine Ross was building in his mind. This distinction crystallized in the spring of 1924, when Ross was offered a job as coeditor (with Norman Anthony) of *Judge*. He took it and stayed for five months, he later said, "to get a toehold in the humorous-magazine business." In his brief tenure he was offered a funny Corey Ford piece about New York's snow removal problems but had to turn it down because its appeal was too limited for a national audience. The experience brought to the surface his growing conviction that the wide geographical circulation of *Judge* and *Life* and also *Vanity Fair* was in some significant ways a liability. "My theory was that the more local humor is, the better it is within its limited circle," he explained later. "Hence the idea of a local magazine." And not just any locality: this was, after all, New York, with 9 million inhabitants—more than most states and many countries—and in its moment of glory. It all made commercial as well as editorial sense: limiting oneself to a New York circulation would also open the magazine up to hundreds if not thousands of shops, restaurants, and services whose proprietors would love to catch the eye of potential customers and would not be inclined to waste advertising dollars reaching readers who lived thousands of miles away.

It was a wide-open field. The only local journal doing anything like what Ross had in mind was the *New York World* of Herbert Bayard Swope. Swope had been named editor in 1920 and had transformed Joseph Pulitzer's yellow sheet into a paper of estimable style and wit. Especially notable were its op-ed page (Swope invented the concept, if not the term) and its Sunday edition, which had become the editorial home of Broun, Adams, Sullivan, Woollcott, and Deems Taylor, with frequent contributions by Parker, Ford, Lardner, Elinor Wylie, and numerous other members of Ross's circle. For a few brief years, the newspaper was a circle all into itself—in Swope's words, "an atmosphere as well as a specific product." But it *was* still a specific product, a daily newspaper, with an obligation to cover yesterday's baseball games and congressional actions and tomorrow's weather. It would be possible, Ross could see, to skim off the cream and serve it up weekly on glossy paper.

When he linked up with Fleischmann, Ross had already worked up a business plan and a mock edition, or "dummy," of his still unnamed weekly. The baker agreed to pony up $25,000, a figure that would increase manyfold over the next few years; Ross and Grant, according to different accounts, either matched that same amount or pitched in $20,000. Now a name was needed for the magazine, and after many bad or dull ideas, including *Manhattan, New York Life,* and *Our Town,* it was immediately clear that publicist John Peter Toohey's suggestion, *The New Yorker,* was a good one. To assuage Fleischmann's trepidations, Ross got ten of his cronies to agree to be listed as a wholly ceremonial "advisory board": Ralph Barton, Heywood Broun, Marc Connelly, Edna Ferber, Rea Irvin, George S. Kaufman, Alice Duer Miller, Dorothy Parker, playwright Lawrence Stallings, and Woollcott. Ross put their names on the bottom of a prospectus that he wrote and, in the fall of 1924, sent out to potential subscribers and investors. This is what it said:

> *The New Yorker* will be a reflection in word and picture of metropolitan life. It will be human. Its general tenor will be one of gaiety, wit and satire, but it will be more than a jester. It will not be what is commonly called highbrow or radical. It will be what is commonly called sophisticated, in that it will assume a reasonable degree of enlightenment on the part of its readers. It will hate bunk.
>
> As compared to the newspapers, *The New Yorker* will be interpretive rather than stenographic. It will print facts that it will have to go behind the scenes to get, but it will not deal in scandal for the sake of scandal nor sensation for the sake of sensation. Its integrity will be above suspicion. It hopes to be so entertaining and informative as to be a necessity for the person who knows his way about or wants to.
>
> *The New Yorker* will devote several pages a week to a covering of contemporary events and people of interest. This will be done by writers capable of appreciating the elements of a situation and, in setting them down, of indicating their importance and significance. *The New Yorker* will present the truth and the whole truth without fear and without favor, but it will not be iconoclastic.

Amusements and the arts will be thoroughly covered by departments which will present, in addition to criticism, the personality, the anecdote, the color and chat of the various subdivisions of this sphere. *The New Yorker's* conscientious guide will list each week all current amusement offerings worthwhile—theaters, motion pictures, musical events, art exhibitions, sport and miscellaneous entertainment—providing an ever-ready answer to the prevalent query, "What shall we do this evening?" Through *The New Yorker's* Mr. Van Bibber III, readers will be kept apprised of what is going on in the public and semi-public smart gathering places—the clubs, hotels, cafes, supper clubs, cabarets and other resorts.

Judgment will be passed upon new books of consequence, and *The New Yorker* will carry a list of the season's books which it considers worth reading.

There will be a page of editorial paragraphs, commenting on the week's events in a manner not too serious.

There will be a personal mention column—a jotting down in the small-town newspaper style of the comings, goings and doings in the village of New York. This will contain some josh and some news value.

The New Yorker will carry each week several pages of prose and verse, short and long, humorous, satirical and miscellaneous.

The New Yorker expects to be distinguished for its illustrations, which will include caricatures, sketches, cartoons and humorous and satirical drawings in keeping with its purpose.

The New Yorker will be the magazine which is not edited for the old lady in Dubuque. It will not be concerned in what she is thinking about. This is not meant in disrespect, but *The New Yorker* is a magazine avowedly published for a metropolitan audience and thereby will escape an influence which hampers most national publications. It expects a considerable national circulation, but this will come from persons who have a metropolitan interest.

In August 1924, Ross quit his job at *Judge,* and he and Fleischmann took small offices on West Forty-fifth Street, which was in the very center of the emerging print capital. (The *Smart Set* and *Saturday Review* were in the same building, *Judge* and the *New York Times* were on West Forty-third, *Vanity Fair* on West Forty-fourth. Among book publishers, the Modern Library was on West Forty-fifth Street, Boni & Liveright on West Forty-eighth, and Charles Scribner's Sons on nearby Fifth Avenue.) They hired a skeleton staff, just two or three men each on the editorial and business sides. Contributions were solicited and received from Round Table associates of Ross's including Woollcott, Dorothy Parker, and Herman Mankiewicz. FPA agreed to come in a day or so a week to choose the light verse. A *New York Times* reporter named Elmer Davis suggested Caslon as the typeface for the text. Most important, Rea Irvin, a San Francisco native who had been art director of

Life until the previous year, signed on as art consultant and designer. He contributed the layout and the headline type (known ever after as Irvin type), as well as the cover of the first issue, dated February 21, 1925, which depicted an early-nineteenth-century fop in a high collar and top hat, peering superciliously through a monocle at a green-spotted butterfly. On the top of the first editorial page, Irvin designed a logo depicting a stylized New York skyline, flanked on one side by the fop from the cover, quill pen and manuscript paper in hand, and on the other by a winking owl. Odd juxtapositions all, but they seemed successfully to invoke the sophistication, lightness, and urbanity Ross was aiming for.

The response to that first issue was not overwhelming, however. In "The Diary of Our Own Samuel Pepys," FPA gave it a single, uncharacteristically critical sentence: "So to H. Ross's, and he shewed me a copy of *The New Yorker*, which is to be issued on Tuesday, but most of it seemed too frothy for my liking." (Adams himself had contributed an extremely frothy humorous exercise called "Short-Story Scenarios.") *Time* magazine purported to have solicited the reaction of an old lady in Dubuque—Ross's proposal and a sentence in the issue both having noted that the magazine was not edited for her—who supposedly responded, "The editors of the periodical you forwarded are, I understand, members of a literary clique. They should learn that there is no provincialism so blatant as that of the metropolitan who lacks urbanity."* George Horace Lorimer, editor of the *Saturday Evening Post,* told Jane Grant the first issue upset him so much that he threw it across the room.

But readers seemed to be willing to give the weekly at least a chance. A form letter that went out to contributors reported, "The first issue virtually sold out in New York City in the first thirty-six hours and we were as surprised as the next one." The print run was increased from thirty thousand to forty thousand. According to a similar letter two weeks later, "High per centage of sale reported but no definite figures."

Even so, Ross—as he would later say in a very different context—was encouraged to go on.

---

*The article was actually written by Fillmore Hyde, whom Ross would later hire as a staff writer.

CHAPTER TWO

HARD QUESTIONS
1925~31

"A MAN IN A CANEBRAKE"

In the July 19, 1930, issue of the *New Yorker*, an article appeared under the title "Answers-to-Hard-Questions Department." It began this way:

> To the Editors of THE NEW YORKER
> Sirs:
>   Recently we have received a number of requests from our readers concerning the exact editorial requirements of THE NEW YORKER. May we have an article from you concerning this and any other information which you may care to include?
>   *Yours sincerely,*
>   THE WRITER'S DIGEST. *A Journal for Ambitious Literary Folk.*

Readers accustomed to magazines other than the *New Yorker* would have found this odd. Typical magazines did not generally publish their business correspondence—as the request from the *Writer's Digest* appeared to be—and they put conventional letters to the editor in a section so designated. In the five years and five months of its existence, the *New Yorker* had never had such a section. The early months of the magazine were so improvisationally chaotic that the most likely initial reason for the failure of Ross and his revolving-door staff to institute one was that it slipped their minds. As the magazine stabilized, prospered, and developed a strong identity as a "sophisticated" voice of the urban and urbane, the idea did come up for discussion. In the early thirties, E. B. White, by then established as the writer of Notes and Comment—the first paragraphs in every week's issue—asked Ross in a memo, "Why don't we make more of a thing of the letters we get? I love to read published letters—nutty, serious, inflamed, dumb—any kind, almost, if amusing." Ross wrote back, the same day, "We don't get any good letters. . . . I suspect that our audience is more blasé and diffident than that of any other magazine and that, therefore, we get fewer letters."

This was not, strictly speaking, true. The magazine actually received a great deal of mail from readers who wanted to commend or take issue with what had been published, point out errors, or merely to say, as a correspondent did in 1928, "What a satisfaction to know a magazine like the *New Yorker* is being published weekly! I have all my secret joys and dreams about New York that I do not talk to anyone about. Yet, why should I. The *New Yorker* writes about them just as I see them. Oh! Source of boundless delight that the *New Yorker* gives to me. Without it my life would lack seasoning." The real reason the *New Yorker* didn't establish a letter page, it would appear in retrospect, is that it had never *had* a letters page. The magazine, as Ross was beginning to define it, would be constitutionally resistant to certain kinds of change.

Within a year of its founding, the look, the editorial and graphic components, and the feel of the magazine would be more or less in place; after that virtually any alteration or innovation would be made *within* those constraints. An example is the magazine's custom of placing author credits at the end rather than the beginning of articles. At the outset, it made perfect sense. To begin with, most of the bylines were initials or pseudonyms anyway, since the authors were New York newspaper and magazine staff members who couldn't be seen contributing to an upstart competitor. Also, the convention sounded a subtle but sure echo of one of the *New Yorker's* most important models, *Punch*. And finally, since few of the articles were more than one page long and none was more than two, a reader embarking on one could discern the byline with merely a glance to the right. Quickly, the *New Yorker* acquired a stable of its own writers who were happy to sign their names; quickly, the emotional and thematic range of its contents strikingly broadened; quickly, the articles got much longer. A move of the authors' names to the beginning of the pieces gathered a more and more powerful logic, and Raoul Fleischmann, who had served as publisher of the magazine from the start, eventually suggested it to Ross, remarking, "Quite a few readers find it a source of irritation to search for the name, because after all many readers do not go through the book 'from cover to cover' but just read the articles by people they know and like. Furthermore, we have good pieces by good authors and it seems to me we hide too much beneath the bushel." The editor replied:

> I am violently against any such change. I think it would be a foolish mistake, would violently impair the whole personality of the magazine. I don't think there is any argument in favor of it whatsoever. I have noticed lately

considerable interest in several such radical proposals. I am against them all. My definite conviction is this: the format of *The New Yorker* is all right; it's been adequately proven all right by several years of signal success. All attempts to "high power" the magazine ought to be kicked in the teeth.

Of course, the inconvenience for readers of having to hunt for authors' names—more pronounced as articles grew to five pages, then ten, and then longer—could have been assuaged by the institution of a table of contents, a feature of almost all other magazines. Fleischmann for years advocated doing so, but got nowhere even after Ross's death in 1952, when William Shawn became editor. Fleischmann wrote to a semiretired editor in 1961, "I would be *delighted* if you and maybe a couple of your influential pals could persuade that little devil—pardon me, little angel—to put in an index. I am sure it would help a good deal because there are lots of things that our steady readers want to read, but when they get a 60 or 70 page Fact piece . . . they are liable to get bored with the whole thing and say the hell with it, and throw the magazine across the room." Finally, in 1969—forty-five years after its founding—the magazine began printing a table of contents, and even then it was a controversial move.

To be sure, there was logic as well as tradition to the *New Yorker*'s surface inscrutability. Ross had a newsman's conception of the magazine as somehow transcending the individuals who contributed to it. In his years of writing Notes and Comment, White frequently chafed at the anonymity of the style it had developed and once, in 1935, suggested it be extracted from The Talk of the Town to stand alone as a signed column. Ross, not surprisingly, disagreed, writing White, "I think . . . your page is stronger anonymous, as an expression of an institution, rather than an individual. I feel this very strongly. I feel that the strength of the *New Yorker* is largely that strength." The institutional voice of Notes and Comment and The Talk of the Town expressed itself in the first-person plural: as *we*. The logic to this convention lay in the conceit that the section was written by "The New Yorkers," who "signed" it at the end. That tag line was dropped in 1934, but *we* stayed around until 1992, when Tina Brown arrived as editor. (In the same 1935 memo to White, Ross addressed the issue of printing a masthead, or a list of significant editors, as virtually all other magazines did: "The reason such a list was never run in the early days of the magazine was, first, there were no proven editors; second, I was encouraging people to write for a magazine that used pseudonyms and initials, signed pieces at the bottom, and didn't play up writers in any way; and, third, because I wanted to avoid a great mass of mail coming in here addressed to me." Now, remarkably enough, Ross professed himself willing to institute a masthead "if there is any popular support for same." Apparently there was not: as of 1999, there was still no masthead in the *New Yorker*.)

But the conservatism of the *New Yorker* was in large part superficial—not surprising given that Ross himself had drifted from job to job, from city to city, in the first thirty-three years of his life and was now putting out a magazine named after and purporting to represent a city in the midst of dizzyingly momentous social, cultural, and economic shifts. In the first few years, readers could never be sure whom or what they would encounter in the magazine's pages: in its ten months of publication in 1925, no fewer than 282 individuals—not including artists—had at least one contribution in the magazine. Nor was there any certainty as to who would be occupying the editorial offices. Ross went through subeditors at a furious pace, being especially manic in his quest for a managing editor who could administer some order to the chaos he seemed to need to perceive. Ross's obsessive hiring and firing of these men soon became a staff joke; the current incumbent was known as the latest "genius," eventually corrupted to "jesus." Looking back years later, Wolcott Gibbs, a fiction editor and prolific contributor who wisely resisted any suggestion by Ross that he sit in the genius chair, could name twenty-two different people, including Ralph Ingersoll, James Thurber, Ogden Nash, and James M. Cain, who in just the first dozen years of the magazine's existence had made the mistake of accepting. Ross was, at least, capable of gently mocking his tendencies. When one candidate accepted a position but asked for a delay in starting work, Ross wrote to him, "Briefly, all right, with this considerable reservation: If some boy wonder comes along in the next half hour he will have his whirl at the job."

A young writer named Robert Coates was hired as a part-time Talk of the Town reporter in 1928 and went on to write short stories, art criticism, and more words for the magazine than anyone else, with the possible exception of White and Gibbs. Decades later, he recalled that on the day he met Ross, workers were tearing down partitions in the *New Yorker's* original offices on West Forty-fifth Street. This was hardly an unusual occurrence. They went up and down so often that James Thurber, also a Talk writer at the time and later a prodigious contributor of humorous pieces, put up a sign that said, "Alterations going on as usual during business." Coates found all the construction "symbolic":

> Those early days represented a period of experimentation and change, and for some time thereafter not only partitions but editors and just about everything else came and went or were shifted about almost constantly. We used to joke about it at the time, as another evidence of Ross's restlessness, but as I see it now, something deeper was involved. Ross, I think, had begun with a certain ideal of his magazine—and a wholly new kind of magazine, at that—fairly clearly fixed in his mind. The image was clear, but it was distant and meanwhile, and in between, there were all the thousands of technicalities

involved in putting out a weekly illustrated magazine . . . on time. In that sense, Ross's sudden changes of plan and direction were like the chargings-about of a man in a canebrake, trying blindly to get through to the clearer ground he is certain must lie beyond.

The chaos was salutary, for as late as 1930, when it printed the "Hard Question" from *Writer's Digtest*, the *New Yorker* was still—sometimes clumsily, sometimes decisively, sometimes haphazardly—constructing an identity. In Coates's terminology, Ross and his associates were still charging blindly about, trying to get to the clearing they knew lay just ahead. They frequently found it convenient or helpful to conduct their navigation in the

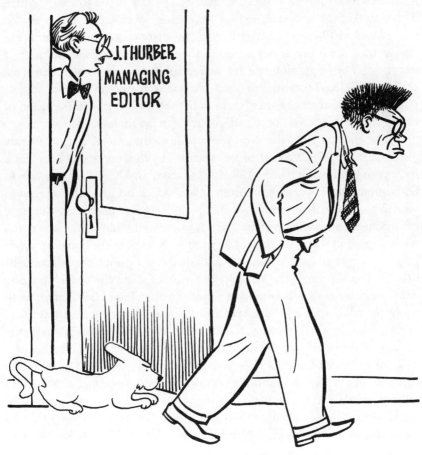

For six painful months in 1927, James Thurber was one of the "geniuses" Ross charged with bringing administrative order to the *New Yorker*. In this unpublished drawing, Carl Rose evokes a sense of what the disaster felt like. Note the Thurber dog at lower left.

very pages of the magazine. The result was a roving and determined self-consciousness in the *New Yorker*. In addition to stories, sketches, humorous pieces, journalistic articles and profiles, cartoons, and reviews, its readers could find a running commentary on and sometimes dialogue about the magazine itself. The reflex gave rise to the not unjust charge that the *New Yorker* could be precious or cute. But what Ross and his colleagues were doing was hanging up a series of mirrors in the hallway of the magazine's childhood and early adolescence, hoping to catch from time to time an accurate and becoming reflection.

The process began in the very first issue, dated February 21, 1925, in the opening section, a collection of paragraphs titled "Of All Things" (the designation would soon be dropped in favor of The Talk of the Town), in which THE NEW YORKER is mentioned no fewer than seven times, the reiterated capped and small-capped letters having the effect of presenting the magazine as no less worthy of our attention than were the ostensible subjects of its articles. The impression was intensified the following week, when most of "Of All Things" consisted of a self-critique of the premiere issue, regretting, among other things, that "there didn't seem to be much indication of purpose and we felt sort of naked in our apparent aimlessness."

A few months later, the *New Yorker* printed the first of twenty weekly installments of "The Making of a Magazine," by the humorist Corey Ford. Ross commissioned it, Ford recalled in his memoir, *The Time of Laughter*, to fill "a gaping hole on the inside front cover," which no advertiser seemed to be willing to buy; Ross remembered hoping the series "would take the curse of smallness out of the magazine, which was awfully thin then." But Ford's work so pleased Ross that he kept it going in the back of the book even after page two began to be sold and later published it as a pamphlet with the subtitle "A Tour Through the Vast Organization of *The New Yorker*." Writing it in the manner of a boosterish company report, Ford constructed, week by week, a facetious and wholly fictional origin, history, and business and editorial profile for a magazine referred to as *The New Yorker*. Here, the process of definition was by negation: the magazine in "The Making of a Magazine" was all the things the actual *New Yorker* was *not*. (On the other hand, the series was an uncannily accurate *predictive* satire of the imperious self-congratulation found in Henry Luce's eventual magazine empire, in which *Time*, two years old in 1925, would soon be joined by *Fortune* and a new *Life*.) In one installment, "Securing Paper for the New Yorker," Ford—gently mocking Ross's already apparent predilection for statistics and facts—wrote, "In order to realize the number of trees which must be felled each week, for one issue of THE NEW YORKER, the reader should try to visualize a vast forest of 8,657,000 trees, or sufficient trees when divided by 10 to equal 865,700 trees. In other words, if the reader will picture one tree, and then multiply that tree by 10% of 86,570,000 trees, he may perhaps form some idea of how many trees 8,657,000 trees are. It is typical of the great New Yorker organization, that it owns and operates today the biggest paper forest in the world, covering 29,000,000 or so acres in Canada, Maine, and northern New Jersey, under the close supervision of The New Yorker's field superintendent, Mr. Eustace Tilley." Tilley was the name Ford gave to the top-hatted fop with a monocle who had occupied the first issue's cover. It caught on, and soon there were bountiful Tilley references inside the magazine—including pieces supposedly written *by* Tilley—and outside it.

A thin magazine with few ads is a magazine in financial trouble, and the *New Yorker* went through some tough times in the spring and summer of its first year. One day in April, Karl Kitchen's popular *Evening World* column, "Mr. Manhattan," began, "I found Mr. Manhattan reading the latest issue of 'The Gothamite' when I dropped in at his apartment yesterday afternoon.

" 'So you're the one who bought the copy,' I said as I helped myself to a proferred cigaret."

Mr. Manhattan goes on to predict that *The Gothamite*—unmistakably the *New Yorker*—is doomed to fail because its backers did not get the support of "the Bellwethers of Broadway"—the ninety-five men and women who "set the tempo and make the pace."* By the end of the summer, this prediction seemed about to come true, as circulation was just twelve thousand and some issues were only twenty-five pages long, with three and a half pages of ads—which, at a rate of $150 per page, did not make for much revenue. At one point Fleischmann came close to folding. His decision to persist was vindicated in the fall, when advertising and circulation both rebounded, a turnaround traditionally linked with the publicity garnered by an anti–High Society *New Yorker* article by Ellin Mackay, daughter of the mining heir, philanthropist, and pillar of society Clarence Mackay. Equally significant was that the magazine rolled out an extensive and effective advertising campaign for the first time.

Naturally, the magazine chronicled its own financial fortunes, as in this Comment item from November: "Observed on the elevated newsstand at Forty-second Street was The New Yorker prominently displayed between *True* and *Snappy Stories*. This, says the circulation manager, is very, very good

---

*Mr. Manhattan's interlocutor goes on to protest that "the founders of 'The Gothamite' are among the best known log rollers in town."

"I'm coming to that," said my host, lighting another cigaret. "Log rolling in New York is an old story. It's firmly entrenched and recognized as quite the usual thing. But it is not enough for one clique of New Yorkers to roll the logs among themselves. That doesn't get them anywhere. . . . The trouble with 'The Gothamite' is that the members of its group of writers only boost each other. And that's why they never have got and never will get very far. For in New York, Oswald, if you want to break through to important money, you've got to get a gang."

news. Suicide Day for sincere member of the staff has been set for next Tuesday."

In the public mind, even more strongly associated with the *New Yorker* than Eustace Tilley was a line from Ross's 1924 prospectus: "The *New Yorker* will be the magazine which is not edited for the old lady in Dubuque."* The force and speed with which the phrase entered the general consciousness suggests that Ross could have been as successful an advertising man as he was a magazine editor. Indeed, the advertisement for the first issue of the *New Yorker* in two newspapers, the *World* and the *Herald Tribune,* prominently featured the phrase. The *New Yorker's* competitor, and Ross's previous employer, *Judge* magazine noted the launch of its new competitor with an item in a regular column: "Judge Wants to Know . . . IF the *New Yorker* is going to be edited for the old lady in the Algonquin?" Ads (in the *New Yorker*) for John Gunther's 1927 novel, *The Red Pavilion,* declared that *it* was not for the old lady from Dubuque. Needless to say, the *New Yorker* itself was not shy about joining in. Reviewing a novel called *Cover Charge,* an anonymous critic professed to be "far less certain than Mother Dubuque would be that it's just your dish, as a NEW YORKER reader, in the line of Night Life fiction."

The richest vein of reflexive commentary flowed through Newsbreaks, those little reprints of comical solecisms, gaucheries, or typos (along with someone's—usually White's—droll response) that filled space at the end of columns. *Life* and *Judge* had long used fillers, but these were invariably of the "gag" type—sometimes original, sometimes picked up from other publications—that went over big in Dubuque and were despised as hopelessly corny by Ross: "Blackmailing them, is he?" "Yes, he has a skeleton key to the closet." Ross outlined his notion of his version in a form letter that went to all contributors after the magazine had been out for a month: "We have in mind a department of bunk, blah, etc. interesting newspaper headlines, super-unctuous press agent announcements, typographical errors, etc." Their first appearance was in the March 21, 1925, issue, where they were lumped together in one page, as in the "Americana" section of Mencken's

---

*The small, landlocked city thus contrasted with the *New Yorker's* "metropolitan" approach was not chosen out of a hat. Edmund Wilson, subsequently the *New Yorker's* book critic and in the twenties a staff member at Frank Crowninshield's *Vanity Fair,* recalled years later in a letter to James Thurber, "Crowninshield used to say, when confronted with something that he feared was too esoteric: 'Remember, there's an old lady sitting in Dubuque, and she has to be able to understand everything we print.' I do not think he invented this idea: he did not really take it seriously, treated it as more or less of a joke. I thought it was some old cliché of New York editorial offices. The slogan of *The New Yorker*—that it was *not* intended for the old lady in Dubuque—was, I think, simply a defiance of this cliché." Crowninshield may have taken the figure of speech from Bert Leston Taylor, who, as "B.L.T.," wrote a column called "A Line o Type or Two" for the *Chicago Tribune* from 1909 to 1921.

American Mercury. They soon found their rightful place at the bottom of columns. In 1926, they found their poet, in White, who commented a decade later, "I still regard newsbreaks as the thing I came to earth for," and continued to produce them into the 1970s. When the *New Yorker* was still formless and in flux, Newsbreaks were its perfect manifestation, not only because of White's genius, but because they took the most difficult creative questions off the table. In the prospectus, Ross had written that the *New Yorker* would "hate bunk"; but publishing bunk-free humor was an extremely tricky and daunting endeavor. Certainly, puns and other word-play, and anything else that hinted however faintly of the cracker barrel or the poke in the ribs, were out. They constituted the "influence which hampers most national publications" cited and rejected by Ross in the prospectus. What the Newsbreaks shared with the other immediately successful component of the magazine, the captioned cartoons, was humor flowing wholly from *others'* blunders, gaucheries, or inadvertent self-revelations. This sardonically mimetic stance was the first and perhaps the most important element of the *New Yorker's* "sophistication." The Newsbreaks and the cartoons subtly but surely fed a sense of superiority on the part of readers, and from the start the *New Yorker's* appeal to many was a clubby sense of not so much social but verbal privilege: to belong, you had to "get" the jokes, and they were not always self-evident. It was not just a stylistic affectation that The Talk of the Town should be written in the first-person plural; there *was* a "we," and they knew who they were. Sometimes this attitude became explicit. An unsigned 1926 review of a biography of George Washington takes the author to task for iconoclasm, observing that "because heroes aren't worshipped anymore, we are all very skeptical about them. On reflection, the population is not entirely composed of—well, readers of THE NEW YORKER." The Newsbreaks, in any case, were taken to so rapidly and enthusiastically that, unsolicited, readers began inundating the office with the clippings that served as raw material for White's comebacks and headings. In 1930, Ross wrote to a contributor, "There is no limit to the supply that comes in here. They arrive by the hundreds—by the thousands, I guess."

It did not take long for the *New Yorker* to start printing Newsbreaks about the *New Yorker*, preceded by the heading GO CLIMB A TREE DEPARTMENT (if negative), HOOPLA DEPARTMENT (if positive), or OUR PSHAW DEPARTMENT (if concerning a *New Yorker* error), or followed by White's comment. One quoted a lecture at Yale by Professor William Lyons Phelps: "Many people would rather read the *New Yorker* than they would *Hamlet*. They think it wittier, you know." The comment: "Oh, we're not out to kill Shakespeare." The self-consciousness went a step further when Newsbreaks started to quote the *New Yorker* itself, as in this one from 1927:

OUR PSHAW DEPARTMENT

It is, to say the least, an unusual composition, scored for eleven mechanical pianos, one of them mechanical.—*The New Yorker*

So many people have told us that that sentence didn't make sense, that we are getting round to the opinion ourself.

Another took the rather remarkable step of poking fun at a *New Yorker* advertisement that had talked of prices being $25 "and forward" ("Forward like a kite," White wrote).*

Another form that had almost no chance of being bunk was parody, which in the hands of writers such as Donald Ogden Stewart and Corey Ford was already going through a small renaissance in the early and mid-1920s. It was no surprise that the *New Yorker* would successfully and adeptly join in. What was rather remarkable, and perhaps unprecedented, was its decision to print a parody of *itself.* The Talk of the Town evolved over the years from a collection of arch paragraphs to a series of short journalistic articles that consisted of, took pleasure in, and frequently wrought humor presenting many facts about a person, place, thing, or phenomenon. At times (generally when they overdid the first-person plural), Talk pieces flirted dangerously with preciousness. For example, here is the first paragraph of a 1931 Talk piece called "No. 1 Man":

Whether you believe what they say or not, somebody has to paint those big signboards on Broadway. Usually Mr. Gus Palmer does, because he is No. 1 staff artist of the General Outdoor Advertising Company, and the most outdoorsy artist alive. He painted the Camel Cigarette ladies with the seven-foot foreheads and the thirty-six-inch mouths, and he painted the Kellogg Corn Flakes kiddy with the forty-two-foot brow. We have found out, by the simple process of asking, how he does it.

---

*Not too many years later, when the *New Yorker* had begun to occupy a position in the culture such that the mere mention of it in a work of fiction or journalism could invoke any one of a number of things, the GO CLIMB A TREE DEPARTMENT took frequent note. For example:

[*From* The Liberals *by John Hyde Preston*]
Their home was general headquarters for ... not-so-young ladies who had bright eyes for anything that could be reduced to the level of *The New Yorker.*

[*From "A Sea Island Lady," by Francis Griswold*]
He glanced through *The New Yorker,* hoping for a slight touch of nostalgia, but all it had was a stale flat taste, like a morning-after living-room glutted with ashtrays and dead glasses.

Less than three months later, the *New Yorker* printed an accurate, cutting, and funny takeoff on the form, "Cloth Collector," by Archibald Pyne, which appeared with the bracketed preface, "This article, originally intended for the 'Talk of the Town' Department, had to be used elsewhere, on account of differences of opinion and ill-feeling among the editors." It began, "As you probably know, all the weatherstripping for children's dollhouses is done by a Mr. Josepy. Mr. Josepy was born in Germany, came here when he was two, went back, came back here again, returned home once more, and is now back." A later sentence was "Incidentally, Mr. Josepy is not half so interesting as Karl L. ('Rabbit') Hutches, who is more than twice as interesting."

The advertisements in the *New Yorker* frequently mentioned the *New Yorker*. An ad for the Paramount announced itself as "The *New Yorker's* Favorite Theater." A footnote explained that what was meant was "The *New Yorker's*, not *The* New Yorker's." And a fur-storage concern actually reprinted the Talk of the Town logo and an item from this section that had dryly complained of the difficulties of storing woolens, supplemented by its rejoinder. The spots for Lewis and Conger, a department store, introduced a character named Aunt Prue, who, they explained, "is not the Old Lady from Dubuque."*

Letters to the editor are the easiest way a magazine can drag itself into its pages' discourse, and this very quality was another likely reason Ross resisted a letters page. That would have lumped them together in a kind of gray holding pen. Instead, with increasing frequency, a selected item would be plucked out of the mailbag, buffed up, and—the better to further the definition process—displayed under its own mock-official heading, such as "Our Disillusioned Readers," "Department of Amplification," "We Stand Corrected" (for letters pointing out errors), or "Our Captious Readers." Under the last, on March 13, 1926, there appeared this:

THE NEW YORKER.

GENTLEMEN:

Very seldomly, let me assure you, am I goaded into the undignified position of writing to a magazine. On the other hand, it is even seldomlier that a magazine takes the trouble to attack me personally but when it does so, I fight.

---

*Perhaps because cartoons were so quickly recognized as working so well, they were understood to be off-limits to what Ross called "intramural" references; the *New Yorker* did not print a cartoon that referred in any way to the *New Yorker* until 1992. Ross himself was similarly protected. In 1932, when Frank Sullivan was putting together the first "Greetings, Friends" annual Christmas poem in which several dozen prominent names would be rhymed together, Wolcott Gibbs warned him to leave Ross out because he "could not bear to be mentioned." In fact, Ross's name did not appear anywhere in the magazine until White's obituary of him in 1951.

Granted that you have the right to be pleased with yourselves, you nevertheless have taken and are still taking an unwarranted step in your nauseating advertising campaign, particularly in the theatre programs. That smart New Yorkers read your confounded paper may be true. But why imply that decent people would become smart if they read it? Dammit, I read it. And I am a bootlegger. And practically all bootleggers and others with a sense of humor read it.

Accept my sincerest expressions of disgust. THE NEW YORKER is not smart. Please have the decency to cease from accusing the honest people who support your senseless waggery with their good cash of vices they don't possess. We may not be perfect but God knows we aren't smart.

So there,

RYE FACE*

The 1930 letter from *Writer's Digest* was placed in the "Answers-to-Hard-Questions Department," a heading designed for certain incoming letters that actually requested an answer, followed by a humorous response. The striking thing about the answer given to the *Writer's Digest* in July 1930, once you looked beyond some arch wording and absurd examples, was how serious it was. The continual self-reference of the last five and half years had not led the magazine to a clear and complete sense of exactly what its editorial requirements were; in fact, the letter arrived at a time when the magazine was clearly being pulled in several different and possibly mutually exclusive directions. For half a decade, a number of factors had allowed it to survive its contradictions and even thrive despite them—starting with the excitement of a launch, and the staff's and contributors' delight at their own cleverness. In some handwritten notes White scribbled decades later for a book he briefly considered writing about the *New Yorker*, he commented, "Ross started mag. more *in contempt* of what was being published than with any

---

*The relevant definition of *smart* in the *OED* is "fashionable, elegant, especially in a very high degree. (Common in recent use, from *c* 1882.)" The dictionary goes on to note, "The reappearance of the word in this sense was the subject of much comment in criticism in newspapers, etc., from about 1885, and the phrases *smart people, smart society, the smart set,* etc., have been commonly used as a general designation for the extremely fashionable portion of society (sometimes with the implication of being a little 'fast')." *The Smart Set: The Magazine of Cleverness* was founded in 1900, coedited by H. L. Mencken and George Jean Nathan from 1914 to 1923, and was a significant precursor to the *New Yorker*. But another definition of *smart,* as a synonym for *intelligent,* was also in wide usage when "Rye Face" wrote his letter. Would the *New Yorker* prove to be smart in either sense of the term, and if so would that mitigate against its "senseless waggery" and make it less palatable to readers with a "sense of humor"? In 1926, the question was open.

notion of how to improve it"; merely being contrary was good for a few years' momentum as well. And, of course, Ross created a further diversion by fiddling with administrative flow charts and office floor plans.

But now there was a sense of being at an impasse. Katharine White, who as Katharine Angell had been hired as a manuscript reader in 1925 and by the time of her marriage to E. B. White was chief literary editor of the magazine, tried to alert Ross to the gravity of the problem in a 1931 memo:

> What the magazine needs more than an organization of routing and track-keeping red tape is ideas, discussions, a getting together of the people who write the magazine and think about what should go in it. I still harbor the illusion I have every time I go away, that the scattered and now wandering nucleus of people you once had working excitedly over ideas that would be good on a certain week, can be called together and revivified and set working on the old basis again.

She wrote as if the golden-age "nucleus" had scattered to the four corners of the earth. But except for Ralph Ingersoll, an early jesus who did much to shape the content and character of The Talk of the Town but had left in 1930 to join Henry Luce's business magazine, *Fortune* (and would later found the newspaper *PM*), they were all still on the premises. In fact, they comprised the editorial heart, soul, mind, and conscience of the magazine. Besides herself, her husband, and Ross, she mentioned Wolcott Gibbs and James Thurber, an Ohioan who had joined the staff in 1927 and, after a brief and even more unsuccessful than usual tenure as managing editor, had become the principal Talk of the Town rewrite man and a prolific writer of humorous essays, sketches, and stories. The quintet, whose sensibilities were otherwise wildly dissimilar, had two things in common: uncommon intelligence and a visceral abhorrence of anything that suggested the reflexively modish, the cornball, or the clichéd. This, again, was fine to start out. But now even the nucleus of five was pulling the *New Yorker* in divergent directions.

Gibbs was the *New Yorker*'s jack-of-all-trades, and it fell to him to compose the reply to the *Writer's Digest* question, it was signed "Mr. Winterbottom (for THE NEW YORKER)." But this task was beyond him. After some facetious throat-clearing, he admitted, "At best my message to your subscribers will have to be more or less negative. I myself have only the vaguest idea what sort of manuscripts THE NEW YORKER wants. I have, however, a pretty clear idea what it *doesn't* want, and I take great pleasure in passing this information . . . along." The list included "epigrams . . . jokes, pointed paragraphs, quips from the shoulder, etc." Also, "there is a certain detachment here about fables, parables, and philosophic conversations among the illustrious dead. An editor, opening a manuscript and encountering the phrase, 'The scene is in heaven,' or observing that it is concerned with characters called 'Mr. Wiseman' or 'Miss 1930,' *always* puts on his hat and goes out to lunch. In this con-nection I might also observe that, for THE NEW YORKER's purpose, funny names do not make funny stories, and the above procedure is also followed in the case of manuscripts dealing with people called Joe Boopus or Miss Glitch." (No mention was made of Mr. Winterbottom or Eustace Tilley.)

That was the easy part. What the *New Yorker* did *not* want was the sort of material that could appear in *Life* or *Judge* or the *Saturday Evening Post*. But neither Mr. Winterbottom nor anyone else could say exactly what *would* meet with approval. The hardest, still unresolved, question had to do with seriousness and humor. In the second issue's critique of the first one, some-one (probably Ross) wrote, "We were astonished and alarmed as much as anybody else at the tone of levity and farce that seemed to pervade it and we hadn't intended it to look so much like *Judge* and *Life*. . . . Above all we don't want to be taken as a humorous magazine." But that was precisely what it was universally and unanimously taken for for the first half dozen years—and, for many people, until World War II. Almost from the start, per-ception and reality clashed, as some elements of the magazine, notably White's Notes and Comment and the Reporter at Large dispatches of a former newspaperman named Morris Markey, were informed by an unmis-takable underlying seriousness. The outsize talent and ambition of the edi-tors and contributors, the growing sense (starting with the stock crash of October 1929) that the economic good times of the twenties were at an end, the mere passage of time—all these factors made it harder to suppress the impulses toward gravity, art, and significance that kept welling up.

The first time the magazine purposefully acted on them was in 1928, when the then Katharine Angell wrote letters to short-story writers asking them to submit serious fiction, resulting in stories by Morley Callaghan, Louise Bogan, Sally Benson, and Kay Boyle that were wholly lacking in lev-ity. The next year Angell began to solicit "serious" poets, who were some-times taken aback upon hearing from her. William Carlos Williams responded, "Really I didn't know that *The New Yorker* was interested in poetry as poetry." Someone more in the *New Yorker's* traditional line was Grace Hazard Conkling, a Smith College professor described in *The Oxford Companion to American Literature* as being "known for her gentle nature poetry." But the magazine's shifts in direction wrong-footed her. Explaining her recent lack of submissions, Conkling wrote to Katharine Angell in 1929, "One feels a certain quality in the *New Yorker* whether its verse or prose: I find it a little baffling. I could not define it, and it is difficult to write with the magazine in mind."

The editors sometimes seemed baffled, too. Mrs. White's groping rejec-tion of a 1929 Callaghan story, "In the Charming City," displays the general uncertainty:

It is very difficult for me to write you about this last story of yours.... It is a most striking and interesting story and it has aroused great dissension in this office. We want fiction and we want short stories, and yet when it comes right down to it Mr. Ross feels that the short stories we use have to be quite special in type—*New Yorker*-ish—if that word means anything to you, and he fears that this is not just the short story we could publish, perhaps because it is not this way.

Even Mr. Winterbottom had only one thing to say about serious fiction, which was essentially that the magazine would not publish latter-day O. Henrys: "THE NEW YORKER does not favor what is known as the 'surprise' ending. Final paragraphs in which a character, previously unidentified, suddenly turns out to be a water spaniel, or a child, or President Hoover, do not surprise the editors."

He concluded: "While the above summary does not pretend to be exhaustive, I feel that it ought to give your readers at least a general idea of the sort of material that is *not* suitable for THE NEW YORKER. What *is* suitable, as I said before, is another and far more intricate matter. My own feeling is that, even if I knew, I would be doing your readers a poor service by telling them. Life would be a pretty dull business without a certain amount of struggle. At least it seems that way to me."*

SOPHISTICATION, NEW YORK, CLASS, TALK

But the magazine's sense of uncertainty was about to be resolved. By 1934, its tenth year of publication, the *New Yorker* was a fixture on the American literary and cultural landscape, a periodical whose graphic and verbal humor, fiction, and journalism were not only universally deemed outstanding but

---

*It goes without saying that no one on the *New Yorker* sent a reply directly to the *Writer's Digest*. Three years later, this Newsbreak appeared in the *New Yorker*:

> The New Yorker, 25 West 45th Street, New York. Read by persons who consider themselves superior to the riff-raff.—*Writer's Digest*
> Many of them not without reason.

It is worth noting that Gibbs's negative definition of the *New Yorker's* requirements was shared by one of its prolific contributors. John O'Hara's brother, Tom, was an aspiring writer, and in 1932 O'Hara gave him some advice on how to break into the *New Yorker*.

"Don't bother sending them anything that mentions the name of a celebrity, like F.P.A.; don't send them anything pertaining to journalism or advertising, no Greenwich Village stuff, nothing with a trick ending. . . . Be careful not to send them anything too long, and don't send them too many pieces. Write every day, if you can, and send *The New Yorker* your best. (I'm a swell one to talk, who just got back two pieces.)"

were absolutely singular and undeniably all of a piece. That year, former editor Ralph Ingersoll wrote for his current employer, *Fortune,* a long article that put the *New Yorker* in the national consciousness for the first time. In it he declared Ross and the other editors had done "a magnificent job. The *New Yorker* has changed the wit of a generation. . . . With its delicately barbed quill, it has battled nobly if ineffectively with a world that is far from perfection." And in fact, if the *New Yorker* has had a golden age, it was the decade preceding Pearl Harbor—a time in its history when it was poised gracefully between the formless and sometimes brittle levity that came before and the unquestionably meritorious, occasionally splendid, but frequently solemn, ponderous, self-important, or dull magazine that stretched from the Second World War on up to the 1980s. The way it took shape in the early thirties was not merely a matter of happenstance or luck, but rather was an organic process. Looked at in retrospect, it seems inevitable. It was not.

A short list of elements of continuity marked the *New Yorker* from its conception in Ross's and Grant's heads, through its dicey infancy, to its triumphant adolescence. One was a word: *sophisticated.* Ross had written in the prospectus that the magazine would "be what is commonly called sophisticated, in that it will assume a reasonable degree of enlightenment on the part of its readers," but that could not explain the utter predictability with which the adjective and its variants were invoked in outside references to the magazine in the first two decades of its existence (and not infrequently after that). In 1932, Gilbert Seldes called the *New Yorker* "the semi-official organ of sophistication." The next year, a *Vanity Fair* article about humorous magazines called the *New Yorker* sophisticated in two sentences in a row. When the word was used in a critique of a Benchley theater review, he replied in a subsequent column: "For some strange reason, anyone writing in this magazine, or any magazine with funny pictures in it, is labeled 'sophisticated.' Just what is meant by the word in this connection is not clear, but the implication is unflattering, I am sure."

Benchley's bemusement was understandable; as the critic Dixon Wecter wrote in a 1935 essay called "A Brief History of Sophistication," "The word is now so slipshod that it can suggest anything from painted finger-nails to intellectual urbanity." The *Oxford English Dictionary* gives the original meaning of *sophisticated* as "mixed with some foreign substance; adulterated; not pure or genuine" and traces the metaphorical form ("altered from, deprived of, primitive simplicity or naturalness") to 1603, but, startlingly, does not recognize any favorable connotation. It was and is used that way much more commonly in the United States; the first definition in the current *American Heritage Dictionary* is "having acquired worldly knowledge or refinement." According to Wecter, *sophistication* "as an epithet of praise" dated from its use by Gertrude Atherton in her popular novel of 1923, *Black*

Oxen. Subsequently, "the advertisers were quick to see its appeal for an aspiring and prosperous middle-class; and the bright young people of America, in their myopic search for wisdom, seized upon sophistication instead." By the time he was writing, he asserted, it was clear that sophistication had become "the beau ideal of our time, as *'ton'* was to the eighteenth century, 'elegance' to the Regency, and 'culture' to the Victorians."

The *New Yorker* was sophistication in the form of a weekly magazine; its early incarnation was animated by the qualities embodied in the word. It was knowing, a trifle world-weary, prone to self-consciousness and irony, scornful of conventional wisdom or morality, resistant to enthusiasm or wholehearted commitment of any kind, and incapable of being shocked. The limitations of this attitude would eventually become apparent, but in the early years it served the magazine well as a foundation, so essential and solid that it went without saying.

A second (and related) continuing theme was the city itself: not so much a celebration of New York as an unstinting *attention* to it. Just months after the first issue, Ross wrote to an old army buddy, Hugh Wiley, "Your first advice, to stick to a covering of New York, has been adopted. . . . I became convinced of that some time ago and we stopped fiddling around on extraneous things." Informing this conviction, on some level, were marketing as well as editorial concerns. In the middle 1920s "New York" represented to America and the world a panoply of desirable qualities: sophistication, wealth, the new. The amazing thing was that this last element—a word advertising writers had recognized as one of the most effective, if not *the* most effective, selling points in existence—was right there in the name of the city and the magazine. So to indicate the excitement inherent in both, one merely had to mention them.

The magazine played the New York note so often in the early years that it turned into continuous background music. A humorous mock-history series beginning in the first issue was "The Story of Manhattankind." Soon there were continuing features inviting reader participation with the titles "Are You a New Yorker?" (a local-trivia quiz) and "Why I Like New York." In 1926, the heading "YOU CAN ALWAYS TELL when a man is a New Yorker because he—" was followed by ten sure signs, the first being, "Never complains about the subway, nor uses it as an alibi when late!" The next month, inevitably, came a self-parody, "What Kind of New Yorker Are You?" with mock questions like "Why do municipal ferryboats have Irish names? Can you blame the ferryboats?" The poet and satirist Baird Leonard instituted a series of sharply etched portraits in blank verse, "Metropolitan Monotypes." Morris Markey wrote several articles under the heading "New York Interiors," and various authors remembered in "A New York Childhood." Charles G. Shaw exercised his nostalgia in a series called "I Knew the

Town," and more general historical pieces went under the heading "That Was New York."* In 1926, an untitled poem by Herman W. Alpert took this tendency about as far as it was possible to go.

> That old New York
> That old New Yorkers
> Knew, that knew New York,
> Was no New York
> As now New Yorkers
> Know, that know New York.
>
> But no New York
> But new New York, New
> Yorkers ever knew;
> For that New York
> That old New Yorkers
> Knew, to them was new.

In all, thirty-nine pieces of prose and poetry whose titles began either with "New York" or "New Yorker," and fifteen starting with "Manhattan" or "Metropolitan," appeared in the magazine between 1925 and 1930.† Advertisement after advertisement compulsively named the city, too, as if merely by iterating the term *New Yorker* one was paying obeisance to its citizens' taste and sophistication. A two-page spot for *Harper's Bazaar* in 1926 (to pick one example from dozens) was headed "Advertisement for New Yorkers—and other knowing people."

Interestingly enough, even as the magazine was obsessing over its home city, readership was beginning to spread out beyond it—confirming the prospectus's prediction of "a considerable national circulation." It didn't happen immediately. The new "out of town subscribers" named in a summer 1926 memo to Ross hailed from such New York suburbs as Pelham, White Plains, and Garden City, and a promotional pamphlet called "Aces!—All Aces" put out the same year said that "only a fraction" of the magazine's circulation went to "outsiders—to a certain number of bright people who ought to live here but can't." But by 1930, a full 30 percent of the *New Yorker's* eighty-two

---

*Shaw's series got its inevitable takeoffs in pieces called "And I Knew the Town," "I Never Knew the Town," and Herman Mankiewicz's "I Also Knew the Town": "I knew the town in the days of short skirts, bobbed hair, chop-suey restaurants, sandwich bars, and midnight sailings. . . . I knew the town when Charles G. Shaw was a young man with a black moustache."
†By contrast, only eleven and five so-titled pieces appeared between 1931 and 1940, suggesting that by that time, the city and the magazine had both achieved a comfortable sense of their identity.

thousand readers lived outside the metropolitan area. Two years later, the figure passed 50 percent, and it continued to climb, reaching 73 percent in 1945. A 1940 *New Yorker* promotional publication archly titled "Rebuke from Dubuque" noted that even in the Iowa home city of the fabled "old lady," the magazine was selling thirty-five copies a week, but averred that even their purchasers, on some important level, were New Yorkers:

"You cannot keep *The New Yorker* out of the hands of New York–minded people, wherever they are. For, unlike the myriad points in which New York–minded people live, New York is not a tack on a map, not a city, not an island nor an evening at '21.' *The New Yorker* is a mood, a point of view. It is found wherever people are electrically sensitive to new ideas, eager for new things to do, new things to buy, new urbanities for living."

Ross and his colleagues were obviously conscious of the New York emphasis in the magazine, though they would probably have been surprised by how frequently the theme was struck. Their letters, memos, and subsequent memoirs indicate that they were not so aware of something else animating the magazine's first five years, a subject returned to so often it amounted to a leitmotiv. This was class. The changes New York had undergone in the first quarter of the twentieth century clearly contributed a sense of vibrancy to the city, but below the surface they also stirred uncertainty, anxiety, and tension. Statistics tell part of the story. In 1890, New York was 48.8 percent Protestant, 39.2 percent Roman Catholic, and 12 percent Jewish. In 1920, the Protestant and Catholic proportions had both fallen, to 34.6 percent each, while the Jewish percentage had more than doubled, to 29.2 percent. Since the Protestant figure included the overwhelming majority of black New Yorkers (3 percent of the total population), white Protestants were now outnumbered by Catholics and barely more numerous than Jews. But the changes involved more than numbers. Over that period the old white Protestant aristocracy of New York was eclipsed in prominence and, to a measure, power—not simply by Jews and Catholics, but by an entire new class of New Yorkers who had earned rather than inherited their money and who expected to earn their way into society on their merits.

Architecture made the changes solid. In the teens and twenties New York saw a simultaneous building and wrecking boom. To make room for the new skyscrapers, retail stores, and Park Avenue apartment buildings, in which the new class plied their trades, made their purchases, and rested their weary heads, the symbols of the older New York were demolished one by one: the Madison Square Presbyterian Church in 1913, the New York Herald Building in 1921, Madison Square Garden in 1925. Most dramatic was the demolition of the Fifth Avenue mansions of the moneyed class, culminating in the loss, in 1924 and 1925, of the houses of Cornelius Vanderbilt, W. K. Vanderbilt, C. P. Huntington, and William Astor. *Vanity Fair* noted with regret that the properties had been sold "to speculators and traders who only ten years ago boasted of no fortune at all. . . . To old New Yorkers, the real melancholy of the situation comes, not from the fact that the houses are soon to crumble into dust, but that the old and well ordered social fabric . . . has itself crumbled and vanished utterly from view. In place of a society restricted to a few hundred people of good breeding, we now have a social fabric mounting into the thousands, most of whom have inherited no very definite traditional creed of conduct or behavior." (The caption to a drawing of the Astor house noted, pointedly but without comment, that "it was recently sold to a Jewish real estate man for $3,000,000.")

These changes were the subtext of the *New Yorker's* first five years, and to say that the magazine was ambivalent about them would be an understatement. Ross, of course, had the social standing (and social graces) of a domesticated animal, yet in a bow to the conventional magazine wisdom that demographics are destiny, he continually struggled to get more Society into the magazine—and never more so than in the early years. In the first months, a form letter went out to contributing artists, noting that while covers have been "consistently good . . . the tone has been scattered, due, perhaps, to the wide choice of subjects. From now on, we feel we should tend strongly toward the elegant—that is to say, the fashionable and smart—the dinner jacket, rather than the sailor's uniform. Interiors of clubs, theatres, etc., situations built with a background of smart social situations, rather than character studies of the social classes." But these efforts to tone up the magazine—and there were many of them—never seemed to bear fruit. By 1927, Ross was complaining to Fleischmann, "The fact is that none of the writers or artists know anything about the clubs of New York and what the Upper Crust does. That is the great difficulty in *The New Yorker.*" This should not have been a surprise. As White pointed out years later, "Oddly enough (yet it really isn't odd at all), only two staff people in the early days of *The New Yorker* had a background of Society: Ralph Ingersoll and Fillmore Hyde. [Hyde was the main Talk of the Town writer before being replaced by Thurber.] The rest of us just popped out of the subway somewhere."

Of course, if the staff and contributors *had* been insiders, the magazine probably wouldn't have lasted five years, much less three-quarters of a century. As it was, the very uncertainty and tension over issues of class animated the *New Yorker's* early years, providing a consistent conversation regularly audible through the cacophony. The article commonly credited with turning the magazine's fortunes was "Why We Go to Cabarets," published in November 1925 and written by Ellin Mackay, a young socialite in New York. The essay danced on the surface of the issue, comparing, in heavily coded language, the relative merits of nightclubs and society balls. Mackay and her set *did* frequent the former, she acknowledged, but not "as our elders would have it, because we enjoy rubbing elbows with all sorts and kinds of people. We do not particularly like dancing shoulder to shoulder with gaudy and fat drummers. We do not like unattractive people." But as opposed to the cabarets, where she does not *have* to dance with such specimens, society parties force her to consort with such types as "the young man who is well-read in the Social Register, who talks glibly of the Racquet Club, while he prays that you won't suspect he lives far up on the West Side" (a Manhattan neighborhood that was known as the home to social-climbing Jews). At one leap-year party at the Colony Club, the girls outnumbered the men four to one, "and the hostesses never knew where the majority of the feminine stag line came from—some suspected the Bronx." (This was the borough where Jews lived before they made it to the Upper West Side.) Mackay and her cohort went to cabarets, she concluded, "because we prefer rubbing elbows in a cabaret to dancing at an exclusive party with all sorts and kinds of people." Grant, with her newspaper connections, got front-page coverage of the article in the *Times,* the *Herald Tribune,* and the *World.** The following year, in a real-life tableau of class, ethnicity, and the changing times, Mackay stunned Society by marrying the songwriter Irving Berlin (né Israel Baline, born in Russia and raised on the Lower East Side, where Jews lived before moving up to the Bronx). Her parents were so mortified by the union that they refused to acknowledge it.

Mackay's pieces were only the most famous of the many hundreds of drawings and written pieces that attended to these issues. Of the few *New Yorker* sketches in the early years that had any pretensions to seriousness, a disproportionate number were driven by the ironies and anomalies of class. Marc Connelly's "Barmecide's Feast" (1927) and "The Dear Old Couple" (1928) and John Mosher's "The Black List" (1929) display the emptiness of some upper-class lives, put into focus by the characters' callousness toward their servants. In Dorothy Parker's somewhat heavy-handed "Arrangement in Black and White" (1927), a woman "with the pink velvet poppies wreathed around the assisted gold of her hair" attends a cocktail party in honor of a Negro baritone and by her condescending comments reveals her prejudice. Mosher's "A Marriage of Convenience" (1930) is about an interclass marriage forced by the economic slump.

Realistic fiction thrives in periods of social ambiguity and flux, and the

*Nor did the matter stop there. The next day, the *Times* ran a follow-up story with a quote from the president of the Junior League, a Mrs. Pleasants Pennington ("Frankly, it amused me very much"), as well as an editorial regretfully commenting that today, "society, so-called, is a thing of rented ballrooms and public caterers." The next week the *New Yorker* ran an article by a "stag" defending his fellows—which was duly reported by the *Times*—and the week after that came Mackay's last word on the subject, "The Declining Function: A Post-Debutante Rejoices."

attention to class was one of the factors working to propel *New Yorker* writing from two-dimensional sketches to fleshed-out short stories. A key transitional work was "But for the Grace of God" (1928), by Thyra Samter Winslow, an Arkansas native who had developed a reputation for her sharp, well-observed short stories in magazines like the *Smart Set*. She was married to *New Yorker* staffer Fillmore Hyde, and she contributed close to a dozen pieces to the magazine in 1927 and 1928. "But for the Grace of God" is about an unnamed young woman who, to her chagrin, is forced to take the subway because she is late for a cocktail party. Descending into the station, she is "uncomfortably conscious of the people around her. Did these people use the subway every day?" After getting on the train, "she sat on the edge of her seat, trying not to touch anyone, not to see these dreadful people. Their noses were all long." Presently, a girl gets on the train, wearing "a decent brown coat, the kind you buy when you don't want the dirt to show." By the main character's fixation on this young woman, we come to understand that she sees her former self in her, that once, before beginning her social ascent, she had ridden the subway and had a "young fellow who didn't have a cent and wanted to marry her and start on nothing at all." A phrase pops into her mind, something that she had read somewhere, when she still read: "There but for the grace of God." Arriving at the party, she drinks more than she should, gets teary-eyed, and tells her friends that when she took "the underground," she saw a girl she used to know a long time ago. The story poses no challenge to Chekhov or de Maupassant, but in its carefully selected details, its mild epiphany, and its attention to the potency of class, it is an accomplished and poignant piece of short fiction.

The locus of the character's confrontation with her past was telling (as was White's comment, "The rest of us just popped out of the subway somewhere"), for the subway was the best symbol in 1920s New York of the sense that the old lines of class demarcation had irrevocably blurred. The first segment of the Interborough Rapid Transit opened in 1904, and by the twenties the subway was an inescapable presence that, by providing transportation to the multitudes who worked and lived in them, effectively permitted the boom in skyscrapers and high-rise apartment buildings. The subway was the strongest and least refutable democratizing force New York had ever seen. That is, unless they were willing to waste hours sitting in traffic jams in taxicabs, Wall Street bankers were forced to share the same straps and breathe the same stale air as immigrants and garment workers. Part of its power as a symbol, perhaps, was that it was subterranean and thus stood in stark contrast to the extended metaphor of ascendance that otherwise dominated the culture.

In any case, the interclass juxtapositions the subway generated were everywhere in the *New Yorker,* most prominently in the anecdotes featured every week in The Talk of the Town: between 1925 and 1930, twenty-three of these were set in the stations, cars, and platforms. There was the lady who was commanded by the guard to "Step lively!" on entering the subway and replied, "I have no wish to tarry, sir"; the mother who tells the boy he doesn't have to remove his hat because "you don't have to be a gentleman in the subway"; the subway guard who picks up a discarded newspaper, puts a monocle in his eye, and scans the news; and this rich interchange from 1932, set down by James Thurber:

> An East Side subway train banged into the Brooklyn Bridge station on a frosty morning and came to an impatient stop. The doors slid open and brought face to face a little Italian woman, who stood on the platform holding a child in one arm and a bundle in the other, and a tall, dignified elderly gentleman who was standing in the car near the door. "Upatown? Upatown, Mista?" she squealed. The gentleman bowed gravely. "Yes, Madam," he said. "Ah—won't you come in?"

New Yorker cartoons can be seen as illustrated anecdotes, and the subway was a rich milieu for them as well. In several early drawings, newspapers crystallize the subterranean class uncertainty: the gentleman reading a low-class seatmate's tabloid over his shoulder, the tough guy looking up from his paper to remark to the dignified gent, "Well, I see where Little Orphan Annie has wound up behind the eight-ball again." In an Alain cartoon from 1936, a man in formal attire riding the subway late at night, surrounded by sleeping bums, says to the begowned woman with him, "We must seem like creatures from another world."

Also beneath the surface was one of the most celebrated of the New Yorker's many running gags, Otto Soglow's 1929 manhole series, the drawings showing the same open manhole in the same city street varied only by each week's comment from one of the workers below. The seemingly inexhaustible humor—there were thirty installments before the workers, Joe and Bill, finally emerged early in 1930—came from the conceit that the laborers spoke with the same assumptions and in the same catchphrases as those with "higher" places in society: "Oh, I had to go. I was the guest of honor." "I drifted a long while before I found myself." "The trouble with you, Bill, is you got your head in the clouds."*

---

*In October 1929, Katharine Angell wrote a memo to Ross laying out the "more familiar art ideas," and number two on the list was "all drawings similar in idea to the manhole, men talking beyond their station, etc. Example: Gents on garbage truck: 'But Gauguin is so brutal, Bill!' " Number six was "wrong answers on telephone and wrong persons answering telephone theme. Example: Tough gent at the phone: 'Yeah, this is Mlle. Modiste speaking.' " The telephone wires were something else shared by all the classes.

A 1928 cartoon by Leonard Dove asked, succinctly and eloquently, the question on everyone's mind. A society lady, relaxing on the beach, turns to a questionable-looking gentleman, wearing a boater and munching a banana, and says, "Excuse me, are you one of *us*?" At this point in New York's social history, it was hard to say precisely who "we" were.

Remarkably enough, however, the *New Yorker* began to answer this question significantly more democratically and inclusively than one might expect. Not many months after the magazine started, a trumpet-playing recent Yale graduate named Curtis Arnoux Peters appeared in the office, wearing sneakers and bearing drawings signed "Peter Arno," to protect the family name. He was the son of a prominent judge, and though his early work was stiff and rather uninteresting, especially in comparison to the stunning energy and fluidity of his mature work, his dinner-jacketed swains had the ring of truth, and Ross, always eager to tone up the magazine, regularly bought them. Ross had assigned a young staffer named Philip Wylie to be liaison to the artists. Decades later, writing to James Thurber, Wylie described looking through Arno's weekly portfolio when he came upon "two half-shot, bellowing old bats about to charge obliviously into a trap—made by the rise of a sidewalk elevator; under this Arno had written, 'Tripe? I'd do almost anything for a bit of tripe!' It greatly amused me. Arno rather uncomfortably said he hadn't meant to show it— just something he knocked off idly." The "old bats," who came to be known as the Whoops Sisters for their habit of following roughly every other sentence with that exclamation, created such a sensation that they were featured nearly every week in 1926 and brought Arno to wide attention for the first time. Their dialect, their coarse explicitness, their predilection for tripe, their antique dresses, and their muffs excluded them from the upper class, yet they were not from any identifiable lower one, either. They were a kind of sociocultural wild card, blowing through New York (to switch metaphors) like a sudden, hard, and invigorating wind. Readers saw them on the subways (naturally), at the circus, at a society gathering: "I hope we ain't intrudin'?"

They *were* intruding, but the process was salutary. Though their creators had little in common as artists, the Whoops Sisters led the way to William Steig's citizens of his native Bronx, who began appearing in the magazine in 1930. (Steig was soon followed by Syd Hoff, whose milieu, drawing style, and sensibility were strikingly similar, but who lacked Steig's sublime and subtle gift for characterization.) Previously, identifiably Jewish characters had appeared in cartoons, but the drawings had never been executed from their point of view; they were at best outsiders, at worst stereotyped caricatures. Steig and Hoff gently and sympathetically poked fun at their characters, the same way Helen Hokinson, Alice Harvey, Garrett Price, Gluyas Williams, and

Perry Barlow pricked the pretensions of the upper-middle and upper classes. (There was never anything gentle or sympathetic about Arno.) The Steig of prose was Arthur Kober, a press agent for the Shuberts and other theatrical personages (and also the husband of Lillian Hellman), who began contributing first-person sketches to the magazine in 1926. His early monologues all sprang from the Broadway world, and most had identifiably Jewish characters, but in a 1931 reminiscence piece called "Mrs. Gittleson," about a candy-store owner from his childhood, he staked a claim in virgin territory (for the *New Yorker*)—the immigrant Bronx. Shortly thereafter he created Bella Gross, the young woman from that borough whose one goal in life was to find Mr. Right, and who would be a *New Yorker* fixture in Kober's dialect stories for two decades.* Steig's and Kober's ascendance ran counter, of course, to Ross's pleas to tone up the magazine, but these had in fact grown more muted and occasional with the years. As he undoubtedly realized, the magazine was attracting readers who had grown up in the Bronx—and in Iowa, for that matter—and there was no reason to expect these people to be inordinately interested in the lives of the 400.

In the early years, the *New Yorker*'s art was its most successful component. In October 1925, Ross was writing to Hugh Wiley, "Everybody talks of the *New Yorker*'s art, that is its illustrations, and it has been described as the best magazine in the world for a person who can not read." There was certainly some frustration in this for a word man like Ross, and Philip Wylie recalled, "The one thing Ross had demanded till all heads rang with it— from early 1925 until it began to become fact, a year or so later, was this: *'Get the prose in the magazine like the art!'* " But the *drawings* (the word that was preferred to the more mundane *cartoons*) still took precedence through the twenties. In 1928, the magazine issued the first of what would be fourteen consecutive "Scrapbooks" containing the best of the year's drawings, and the *New Yorker* cartoon was on its way to becoming a singular American art form.

There were several reasons for the immediate success of the art. Wylie attributed it, most of all, to the influence of Rea Irvin: "Irvin rubbed most of the uncouthness and corn-love out of Ross's mind in the all-afternoon Tuesday [art] conferences. Irvin then was modest and twinkling, quietly gay—and

---

*It has to be said that it would be many years before *New Yorker* art or prose would be as inclusive for Americans whose ancestry was neither Northern European nor Jewish. The magazine did print some biting cartoons on racial prejudice, but never one from a black person's point of view until the 1970s. As for writing, only authors still living abroad or recent immigrants seemed to be exotic enough to break through. Thus the *New Yorker* published countless autobiographical stories by Arturo Vivante and Niccolo Tucci, both of whom had immigrated to the United States as adults, but little or nothing by Italian Americans who had grown up here.

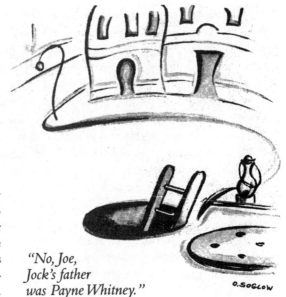

One of the thirty installments of Otto Soglow's hugely popular manhole series. The caption to this one was contributed by the composer Cole Porter.

"No, Joe, Jock's father was Payne Whitney."

O. SOGLOW

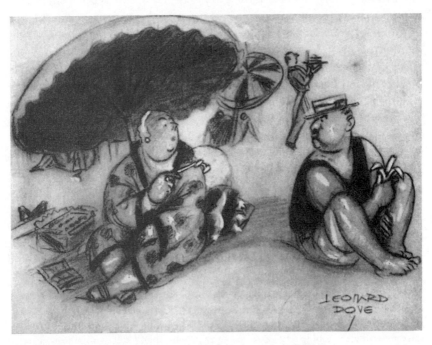

"Pardon me, sir, but are you one of us?"

The society matron's question in Leonard Dove's 1928 cartoon was an ongoing subtext in the early *New Yorker.*

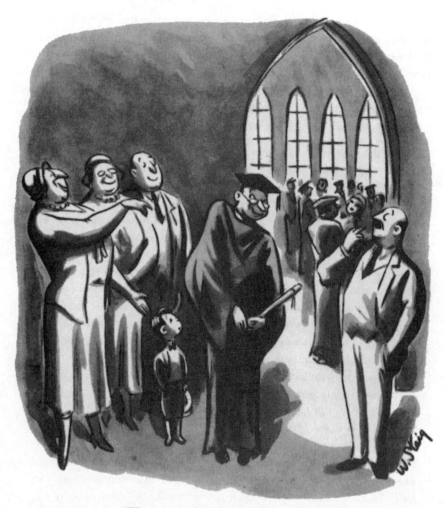

"Turn around—show Aunt Sophie!"

Besides being a master draftsman of facial expression, William Steig opened the *New Yorker*'s pages to sympathetic portrayals of a different class of people. This 1931 drawing wryly reflected the social and educational mobility of first-generation Jewish New Yorkers.

his sense of humor was as fast and subtle as variegated."* And, certainly, whether Ross or Irvin was primarily responsible, the New Yorker irrevocably broke the Life-Judge, he-she pattern and finally established a twentieth-century model for the magazine cartoon. Ross once shared some of his thoughts on the matter with a cartoonist named Alice Harvey, who was upset because the magazine had solicited, then killed, one of her drawings.

"For years and years," Ross wrote,

> before the New Yorker came into existence, the humorous magazines of this country weren't very funny, or meritorious in any way. The reason was this: the editors bought jokes, or gags, or whatever you want to call them, for five dollars or ten dollars, mailed these out to artists, the artists drew them up, mailed them back and were paid. The result was completely wooden art. The artists' attitude toward a joke was exactly that of a short story illustrator's toward a short story. They illustrated the joke and got their money for the drawing. Now this practice led to all humorous drawings being "illustrations." It also resulted in their being wooden, run of the mill products. The artists never thought for themselves and never learned to think. They weren't humorous artists; they were dull witted illustrators. A humorous artist is a creative person, an illustrator isn't. At least they're not creative as far as the idea is concerned, and in humor the idea is the thing.
>
> I judge from your letter that you apparently don't realize that you are one of the three or four pathfinders in what is called the new school of American humor. Your stuff in Life before the New Yorker started might well be considered the first notes of this new humor. I remember seeing it and being encouraged by it when I was thinking of starting the New Yorker. It had a lot to do with convincing me that there was new talent around for a magazine like this. And now you speak of "illustrating jokes"! The very words in your letter to me. I always see red when an artist talks of "illustrating" a joke because I know that such a practice means the end of the New Yorker, the new school of humor, and all. Unless an artist takes ahold of an idea and does more than "illustrate" it he's (she's) not going to make a humorous drawing.

The resounding and almost immediate success of New Yorker cartoons was directly tied to a fourth unifying theme of the magazine's first five years, besides sophistication, New York, and class. This was talk. The most distin-

---

*In addition to his work on the cartoons, Irvin oversaw the look of the magazine as it subtly evolved week to week, before finally settling into its more or less final state in 1928. Katharine White described one of those small changes: "At first the magazine was brought out with a straight mechanical rule between the columns. Ross thought this was too formal and he wanted an irregular rule that would be more informal. Rea was very patient and must have drawn hundreds of what we called 'the wiggly line.' He did a lot of wavering lines and finally he did one that Ross accepted and that has been used ever since."

guishing characteristic of the drawings was that their captions represented something close to the way people actually spoke. This was not immediately the case: in the first issues, the most successful pieces were uncaptioned conceptual (rather than character) drawings and caricatures by such accomplished artists as Ralph Barton, Al Frueh, and John Held Jr. But wonderful as some of these were, they were the equivalent of silent-film comedy, with broad gags and with titles instead of captions. Ross and Irvin knew they were after something else. In June, artists interested in contributing began to get a form letter stating that while initially the art had been chosen on its "artistic and decorative merit," now the magazine was looking for "character stuff, with a situation." Another (undated) form letter explained, "Generally speaking, ideas should be satirical without being bitter or personal; our secondary need being for ideas that are unusual, extravagant or 'nutty.' Situations should be plausible. Ideas should be literal and show how, unconsciously by their speech and acts, individuals of every New York type show up their hypocricies [sic], insincerities, false fads and absurd characteristics."

The artist who first and most successfully realized these goals was Helen Hokinson, an Illinois native who in 1925 was drawing a daily comic strip called *Sylvia in the Big City* and had contributed illustrations to *Vanity Fair* and other magazines. From the beginning, Ross recognized that her work had the casual yet solid feel he was striving for. In the words of Lee Lorenz, the art editor of the magazine from 1973 until 1997, "Coming upon her first, quiet sketches in the sideshow atmosphere of Ross's early magazine is like being handed a cool glass of water in a steambath." Hokinson's world was a nearly all-female one (with the occasional appearance of a little boy or a butler), and though she dabbled in flappers at the beginning, she was quickly drawn to the rounded society matrons with whom her name was ever after identified, sketching them with a humor that was as respectful as it was pointed.

Hokinson's cartoons, like the best of Arno, Harvey, Barbara Shermund, and Mary Petty, gravitated to the one-line caption—a device hitherto used most frequently in, of all places, the left-wing magazine *The Masses.* That was because these artists' drawings captured a point in time, and that extra line would have elongated it beyond plausibility. Streamlining the caption also let the picture and text work together like a well-oiled machine. The best *New Yorker* cartoons, as one critic put it in the 1940s, "present an idea or predicament that screams for clarification. The drawing alone, more often than not, is enigmatical, but in conjunction with the surprising title it becomes explosively funny." And the shorter captions were somehow more audible. That is, you could almost *hear* the lines of dialogue, as they picked up on the cadences of the streets and the living rooms, the nightclubs and the boardrooms. (In retrospect, the decision—presumably Irvin's—to put the captions in italics, with quotation marks around them, added to the sense of freshness. Traditional captions were in capital letters and small caps, without quotes, producing a subtly static quality.) In the case of what for years was the *New Yorker's* most famous cartoon—published in 1928, just before the two-line caption was banished for good—the process was reversed, and the vox populi took a cue from the magazine. A little girl and her mother are at the dinner table. The mother says, "It's broccoli, dear." The girl says, "I say it's spinach, and I say the hell with it." E. B. White's spinach line—the drawing was by Carl Rose—immediately became a catchphrase and was eventually used as a song title.*

The magazine was picking up on something in the culture: it was a moment when the air reverberated with the sound of speech. The trend had started in the early years of the century, in comic strips like *The Katzenjammer Kids,* where dialogue appeared in balloons coming out of the characters' mouths. Later cartoonists such as Milt Gross and Thomas A. Dorgan (*Tad*) were connoisseurs, and sometimes creators, of slang. In the midtwenties, Gross published *Nize Baby,* a novel, and *Hiawatta,* a rendering of Longfellow's poem in his fractured Yiddish cadences—"Smoked de chiff a pipe tebbecca"—and attention was paid even in the higher realms of culture. The freshness and vitality of the vernacular was the raw material of the poets of Tin Pan Alley, lyricists such as Ira Gershwin, Irving Berlin, Cole Porter, and Lorenz Hart—think of the song titles "S'Wonderful," "I Should Care," "I Get a Kick out of You," and dozens more. Under the partial influence of the songwriters and the cartoonists—and with a nod back to Twain's *Huckleberry Finn*—"serious" writers had begun to utilize and experiment with voice. Sherwood Anderson's influential 1922, first-person story "I'm a Fool" went in and out of the vernacular, and John Dos Passos's 1925 novel, *Manhattan Transfer,* was saturated with slangy dialogue. Even though Fitzgerald and Hemingway were after other game, it is worth noting that their most artistically successful novels of the twenties, *The Great Gatsby* (1925) and *The Sun Also Rises* (1926), were both written in the first person, which has always had more of the sound of speech than the third. The key figure here was a writer universally admired by the Algonquin set, Ring Lardner. He had made his reputation in the teens with first-person works like *You Know Me, Al* and *Own Your Own Home,* in which the narrator was

---

*Ross later wrote that after the cartoon had been created and submitted, "I didn't think it was anything special and put it aside for two or three weeks, largely because of the word *hell* in it. We get so much profanity in our captions that I usually hesitate over a *hell* or a *damn.* Anyhow, I didn't think it was anything very hot. I went away to Florida and Mrs. Katherine [*sic*] White ... who always insisted it was hilariously funny or something, printed it. It very shortly became a by-word much to my surprise."

supposedly writing down the story. While effective, the technique was something of a cheap shot, since these characters were not at home with the written word. But by the end of the decade and on into the twenties, Lardner had made a daring, significant, and artistically rewarding shift: books like *Gullible's Travels* and *The Big Town* and stories like "The Golden Honeymoon," "Who Dealt?" "Haircut," and "Ex Parte" proceeded from the notion that the narrator was *speaking* the story. (All these developments set the stage for the end of the decade, when radio and sound motion pictures would generate and disseminate more talk than anyone would have thought existed. Oddly, dialogue in the theater was still under the sway of artifice, and a more naturalistic rendering of speech would not occur until the arrival of the Group Theater in the middle thirties.)

In the *New Yorker,* the cartoons led the way, to be sure, but from the first section (called The *Talk* of the Town, remember), with its famous anecdotes, to the end, the magazine was filled with the sound of voices. In fact, if the *New Yorker* of the twenties could be said to have specialized in a certain kind of written piece, it was the monologue. Arthur Kober wrote more than three dozen of them in just three years, and not close behind was Zelda F. Popkin, also a theatrical press agent. In her series "Reflections of Silent New Yorkers," we were made privy to the inner voices of a taxi driver, an apartment-house super, and so forth. A writer named J. P. Grover contributed a series done entirely in criminal slang, with "translations" on the side. An additional twenty monologues and dialogues appeared between 1927 and 1929 under the heading "Overheard." As early as the summer of 1928, Katharine Angell was writing to a contributor, "We are growing wary of the monologue form; it has been done so often."

Four of the "Overheard" pieces were contributed by a brash young Pottsville, Pennsylvania, native named John O'Hara. In early 1928, O'Hara, twenty-three, was floating from one newspaper job to another (he was generally fired in a matter of months), living in various furnished rooms, and inundating the *New Yorker* with submissions, proposals for profiles, even cartoon captions. Back in Pottsville, O'Hara had been published in "The Conning Tower," and on his arrival in New York, FPA had effected an introduction to Ross. The editor thought enough of the young man's work to maintain a personal correspondence, but not enough—at first—to publish him. "This isn't it yet," Ross wrote O'Hara in March. "You haven't got enough to this stuff. Try some more. We are a hard market but good when you get going." A few weeks later, presented in the magazine's offices to Katharine Angell, O'Hara was so excited he didn't catch her name. He thanked Ross for the introduction to "Miss X" and commented, "Really it will be a pleasure to have manuscripts turned down by her, which is a compliment if ever I gave one." But three days later Mrs. Angell wrote O'Hara that the magazine was taking two pieces. The first to be published, "Alumnae Bulletin," supposedly expressed the thoughts of a Seven Sisters graduate as she peruses her class notes; the second was "Overheard—In a Telephone Booth." O'Hara had found a way into the *New Yorker*, and it was through his uncanny ability to reveal the character of all kinds of characters through speech. Later in the year, he embarked on two long-running series. The first purported to be transcripts of the proceedings of a New Jersey women's group called the Orange County Afternoon Delphian Society, which was patterned after a club his mother belonged to in Pottsville. In the second, the manager of a Manhattan paint-manufacturing company addressed his staff. Here, with the firm about to move, he starts to divide up the new offices:

> Now that leaves seven windows on Park Avenue. Six, really, because I have the one next to F.W.'s, naturally. I don't think—well, I don't think there'll be much questioning of that, because I'm in F.W.'s office practically every minute of the day when he or I isn't otherwise engaged, so of course I had to take the office next to his. I could have taken an office on the Forty-sixth Street side, but—well, we won't go into that. Yes, maybe we will. If there's anybody thinks the assistant to the president and office manager, which I am, isn't entitled to a Park Avenue window, why let them give reasons. I'm being perfectly square about this. If anybody here really thinks that I'm not entitled to one of those offices, why if they give a good enough reason, I'll take an office over around the other side of the building. . . . Well, that's settled.

O'Hara's rightful place was deemed to be in the back of the book—BoB in the *New Yorker's* parlance—the place in the magazine, after the featured casuals and journalistic pieces, where the sketches and reminiscences deemed as slighter or nonmetropolitan were placed. From May 5, 1928, through the end of 1930, O'Hara had fifty-eight pieces in the magazine, only seven of which appeared before page 40; virtually all were monologues or dialogues. O'Hara's friend and editor Wolcott Gibbs (after whom the author would name Gibbsville, the stand-in for Pottsville in his fiction) later called these "finger exercises," and O'Hara would affect disdain for "those dreadful little potboilers in the back of the book." But indisputably the discipline and tools he acquired in writing them led directly to his extraordinarily successful conventional short stories, the first of which, "Mary," appeared in the *New Yorker* on May 2, 1931.

"A SORT OF NATURAL DRIVE IN THE RIGHT DIRECTION"

Thomas Kunkel's biography of Harold Ross is aptly titled *Genius in Disguise,* and the final factor unifying the *New Yorker* in the chancy early years was the unexpected brilliance of Ross himself. Two particular qualities suggest themselves as critical. The first was his patience in not forcing the magazine to define itself before it was ready to do so; he was able and willing, for a time, to accept some editorial flailing about. E. B. White's obituary of Ross noted the editor's "scholastic deficiencies" but observed that he "had a thing that is at least as good as, if not better than, knowledge: he had a sort of natural drive in the right direction. . . . He was like a boat being driven at the mercy of some internal squall, a disturbance he himself only half understood, and of which he was at times suspicious." Second, Ross had a truly remarkable ability to recognize and appreciate the not always immediately evident talents of others, just as he had with O'Hara. Generally gruff in person, Ross could be eloquently and amusingly effusive in memo or correspondence, never more so than when he was writing to someone he felt the *New Yorker* needed to have in its pages, and especially when he perceived that writer or artist was given to self-doubt.

Thus Ross to Dorothy Parker, February 26, 1927: "The verses came and God Bless Me! If I never do anything else I can say I ran a magazine that printed some of your stuff. Tearful thanks. Check, proof etc. to follow." (Ross went on to advise Parker that "it is better . . . to spread your stuff out because it reminds people of you oftener and will help you sell your book. I'm nothing if not practical, and one of the leading men in New York though still in my early thirties.")

And Ross to Ralph Barton, April 6, 1928: "The piece is amusing, unique and distinguished, something we will be proud to print. I will pray practically nightly hereafter that you will keep up your writing because you are one of the ablest, most intelligent and civilized people there is."

Ross to Emily Hahn, August 6, 1929: "In our judgment you undoubtedly have the gift to write which I am coming to believe is very rare, and if you can just be a little clearer, you ought to be quite successful."

Ross to Gluyas Williams, August 14, 1929: "That 'Will Somebody Pick a Card' drawing may be of a kind different from your usual ones but you did it better than anyone else would have done. We'll continue to send up slightly different ideas, or somewhat different ones and—who knows?—you will probably find entirely new fields. You don't know your own strength. Its receipt was much appreciated by me as most of our artists have taken to killing themselves, getting shot at by Vanderbilts and so on. Beware of Vanderbilts."*

*"I've been in California for a month," Ross's letter to Williams concluded. "I was returning bronzed, muscular, and tawny, and got a cinder in my eye west of Chicago which left me half blind for a week. I'm fully recovered now and will try to find some ideas." Incidentally, his line about artists killing themselves chillingly prophesied the 1931 suicide of Ralph Barton. In an undated letter, Barton had written to Ross, "Try to cling to a little of your faith in me. It is my only light in the darkness."

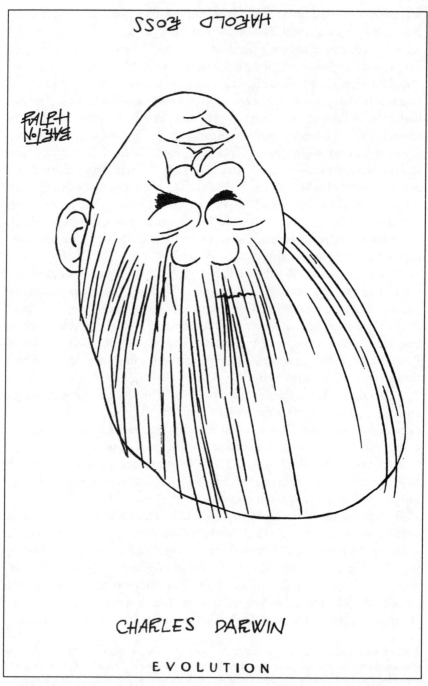

CHARLES DARWIN

EVOLUTION

For Ross's birthday in 1926, the staff and contributors of the *New Yorker* put together a parody issue of the magazine. This inventive caricature was by one of Ross's favorite artists, Ralph Barton.

Ross to William Steig, October 19, 1933: "The picture you did of the lady watching the accident, is in my judgment, one of the best that has come through in a long time. A very delicate, subtle, and masterful job, if I may say so."

And finally, Ross to Frank Sullivan, an old friend, March 29, 1929: "Your piece was on my desk (as we say here) when I arrived at my office today. I was right on the verge of my morning movement and I took the play with me to read. I can't say which I enjoyed more, the play or the passage of my bowels. Looking back on it now, I guess it was the combination. The piece sort of relaxed me. I think your stuff has this effect, Frank, and that if you would do one a week for us awhile a lot of people in this town who are taking pills, now, would stop taking them."

In Ross's mind, at least, even his rough-and-ready interpersonal style was salutary. In 1941, a young staff writer named Brendan Gill developed the notion that the editor had a grievance with him and had tried to "scare" him. Ross explained that this wasn't the case:

"I don't try to scare anyone, although occasionally I don't give a damn if I do probably. Anyone I can scare must scare easily, so easily you can't help scaring them. There are, I suspect, some such. I didn't try to scare you. The profanity was natural. My manner is not orthodox, but I've given up trying to curb it, for often as not it serves (astonishingly) to put people at their ease. I think it relaxes more people than it excites. I hope so anyhow."

Ross was not unerring as a talent-spotter, but he was damned good. He needed to be in the first years, because budget restrictions meant that even big-name writers who were sympathetic to the magazine's enterprise, such as Lardner, Hemingway, Fitzgerald, Benchley, and Don Marquis, only submitted the occasional piece that was too slight or eccentric for high-paying mass-market magazines. (In the first five years, Hemingway contributed one and Fitzgerald two forgettable pieces.) Of the Algonquin heavy hitters, only Dorothy Parker published frequently from the start, which helps to explain Ross's abject gratitude to her in his letters. Possibly even more important to the magazine than her justly famous stories and light verse were her superb and sometimes scathingly funny book reviews, signed "Constant Reader" and inaugurated in October 1927. At the time, the film, literary, art, and music criticism in the magazine was generally undistinguished—at best middlebrow and at worst philistine—with the burden of the review more often than not being whether the work under discussion excessively taxed the listener, viewer, or reader. (An anonymous book critic in the first issue said of a Joseph Conrad collection, "Four, all admirable and easy to read, and you needn't be a seasoned Conradian.") But when Parker came on, readers would pick up the magazine and turn to her first, thus inaugurating a long tradition of ostentatiously distinguished criticism that would extend through

Robert Benchley (starting in 1927) and A. J. Liebling on the press; Benchley (1929), Wolcott Gibbs, and Kenneth Tynan on theater; Lewis Mumford on architecture (1931) and art (1932); Edmund Wilson on books; Harold Rosenberg on art; Whitney Balliett on jazz; Arlene Croce on dance; and Pauline Kael on film. Ross certainly recognized Parker's importance, writing to White a decade later that "Constant Reader, in the early days, did more than anything to put the magazine on its feet, or its ear, or whatever it is today."

Ross did have a little more leeway in hiring critics and regular contributors than in engaging the top freelancers, and in 1925 he made some sterling personnel decisions that would pay great dividends in the decades ahead. In the spring he hired Morris Markey away from the *New York World* to write regular journalistic pieces that would eventually appear under the rubric "A Reporter at Large." In a long dedication to Ross in a 1927 collection of his pieces, Markey recalled being thunderstruck by a piece of instruction the editor gave him at their first meeting: that he should "be honest at whatever cost."

Markey went on, "It was entirely novel to be told such a thing. I had written for newspapers, and newspaper writers can never be wholly honest, no matter what their editors say, for the reason that they can never allow themselves to be bored, or indifferent, or excited, or angry, or to forget the caution instilled into them by the fear of violating good taste." Markey didn't only display his emotions in his stories—he displayed *himself,* habitually structuring them around the act of reporting. This near-revolutionary unveiling of the traditionally invisible reporter prefigured the "new journalists" of forty years hence. Markey's topics were notable as well. By the end of 1926, he had visited the Tombs prison, a boxing match, a baseball game, Bible-thumping churches, a Harlem dance hall, and an East Side speakeasy; both the low-life subject matter and the sober eloquence of the prose offered a welcome gravity countering the airiness of the rest of the magazine.

In the summer of 1925, Ross had Jane Grant write a friend of hers, an American expatriate in Paris named Janet Flanner, with a proposition: "He wants anecdotal and incidental stuff on places familiar to Americans and on people of note whether they are Americans or internationally prominent— dope on fields of the arts and a little on fashion, perhaps, although he does not want the latter treated technically; there should be lots of chat about people seem [*sic*] about and in it all he wants a definite personality injected. In fact, any of your letters would be just the thing." Flanner inferred volumes from this charge: specifically, that her writing was to be "precisely accurate, highly personal, colorful, and ocularly descriptive; and that for sentence style, Gibbon was as good a model as I could bring to mind, he having been the master of antithesis, at once both enriching and economical through his use of opposites." Her first "Letter from Paris," signed "Genêt," appeared in September. She would continue to file them for another five decades, doing as much as anyone to establish essay-journalism as a *New Yorker* tradition, one subsequently practiced by the likes of Rebecca West, Edmund Wilson, Jane Kramer, Andy Logan, and Janet Malcolm.

Also in the first year, Ross brought on Lois Long, a twenty-two-year-old Vassar graduate, late of *Vanity Fair,* to review nightclubs. Long's "Tables for Two" column ended with the twenties, but her first-rate fashion criticism, under the rubric "On and Off the Avenue," continued until 1969. Long, a member of the school of Parker, was a true groundbreaker in fashion writing, having simultaneously a strong knowledge of the subject, excellent taste, the good sense not to take it seriously, and the writing ability and wit to carry it all off in print. Ralph Ingersoll, in his 1934 *Fortune* article on the *New Yorker,* credited "On and Off the Avenue" with being a "magazine sensation" that "broke a fifty-year-old tradition that commercial names—let alone addresses and prices—should never be mentioned in polite publishing." In 1931, Long inaugurated a series of cranky, biting, and funny personal essays, under the running heading "Doldrums," that, minus some topical references, could have been printed sixty years later with no trouble under the byline Fran Lebowitz or Nora Ephron. (After "Doldrums," unfortunately, Long stuck to fashion, but connoisseurs of good writing knew they could find her there.)

For all Ross's comic-opera hiring and firing of "jesuses," he also was sometimes capable of good judgment in retaining and promoting editors. There were two spectacular examples of this in the *New Yorker's* history. The second was William Shawn, who, between 1933 and 1939, rose from a freelance reporter for The Talk of the Town to the managing editor for fact (the position he held until assuming the editorship in 1952). The first was Katharine White, whose contribution to the magazine was equally important. An upper-middle-class New Englander, educated at Bryn Mawr and spectacularly intelligent, Katharine Sergeant Angell, then thirty-two years old, was hired as a part-time manuscript reader in August 1925. Perceiving her outstanding qualities, Ross quickly moved her to full-time; within a year, she was the magazine's top literary editor, responsible for the majority of every week's copy. In retrospect, it may seem odd that Ross, a man's man almost to the point of caricature, would see to it that no glass ceiling halted Mrs. Angell's progress. But remember that he was married to an ardent and vocal feminist; though he and Grant would separate in 1927 and divorce two years later, he never showed any indication of turning his back on her ideas about equal treatment of and opportunity for women. From the beginning, female and male writers were published in the *New Yorker* in roughly equivalent number. The entire magazine, in fact, was solicitous of readers of both genders—an unusual stance, then as now. Columns about motorcars and sports coexisted peacefully with ones about fashion and shops, and the range of advertisements reflected the sense that both men and women were in the reading audience.

Mrs. Angell's particular and everlasting early contribution was making the magazine hospitable to serious fiction and poetry, neither of which held any appeal for Ross (though he was a perceptive reader and judge of the former). In 1928, she began to actively solicit fiction, writing to Morley Callaghan, for example, shortly after he had two short stories published in a single issue of *Scribner's* magazine, the preeminent showcase of the day:

"We have read with much interest and pleasure your stories in *Scribner's*, and we wonder if by any chance you have on hand any short sketches (from 1000 to 1500 words) which you would care to let us see.

"We do not necessarily, you know, publish only 'funny' stuff, but we do like a great deal such vivid character sketches, though they must of course be pretty short."*

Poetry (as opposed to the light verse that had been a feature of the magazine since the outset) was a tougher sell, but by late 1929 she had persuaded Ross to let her recruit serious poets. Meanwhile, she was keeping an eye out for potential contributors of all kinds, and she tended to spot the kinds of writers Ross would miss. One such was Lewis Mumford, a widely published young cultural and architectural critic, whom she noticed writing for the *New Republic* and who, she said in a 1931 memo to Ross, "is the man who ought to be doing our Skyline [column]. He is the only person in the country writing important criticism on architecture today." Ross had the good sense to agree, as well as the skill to pursue Mumford until he had hooked him, as this exchange of letters shows:

Ross to Mumford, April 23, 1931: "I would very much like to see you before you go abroad and talk to you generally about the possibility of your doing some writing for us occasionally."

Ross to Mumford, May 5, 1931: "Please remember we are willing to entertain a suggestion for a story on the Rockefeller City."

Mumford to Ross, May 6, 1931: "Your note found me surrounded by three thousand words I had written this morning on Radio City: and I have just thrown them into the waste basket. After persistent groping one discovers that there is no architectural story on Radio City. All its possibilities went flat from the moment they decided to make it, not a public project,

---

*Callaghan responded with a submission, and two weeks later Mrs. Angell was writing him, "We were more delighted than we can say to receive your short story 'An Escapade' and we are honored to publish it. A short story of this sort is always new material for us and we have always, more or less, been in a quandary as to whether or not to publish straight fictional material but when anything as good as 'Escapade' comes along we are glad to take the plunge into a new field."

but a good piece of private business: which means as near like the rest of the city as possible. Perhaps they are a little short-sighted, even on those terms: but the *New Yorker* isn't the place to enter into the fallacious economics of the tall building."

Ross to Mumford, May 7, 1931: "I am very sorry. I wonder if you couldn't retrieve those 3,000 words from the waste-basket and let me see them. I am not convinced there is not a story in it. I should like to read what you have to say about Radio City even if it is in the form of rough notes or random thoughts."

Mumford's blistering critique of the Radio City office complex appeared in May and was one of the most talked-about pieces in the magazine's brief history. He continued to write the Skyline column until 1963 and reviewed art for the magazine from 1932 to 1937.

By the early thirties, Mrs. White's importance to the *New Yorker* had transcended her specific duties; in Brendan Gill's terms, she had become its "intellectual conscience." In 1933, Ross remarked in a memo to Fleischmann, "I regard Mrs. White as essential to the magazine, along with White, more essential than the entire business organization put together, and most of the editorial, for instance. She is irreplaceable, which very few other people are."

It would be hard to imagine a more mismatched pair than Ross and Mrs. White. In a letter to Thurber years later, Edmund Wilson wrote, "I always felt that the real riddle of the *New Yorker* was whether its elegance and literary correctitude represented some genuine ideal of Ross' or were entirely the creation of Katharine and the rest of you. Was it merely—as he at times seemed to imply—an accident that he was the editor of the *New Yorker* and not some other different kind of magazine?" It was no accident: the quality of the magazine emerged from the combination of these two diametrically different sensibilities. In a *Paris Review* interview, E. B. White explained:

> Ross, though something of a genius, had serious gaps. In Katharine, he found someone who filled them in. No two people were ever more different than Mr. Ross and Mrs. Angell; what he lacked, she had; what she lacked, he had. She complemented him in a way that, in retrospect, seems to me to have been indispensable to the survival of the magazine. She was a product of Miss Winsor's and Bryn Mawr. Ross was a high school dropout. She had a natural refinement of manner and speech; Ross mumbled and bellowed and swore. She quickly discovered, in this fumbling and impoverished new weekly, something that fascinated her: its quest for humor, its search for excellence, its involvement with young writers and artists. She enjoyed contact with people; Ross, with certain exceptions, despised it—especially during hours. She was patient and quiet; he was impatient and noisy.

The man who composed those words was christened Elwyn Brooks White in 1899 and grew up in the New York suburb of Mt. Vernon. His father was the chief executive of a successful piano-manufacturing company, interesting since White himself, though not musical, was sublimely attuned to the sounds of the language. In 1925, he was living with his parents, working unhappily for the Frank Seaman advertising agency in Manhattan, and contributing frequent light verses to FPA's "Conning Tower." The glory of these publications (there was no fee) and his mere proximity to the eminences of the moment fed White's soul. He wrote in retrospect:

> I burned with a low steady fever because I was on the same island with Don Marquis, Heywood Broun, Christopher Morley, Franklin P. Adams, Robert C. Benchley, Frank Sullivan, Dorothy Parker, Alexander Woollcott, Ring Lardner, and Stephen Vincent Benét. New York hardly gave me a living at that period, but it sustained me. I used to walk quickly past the house at West 13th Street between Sixth and Seventh where F.P.A. lived, and the block seemed to tremble under my feet the way Park Avenue trembles when a train leaves Grand Central Station.

It was in Grand Central Station, through which he passed in his commutes to and from Mt. Vernon, that White saw a copy of the first issue of the *New Yorker*. He recalled that he "was attracted to the newborn magazine not because it had any great merit but because the items were short, relaxed, and sometimes funny. I was a 'short' writer, and I lost no time in submitting squibs and poems." White's first published piece appeared April 11, titled "A Step Forward" and signed "E.B.W." In it White imagined the results when "the advertising man takes over the VERNAL account." The first two of his six examples will give the flavor of his conceit:

> A Million a Day
> If the new 1925 crocuses were not the most remarkable VALUE in the field, they wouldn't be appearing at the rate of a million a day.
> Nothing satisfies like a good crocus!

> New Beauty of Tone in 1925 Song Sparrow
> Into every one of this season's song sparrows has been built the famous VERNAL tone. Look for the distinguishing white mark on the breast.

There were three noteworthy things about this piece. All would have profound implications for the *New Yorker* in the ensuing decades, when White, as the writer of Notes and Comment, the first paragraphs in every week's issue, would be the magazine's strongest and most identifiable voice. First, it showed White's utter disdain for his soon-to-be-former employer, the advertising industry. It wasn't just that advertising was based on distortion and sometimes outright deception; advertisers'"weapons," as White put it in a 1936 Comment, "are our weaknesses: fear, ambition, illness, pride, selfishness, desire, ignorance." Bemusement sometimes bordering on contempt toward advertising would be one the strongest continuing themes of both Notes and Comment and White's Newsbreaks. (The appearance of these positions in a magazine that depended on advertising for its revenue, and thus to pay his own salary, was a paradox White never addressed.) Second, "A Step Forward," slight as it was, showed White's perfect-pitch ear for advertising's abuses of the language. More than any other writer of his generation, he *heard* the words he wrote and he read, and he brought that quality to the *New Yorker* as well. The third significant aspect of the piece was that it was about the coming of spring—crocuses and sparrows, and also daffodils, fertilizer, earthworms, and grass. It was so funny and on-the-mark that no one would have noticed at the time, but these subjects ran diametrically counter to the magazine's urban, steel-and-concrete view of the world. White, child of suburbia though he was, was as deeply attuned to the natural world—even in Manhattan!—as he was to the linguistic one, and over the years this was another gift he would pass on to the *New Yorker.*

White continued to contribute occasional pieces over the next year. According to his biographer Scott Elledge, two sketches he published in May 1926 prompted Katharine Angell to suggest to Ross that White be offered a job as a staff writer. These pieces—"Always" and "Lower Level"—were significant as well. The former was a portrait of a bum in Union Square, the latter of a drunk on a commuter train, both of them lowlife studies not at all out of keeping with the young magazine. But their perspective was completely fresh. Where the prevailing tone had been brittle and sardonic, White was ironic yet sympathetic toward his subjects and added a layer of complexity by foregrounding his own alternately amused and bemused reactions. Ross and Mrs. Angell may not have been able to put it into words, but they clearly realized that here was someone who could humanize their magazine.

Constitutionally independent, and still smarting from his advertising-business experience, White turned the offer down. But more and more of his efforts began to revolve around the *New Yorker.* From their inception, Newsbreaks writing had been a kind of joint enterprise, up for grabs by any staffer or contributor who wanted to take a crack at them. In the fall of 1926, Ross sent a batch to White and, upon receiving them back, immediately phoned the writer to ask him to take charge of the department. "I had never heard such a loud voice over the telephone," White recalled, "and I had never been encouraged before by an employer, so it was a memorable occasion." Shortly afterward, White accepted a $30-a-week, part-time job writing Newsbreaks, rewriting Talk of the Town pieces, and writing or "tinkering" with cartoon captions. This was all anonymous work, so his contributions cannot be pin-

FILE

E.B White

August 6, 1929

Dear Whites

A brief discussion this morning between Gibbs and myself,(you will note we are still carrying on down here) followed by a hasty calculation, led to the following intricate decision about your pay while you are away. We divided up your $150 weekly pay thus:

                    For Comment .... $ 90.00
                    For Newsbreaks 40.00
                    For office work ...   20.00
                    (including spinach
                     captions, etc.)

Your pay for office work is stopped. We will deduct from your Comment pay temporarily, the amount paid to other people contributing to this department, and we will deduct each week, $3.33 1/3 for each non-White newsbreak used. This, you will undoubtedly see, is 1/12 of 40 — the average number of newsbreaks used per issue.

Trusting you are the same,

                                        H. W. Ross.

P. S.   On second thought (after further discussion and

?.

figuring, we have decided it is simpler to pay you per inch
for your Comment as used, at a rate of $4.50 an inch.

H. W. R.

E. B. White, Esq.

One of Ross's attempts to pin down the notoriously elusive E. B. White.

pointed, but Lee Lorenz notes that after White's arrival, "the gag lines showed an immediate improvement" and nominates him as the person responsible for muscling into shape the one-line captions for which the *New Yorker* would become famous. Lorenz's supposition has the ring of truth. It is also supported by circumstantial evidence: White now selected the overwhelming majority of Newsbreaks and composed their tag lines, and they possessed the same completely unlabored, conversational, funny perfection of diction and tone that presently began to be seen in the captions.

White took over Notes and Comment—hitherto open to any contributor or staffer with something on his or her mind—in the final issues of 1926 and, except for a six-year break commencing in 1937, was its principal proprietor for the next thirty years. His approach and his prose, as Thurber put it, "struck the shining note that Ross had dreamed of striking," and the editor recognized this right away. Ralph Ingersoll, the managing editor, reported to Harrison Kinney, Thurber's biographer, that Ross "took to White instantly, sheltered him from the day of his bewildered arrival. White could do no wrong." In his own five years at the *New Yorker,* Ingersoll said, the only pieces Ross found "just right" were written by White. In the late thirties, the Whites left New York for Maine, and E.B.'s contributions to the *New Yorker* slowed. During World War II, Ross, desperate to get him back, wrote to Katharine, "Would he want to do anything else, do you think, or some special kind of writing? Whatever White wants to do he can do, as far as I am concerned. He's the one man I'll make any kind of deal with that he can name."

White, for his part, recognized that the *New Yorker* was the home where he was destined to settle, but, characteristically, he realized it rather slowly. In 1929, he wrote to his brother Stanley that the magazine was the first place that seemed amenable to the "impertinences and irrelevancies" by which his sensibility operated. In his *New Yorker* pieces, he went on, "Sometimes in writing of myself—which is the only subject anyone knows intimately—I have occasionally had the exquisite thrill of putting my finger on a little capsule of truth, and heard it give the faint squeak of mortality under my pressure, an antic sound."

Ross's immediate embrace of White really does seem like an act of genius, if only because the two men were superficially and inherently so different: the one profoundly loud, the other profoundly quiet; the one a tramp newspaperman, the other a self-confessed "flop" as a reporter; the one a Westerner who struck out on his own at fifteen, the other a Westchesterite who still (as of their first meeting) lived with his parents. After Ross's death, White wrote to their mutual friend Frank Sullivan:

> The things that matter a great deal to me, most of them, were not of much
> interest or importance to Ross, and vice versa, and we only met at a rather

special level and at one place—like a couple of trolley cars hitched together by a small coupling. The thing I thank God for is that the connection proved flawless and was never even strained, not even in the middle of Ross's towering rages. His rage, actually, was one of the sustaining things at the magazine because it was usually a sort of cosmic rage directed not at the person he was shouting at but at the enemy. Ross's private enemy is a study in itself. In retrospect I am beginning to think of him as an Atlas who lacked muscle tone but who God damn well decided he was going to hold up the world anyway.

As it was originally conceived, Notes and Comment was in the tradition of the collection of editorial paragraphs, a staple of American journalism dating, according to Scott Elledge, from Eugene Field's "Sharps and Flats," which ran in the *Chicago Daily News* from 1883 to 1895. Contemporary examples in New York, besides FPA's "Conning Tower," were Christopher Morley's "Bowling Green" in the *Post* and Don Marquis's "Sun Dial" in the *Sun*; in England, *Punch* led off with a section of blithe pronouncements called "Charivaria." The *New Yorker's* version was anonymous but otherwise resembled its counterparts in offering up an assortment of usually unrelated bons mots, observations, ironies, and bits of intelligence or whimsy, each kicked off by an initial capital letter. Here are some selections from a Notes and Comment from early in 1926:

> While not one of those fortunate creatures whose minds are like a rose garden and who can find joy and beauty in everything, we nevertheless agree with the man who does not mind the shortest day in the year if it means that the Woolworth Building is illuminated that much longer.

> Recently we have ceased to be able to overlook the vegetable broccoli. We successfully overlooked Hearts of Palm—excepting as an occasional vehicle for hollandaise—but broccoli is more persistent. Be it noted that we will eat broccoli only when we have eaten up all the cauliflower.

> During the week, Mr. Eustace Tilley found himself with three gentlemen of legal bent. Suddenly said one of them, "Did you go to the F.P.A. dinner?" The ladies present, like almost all ladies, having written at some time for the Conning Tower, pricked their ears. But no. It was the Foreign Policy Association.

> Christmas Eve at four-thirty the policeman at Fifth and Forty-ninth Street solved the traffic problem. Everything was jammed and there was no place to go. Yet when the lights changed, a taxi moved. "Where you going?" bawled the policeman. "Can't you see there ain't no traffic?"

In White's hands the paragraphs became longer and deeper. He was a great admirer of Thoreau (one of the few authors he took to his heart), the

Thoreau who wrote in *Walden,* "I once had a sparrow alight on my shoulder for a moment while I was hoeing in a village garden, and I felt that I was more distinguished by that circumstance than I should have been by any epaulette I could have worn," and, in his journals, "The perception of beauty is a moral test." To an extent not seen anywhere in the *New Yorker* before, White's Notes and Comment was cognizant of and attuned to the natural world, even if in Manhattan this manifested itself in such forms as the birth of a son to his pet snail and the unexpected cactus plants seen in many florists' windows one winter. The last led White to muse, "From our seat overlooking the city's canyons of tinsel and remorse, we like to think that on the window sill of many a little stenographer's bedroom there sits a tiny cactus plant, emblem of horsemanship, love, fresh air, and virtue triumphant." Nature in turn directed his attention to its two great themes—beauty and death. The Thoreauvian parallels continue. White was a militant individualist who valued freedom, especially his own freedom, above all other virtues. He was admittedly focused on himself, sometimes to the point of solipsism, and always precluding the awareness of and interest in others that would permit him ever to write adult fiction. (Thoreau wrote in *Walden,* "I should not talk so much about myself if there were anyone else I knew as well.") But for White's literary purposes, his self-consciousness was fertile and benign. In the foreword to his collected essays, he wrote:

> I have always been aware that I am by nature self-absorbed and egotistical; to write of myself to the extent I have done indicates a too great attention to my own life, not enough to the lives of others. I have worn many shirts, and not all of them have been a good fit. But when I am discouraged or downcast I need only fling open the door of my closet, and there, hidden behind everything else, hangs the mantle of Michel de Montaigne, smelling slightly of camphor.

When he had been conducting Notes and Comment for nearly five years, White received a questionnaire from a professor writing a textbook on American magazines. One of the questions asked, "Does your periodical endeavor to render public service or to wage crusades? If so, kindly list some of the projects in which your publication has been interested, past and present." As with Wolcott Gibbs in "Answers to Hard Questions" the year before, this became grist for White's editorial mill. Unlike Gibbs, he had no trouble responding.

"The answer is Yes," White wrote.

> Crusaders we. Our sword is forged not of steel (which fluctuates in the open market) but of the soft tinfoil wrappers of Tutti-Frutti gum, which bend to every thrust, neither injuring our opponent nor breaking our own wrist. Our

protagonist is Cyrano, in a three-button suit. We lie in wait for popular philosophers who gather into small salable books the profundities. We attend fires, particularly those of the Harvard Club. Verbosity we cut down with a single stroke. We attend teas, fêtes, balls, ribbon-cuttings, and coronations, attempting to describe such affairs in the manner in which they appear to us. We are against capital letters, and war. We are the head of a society for the preservation of Ed Wynn. Poets we discipline, and we are on the side of snow, and against its removal. We abhor and attack the garnished utterance of the public character. In a crusading spirit we aim to interpret the dreams of our warriors by correct spelling, and correct punctuation. We pay them just enough to live on. We go about burning all second-class mail matter. We refrain from calling a spade a spade if it is dull anyway. We are against the spirit of advertising in radio, which attempts to direct notice to a chocolate bar by the singing of a love lyric. We succeeded in getting the information booth at the Pennsylvania terminal moved out into the middle of the floor, and then discovered there was no information we needed. We are in favor of the sublimation of cross-town traffic in art, and of the sublimation of art in inactivity. We pointed out a year ago that the extra number in the telephone system would be the beginning of the end. Go ahead and list us in your book as a crusading publication, but watch out! Our sword, already bent double, is doubling back upon our breast!

The final piece of this particular puzzle was James Grover Thurber, a native of Columbus, Ohio, who, in June 1926, was deposited in New York after a year's sojourn in Paris. He had some experience as a newspaperman, but his aspirations were literary and comical, and he began peppering the *New Yorker* with submissions. After being rejected twenty times in a row, Thurber was seriously considering returning to Ohio, deciding to stay only when FPA devoted an entire "Conning Tower" to one of his *New Yorker* rejects. Soon after that he took a reporter's job at the *New York Evening Post*, and soon after *that* the *New Yorker* finally bought something he had written. The circumstances of that first acceptance are telling. The writer Joel Sayre, a close friend from Columbus, told Harrison Kinney, "I was lounging on a sofa in the Thurbers' apartment one Sunday afternoon in January 1927. Thurber had been working away at his typewriter on something he hoped to sell the *New Yorker*. Althea [Thurber's wife] said to him, 'Aren't you spoiling your stories by spending too much time on them?' She suggested, half in fun, that he set an old alarm clock to ring in forty-five minutes and try to finish his article within that time. Thurber did. Then he retyped it cleanly and sent it off to the *New Yorker*. He received a check for forty dollars."

The rejected pieces are lost to history, but Sayre's anecdote suggests that their problem lay in their being labored, obvious—not casual. The accepted one, titled "An American Romance," was so brief and offhand that few people reading the issue of March 5, 1927, probably even remembered it into the next day. But in the light of literary history it has an air of absolute inevitability. The piece begins:

"The little man in an overcoat that fitted him badly at the shoulders had had a distressing scene with his wife. He had left home with a look of serious determination and had now been going around and around in the central revolving door of a prominent department store's main entrance for fifteen minutes."

The little man continues to go around for two hours more, attracting, in turn, a crowd of onlookers, a pack of newspaper reporters, and an assortment of offers from motion picture companies. The whole ridiculous tableau mildly satirized the odd 1920s trend of English Channel–swimming, flagpole-sitting, and the like. But the theme is immaterial. The astonishing thing about the piece is the way that first paragraph points the way to James Thurber's contribution to the *New Yorker* and to American literature. "The little man"—ineffectual and quietly resentful in the face of the forces ruling his life—would become the best-known creation of Thurber and, by extension, the *New Yorker,* culminating in the 1939 "The Secret Life of Walter Mitty." The throwaway reference to a "distressing scene with his wife" retrospectively sounds the starting pistol for Thurber's exhaustive, merciless, and meticulous three-decade chronicle of the war between men and women, especially between husbands and wives. Without Thurber's dispatches, the Maple stories of John Updike would not be imaginable. Less apparent, but possibly more daring, is the way, by matter-of-factly positing an absurd but resonant premise and doggedly pursuing its logical consequences, the story prefigures another later *New Yorker* writer, Donald Barthelme. It is a Kafka sort of method, and it can be seen as representing the *New Yorker's* first brush with literary modernism of any kind.

Over the next few weeks, Thurber sold another casual and two poems to the magazine. Meanwhile, he met E. B. White, with whom he shared a mutual friend. Apparently laboring under the misapprehension that the two were boon companions of long standing, Ross summoned Thurber to the *New Yorker* office and, to the writer's shock, hired him as the latest Central Desk man charged with bringing order to the magazine. Thurber was perhaps the least likely "jesus" in the magazine's history, in that he possessed virtually no administrative, organizational, or managerial skills. After about six months (actually, a longer stint than usual), Ross relieved him of his editing duties and assigned him to the post of rewrite man for The Talk of the Town.

By this time Thurber and White really had become close friends. They shared an office (White recalled in a touching obituary he wrote for Thurber in the *New Yorker*) "the size of a hall bedroom. There was just enough room for two men, two typewriters, and a stack of copy paper. The copy paper disappeared at a scandalous rate—not because our production was high (although it was) but because Thurber used copy paper as the natural receptacle for discarded sorrows, immediate joys, stale dreams, golden prophecies, and messages of good cheer to the outside world and to fellow-workers. His mind was never at rest, and his pencil was connected to his mind by the best connective tissue I have ever seen in action." Their tiny work space was such a petri dish of literary creativity that it is impossible to chart precisely the two men's influence on each other, but the movement in each direction was surely considerable. Comically extravagant in person and on the page, and connected to an imagination that if anything was too fertile, Thurber profitably adopted a measure of his officemate's controlled approach. He observed in the 1950s, "The precision and clarity of White's writing helped me a lot, slowed me down from the foxtrot of newspaper tempo and made me realize a writer turns on his mind, not a faucet." And White—though he had by this point committed to the path of his own choosing—was too smart not to observe and absorb from Thurber some of the rewards of occasional literary risk-taking.

Under Thurber, The Talk of the Town became a literary highlight of the magazine. The department was originated by one James Kevin McGuinness and, after a series of adjustments over the first year, took the shape it would retain for another sixty-five. The "Van Bibber III" signature was dropped almost immediately in favor of "THE NEW YORKERS"; italicized titles for the individual pieces showed up in March and in August began to be limited to one or two words, in the manner of the slugs newspaper reporters use on their copy; and in the same month Notes and Comment made its first appearance as a series of leadoff editorials. Ross would always take a strong interest in the section, but Ralph Ingersoll (in a letter to Thurber after *The Years with Ross* was published) claimed:

> It was I who invented—literally—the *form* of the Talk Department. Not the style, God forbid, nor the polish—but the form: of alternating short essays with anecdotes; inventing the several different essay forms . . . consisting of "visit pieces," miniature Profiles, dope stories (background pieces to newspapermen) etc.; the whole anecdotal warp and short essay woof to be woven into a disguised but discernible pattern to cover those fields of Metropolitan interest which were our special province: each of the arts, Park Avenue and a touch of Wall Street, the beginnings of what's now known as Café Society, etc.
>
> It was my idea that the department be run by spot news coverage backed by a bank of material which, ideally, should include an inventory of visit, personality and dope pieces in *each* field—and anecdotes, ditto—so that a given

week's departments could be put together with each of the dozen-odd components laid in a different sphere of interest. Done right, the whole would give the reader—unobtrusively—the feeling that he had been everywhere, knew everyone, was up on everything. And each week a different locale and subject pattern—so that over, say a month or six weeks with Talk, a reader did really get around.

Before Thurber's arrival, the principal writers for the section were Fillmore Hyde and Russel Crouse, later a prominent playwright. Ross's notion was always that Talk would sound like "dinner-table conversation," and Thurber—a virtuoso raconteur among friends—took over the task of taking reporters' raw notes, running them through his typewriter, and emerging with polished gems. Talk had to have a consistent tone, and until he gave up the job to go freelance in 1935, Thurber (or sometimes White, Coates, or Ross) would rewrite everyone who contributed to the section. Thus, when Henry Pringle, one of the top journalists in the country and a regular writer of New Yorker Profiles, sent in a sketch about an influential City Hall financial staffer named Duncan MacInnes, Thurber cut it by a third, eliminated Pringle's lead—a long anecdote about a past municipal investigation—and cast the whole in the sort of stately but light understatement for which The Talk of the Town soon became known. Thurber also wrote numerous Talk stories on his own. In their richness of observation, humor, and high style, the best of these—accounts of a walking tour he took of cemeteries in lower Manhattan, of the area around the docks on the West Side of the city, and of the length and breadth of Fourteenth Street; a consideration of O. Henry's last years in New York; visit pieces on an early network-radio broadcast, a bridge tournament, and a Gertrude Stein autographing session; and personality pieces about the prizefighter Jack Johnson and Huey Long—suggest that, in the traditional news feature no less than in other forms, Thurber was an artist and innovator of rare quality.

Something else that set Thurber apart from White was his complicated romantic life. (White's, always manageable, was permanently set after his marriage to Katharine Angell.) Although Thurber had been married to the former Althea Adams since 1921, the couple periodically separated, and Thurber pined for, among other people, Eva Prout, whom he had known since the third grade in Columbus and who was now a dancer in vaudeville. In the spring of 1928, when Prout and her husband were performing in New York, they stayed at a Times Square hotel, and Thurber would visit them every night when their show was over. The little group would play popular records on the Victrola, send out to the delicatessen for sandwiches, and then Thurber would make his way home to his Greenwich Village apartment in the small hours. Out of these elements Thurber fashioned a story, "Menaces in May," which the *New Yorker* published on May 26, 1928. In his book *The Years with Ross,* Thurber said Ross consented to print it only after White urged him to do so, and the editor's reluctance is understandable, for "Menaces in May" is a powerful, daring, and shrewd piece of fiction. Thurber refers to it as "my first serious casual," but in fact it was the first serious short story published in the *New Yorker* and as such opened the door for Morley Callaghan (to whom Katharine White would write five months hence) and hundreds of distinguished works of fiction over the next seven decades.

Composed in the present tense, the story tracks the consciousness of Thurber's alter ego (described as a playwright but referred to only as "the man") as he leaves the hotel and goes home through menacing Manhattan street scenes; his mind careens from the torch he carries for "Julia," to his troubled relationship with his wife, to his Mittyesque fantasies of subduing a drunken sailor on the subway. It is pure autobiography, as anyone who knew Thurber would immediately recognize, not only in particulars but in the merciless way he catches his own habit of alternating among self-mockery, self-aggrandizement, and self-pity. That stance shows a true sophistication beyond anything that had appeared in the *New Yorker*, as does the way the snatches of conversations "the man" has overheard and the lyrics to the romantic songs played on the hotel-room Victrola reverberate in his head, providing a running and ironic counterpoint. At the end, as he falls into bed, "He tries to keep his mind fixed on the dark sheen of a whirling Victrola record. 'What a day was yes-ter-day for yes-ter-day gave me you-u-u ... the hell ya ever bin in love the hell ya bin in love the hell ya have ...'"

By now, in addition to Talk duties, Thurber was a frequent contributor of signed pieces, selling thirteen each in 1927 and 1928, twenty-three in 1929, and twenty-six—an average of one every other week—in 1930. Many of them were protypical humorous casuals, identifiably different from what Robert Benchley, Frank Sullivan, and Wolcott Gibbs were contributing only in Thurber's noticeably more elevated frame of literary and cultural reference. He would frequently mention or allude to Proust or Henry James (always a favorite of his); in an exercise called "More Authors Cover the Snyder Trial," he imagined how tabloid journalism would be perpetrated in the hands of James Joyce and Gertrude Stein. And in a series of a dozen pieces called "Our Own Modern English Usage," he delightfully skewered H. W. Fowler's *Modern English Usage,* the 1926 handbook that had already become Ross's bible in matters of diction, grammar, and punctuation. From Thurber's essay "Who and Whom":

> The number of people who use "whom" and "who" wrongly is appalling.
> The problem is a difficult one and it is complicated by the importance of

tone, or taste. Take the common expression, "Whom are you, anyways?" That is of course, strictly speaking, correct—and yet how formal, how stilted! The usage to be preferred in ordinary speech and writing is "Who are you, anyways?" "Whom" should be used in the nominative case only when a note of dignity or austerity is desired. For example, if a writer is dealing with a meeting of, say, the British Cabinet, it would be better to have the Premier greet a new arrival, such as an under-secretary, with a "Whom are you, anyways?" rather than a "Who are you, anyways?"—always granted that the Premier is sincerely unaware of the man's identity. To address a person one knows by a "Whom are you?" is a mark either of incredible lapse of memory or inexcusable arrogance. "How are you?" is a much kindlier salutation.

In late 1928 and 1929, while writing "Our Own Modern English Usage," Thurber was also contributing another series, one that represented a true creative leap. In eight stories about a couple called Mr. and Mrs. Monroe, Thurber took the autobiographical impulse of "Menaces in May" but recast it in the dark comic tones that would henceforth be known as Thurberesque. Mr. Monroe is a Thurber alter ego beset (as the author was) by having to deal with machinery, workmen, bats, strange noises in a country house at night, and not least, the supercilious Mrs. Monroe, who haunts and torments him even during her frequent absences. Mr. Monroe acknowledges that she can read him like a book, but maintains that while she has the details right, she has missed the deeper themes. Thurber's striking achievement in the stories is to unfacetiously make fun of himself, presenting Mr. Monroe as a prisoner of the resentments, neuroses, small fears, and overheated imagination Thurber knew so well.

Also in that astonishingly productive year, 1929, Thurber and White collaborated on a book. Titled *Is Sex Necessary?* it was a takeoff on the sex manuals and self-help books that were proliferating at the time, and it was a great success, staying on the best-seller lists for weeks and putting the authors on the road to celebrity. The whimsical content would be forgettable today were it not for one thing. During their joint tenantship of a *New Yorker* office, White had noticed that Thurber habitually made drawings—mostly of people and dogs—during pauses in his writing, the way other people would scratch their chin or light a pipe. Unlike anyone else, including Thurber, White saw merit in the pictures and insisted that his coauthor contribute the illustrations to the book. They were undeniably expressive and comical, yet so unconventional in their spare abstraction that White felt obliged to contribute, as an afterword, "A Note on the Drawings in This Book," in which he prophetically identified some of the characteristics of the Thurber style:

> When one studies the drawings, it soon becomes apparent that a strong undercurrent of grief runs through them. In almost every instance the *man* in

the picture is badly frightened, or even hurt. Those "Thurber men" have come to be recognized as a distinct type in the world of art; they are frustrated, fugitive beings; at times they seem vaguely striving to get out of something without being seen (a room, a situation, a state of mind), at other times they are merely perplexed and too humble, or weak, to move. The *women,* you will notice, are quite different: temperamentally they are much better adjusted to their surroundings than are the men, and mentally they are much less capable of making themselves uncomfortable.

On White's urging, Thurber had submitted a drawing to the magazine shortly before the book came out. This was the time when Admiral Byrd and others were exploring the polar regions, and the cartoon showed a seal on a rock, looking at some figures in the distance and saying, "Hmmm, explorers." Thurber remembered, "It came back with a note and sketch from Rea Irvin, the art director . . . showing how a seal's whiskers look. White resubmitted mine, saying this was how a *Thurber* seal's whiskers look, but Ross turned me down. After the book was a success, he denied that he had seen it. He asked me for it, but I'd thrown it away. He wanted me to do it again, but more than a year went by before I tried it."

By this time, the *New Yorker* tradition of plausible, realistic cartoons had been established. And so it was ready to be imploded and brought to a higher level of truth by Thurber. In the new version of his seal cartoon, Thurber found, to his surprise, that instead of a rock, the seal's perch was starting to look like the headboard of a bed. So Thurber made it a headboard and followed that with a Thurber man and a Thurber woman in the bed proper. In his caption, the woman looks angry, the man looks beleaguered, and she is saying to him:

"All right, have it your way—you heard a seal bark."

CHAPTER THREE

LOWLIFE ASCENDANT

1931~41

SUCCESS STORY

Hawley Truax tells me that he went into some clothing firm, Tripler, I think, to buy some trousers advertised in a recent issue of the *New Yorker*. The salesman said, "We are all sold out." Truax said, "All out of my size?" "No," said the salesman, "entirely sold out of the whole stock. I suppose you saw them advertised in *The New Yorker*." "Yes," said Mr. Truax.

—Harold Ross to Raoul Fleischmann, July 27, 1927

~~~

I think it is essential that all members of the advertising staff be tactfully but firmly taught that they are in no wise to have direct contact with the members of the editorial staff or with me—that they are to deal with the editorial department only through the head of their department.

In my opinion this is most important. Unless stern measures are taken my present efforts to keep the editorial department independent, uninfluenced, honest and—more important than all—slightly aloof, will be more or less defeated. I do not want any member of the staff to be conscious of the advertising or business problems of *The New Yorker*. If so they will lose their spontaneity and verve and we will be just like all other magazines. In my opinion it is this burdening of practical problems on editorial departments that makes them timid, self-conscious and afraid and produces a flat book. In this kind of publication the flavor is practically the whole thing.

—Ross to Fleischmann, April 17, 1926

~~~~

Near the top of any list of significant points about the *New Yorker* would have to be its success, which was quick, substantial, and, for about forty-five years, virtually unrelenting. Growth was especially dramatic in the first three decades. Circulation hit a nadir of fifteen hundred copies in the grim summer of 1925, but then increased at a redoubtable steadiness. Consider the following year-end circulation figures:

YEAR	SUBSCRIPTION	SINGLE COPIES	TOTAL
1925	3,375	10,689	14,064
1926	25,069	21,377	46,446
1927	31,963	29,090	61,053
1928	34,008	35,509	69,517
1929	36,333	45,844	82,177
1930	43,803	61,205	105,008
1931	49,620	69,093	118,713
1932	56,751	55,838	112,589
1933	60,491	56,116	116,607
1934	63,526	60,847	124,373
1935	67,267	60,943	128,210
1936	73,335	60,943	134,004
1937	78,459	55,384	133,843
1938	85,016	49,791	134,807
1939	90,744	55,838	146,582
1940	96,769	59,779	156,548
1941	105,105	66,560	171,665

The progression is all the more impressive when one goes behind the numbers. First, it was achieved with minimal advertising or promotion (except in 1926, when, according to Ralph Ingersoll's 1934 *Fortune* article, about $125,000 was spent—and well spent, too, in view of the more than 300 percent circulation increase that year). Nor did it benefit from the discounted subscriptions or contests traditionally used to gain readers. A newspaper ad the magazine ran on its second anniversary boasted, "Without premiums, short term offers, clubbing, guessing or prize contests, the bright Manhattan public have taken us up because they like us." There was truth behind this hype.

According to Ingersoll, some 60 percent of *New Yorker* subscribers consistently renewed every year, historically a high figure in the magazine industry. Those not renewing were replenished, and then some, from the pool of newsstand buyers of single issues. This was an impressively large pool, roughly equivalent in number to subscribers until the late thirties, when it dipped and, not coincidentally, circulation as a whole temporarily stagnated. (Subscription sales doubled newsstand sales for the first time in 1944, tripled them in 1961, and quadrupled them in 1967. In the six months ending June 30, 1997, subscription sales averaged 755,771 and single-copy sales 43,272—the latter being lower than the corresponding figure for 1929.)

Advertising traditionally follows circulation, and so it did in the *New Yorker*. In every year between 1927 and 1940, it was one of the top three American magazines in number of advertising pages sold. (Interestingly, it was first only once, in 1934.) It had the advantage of being a weekly, of course, but so did *Time* and the *Saturday Evening Post*. Although those two magazines had vastly higher circulations, the nature of the *New Yorker's* readership set it apart. It was the inevitable choice for anyone seeking to reach a certain class of New Yorkers. Ingersoll's *Fortune* article set out some numbers that made this clear: *Vogue* had 28,000 readers in New York, but to speak to them, an advertiser had to spend $1,500 a page. A page in the *New Yorker*, with half of its 125,000 readers living in the city, cost $850. (The magazine had also inaugurated a two-edition policy with the "out-of-town" edition containing marginally less copy than the "metropolitan" one. One could buy a page in the New York edition alone for $550, a "bargain price" that, in Ingersoll's view, "saw the magazine through the depression.") On the other side of the spectrum, the *New York Times'* circulation was 389,000, but it cost $2,131 a page to reach readers on all levels of society.

The advertising community took heed, and, again, figures tell the story.

YEAR	ADVERTISING INCOME	AFTER-TAX PROFIT
1925	$36,000	$(66,000)
1926	389,000	(330,000)
1927	1,047,000	(276,000)
1928	1,476,000	287,000
1929	1,929,000	486,100
1930	1,922,000	361,600
1931	1,797,000	371,700
1932	1,448,000	175,100
1933	1,491,000	263,000
1934	2,250,000 (est.)	619,400

The magazine's growth and earnings in its first five years were spectacular, but its consistent profitability in the thirties—the decade of the Great Depression—was even more remarkable. Profits didn't even take a hit until 1932; they not only recovered but shot ahead in 1934 because of the repeal of Prohibition the year before. According to an internal New Yorker document, liquor advertising represented about 17 percent of the 1934 gross and 40 percent of the increased volume. The magazine did so well during the years of the slump that White later admitted to a friend, "I have lived all my life with a guilty feeling about the depressed years. The New Yorker was, of course, a child of the depression and when everybody else was foundering we were running free, and I still feel that I escaped the hard times undeservedly and will always go unacquainted with the facts of life."

Despite continuing gains in circulation, profits did subsequently decrease, leveling off at about $200,000 in 1939 and 1940, due in part to continually increasing manufacturing costs and a rise in the federal corporate income tax from about 12 percent when the magazine started to 31 percent in 1941. As a result of the European war in the late thirties, travel ads dropped off markedly. In addition, with the magazine firmly on its feet, Ross began using some of the revenue to significantly increase hitherto meager contributor payments and staff salaries; through the mid and late thirties, the editorial budget consistently rose nearly 10 percent a year. The spending strained Ross's already testy relationship with Fleischmann, who in a 1941 memo complained, "It is not benighted capitalistic hoggishness that makes me anxious as hell, but a realization that if the Editorial Department does not call a halt somewhere and sometime, the lines of rising costs will reach a point where any recession in business will bring us into the red and any important recession for any length of time will put us out of business."*

Also a source of tension, and also a drag on the bottom line, was Ross's unusual notion that the magazine should be as selective about the ads it ran as it was about the articles and drawings it printed. He exploded at anything that hinted of the cheap or fraudulent, a category in which he included the full-page ads for Fleischmann yeast asserting that the product was a virtual panacea, and endorsements of coffee featuring the likenesses and testimony of New Yorker contributors Alexander Woollcott and John Held Jr. Concerning the latter, Ross fired a memo to one of Fleischmann's aides that impressed then-editor Ralph Ingersoll so much, he preserved it in his scrapbook:

---

*Fleischmann made no mention of another drain on profits, his investment, in the late thirties, of an estimated $750,000 of the magazine's money in a glossy entertainment magazine called Stage. Ross found out about this in 1938 and threatened to quit if the New Yorker did not abandon its bankrolling of this money-losing competitor. Fleischmann complied.

Well, I am as bitter as ever about some of the advertising we have been carrying lately, and since the situation has recently led to embarrassing complications, I think we ought to do something definite about it. I propose as follows: that we will not use any endorsement advertising containing a palpable lie, or a statement we are morally certain is a lie.

...Our readers, or the readers we hope to hold and get for the *New Yorker* are intelligent enough to know that this stuff is the bunk (Woollcott and Held endorsements). We are being shortsighted in running it. We have an opportunity to live honestly. We also have the great privilege now of being in a position to lead the advertising industry for Christ's sake. Let us no longer pussyfoot. Let us be really honest, and not just slick. I think that in our present prosperous condition we could afford to suffer even a temporary small loss in revenue to keep our conscience clear.

Ross also resisted ads that had any connection with bodily functions or patent-medicine cures. This position stemmed not only from the traditional disreputableness of such products but from his own notorious squeamishness, in part a function of the ulcers and other stomach problems that afflicted him. He once boasted to Ralph Barton that the magazine had never run halitosis advertising.* ("I am forced to acknowledge," he went on, "that we carried an ad for a belching preventative two or three weeks ago but that was because the advertising manager was asleep.")

Taste was a concern in editorial as well as advertising decisions. Ross, predictably, would not countenance any reference to what he called "the filthy excretions of the body." Sexual frankness was less of a problem, and in fact the magazine was known in its early years for its daring. The journalist Elmer Davis observed to Ross in 1926 that the *Saturday Review* "seems to be getting a little more lubricious, inspired by the example on the floor above. So is *Life*, by the way, and I doubt not you started them off too. The *New Yorker*, whatever its other achievements, can certainly be set down as having expanded the pomoerium of periodical frankness." To the extent that this was true, it was mainly the result of the cartoons, which often treated carnal matters explicitly—but usually resisted the leer or wink. It was an oddly selective explicitness, fixating on the relationships between stuffed-shirt sugar daddies and chorus girls and other kept women, but was no less funny or knowing for that. Of the two men who mined the territory most productively, Peter Arno got the most attention, but the little-remembered William C. Galbraith was probably the sexiest artist in the magazine's his-

*That particular issue was still a concern in 1940, when managing editor Ik Shuman wrote in a memo to Fleischmann, "Mr. Ross, Mr. Shawn and I felt that any ad which implied bad breath should be barred from magazine because they are in bad taste, disgust many readers and lower the tone of the magazine."

tory. Arno was justly appreciated for the almost palpable sexual energy his drawings gave off, but his cartoons were identifiably *cartoons,* with comical white-mustached suitors and chorines whose estimable breasts pointed toward the stars. Galbraith's charcoals and wash gave his full-page drawings a rich chiaroscuro, his scantily (and sometimes not-at-all) clad women were the stuff of adolescent fantasy, and the dark areas in the backgrounds and corners suggested something of the not always pleasant or easily discernible regions of carnal knowledge. Sex would always be a subtheme of *New Yorker* cartoons (and Whitney Darrow Jr. and Sam Cobean, who began contributing in 1933 and 1944, respectively, would make the nude female figure a specialty), but it subsided in the late thirties, partly because *Esquire* magazine hit it so hard; next to the color illustrations of George Petty and E. Simms Campbell, even Galbraith's stuff seemed tame.

From the evidence of Ross's memos and letters, language was a more frequent sticking point than sex. No one as sensitive as he was to the written and spoken word could fail to recognize how close to necessary "profanity" sometimes was; the brilliance of the famous spinach caption was "and I say the hell with it." But Ross kept a close eye on every such word that went into the magazine. Here is a characteristic 1930 memo to Rea Irvin, about an unidentified cartoon:

"Cut our throats if you will, but we changed that 'damn' in the caption to 'you idiot,' as several of us thought that was better. We have too much profanity in the book. We had six 'hells' in one issue lately, and probably a couple of 'damns' also."

Sensitivity to language is a curious and continuing feature of American puritanism, and 1930 was in fact a benchmark in its long history. In that year Hollywood instituted its notorious Motion Picture Production Code, which would eventually list forty-three prohibited words and phrases—including *broad, cripes, fairy* ("in a vulgar sense"), *hot* ("applied to a woman"), *in your hat, nerts,* and *tomcat* ("applied to a man"). Cultural gatekeepers such as magazine editors were compelled to address this issue head-on, and in 1933, *Vanity Fair* editor Frank Crowninshield wrote Ross asking for advice:

> We are a little in a quandary here as to how far it is wise for *Vanity Fair* to go in the direction of tabooed words. I often feel that I am more than a generation behind the trend of the day, when I read the manuscripts that are sent us, go to the movies, glance at the tabloids, or read the novels of Faulkner, Hemingway et al.
>
> Would you, as a favor, tell me whether or not you permit, in your pages, such words as *Christ* (used as an expletive), *bitch, bastard,* or *Lesbian?* I find an increasing insistence on these words in the manuscripts that are sent me by young and often really promising writers. . . .

Ross's reply was a revealing document, given added piquancy because the time he himself had spent in newsrooms and barracks was not wasted: his own speech was profane in the extreme. "The use of daring words is one of our most serious problems, or at any rate, one of my most serious concerns," he began.

> I, too, suspect frequently that I am a generation behind. Much of my activity the last couple of years has been fighting the use of words which I think are shocking in print. I am completely disqualified as a judge of what is shocking. That is my difficulty in the present situation. I am an old-fashioned double-standard boy who is shocked at nothing, absolutely nothing, in a stag gathering, but who is embarrassed poignantly at any word or reference which used to be called off-color, in mixed company....
>
> A magazine is certainly something for circulation in mixed company and I always keep in mind *The New Yorker* will be left around the house where it is available to women and children. That is a practical consideration and, it seems to me, a very important one.... On the other hand, I am theoretically in favor of a certain amount of frankness, sex freedom, and all the other things talked about today. This is intellectual and not instinctive. I cannot dismiss my puritanical inheritance and training....
>
> We were very out-spoken, more so than any other publication, I think, a few years ago, allowing writers to use "hell" and a few words like that, but from the stuff we get in here today you would think the young writers were having a field day with dirty words. I fight it all I can, killing all profanity and all obscenity when they are not absolutely justified. At that, I went through one issue recently in which we had five "hells": in five pages, all of them justified artistically, but the net impression was nevertheless, pretty bad, I think.

A corollary to Ross's standards concerning taste in advertising was his determination, arrived at early on, that the prospect of either gaining or losing ads would never influence the magazine's contents. That kind of aggressive independence from business concerns was common in the newspaper world that schooled him, but much less so in commercial magazines, which were expected to present at the very least a *climate* conducive to consumption and in many cases dealt with explicit quid pro quos: editorial mentions in exchange for space bought. To prevent even the appearance of such arrangements, Ross was adamant that strict lines of demarcation be kept between the editorial and business departments, demanding in a 1926 memo to Fleischmann that "the members of the advertising staff be tactfully but firmly taught that they are in no wise to have direct contact with the members of the editorial staff or with me." This "separation of church and state" would come to be one of the most famous characteristics of the magazine, adhered to so strictly that men and women who worked in the respective departments (physically separated by only one floor at 20 West Forty-third Street) for decades would retire never having met one another.

On this point, Ross got no argument from White, who was still fighting the good fight in 1976, when the Xerox Corporation announced plans to pay journalist Harrison Salisbury a substantial amount to write an *Esquire* magazine article about a trip across America. In a letter to one of the copier-machine company's minions, White recalled the days when Ross

> was having a tough time finding money to keep his floundering little sheet alive, yet he was determined that neither money nor influence would ever corrupt his dream or deflower his text. His boiling point was so low as to be comical. The faintest suggestion of the shadow of advertising in his news and editorial columns would cause him to erupt. He would explode in anger, the building would reverberate with his wrath, and his terrible swift sword would go flashing up and down the corridors. For a young man, it was an impressive sight and a memorable one.

A WINNING FORMULA

During all the early part of my life I was kicked around by art editors who used type merely to frame pictures, or give them a background, and who made writers write to fit layouts of their concoction, etc., and I'm violently against them. When I started this magazine I didn't allow an art editor within three blocks of the premises and gave the type the right of way.

—Harold Ross to Lucius Beebe, February 25, 1948

P.S. I forgot to say that we would like to get further pieces from you—anything, including things on your father. We would be very glad to run a little series on him if you saw fit, which is a very bright idea for an editor to have.

—Harold Ross to Clarence Day, December 12, 1932,
in a letter accepting "Father and the French Court,"
Day's first "Life with Father" piece in the *New Yorker*

As the *New Yorker* gained more readers and sold more advertising, it was obliged to print more pages of editorial material. It would have been easy and justifiable to take up substantial parts of this space with photographs or large graphic displays, but Ross, instead, chose to commit himself to text. In retrospect this shines as another stroke of genius. Flashy graphics—and even substantial amounts of white space—would have distracted readers from the writing and the cartoons to which Ross was committed. A side benefit was that an editorially gray and subdued magazine offered no visual competition to colorful big-splash advertising; the New Yorker's format, as well as its readership, was an important reason for its success on Madison Avenue.

The magazine filled its space by printing more articles and longer articles. The expansion was not dramatic in the case of casuals and short stories. Up until 1930, the unofficial limit for these was two thousand words. By 1935, Katharine White was writing to a new fiction contributor, Sylvia Townsend Warner, that stories generally ran "three thousand words or less." And in the late thirties, several notable stories, including Robert Coates's "The Net," Jerome Weidman's "The Explorers," Irwin Shaw's "Main Currents of American Thought" (and other Shaw stories), and Daniel Fuchs's "Love in Brooklyn," approached or surpassed four thousand words. Nonfiction pieces grew quickly, so much so that they soon had to be broken up over two or more issues. John K. Winkler's Profile of William Randolph Hearst ran five parts in 1927, Niven Busch's of Henry Ford the next year took four, and the multipart Profile was off and running.* A 1931 Reporter at Large set in an emergency room covered eight pages. In 1940, Geoffrey Hellman wrote a three-part, twenty-thousand-word Profile of the Metropolitan Museum of Art—one of the first Profiles of an institution rather than an individual, and the longest piece the magazine had published to that point.

---

*A handwritten note preserved in the New Yorker Records shows Ross grappling with what to put at the end of the initial installments of the Hearst Profile: "To be continued??—Or, 'This is the first of a series of five articles. . . .' " The second option won. From close to the very beginning of the magazine's history, incidentally, there was carping that its articles were getting too long. Newspaper publisher Joseph Pulitzer Jr. wrote Ross in 1926, "In my judgment 'Profiles' is still one of your best features but that is no reason why you should begin letting it run over two and almost three pages. . . . I thoroughly enjoy it all, but for some weeks I have been getting the feeling that prosperity was going to your heads a little with the result that you are giving us too much. It takes a pretty long time to read the New Yorker all through. I don't give a damn for your intermediate articles, with a very few exceptions." Four years later, Lawrence Winship, the editor of the Boston Globe, wrote, "I think it is a mistake for you to divide a 'Profile' into two installments. Even as well-written a piece as [Alva] Johnston's on [Nicholas Murray] Butler would have been much better in one installment, I think." This point of view would continue to be expressed. In 1941, Katharine White wrote to Ross in a memo, "It seems to me that our profiles and other factual stuff is becoming increasingly unreadable and long, long, long. I hear this from all around. People who always used to read profiles and reporters have given them up because they are in so many parts and are so complete and so dreary. We have got away from what the very word 'Profile' means—It was meant to indicate a portrait that gave just one side to a person—not a full face, a profile."

The need to fill space was also one important reason for the *New Yorker's* predilection in the thirties for continuing series. Ross had always tried to provide some continuity to his weekly, but in the early years it tended to be in the form of gimmicky features such as "Are You a New Yorker?," snatches of conversation from the likes of O'Hara's familiar paint-company executives, or running gags such as Otto Soglow's workers below the manhole covers. Ross would continue to keep an eye out for these, as in 1935, when Frank Sullivan wrote a hilarious casual about Mr. Arbuthnot, the "cliché expert." Two months later, Ross wrote Sullivan, "I favor your immediately doing another piece on clichés. I have favored your doing a whole series of these for the last seven years, as you well know, and the one you did merely made firmer my conviction that they would be a great success." But in the thirties the continuity came mainly from *character,* in multipart reminiscences and linked stories. The first notable series came from Clarence Day, who was so important to the magazine that Sullivan remembered Ross remarking, "If I had never done anything but publish Clarence Day, I would be satisfied." An upper-class native New Yorker, Day had embarked on a life in finance but, in his early middle age, was crippled by a severe case of arthritis and henceforth confined to his Manhattan apartment. There he watched his (highly successful) investments, but simultaneously embarked on a career as a humorous writer. In 1920, he wrote a book called *This Simian World,* which displayed much of the ingenuity, imagination, and light-handedness that would characterize the best of the decade's humor writing. Although he wrote many casual essays that would have been perfect for the *New Yorker,* his first piece in the magazine, "Father and the French Court," a funny extended anecdote about the stiff and proper Clarence Day Sr., did not appear until January 1933. In the next five years, the *New Yorker* would publish forty-four of Day's sketches about his father, an especially remarkable number considering that the author died in the last week of 1935, with a number of completed or nearly completed stories on his desk. In retrospect, Ross's enthusiasm bordering on veneration for Day (with whom he became close friends, making frequent visits to his apartment) makes perfect sense: not only were his pieces casual, funny, and plentiful, but their indisputably authentic atmosphere of upper-class turn-of-the-century New York was just what the magazine had always been looking for.

Characteristically, Thurber took a look at what Day had done and transposed it to something strange, new, and wonderful. Just six months after the first "Father" story, Thurber weighed in with six consecutive reminiscence pieces of his own. The tradition in which he was working was more the Paul Bunyan tall tale than the traditional memoir, so hyperbolically did he stretch the eccentricities and mishaps of his Ohio youth. The pieces made an immediate impact, and their collection the following year, as *My*

Life and Hard Times, was the occasion for the first general recognition of Thurber as a significant humorist and possibly a significant *writer.*

Other series fell short of this level of invention and wit, but did serve at least three other important functions: they provided reams of copy, year after year; they added to the sense that the *New Yorker* was a unified and continuing entity, not (like the *New Republic* or the *Atlantic Monthly*) merely the receptacle for a discrete group of articles; and they expanded the magazine's geographic and cultural horizons, introducing characters and settings that would not otherwise have been welcome in its pages. They also established genres in the magazine that would later be taken up and artfully transformed by such writers as Vladimir Nabokov, S. N. Behrman, Joseph Wechsberg, Mary McCarthy, and Ved Mehta in memoir, J. D. Salinger, Gilbert Rogin, Renata Adler, and John Updike in linked stories. The list of the *New Yorker's* 1930s series, in any case, is striking in its length, familiarity, and distinction:

- O'Hara's Lardneresque letters from a heel of a singer, "Pal Joey."
- Ruth McKenney's series about the adventures of her and her eccentric sibling, later collected as *My Sister Eileen.*
- Two groups of linked stories from Sally Benson—the recollections of her childhood, collected as *Meet Me in St. Louis,* and the stories of a preadolescent girl, collected as *Junior Miss.*
- The stories about H*Y*M*A*N K*A*P*L*A*N, a Jewish immigrant struggling to learn English in an adult-education program, signed by "Leonard Q. Ross," a pen name for Leo Rosten.
- H. L. Mencken's reminiscences of his youth, later included in the books *Happy Days, Newspaper Days,* and *Heathen Days.*
- Arthur Kober's tales of Bella Gross and of Hollywood agent Benny Greenspan.
- Emily Hahn's series about the footloose Chinese gentleman Pan Heh-ven (he was based on the publisher Sinmay Zao, with whom Hahn had a scandalous love affair in 1930s Shanghai).
- Ludwig Bemelman's recollections of his youthful days working in Manhattan's Hotel Splendide.
- Christopher La Farge's series of stories about a middle-class Rhode Island family called the Wilsons.
- Richard Lockridge's accounts of the gentle sparrings of Mr. and Mrs. North (a kind of Mr. and Mrs. Monroe "lite," later turned by Lockridge into detectives in a seemingly never-ending series of mystery novels).
- The brilliant John McNulty's dispatches from the world of Third Avenue taverns. Edward Newhouse also set a series in a Manhattan barroom, manned by a bartender named Jake.

The tradition was so firmly established by 1939 that after cartoonist Charles Addams published a drawing peopled by a macabre "family," Ross urged him to make it into a series. Addams complied, with famously triumphant results.

Continuing characters and reminiscences not only became specialties of the magazine, but they brought it to a wider world. Except for the La Farge and the Newhouse, each of the series mentioned above was eventually collected in a book (and in some cases multiple books); when they were advertised or reviewed, their origin in the New Yorker was invariably mentioned. Between 1940 and 1942, five plays based on New Yorker series ran on Broadway: Pal Joey, My Sister Eileen, Life with Father (still the longest-running straight play in Broadway history), Mr. and Mrs. North, and Junior Miss.*

To accommodate all the copy that found its way into the New Yorker each week, an accordion-like format was in place by 1927, capable of expanding and contracting according to the amount of advertising sold. The front section—The Talk of the Town, followed by a section containing two to three casuals and one or more poems, and then a Profile—would have plentiful cartoons and no ads. Then, in a back of the book filled with ads, there would alternate the slighter casuals; one or more reporting pieces topped by any of a growing roster of rubrics—A Reporter at Large, Onward and Upward with the Arts ("the arts" being so loosely defined that it could include greeting-card design and radio soap-opera production), Annals of Crime, and Our Footloose Correspondents (for pieces set outside the city); foreign Letters; the one-page column Shouts and Murmurs, which Alexander Woollcott contributed from 1929 through 1934; and several critical departments from a likewise growing number of reviewers. The issue would conclude with a book-review section, conducted after Parker by Robert Coates and, from 1933 to 1943, by Clifton Fadiman. In the back of the book, a cartoon might or might not appear on the opening page of pieces; the continuations would be one or two columns wide, so as to allow for two- or one-column ads.

The format, which was retained with minor variations until 1992, was developed and initially maintained by a young staff member, Rogers E. M. "Popsy" Whitaker, followed in the early thirties by Carmine Peppe, who continued as makeup editor until his retirement in 1977. Peppe had no artistic training and had started at the magazine in its first year as an office boy, but he served as the New Yorker's de facto art director, and his weekly

---

*Also on Broadway in this period were The Male Animal, cowritten by Thurber and his childhood friend Elliott Nugent, a well-known actor and producer, which was not based on New Yorker material, and The Man Who Came to Dinner, whose main character was modeled after New Yorker contributor Alexander Woollcott.

orchestration of articles, poems, Newsbreaks, and subliminal "spot" drawings so that everything would fit, precisely and elegantly, was truly remarkable—all the more so because the *New Yorker's* veneration of text deprived him of the makeup editor's traditional recourse, cutting from or adding to the copy. As William Shawn noted in a 1985 *New Yorker* obituary of Peppe,

> He was truly a mythical figure in our office. . . . When insoluble makeup problems arose, Carmine Peppe resorted to magic. If a piece of writing ran longer than had been anticipated, he was able to pull extra columns of space out of the air. If something ran short, he was able to produce the illusion that it didn't. His aesthetic instinct for what drawing should appear on what page and what size it should ideally be was faultless. If, say, a drawing was an eighth of an inch too wide, he saw it as jumping off the page, and he was right. . . . In the last analysis, it was Carmine who determined, early in our history, how the pages of *The New Yorker* should look, how the magazine as a whole should look. Since what he designed for us was appropriate to our intentions and was classic, we stayed with what he gave us.

Though they got less attention than the up-front material, the back-of-the-book department pieces constituted the bulk of the magazine from week to week. Some of them were unquestionably first-rate. Janet Flanner was instantly recognized as a distinctive and valuable voice; in the second half of the decade, when war clouds began to gather over Europe, her dispatches took on an authority and weight they would retain for the rest of her long tenure. Woollcott was probably the least *New Yorker*-like regular contributor the magazine ever had. Ross was a devotee of the plain style; his old army pal was ornate to the bone. "Woollcott had mannerisms in writing," White observed. "He liked to talk about 'these old eyes' and he liked words like 'reticule' and 'tippet'—words that made Ross retch." The Shouts and Murmurs column even *looked* different. It was always exactly one full page, with no illustration, and each week Woollcott's copy had to be cut or stretched to fit. This was standard practice in other magazines and newspapers, but with Ross (and his successors) it was a point of pride that the *New Yorker* should adapt to fit the writing.

As for the critics, Lewis Mumford was, as noted, a cogent and influential observer of architecture and art. The level of discourse was also raised by H. L. Mencken's Onward and Upward with the Arts pieces on the American language in 1935 and 1936. Most significantly, Louise Bogan, a fiercely intelligent poet and fiction writer, and the wife of staff member Raymond Holden, contributed a semiannual review of poetry books, beginning in March 1931 (and continuing to 1969). Bogan was a serious and eloquent critic, and her essays brought a newfound respect to the magazine. Several years later, W. H. Auden called her the best critic of poetry in America.

The book reviewer, Clifton Fadiman, was more of a literary reporter than a critic; he once remarked in print, "To the best of my knowledge and belief I have never written a word of literary criticism in my life." Fadiman had originally caught Ross's eyes with a *Nation* essay, "Ring Lardner and the Triangle of Hate," that praised Lardner as a writer but pointed out that at the bottom of his works was a profound misanthropy. As Fadiman later recalled, Ross gave him no instruction whatsoever, which seemed to him typical of the editor's attitude: he trusted writers completely, but if they didn't produce surprising and brilliant prose, he simply fired them. Fadiman was knowledgeable, fluent, and generally sensible in his judgments; but he was not as surprising or brilliant as Dorothy Parker, who, in addition to her other attributes, looks in the light of history almost always to have been *right*. Fadiman took some notorious whiffs. Reviewing Faulkner's *Absalom, Absalom!* in 1936, he began by stating "in all humility" that he did not understand the book, but he was prepared to say that it was "the most consistently boring novel by a reputable writer to come my way during the last decade." Four years later, about another Faulkner classic, *The Hamlet,* he wrote: "All in the line of duty, I have spent part of this week weaving through *The Hamlet.* From the intense murk of its sentences I emerge, somewhat shaken, to report that the author apparently continues to enjoy as lively a case of the 'orrors as you are apt to find outside a Keeley-cure hostelry." Even when his judgments stand up, they are sometimes weakened by his readiness to apologize at the mere possibility of sounding pompous. He wrote of *Of Mice and Men,* for example, "The real subject of the book, banal as the phrase is going to sound, is human solitude."

In a 1937 essay about the *New Yorker* in the new left-wing journal *Partisan Review,* Dwight Macdonald wrote, "The chief quality of *New Yorker* criticism is its amiability." He must have been thinking of Benchley, the magazine's drama critic until 1940 (Gibbs replaced him), who almost always *wanted* to like the plays he saw. A classic case is his review of Clifford Odets's 1935 proletarian drama *Paradise Lost,* where Benchley confessed he had no idea what the work was about. "A certain mental torpor is not without its advantages in theatregoing," he observed in a memorable, strikingly good-natured expression of the creed of philistinism.

> You have a much better time if you can merely sit in your seat and let the impressions blow through your hair like a sea breeze, reacting slightly now and then with a short, musical laugh or a barely audible catch in the throat, but without trying too hard to figure out what it is all about. . . . [If] you have achieved this elementary state of thought suspension, you will find yourself at the end of a play as fresh as a daisy, after possibly having had a very good time in the bargain, while the ratiocination mob are leaving with their brows still

furrowed and their programs twisted damply into their pockets for further study at home.

Macdonald went on, "Since to Park Avenue, art is important chiefly as a means of killing time, what is required is not critics but tipsters." With the exceptions noted above, this was a legitimate appraisal, as one could discern even from the *New Yorker* critics' writing style. Their prose favored the first person (characterized by subjective reactions) or the second person (speculating on what "you," the reader, would think—as in a consumer guide). Strong critics (such as Parker and Mumford and Bogan in the *New Yorker*), by contrast, work by alternating generalizations with judgments or observations about the work under review—a third-person attitude.

Interestingly, Benchley's "Wayward Press" column was much more informed and rigorous than his theater reviews; possibly "Guy Fawkes," the pseudonym he used for it, relieved him of a self-imposed obligation to be unfailingly funny. He was especially sharp in pointing out instances in which the newspapers seemed to be in league with moneyed interests, as when he complained about all the "reassurances" that the newspapers printed in the weeks after the stock market crash of 1929: "That any group of citizens can get together behind closed doors and decide what is best for the rest of the citizens and then count on the Press of the country to help them disseminate their propaganda (for it is nothing but propaganda) is somehow bad." A little more than three years later, he discerned a conspiracy of silence in the lack of coverage of President Roosevelt's bank holiday: "During the first three days of March, when the rest of the country was echoing to the sound of closing bank doors, readers of New York journals knew nothing of the situation unless they delved into the back pages of their newspapers."

Some semiprecious gems could be found in the *New Yorker's* back pages if you knew where to look for them. In 1926, Ross had hired a young roué named George T. Ryall, who, under the pen name Audax Minor, wrote a dry and oddly entertaining racetrack column that would appear in the *New Yorker* for the next fifty-two years. The radio column Ring Lardner wrote in 1933 (while bedridden with what turned out to be his terminal illness) was prime Ring. Lois Long retained her special touch in writing about fashion, but with the success of the magazine, On and Off the Avenue was expanded to include sometimes quite long sections on men's clothing, housewares, food and drink, and other consumables. In addition to taking up space, these were valuable in providing a favorable "environment" for advertising, but Ross freely admitted that they were not in keeping with his original vision of the magazine. In 1930, replying to humorist Don Marquis's complaint about the increasing fashion coverage, Ross wrote:

As a boy, I never dreamed I would have to deal with any publication running critical pieces about women's underwear. Here I am though. My viewpoint on these departments is that they are necessary evils. I wanted to make sure that the *New Yorker* would succeed economically, and I therefore realize it has to be of some use; that you just cannot start a magazine such as *Punch* in this country in this century. I regard these departments as more or less of a nuisance, and as a matter of fact have paid little attention to them over the last year or two, trying to build up the other part of the magazine, which, as a matter of fact, is the only thing that interests me.

As for the back-of-the-book casuals, *filler* is a harsh word, and it implies, in any case, a lack of quality the *New Yorker* rarely if ever countenanced. But the fact remains that the magazine published many hundreds of pieces whose main virtue was that they inoffensively took up space. The bound volumes of the thirties abound with supposedly humorous pieces (some of them in the *front* of the book) balanced on the most negligible conceit imaginable, and essays so casual as to be nearly asleep. They were written by the likes of Richard Lockridge, Francis Steegmuller, Frances Crane, Frances Warfield, James Reid Parker, Donald Moffat, and many, many other less notable practitioners. The same slightness characterized the light verse of Frances Frost, Stanley Jones, Hortense Flexner, David McCord, Martha Thomas Banning (Patience Eden), Jean Batchelor, Elspeth O'Halloran (Elspeth), Leslie Nelson Jennings, and *their* capacious cohort. (Verse had the additional advantage of being able to fit into tight spaces and thus relieve the burden placed on Newsbreaks.)

But this lightweight stuff was only one part of the whole package, which points to a distinguishing feature of the *New Yorker* almost from the beginning: its multiplicity. Over the years this has quietly confounded critics and commentators seeking to assess the magazine. For the articles and poems and stories and Newsbreaks and casuals it published—more and more and more of them as the weeks, then the years, accumulated—were by no means all of a piece, and generalizing about them is a perilous enterprise. In truth, the magazine anticipated a commonplace in modern literary theory: the notion that texts conduct civil war with themselves. Matters are further complicated in the *New Yorker* by the advertisements, which are indisputably a part of the "text" yet embody assumptions, values, and implications that were frequently and increasingly at odds with the articles and stories. Like Whitman, the *New Yorker* contradicted itself because it contained multitudes.

A prime example would be the *New Yorker's* response to the Depression. The conventional wisdom, then and now, would be that the magazine blithely ignored the hard times, just as its balance sheet barely took a hit from them. Evidence for this view can be found in the magazine's public face, its covers: not until March 11, 1939, did it publish one that even hinted that a record number of Americans had been hungry and out of work for the better part of a decade. (This was a Constantin Alajalov cover showing an unkempt candy-and-apple salesman insinuating his wares into an aristocratic couple's limousine.) Inside the magazine, a generalized sense of remoteness from the political fray prevailed, especially striking given that this was the decade of the "committed" American writer, a time when magazines such as the *New Republic* and the *Nation* set up their barricades firmly on the left, and intellectual life was generally politicized. The *New Yorker*, animated by the twenties spirit of ascension, had a powerful resistance to coming down to earth. A White comment from the early thirties boasted that the magazine had taken only one political stand in its history: strongly opposing a proposed relocation of the information booth in Pennsylvania Station. It is true that, in the late twenties, there were frequent comments on the Scopes trial, but taking shots at rural know-nothingism hardly constituted political engagement. On the Sacco and Vanzetti trial and execution, a contemporaneous and much thornier issue, the magazine was for all intents and purposes silent.

On the other hand, in 1930 there was a Jose Schorr casual accurately titled "How to Pass Time in a Bread Line." ("Ponder on the statements issued to the press by business leaders blaming your plight on overspeculation in the stock market. Count on the fingers of one hand the number of times you have ever telephoned to a stockbroker. Try to name one business leader who has thought of blaming himself for hard times.") A year later the *New Yorker* published the scathing "It's About Time Department": six columns' worth of quotations uttered by business leaders, politicians, economists, and pundits since the stock market crash averring that the bottom had been reached, the corner had been turned, and in the words of Ambassador Charles Dawes in September 1930, "Nothing is more certain than the coming of business recovery." Morris Markey, in A Reporter at Large, regularly and with great empathy chronicled the destitute and the bureaucratic apparatus that was growing up to serve them. Even White, he of the don't-move-the-information-booth politics, occasionally weighed in with a direct statement about the plight of the nation. In December 1933, after Franklin D. Roosevelt's New Deal had been in place for close to a year, White took a swipe at business interests who were beginning to complain that "fellows like this Rexford Tugwell, with his foreign name and his foreign ways, are trying to put over a pure-food-and-drug regime that would take all the vital monkeyshines out of American initiative." He concluded with a paragraph that, in the *New Yorker* context, qualified as pure Red propaganda:

We have been waiting for this. We knew that the new program wasn't going to satisfy the old school, as soon as the old school was able to be up and around. Well, maybe it *is* time ... to return America to the Americans.... But then again, maybe we better let the foreigners down at Washington keep the country a while longer. They seem to have plans for an order based on social equilibrium; and whether they can make it work or not, we say God bless them and Merry Christmas!

Indirectly, the Depression was a significant period indeed in the *New Yorker's* history, as the shrinking cost of living permitted the magazine's three most significant employees, after Ross, to leave the staff by the end of the decade. Thurber departed at the end of 1935, though he continued to contribute many casuals and cartoons. In August 1937, White commenced what was intended to be a year's leave of absence from the magazine, to travel and write without the burden of a weekly deadline. Before the year was over, however, he—and Katharine—had decided to leave New York and live year-round in a cove-side Maine farmhouse on forty acres of land they had bought in 1933 for $11,000. White went on to do Newsbreaks, casuals, and occasional Notes and Comments for the magazine, but his main literary endeavor for the next five years was "One Man's Meat," a monthly column for *Harper's* magazine that finally let him substitute the first-person singular for the first-person plural. Katharine, meanwhile, arranged with Ross to be a part-time, long-distance fiction editor.

The Depression had an unmistakable and global effect on the magazine's contents as well. In the thirties, to a greater or lesser degree, the humor, cartoons, journalism, and fiction in the magazine all acheived great distinction—and they did so, in striking contrast to 1920s ascendance, by looking *down*. The changes in the outside world opened up new subjects and new approaches, and most of them shared an earthiness that suited the decade.

FUNNY STUFF

A further suggestion: Write a lot more of those verses for us. They are about the most original stuff we have had lately.
—Harold Ross to Ogden Nash, August 6, 1930

~~~~

This is a magnificent piece, although confusing.
—Wolcott Gibbs to S. J. Perelman, January 23, 1933

~~~~

I must say I was surprised meeting Ross, as I had expected a much older man. Our interview was satisfactory enough except that he kept tugging at a rubber nipple and murmuring "Gloo, gloo," which I ascribed either to teething or heat rash. But he is a very enterprising fellow, make no mistake about it. (This in case you were thinking of making some mistake about it.)

—Perelman to G. S. Lobrano, 1940

The great thing about the *New Yorker*, as it had evolved by the early thirties, was its openness to genius. That is, it had instituted certain forms or genres of writing and art that, within the context of the magazine, "worked." Depending on the week, the specific text or drawing could be provided by someone who merely understood the requirements of the form. Or it could be filled by someone who took the form and was able to transform it into something surprising, personal, and wonderful—just as White had transformed the "paragraph" and Thurber had the casual and the reminiscence.

Not that it was always easy for the editors to recognize or appreciate such a genius. A classic case is Sidney Joseph Perelman, who is now identified as a *New Yorker* writer but whose road to the magazine was bumpy and long. After leaving Brown University (just short of graduation) in 1925, Perelman began publishing in *Judge* humorous pieces and pseudo-antique drawings that showed the clear influence of John Held and Ralph Barton. In 1929, he started a sideline of writing for the movies, something he would continue doing through the 1950s. He published a handful of pieces in the *New Yorker* in 1930 and 1931, but had many more rejections: he didn't fit comfortably in the magazine. His writing was about as far from "casual" as possible: dizzy, nervous, sprinkled with Yiddish words, obsolete adjectives, and references to obscure Tin Pan Alley songs and Victorian memoirs, all of it propelled by a tightly wound verbal energy. It was humor as performance—not at all the *New Yorker*'s style. Still, his talent was unmistakable and the editors, to their credit, kept an eye on him. In March 1932, Mrs. White sent Wolcott Gibbs a memo: "Will you please follow up S. J. Perelman and get him to write some pieces for us?" Gibbs, already chafing at the magazine's strictures, replied, "Why? We just reject them." (Although this question was clearly rhetorical, Mrs. White felt the need to come back with, "Because Mr. Ross wants you to.")

The next year, Perelman submitted "The Island of Dr. Finkle," a typical mixed metaphor of a piece that took as its jumping-off point H. G. Wells's horror novel *The Island of Dr. Moreau,* recently adapted into a film. In the exchange of memos among the bemused editors, one can feel them straining, first, to "get" Perelman and, second, to envision a place for his antics in the magazine:

Katharine S. White to Gibbs: "Not having seen the Island of Dr. What's His Name I don't know whether this is any good. He seems to be burlesquing a dozen things at once also??"

Gibbs to KSW: "I didn't know there was any such book. Thought this was just a burlesque of those old clubmen talking about India stories. Anyway it rather amuses me as an altogether wild one, and I'm for it. Object to one or two of the worst gags, but other wise O.K. By the way, Donald Stewart and Thurber have both done things like this, if it matters."

John Mosher—the magazine's principal first reader and movie critic up until his death in 1943, and also a writer of urbane and subtly ironic casuals—could barely countenance Perelman's excesses, writing to Mrs. White: "Awful humor—this dry, synthetic stale style—central idea about island is rather funny perhaps. . . . I can't stand these trick phrasings—jumpy nervous nasty things."

Mrs. White summed up the responses to Ross: "While there are some funny lines, it's so dizzy it ceases to amuse me, and he tries to burlesque too many things at once

"1) The H. G. Wells novel and movie
"2) Clubmen stories in general
"3) A touch of Sherlock Holmes burlesque (isn't there?)"

In rejecting the piece, Ross advised Perelman, "I think you ought to decide when you write a piece whether it is going to be a parody, or a satire, or nonsense. These are not very successfully mixed in short stuff; that has been my experience. You have some funny lines in this, but on the whole, it is just bewildering. . . . You have got too much of a mouthful for one piece and the germ of five or six pieces, it seems to me."

Needless to say, "mixing" genres and being "dizzy" and "bewildering" was part of Perelman's special art. It was almost as though, to adapt to it, Ross and his colleagues first had to shun it. In any case, after rejecting "The Island of Dr. Finkle" (which, alas, does not survive) the magazine began accepting Perelmania with increasing regularity, signing him in 1937 to a contract for a set number of casuals annually. That same year he published a collection, *Strictly from Hunger,* with an introduction by Benchley, who wrote that Perelman had put him and other writers of short humorous pieces based on madcap free association out of business: "It was just a matter of time before Perelman took over the dementia praecox field and drove all of us to writing articles on economics for *The Commentator.* Any further attempts to garble thought-processes sounded like imitation-Perelman. He did to our weak efforts at 'crazy stuff' what Benny Goodman has done to middle-period jazz. He swung it. To use a swing phrase, he took it 'out of the world.' And there he remains, all by himself." By the time of his death, in 1979, Perelman had contributed close to three hundred casuals to the *New Yorker*—an unsurpassed and, considering their standard of quality and inventiveness, astonishing number.

The path to acceptance was smoother for the magazine's other important new humor contributor in this period, Ogden Nash. Ross initially met him through Nash's work as an editor at Doubleday Doran, which published the annual albums of the magazine's cartoons. Late in 1929, Nash began submitting, and selling, humorous poems. Ross and his colleagues could barely help recognizing in Nash an antidote to the fatally mild, buttoned-up light verse of the day, which had been amply represented in the magazine since its inception. Like Perelman (with whom he would later collaborate on an unproduced screenplay and the Broadway musical *One Touch of Venus*), Nash was a linguistic prestidigitator, and his diction and rhymes were unexpected, strange, often neologistic, and delightful. To counter the prevailing singsong quality of light verse, he spun out endless lines, in the manner of Whitman, thereby banishing all hope of rhythm, or sometimes braked them to a halt after a single word. Both techniques are on display in "It Must Be the Milk," a *New Yorker* poem from 1936, which takes a rather commonplace observation and elevates it to high entertainment through Nash's distinctively skewed expression. It begins:

> There is a thought that I have tried not to but cannot help but
>   think,
> Which is, My goodness how much infants resemble people who
>   have had quite a bit too much to drink.
> Tots,
> Sots;
> So different and yet so identical!
> What a humiliating coincidence for pride parentical!
> Yet when you see your little dumpling set sail across the nursery floor,
> Can you consciously deny the resemblance to somebody who is
>   leaving the tavern after having tried to leave it a dozen times
>   and each time turned back for just one more? . . .

Sterling as they were, Perelman and Nash stood alone in the ranks of important new *New Yorker* humorists in the thirties. To be sure, the magazine continued to print humor, by the estimable likes of White; Benchley; Sullivan, who contributed a dozen "cliché expert" pieces in the late thirties and the tour de force "A Garland of Ibids for Van Wyck Brooks" in 1941; and Thurber, in such classics as "If Grant Had Been Drinking at

Appomattox," "The Catbird Seat," "A Couple of Hamburgers," and "The Secret Life of Walter Mitty." Two reliable founts of cleverness were Gibbs—who specialized in dead-on parodies and was also the main writer of Notes and Comment following White's departure—and a newcomer named Russell Maloney, who took over Thurber's Talk of the Town rewrite job in 1935 and also wrote or edited hundreds of cartoon captions. But comic inspiration no longer flowed so wide, fast, or pure. That was not so surprising, given that the world was a very different and noticeably less amusing place than it had been just a decade before. In the words of Corey Ford's title, "the time of laughter" was over and it didn't seem likely to return.

CARTOON CAVALCADE

In re Art Bank
... Some types of pictures always tend to be overdone, such as workmen on girders of skyscrapers, boxers or wrestlers making irrelevant remarks, and men sitting at desks; of the latter we have on hand 12. Bums on park benches get pretty well overdone each year; we are starting May with 3 on hand.

A count of some of the other classifications (overlapping) shows:

Animals 15; Art and artists 6; Architecture 6; Babbits 17; Baths 3 (comparatively low); Barbers-beards 9; Books only 2 (need for book page currently); Crooks, crime and bums 9; Cops 8; Medical 7; Jews 4; Man or woman at phone 7; Renting and moving 5; Workmen 18 ...

—Bill Levick to Harold Ross, April 8, 1931

I noticed an interview with Bateman in the morning paper. He commented on various artists, mentioning mostly fellows who draw for the *New Yorker*. He said they weren't setting down the times, weren't commenting on it. Of course he's right. Not since the days of you and Boardman Robinson has there been a cartoonist who had a single idea about social or political affairs and handled it in a forthright manner. There hasn't been a direct commentator. Some of the boys get quite a bit of comment in their stuff, but it is indirect. I am talking here about magazine artists, and I make one exception, Ralph Barton. He had theories and intelligent ideas and he could put them on paper, but he was so twisted up mentally that very little real stuff came out of him.

—Ross to Art Young, January 20, 1932

~~~~~

Once again I am completely flabbergasted by the editorial deci-sions. Out of a group of drawings expounding a particular idea one is chosen with the recommendation that the situation be reversed. . . . Don't you think it would be fairer for me to refuse them flatly? Frankly I don't want any collaborators. Would you? Would you like someone to suggest that you select a paragraph from one of your stories, change it so that it becomes the oppo-site of what you intended and throw away the rest? I appeal to you as a fellow human-being. Is the whole world going mad?

—William Steig to William Maxwell, June 1937

~~~~~

One of your roughs—the one about the father breaking the unbreakable doll—seemed to us a possible idea, but Mr. Ross is troubled by the fact that a man wouldn't use a sledge hammer in the house, and thinks the scene had better be in the back yard with the doll placed on a large stone, or on the floor of the garage. Also he thinks it would be better if the mother were dis-tressed and the child were in tears.

—William Maxwell to Chon Day, July 7, 1938

~~~~~

[After the same idea was given to artist Richard Decker] I have taken the liberty of drawing two lines on your drawing to indi-cate a plain cement sidewalk going straight out from the door-way. Mr. Ross thinks it would be better to have the doll broken on cement rather than on stepping stones because the broken pieces will show up better. Also, you'll have to move the father back a couple of feet, and the box, he thinks, doesn't have to have the letters "Unbreakable Doll" on it . . . ?

—Maxwell to Decker, September 23, 1938

~~~~~

If this drawing is not funny, and is not a swell drawing, I shall engage to eat it, and with it all of Price's fantasies that just miss, all of Taylor's S. Klein women, and all eleven versions of every drawing Day does of two men in a restaurant. I will also eat every drawing of a man and a woman on a raft, every drawing of a man and a native woman on a desert island, and every drawing of two thin women in big-backed chairs. . . . I will also eat every drawing of a small animal talking to its parents, and every drawing of two large animals talking about their young.

—James Thurber to Daise Terry,
resubmitting a rejected drawing, 1937

~~~~~

Hokinson has done the two funniest pictures in a long while: the winking man one and "*I'm* the one that should be lying down." Who blunted the glory of that caption by adding "somewhere" to it? Did the Art Conference think that people would figure the lady wanted to lie down in the cage? Have we got to that point? . . .

I close with an Imaginary Art Conference meeting, the subject being "Is the Caption of the Hokinson Winking Man Picture Right?"

A: She just says she wants to report a winking man. She doesn't say who he was winking at.

B: I agree. She is obviously too old and unattractive to have a man winking at her.

C: Yes, you're right. What about "I want to report a man I saw winking at a young lady"?

A: Much better.

B: Why just winking. How about "I want to report a man who has been annoying young women"? Takes in more territory, applies to more people. Many of our readers are young women who are annoyed.

A: Much better.

C: Shouldn't the woman in the drawing *be* this young woman? How about letting Garrett Price do the thing over, with a pretty girl?

A: Much better.

B: No. I'd say have this same oldish woman drag the man she is talking about up to the officer and say "This man has been annoying my niece."

—Thurber to Daise Terry, 1938

~~~~~

We need pictures showing normal people in normal places doing normal things. We are acutely short of high life people doing or saying something plausable [*sic*] (as opposed to them doing eccentric and grotesque and unbelievable, though very amusing things).

—*New Yorker* form letter, addressed
"To Our Artists," November 1939

～～～

In 1932, when he was twenty years old and an art student in New York, a native of Westfield, New Jersey, named Charles Addams sold the *New Yorker* a spot drawing. These visual fillers were the traditional point of entry for *New Yorker* cartoonists: James Thurber and George Price, for example, and in later years Charles Saxon and James Stevenson. But in the next couple of years, Addams had only a handful of cartoons accepted, none of them outstanding or particularly distinctive. In 1934, the administrator of the art department, Daise Terry, took pity on the young man, still living back home in Westfield, and tried to get him a job assisting Eugene Kinkead, a Talk of the Town reporter. Nothing came of it, and Addams eventually took a position with a true-detective magazine touching up the photographs of corpses. It may have been that macabre environment that inspired a cartoon he submitted early in 1935. Executed in his customary line-drawing style, it showed a newspaper press turning out copies of the *Herald Tribune*. A pressman suddenly notices to his alarm that among the hundreds of *Herald Tribunes*, their gray columns of type illegible, is one copy of the tabloid *Daily Mirror* with the screaming headline: "SEX FIEND SLAYS TOT."

As with all cartoons accomplished enough to be considered for publication, this one was dispatched to the Tuesday-afternoon art conference, a weekly event since the magazine's inception (and still one today). Beginning at 2 P.M., Ross, Rea Irvin, Katharine White, and Wolcott Gibbs gathered to assess and critique, accept and reject, the week's crop of sketches, finished cartoons, and ideas. (Gibbs was assigned to convey the verdicts and instructions to the artists; he would shortly be succeeded in these duties, to his immense relief, by William Maxwell.) As Ross pointed out each drawing's weak spots with his knitting needles, Daise Terry took notes, and later typed up a sort of minutes that was circulated to the participants. The meeting took its lead from Ross, who in cartoons as much as in text was attuned not to larger questions of humor and art but to matters of detail and plausibility. Who, he famously and repeatedly wondered, is talking? James Geraghty, who took Maxwell's place and then, in 1939, assumed the new position of cartoon editor, wrote in an unpublished memoir, "Ross approached drawings in the mood of those quasi-educational drawings that appeared in the *Book of Knowledge*. 'What is wrong with this picture? The artist made twenty mistakes. See if you can find them.' " Nearly as often, the art conference would offer infuriatingly vague advice, sometimes simply, "Make funnier."

The meeting of February 5 was characteristic. Thirty-two sketches were assessed, and Terry's minutes noted about a few of them:

PRICE, Gar.: Man and two small boys in picture gallery; man has stopped before nude painting. One of the small boys is saying to the other, "There's something about it gets the old man every time."
Not right type of people; should be smart people.
SHERMUND: Scene in beauty parlor; masseuse is massaging the back of a woman's neck and saying, "You're one of the lucky few who have a normal skin, Madame."
Make better drawing; this too unpleasant.
DUNN: Couple looking at grandmother in next room mixing herself a whiskey and soda. "Just because it's Mother's Day she thinks the lid is off."
Better whiskey bottle.

Addams's newspaper-press cartoon was also scrutinized, and Terry recorded this suggestion to be directed to the artist: "Make it N.Y. Times; look at press and make it authentic." The finished drawing, published in the issue of March 23, 1935, shows that Addams did change the *Trib* to the *Times,* which was considered a duller paper and thus offered a sharper contrast with the blaring tabloid. And the press appears extremely authentic, not surprising in retrospect, given Addams's love for architectural and mechanical details. Unremarkable in itself, the cartoon seemed to turn on a creative switch of some kind in Addams, and a couple of months later he sold a drawing (this one in wash rather than line) of two eastern swamis with beds of nails. One of the men hoists a small rectangle, also covered with nails, and says, "Let's have a pillow fight." There followed, in the next two years, cartoons of cleaning ladies on broomsticks, Medusa in a beauty-parlor chair, an Eskimo ice-fishing at a hockey game, a Salvation Army band attracting hundreds of mice, Rip van Winkle's dwarfs at a modern bowling alley, and several revolving around wives who either want to murder or have murdered their husbands. By the end of the decade, Charles Addams was a national institution.

Unlike S. J. Perelman, Addams was not alone as an outstanding 1930s newcomer. I have already mentioned Thurber and William Steig, both of whose first cartoons were published in 1930. Following them, in short order, were George Price, Richard Decker, Robert Day, Richard Taylor, Syd Hoff, Alain, William Galbraith, Chon Day, and Whitney Darrow. They joined Arno, Hokinson, Gluyas Williams, Otto Soglow, Al Frueh, Rea Irvin, Mary Petty, Alan Dunn, Carl Rose, and other holdovers from the first half decade. Indeed, perhaps even more than in the early years, the jewel in the *New Yorker's* 1930s crown was the art. The cartoons served multiple purposes. First, they were a point of entry. Over and over again, longtime *New*

Yorker readers say that at first they only looked at (or understood) the cartoons, which provided a sort of safe harbor until they were ready to move on to the articles and stories. The cartoons were also widely reprinted in advertisements and in other publications—by the end of the decade, the top artists were habitually receiving twelve to fifteen reprint requests a year, and sometimes as many as forty—and thus were visual ambassadors for the *New Yorker.* The most subtle function they served was within the magazine's pages. In the absence of photographs, color, and for the most part, even illustrations, the cartoons had to provide virtually all visual interest and continuity. They did this admirably, once readers adjusted their eyes to the monochromatic editorial landscape. Artists such as Arno, Richard Decker, Robert Day, Charles Addams, Gluyas Williams, and William Galbraith were wonderfully accomplished draftsmen, whose pictures rewarded close and extensive inspection. And the difference in style among the cartoonists—the line drawings of Williams or George Price, the energetic line and subtly varied washes of Arno, the distinctive charcoal of Alan Dunn, Galbraith's chiaroscuro, and Thurber's minimalism—afforded tremendous visual variety.

Eventually, recognition came that the cartoons had some distinction beyond being accessible, amusing, and pleasing to the eye. Both Thurber and Arno had gallery showings of their work in the early thirties, and comparisons were made (respectively) to Matisse and Rouault. Initially, the prefaces to the annual cartoon "Albums" were facetious noodlings by White, Thurber, Lardner, or Benchley, but for the 1935 edition, the editors solicited for the first time a piece by a serious art critic, their own Lewis Mumford. This turned out to be a bad move. Mumford, who was notoriously independent-minded, criticized *New Yorker* drawings as a whole for being "less interesting than the ideas," described them as "elfin, dissociated, abstract," and complained that they failed to capture "the subway face, the Library face, the luncheon face," and the other visages of present-day New York. He regretted that in the magazine's pages that was no new Daumier or Hogarth who would give us "wise, swift, mocking accounts of our contemporaries."

One sees the point. In 1935, as ten years earlier and fifty years hence, a substantial proportion of *New Yorker* cartoons were almost triumphantly superficial. There were the hundreds upon hundreds of cartoons that—far from "mocking . . . our contemporaries," as Mumford wanted—in a subtle but unmistakable way *fortified* the magazine's bourgeois readers in their very bourgeoisness. In these cartoons, women are always late, men tend to be stuffed shirts, and the general mood is, yes, we can all have a good laugh at our own expense, then immediately go on to something else. This was the special province of the artist Perry Barlow. Ross once wrote Barlow that he and Hokinson were the "only two first-class character artists in the United

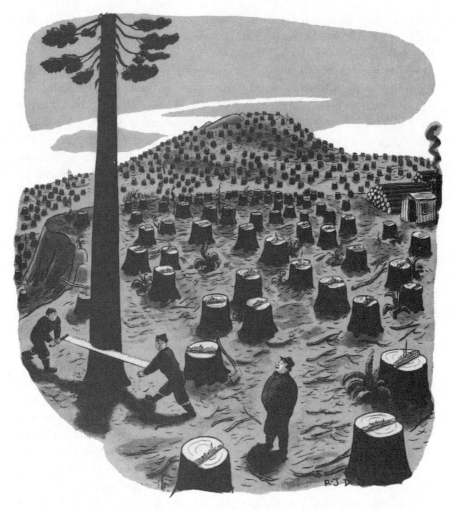

"When you finish this one, boys, I'd like a word with you over at the office."

Three cartoon masters came into their own in the 1930s. *(Above)* Robert J. Day, like his colleague Richard Decker, was a virtuoso of the panoramic full-page gag. In his unmistakable line drawings, Gluyas Williams *(opposite, top)* cast a cold eye on the foibles of the upper-middle class. Helen Hokinson saw (and used) more of the grays in depicting her inimitable clubwomen, who always seemed to be grappling with difficult questions.

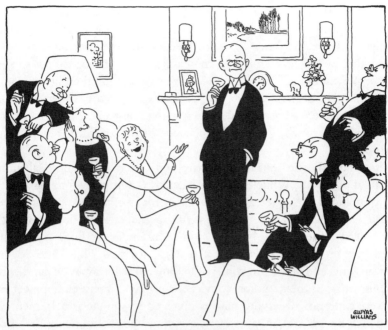

RACONTEURS

"Honestly, you would have died laughing at Joe. Give him two cocktails and he thinks he's Sir Walter Raleigh or somebody. Well, when this woman at the next table drops her bag, up jumps Joe, and you know how clumsy he is anyway, and . . ."

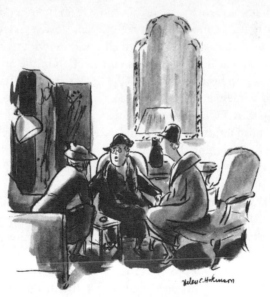

"Which would be the most restful—go to the movies and then have dinner, or have dinner then go to the movies?"

States," and indeed Barlow was a graceful and assured draftsman, whose free and easy washes provided a satisfying contrast to, say, the precision of Gluyas Williams, the naturalism of Richard Decker, and the controlled energy of Arno. Barlow poked such gentle and casual fun at his upper-class subjects, and made them look so attractive, while never questioning any of the underpinnings of their world, that his cartoons could only serve to make the comfortable readers who identified with them feel even more comfortable. One can see why Ross so appreciated him; he was the Clarence Day of cartoons.

Another subgenre was less palliative and generally a good deal funnier but no more biting. While Ross's initial exhortations were for artists to base their situations in character and plausibility, many of the best cartoons were, in the magazine's parlance, "tricks": sight gags that based their humor not on any social observation but on some misunderstanding, incongruity, mechanical mixup, or reworking of a stock situation. Thus Otto Soglow's famous king, and all the drawings of talking animals, castaways on deserted islands, artists in their studios, convicts or priests in conversation, scenes in heaven, explorers observing natives involved in strange rituals, men with sandwich boards and, in later years, carrying signs announcing the end of the world.

The work of Richard Decker, Carl Rose, and especially Robert Day amplified this subgenre to the level of tour de force, with full-page drawings, often panoramic landscapes, that were stunning in their detail and execution. Much of these cartoons' impact came from their frequently dizzying scope, with the full humor not felt till one has slowly taken it all in. Thus Day's drawing of the mammoth football stadium, with every one of the hundreds of meticulously drawn rows empty. High in the press box, a radio announcer says into his microphone, "Well, folks, here it is starting time! . . . One moment while we take a look at that little old schedule." (The insufficiently recognized Day, who contributed cartoons up until his death in 1985, was so productive that he would often have more than one cartoon printed in an issue, signing the second with his initials, R.J.D.) The pleasure also comes in part from the perfection or near-perfection of the execution, as in a gag in a Buster Keaton movie. An example is Decker's drawing of an idea by Richard McAllister, who began submitting gags to the New Yorker in the thirties and has at this writing sold more than four thousand of them. We first see a workman high on a ladder (even indoors there is the element of the sublime), then take in that he is in a church, repairing a stained-glass window. Our eye then goes to the ground, where we see another annoyed-looking worker rubbing his head, and then to the hammer on the ground beside him. Having taken in what has happened, we notice a white-collared clergyman standing next to and observing this little scene, and only then are we ready for the caption: "Gee, Jack! That was very careless of you." Not a word or comma could be changed to make this better, nor a single detail in the picture.

Yet *New Yorker* cartoons were much more than a series of polished gags. Admittedly, any deeper import was not achieved through the offices of the art conference, which kept its attention resolutely on the surface issues of plausibility and gag construction. The artists explored this territory on their own, and sometimes, no doubt, unwittingly—but they did it. To start, there *was* in the magazine a bit of the corrosive quality Mumford found lacking—admittedly less so since the death, in 1931, of Ralph Barton. It could still be found in the work of Reginald Marsh, whose scenes of breadlines and saloon interiors were a creditable try at putting the city down on paper, and in the occasional appearances of the veteran Wallace Morgan. (Marsh's most biting cartoon of the thirties was set in the rural South: a woman in a crowd lifts her toddler high, explaining, "It's her first lynching.") And, if it was faces Mumford was interested in, where better to look than William Steig, who in his magnificent series "Small Fry" could economically evoke character—with a minute adjustment to an eighth-of-an-inch-long eyebrow—like no cartoonist before or since?

Gluyas Williams, while admittedly not a Daumier or a Hogarth, *was* a sort of Brueghel in line drawing for the early-twentieth-century gentry. His carefully worked-out, detail-filled tableaux did not attempt to disparage or exalt upper-middle-class life; they merely took a long, unblinking look at it. They were not without affection, but that made them harder to dismiss and ultimately stronger. Williams was a master of the more intimate portrait as well, and his most brilliant came in continuing series such as "Raconteurs" and "The Writing Public." His drawing of a woman at a party mocking her husband for an attempted act of gallantry is almost breathtaking in its perfect execution. And, while Williams's touch is exquisitely light, the drawing is about as corrosive a commentary as you could ever hope to see on the debasement of marriage, morals, language, and humor.

Such piercing and potentially subversive glimpses into the readers' own world were admittedly rare; they seemed to demand a long running start, on the part of artist and audience alike. Thus it took a long spell of looking at Helen Hokinson's clubwomen as cute and mildly amusing before one began to see that Hokinson and James Reid Parker, who wrote most of her captions, were effecting comic commentary on a high level indeed. Like all the best comic artists, Hokinson created a world of her own. It was a world (one could sense if one attentively peered into it) whose inhabitants were in a continual battle against the banality and idleness that seemed their lot. The Hokinson woman had no occupation—no job, no children (possibly they had grown up and moved on; in any case they were never mentioned), no apparent religion, not even any housework (the maid in the background took care of that). Her rounded-off figure and the infrequent appearance of her husbands gently suggested that her life lacked intimacy as well. Looked at in this light, her whirlwind of activity—at club meetings and community dramas, her usually fruitless attempts to find the right wine or the perfect mystery novel, to take off a few pounds, or to correctly understand what she is presented with at the art gallery or the opera—appears as a heroic struggle, against all odds, for some kind of transcendence.

The *New Yorker's* pay scale, for cartoons as well as text, was almost defiantly byzantine and does not reward close analysis. But in a chart that was circulated internally in 1947, Hokinson, Arno, and Williams were at the top of the scale, in a "special" category. Clearly, this was not only because of their excellence but also their high-life subject matter. But as befits the decade of the Depression, the true geniuses who arrived in the thirties—Steig, George Price, and Addams—were masters of lowlife. (I except Thurber as being in a category all his own.)

George Price, also a New Jersey native, was eleven years older than Addams and, during the twenties, had contributed cartoons to *Life, Judge, Collier's,* and the *Saturday Evening Post.* Maybe that explained why he came to the *New Yorker* with a fully formed sensibility. A drawing from 1933 (a year after his first appearance) is pure and classic Price. We see an apartment room in which water has risen to the level of roughly three feet. Considerably less alarmed than they should be, a man shaves, a little boy and his dog frolic, and a woman, frying pan in hand, explains it all to a lady friend (such a visitor, a stand-in for the presumably befuddled viewer, is a frequent presence in Price). Price's adjustments over a decade or so were subtle but unmistakable: the artist's line would become more angular; the apartments he drew would become shabbier (typically with cracks in the plaster), smaller (with no additional room visible), and more tightly packed with only vaguely recognizable machinery and memorabilia; the families inhabiting them would become more aggressively eccentric and large. The world of Price was absolutely novel, with no suggestion of stock lowlife characters or situations. What elevated his work to a high level was, first, the vigor and imagination with which he executed it, and, second, the implicit contrast it offered to everything his readers held dear. During the six decades in which Price contributed to the *New Yorker,* the magazine's readers were moving up, socially, economically, and occupationally. They typically had two children, or perhaps three. (In 1960, the mean income for families with six or more children was $19,564; for families with two children it was more than 50 percent higher—$29,606.) They most certainly did not live with their aged parents or in-laws. They moved from city apartments to houses in the suburbs. They answered, each in his own way, the siren call of conformity.

Price's characters resolutely, unapologetically, and rather nobly stayed put, kept breeding, and got stranger and stranger. The joy of his best cartoons is a kind of reverse spin on the shock of recognition.

If Price put the public fears of the *New Yorker*'s readers on display, Addams's best work took as its special province their private ones. Looked at one way, Addams simply offered a fresh wrinkle to the school of Robert Day and Decker, pushing the incongruity of the pictured situation resolutely in the direction of the macabre or the uncanny. In the "Addams family," a straight-A report card is greeted with disconsolate sighs, and the reaction to a monsoon out the picture window is "Just the kind of day that makes you feel good to be alive!" These are mere reversals of convention, done in a cartoony manner. But Addams's best work went deeper. In the cartoon captioned "Tell me more about your husband, Mrs. Briggs," the setting is a drab apartment out of Price; the wife has had to fashion a makeshift ironing

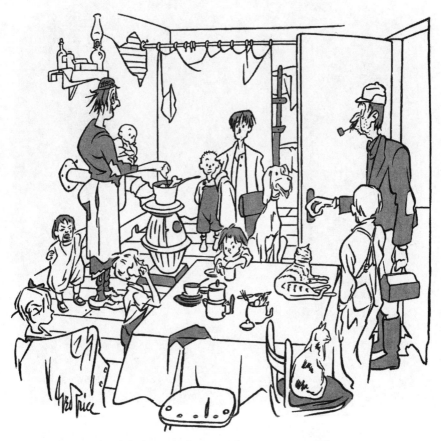

"Boy, did I have an afternoon! The census man was here."

board and to plug in her iron to a bare light socket. The timing is masterful as we progressively notice the clump of bananas on the wall, the oddly shaped suits hanging up, and—the best touch—the rings suspended from the ceiling, and share the visitor's mortified bewilderment. Addams has ratcheted the joke from mere sight gag to the consideration of a notion well beyond taboo. Even more chilling is his famous 1940 cartoon in which a hospital nurse tells an exceedingly strange-looking gentleman, "Congratulations, it's a baby." We find ourselves grateful that the nurse appears so cheerful and competent, the hospital walls so spotlessly white, the floor tiles so geometrically regular, and that the door she holds is so substantial and dark: we would give a great deal, we feel, not to have to see what is behind it.

Through the years, until his death in 1988, Addams alternated wonderful gags—the ski tracks that mysteriously straddle a tree is the classic example—

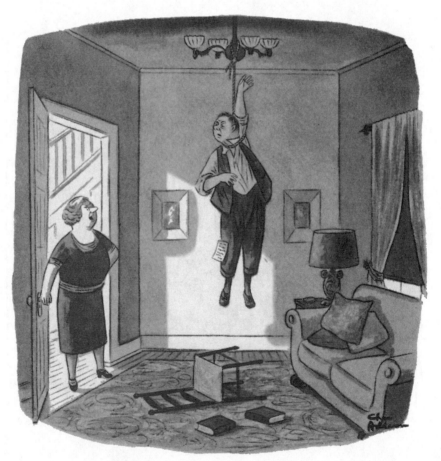

"For heaven's sake, can't you do __anything__ right?"

with cartoons that, in his unique way, blended the truly horrifying and the deeply comic. In his 1949 "For heaven's sake, can't you do *anything* right," the perfection of the details (the tidy symmetry of the room, the eye-level placement of the note, the two books on the floor, the closed window shade, the plausibly misplaced rope) may initially distract us from the terrible beauty of the caption. But if we ponder it long and hard enough, it will sink in and offer a depth of laughter that only the highest comic art provides.

"WE'VE GOT TO HAVE MORE JOURNALISM"

Quite obviously I can't do that cop profile; but I've got the very guy for you. His name is St. Clair McKelway, an old stablemate of mine, who went off to edit the King of Siam's paper about six years ago, and has just returned. He is very anxious to do some business with you. . . . Honest to Jesus, Kay, I do wish you'd take him under your wing. He's the best un-magazine-published writer I know, a great guy, and needs money terribly. . . . He's really better than [John] Lardner, [Edward] Angly, or any of those other *Trib* people.

—Joel Sayre to Katharine S. White, 1933

The *New Yorker,* which has been enormously successful, has demonstrated that a smart, casual style, coupled with a sophisti-cated viewpoint, does anything but repel the reader. The weekly is the product of the peculiar genius of Harold Ross . . . a shrewd merchant of news. He prints Profiles which sometimes are mod-els of the art of biography. The Roving Reporter feature often is brilliant and timely and would not be out of place in the news columns of any daily paper. Moreover, the *New Yorker* is admirably conscientious in checking its facts and getting the minute, reveal-ing details. It has made money by treating its readers, not as pathological cases or a congregation of oafs, but as fairly intelli-gent persons who want information and entertainment.

—Stanley Walker, *City Editor,* 1934

It is a legend that it is dangerous to telephone during a thunder storm. Is this true in New York what with all the wires being underground, or practically all the wires? Come to think of it, are all wires underground in New York? I suppose they are in

Manhattan. To what extent is the telephone company's business cut during a thunder shower?

—Harold Ross, memorandum, May 12, 1933

The thirties may have been an unexceptional time for the *New Yorker* humorous casual, but the *New Yorker* continued to be a very funny magazine. One, possibly unexpected, place readers could find humor was in the magazine's journalism, which benefited from a modest renaissance under way in newspaper writing at the time. A key figure in this was Stanley Walker, a native Texan who as city editor of the *New York Herald Tribune* followed up on the innovations of the *World,* which had folded in 1931, and encouraged a literate and sometimes literary approach to covering the news. Soon after setting out his creed in his book *City Editor,* Walker, a pal of Ross's, was hired as the latest jesus. His stint turned out to be even briefer than the norm, but while on board he cemented a pipeline bringing in first-rate reporters and writers to the magazine. Joel Sayre was one, and as Sayre hoped, St. Clair McKelway soon followed. In due time, the *New Yorker* took in a remarkable list of writers and editors who were originally hired or recruited by Walker: Don Wharton, Sanderson Vanderbilt, Joseph Mitchell, John McNulty, Richard Boyer, Jack Alexander, Alva Johnston, and John Lardner. There were other pipelines as well. Meyer Berger came over from the *New York Times,* and A. J. Liebling from the *World-Telegram.* Simply put, the *New Yorker* was a player in New York journalism in the thirties: competing with the newspapers for reporters, stories, and literary élan, all of which were heatedly discussed over drinks and "the match game" at Bleeck's and Costello's saloons.

But for all the journalistic cross-pollination, *New Yorker* fact writing (as it began to be called at the magazine) was noticeably different from what you would find in the newspapers. The singularity stemmed in large part from the inordinate respect, bordering on reverence, Ross had for two things: facts and humor. This in itself was not exceptional. What *was* was the way *New Yorker* writers under him combined the two. In an appreciation of Ross that William Shawn contributed to Brendan Gill's *Here at the New Yorker,* he wrote, "I have never been sure just what Ross really thought about facts. All I know is that he loved them. They were an end in themselves; they were self-justifying. . . . Facts steadied him and comforted him. Facts also amused him. They didn't need to be funny facts—just facts. A series of factual statements set down with complete gravity could make him laugh because they took him by surprise or amazed him in some inconsequential way."

Nothing gave Ross more pleasure than wrapping his mind around a new and preferably unexpected nugget of information, and his curiosity was prodigious. Most commonly it expressed itself in ideas for Talk of the Town pieces. The bulwark of the department grew to be the "dope" piece—a collection of facts about a person, thing, process, or enterprise the reader may have been interested in or could be expected to be interested in. The Talk section for April 11, 1931, for example, contained pieces about the fake-fur racket, the mail chutes in skyscrapers, how the ice gets changed in Madison Square Garden, and the canal-boat headquarters. As the data flowed through the typewriter of rewrite man Thurber, and later Russell Maloney, the numbers and precise declarative sentences accumulating in paragraphs that grew longer with the years, it uncannily acquired a comic feel. That voice was the New Yorker's alone.

The dope was collected by a growing staff of reporters that included such eventually important figures at the magazine as Geoffrey Hellman, William Shawn, and A. J. Liebling. Ross demonstrated the importance of these men's work by actually paying them salaries, a courtesy he did not extend to his "staff writers," who had to write their pieces on speculation, like a freelancer off the street, and were paid weekly "drawing accounts," money advanced against the eventual acceptance of their work. ("Departmental" writers—including Morris Markey, Janet Flanner, and the critics—were spared having to write on speculation.) The facts these reporters hunted down for Ross were unending, but limited in kind. Perhaps sensibly, his curiosity gravitated toward questions that had definite and obtainable answers. Thus a great many Talk pieces were about the workings of telephones, skyscrapers, the subway, and the radio, and virtually none were about human relations or large political or economic questions.*

Ross used to type out idea sheets for Talk, sometimes a half a dozen or more a day, and a selection of these from the early thirties gives a window into the workings of his mind:

December 17, 1930
Who is Mr. Donovan who inspects all the elevators? Everyone in town must have read his name and he would be a good freak personality, together with a paragraph on elevator inspection.

April 12, 1932
Investigate "The Only Original Morris Mike & Meyer, Inc." at 29 Bayer St. A very funny and mysterious listing in the telephone book—immediately following The New Yorker in the T's.

---

*One observer who picked up on this fixation on mechanical processes was Jean-Paul Sartre, who noted in 1947, "The respect for science, for industry, for positivism, and a fanatical delight in the gadget go hand in hand with the grim humor of The New Yorker, which makes bitter fun of a mechanical civilization and of the 100 million readers who try to satisfy their need for the marvelous by reading the incredible adventures of Superman or Mandrake the Magician."

November 19, 1932
Baptism of new members of Colored Baptist Church in the Harlem River. Done periodically.

January 24, 1934
What is on the radio and in electronic sound transmitting devices the equivalent of "Now is the time for all good men to come to the aid of their party"? Has the radio a set phrase to try out enunciation of announcers and performers? I am told that the Bell Telephone Laboratories have a set piece, if no one else has. It is (from the memory of my source) something like: "Joe put father's shoe bench out; she was waiting at my lawn."

April 27, 1934
What is the record distance from which the Empire State Building Tower can be seen? . . . How far can airplanes see it? Airports would have this dope.

February 18, 1935
What does the term "hard labor" mean in the sentences of criminals? When is it included in sentences—at the judge's discretion, by law, or how? How does the treatment of such a convict so sentenced differ from one not so sentenced?

May 20, 1935
Kosher Coca Cola. Mr. Thurber had the top from a bottle of Coca Cola which had some kind of Jewish assurance on it.

September 23, 1935
There's a legend that a man once went into the Coca Cola offices and said he had an idea which would make millions for them and would reveal it on payment of $50,000. After a solemn agreement had been drawn up he gave them the idea in two words: "Bottle it." I've heard this legend for years. Any truth in it? There are a lot of other legends of the kind that could be bunched with this one, if only to explode them all.

November 20, 1935
Do the candy stores, restaurants, etc. which exude the saliva-starting odors do it intentionally or is it an inadvertent bit of advertising? Have they got a machine to create smells on the sidewalk? I suspect they have after walking through 42nd Street, uptown side, from Lexington to Fifth Av. this morning. You could smell the Schraft [sic] place there for the entire block.

As for the long fact pieces, they came in two kinds. Markey continued to be the principal proprietor of A Reporter at Large until 1936 (when the rubric became open to any of the magazine's writers), and his tended to be what Ross called "color" pieces—impressionistic, sometimes technically daring, inherently serious. A later term for Reporters was the "long visit" story, and the key to them was that the reader experienced everything through the reporter, who commonly made himself a presence in the story and set down the events he witnessed and impressions he arrived at with little apparent artifice.

The other category was the Profile. The term now appears in the dictionary with the definition "concise biographical sketch" and is universally used in journalism to refer to any article about a person, so it is easy to overlook that the early *New Yorker* staffer James Kevin McGuinness coined it. Similarly, so inescapable are such articles today that it is likewise hard to believe that when the *New Yorker* started publishing these pieces, they were considered unusual. In 1938, writing to Clifton Fadiman, who had been assigned to write a preface to an anthology of *New Yorker* Profiles, Ross staked a claim for innovation:

> The *Saturday Evening Post* and other magazines used to use a lot of personality stuff in the old, pre–*New Yorker* days, but it was mostly of two kinds— the *American Magazine* kind, which was practically Horatio Alger done in fact or near-fact stuff, and the josh stuff. . . . After *The New Yorker* started, other magazines got onto the fact that it was possible, notwithstanding libel laws, personal taste, etc., to write history about living people, or write at it, and so help me God, most of them seem to be doing it.

In the very early days, the Profiles tended to be written by young literary types like Gilbert Seldes, Niven Busch, and Waldo Frank (who signed his pieces "Search-Light"), the last two of whom published collections of their Profiles in the late twenties. The pieces were characteristically brief and arch, with an emphasis on getting an acute "angle" on the subject. Katharine Angell wrote to a prospective contributor, "We want the main biographical facts brought in incidentally but the most important thing is to give an intimate picture of the man—something more intimate and personal than the average Sunday magazine newspaper write-up." In keeping with the pictorial metaphor of the title of the department, the emphasis was on getting a sidelong rather than a direct view; "sometimes," Ross told another potential Profiler, "it is not even necessary to see the subject himself at all." The finished products consisted of anecdote and attitude; in striking contrast to later profiles, in the *New Yorker* and elsewhere, rarely would you see a direct quotation from the subject.

Presently a new wave of Profile writers arrived in the persons of John K. Winkler, Alva Johnston, and Henry F. Pringle. All three were newspapermen, and they brought a new level of factual rigor and density to the form. Indeed, one trouble was that reporting and writing Profiles to the new specifications took so much time that it became an economically unrewarding enterprise. Yet the magazine had become something of a literary showplace, and for ambitious literary journalists a kind of loss leader. Winkler complained to Mrs. Angell, "Gosh, Duchess, you don't realize how much striving and straining there is in these Profiles. When the wolf howls I can run off a yarn for a monthly tabloid in a few hours and throw six or eight hundred in the animal's face. Would I do a piece for the *New Yorker* in three or four hours? Sure I would. Would it get past the Angell-Ross outpost? Nope."

The most important of these new contributors was Johnston, a veteran newspaperman, the winner of the 1923 Pulitzer Prize for Reporting, who moved from the *Times* to the *Herald Tribune* in 1928. That same year he wrote his first freelance Profile for the *New Yorker,* and Ross, typically perspicacious, pegged him as the man who could finally yoke facts and humor together in long form. In 1932, when a new jesus named Bernard Bergman came on board, Ross mentioned that he'd long wanted Johnston to come to the magazine full-time. Bergman asked how much money Ross had offered Johnston. Ross said, "Oh, we never discussed money." Bergman proposed putting a $300-a-week drawing account on the table, and Ross said, "Bergman, you're a genius. I never thought of offering him money." Genius or not, it worked, and Johnston came over.

Johnston's *New Yorker* colleague A. J. Liebling once referred to the older man's "technique of defining character by a series of anecdotes on an ascending scale of extravagance, so that the reader of the sixth installment wolfed yarns that he would have rejected in the first." This was on display in two five-part Profiles, written ten years apart, that connoisseurs of the form count among the *New Yorker's* finest: a series in 1932 on the phony Russian prince Mike Romanoff and one in 1942 on the prodigious con man and aphorist Wilson Mizner.*

Speaking to a Princeton Tiger banquet in 1950, two years before Johnston's death, John O'Hara said, "The perfect *New Yorker* Profile in form and style was achieved . . . by Alva Johnston. . . . All good Profiles, and copies of Profiles that you see in *Collier's* and the *Saturday Evening Post,* are modeled after the Johnston originals." Johnston's "form and style" was the product of several attributes infrequently combined in one individual: an inclination to pursue and an ability to carry out extensive reporting; a sharp and interesting critical intelligence that was drawn to the comic or at least the ironic aspects of his subjects; and the ability to impart his material and observations

---

*Johnston would eventually write several more Profiles of Mizner and his brother Addison, famous as a Florida architect, and collect them into the 1953 book *The Legendary Mizners.* John McPhee has said that reading one of Johnston's late pieces on the Mizners inspired him to try to become a *New Yorker* writer. In 1999, Stephen Sondheim was working on adapting *The Legendary Mizners* into a musical comedy.

in well-modulated declarative sentences whose subtly elevated diction and syntax contrasted with their subject to great effect. Consider this characteristically capacious paragraph from his 1934 Profile of movie producer Darryl F. Zanuck, who had made his name by bringing gangster stories to the screen for Warner Brothers; in it Johnston develops his thesis that "Zanuck is primarily a great journalist using the screen instead of the printing press":

> Zanuck became the chief interpreter of the Hardboiled Era. He backed his own newly acquired hardboiled mood against all the canons of the American screen by producing *Doorway to Hell,* a cold and gory picture, which had an unhappy ending, no hero, no major character that inspired sympathy. The Warners regarded it as a reckless experiment and allowed Zanuck to spend only a small sum in making it, but it was a box-office hit. Zanuck's masterpiece of movie journalism was *The Public Enemy,* in which the star roughly handled his mother, hit one girl in the face with a grapefruit, punched another in the jaw, shot a horse for kicking and killing a man, and wound up being taken for a ride and delivered as a corpse at his mother's door. The picture was almost straight news-reporting, the horse-shooting incident and nearly every other bit of action being based on real events which had appeared in the press. Zanuck's greatest pioneering feat was probably the lady-socking. Previously it had been allowable in the films to shoot a woman, to poison her, to rob her, to wrong her in almost every conceivable manner, but not to sock her. Zanuck had turned hardboiled enough to appreciate a hussy-slugging scene; so had the public. This novel touch was greeted with universal cheers, and wallops on the chins of America's sweethearts grossed millions for Hollywood before they became so monotonous that the fans became bored.

Following Johnston's lead was Meyer Berger, who in the early thirties was unanimously deemed the best reporter on the *Times.* Berger's specialty was the "lowlife story," told with a feathery touch. Between 1933 and 1935 he wrote *New Yorker* Profiles of a Broadway "chiseler" whose principal source of income was the manufacture of slugs; of a woman named Anna Lonergan whose brother, first husband, and second husband had all been shot to death in the waterfront wars of Brooklyn; and on March 25, 1933, of a bail-bondsman with an improbable and ultimately inexplicable name. It began:

> The original Stitch McCarthy, a pug-nosed Irish boy who worked in the pressroom of the *Sun* back in 1895, has been one with the dust these many years. He was bantam-weight champion of Jersey City.
>
> For the past thirty-eight years the title has been held by a wizened, cross-eyed little man who looks Irish, but isn't by a good many miles. The current

Stitch McCarthy, a Roumanian Jew, is one of the shrewdest and most affluent bondsmen in the city. His real name, which appears only on bail bonds, is Sam Rothberg.*

Traditionally this kind of subject matter was not highly regarded at the *New Yorker.* After all, the magazine's genesis had been based to a large extent on the 1920s ethos of ascendance, architectural, literary, and social. Whenever a choice was offered between "high" and "low," the choice would always be to go up. Berger, Johnston, and others were permitted to begin to make exploratory descents for two reasons. First, as a result of the Depression, there was a lot more lowlife around. Second, the realization had begun to sink in that highlife tends to be dull. In a 1930 letter to Ross, Don Marquis warned that the Profiles "are going to get too much like the stuff in *American Magazine* if you don't watch them and break the series with something more in accord with your own essential pervading one. They might belong anywhere, the turn they are taking; they need a jab of the needle that will make them your own peculiar stuff again." This was a great period of New York street life, mined, in a different way, by Damon Runyon's tales of guys and dolls, and the *New Yorker* finally saw its potential as the stuff of journalism. Over the course of the decade the pendulum swung the other way, and there were many Profiles of hustlers, large and petty criminals, Broadway characters, Jews, and despite Ross's racism, even a few blacks. Eventually, in answer to a Katharine White complaint, Ross had to admit, "You're right in saying we've gone in for too many obscure, freak people. The boys like to write about them because they're easy to write about and sometimes make better stories."

St. Clair McKelway (the accent in his last name was on the *Kel*), who came over from the *Herald Tribune* late in 1933, was drawn to lowlife as well, especially that part of it associated with crime. His first Profile was of a tong leader in Chinatown, his second, of an "average cop"; by 1936, a new fact rubric, "Annals of Crime," was devised to accommodate his dispatches. (They were eventually collected in a book called *True Tales from the Annals of Crime and Rascality.*) As Joel Sayre had predicted, McKelway was an ideal *New Yorker* writer, a little more modulated than Johnston but possessing the same mix of reportorial rigor, verbal mastery, and ironic point of view. In a 1936 Profile of a New York Fire Department official in charge of apprehending arsonists, he

---

*After freelancing for the magazine for a few years, Berger left the *Times* and joined the *New Yorker* staff in 1938. In addition to finding that he missed the newsroom and the daily deadlines of a newspaper, he was bemused by some of the peculiarities of the *New Yorker,* and he resigned within the year, returning to the *Times* for good. "One of the reasons Mike Berger left was this notion that we were all classified as 'lowlife' writers," Joseph Mitchell said in a 1995 interview. "And he couldn't stand all of Ross's queries."

wrote a characteristic sentence that, for its purposes, was more or less perfect: "Professional firebugs regard themselves as upright citizens and their calling as one that is made necessary by the exigencies of competition in the business world." Ross soon decided to make him an editor, which would have been tougher to predict—since McKelway mumbled (so egregiously that it completely escaped Philip Hamburger when McKelway hired him as a Talk reporter), and since he suffered from a severe manic-depressive condition. But McKelway had shown a rare knack for editing from his first weeks at the magazine and thereafter spent a couple of days a week handling copy. In 1936, Ross named him to a new position, managing editor, with the charge, "We've got to have more journalism." The appointment was historic. It marked, first, the end of the parade of jesuses, McKelway having insisted that he would do no administrative work, and, second, the formal and institutional separation of the fact and fiction departments.

McKelway served in the job for just three years: late in 1939, he went back to full-time writing and was replaced by his assistant, William Shawn. But in that time he solidified *New Yorker* fact-writing style, through example, editorial instruction, and the recruitment of Berger, Sanderson Vanderbilt, Jack Alexander, Richard Boyer, John McNulty, Joseph Mitchell, Margaret Case Harriman, and, as Talk of the Town reporters, the youthful E. J. Kahn Jr., Brendan Gill, John Bainbridge, Philip Hamburger, and David Lardner, who was Ring's son and John's brother. The concentration of talent and the encouragement of journalistic excellence made the magazine, at that moment, an exceptional place for a reporter to be. "In those days, two magazines were reporter's bibles, the *New Yorker* and the *American Mercury*," Mitchell recalled. "Everybody wanted to write for the *New Yorker*." At the office and over lunches at Stouffers, he went on, the reporters would debate the merits of Thomas Mann's fictions and Edward Gibbon's paragraphs. It almost went without saying, in their minds, that the journalism at the *New Yorker* was better literature than the fiction. "We could see the reliance on Katherine Mansfield—the stories that ended nowhere," Mitchell said. "Later, there were all those Westchester stories. The reporters certainly reflected the Depression more than the fiction writers did."

In the classic Profile under McKelway, the edges were smoothed out, and all effects—the comic, the startling, the interesting, and occasionally, the poignant—were achieved by the choreography, in characteristically longer and longer (but never rambling) paragraphs filled with declarative sentences, of the extraordinary number of facts the writer had collected. The Profile metaphor, with its implicit acknowledgment of limited perspective, was no longer appropriate. Instead, it was as if the writer were continually circling around the subject, taking snapshots all the way, until finally emerging with a three-dimensional hologram. This form proved durable, as Geoffrey Hellman, Kahn, Bainbridge, and Hamburger refined it in their multi-decade careers at the magazine and such later arrivals as Robert Lewis Taylor, Calvin Trillin, John McPhee, Mark Singer, and Alec Wilkinson found it amenable and carried it on to the time of this writing.

The form was also strikingly adaptable, suiting lowlife and highlife (this was Hellman's bailiwick, as he wrote about corporate tycoons, society personages, and cultural institutions). Margaret Harriman, a sprightly writer, took show business for her principal beat. From Europe, Janet Flanner contributed Profiles that were noticeably different from her reflective and impressionistic Letters. In 1936, she wrote a three-parter on Adolf Hitler, which almost, but not quite, managed to do justice to evil through the ironic and dispassionate juxtaposition of facts. The Profile began, "Dictator of a nation devoted to splendid sausages, cigars, beer, and babies, Adolf Hitler is a vegetarian, teetotaller, nonsmoker, and celibate." (But the piece did lay out some of Hitler's crimes, and Flanner subsequently wrote to Katharine White, "The only job on the magazine that I am really proud of was the fact that I had sufficient apprehension, three years ago, to propose to write about Hitler as an important man.") The Profile *could* easily manage with the merely venal and corrupt, as John McCarten proved with his remarkable 1938 dissection of Jersey City mayor Frank Hague, "Evolution of a Problem Child." Equally impressive are the goods McCarten has gotten on Hague and the mastery with which he lays out his case. The piece begins in characteristic form, with a confidently attention-grabbing lead, followed by an almost perversely long second paragraph, in which long sentences, short sentences, significant facts, and seemingly trivial ones are alternated with stately rhythm and punctuated by brief and pungent quotes:

> Possibly nobody in the country, with the possible exception of Donald Duck, is as persistently indignant as Frank Hague. In the twenty years that he has been Mayor of Jersey City and Democratic boss of New Jersey, Hague has been indignant about practically everything from brothels and poolrooms to Roosevelt and Republicans. At the moment he is beside himself because the C.I.O. wants to organize the workers of Jersey City.
>
> To keep himself in proper emotional fettle, Hague broods a good deal about the plots his enemies are hatching against him. One of his favorite words is "sinister," and he uses it continually in describing the machinations of his opposition. Actually, for the present, at least, he appears to have very little opposition, sinister or otherwise. The Governor of New Jersey, A. Harry Moore, is his protégé. The state is represented in the United States Senate by a couple of loyal Democrats. As for Jersey City, Hague at the moment seems more secure there now than he ever was before. Last May he was elected head man in the city for the sixth time in a row by the almost unanimous vote of

110,743 to 6,798. Nevertheless he goes right on seething about the people he thinks are trying to get him. He makes no attempt to hide his feelings. His characteristic facial expression is one of confused resentment, as if he had just been insulted or expected to be any minute. Even when he draws himself up to his full six feet, folds his arms, pulls back his head, and announces that he is "the leading citizen of New Jersey," he looks gloomy. His pale-blue eyes are heavy-lidded and suspicious, his long, thin lips curve morosely downward, his chin sets pugnaciously in the folds of the dewlaps that dangle over this high, Berry Wall collar. In this "leading citizen" pose, Hague has the air of a right-eous dominie in the midst of a world of sin. He never sounds like one, though. His voice is loud and confident. His conversation is profane and tough. When he wants to be emphatic he claps his hands or pokes his fore-finger challengingly at his listener's chest. He constantly breaks the thread of his remarks to assert aggressively, "You know I'm right!" He is as slovenly in his grammar as he is meticulous in his dress. He wears dark, well-tailored suits, high topped shoes of Vici kid that he gets, at a bargain, for twenty-five dollars a pair, and rich, quietly patterned ties. His hats are by Dobbs, his col-lars by Sulka. He is particular about the placement of his tiepin and the posi-tion of his shirt cuffs. If he changed his shirts daily instead of wearing them for two days at a stretch, he would be impeccable. He is proud of his power-ful figure and likes to be told that he looks youthful. At sixty-two he is often taken for forty-five. When he poses formally for photographs he usually wears a hat to hide the fact that he is rather bald. He keeps the gray hair that borders his domed head carefully trimmed. In his speeches he frequently says that his appearance offers a fine example to the youth of Jersey City. His advice to the young ones is forthright and elementary. "If you will keep clean and work hard and stay honest like your Mayor," he says, "you can grow up like him and be respected as the first citizen of your city."

With the style in place, it was open to transformation by genius. This arrived in the persons of Joseph Mitchell and Abbott Joseph Liebling, who signed his work "A.J." Although Mitchell was from rural North Carolina and Liebling was a native New Yorker, and although Mitchell's writing was as quiet as Liebling's was loud, the two men otherwise had a lot in common. They were both called Joe, they both worked at the *New York World-Telegram* (where they became close friends), they both militantly believed that jour-nalism could be just as creative and artful as fiction, both were devoted to lowlife and its chroniclers—Villon, Rabelais, Sterne, and Dostoyevsky—and both started their association with the *New Yorker* in 1933. Liebling, twenty-nine at the time and the older man by four years, had the rougher path. He did freelance reporting for The Talk of the Town, but had a hard time working up the right tone for long pieces. In the summer of 1933, an editor at the magazine wrote him that five stories were "reserved" for him (the closest the magazine came to giving an assignment): "Africa, Big Game Hunting In; Billiardists, Finger-Technique, Exploits; Mining Pans, Manufacture of"; and two Profiles. I don't know if any of these pieces was ever written; I am certain none was published. Early in 1935, he submitted a piece on vaudeville for Onward and Upward with the Arts, only to have it turned down by McKelway, who wrote him, "Everybody here seems to feel it lacks the satirical slant which seems to be required in the Onward and Upward department." Liebling took a staff job with the magazine that summer, doing Talk of the Town reporting, but still was unable to get anything published over his byline, and even had trouble getting his own stories into Talk. He later attributed this to his newspaper mind-set: "I brought to [the New Yorker] a successful newspaper short-feature method that was not transferable to a magazine, especially in long pieces. It would have been like running a mile in a series of hundred-yard dashes." William Shawn gave a different explanation in an interview with Liebling's biographer, Raymond Sokolov:

> His problem was one of tone or style, not length. At the time the "Talk" stories all had a fairly accepted tone. They sounded pretty much like Thurber or White. Liebling, who was very individual, had his own style. . . . He had trouble finding his way that first year. But Liebling, more than almost any writer I've known here at the magazine, improved his writing. He had trouble putting sentences and paragraphs together, but he learned in a remarkable fashion. I don't know how. He absorbed something—he wasn't taught. Something developed in him. He became fluent and extremely stylish, a master in journalistic terms.

Whatever the exact cause of Liebling's troubles, what clearly turned him around was his work on a three-part, fifteen-thousand-word story called "Who Is This King of Glory?" which was published in June 1936. It was an exposé of an African-American preacher who, as the lead put it, "has said on more than one occasion that he is God," and who operated on the understanding that his many disciples would hand all their assets and earnings over to him. Liebling traced Father Divine back to his early years in Baltimore and discerned, in painstaking detail, the precise ways in which he exploited his followers. Unfortunately, while working on the story, Liebling got so wrapped up that it threatened to turn into "a million-word book on comparative religion." "Everybody agreed it was wonderful stuff," recalled McKelway (who had not yet been named an editor), "but nobody could see how to teach Liebling how to do it right. . . . Ross finally asked me to read it and see if I could edit it into shape. I said I couldn't, that it would have to be entirely reorganized and heavily rewritten, using it as source material and sometimes using whole pages exactly as they were." The piece, published over a double Liebling-McKelway byline, remains one of the classic Profiles. After that, Liebling's troubles were over. From the Father Divine piece until 1939, when he convinced McKelway to send him to France to cover the war in Europe, he contributed a series of magnificent lowlife portraits, taking what Meyer Berger and Alva Johnston had done one step further through the sheer gusto of his prose. He was a large man, prone to laughing at the typewriter over his own formulations, and he seemed to embrace his subjects. He wrote about Broadway tummlers, boxing cornermen and sparring partners, bookies, hatcheck concessionaires, and professional-wrestling promoters. The Profile of the cornerman Morris "Whitey" Bimstein appeared on March 20, 1937, and it displays Liebling pretty much at his best, combining precise and detailed descriptions of Bimstein's trade with moments of ripping humor. Describing a typical Bimstein day, Liebling writes that in setting up his equipment at Stillman's Gym, "he is assisted in this by a satellite, a Mr. Emmet. Mr. Emmet, a Bostonian, is so called because, as he explains, 'I always hanged in Emmet Street.' He has forgotten his former name, which was polysyllabic."

The world paid attention. In 1938, Sheridan House brought out a collection of Liebling's pieces from the *New Yorker* and the *World-Telegram*, under the title *Back Where I Came From*. The next year, in a memo discussing salaries, Ross commented to the administrative editor, Ik Shuman, "Liebling is the big success of the year, I think." France and England declared war against Germany on September 1, 1939, and Liebling, who had the reporter's heliotropism toward the big story, determined that Europe was where he wanted to be. Janet Flanner was on home leave, and Liebling convinced McKelway and Ross to let him take her place, even though, he later wrote,

> I knew very little about Lady Mendl, Elsa Maxwell, Mainbocher and Worth the dressmakers, Mr. and Mrs. Charles Badeaux, or a number of other leading characters in Genêt's Paris dispatches. But since it seemed probable that they would lam anyway, Ross was willing to overlook this deficiency and even agreed in a halfhearted way with McKelway's idea that I write about the reactions to the war of ordinary French people. "But for God's sake keep away from lowlife," Ross said.

When Liebling returned home in 1941 (he would go back to Europe twice more before the war was over), he wrote his lowlife masterwork, "The Jollity Building," a three-part Profile of a Times Square office building populated by what Liebling called "the petty nomads of Broadway—chiefly orchestra leaders, theatrical agents, bookmakers, and miscellaneous promoters." ("The term 'promoter,' " Liebling explains, "means a man who mulcts another man of a dollar, or any fraction or multiple thereof.") By that time McKelway had been replaced by Shawn, who was much less sympathetic to marginal personalities and themes than McKelway had been and, until Liebling's death in 1963, tried to encourage him toward elevated subjects, with varying degrees of success. Philip Hamburger recalled having lunch with Shawn on the day of Liebling's memorial service, where Hamburger was to give a eulogy. Shawn's last words as Hamburger departed were, "Watch out for lowlife."

Joseph Mitchell got published in the *New Yorker* before Liebling—initially, with a 1933 Reporter at Large from Elkton, Maryland, where more marriages were performed than in any other city in America. Over the next half decade, his *World-Telegram* features and his occasional *New Yorker* freelance contributions put him—with Meyer Berger and a couple of others—into the highest rank of newspapermen in the city, and his pieces were collected in 1938 in a book called *My Ears Are Bent*. "I guess he must be about the best interviewer in the world," Fadiman said in his *New Yorker* review, "though on the surface it seems he does nothing but let people talk. Every Joe Mitchell story I have ever read has been—in its own way—a work of art, a fact of which the author is doubtless perfectly unaware."

That "doubtless" was whistling in the dark, for art was very much on Mitchell's mind and prompted his acceptance, later that year, of McKelway's offer to come to the *New Yorker* full-time. He did so on the condition that he would be on a straight salary rather than a drawing account, and for half a century he was the only *New Yorker* journalist with this arrangement. "I had written about a great variety of people, and, working for an afternoon newspaper, I had had to work very fast," Mitchell said in a 1995 interview. "But there was this anomaly: you can write something and every sentence in it will be a fact, you can pile up facts, but it won't be true. Inside a fact is another fact, and inside that is another fact. You've got to get the *true* facts. When I got here, I said to myself I don't give a damn what happens, I am going to take my time."* Once on the staff, he found a group of likeminded writers—Liebling and Berger and Richard Boyer—who had the same aspirations he had for a new urban literary journalism. "We would argue endlessly about the ways of writing about New York City," Mitchell said in another interview late in his life. "We talked about Stephen Crane's

---

*In the interview, Mitchell recalled the circumstances of his hiring: "One time McKelway called me and said Mr. Ross wanted to have lunch. We went over to the Blue Ribbon, which was a restaurant that a lot of *New Yorker* people went to. I asked Mr. Ross some questions about when he worked in Atlanta, and he talked the whole lunch through about himself, about newspaper work. And then at the end he said, 'If you want to come to work, speak to McKelway.'"

Maggie: A Girl of the Streets, about how we were disappointed in Dos Passos. We never thought of ourselves as experimenting. But we were thinking about the best way we could write about the city, without all the literary framework."

After initial contributions that were first-rate, but not dramatically different from what others were doing, Mitchell developed into a peculiar genius. That flowering can be pinpointed to 1940, when he published a breathtaking trio of lowlife Profiles: "Lady Olga," about a circus bearded lady; "The Old House at Home," about a lower-Manhattan barroom called McSorley's; and "Mazie," about the ticket-taker and part-owner of a cheap movie house on the Bowery. These are appropriate subjects for a newspaper feature article, or even a standard *New Yorker* lowlife piece, but Mitchell wholly resists the condescension, breeziness, or easy irony those genres are heir to. His humor is of a singular kind, not unlike that of Charles Addams among the cartoonists. "Graveyard humor is an exemplification of the way I look at the world," Mitchell explained in the introduction to his collected writings, *Up in the Old Hotel.* "It typifies my cast of mind." (Another similarity was pointed out by Ross in a 1946 memo about payments to contributors: "Mr. Addams is a special problem, somewhat like Mr. Mitchell among the writers—excellent quality, low productivity.") For Mitchell, graveyard humor meant, in part, giving the grotesque, the macabre, or the eccentric the respect it deserves. Here is a paragraph from "Mazie," about the title character's place of business:

> The Venice is a small, seedy moving-picture theatre, which opens at 8 A.M. and closes at midnight. It is a dime house. For this sum a customer sees two features, a newsreel, a cartoon, and a serial episode. The Venice is not a "scratch house." In fact, it is highly esteemed by its customers, because its seats get a scrubbing at least once a week. Mazie brags that it is as sanitary as the Paramount. "Nobody ever got loused up in the Venice," she says. On the Bowery, cheap movies rank just below cheap alcohol as an escape, and most bums are movie fans. In the clientele of the Venice they are numerous. The Venice is also frequented by people from the tenement neighborhoods in the vicinity of Chatham Square, such as Chinatown, the Little Italy on lower Mulberry Street, and the Spanish section on Cherry Street. Two-thirds of its customers are males. Children and most women sit in a reserved section under the eyes of a matron. Once, in an elegant mood, Mazie boasted that she never admits intoxicated persons. "What do you consider a person intoxicated?" she was asked. Mazie snickered. "When he has to get down on all fours and crawl," she said. In any case, there are drunks in practically every Venice audience. When the liquor in them dies down they become fretful and mumble to themselves, and during romantic pictures they make

loud, crazy, derogatory remarks to the actors on the screen, but by and large they are not as troublesome as a class of bums Mazie calls "the stiffs." These are the most listless of bums. They are blank-eyed and slow-moving, and they have no strong desire for anything but sleep. Some are able to doze while leaning against a wall, even in freezing weather. Many stiffs habitually go into the Venice early in the day and slumber in their seats until they are driven out at midnight. "Some days I don't know which this is, a movie-pitcher house or a flophouse," Mazie once remarked. "Other day I told the manager pitchers with shooting in them are bad for business. They wake up the customers."

You can sense the writer taking the familiar "grammar of facts" (as Malcolm Cowley called a *New Republic* review of Mitchell's 1943 collection of *New Yorker* articles, *McSorley's Wonderful Saloon*) and using it in altogether new ways. His amalgamation of humor and profound sadness was new, and so was the way he tried to write nonfiction "stories," with beginnings and endings. At first these attempts met with some resistance at the *New Yorker*. "The conventional way of reporters when I began was to write a lead and then hang from it the details connected with the lead," Mitchell said years later. "And that dominated Mr. Ross's ideas for a long time—he wanted everything in the lead, just like in the newspaper. He'd write some query about some missing information in the beginning of the story, and my response would be, 'What do you want me to do, tell the whole thing in the first paragraph?' Then he began to see that the surprise and development of the thing was part of it."

In Mitchell's 1940 pieces, the surprise and development was the notion, subtle at first but more insistent as each one went on, that their subjects were not isolated eccentrics but representative of something deeper and more universal. Every night after the theater closes, we are presently told, Mazie goes on a two-hour tour of the Bowery, giving dimes and quarters to homeless men; in cold weather, she rouses them from park benches and manhandles them into flophouses, where she takes off their shoes, loosens their collars, and puts them into bed. From a lowlife sketch, the story becomes an examination of the possibilities of doing good. As Mitchell observed her while reporting the story ("When I was writing about Mazie and the bearded lady, I spent so much time with them that I drove them crazy," Mitchell said), the comparison that came to mind was with Alyosha, the most pure of the Brothers Karamazov. "Her devotion to those poor fellows, you know," he said. "Maybe I got some indication of it in there."

Similarly, "The Old House at Home" may initially seem merely a portrait of a colorful New York institution. Before long we realize that McSorley's is an emblem for all the bulwarks we think we have against death and what

Mitchell, in the piece's penultimate sentence, calls "the dreadful loneliness of the old and alone." At the *New Yorker,* another term for lowlife was *freak,* and "Lady Olga" took that literally. The first part of the Profile is animated by the humorous contrast between the highly unusual appearance of the bearded lady, Jane Barnell, and the profound conventionality of her world-view and her life away from the circus, which is devoted to her cat, her husband (a former clown nineteen years younger than she), and her conviction that New York City tap water contains a lethal acid, removable only by boiling. Gradually, and with his characteristic subtlety, Mitchell asks us to consider the pain Barnell has undergone in her sixty-nine years. By the end of the story, this is something we cannot ignore, and by the time we get to her stunning final quotation, we have been prepared to accept it as categorically true. Leading up to it, Mitchell says that, unlike some of her colleagues, Barnell does not object to being called a freak:

"'No matter how nice a name was put on me,' she says, 'I would still have a beard.' Also, she has a certain professional pride. Sometimes, sitting around with other performers in a dressing room, she will say, with a slight air of defiance, that a freak is just as good as any actor, from the Barrymores on down. 'If the truth was known, we're all freaks together.'"

BENSON, O'HARA, SHAW, ET AL.

Everyone likes the way you've done it, but these long straight stories are about the worst problem we have. We have about sixteen on hand now, and for mechanical reasons they're poison to work off. We feel, too, that they're really pretty much out of key in a magazine such as this. Consequently we've had to tighten up a lot on them, making it a virtual rule that we couldn't use them unless they were definitely set in New York City. . . .

—Wolcott Gibbs to Joel Sayre, July 31, 1931

~~~

Somehow, we feel that the effect of your other story ("Apartment Hotel") was in the lack of elaborateness, the lack of plot, and I think the less elaborate you make this the better.

—Katharine Angell to Sally Benson, February 5, 1929

And if you think these things are getting to be what might be called vignettes, tear them up.

—Benson to Katharine White, 1930

Here's another. It's good. By the way, what do you do with my pieces. I *think* I know, but want to be sure.

—Benson to Wolcott Gibbs, undated

For God's sake, can those little *New Yorker* pieces and spread out. The magazine, excellent as it is, is devoted to precociousness, which means it is got out by a lot of precious amateurs, who are not the less amateurs because they are very gifted.

—James M. Cain to Benson, August 25, 1934

I have been feeling a little silly lately because it seems I am being considered literary, whereas you know and Gibbs knows that most of my simplicity is due to an appalling ignorance in the use of adjectives and a blank spot in my brain where grammar should be. I hope both of you have the decency to keep quiet about it.

—Benson to Katharine White

~~~

It does seem the greatest of pities that you can't spend a little more time on your manuscripts for *The New Yorker*. Take these three, for example: they all have something and come near to being very good stories, but each one of them seems to fail and we are under the impression that the reason they fail is that you haven't spent enough time or thought on the material you are using.

The small boy's letter is probably authentic, but it doesn't seem to us to come off as completely amusing. But this manuscript is a less good example of what I mean than the other two which seem rather inconclusive, more like synopses for stories yet to be written, or perhaps like chapters out of a book. They don't seem to start anywhere or get anywhere, and the general idea is hard to follow.

I go into all this detail because we are really so very anxious to have contributions from you and understand your fatigue with the Afternoon Delphians, the Paint and Varnish Company and all the rest of them. Your story in—was it *Scribner's*—which I read seemed to me a much more finished piece of work, well conceived and thought out from beginning to end. I don't mean by this that we want always a finished short story, as you know we tend to the more unconventional rather than the plotted form, but at least we think a story should have some unity of idea.

—Katharine White to John O'Hara, January 21, 1932

I can't help thinking that it is fine to regard the *New Yorker* as an experimental medium, but that when nobody, nobody at all, understands just what a writer is driving at that is an unsuccessful experiment from our point of view. And if the general mind here is the Scarsdale mind it is a tough break for the author, but I don't know what anybody can do about it.

—Wolcott Gibbs to O'Hara, April 3, 1936

Okay, kill the old ending in Ideal Man. If the ending hadn't been there, Ross would have rejected it. It's there, so he doesn't want it. Ross wants to be a writer.

—O'Hara to William Maxwell, February 8, 1939

I want more money I want more money I want more money I want more money I want more money I want more money I want more money I want more money I want more money I want more money I want more money.

—O'Hara to Harold Ross, October 6, 1939

If I were you I'd howl for a raise, if my inference is correct and you are to "handle" my contributions and me. You saw what I did to Maxwell, and he was a wiry fellow.

—O'Hara to Gustave Lobrano, March 1940

~~~

We don't feel that LET-DOWN as you have done it over entirely succeeds. You have made the story clearer at the start, but the final decision is that as a whole it is just too hard to follow— at least too hard to follow for our type of reader. Perhaps it belongs in some other magazine.

—Katharine White to Louise Bogan, June 9, 1931

~~~

I buy most magazines for their fiction. In most instances, I know what to expect for my money: thus *Harper's* gives me idylls about suburban matrons who discover to their amazement that they still love their husbands; *Cosmopolitan* supplies me with de luxe broker-stenographer romances; *The New Yorker* offers whimsies concerning frustrated little Milquetoasts; and so on.

—Stephen W. Calkins, letter to the editor, *Vanity Fair,* 1933

~~~

The reason against this one is that it is a somewhat conventional story, too consciously smart and sophisticated for us. We think it would go far better in *Vanity Fair* or *Harper's*.

—Katharine White to Maxim Lieber,
literary agent, rejecting Tess Slesinger's
"For Better and for Worse," June 21, 1935

~~~

I have been reading the *New Yorker* for years, with such veneration that it has never occurred to me that I could write for it. Now that blasphemous thought has lodged itself in my head.

—Sylvia Townsend Warner to Katharine White,
December 26, 1935

However pleased the *New Yorker* may have been to get "Two Minutes Silence," it cannot possibly have been as pleased as I was to get your letter of acceptance and your check for seventy dollars. "Princely," I said to the cat. . . . I shall probably have "contributes to the *New Yorker*" embroidered on my handkerchiefs. Your paper is one of the lights of my eyes, and I lend it to deserving sickbeds in this village; then they, may be, admire the advertisements most, and enquire with their last breaths about your currency.

—Warner to Katharine White, February 16, 1936

~~~

. . . the great flood of casuals that begin like this

1) It was snowing a little when Mr. Prentice set out for the drugstore . . .

2) When Mr. Birdseed took hold of the table runner, a tiny shower of sequins from his dead wife's party gown sifted to the floor.

3) Mr. Applegate walked out on the back porch, sniffed the first fine cold air of winter, and sighed. He walked on down to the drugstore, noticing, as he stopped for a moment in front of the Whitney's gate, that the fine cold air was there, too. Vaguely uneasy, he . . .

We've had an awful lot of the sad drifting little men, muddling gently through the most trivial and impalpable of situations, ending up on a faint and, to me, usually evasive note of resignation to it all, whatever it all is.

—James Thurber to Katharine White,
January 22, 1938 (ellipses in original)

We have great hopes for Cheever and feel that even in this story there is that special quality which he gives to his things and which is exactly right for *The New Yorker.*

—William Maxwell to Geraldine Mavor, literary agent,
October 20, 1939

"The Way Some People Live" has some very touching things in it, but it remains a little on the sordid side, it seems to us, and is also a little melodramatic.

—Maxwell to Mavor, November 17, 1939

There are thirty sketches in this volume; all of them are worth at least five minutes of your time, even though the majority are exercises in marital disruption, hag-ridden dipsomania, poverty, or plain and fancy jitters. Most of them appeared between the covers of *The New Yorker.* Perhaps this accounts for their peculiar epicene detachment and facile despair.

—William Du Bois, review of John Cheever's
The Way Some People Live, New York Times Book Review,
March 28, 1943

The new story I have just returned to Miss Nowell [literary agent Elizabeth Nowell]. It's what is known around here as a "mood piece," meaning that what people do is determined by the frame of mind they're in at the time the story opens, and you can tell a mood piece very easily because they nearly always begin with somebody standing and looking out of the window. Yours does. . . . If you are serious about doing more *New Yorker* pieces, and I hope to God you are, will you remember to start them with something happening instead of somebody in the dumps.

—William Maxwell to Nancy Hale, November 17, 1939

Whenever I read anything of yours, in manuscript here, or at my dentist's, I am convinced against a mountain of evidence to the contrary that there is such a thing as the human heart.

—Maxwell to Hale, May 16, 1941

~~~

I'm writing to you because I saw your name on a letter written to Mr. Jacques Chambrun about a story of mine submitted to (and rejected) by the *New Yorker*. The story was called "The Wedding."

Since that time I've submitted a few things on my own hook, since I feel that Mr. Chambrun is merely humoring me when he handles what even I can see is not commercial writing. Until I turn up with something that I think is acceptable for the *Saturday Evening Post* or *Esquire*, I don't intend to bother Mr. Chambrun.

The unfortunate thing about my lone ventures in contributing to the *New Yorker* is that all my stories come back in the next morning's mail. I leave something late Wednesday afternoon and the postman hands it to me at nine o'clock on Thursday. While this might be evidence of an admirably efficient corps of readers in the *New Yorker* office, it is somewhat dispiriting to a young and purely undiscovered writer. On occasion I have doubted that my manuscripts have been touched by a reader's hand.

It is to dispel these doubts that I have taken the liberty of addressing this latest story of mine to you. I would like to have the assurance that my manuscripts get at least one step further than the *New Yorker*'s tireless shipping clerk.

—Irwin Shaw to John Mosher, December 15, 1935

There's something I don't want to happen to my stories . . . (and if it ever does happen, please tell me) . . . I don't want my things, in between the dialogue, to sound like a typical *New Yorker* story.

—Irwin Shaw to G. S. Lobrano, undated letter

In the typical *New Yorker* story everything occurs at one place in one time, and all the dialogue is beside the point.

—Irwin Shaw, quoted by William Maxwell, 1981 interview

~~~

Tell him that if he ever writes a short story that he thinks the *New Yorker* ought to have, for God's sake to send it in to us. In the early days I never went after him because we didn't pay anything. We don't pay much now, but we pay more than *Esquire* (although not using fishing stuff).

—Harold Ross to Martha Gellhorn
(Ernest Hemingway's wife), February 15, 1943

Although the *New Yorker* began to publish identifiably serious short fiction in 1928 and then continued to do so regularly, it took the world at large a fairly long time to digest this fact. Every year beginning in 1915, Edward O'Brien put out a book called *The Best Short Stories* (or some variant thereof) and assessed the state of the genre in an introduction. The *New Yorker* made its first appearance in the 1930 edition, when O'Brien included three stories from the magazine (by Morley Callaghan, Emily Hahn, and Dorothy Parker). But in no year in the rest of the decade did he select more than one, and never did he mention the *New Yorker* in an introduction. The magazine fared even more poorly in a competing anthology, *The O. Henry Memorial Award Prize Stories,* where it was ignored until 1935.

The eventual recognition that *New Yorker* stories were in fact short stories, and had substantial value as such, can be traced to a single event: the publication, late in 1940, of the magazine's own anthology, *Short Stories from the New Yorker.* This was a project directed by Mrs. White, and she clearly saw it as a way to announce that, yes, the *New Yorker* was a forum for first-class fiction. In a 1939 memo to Ross, she wrote, "What this book should be, as I see it, is a distinguished collection of short stories which, though we didn't set out to do it, we seem to have amassed during the years. It would be mostly savage, serious, moving, or just well written fiction with some that are funny in part." To underscore this point, she omitted from the book reminiscences, humorous casuals, and stories that were parts of series—all the things, in other words, for which the *New Yorker* was best known. The strategy worked. Reviews of the anthology invariably noted, with surprise, the high quality of the fiction, and in 1941 Edward O'Brien chose three *New Yorker* stories for *Best American Short Stories.* O'Brien died before the next edition, and his successor, Martha Foley, took four selections from the *New Yorker.* She rhetorically wondered in her introduction if the reading public was aware of "the fine character of the fiction published by the magazine."

Why, at this late date, was there any doubt? One reason is that the strength of the magazine's identity as a humorous publication—an identity bolstered by the cartoons, the Newsbreaks, the ironic Talk of the Town pieces and Profiles, and by all the light casuals and reminiscences—created a sort of literary camouflage in the midst of which writing of a very different kind tended to go undetected. At the same time, the "serious" short stories were sent out to the world under their own protective coloration. No visual cue alerted readers to a dark piece by Morley Callaghan or Kay Boyle or Robert Coates—it would have the same position in the magazine, the same typographical treatment, more or less the same length, and the same lack of illustration, labeling, byline, subheading, or any other graphic apparatus as a casual by Benchley or Perelman. In other words, readers had to *work* to orient themselves in a piece of writing—a sharp contrast to most other magazines, then and now, where they are led by the hand and sometimes elbowed in the ribs lest they miss the point. Ross's notorious insistence that the circumstantial elements of a piece, fact or fiction, be identified or "pegged" in the first one or two paragraphs was surely in some measure designed to ease this hard labor.

But the lack of recognition also had to do with the stories themselves. One of Ross's articles of editorial faith, a hardy holdover from the *Judge/Life* model, was brevity, and the stories grew in seriousness and heft much more quickly than they did in length. But readers and critics looked to short stories for the experience of settling into a narrative and some people's lives, and in a piece of three thousand or even four thousand words, after setting, character, and mood had all been established, there was hardly room left for incident. Similarly restricting, as Irwin Shaw observed, was that *New Yorker* stories usually observed an Aristotelian unity of setting. (One of the several groundbreaking aspects of Shaw's 1939 "Sailor off the *Bremen*" was its multiscene structure.)

It was not only a matter of length. Part of Mrs. White's creed was that plot, on the whole, was bad, and when it reared its head in a short story under consideration, all kinds of flags went up. Her stance was not surprising. The late teens into the thirties was a boom time for American short stories. They were the main editorial fare at dozens of magazines and provided a good livelihood for hundreds of writers. One scholar has calculated that during the twenties alone, more than one hundred handbooks were published, each promising to reveal the secrets of how to write salable short fiction. The inevitable parallel, half a century hence, is with television. Also like television, short stories for the most part were characterized by melodrama, sentimentality, heavy-handed irony, contrivance and/or patent improbability. In strikingly familiar terms, they were vilified in the upper realms of the culture. Writing in the *Dial* in 1922, Gilbert Seldes proclaimed, "The short story is by all odds the weakest, most trivial, most stupid, most insignificant art work produced in this country and perhaps in any country." Similar, too, was some of the imagery used to describe the effect of short stories on their readers. "Overindulgence in the short story is a dissipation which produces an inevitable reaction; it leaves the mind in a jerky state," wrote a critic. An essay by Helen Hull about the short-story boom was titled "The Literary Drug Traffic." Both the appeal of short stories and their artistic weakness, it was generally agreed, originated with plot, which was still under the influence of O. Henry's picturesque characters and surprise endings (ten and even twenty years after his death in 1910), but without any of the feeling and freshness of approach even his detractors admitted he brought to the genre.

In this climate, the *New Yorker*, hypersensitive as it was to gaucheries and hokum, could scarcely be expected to begin printing "conventional" short stories. Instead, it quietly created its own category. The more perceptive observers of the literary scene recognized this. Writing in 1934 to the psychiatrist treating his wife, Zelda, F. Scott Fitzgerald observed, "She writes a brilliant letter and has made marked success in short character studies and has an extraordinary talent for metaphor and simile. Along that line, and with the realism of having to write her stuff to sell she could be, say, a regular contributor to the *New Yorker* and such magazines that publish short pieces." The note of condescension is hard to miss; after all, Fitzgerald did not consider the *New Yorker* a suitable market for himself, contributing just five pieces, all either humor or light verse, before his death in 1940. (He would doubtless have written more if the magazine's top rate of pay for much of the thirties had not been just ten cents a word, a small fraction of what he could get from *Collier's, Esquire,* or the *Saturday Evening Post.*) In the introduction to the 1940 O. Henry collection, the editor, Harry Hansen, sniffed, "In recent years the ironic sketch has been highly developed in the pages of the *New Yorker,* but only rarely does it contain that conflict and progressive development that would make it a short story."

Whatever the qualities of the serious short stories in the magazine, for the greater part of the decade they were far outnumbered by the casuals and reminiscences. To be published in the *New Yorker,* a piece of serious fiction had to run a gauntlet of editorial standards. Besides literary quality and relative brevity, there was just one absolute requirement: clarity. But if a story took place outside New York, if it had a lowlife setting or characters, if it was downbeat or grim, it had to be perceived as having great merit indeed to make the grade. Those that did were deftly characterized by Stanley Edgar Hyman in his 1942 *New Republic* essay on the *New Yorker* as "tight, objective sketches with a strong undercurrent of emotion, aimed at capturing a mood, a feeling or a situation." One can offer some additional characteristics. They had plentiful dialogue (thus carrying forward the "talk" theme of the early years) and an unmistakable journalistic quality. They offered little in the way of flights of fancy, displays of emotion on the part of characters or author, or identifiable literary style, other than the faint irony of flatness—second-generation Hemingway. Instead, there was precision, detail, and a tough-minded authenticity. On examination, they bear a striking resemblance to the matter-of-fact epiphanies and meticulously observed slices of life in the short stories generally recognized as bringing modernism to the genre: James Joyce in his 1914 *Dubliners* and Katherine Mansfield, in several collections published before her death in 1923, as well as to those writers' common ancestor, Anton Chekhov. American writers seeking to create "modern" short stories, such as Sherwood Anderson, Hemingway, and (though he may not have realized it) Lardner, tended to push emotion more roughly to the surface. In the words of the critic Andrew Levy, the more genteel strain of modernism slipped into America "through the back door," courtesy of the *New Yorker.*

One can get a sense of the way a manuscript turned into a *New Yorker* story from a 1936 submission from Arthur Steig (William's brother), who wrote under the name Henry Anton and had been trying to break into the magazine for some time. This story was about a young jazz trombone player whose "respectable" girlfriend gives him an ultimatum—music or her. He chooses music, she breaks up with him, and at the end, as he gets ready to play the late show, we are given to understand that, irony of ironies, he isn't a very good trombonist. Mrs. White wrote to Anton's agent:

> Three of us here have pondered considerably over this Anton story. We like it very much, better in fact than anything he has written thus far and we want to buy it, but we have a problem on it that we hope you will put up to him. The problem is that we don't know whether his ending as it now stands is better than an ending which would not be so pat and trick—which would not have a surprise ending, in other words. Will you ask him to think this over and see whether he thinks the story would be sounder and better if he let the piece end with the old trumpet player a bust without his knowing it. In general, the patter the ending, the more conventional the short story, and you know we try to avoid a snap finish for this reason. However, I think there is a real argument on the other side and that in this case the story might be more conventional if it were purely a sob story than with this trick. . . .
>
> We are really puzzled about it and there are two schools here on the matter, so please ask Mr. Anton to give it his best thought. . . . We certainly want the story but are putting this problem up to him as an artist and we hope he will take that amount of interest in his own work, and realize we only want to make the story as good as possible.

Anton knew it was a buyer's market, and so it's not surprising that "Trombonist Extraceptional" was published, on September 26, 1936, without the "snap finish"—that is, as a "sob story." It is interesting that Mrs. White would have invoked the latter phrase. Normally used derisively, it had an undeniable aptness for *New Yorker* fiction. (In a 1939 review of Irwin Shaw's short-story collection *Sailor off the* Bremen, Alfred Kazin dismissed Shaw's "creamy sob stories from the *New Yorker*.") Ross and the other editors were sensitive to the charge. John Cheever remembered, "He'd say, 'Goddammit, Cheever, why do you write these fucking gloomy goddamm stories?' And then he'd say, 'But I have to buy them. I don't know why.'" In a letter to Christopher La Farge, accepting his story "Mary Mulcahy," Ross wrote, "The only thing I have against it is that it falls in the 'gloom' category. Even the most light-hearted writers of nonsense have collapsed in the face of world conditions, and my literary life is spent in a cloud of dissatisfaction and suffering. Geniuses even greater than I are bringing this about and the only thing to is be patient."

The gloom Ross sensed everywhere was rarely a matter of out-and-out pathos. That would have required the kind of sympathy for and identification with characters that the quasi-journalistic editorial approach discouraged. William Maxwell, who was hired as a fiction editor in 1937 and, alone among his colleagues, sometimes took a professorial tone with writers, spent months trying to convince Mark Schorer that his approach was too "intuitive" and insufficiently "comic" for the *New Yorker*'s purposes. Schorer finally saw the light, writing Maxwell, "If it is chiefly a matter of point of view, of looking at rather than getting into the characters, then I think I understand now." The gloom and sadness came, instead, from the angle of vision. Without plot to serve as distraction, and with what action there was not permitted to come to a standard resolution, *New Yorker* stories exposed their characters' lives and social settings in a harsher, more unforgiving light than readers were used to. Again, this is a characteristic of the modern "art" short story generally. Frank O'Connor in *The Lonely Voice* remarked that perhaps the most salient characteristic of the form is "an intense awareness of human loneliness."

The critic Lionel Trilling took note of this quality—and of its contrast with the rest of what was in the magazine—in a 1942 review of *Short Stories from the New Yorker* in the *Nation*:

> The *New Yorker* publishes along with its more genial contents, with its anecdotes, its comic drawings, and its excellent journalism, a kind of short story, the main characteristic of which is its moral intensity. Every week, at the barber's or the dentist's or on the commuting train, a representative part of the middle class learns about the horrors of snobbery, ignorance, and insensitivity and about the sufferings of children, servants, the superannuated, and the subordinate, weak people of all sorts.

Trilling went on to accuse the short stories of a characteristic "cruelty": the authors "do not condescend to attack at all, they merely lay traps of situation into which the doomed characters must inevitably fall. In these stories immorality is exposed not by the author's aggression but by the character's unwariness."

Some of what Trilling was referring to could certainly be found in the work of Sally Benson, who vied with Robert Coates for the position of second most prolific all-time *New Yorker* fiction writer, after John O'Hara. Between 1929 and the end of 1941, she published ninety-nine stories in the magazine, including nine signed "Esther Evarts," a nom de plume she adopted in 1939 to counter the impression that she may have been going to the well too often. James Thurber once remarked that the "fastest writers I know are Sally Benson and John O'Hara," and Benson's speed was sometimes scary indeed. "Once I was having lunch with Sally and [fiction editor] Gus Lobrano," recalled Edward Newhouse, himself a prolific short-story writer for the magazine. "Gus told us how he had once told his daughter, Dottie, when she was in the eighth grade, that one of their ancestors was Jean Lafitte, the pirate, and Dottie had written a report for school called 'I Am Partially Pirate.' When we went back to the *New Yorker*, Sally went into an office for five hours and came out with a publishable story based on what he'd told us." The story was printed in the magazine as part of Benson's "Junior Miss" series.

Benson, who was born in St. Louis in 1900 and came to New York as a teenager to study dance, was introduced to *New Yorker* editors socially in the late twenties. She was a sort of found talent; what she called "an appalling ignorance in the use of adjectives," looked at another way, was a pure literary objectivism. Her sketches and stories were narrative versions of Baird Leonard's blank-verse series "Metropolitan Monotypes," informed, in some measure, by the anguish she felt from her recurrently disabling alcoholism.

Benson showed growth. Her early pieces were rather one-dimensional, withering glances in prose. "Pour le Sport," published on November 14, 1931, takes aim at an easy target, an airheaded, motormouthed girl watching a football game. But Benson destroys her with a subtly devastating effectiveness. We immediately note the way the (unnamed) young woman takes far more of an interest in fistfights in the stands and in injuries than in the game, misuses (twice) the adjective *modernistic*, and muses, "Muscular people weigh heavier." But only after looking closely at the piece do we see that most of what her date, Charlie, has to say is paraphrased rather than directly quoted, so as to highlight the inanity of her own remarks (when we do hear his exact words, they are completely uninflected, for the same effect), or that Benson withholds from us any clue to Charlie's reaction to her, so that ours can organically arise. Just as Joseph Mitchell was striving to write journalistic stories with beginnings, middles, and ends, *New Yorker* fiction writers of the thirties tried, within the constraints handed to them, to present a progression or development rather than a static sketch. "Pour le Sport" builds to a statement, characteristically simple, that puts everything beforehand into focus; Ross would probably have wanted it in the opening, but Benson withholds it until the last sentence of the fourth paragraph from the end. Even though the game is exciting, the girl wants to get a sandwich before halftime to beat the crowd:

> They squeezed past the line of knees again and walked down to the cinder path. She was clinging to his arm and looking up brightly into his face. She was a very pretty girl.
> "You were a dear to take me today, Charlie," she told him. "I love to go. I haven't missed one Saturday this year."
> "Oh, that's all right," he said.
> There was another terrific cheer from the stands. She edged closer to him and gave his arm a little squeeze. "What are we going to do afterwards?" she asked.

Benson's 1938 story "Little Woman" casts the same cold eye on its characters and has the same controlled prose, but here she is working with a much more extensive palette and on a broader canvas. It is about Ralph and Penny Loomis, whose initial attraction and ten-year marriage, we are led to understand, is based to an alarming extent on Penny's physical slightness. After their first meeting:

> There were three months of being engaged, of dancing night after night, attracting attention because Ralph was so tall—over six feet—and she was so tiny. He was enchanted with her daintiness and made jokes about it. "Now where," he would ask, looking over her head and pretending he couldn't see her, "did I put that woman I had with me?"
> Everybody would laugh, especially Penny. "Big silly!" she would say. "Take me home!"

The progression in the story, inevitably, is Ralph's realization—deftly suggested by Benson—of the hollowness, not to say the perversity, of their bond. (Penny habitually wears little-girl-style clothing, and "boy's denim trousers" when Ralph takes her fishing.) But "Little Woman" is more than a well-made story. First, in the least likely setting and time for a feminist commentary, it manages to be a sort of parable about the infantilization of women in middle-class society. It is also a subtly reflexive nod to the genre of the *New Yorker* story itself, which, following the Thurber of Mr. North and Walter Mitty, was widely if not especially accurately characterized as being inordinately concerned with "little men." A story about a little woman made for an intriguing variation on the theme. Finally, Benson uses the central notion of smallness to push up against the bounds of realism, anticipating the later work of John Cheever and corresponding to what Charles Addams was doing in cartoons. Through the story, she uses bird imagery to describe Penny, so that when she finally makes the explicit comparison, at the very end, we feel a level of horror mere metaphors rarely communicate. For most of the story, Benson shrewdly doesn't tell us, in feet or inches, exactly how short Penny is, and without a guideline our imagination keeps shrinking her well past the point of plausibility. Ralph takes up this task in the penultimate paragraph: "As he looked at her, she seemed to grow smaller and smaller until there was nothing much left of her but a pink taffeta dress and a pink taffeta ribbon."

John O'Hara and the *New Yorker* had a turbulent thirty-eight-year relationship, punctuated by one long separation and several brief but no less bitter ones. The magazine was continually urging him to be less explicit sexually and more explicit thematically. When he found this too much to take (or when he chafed at its low rates and refusal to guarantee any acceptances), he would announce he would never write for the *New Yorker* again. But until the final rift, which lasted from 1949 till 1960, he always came back after a brief cool-down period and managed to find productive common ground with the editors. By 1931 and 1932, O'Hara was branching out from the monologues—the "dreadful little potboilers in the back of the book"—with which he had made his name. Animating these transitional works is a strong sense of O'Hara as a storyteller bursting with tales to tell. In "Mary," published May 2, 1931, someone who appears very much like O'Hara—to the extent of having the same nickname, Doc—narrates a brief biography of a coal-town Pennsylvania girl who becomes a woman-about-town in New York, but still talks about one of her beaus having a grand sense of "yoomer." "Ella and the Chinee," published eight months later, begins, "Ella will tell you to this day that no matter how hard up she was, she wouldn't of took that job if she'd of known the place was run by a Chinee." A mean Bronx girl, Ella decides to keep her job in Mr. Lee's lunchroom, hoping that it will lead to exotic experiences. But Mr. Lee is a boss like any other, not even important enough to belong to a tong. The restaurant goes out of business, and on her way out, Ella lifts five dollars from the cash register. You sense someone is telling you this story, but there is no "I"; rather, O'Hara is deploying something like the collective voice of Ella's world.

The balance of power in the O'Hara–*New Yorker* relationship, hitherto strongly tilted in favor of the magazine, was at that moment changing. In 1931 and 1932, *Scribner's*, the most prestigious literary journal in the country, printed two long O'Hara stories, which he always felt made the *New Yorker* take him seriously for the first time. And in 1934 and 1935, O'Hara came out with *Appointment in Samarra* and *Butterfield 8*, critically and commercially successful novels that immediately elevated him to the top rank of American writers. Working on long fiction had a salutary effect on his short fiction. In December 1934, the *New Yorker* published "Over the River and Through the Trees," a recounting of an old man's progressive humiliation and one of O'Hara's and the magazine's greatest stories. For the first time in a *New Yorker* piece, his narrative is omniscient, an adjective that takes on new meaning when applied to this writer. At his best—and O'Hara was at his best in his mid and late thirties *New Yorker* stories such as "Over the River . . . ," "Olive," "Price's Always Open," "Are We Leaving Tomorrow?" "The Gentleman in the Tan Suit," "Saffercisco," and "Bread Alone"—he really did seem to know everything, easily crossing socioeconomic and ethnic lines that would halt anyone else. The stories just mentioned had to do, respectively, with the dark secrets of an upper-class Massachusetts family; the day telephone operator at a modest Manhattan hotel; the conflict between summer people and a young townie at an unnamed waterfront village; a pair of unusual guests at a Florida resort in March; the amorous entanglements of some Hollywood movie people; a New York secretary who is visited by relatives from San Francisco; and a black garage worker's wonderful day at Yankee Stadium. Through the right dialogue and detail, through occasional digressions and asides, and through the absolute authority of the narrative, O'Hara gives the sense that he is privy to a great deal more about the people in these stories than he has set down—that he could supply their family trees and childhood pastimes and secret wishes, if necessary. More than any other *New Yorker* writer, O'Hara could take in his stride the necessity for brevity and the strictures against "plot" and present the old-fashioned tableau of a born storyteller, gesturing to his listener to sit down beside him and pay attention.

Benson and O'Hara exemplified an evolutionary redefinition and expansion of "the *New Yorker* short story." More abrupt deviations, as with Thurber's "Menaces in May," tended to be wrought by writers already associated with the magazine. Between 1931 and 1935, Louise Bogan contributed a dozen short pieces, including "Hydrotherapy," "Let-Down," "Journey Round My Room," and "The Short Life of Emily," which E. B. White considered the best short story the *New Yorker* had published to that point. The strongest of them were less short stories than artistically heightened personal essays in which Bogan confronted her demons and depression. They had overtones of Dorothy Parker but were more introspective, tough-minded, and ahead of their time: there is a direct link from Bogan to, say, Joan Didion's essays of the 1970s or Renata Adler's *New Yorker* pieces collected in *Speedboat*.* Robert Coates, the art critic, erstwhile book critic, and all-around friend of the magazine, aside from many conventional sto-

---

*The editors appreciated Bogan's pieces, especially Mrs. White, who wrote her, "The day a casual from you arrives is always a Red Letter day in the office." But art linked that closely to personal travail cannot be depended on as a commodity, and from 1935, Bogan never wrote another piece of fiction.

ries, wrote dark psychological studies such as "The Net," the story of a murder told from the point of view of the murderer, and "The Fury," which, incredibly enough, was about a child molester who ends up throwing himself under a subway. It is safe to say that if these stories were written by an outsider, they would not have found a home in the *New Yorker*. But they did, and they opened the door for the work of Albert Maltz, a self-identified left-wing writer, who contributed strikingly grim urban tales in the late thirties and the forties. Nancy Hale, the granddaughter of the nineteenth-century author Edward Everett Hale, came from the same upper-class Massachusetts world as Katharine White, who became a close friend of hers and accepted her lyrical if somewhat overwrought pieces such as "Midsummer" and "Last Summer." Kay Boyle, similarly impressionistic in style, had no connection to the magazine but published nineteen pieces there in the thirties and added considerably to the ever-broadening definition of what kind of fiction one could find in the *New Yorker*.

So did Sylvia Townsend Warner and John Collier, British writers who began contributing frequently in the late thirties. Warner was able to slip in, most likely, through the offices of a mild Anglophilia that had been a characteristic of the magazine almost since the beginning. Her marvelously subtle, witty, and uncanny stories, about parsons, retired military officers, elderly ladies, and other deeply eccentric characters in the English countryside, would otherwise probably have been too stylized and indirect for the *New Yorker*. Having established herself, she became a fixture at the magazine, and at the time of her death, in 1978, had published 144 stories there, the last ones being fantasies set in the elfin world. Collier, the author of a highly successful 1930 novel called *His Monkey Wife* (the title was literal), was more accessible, but his macabre stories, following Saki and predating Roald Dahl (also a *New Yorker* contributor), struck an equally new note. He was the Charles Addams of fiction, his narratives of betrayal and murder among spouses striking a similar tone of deadpan comedy.

Editorial personnel changes also affected the quality of fiction. In 1937, the year fact and fiction became separate departments, Katharine White hired a young English professor from Illinois named William Maxwell, initially to succeed Gibbs (who had wearied of the task) as the staff member charged with communicating the art meeting's decisions and recommendations to the cartoonists. In due time Maxwell was given manuscripts to consider, and then ones to edit, and he remained at the magazine for the next forty years, minus the time he would periodically take off to work on his own novels and short stories. He was, in fact, the first *New Yorker* fiction editor who was a serious writer in his own right, and where editorial dealings with all but the most favored authors had traditionally been marked by a certain brusque or passive-aggressive superciliousness, Maxwell's correspondence with writers exudes a palpable empathy. He understood their struggles, shared in their triumphs, and agonized over rejections; when these couldn't be avoided, he always gave them to understand that the fault was at least partly the magazine's. Maxwell would develop intimate relationships with a number of contributors—Sylvia Townsend Warner, Frank O'Connor, Eudora Welty, John Cheever, Mavis Gallant, John Updike, Larry Woiwode—and they would come to think of him as a true collaborator.

In 1938, when the Whites moved to Maine, Katharine White handed the fiction department to Gustave "Gus" Lobrano, a college friend of her husband's who had previously worked as an editor at *Town and Country* magazine. In a carryover from the days when everyone did everything, Mrs. White's duties had always been spread through many precincts of the magazine; Lobrano, concentrating completely on fiction, raised its profile. One important step was his institution of the "first reading agreement," by which regular contributors received an annual bonus payment if they agreed to let the *New Yorker* see all their work before any other magazine. (A few years later came a refinement: a further bonus was paid if they were able to sell more than a set number of stories during the year.) There was still no guarantee that the magazine would accept anything they wrote, but the innovation gave them the sense that they belonged to a sort of family.

Compared to Maxwell and Mrs. White (and for that matter, later fiction editors such as Roger Angell and Rachel MacKenzie), relatively little of Lobrano's correspondence survives, and what does is more matter-of-fact than inspirational. More than his colleagues, Lobrano tended to bond with his writers in person, and soon after arriving at the magazine, he formed friendships with the first two authors he was given charge of—John Cheever and Eddie Newhouse—and eventually, a whole new crop of male authors in their late twenties and early thirties who lived in and around New York. Cheever, Newhouse, Irwin Shaw, Jerome Weidman, Walter Bernstein, S. J. Perelman, and the Talk of the Town writer E. J. "Jack" Kahn played tennis and squash and badminton and fished with him and saw him as a kind of older-brother figure (a decade hence, he would form a similar relationship with a new contributor named J. D. Salinger).* All of those mentioned would eventually dedicate at least one book to Lobrano, as would John Collier. "Gus was the person primarily responsible for making the *New Yorker* a home away from home for an awful lot of us," Newhouse

---

*Interestingly, all of these writers were Jewish except Newhouse (whose parents were Hungarian immigrants) and Cheever. Mrs. White was by no means overtly bigoted—and in fact came to value Lobrano's stable—but wore her upper-class Anglo-Saxon background on every inch of her frame and would not independently have championed this new crop of ethnic writers.

said in an interview. "He would say, 'Let's have lunch,' to three people simultaneously. I'd come in for lunch and see that he'd also invited Sid Perelman
and Ogden Nash, and, just as Gus planned it, we became friends."

A sign of Lobrano's impact is the 1940 anthology *Short Stories from the
New Yorker*. Although it covers the first fifteen years of the magazine's existence, a comfortable majority of the contents were published in Lobrano's
brief tenure—1938, 1939, and the first half of 1940.

The first selection in that book is "The Girls in Their Summer Dresses,"
by Irwin Shaw, initially published in the *New Yorker* in February 1939. Two
additional stories of Shaw's were chosen, tying him for top honors with
Benson and O'Hara. Born in Brooklyn in 1913, and a graduate of Brooklyn
College, where he played varsity football, Shaw made his way in the literary
world by force of both his magnetic personality and his talent. He broke
into the *New Yorker* in 1937, by which time he had written radio serials (an
experience on which he based his 1939 story "Main Currents in American
Thought") and the successful Broadway play *Bury the Dead*. Some six
decades later, his *New Yorker* stories of the late thirties and the forties call
immediate attention to themselves. It is not that they are so good, though
the best of them are very good indeed. "The Girls in Their Summer
Dresses," for example, is a smashing and chilling encounter, taking place
over several hours, between a husband who is a case study in what feminist
theorists half a century later would call "the male gaze" and a wife who
comes to understand that their marriage is over. It has splendid dialogue—
Shaw's early years in the theater would always serve him well—and one of
the most devastating last lines in American fiction. But it is not a stretch to
think that O'Hara or Benson could have written it.

Other Shaw stories were revolutionary, not evolutionary. More than anything else, in an editorial environment where understatement and subtlety
had always been hallmarks, they stood out then and stand out today because
they pushed emotion and story and meaning. Where not explicitly autobiographical, they were usually romantically self-concerned, in the manner of
Hemingway, Thomas Wolfe, and the lesser Fitzgerald. Even Shaw's titles had
a lyricism that called attention to themselves. All that commotion could
rarely be fit into the traditional three thousand words, and Shaw almost
single-handedly stretched out the *New Yorker* story, to four thousand, five
thousand, and eventually six thousand plus. Essentially to accommodate
him, the magazine instituted what it called an all-fiction issue, meaning that
a long short story was printed in place of the traditional Profile. Sometimes,
admittedly, Shaw pushed to the point of bathos, self-absorption, melodrama, and/or schematic morals. But even his less successful stories brought
to the magazine a welcome vitality. Brendan Gill, a young Talk of the Town
reporter who really aspired to write fiction, told Shaw's biographer, "We

would gasp at how many inches his stories took up in galleys....We were all thrilled by his stuff; we would all wonder what he'd do next." In time—just as they would with the work of J. D. Salinger ten and fifteen years later—people bought the *New Yorker* and immediately looked to see if a Shaw story was in it. In recognition of the effect Shaw was having, Edward O'Brien dedicated the 1940 edition of *The Best American Short Stories* to him.

Shaw's first groundbreaking story was "Sailor off the *Bremen*," published just three weeks after "The Girls in Their Summer Dresses." It was not nearly as distinguished artistically, but far more of a departure for the magazine. The first thing one has to contend with in the story is its complicated plot. The opening scene is the New York City apartment of an artist named Ernest, where a variety of characters eat pancakes and talk. Some days before, we come to understand, a Communist-organized anti-Nazi demonstration occurred aboard the German ship *Bremen,* currently in port in New York. During it, Ernest, who was one of the demonstrators, was badly beaten by a ship's steward. Now Ernest's friends, his wife, and his brother plot revenge against the steward. The scene shifts to a Manhattan street corner where the revenge is meted out: the wife lures the steward to a dark spot under the el, and Ernest's football-playing brother brutally beats him up. And so not only did "Sailor off the *Bremen*" have a plot, it had a frankly melodramatic one resolved by violent action. Moreover, its backdrop was the global political turmoil, something rarely alluded to and hardly ever directly confronted in the *New Yorker*. In fact, after writing the story Shaw assumed the *New Yorker* wouldn't be interested and submitted it to *Esquire*. But he had the manuscript in his pocket while visiting Maxwell, who asked to read it, then bought it.

With the events in Europe on every front page, it was no longer possible to ignore them. The sense of being powerless at the prospect of an inevitably looming conflict informed many *New Yorker* stories of the period. As Shaw said in an interview years later, "In almost everything I wrote, even these simple stories, little sketches really, of the young men and girls in New York, this thing was hanging like a backdrop."

This is a perfect description of "Weep in Years to Come," more of a "sob story," which takes the ironic man-woman dialogue of "The Girls in Their Summer Dresses" and sets it against a backdrop of impending war. As Paul and Dora, lovers in the first flush of their affair, come out of a movie, they hear a newsboy shout, over and over, the single word "Hitler!" They walk slowly uptown, window-shopping, dancing around the subject of what war will do to them, singly and together. The story was published in July 1939, and the next month saw the signing of the Stalin-Hitler pact. It was immediately followed by the German invasion of Poland, and France's and Britain's declaration of war against Germany. Those events focused the country even more intently on issues of action and inaction, and with them as a backdrop Shaw contributed a first to the *New Yorker*, a frankly political parable. This was "The Dry Rock" (May 31, 1941), about the Fitzsimmons, a well-to-do Manhattan couple whose taxi has a minor accident while they are on their way to a dinner party. The other driver, unprovoked, punches the cabdriver in the nose, and the cabbie, a Russian immigrant named Leopold Tarloff, wants to settle the matter at the police station. Now the dinner party is well under way, and Helen Fitzsimmons is impatient to get there, but Claude Fitzsimmons—read, the United States—sees standing up and bearing witness as the least an honorable man can do. It sounds schematic in summary, but Shaw's dialogue and pacing are so expert that the story works as a realistic narrative as well as a call to arms.

Shaw, who was Jewish, played a significant role in the ethnic development of the *New Yorker*. Other Jews had written for the magazine, of course. But Arthur Kober and Leo Rosten wrote affectionate burlesques, and though the stories of Daniel Fuchs and Jerome Weidman in the late thirties had a broader emotional range, they took place in a self-enclosed and segregated urban culture. Shaw in no way denied his Jewishness, but he was almost militantly assimilated, in life and in art. Thus Claude Fitzsimmons, Paul Triplett (of "Weep in Years to Come"), and a great many other of his protagonists were identifiably Gentile. Jewish characters in Shaw's stories ventured out into and confronted a sometimes hostile world. In "Select Clientele" (August 17, 1940), a young Jewish writer, his wife, and their friend, guests at an artists' colony in the country, are stopped while bicycling by a handful of local youths who are planning to shake them down. They have no money on them, but as they are pedaling away, the locals throw stones at them, one shouting, "Lousy Jew bastards." The writer, Sam, tells himself not to take the "four hoodlums" too seriously. But then he thinks again:

> Day by day the American people were becoming like them. Men and boys selling Father Coughlin on the street corners and the mean little middle-aged ladies buying him. The undernourished, baleful faces on those newsboys and their customers. The disease was growing stronger in the veins and organs of America. All the time there were more hotels you couldn't go to, apartment houses right in New York you couldn't live in. Sam sold stories to magazines that published advertisements for vacation places that said "Distinguished clientele" or "Exclusive clientele" or "Select clientele." A hotel advertises that its clientele is exclusive, Sam thought, if it allows in everybody but six million Jews and fifteen million Negroes. It's exclusive for a hundred and ten million people. All right, Sam thought, you had been able to overlook it, it was static, a condition of existence, there was still room to breathe. It wasn't static any more.

It was an amazing paragraph. The magazine Sam wrote stories for, of course, was the *New Yorker*, which in one issue that same summer of 1940 ran ads for the Sea Spring Inn in East Hampton ("Discriminating clientele"), the Forest Hills Hotel in Franconia, New Hampshire ("Restful, homelike—modern facilities, excellent cuisine. Restricted clientele"), and the Monmouth in Spring Lake, New Jersey ("restricted clientele").* Anyone who paid attention could tell the story was picking a fight with the very publication in which it appeared. Actually, Shaw had taken up the fight three weeks earlier, in a story called "Free Conscience, Void of Offense." It was set during the week in 1938 when the Munich pact was signed. A young Anglo-Saxon woman having dinner with her father notes a group of well-heeled patrons at the bar, giddy because Chamberlain's appeasement has apparently averted war. Her disdain turns to shock when they begin to sing, "Heigh-ho, heigh-ho, I joined the C.I.O., I pay my dues to a bunch of Jews, heigh-ho, heigh-ho." She turns to her father and sees that he is laughing along:

> Margaret looked carefully at him, as though he were a man whom she had just met. Her father's face was not fat, Margaret noticed, but almost so. His gray suit was double-breasted and his collar was sharp, starched white. The heavy silk necktie flowed like a spring from his lined though ruddy throat, and his shoes looked as though they had been brought from England for carefully custom-built feet. She looked at his face, like the faces of all the fathers of her friends, the men who had been graduated from the good colleges around 1910 and had gone on to stand at the head of businesses, committees, charity organizations, lodges, lobbies, political parties, who got brick red when they thought of the income tax, who said, "That lunatic in the White House."

That is a good description, also, of the audience the *New Yorker* had been courting since its founding, some of whom, no doubt, were reading "Free Conscience, Void of Offense." They could not think of the story as a mild satire, along the lines of a Hokinson or Arno or Barlow cartoon. No, this was an indictment, and its presence in the magazine—indeed, the very

---

*Someone at the magazine was shrewd enough to make sure no such ads appeared the week "Select Clientele" appeared. In a Comment four years earlier, White had noted, "Practicing American Christians feel bitterly about the way Germany treats the Jews. We notice he is gratified to receive a booklet from a Florida hotel advertising 'a refined Christian clientele.' Americans' philosophy seems to be that it is barbarous to persecute Jews, but silly to suppose that they have table manners. Of the two types of persecution, Germany's sometimes seems a shade less grim." Needless to say, advertisements in the *New Yorker* were never so blatant as to include the word *Christian*.

ascendance of Irwin Shaw there—was a striking instance of the *New Yorker* countenancing a kind of civil war in its pages. To the great credit of Ross, Lobrano, and Maxwell, they let the battle rage on—even, it sometimes seemed, encouraged it. They trusted in the process.

As the real-life war began to seem more and more inevitable, it appeared that Shaw was winning the battle in the *New Yorker*. On August 30, 1941, the magazine printed his "The City Was in Total Darkness," which at some six thousand words was the longest story it had ever run.* It was set on the day that France and Britain declared war on Germany. The author's alter ego this time around is a cynical screenwriter-novelist named Dutcher, who is persuaded by some friends to tag along on an overnight trip from Los Angeles to Tijuana. If the traditional *New Yorker* short story was a chamber piece, this was a symphony. Not in the sense of melodramatic crescendos: Dutcher and his lonely friends speed along the dark roads, stop to have drinks and then eat waffles in San Diego, negotiate who will share a room with whom at the hotel in Mexico. But the uneventful foreground plot is perfect counterpoint to the momentous news from Europe continually coming over the radio, to the conversation that keeps returning to the subject of war, and to the emotions, dreams, and anxieties swirling in Dutcher's head.

"The City Was in Total Darkness" was a full-fledged short story, without qualification, apology, or pulled punches of any kind. There were still limitations to the kind of fiction the *New Yorker* would print, of course. But thanks to a combination of circumstances—the sensibilities of Gus Lobrano and William Maxwell, the good sense of Harold Ross, the force and talent of Irwin Shaw, the coming of the war, and sheer artistic momentum—the door was open immeasurably wider than it had ever been before.

---

*Shaw broke his own record with "Gunner's Passage," which ran sixty-eight hundred words, in July 1944. But that lasted only two months before Mary McCarthy topped it with "The Weeds," at more than nine thousand words.

CHAPTER FOUR

SOPHISTICATION
AND ITS DISCONTENTS
1938~51

DRUMBEATS

We predict that there will be no war in 1936, 1937, 1938, 1939, and 1940. There will be a small war in 1941 between Cambodia and Alberta over a little matter of some Irish Sweepstake tickets, and then there will be no war in 1942, 1943, 1944, 1945, and 1946. Our prophecy is no mere wish-fulfillment—it packs a heap of personal good feelings toward nations. In 1947 there will be a general war to end war. It will be fought, appropriately enough, in the Scilly Isles, and will continue for three hundred years, being unable to end even itself. Through it all we predict the survival of capitalism, diptheria, Wash Monday, the Automobile Show, plant lice, Catholicism, tired and aching feet, monogamy among pigeons, tidal currents, publishing houses, love, Minsky's, west winds on clear days, motherhood, *Punch,* the tile floor in the Brevoort Grill, gray squirrels, and the Sleepy-Tyme comforter—a high grade product.

Note: This prophecy voids all previous prophecies made in this column.

—E. B. White, Notes and Comment, the *New Yorker,* April 6, 1935

~~~~

Recovering against our will after a night of seasonal gaiety, we would like to say that, in general, 1938 will be a year of unparalleled national confusion and private woe. It may even be that many clouds too long gathering, purple in the western sky, will burst in deluge—the year of cataclysm, the hour of the rat. We have no idea what shape disaster is likely to wear, whether it will be war or the final collapse of an implausible economic structure or simply the slow piling up of little burdens and anxieties until they are intolerable and the nation, as one man, marches down to the sea and drowns. The details are unimportant; you can be very sure that the total will be unpleasant. Happy New Year, everybody!

—White, Notes and Comment, January 1, 1938

~~~

Great pressure is being put on me to have *The New Yorker* swing over strong to preparedness and the hop-right-over-and-aid-the-Allies viewpoint. Wish you were here.

—Harold Ross to White, May 31, 1940

~~~

An hour or two ago, the news came that France had capitulated. The march of the vigorous and the audacious people continues, the sound is closer, now, and easier to hear.

To many Americans, war started (spiritually) years ago with the torment of the Jews. To millions of others, less sensitive to the overtones of history, war became actual only when Paris became German. We looked at the faces in the street today, and war is at last real, and the remaining step is merely the transformation of fear into resolve.

The feeling, at the pit of every man's stomach, that the fall of France is the end of everything will soon change into the inevitable equivalent human feeling—that perhaps this is the beginning of a lot of things.

—White, Notes and Comment, June 22, 1940

~~~

In any number of ways, the Second World War was a turning point for the *New Yorker*. The war thrust it, not necessarily willingly, onto a wider stage, forever removed from it the label of "humor magazine," robbed it (as even the Depression had not) of the comfortable luxury of noncommittal politics. This last process began well before Pearl Harbor and found one of its first expressions, interestingly, in reaction against the anti-Semitism of Nazi Germany. Adolf Hitler came to power in January 1933, and shortly afterward came the first acts of persecution against Jews. In a Comment published on April 8 of that year, E. B. White noted some of the grim happenings and remarked, "Thus in a single day's developments in Germany we go back a thousand years into the dark." The statement does not seem remarkable or daring today, but that early in the Nazi regime—and for a depressing number of years thereafter—such a definitive condemnation was rare in the American press. Each successive year, of course, the news from Germany was darker. In a Comment looking over the events of 1938, Wolcott Gibbs wrote that "in Germany ... a helpless minority suffered a shameful and brutal persecution unequaled in the memory of any man alive. It is unlikely that we have seen the end of that. ..."

Condemning anti-Semitism and calling for any form of U.S. intervention in European affairs are very different, however, and for a long time the positions expressed in Notes and Comment on these matters were marked by bemused ambivalence. Such evenhandedness became more difficult to sustain in 1938, when Germany invaded Austria and then Czechoslovakia, and close to impossible after the invasion of Poland, and the subsequent declaration of war by Britain and France, in September 1939. On the staff, the interventionists included Thurber, Shawn, and Frank Sullivan, who wrote of Hitler in his 1939 end-of-the-year "Greetings, Friends" poem, "*Lebensraum* he wants? So! Well, / Let's hope he gets it soon, in hell." White was of their number as well, but after his move to Maine in 1938, his familiar voice was less frequently heard in the magazine. His replacement, Gibbs, tended to be much more skeptical—but then, as Ross noted in a letter to White, "Gibbs is, of course, skeptical of everything." In a Comment published on February 11, 1939, Gibbs took President Roosevelt sharply to task for supposedly directing threatening remarks to Germany: "We believe that until the German and Italian governments perform legally hostile acts against us as a nation it is indefensible for the President to give his official sanction to attacks on their internal policy, no matter how cruel and shameful it may *appear to him personally*. Mr. Roosevelt, in our opinion, is not employed to express moral attitudes; his first duty is the well-being of this country, a duty which includes doing his utmost to keep it out of avoidable wars" (emphasis added). Ross himself was professionally (the newspaperman's resistance to "editorializing"), geographically (his native West was the bastion of isolationism), and constitutionally opposed to beating any drums. But White, even in absentia, was his editorial conscience, and in June 1941, at a point in the European war when sitting on the fence had become a nearly impossible balancing act, the editor sent a sort of defense of editorial neutrality up to Maine:

> I have been strongly suspicious that you disapproved of what we have been doing in the Comment page and elsewhere in relation to the international sit-

uation. I am not positive of this, of course, but I gather you would have gone a lot further. My decision is that we have been doing it right and that we ought to go on as we have been going, call it slacking, call it escapist, call it what you will. I will be God damned if I've got the slightest bit of confidence in the opinions and emotions of all the people who have advised me, denounced me, ridiculed me, tried to lead me, etc. Nor have I any in myself. I have been an earnest clutcher for a straw but I haven't got ahold of a straw yet. I doubt if there is any mind on earth that work [*sic*] out a solution to the present situation or tell me what to do. I am, therefore, for drifting. After a great deal of thought, I think the thing for American publications to do is follow the President, for better or worse. That's all I see to do. He knows more than anyone else here and presumably is in the position to make the wisest decision.

The magazine may have been disinclined to take a strong editorial position on the European hostilities, but they were surely and unmistakably reflected in its pages. Flanner's and then Liebling's dispatches from Paris gave an invaluable sense of how the coming of war, and then the war itself, *felt*, in apartments, offices, and streets. On the day Germany invaded Poland, St. Clair McKelway, the managing editor for fact, considered who might write about the view from Britain and settled on Mollie Panter-Downes, a thirty-three-year-old English novelist and short-story writer who lived in a part of Surrey bordering on Sussex and had contributed to the magazine a handful of casuals and poems, and one Reporter at Large, a 1937 piece about Jewish refugee children arriving at Victoria Station. He sent her this telegram:

CAN YOU CABLE US UP TO TWO THOUSAND WORDS OF HUMAN RATHER THAN POLITICAL EVENTS LONDON AND COUNTRY SOMEWHAT SIMILAR TONE AS FLANNERS STUFF FROM PARIS STOP . . . WOULD YOU BE PREPARED SEND US CABLES AND LETTERS REGULARLY AS OUR LONDON CORRESPONDENT IF THAT SEEMS PRACTICABLE LATER STOP

Panter-Downes initially replied in the negative, since she was expecting evacuees at her house, but their arrival was canceled, and she filed a story two days later—the day Britain and France declared war on Germany—and was published in the issue of September 9. As requested, she stressed the human factor:

All over the country the declaration of war has brought a new lease on life to retired army officers who suddenly find themselves the commanders of battalions of willing ladies who have emerged from the herbaceous borders to answer the call of duty. Morris 10s, their windshields plastered with notices that they are engaged on business of the A.R.P. or W.V.S. (both volunteer services), rock down quiet country lanes propelled by firm-lipped spinsters who yesterday could hardly have said "Boo!" to an aster.

It was clear to everyone who read it that she had found the perfect tone—clear-eyed, good-humored, but never facetious, with an unfailingly firm lip herself—and that she was the perfect London correspondent. McKelway's next cable allowed:

IN FUTURE OKAY DISCUSS POLITICS STRATEGY ETCETERA IF INTER-
ESTING AND YOU FEEL INFORMED.

Thus credentialed, Panter-Downes filed indispensable Letters from London throughout the war, sometimes weekly, sometimes fortnightly. In 1940, the Atlantic Monthly Press published a collection of them, titled *Letter from England*; like the novel and subsequent film *Mrs. Miniver*, they did much to cement in the minds of Americans the image of Britishers as plucky, brave, and fundamentally sound. Panter-Downes continued to contribute dispatches to the *New Yorker* after the fighting was over; her final letter, published in 1984, was her 477th.

In the rest of the magazine the European war was treated with an ambivalence that bordered on schizophrenia. Some cartoonists—notably Rea Irvin, Wallace Morgan, and Carl Rose—used the *New Yorker* as a platform to attack Hitler and the Nazis. Irvin's "A Nazi History of the World," which ran in late 1939 and early 1940, was a particularly biting display of the story of humankind, as Irvin imagined it revised by the Nazis. Covers, the public face, were another story. None referred to the war in any way until Virginia Snedeker's illustration for June 10, 1939, which treated it in a sidelong and facetious manner: a swarthy "proletarian" artist and his wife are lugging a huge canvas containing an allegory of the world in crisis. Indeed, in the entire prewar period, only one cover truly confronted the terrible news from across the Atlantic. This was Christina Malman's, on July 27, 1940, showing monochromatic hat-wearing figures, presumably Jews, being herded by soldiers along a concrete wall. It was a stark and powerful image, all the more so for being completely different from what came before and after.

Oddly enough, poetry was where the *New Yorker* most directly and seriously dealt with the events in Europe and the growing probability of world war. This was odd because the magazine had never been particularly hospitable toward the form. Ten years before, in the late twenties, Mrs. White had convinced Ross to begin printing serious poetry, as opposed to light verse, but the experiment ran aground over one of Conrad Aiken's series of "Preludes." Ross said he did not understand it and therefore would not publish it. "I changed his mind," Mrs. White recalled later, "by saying that it was the sound that mattered here, not the sense, and wondered if it made any difference if he understood it or not. To my astonishment he agreed to buy it." Nevertheless, poetry continued to be a sore spot, offending as it inevitably did Ross's reverence for absolute clarity and lucidity. In 1937, he suggested eliminating it from the magazine's pages. Mrs. White responded with a memo, five single-spaced pages in length, that shrewdly took not the high aesthetic ground but the unassailable approach of pragmatism. For one thing, she wrote, poetry

> is effective as a change in mood and tempo. We use serious fiction to coun-
> terbalance humor for this same reason. Granted that we're a humorous mag-
> azine, I think the very reason we've been able to survive so long, "keep up the
> standard" as the phrase goes, is that we never set out to be exclusively humor-
> ous, like the old *Life,* or *Judge.* . . . *The New Yorker* is a better magazine if it has
> fiction, articles and poetry in it as well as humor and verse. But there's no rea-
> son for our using obscure, heavy, or esoteric poetry. . . . Gibbs says he's for
> abandoning buying "advanced and intellectual verse." If by that he means
> queer, heavy, or obscure poetry I'm with him. If he means he wouldn't buy a
> good Edna Millay sonnet if it came our way, or the Elinor Wylie we published
> in her lifetime, etc., etc., I don't agree.

Ross backed down. His next move took the onus off himself: he decreed that the magazine would henceforth not publish any poem the recently hired William Maxwell didn't understand. Maxwell was never sure why he was chosen for this role, or indeed how seriously to take it. Fortunately, the impending war presently clarified—in two senses of the word—the poetry situation. Probably because their referents were so obvious and their emo-tional underpinning so direct and unmistakable, Ross agreed to publish a number of powerful and unmistakably heavy poems about war, death, and intolerance, some of which didn't even rhyme, including Stephen Vincent Benét's "Nightmare for Future Reference," Harold Lewis Cook's "In Time of Civil War," W. H. Auden's "Song" ("Thought I heard the thunder, rum-bling in the sky, / It was Hitler over Europe, saying, 'They must die.' / O we were in his mind, dear, O we were in his mind"), Harry Brown's "1939," Frederick Prokosch's "Song," Marya Mannes's "Cable from Paris, 1950," Louis MacNeice's "Barroom Matins" ("Mass destruction, mass disease— / We thank thee, Lord, upon our knees / That we were born in times like these . . ."), Judd Polk's "Crisis in the Spring," and "The Portents," by Phyllis McGinley, whose work was beginning to show a new gravity and depth.* It

---

*One poem that unfortunately got away was submitted by Auden on September 9, 1939. He wrote Maxwell, "I know it's rather long and I don't know if it's any good, as I am too upset just now to have any critical judgment about it. But if it should be allright, I would rather it

was an impressive sequence and seems to have inspired Ross to make a new commitment to poetry, for in June 1939, after several in the group had been published, he hired Charles A. "Cap" Pearce as his first editor working exclusively with poets. In his first months on the job, Pearce solicited work from such prominent and serious writers as John Peale Bishop, John Crowe Ransom, Delmore Schwartz, and Marianne Moore. He accepted a poem by Langston Hughes and wrote an encouraging rejection to John Berryman. Also in 1939, Elizabeth Bishop sold the poem "Cirque D'Hiver" to the *New Yorker*, beginning her long association with the magazine.* In the next few years, the *New Yorker* would open its pages to Rolfe Humphries, Karl Shapiro, Theodore Roethke, and John Malcolm Brinnin, while continuing to publish work by Auden, MacNeice, Aiken, Louise Bogan, Mark van Doren, and William Carlos Williams. But if Ross saw the logic and perhaps necessity of this enterprise, he never enthusiastically endorsed it. He once asked cartoon editor James Geraghty if he read the poetry in the magazine. "Yes, but not all of it," was Geraghty's cautious reply. "Well, I don't," Ross said.

Reporters at War

Cecille Shawn practically widowed by manpower shortage in fact dep't. keeps hoping to get Shawn home for dinner some time.

—*The Conflict* (the *New Yorker's* house newsletter
during World War II), January 24, 1943

~~~~~

It gets tougher every week.... We scrape the bottom of the barrel weekly and get to press somehow.

—Harold Ross to Lewis Mumford, March 34, 1943

~~~~~

---

appeared in *The New Yorker* than anywhere, as there is no journal I have ever read which I admire so much." Maxwell wrote back four days later, "Apparently cutting and tampering with 'September 1939' (we tried both) do nothing but spoil it. It is an effective poem but in its entirety not right for us, for reasons which you doubtless appreciate." The poem, retitled "September 1, 1939," was published in the *New Republic* and became a much anthologized classic. It contains the line "We must love one another or die."

*In 1939, Maxwell solicited work from Wallace Stevens, who declined and never in his career published in the *New Yorker*. Stevens once advised Richard Wilbur that publishing in the *New Yorker* would be the worst thing he could do for his career as a poet.

The *New Yorker* is a worse madhouse than ever now, on account of the departure of everybody for the wars, leaving only the senile, the psychoneurotic, the maimed, the halt, and the goofy to get out the magazine. There is hardly a hormone left in the place.
—E. B. White to Stanley Hart White, March 2, 1944

〜〜〜

[Shawn] has taken more than any man I know in this war, and that goes for General Marshall and a lot of others I can name. He has done two-and-a-half jobs for four years, working every night practically and every week end, having been driven in a most inhuman manner. It is heart-rending.
—Ross to Hobart Weekes, August 23, 1945

〜〜〜

One magazine of general circulation stands high above all others in the accuracy of what it prints about the war—the *New Yorker*.
—*Infantry Journal*, September 1944

〜〜〜

The *New Yorker's* coverage of the United States' World War II could be said not to have begun until the issue of March 20, 1943, when it arrived in the form of a Reporter at Large by A. J. Liebling entitled "The Foamy Fields." This is not to say that the conflict had previously been ignored. In the weeks after the bombing of Pearl Harbor, various pieces considered its impact on the native psyche and rhythms of life. (Ross characteristically complained to White that the first week's performance would have been better had the timing of the bombing not sandbagged the magazine: "If the war had started a day earlier than Sunday we'd have had good coverage, or reflection, in last week's issue. Sunday was a bad day.") Moreover, Panter-Downes's letters from London continued; the young staff writer E. J. Kahn Jr., who had been drafted before the attack, contributed "This Army Life," a series that resembled letters home from any mother's son; and there were various reports from the home front. In Goings on About Town, along with the nightclub listings and capsule theater reviews, a section called Civilian War Activities matter-of-factly gave instructions on how to save household fat that would eventually be turned into glycerin: "If you want to help out, strain your pan and broiler drippings and excess deep-frying fat into a clean wide-mouthed can, and keep what you collect in a cool place until you have a pound or more to turn over to your butcher." But for a long time no reports from any fighting front appeared in the magazine. The *New Yorker* was not the sort of publication that could or would speedily dispatch correspondents to cover the battles in Europe. At this point, it had only Liebling, and on December 7, 1941, Liebling found himself on his way back to America aboard an exceedingly slow Norwegian tanker. He was not able to return to Europe until late 1942. He wound up in Tunisia, where the African campaign was in full swing. He began "The Foamy Fields" with this sentence: "If there is any way you can get colder than you do when you sleep in a bedding roll on the ground in a tent in southern Tunisia two hours before dawn, I don't know about it."

The note he struck was authentically new, as far as war reporting was concerned, and he developed it in subsequent pieces—aboard a troop transport ship prior to and during the invasion of Normandy, and then from the battlefields of France. As William Shawn, who edited this and all of Liebling's war pieces, later observed, "Liebling adapted the Reporter-at-Large formula in a most original way to war correspondence." That is, instead of taking one of the traditional routes—grand strategic generalizations or sentimental drum-beating or "human interest" portraits of GI Joe—Liebling, just as he would on Forty-second Street, posited the reporter as the central figure: presenting the facts that he had experienced or been able to determine, and presenting them in his own intelligent and ironic voice. In his definitive history of war correspondence, *The First Casualty,* Phillip Knightley notes the generally low level of most World War II reporting and observes, "Perhaps what was needed was more correspondents of the caliber of A. J. Liebling of the *New Yorker.* Liebling's ability to seize on what appeared to others to be the commonplace and to fit this into its proper context in the war was not part of the equipment of many correspondents."

One who did have it in his arsenal was John Lardner, a son of Ring and a *Herald Tribune* reporter in the glory days under Stanley Walker, who was sent to the war for his employers, *Newsweek* and the North American News Association syndicate. Ensconced on the Anzio beachhead south of Rome for two months in 1944, he found that some of his reporting, experiences, and impressions did not fit into the predetermined forms he had to work with. So he put together a splendid, Lieblingesque dispatch and sent it to the *New Yorker,* for which his kid brother David worked as movie critic and all-around utility columnist. Published February 26, 1944, it began:

> Tenement life is no more congested than life on a beachhead. We took the Germans by surprise when we landed around Anzio, and we quickly collected a wedge of Lebensraum ten miles wide along the seacoast and six miles long at its apex up the road toward Rome. Then the Germans reacted with their customary speed, skill and sureness of touch, and our boundaries became quite firm. Our ships, shuttling up from Naples, kept putting stuff ashore—troops, vehicles, food, fuel, and other supplies—but it was like cram-

ming a month's needs into an overnight bag. The unit I traveled with as a correspondent found an empty farmhouse to its liking the sixth day after we landed, and set up housekeeping there. The next thing we knew, it was like Broadway and Forty-second Street on a Sunday afternoon. Some Army longshoremen from the Pier 80 neighborhood of Hell's Kitchen moved into a lane behind us. Their ship had been shot from under them in the Anzio harbor by a German dive-bomber pilot whom the boys described as "a Colin Kelly with a kraut accent." It seems that the German, his plane set afire by an antiaircraft shell, picked out this ship as the handiest and dove into it, plane, bomb, and all. Four of the longshoremen came in to pass the time of day with us and borrow magazines. "I used to take a drink now and then at Duffy's Tavern on Fortieth Street," said Francis Jay Cronin, a private from Fortieth and Tenth Avenue. "How we coming? Are we anywheres near Rome yet?"

Lardner would go on to file memorable pieces from Iwo Jima and Okinawa; in later years he performed meritorious service as the *New Yorker's* film and theater critic.

Not quite jaunty enough to belong to the school of Liebling and Lardner was a young man named Walter Bernstein, who before the war had sold the magazine several casuals, the first one published before he graduated from Dartmouth. He was drafted in 1941 and continued to contribute short stories and nonfiction pieces to the magazine. After some time in the infantry, Bernstein was assigned to work on the publicity for the show *This Is the Army*. He wrote a humorous piece on the making of the production, but his supervising colonel, unhappy with the disrespectful tone of the article, refused to let Bernstein publish it in the *New Yorker* and furthermore began a transfer of him to some new, presumably unpleasant assignment. At that point Ross, who had maintained some army connections since his World War I days, called General George Marshall, the chief of staff of the army, and arranged to have Bernstein sent to Europe to join the staff of the just-started *Yank* magazine, the World War II counterpart to *Stars and Stripes*. Bernstein's method was to attach himself to units, report on their activities for *Yank* and, often, submit longer dispatches to the *New Yorker* that, with their superb dialogue and well-constructed scenes, stretched the definition of magazine journalism.

In writing his *New Yorker* pieces, Bernstein was working without a net. He composed the stories without any approval from or communication with the magazine, sent them in to William Shawn, and learned if they had been accepted only when he saw them in print. That independence may have contributed to the artistry and daring of a piece like "Search for a Battle," which appeared on September 23, 1944. It began:

> The attack was to jump off at nine in the morning. The objective of my infantry regiment was a long, steep ridge that stood like a door at the head of

the valley we occupied. The pattern of attack was familiar and orthodox: first an hour of dive-bombing to soften the objective, then a half-hour of artillery, and finally the infantry to do the dirty work. It was a pattern that had been followed ever since we had landed in Italy. Everyone was getting tired of it.

Bernstein is supposed to be woken up at two in the morning so he can join one of the attacking battalions, but in a typical foul-up, the message to rouse him gets lost. Waking by himself at daylight, he sets off toward the front to see if he can find the battalion. One clue that his journey is an existential one is the complete lack of place names—omitted less for censorship reasons, clearly, than to suggest universality. Bernstein hitches a ride on a jeep that drives across a field that's "supposed" to be mined, struggles with the temptation to stay put in an observation post where "the grass was soft and only a little wet," presses on, and encounters the wounded and the desperate and black-comic characters out of *Waiting for Godot,* such as two infantrymen "looking very dirty and completely bushed":

> "We just got relieved," the rifleman said. "Only nobody knows where we're supposed to go."
> "I ain't even sure we been relieved," the mortar man said.
> "I'm sure," the rifleman said. "The lieutenant come by and said we were relieved. That's good enough for me."
> "The lieutenant got killed," the other man said.
> "So what?" the rifleman said. "He relieved us before he got killed."

Still separated from the battalion, Bernstein finds himself in a valley under shell attack and is unknowingly in the crosshairs of a German tank until some GIs summon him into their homemade shelter. After the tank retreats, Bernstein sets out again and thanks the soldiers for saving his life. One of them replies: "Hell, he might have missed you." He finally makes his way to the top of the ridge, which has been captured by the regiment after a difficult fight. He drops his bedding roll and carefully looks out over the top:

> Everything was exactly the same. There was the other side of the ridge dropping off beneath me and at the bottom was a green little valley, and then another ridge. Beyond that were more ridges, rising and falling in the same pattern. There seemed to be no end; it was like being in an airplane over a sea of clouds that stretched forever into space.*

---

*Bernstein's articles were collected in 1945 in a book called *Keep Your Head Down,* which is one of the insufficiently recognized classics of World War II reporting. After the war, Bernstein applied his gifts to screenwriting. His most prominent credit is the Woody Allen film *The Front,* which was based on Bernstein's experience of being blacklisted; in 1997, he won an Emmy Award for the teleplay *Miss Evers' Boys.*

Mr. Shuman:

                    Saul
Regarding our artist Steinberg:

He is now in the Dominican Republic. He has no passport. His
Rumanian passport has expired long ago. His agents have pre-
pared some sort of request for permission to enter this country.
Two responsible relatives have guaranteed him financial support.

It is very much to our interest that he come to New York. I'm
confidant that he will become a major artist almost at once.
I'm told he's in his twenties, and a man of ideas.

The question is - can we do anything to help things along; His
agent thinks a word from anyone of importance in Washington to
the immigration people will be a big help. She says it's done
all the time, and she moves in circles where she ought to know.

The name of the agent is:

              Cesare Civita,
              2 West 45th St.,
              New York City.
                    Gertrude Einstein

Civita is now in South America and Gertrude Einstein is handling
his affairs in New York. I understand the relationship between
Civita and Steinberg is that of friends as much as agent and
client.

I also recomend that we sign Steinberg to a first look contract.

                              Geraghty

Art editor James Geraghty, the author of this 1941 memo to administrative editor
Ik Shuman, was eventually successful in helping Saul Steinberg emigrate to the
United States.

By 1944, the *New Yorker's* coverage was humming, with contributions from staffers in uniform (such as McKelway, Kahn, and Eugene Kinkead) and familiar freelancers Lardner, Bernstein, and, in the Pacific theater, Robert Lewis Taylor and Robert Shaplen. The growing number of accredited correspondents would include Daniel Lang, who reported from Italy, Joel Sayre, who spent a year with the Persian Gulf Command in Iran, Philip Hamburger, and Edmund Wilson. Young David Lardner arrived in Europe late in 1944 in relief of Liebling. He had only filed one dispatch from Luxembourg when the jeep he was riding in drove over a pile of mines; Lardner died hours later.

A correspondent who stood apart from the others was Saul Steinberg. Born in Rumania in 1914, Steinberg was in Milan, studying architecture and drawing cartoons, when the war broke out. He fled Europe and in 1941 ended up on the island of Santo Domingo, from where he sent a batch of drawings to the *New Yorker*. James Geraghty enthusiastically appraised them and arranged for the magazine to sponsor Steinberg's entry into the United States. He steadily contributed cartoons (these early efforts seem startlingly conventional in the light of Steinberg's later work) through 1943, when he was drafted, eventually joining the staff of General William "Wild Bill" Donovan of the Office of Strategic Services. Posted to China, he sent the *New Yorker* a group of uncaptioned drawings of what he was seeing and observing, commenting to Ross, "This theatre of war being so far away and unknown has almost no

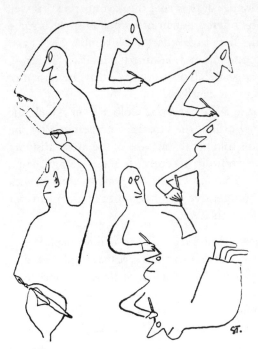

reality, a good alibi for a local magazine to publish it." Over the next year, the magazine printed this and a half dozen other Steinberg portfolios from China, India, and other Asian venues, constituting an exceptional venture into graphic journalism.

Steinberg's experiences in the war seemed to prompt him to stretch artistically. In 1944,

Steinberg started off doing more or less conventional cartoons, but quickly brought something authentically new, something simultaneously antic and meditative to the *New Yorker*. This drawing appeared in 1945.

he declined to execute a sight gag—"a group of short and tall fellows, taking a picture"—that Geraghty had sent him, writing, "I don't feel much like making that sort of drawing for the time being." He added, "I wish you wouldn't print any more of the old stuff like the one I received lately—the man with the surprise box, a drawing made from Santo Domingo and I changed a bit since. It was the period when I had to change from European to American 'style,' so the faces were rather silly and imitations." Steinberg's new, captionless stuff was a unique, profoundly witty, and totally arresting blend of the graphic and philosophical. It was completely different from what any other *New Yorker* cartoonist was doing, yet perfectly in keeping with the tradition of the magazine.

Much significant writing on the war was done from this side of the Atlantic. In 1943, Janet Flanner, who had remained in the United States, wrote a three-part account of the struggles of her friend Mary Reynolds (referred to in the article as "Mrs. Jeffries") to escape occupied Paris and return to America. As the first long, straight "reconstructed" narrative the magazine had printed, it paved the way for the better-known efforts of John Hersey. The following year, her return to Europe still delayed by personal concerns, Flanner wrote a four-part Profile of Marshal Pétain, head of Vichy France. It was a remarkable feat of long-distance reporting, and Ross told Flanner he had never seen anything of its kind in any other magazine: "I don't know what our debutante subscribers will think about this, but our savant subscribers will be profoundly impressed. I think your time was well spent and that probably you'll be offered a chair of French History at some Middle West University." Flanner flew to London in November 1944 as an accredited *New Yorker* correspondent and resumed her Paris letter in December. After the first one appeared, Ross wrote her that the return of Genêt was "a historical moment in journalism."

In March 1945, Flanner wrote a "Letter from Cologne" in which she unflinchingly and extensively described the atrocities perpetrated by the Germans on their prisoners. Ross told her it was "one of the most satisfying and gratifying things that have come in recently" because despite being with a group of other journalists, Flanner was the only one to emerge with the story. Ross's newsman's competitive instincts, mainly dormant for twenty years, had been reignited by the war:

> Please keep this Cologne piece in mind as an example of how simple it is to scoop the world, even if a flock of other journalists have the same facts and the same opportunities. Newspapers don't think such things as visits to Cologne make the sort of story you wrote. God knows why that is, but they don't. You have told me all I know of what the Germans did in Cologne and what the Germans *are* in Cologne, and elsewhere. . . . You are safe in assuming

that, in general, the other correspondents aren't going to cover stories you come upon unless the stories are right in certain well-established journalistic ruts. The war is going to be over and forgotten before any number of real atrocity stories are printed, I'm afraid, unless the *New Yorker* gets around to doing something.*

One senses Ross realizing, possibly for the first time, how outstanding a hard-news platform his weekly had become. There was some public recognition of this, especially when *The New Yorker Book of War Pieces*, edited by Shawn and dedicated to the memory of David Lardner, was published in 1947. A *New Republic* reviewer wrote that it represented "the most detached, least phony and truest account that the war produced"; the novelist and veteran correspondent Vincent Sheean said in the *New York Herald Tribune*, "It would be impossible to find better war reporting than there is in this book." But during the conflict, with the *New Yorker*'s circulation below 230,000 and its war coverage (by Phillip Knightley's count) constituting less than 1 percent of the total reaching the American public, the magazine's achievements were far from common knowledge.

The lack of recognition didn't merely hurt Ross's pride—it threatened the *New Yorker*'s survival, by depriving it of special allotments of paper, correspondent accreditations, and most crucially, draft deferments awarded to "essential" publications. By the magazine's count, of the twenty-five "key" editorial employees at the time of Pearl Harbor (all of whom were men), twelve were in the armed forces by February 1944—and six of the remaining thirteen were eligible for the draft. In its frequent protests to the War Department, the *New Yorker* noted it was devoting a great deal of coverage to the war—with 91 percent of the pieces published in the Reporter at Large between October 1941 and February 1944 pertaining to war subjects. Moreover, Ross and his associates argued, the magazine was also a substantial aid to military morale, because of the abridged and reduced-size "Pony" edition distributed for free to servicemen and -women. This began in 1943 as an idea of Jane Grant, who had been separated from Ross since 1927 and divorced since 1929 but was still a stockholder of and presence at the *New Yorker*. The edition was so popular that within a year it was distributed weekly rather than monthly; by the end of 1944, the circulation was 150,000. (The Pony edition turned out to be one of the greatest marketing moves in the history of magazines. Much of the *New Yorker*'s dramatic post-

---

*Over the next two years, in addition to her Letters from Paris, Flanner would write a series of Letters from Nuremberg, about the Nazi war-crime trials, and "Beautiful Spoils," a remarkable three-part piece about the U.S. army's recovery of artwork stolen and hidden by the Nazis.

war circulation jump came courtesy of returning soldiers who had developed a taste for the magazine, not only from the Pony but from regular editions mailed out after their wives or families had finished reading them and then passed around in the barracks. One estimate was that during the war, service readers outnumbered civilian readers ten to one.)

But Ross's and Fleischmann's pleas fell on deaf ears. In March 1944, after the *New Yorker* was turned down yet again for the essential designation, Ross erupted to Stephen Early, a contact of his at the White House:

> It is my conviction that we have been grossly discriminated against....A certain number of government officials seem never to have heard of the *New Yorker* and don't know what we're talking about when we mention it, and that others definitely dismiss it with a shrug as a mere comic publication printing cartoons with a little text to go around them and not worthy of support in any degree ... Apparently magazines of all sorts have got deferments under the definition, by a liberal interpretation of what is news and information, i.e., its fashion news, for one thing. How are *Vogue* and *Harper's Bazaar* essential if the *New Yorker* isn't essential? How is *Fortune* essential and *The New Yorker* not essential? If it comes right down to it, how are *Time* and *Life* themselves black and the *New Yorker* white? We have printed a vast number of war stories, and important ones. I'll come right out and say that our coverage of the war has been spectacular, that we've printed more good war stories than any other magazine and that throughout the magazine we've been useful, no question about it.

Ross concluded by pleading for deferments for two irreplaceable employees, unnamed but unmistakable from their descriptions. The first was "our make-up, layout, and production man"—Carmine Peppe. Of the other, Ross wrote that he was "thirty-seven, flat-footed, stoop-shouldered, a pill eater, hopeless for any service more deadly than behind a typewriter." This was William Shawn, who succeeded McKelway as managing editor for fact at almost precisely the point when the war in Europe began to heat up.* With the departure for the war of his main subeditors—Hobart Weekes, Rogers Whitaker, and Sanderson Vanderbilt, and of McKelway, who had continued to help out with editing—Shawn came to take on the entire load of the fact department himself, with a significant assist from his

---

*Ross had long feared that Shawn would be drafted, writing to E. B. White in 1942, "Shawn is now highly eligible on paper, but by God I don't think he would make a soldier." But Ross probably needn't have worried. The following year, Shawn wrote to E. J. Kahn, "The army looked me over the other day and quite ambiguously indicated that I belonged in 4F, too, though temporarily they chose to leave me in 3A." This was the classification for otherwise draftable men with dependents, and Shawn was married with a three-month-old son, Wallace.

boss. (After the war was over, Ross wrote to Robert Sherwood that Shawn "really deserves all the credit for our war stuff, although I will say I found I could be pretty helpful in it because I'd worked on *Stars and Stripes* in the last war and knew pretty well what we'd be up against this time, and was in a perfect position to distinguish the phoney stuff from the real, which was not easy, evidently, for anyone who has not been through the mill once.") The workload was especially brutal because of the nature of the articles Shawn was handling. They were not Profiles of society figures or Reporters at Large about Bowery flophouses. They were dispatches from the far corners of the earth—coming in on deadline, at all hours of the day and night, by telex, cable, or telephone, from writers who generally could not be available for consultation, sometimes garbled, sometimes lacking punctuation, almost always in need of substantial editing. A typically vexing example was when a long John Lardner story from the South Pacific still hadn't appeared in the office days after he had filed it. Lardner finally got the article back, with the explanation that the New Yorker Hotel had refused to accept the charges. Though nothing was said about it at the time, Shawn's heroic efforts during the war essentially ensured that he would succeed Ross when the editor eventually stepped down; a year after the fighting ended, a press report noted he was "regarded by some as heir-apparent to the magazine's brusque founder-editor." Writing to Rebecca West in 1947, Ross called Shawn "the hardest-working and most self-sacrificing man I have ever done business with."

THE MAKING OF A CLASSIC

Hersey has written 30,000 words on the bombing of Hiroshima (which I can now pronounce in a new and fancy way), one hell of a story, and we are wondering what to do about it. Shawn has an idea that we should print it all in one issue, and print nothing else that week.... He wants to wake people up and says we are the people with a chance to do it, and probably the only people that will do it, if it is done.

—Harold Ross to E. B. White, August 7, 1946

John Hersey was born in 1914 to two American missionaries in China and spent his childhood there. After graduating from Yale, he spent a year at Cambridge and several months as secretary to Sinclair Lewis, then went to work as a writer for *Time* magazine. He covered the early part of the war for another of Henry Luce's magazines, *Life,* and also managed to write three books: the nonfiction accounts *Men on Bataan* and *Into the Valley* (a riveting first-person account of a bloody "skirmish" on Guadalcanal) and *A Bell for Adano,* a novel about the U.S. occupation of an Italian village, which won the 1945 Pulitzer Prize for fiction. In New York early that year, he and his new wife, the former Frances Ann Cannon, went out with navy lieutenant John F. Kennedy, the son of the former ambassador to England and formerly a beau of Frances's, to see Zero Mostel perform at La Martinique, a supper club. Kennedy told them an abbreviated version of an amazing tale: his and his men's struggle for survival, the previous August, when their PT boat had sunk in the South Pacific and they were stranded in the ocean with no apparent prospect of rescue. Hersey expressed interest in writing about it and later talked more extensively with Kennedy in a Boston hospital where he was receiving treatment for injuries sustained during the ordeal. On Kennedy's suggestion, Hersey got further details from three of the enlisted men. He wrote up the story, but for some reason—possibly because the events described were already almost a year in the past, and there was pressing war news every week—*Life* turned it down. Hersey thereupon submitted the piece to the *New Yorker,* which published it in June as a Reporter at Large, under the title "Survival."

If "Hiroshima" was the most influential magazine article in the history of journalism, the case could be made that "Survival" was second. In detailing Kennedy's amazing heroics—swimming from island to island in search of help, sometimes dragging an injured comrade by a rope held between his teeth, all accomplished calmly, with a wisecrack and a chuckle here and there—it laid the foundation on which his subsequent image would be built. When he ran for the House of Representatives for the first time, in 1946, his father printed up one hundred thousand copies of the *Reader's Digest* reprint of the article and distributed them to Boston voters. "Survival" was the basis for the popular book, and later film, *PT 109.* And in 1959, when Kennedy was preparing to run for president, *U.S. News and World Report* printed extensive selections from the article (without Hersey's or the *New Yorker's* consent, incidentally).

The journalistic precedent it set was no less significant. For several years, Hersey had been fruitfully patrolling the literary borders between fact and fiction. *A Bell for Adano* was based on identifiable characters and incidents, while *Into the Valley* had the suspense, vivid characterization, and memorable dialogue of fiction. In a 1944 *Life* piece, "Joe Is Home Now," Hersey blended dozens of traumatized GI's he'd interviewed to create a composite character, the better to dramatize the difficulty many veterans had in adapting to civilian life. (Tom Wolfe, in the introduction to his anthology *The New Journalism,* would cite "Joe Is Home Now" as a seminal precursor of the genre.) In "Survival," Hersey used a different method, gathering his material through extensive interviews, then telling the story the way a fiction writer would—omnisciently, with scenes and dialogue and incursions into the thoughts of his characters, and without any of the traditional journalistic attribution of sources. Indeed, *all* the familiar apparatus of journalism was tucked away out of plain view. This made the approach highly uncharacteristic for *New Yorker* Reporters at Large, which, under the sway of Liebling, had increasingly been organized around the experiences, actions, and sometimes reactions of the reporter. Factual writing of the novelistic sort was not unheard of (a 1939 book by Hickman Powell, *90 Times Guilty,* had used it to good effect), but it was mainly the province of juvenile biographies, sports stories, and *True Detective* magazine—of the low-rent and the factually suspect. Hersey, who had a novelist's eye and ear and a reporter's work ethic, was the perfect person to blend fictional form with journalistic content; the *New Yorker,* with its reputation for impeccable accuracy, was the perfect place to give this new method respectability. It helped that the piece was superbly written. "Survival" was not much remarked on when it was published, but in reading it half a century later—with Hersey's simple language describing the melodramatic events, his deft choice of detail and perfect-pitch reconstructed dialogue, and the artful rhythm of his scenic structure—it has the feel of a classic.

In 1945, Hersey wrote two domestic pieces for the *New Yorker.* Then, late in the year, he arranged to make a tour of postwar China and Japan; his expenses, in an unusual arrangement, were to be shared by the *New Yorker* and *Life.* Before leaving, he sat down with Shawn and discussed about ten possible story ideas. One of them, suggested by Shawn, grew out of a piece Joel Sayre had been working on the previous spring: to document the Allied bombing of Cologne from the point of view of the German civilians on the ground, who had suffered its effects. But Sayre's story was beset with problems from the outset, and in August, when the war abruptly ended with the bombing of Hiroshima and Nagasaki, it was dropped. Now Shawn proposed to Hersey that he might write in much the same way about the atomic bomb that had devastated Hiroshima.

The notion could be expected to appeal to Shawn. Although he had been a hawk on the issue of U.S. involvement in the war, he was a fundamentally gentle man who abhorred violence, between individuals or nations. Writing to Hobart Weekes in 1943, he remarked how much he hated the word *killing,* and wished that war could be conducted, and written about, without it. But if an unflinching account of the bomb's effects could potentially reduce the likelihood of this weapon's ever being used again, Shawn would gladly sacrifice his sensibilities. Moreover, Shawn was given to brooding about apocalyptic matters. In his career at the *New Yorker,* which spanned fifty-four years, he contributed only one signed (with the initials "W.S.") piece—a 1936 casual called "The Catastrophe," which imagined what would happen if a meteor destroyed the New York metropolitan area. In the years after he became editor in chief, a striking number of the major articles he published wrestled with the issue of various catastrophes man often appears to be bringing upon himself: Joseph Mitchell's "The Bottom of the Harbor," Rachel Carson's "Silent Spring," Barry Commoner's "The Closing Circle," and Jonathan Schell's "The Fate of the Earth." Hersey, though never one to preach, was receptive to these concerns. Looking back on his body of writing years later, he observed that he seemed to have been "obsessed, as any serious writer in violent times could not help being, by one overriding question, the existential question: What is it that, by a narrow margin, keeps us going, in the face of our crimes, our follies, our passions, our sorrow, our panics, our hideous drives to kill?"

Hersey's first stop was China, but from the start the Hiroshima story was on his mind. In March 1946, news came out that the United States would be conducting atom-bomb experiments two months hence. With the typical reporter's fear of possibly missing a news peg, Hersey cabled Shawn from China that he might be able to speed up his trip so as to arrive in Japan in May and file the article from there, to coincide with the tests. But he went on:

STILL THINK IT WOULD BE ADVANTAGEOUS TO WAIT AND WRITE THEM UPON MY RETURN; IN THAT CASE YOU WOULD NOT GET THEM INTO PRINT UNTIL JULY OR PERHAPS AROUND THE ANNIVERSARY OF THE HIROSHIMA BOMB IN AUGUST. PERSONALLY I DON'T SEE WHY THE MAY EXPERIMENTS SHOULD DETRACT FROM THE HIROSHIMA STORY PROVIDED EYE CAN GET IN THE SORT OF DETAIL WE ENVISAGED.

Shawn sent a return cable the same day:

EYE WAS ABOUT TO CABLE YOU URGING YOU TO DO PIECE AS WE ORIGINALLY PLANNED. WE DO NOT THINK THAT MAY EXPERIMENT WILL AFFECT IT. THE MORE TIME THAT PASSES THE MORE CONVINCED WE ARE THAT PIECE HAS WONDERFUL POSSIBILITIES. NO ONE HAS EVEN TOUCHED IT. THINK BEST TO WRITE IT BACK HERE AND TIME IT FOR ANNIVERSARY.

Sailing for Japan in May, Hersey had still not reached a definite decision on how to approach the Hiroshima story. Confined to the sick bay with the flu, he began to read the ship library's copy of Thornton Wilder's 1927 novel, *The Bridge of San Luis Rey*, which looks at a cataclysmic event in eighteenth-century Peru from the points of view of five different characters. He had found his device. Hersey arrived in Hiroshima the evening of May 25 and set about finding his characters. In addition to his interviews with scientists and other experts, he talked to about forty survivors of the blast, emerging with six—five Japanese and one German—around whose experiences he would construct the article. Although the group (which included two physicians and two clergymen) was not socioeconomically representative of the Hiroshima population, Hersey felt their education, articulateness, or knowledge of English lowered the inevitable language barrier and made them the best available subjects.

Hersey returned to the United States on June 12 and produced his article about six weeks later. It was more than thirty thousand words and, if published uncut, would constitute the longest article ever to appear in the *New Yorker*. Hersey had written in the narrative style of "Survival" and shaped it as a four-part Reporter at Large, with the provisional title "Some Events at Hiroshima." Shawn began editing with that in mind, then suddenly had another idea. According to an unsigned *Newsweek* article (filled with such inside detail that one speculates it was written by John Lardner, whose name was prominent on the magazine's masthead) published the same week as "Hiroshima" was published:

> Hersey had, in typical *New Yorker* fashion, refocused on the scene at the beginning of each installment. To Shawn, this made the story lose much of its impact and he went to Ross with a suggestion that was daring even for the *New Yorker*. "This," he said, "can't be serialized. It's got to run all at once."
>
> Ross agreed, but wondered how he might justify substituting a single heavy dish for the *New Yorker* readers' usual varied and light fare. He found an out in the *New Yorker*'s first-issue statement of intentions back in February 1925. "*The New Yorker*," it began, "starts with a declaration of serious purpose . . ." That's as far as Ross read.
>
> For the next ten days, Shawn and Ross locked themselves in Ross's office from 10 A.M. to 2 A.M. daily, while Hersey feverishly rewrote and Shawn and Ross, sidetracking everything else, fed the Hiroshima story to the printers. No one outside Ross's office, except a harried makeup man, knew what was going on. "Talk" reporters turned in their copy as usual and petulantly demanded: "Where are proofs?" when they mysteriously failed to appear. The business office was kept blithely unaware (as it usually is at the *New Yorker*) of what the magazine's advertising would run around.

For Hersey, the most notable aspect of the editing experience were Ross's queries. Over the years, the editor had developed the habit of responding to an article or short story by reading it—sometimes in manuscript, but more frequently in galley proof, after another editor had done preliminary work—and compiling a list of comments or questions keyed to specific points in the piece. Ross stressed that these were truly queries—for the most part, they did not oblige the writer to make any changes—and he made them into a kind of work of art. "It is a pity you never saw any Ross notes," William Maxwell wrote to John Updike in 1960, when he was putting through a long Updike story called "Home." "A story this length would have at least sixty or seventy, and be somewhere along the line apocalyptic, but end up despairing or admiring. It was always uncertain." (Maxwell added: "Nobody could be more graceful at fashioning an acceptable compliment.")

Ross acknowledged that many of the queries were the product of his inordinate desire for complete lucidity, and some were simply a result of his having read the piece too hurriedly to have fully grasped its meaning. But the system seemed to work. Edward Newhouse, who contributed dozens of short stories to the magazine, recalled, "I would sit down with Gus Lobrano and go through Ross's queries. Gus would just cross out twenty for every one he'd say we should address—but that one change would immeasurably improve the piece." In a 1976 interview, John Cheever said much the same thing and cited Ross's suggestions on Cheever's 1947 story "The Enormous Radio":

> A diamond is found on the bathroom floor after a party. The man says, "Sell it, we can use a few dollars." Ross had changed "dollars" to "bucks" which was absolutely perfect. Brilliant. Then I had "the radio came softly" and Ross penciled in another "softly." "The radio came softly, softly." He was absolutely right. But then there were twenty-nine other suggestions like, "This story has gone on for twenty-four hours and no one has eaten anything. There's no mention of a meal."

Ross frequently appended his general impressions of a story to the query sheet, and by the time he had gotten through part two of Hersey's article, he was moved to say: "A very fine piece beyond any question; got practically everything. This will be the definitive piece [or] the classic piece on what follows a bomb dropping for some time to come. I read it very carefully, and have a lot of notes. I probably read it over-zealously, and more than the normal amount of queries are to be discounted probably."

He did indeed have a lot of notes. For Part I alone, there were forty-seven, plus an additional twenty-seven on Hersey's revised version and six more on an additional revise. As usual, most concerned small, even pedantic, points of fact, clarity, consistency, diction, grammar, or logic; many were profane, some were very funny; and all were posed humbly, helpfully and constructively:

> Can a fellow priest be a communicant. (I merely don't know.)

> I should think it would be plural, "streets"; unlikely they'd confine themselves to just one street for blocks, they'd go into the intersecting streets.

> I don't see how a doorway can be said to have strength; a doorway is a hole, a space. A door frame can have strength, and that's what meant. But how

about as marked. As an old air raid and San Francisco earthquake veteran, I know that the idea is that you stand in a doorway and that nothing can (theoretically) fall straight down on top of you. That's probably what this fellow had in mind.

A kimona sleeve isn't a very good example here, seems to me. It stopped me. Kimona sleeves very loose, hardly sleeves at all.

If this pole is slender, should be said here, first mention, but, by God, if it's very slender he couldn't have rowed this boat with it, as nearly as I can make out. I asked Hersey how one could row a boat with a bamboo pole and he said this Jap did it, but I wouldn't trifle with my luck by making it a *slender* pole. I'll say that. Seems kind of ridiculous.

It seems these Society of Jesus gents all went to their rooms, by God, and wouldn't it be better to say so, and make a couple of changes along the line I've suggested. I'll be damned if it isn't amazing that they all went back to bed after breakfast. I've been suspicious of these religious men all along, and envious. Ah to be a member of the Society of Jesus.

But some of the queries were more significant. Ross understood that the strength of the narrative came from looking at the events in Hiroshima from the point of view of the characters—a view from the ground and not from the sky, as it were—and he pointed it out whenever Hersey wavered and indulged in omniscience. For example, when Hersey referred to a fact that the characters would probably not have been privy to, Ross wrote: "Touchy technical point here, and an important one. This is a story throughout of what people see first hand and (except for a few parenthetical remarks) only that. Did this woman see her dead husband and know it that way. If so should be told that way. If not, should be out, as getting ahead of the story, or should be said in parens. Or so it seems strongly to me." Hersey cut the reference out.

One of Ross's queries in the first part read: "Point of considerable magnitude here. The exact minute that this bomb fell is extremely important in a story like this, which is based religiously on a time table. It is of the utmost importance that the time table be right." He listed some chronological discrepancies, and then, "Think Hersey has to pick a minute and stick to it."

Hersey did, and the ultimate precision in matters of time helped give an almost biblical power to the finished piece. Thus the first sentence of the published version: "At exactly fifteen minutes past eight in the morning, on August 6, 1945, Japanese time, at the moment when the atomic bomb flashed above Hiroshima, Miss Toshiko Sasaki, a clerk in the personnel department of the East Asia Tin Works, had just sat down at her place in the plant office and was turning her head to speak to the girl at the next desk."

Watch for revise 8/16.   *Miss Frye*

August 6, 1946

Mr. Wigglesworth:

    Mr. Ross's notes on "Reporter - Some Events At Hiroshima - Part II" by Hersey.

    A very fine piece beyond any question; got practically everything. This will be the definitive piece on the classic piece on what follows a bomb dropping for a long time to come. I read it very carefully, and have a lot of notes. I probably read it over-zealously, and more than the normal number of queries are to be discounted probably.

    I am still dissatisfied with the series title.

    There is, I think, one grave lack in this piece. It may be Hersey's intention that there be. If so, ask consideration for what I say anyhow. All the way through I wondered about what killed these people, the burns, falling debris, the concussion—what? For a year I've been wondering about this and I eagerly hoped this piece would tell me. It doesn't. Nearly a hundred thousand dead people are around but Hersey doesn't tell how they died. Would it be possible—if so, would be wise—to tell on Galley 7 where he gives the 100,000 people how many were killed by being hit by hard objects, how many by burns, how many by concussion, or shock, or whatever it was. Or would this be getting ahead of his story. I haven't read third and fourth parts yet. At one place, away over on Gally 14, a woman with no visible injury dies. Were a lot of the corpses that day without visible burns or injury. How about all the dead that littered the pavement when the Catholics were migrating—what proportion of them unmarked. I think getting a little this into the piece, fairly early, would be a good idea—unless, as I said, it conflicts with Hersey's basic plan.

    One thing, though: I think he ought to mention the vomiting, though. He doesn't mention it at all until Galley 13, where it comes as a considerable surprise to the reader that, more or less generally, the ailing were vomiting. That pretty late in piece to be telling that; several scenes have been described in which there must have been general vomiting. (One thing more: I think that from time to time Hersey might tuck up on the time of day; reader loses all track of the hours.)

    I would suggest (I'm making this as in insert in these notes after completing annotating) that Hersey might do well to tuck up on the time—give the hour and minute, exactly or roughly, from time to time. The reader loses all sense of the passing of time in the episodes and never knows what time of day it is, whether 10 a.m. or 4 p.m. I thought of this half way through annotation and mentioned it several times. If I appear to be nagging on the subject, that's why.)

1. I'd tuck up on the time and the date by all means, repeating wording of first part.

2. The safe place mention here isn't explained, and maybe there's a question as to whether the place was safe, or just a fluke. Anyhow, it wasn't that he was out in this suburb that made the place safe, but the fact, as stated in Part I, that he was between two rocks, pressed again. It was that niche that made him safe, and should be repeated here, I think. The soldiers were practically in same place, but they weren't safe.

3. I raised the question at end of Part I as to whether there were a lot of people in the house. If there were a lot of people and repair made Part I, perhaps should be made here too.

4. Trouble with these Jap quotes. Ordinarily our style has been to follow the foreign word with a dash and then the translation in English. That doesn't work here, because the quote partly in Jap and partly English. I'd avoid this construction, and follow our rule that all such words should be translated. That would mean revision here and several other spots.

Some of Ross's notes on "Hiroshima," as retyped by his secretary.

That sentence is by now familiar: "Hiroshima" was published as a book just months after its appearance in the *New Yorker* and has been continuously in print around the world ever since. An extensive description of it is unnecessary. But a quotation of two paragraphs can give much of the flavor of Hersey's method. The passage comes near the beginning, after he has introduced the six characters (the other one, besides the professional men mentioned above and the factory clerk introduced in the lead, is a tailor's widow), and tells of Dr. Masakuzu Fujii, who at 8:15 A.M. was on the porch of his private hospital, overlooking the Kyo River:

> Dr. Fujii sat down cross-legged in his underwear on the spotless matting of the porch, put on his glasses, and started reading the Osaka *Asahi*. He liked to read the Osaka news because his wife was there. He saw the flash. To him—faced away from the center and looking at his paper—it seemed a brilliant yellow. Startled, he began to rise to his feet. In that moment (he was 1,550 yards from the center), the hospital leaned behind his rising and, with a terrible ripping noise, toppled into the river. The Doctor, still in the act of getting to his feet, was thrown forward and around and over; he was buffeted and gripped; he lost track of everything, because things were so speeded up; he felt the water.
>
> Dr. Fujii hardly had time to think that he was dying before he realized that he was alive, squeezed tightly by two long timbers in a V across his chest, like a morsel suspended between two huge chopsticks—held upright, so that he could not move, with his head miraculously above water and his torso and legs in it. The remains of his hospital were all around him in a mad assortment of splintered lumber and materials for the relief of pain. His left shoulder hurt terribly. His glasses were gone.

In just eleven well-modulated sentences, Hersey shows the transformation of Dr. Fujii's world—from a well-ordered, "spotless" place to one of sudden pain and utter confusion, emblemized, perfectly, by his delayed realization that his glasses are missing. The level of detail (1,550 yards!) and precision, in the description of the pieces of timber that were pinning him, were guaranteed to warm Ross's heart. The writing, meanwhile, struck just the right note—matter-of-fact and lucid, with the simple sentences punctuated by the occasional well-chosen adjective: *spotless* matting, *brilliant* yellow, *terrible* noise, *mad* assortment.

Hersey was able to sustain that same force and control for the entire thirty-one thousand words, as he unflinchingly described what the six suffered and saw in the days following the blast. As its power accumulated page by page and as it set forth its characters' sufferings and struggles to stay alive, the article managed to do something nearly impossible: it took some people from a nation that had been collectively vilified as "Japs" for the past five years and presented them as recognizable, sympathetic human beings. (Racism certainly had something to do with the dehumanization of this particular enemy, and Hersey's Asian upbringing no doubt helped him avoid that pitfall.) And by doing so, it made it immeasurably harder for Americans to ignore the terrible weapon that had been unleashed on the world.

Hersey's article appeared in the issue dated August 31, 1946. When the decision was made to run it in its entirety, there wasn't enough time to change the cover, a blithe Charles E. Martin scene of summer frolicking in a park, but all newsstand copies did carry a white band alerting potential buyers that this was not a typical *New Yorker*. Inside, after the Goings on About Town entertainment and cultural listings, the article—presented as a Reporter at Large with the simple title "Hiroshima" and a subheading for each of the four sections—commenced in the space where The Talk of the Town was usually found, along with a box headed "To Our Readers":

> *The New Yorker* this week devotes its entire editorial space to an article on the almost complete obliteration of a city by one atomic bomb, and what happened to the people of that city. It does so in the conviction that few of us have yet comprehended the all but incredible destructive power of this weapon, and that everyone might well take time to consider the terrible implications of its use.

The article continued until the last page of the magazine, accompanied by only one abstract illustration and uninterrupted by any Newsbreaks or cartoons.

On the day before publication, copies of the magazine were messengered to the city editors of the *Times* and the *Herald Tribune*, along with a letter describing some of the circumstances of the article, pointing out that Hersey had for the first time established the number of casualties—100,000 dead and 100,000 wounded in a city of 245,000—and stating, "We think the story is a terrifically important one." Both papers ran editorials commending the article, as did Ralph Ingersoll's liberal daily *PM*. But the response to "Hiroshima" went far beyond the world of New York journalism. All newsstand copies sold out the day they appeared, and when Albert Einstein attempted to buy one thousand copies of the magazine, he was told none were available. Within two weeks a secondhand copy brought $18 at auction. A reader wrote in to the *New Yorker* to say that "no one is talking about anything else but the Hersey article for the last two days, either in trains, restaurants, or at home." Another commented, "I had never thought of the people in the bombed cities as individuals." In four half-hour installments, the evenings of September 9–12, the American Broadcasting Company presented a reading of the entire text of the article, with no commercial interruptions, and in England the BBC did the same. When the article was published in book form that November, the Book-of-the-Month Club gave a free copy to all of its subscribers because, in the words of its president, "We find it hard to conceive of anything being written that could be of more importance at this moment to the human race."

At the *New Yorker*, which would never again be thought of as primarily a humorous magazine, some quiet pleasure was taken at the unqualified success of Hersey, Shawn, and Ross's bold experiment. As normal operations started up again, friends and contributors sent in their congratulations from around the world. Ross confessed to one of them, Irwin Shaw, "I don't think I've ever got as much satisfaction out of anything else in my life."

POSTWAR PORTENTS

> If thou must choose
> Between the chances, choose the odd;
> Read the *New Yorker*, trust in God;
> And take short views.
> —W. H. Auden, "Under Which Lyre," 1946

〰️

> I think our transition to peace, art, amusement, frivolity, etc., will be gradual, and probably the magazine will never get back to where it was, on account of having gone heavyweight to a considerable extent during the war.
> —Harold Ross to Janet Flanner, June 25, 1946

〰️

> I started to get out a light magazine that wouldn't concern itself with the weighty problems of the universe, and now look at me.
> —Ross to Howard Brubaker, January 22, 1951

〰️

After the war, the United States found itself in a new world. In many if not most respects, it was a grimmer place. Yet, puffed up by military victory and an unprecedented economic boom, the predominant proportion of the country chose not to see it that way. The official version of things was that we had vanquished the forces of evil and, with the help of our friend the atom, were on our way to defeating our new enemies behind the Iron Curtain. To a remarkable and persistent degree, the *New Yorker* resisted this tide of postwar optimism. "Hiroshima" was only one of many expressions of a strong desire to see the world plain.

As Hersey's article would suggest, the magazine was most adamant about recognizing and reporting on the ominous arrival of the nuclear era. The key figure was E. B. White, who with his wife agreed to return to New York and the *New Yorker* in 1943 to reinforce a staff severely depleted by war. Katharine resumed full-time editing and White reclaimed Notes and Comment. Before long it became clear that the Allies would prevail, and much of White's thinking was directed to the contours of the postwar world. The day Japan surrendered, he wrote in a piece published August 18, 1945, he was in the kitchen "putting up string beans" (a quintessential White setting) and trying to "imagine what it will mean to a soldier, having gone out to preserve the world as he knew it, now to return to a world he never dreamt about, a world of atomic designs and portents. . . . For the first time in our lives, we can feel the disturbing vibrations of complete human readjustment." The new world was unsettling yet oddly familiar to White, who had always been bemused or unsettled by technology and whose constitution was finely tuned to sense catastrophe. In the *New Yorker* of September 1, 1945, he wrote, "The Atomic Age is scarcely a month old, yet we feel as though we've been swimming in its dark, radioactive waters for centuries."

The war itself had convinced White of the necessity for world government, and since his return to Notes and Comment, he had consistently beaten the drum for this notion. He understood that causes—especially ones that appeared to be pie-in-the-sky crusades—were precisely the sort of thing Harold Ross had no interest in or sympathy for and, after the first few pieces, checked in with the editor to see if he approved of this new direction. Ross replied in the affirmative:

> Your new world line of comments . . . seem to me to be the most eloquent things you have ever written and magnificent. My viewpoint is that if the people of the earth don't get a new set-up, they are being offered a very remarkable line of writing and thinking anyhow. You (collective) can't lose on that basis. . . . I say dismiss any fear that you might make the magazine a crank publication. Probably that's what it ought to be, if the crankiness is sound; the uncertain factor is how soon will such truths be effective. But aside from all that and from everything else, you made the Comment page what it is, God knows, and I have for long regarded it as yours to the extent that you want to make use of it.

Between 1943 and 1947, White devoted approximately one of every three Comments to the one-world theme. The specter of nuclear war only strengthened his conviction. "Nuclear energy and foreign policy cannot coexist on this planet," he declared. "The more deep the secret, the greater the determination of every nation to discover and exploit it. Nuclear energy insists on global government, on law, on order, and on the willingness of the community to take the responsibility for the acts of the individual."

An objective counterpoint to White's editorials were a series of Reporter at Large pieces and Profiles by Daniel Lang, a young staff writer who had covered the European war and, after the peace, found himself short of ideas. Shawn sent him to Oak Ridge, Tennessee, where the bomb that destroyed Hiroshima had been assembled, to find out how total secrecy had been maintained. Lang subsequently kept on the nuclear story—reconstructing how decisions and discoveries had been made during the war, chronicling how the atom was being exploited during the tense peace, with an attention all the while to the moral dimension of man's actions and decisions—in several dozen articles over two decades. It took Lang some time, he would write, to appreciate "the profusion of ancient themes and modern variations that would unfold as atomic energy and, later, space rocketry engaged us in questions of good and evil, life and death."

There were other unsettling facts of postwar life to consider. In 1945 and 1946, war-crimes trials in Nuremberg revealed some measure of the horrors of the Holocaust, and the New Yorker accorded them ample coverage, in Letters by Joel Sayre, John Winterich, Janet Flanner, and Andy Logan. (Logan was one of the magazine's first crop of female staff reporters, hired by Ross during the war to fill out his depleted staff. Among the others were Lillian Ross and Scottie Lanahan, who was the daughter of F. Scott Fitzgerald.) Flanner also contributed, in 1947, a remarkable three-part piece on the Nazis' plunder of European art, "The Beautiful Spoils."

Some trouble erupted closer to home. Soon after the Allied victory, a series of congressional committees began carrying out investigations of communist influences in Hollywood, unions, higher education, and the government itself; more generally, there developed a climate of suspicion in which the "loyalty" of any American was implicitly under question. At least as much as any other mainstream publication, the New Yorker took offense. Once again, E. B. White was in the lead. The New York Times did not begin to criticize the House Un-American Activities Committee until September 1948, but White fired his first volley on November 1, 1947, a sardonic but relatively mild meditation on whether the New Yorker itself would pass muster from the committee and its chairman, J. Parnell Thomas:

> Our procedure so far has been to examine the manuscript, not the writer; the picture, not the artist. We have not required a statement of political belief or a blood count. This still seems like a sensible approach to the publishing problem, although falling short of Representative J. Parnell Thomas's standard. One thing we have always enjoyed about our organization is the splashy, rainbow effect of the workers: Red blending into Orange, Orange blending

into Yellow, and so on, right across the spectrum to Violet....We sit among as quietly seething a mass of reactionaries, revolutionaries, worn-out robber barons, tawny pipits, liberals, Marxists in funny hats, and Taftists in pin stripes as ever gathered under one roof in a common enterprise. The group seems healthy enough, in a messy sort of way, and everybody finally meets everybody else at the water cooler, like beasts at the water hole in the jungle.... Our creative activity, whether un- or non-un-American, is properly not on a loyalty basis, but merely on a literacy basis—a dreamy concept. If this should change, and we should go over to loyalty, the meaning of "un-American activity" would change, since the American designated in the phrase would not be the same country we have long lived in and admired.

Four months later, the extent of the inquisition was becoming apparent, and White was ready to state the issues more plainly. He described a Town Hall forum in which an audience member asked the moderator, "Isn't it true, sir, that in the last analysis this boils down to the old struggle between freedom and tyranny?" White wrote:

All around him heads nodded gratefully, everyone relieved to have life clarified in a moment of revelation. Anti-Communism is a strong drink. Already the lines are being drawn tighter; already fear produces symptoms of the very disease we hope to fight off: the preoccupation with loyalty, the tightening of censorship, the control of thoughts by legislative committee, the readiness to impute guilt by association, the impatience with liberalism. The tyrant fear, pricking us to fight tyranny.

White kept up the theme, sometimes in strikingly combative language. In a 1949 Comment, he characterized the dismissal of so-called subversives in Hollywood and academia as "a political purge"; in another he referred to "a growing group of American political prisoners." Other contributors followed in his path. Historian Mary Frances Corey has identified an entire subgenre of *New Yorker* casuals in which "a contributor would describe some utterly innocent incident from his own past, which could, in the current climate of fear and distrust, easily place him under suspicion." These pieces were played for laughs, but the underlying point was unmistakable and serious: no one is safe from the inquisition. Strong reporting pieces also implicitly or explicitly protested the political climate: Lang's 1948 Profile of a wrongfully discredited Department of Commerce official; A. J. Liebling's hard-hitting "Wayward Press" columns on some newspapers' eagerness to print undocumented "revelations" from the Un-American Activities Committee; and Lillian Ross's 1948 "Come In, Lassie!" about the climate of fear and capitulation in Hollywood. (The title reflected the fact that Lassie was the only Hollywood star who was above suspicion and thus assured of regular work. One studio executive told Ross, "We like Lassie. We're sure of Lassie. . . . Katharine Hepburn goes out and makes a speech for Henry Wallace. Bang! We're in trouble. Lassie doesn't make speeches. Not Lassie, thank God.") Richard Rovere, a former writer for left-wing publications such as the *New Masses* and the *Nation* who began contributing a regular "Letter from Washington" for the *New Yorker* in 1948, was one of the first journalists to criticize Senator Joseph McCarthy. In a column published April 22, 1950, he compared the senator's use of "the multiple untruth" with Hitler's use of "the big lie." Not until a month later did the *Washington Post* accuse McCarthy of "witch-hunting."

These strong stands did not escape the attention of the country's self-appointed guardians against communism. The red-baiting periodical *Plain Talk*, in an article called "The Wayward *New Yorker*," reprimanded the magazine for "its pro-Communist reporting" and in another issue stated that Liebling was working for Alger Hiss as "a kind of assistant counsel and private detective." More ominously, the FBI was accumulating a file on Liebling, referring to him as a "careless journalist of the *New Yorker* set," as being guilty of "compulsive fellow-travelerism," and of being responsible for "the pinko infiltration of the *New Yorker*."

Clearly, it took some courage for *New Yorker* writers to compose these articles, and some courage for Ross to agree to print them. The editor's case is more interesting. While Ross once described himself as "incapable of having partisan politics" and "completely detached politically; or that's what I claim,"* his biographer terms him "conservative with an isolationist bent." In racial matters he didn't even deserve to be called conservative: he was burdened with the reflexive bigotry common to his generation. Yet Ross had no patience with McCarthyism or any other form of witch-hunt. In the late forties, he assigned Walter Bernstein, who had in fact been a communist, to cover a trial in Yugoslavia. Bernstein recalled in a memoir that Ross told him of receiving complaints that he was too "left-wing" for the assignment, but that he paid them no heed: "Nobody was going to tell him whom to hire, and if he didn't like what I wrote, he would simply not print it."

Moreover, there is no record of Ross censoring any article by a *New Yorker* writer because of his or her political views. In 1950, when staff writer E. J. Kahn wrote a "Wayward Press" column defending two friends who had been accused of communist leanings, Ross said, "Jesus Christ, Kahn, why did you have to write this goddamned piece? Now I have to run it."

---

*Ross continued: "I'm a liberal, though, by instinct. Human, you might say, and a meliorist by belief." The meliorism probably came from the nineteenth-century English philosopher Herbert Spencer, for whom Ross had experienced a youthful enthusiasm.

Richard Rovere recalled Ross using almost precisely the same words about a Rovere column criticizing segregation in Washington, D.C. This despite Ross's writing on the query sheet for the piece that Rovere "plainly doesn't know what he's talking about. . . . I don't see why this magazine has to draw every Abraham Lincoln in New York." Ross's conception of editorial integrity included this notion: if one of his regular writers wrote an accurate, timely, and acceptably literate piece that refrained from blatant editorializing, it was his obligation to run it.*

As Corey has pointed out, the New Yorker writers, editors, and readers had reason to be especially sensitive to the charges and innuendo that were swirling around the country like a foul wind. After all, the targets of this campaign were journalists, actors, professors, civil servants, artists, and intellectuals in general—a rather precise roster of the magazine's readers and contributors. Alger Hiss, accused of spying by Whittaker Chambers in 1948, was a perfect case in point. In the words of historian John P. Roche, Hiss "wore no beard, spoke with no accent, moved casually in the best circles . . . looked like the man down the block in Scarsdale or Evanston, the man in the office across the hall on Wall Street or State Street." Seeing Hiss publicly pilloried for what seemed at worst some youthful indiscretions, many associated with the New Yorker couldn't help but think, "There but for the grace of God . . ."† Yet the element of identification should not diminish what was, for the magazine, an expeditious, strong, eloquent, and courageous protest against a virulent new strain in American life.

*Richard O. Boyer, a longtime staff writer, appears to have been the New Yorker's one political victim. Late in 1949, after Boyer, an avowed communist, was reprimanded by the right-wing columnist Westbrook Pegler for contributing to the Communist Party newspaper the Daily Worker, he found his articles no longer accepted by the New Yorker. He wrote to Ross promising not to "permit my views to embarrass the New Yorker in any way, shape or form, and, specifically, that I will not write for The Daily Worker." But he declared that the magazine would "be hurt and in the long run badly hurt if it starts firing people because of their political views." To his lasting discredit, Ross responded only to a minor and technical point: ". . . you can't be fired. . . . Our relationship with a free-lance writer is that we buy his stuff when it's done, if we like it, and that's that" (emphasis added). A letter written (but never sent) by White to someone who had protested the incident acknowledged that the New Yorker had "frozen up" as far as Boyer was concerned and said this was because the Party had shown "signs" of wanting to "exploit" his connection with the magazine. White went on, "When Boyer wrote (for the Daily Worker) some reportorial articles that experienced editors like Bill Shawn and Harold Ross regarded as thoroughly nonobjective, it didn't raise his stock any with the magazine. If there is one thing The New Yorker takes a dim view of, it's a reporter playing footsy with his facts." The talk around the office was that Boyer had conducted political business using New Yorker stationery. Boyer had one article in the New Yorker in 1950 and after that never appeared in its pages again.

†In the 1960s, Hiss's son, Tony, would come to work for the New Yorker as a staff writer.

Fussing as an Art Form

Lobrano says that my query No. 9 is nonsense, that a person can mumble prayers while biting on a bullet. I bit on my lead pencil just now and mumbled a prayer, but I didn't do it *between bites*. I exerted a constant pressure.

—Harold Ross to Samuel Hopkins Adams,
March 25, 1947

~~~

I urge that every time it is said or implied in a story that a man is dead that this statement or implication be checked. I would extend this to such people as Napoleon but would especially be interested in lesser people, or more recent people.

—Ross to Frederick Packard, undated

~~~

In the Comment on Life's storage wall, I wrote: "a pretty good case can be made out for setting fire to it and starting fresh." Some studious person, alone with his God in the deep of night, came upon the word "fresh" and saw how easily it could be changed to the word "afresh," a simple matter of affixing an "a." So the phrase became starting "afresh" and acquired refinement, and a sort of grammatical excellence.

I still think people say "start fresh." I shall continue to write "start fresh," to say "start fresh," and, in circumstances which require a restart, I shall actually *start* fresh. I don't ever intend to start afresh. Anybody who prefers to start afresh is at liberty to do so, but I don't recommend it. An afresh starter is likely to be a person who wants to get agoing. An afresh starter is also likely to be a person who fells acold when he steps out of the tub.

—E. B. White to William Shawn,
February 1945

~~~

Just cross out all the proposed changes you don't agree with, including the several inserted commas if you don't want them. This magazine is over commaed. They are out of control.

—Ross to H. L. Mencken, August 18, 1948

~~~

We have carried editing to a very high degree of fussiness here, probably to a point approaching the ultimate. I don't know how to get it under control.

> —Ross to Mencken, November 10, 1948

~~~~

The *New Yorker,* superbly edited, is what is called a "wonderful job"; most writers who write for it are edited (or edit themselves) almost out of existence so that everything in it appears to be by an anonymous body called the *New Yorker.*

> —Stephen Spender, "The Situation of the American Writer,"
> *Horizon,* March 1949

~~~~

The queries that "Hiroshima" (and every other article and story the *New Yorker* published) elicited from Ross were only the final stage in a long, multifaceted, sometimes tedious, and completely distinctive process of editing. The process was not completely in place until the late thirties, but from the early days of the magazine, it was understood that contributions were subject to queries, changes, and sometimes wholesale rewriting. An example of the last was a 1931 Profile of the Prince of Wales by an English writer named Anthony Gibbs. After he had submitted it, Katharine White wrote him allowing that it was "the foundation of a very good piece" and wondering if Gibbs would "let us have the Profile on a re-write basis, hinging our piece on yours, but rearranging it somewhat?" It fell to Wolcott Gibbs (no relation) to put the piece "through the typewriter," as the office parlance had it, and it was so much his product that when it was about to appear, Anthony Gibbs wrote to Mrs. White, "I am still a little nervous about having my name on the profile.... But perhaps we had better let it go. I suppose it couldn't be qualified in some way—'By Wolcott and Anthony Gibbs,' or simple 'School of Anthony Gibbs.'"

This was admittedly an extreme example, but every contributor had to be prepared to answer innumerable questions and to respond to suggestions for changes large and small. Sometimes, the changes would be made unilaterally, and it would be up to the author to recognize them on galleys and protest if so inclined. Generally, the assumption among the editors was that substantial editing was almost always necessary—an unexalted view of authorial sovereignty that Ross carried over from his newspaper years. At the *New Yorker,* it was consistent with the bylines being at the end of pieces, the lack of a table of contents, and the anonymity of Notes and Comment and The Talk of the Town. The ethos was mostly unspoken, but was given voice in "Theory and Practice of Editing *New Yorker* Articles," a remarkable and only minimally facetious document Wolcott Gibbs prepared for Gus Lobrano in 1937, when Lobrano was about to join the staff as a fiction editor. It began: "The average contributor to this magazine is semiliterate; that is, he is ornate to no purpose, full of senseless and elegant variations, and can be relied on to use three sentences where a word would do." There followed thirty-one numbered points, all pertaining to literary excesses, clichés, faux pas, or plain blunders that contributors should not be allowed to get away with. Some of the strictures made sense; some amounted to not much more than rather arbitrary prejudices. For example:

> 10. To quote Mr. Ross again, "Nobody gives a damn about a writer and his problems except another writer." Pieces about authors, reporters, poets, etc., are to be discouraged in principle. Whenever possible the protagonist should be arbitrarily transplanted to another line of business. When the reference is incidental and unnecessary, it should come out.

> 28. It has been one of Mr. Ross's long struggles to raise the tone of our contributors' surroundings, at least on paper. References to the gay Bohemian life in Greenwich Village and other low surroundings should be cut whenever possible. Nor should writers be permitted to boast about having their telephones cut off, or not being able to pay their bills, or getting their meals at the delicatessen, or any of the other things which strike many writers as quaint and lovable.

For many contributors, used to writing for intellectual weeklies or literary journals, where their copy would be edited for spelling, consistency of capitalization and abbreviation, and possibly grammar, but otherwise left unchanged, the editorial processes at the *New Yorker* were a source of mild or pronounced bemusement. In 1931, after the appearance of his first "Skyline" column, on Radio City, Lewis Mumford wrote to his friend and fellow contributor Babette Deutsch: "Oh these good editors! I respect them so deeply and they are so bothersome! They tempt one with their high rates, and by the time one has met them, debated with them, struggled with them, and finally come to a diplomatic understanding, one has spent enough time and energy to have written half a dozen articles for less competent and therefore more easily pleased editors!" These sentiments would be frequently echoed in the years to come.

The roots of *New Yorker* editing were deep. One might start with Ross's mother, Ida, who came from old New England stock and was at the time of her marriage a schoolteacher in Kansas. Ross's biographer, Thomas Kunkel, tells us she supplemented young Harold's education with evening grammar lessons at home, in which he was required to parse sentences. There was probably also an element of overcompensation. "I am frequently regarded as ignorant," Ross once wrote, "I guess, because I haven't a conventional college education, but I have a vast knowledge of a great many things that never could have been got in college that, in this job, has proved about twenty times as valuable as a college education, because I complement the college educations that almost totally surround me. It used to bother me to be sneered at by college pups but it long ago ceased to bother me." Actually, Ross never graduated from high school, much less college, and he may unconsciously have become a stickler and scholar on matters of grammar and usage as a sort of substitute for other kinds of book learning. He certainly took to *A Dictionary of Modern English Usage,* a book by the British grammarian and lexicographer H. F. Fowler published the year after the *New Yorker* began. Ross always had a copy of Fowler (as the volume was eponymously called) within reach, and in 1937 Wolcott Gibbs referred to it as "our reference book." Ross valued Fowler less for its specific strictures (although he was inordinately fond of the four-page discussion of the difference between *which* and *that* and distributed copies of it to contributors) than for the sense permeating it that to communicate successfully in the English language, one must be attuned to moral and historical matters, as well as the merely technical ones.*

Ross's—and by extension the magazine's—editing was also highly attuned to accuracy, and this can be traced in part to his days as a reporter. In one of his reminiscences first published in the *New Yorker* and later in the book *Newspaper Days,* H. L. Mencken wrote that when he was on the staff of the *Baltimore Sun* in the early years of this century, he and his fellow reporters felt "hobbled by the paper's craze for mathematical accuracy," which resulted in reporters "who tended to write like bookkeepers." Ross had been a newsman in this same era, and in the *New Yorker's* famous system of fact-checking seems to have attempted to apply "the craze for mathematical accuracy" on an institutional scale. The system began, Katharine White subsequently recalled, in 1927, when a profile of Edna St. Vincent Millay was so riddled with errors that the poet's mother stormed into the magazine's offices and threatened to sue if an extensive correction was not run. (The magazine ultimately printed her lengthy letter under the heading "We Stand Corrected.")

From its beginning in 1924, *Time* magazine had had a group of female researchers, known in the office as "checkers," who verified all facts in sto-

---

*The reliance on the book continued long after Ross's death. In 1958, soon after Kenneth Tynan began writing theater reviews for the magazine, he wrote to a friend: "The *New Yorker* is madly hospitable but has a sort of Fowler fixation that makes it jump on the tiniest vagaries of grammar, syntax and punctuation. It's also a bit anti-sex. Once out of the office I curse and mutter obscenities and say 'ain't,' just to let off stream."

ries prior to publication. Whether or not it was consciously following *Time*'s lead, the *New Yorker* put a similar system into place. Initially, Mrs. Angell supervised the process; in 1930, Ralph Ingersoll received a memo from Ross instructing him, "Add Fact Checking to your list of chores." Ingersoll left the following year and was succeeded as chief "checker" by Rogers Whitaker, who by 1933 was spending so much time supervising two underlings and fact-checking himself that he relinquished his makeup duties to Carmine Peppe. Frederick Packard took over the department in 1936 and ran it for two decades, as it became an institution, famous for its Canadian Mounty–like determination to hunt down any fact, no matter how obscure. By 1941, *New Yorker* fact-checking was so well known that Gibbs could make sport of it in a theater review and count on knowing laughs from his readers: "Once, in a spirit of sacrilege, I named my own five favorite Hamlets, suggesting they might get up a ball team. The list was composed of Forbes-Robertson, Mantell, Hampden, Barrymore, Geilgud, Howard, Tinker, Evans and Chance, and after a dusty afternoon in the Library, the most scholarly of the *New Yorker* proofreaders came back to report than as far as existing records showed neither Mr. Tinker nor Mr. Chance had ever played Hamlet in his life."

Fiction and poetry as well as factual pieces were checked, to make sure, first, that all characters were consistently named and described and, second, that all locations and other details were accurate. In 1948, the magazine was prepared to accept its first poem by the young writer Richard Wilbur, "Museum Piece." But it included an anecdote about the painter Degas hanging his clothes on an El Greco, and the fact-checkers could not verify it. Poetry editor Peter DeVries suggested changing the phrase "Edgar Degas purchased once ..." to "It's said that Degas once possessed ..." Wilbur said no, because "to remove the abruptness" would "greatly injure the subtlety of the sequences of associations which constitute the poem." DeVries thereupon rejected the poem, explaining, "This magazine is notoriously fastidious about points of fact, and we feel the same way about poetry, whether rightly or wrongly."

When attempting to explain or defend the level of fussiness at the *New Yorker*, Ross usually took the tack he did as early as 1927, six weeks after the Millay Profile was published, in a memo to Fleischmann: "What with our making fun of the mistakes in other publications and what with the nature of the magazine, *The New Yorker* ought to be freer from typographical errors than any other publication. . . . A SPECIAL EFFORT SHOULD BE MADE TO AVOID MISTAKES IN *THE NEW YORKER.*" This was true enough. But it did not account for the terror Ross seemed to feel that an error should slip in, or that any statement in the magazine might be at all ambiguous, misleading, or unclear. Ross's famous query "Who he?"—written next to any bald naming of a person who would not, he suspected, be immediately known to virtually every reader—was a case in point. (As a gag, A. J. Liebling once had "Who he?" painted under his name on his own office door.)

So was Ross's unshakable belief in the need for what he referred to as "pegging"—the establishing, as early as possible, preferably in the first paragraph, of a story's setting. Ross's query sheet on a 1949 Frank O'Connor story called "The Idealist" began, "This pretty darned good story. Must be pegged, of course. I see place allowed for it at (1). Suggest further that another place to get in a natural peg would be at (1a). Could put in Irish-sounding name here, and then say at (1a) something along line *us lads in Ireland* or *us Irish lads.*" An equally literalistic—and, upon reflection, silly—corollary to this was the principle, formulated early at the *New Yorker,* that stories and poems that took place in or concerned a particular time of year must be *published* at that time of year. If a spring story didn't manage to get in the magazine by the time June had run its course, it had to wait till the following March. (A decade later, John Updike would plead to Maxwell that a Christmas story submitted in February not be held till the following December, explaining, "There is something repellent about holiday stories that appear on the holiday; they have a quality of being trumped up for the event, like spectaculars on TV and decorations in dept. stores.")

In his memoir *The Years with Ross,* Thurber complained that his employer "sometimes seemed to be editing Talk for a little boy or an old lady whose faculties were dimming" and had a "profound uneasiness with anything smacking of scholarship or specialized knowledge." To prove his point, Thurber reproduced a Talk piece he had written about the Metropolitan Museum of Art, with Ross's insertions in italics:

> For those who exclaim over armor, *a thing pretty rare with us,* the three new suits the museum has just come by will prove enthralling. One of them, a richly ornamented Spanish war harness, has more pieces of re'change, *or you might say accessories,* than any other battle suit in the world. . . . Among other prizes of the New Accession Room is the lid of an amphora, *but we never did find out what an amphora is.*

In general, the magazine had a pronounced inclination toward qualification or understatement, as if taking a strong stand or displaying raw emotion were somehow unseemly. Probably the chief culprit was Gibbs. In one of his theater columns, the following qualifying phrases were found: "I found myself wondering," "I imagine," "I wouldn't be surprised," "I have an idea," "I'm afraid I can't say that," "I doubt it," "I think," "I'm embarrassed to say," "I can only say that," "reminding me somehow," and "I can only agree with." Ross was certainly aware of the tendency and eventually banned the use of *a little* or *pretty* as adverbs.* But such a rearguard action did not solve the underlying problem, as one sees in a 1948 letter to Ross from Kay Boyle, a veteran *New Yorker* writer. She noted that she had not once used the word *little* in her new novel

> —which may be, in part, the explanation of why material submitted to you is over-run with "littles." When I write with the *New Yorker* in mind, I am (a little) leary of emotion. When I set down in my book: "He looked desperately around him" I write it just like that, without a thought of qualifying it. But if that phrase should be written in a story destined to submit to you, I would immediately qualify it, writing it: "He looked *a little* desperately around him." If my hero wished to tell the girl he loved her, he would say so, right out, in my book—but for the *New Yorker* I am certain I would write "I love you, I think, somewhat"—or "It feels a little like love."

Thurber was particularly vehement in protesting this tendency. He frequently complained about the last sentence in the magazine's obituary of David Lardner, which as originally composed by Gibbs, read, "We have never written a paragraph with more regret." Thurber himself insisted that *regret* be changed to *sorrow.* "The curse of our formula editing," he wrote to Ross in 1949, "is that uniformity tends toward desiccation, coldness, and lack of vitality and blood. It is the New York and New Jersey boys and girls, with the honorable exception of White, who set this well-dressed, well-mannered English detachment kind of thing. We are afraid of warmth, as we are afraid of sex and human functions. Our only true boldness lies in the use of 'Jesus Christ' to show we're not afraid of the Catholic Church."

Point 18 of Gibbs's "Theory and Practice" read: "I almost forgot indirection, which probably maddens Mr. Ross more than anything else in the world. He objects, that is, to important objects, or places or people, being dragged into things in a secretive and underhanded manner. If, for instance, a Profile has never told where a man lives, Ross protests against a sentence saying 'His Vermont house is full of valuable paintings.' Should say 'He has a house in Vermont and it is full of paintings.'" One sees Ross's point, but his and his editing staff's attempts to banish indirection from the magazine came to reach absurd proportions. For example, the word *the* was queried when it preceded a noun whose existence had not previously been established. This was, in Ross's view, an underhanded way to import information,

---

*This was formalized in a document entitled "Style Rules," written in 1942 by Ik Shuman. Among the other words or phrases "to be avoided or queried" were: *brooding; wistful, wistfully; vague, vaguely; allergic; -ish* ("as in 'smallish, prettyish,' etc."); *faintly; oddly enough; we dropped everything* "(in Talk)"; *God knows* "(permissible in moderation)"; — *to you* "(As, 'the bow of the ship (the front to you)')"; and "overuse of 'Gadget.'"

and it occasioned his most famous indirection query. The piece was "Lantern Slides," a 1950 reminiscence by Vladimir Nabokov, a Russian émigré who had been publishing poems and casuals in the magazine since 1942, shortly after his arrival in America. In a sort of composite memory of his blissful childhood in St. Petersburg, Nabokov had recalled

> voices speaking all together, a walnut cracked, the click of the nutcracker carelessly passed, thirty human hearts downing mine with their regular beats; the sough and sigh of a thousand trees, the local concord of loud summer birds, and, beyond the river, behind the rhythmic trees, the confused and enthusiastic hullabaloo of bathing young villagers, like a background of wild applause.

Ross's query was "Were the Nabokovs a *one*-nutcracker family?"

The ban on indirection had a subtle but distinct effect on the *New Yorker's* prose. Most notably, it led to a proliferation of nonrestrictive clauses. That is, "He walked inside his three-story house" would be changed by the *New Yorker* to something like "He walked inside his house, which was three stories high." (If the man in question owned several houses, only one of which was three stories, and this fact had already been established, the original sentence would be restrictive and correct as written.) Such a clause is preceded by a comma, a form of punctuation Ross had long been drawn to, thinking perhaps that if the elements of a sentence could be rigorously separated, the chances of confusion or misunderstanding might be reduced. Jane Grant recalled that during World War I, he gave one of his associates at *Stars and Stripes* a page of commas as a Christmas present.

At the *New Yorker,* one of the first style rules Ross established was the serial comma—that is, "red, white, and blue" instead of "red, white and blue." Here he was following his friend Franklin P. Adams, himself a notorious stickler, and Fowler, who argued that since omitting the serial comma sometimes led to confusion as to whether the last two elements in the series are to be taken separately or together, it should always be used.* The usage was occasionally objected to as extraneous and stilted, but Ross held firm. "The serial comma is important because it is almost exclusively the *New Yorker's,* and is a mildly controversial thing," he once wrote to Fleischmann. "But we're right, and all the rest are wrong."

But a continual interlarding of commas can lead to halting, stammering prose. As time passed, *New Yorker* editors became more vigilant in guarding against the underhanded importing of information and inserted commas ever more aggressively. The following two sentences are characteristic:

---

*Fowler also favored inserting a comma *after* a series, as in "He spoke to every man, woman, and child, in the room"—without the comma, one cannot tell whether *in the room* modifies *man* and *woman* and *child,* or only *child.* Ross did not follow him that far.

(1) "After being graduated from Harvard, Perkins worked for three months, in Boston, in a settlement house on Salem Street." (from a 1944 Profile of Maxwell Perkins by Malcolm Cowley)

(2) "When Uncle Ruka died, in 1916, he left me what would amount nowadays to a couple of million dollars and his country estate . . ." (from the 1948 reminiscence "Portrait of My Uncle" by Vladimir Nabokov)

In (1), the comma after *months* is meant to indicate that Perkins worked his three-month stint only in Boston; the one after *died,* in (2), that Uncle Ruka did not die at any other time besides 1916. But in both cases the meaning would be unmistakable without the commas, and copyeditors on no other publication would think to insert them. That the *New Yorker* did so was, ultimately, a stylistic affectation. It was noticeable only on a subliminal level in the above examples, but sometimes (generally in the case of undistinguished writers, who were heavily rewritten) it became blatant, almost to the point of self-parody. One sentence from a 1948 casual had seven commas in just forty-six words: "When I read, the other day, in the suburban-news section of a Boston newspaper, of the death of Mrs. Abigail Richardson Sawyer (as I shall call her), I was, for the moment, incredulous, for I had always thought of her as one of nature's indestructibles."

In a *Paris Review* interview, E. B. White remarked, "Commas in the *New Yorker* fall with the precision of knives in a circus act, outlining the victim."

In the forties, the adjective *sophisticated* was still reflexively being attached to the magazine. But in fact the literalness of the editing, the intolerance for the most minor solecism, ambiguity, or inaccuracy, even the requirement that the stories conform to the season—all seemed to presuppose ignorance or slow-wittedness on the part of the readers and thus represented something like the opposite of sophistication. Ironically, the cartoons—the entry point to the magazine for children and other new readers—achieved true sophistication more consistently than the text, since the better ones were based on inspirations that were not subject to clarification, explanation, or editorial "improvement."

If they understand anything, writers know that the world is not characterized by absolute clarity. And so *New Yorker* contributors could be expected to resist *New Yorker* editing. To be sure, the query system meant that no writer was compelled to assent to any particular change or suggestion, and the stronger-willed among them just said no, continually. In one Sally Benson story, a man happened to live in a mountainside cabin. To Ross's query "How he come to be living on mountainside?" Benson replied in pencil: "I don't know how he came to be living on a mountainside. This is just a story that I made up, and I didn't make up that part." But few writers have the patience or the stomach to go to battle over comma after comma in a story, or to resist each inserted explanatory passage. A number of contributors—including Kay Boyle, Jean Stafford, Peter Taylor, Elizabeth Taylor, Joseph Wechsberg, Vladimir Nabokov, and Roald Dahl—took the sensible route of generally acceding to the *New Yorker* editors' wishes and, when it came time to publish the story in book form, restored the original version.

And they and others exercised their right to complain, often with considerable ire and wit, as this sampling demonstrates:

> If Mr. Ross wants the house in "Conversation Piece" placed on the north side of 37th Street, and described in detail as a "large old-fashioned brownstone mansion, with a stoop," I'm afraid someone else will have to write that in for me, because I certainly don't see any sense in writing it in, as myself. I've placed the house in New York (as opposed to Jersey City) and even the most bewildered person in the world, in the sense of the person most prone to bewilderment ought to be able to read the rest in.
>
> —Louise Bogan to Wolcott Gibbs, March 28, 1933

> This is submitted with fear & trembling. I must refuse at the very outset to put a date-line on it, or tell what time of year it is, or the names of the parties involved, or anything else about it. It is so slight a piece that it has to be read in its entirety for it to have any point, and if Ross wants to make what is only a mood read like a Reporter piece, he can send it back.
>
> —John O'Hara to Wolcott Gibbs, 1935

> Somebody has taken liberties with my style that make my hair stand on end. My eye lit on "the pool, WHICH was round, deep [*sic*] and lined with cement," and I thought, "My God, have I done this after all!" Then I knew that, drunk, dreaming or unconscious, I could not have used this sentence structure. . . . I seriously doubt if you can find a single "which" or "who" in any one of my books, and I guarantee that you could not find a half dozen examples in everything I have written. This particular syntax is anathema to me. I think that any editing that makes for more complete articulation is good. Any editing that substitutes another's style and syntax for the author's is a shooting matter. Only distance prevented my going gunning for someone on your staff.
>
> —Marjorie Kinnan Rawlings to G. S. Lobrano,
> January 22, 1941

> Kay Boyle . . . says she's never been able to read a story of hers in the *New Yorker* because of the way we edited, etc. Says . . . that her books always specified that her original Mss. be used, not the reprint of the *New Yorker*, etc., etc., etc. Amazing.
>
> —Harold Ross to Katharine White, January 22, 1942

I'm sorry I can't see the proofs, as they almost inevitably cut out the best line of the story, besides changing delicately balanced sentences to make them sound more as if Geoffrey Hellman had written them.

—Irwin Shaw to his agent, Frances Pindyck, May 11, 1944,
on his story "Oh, to Be in England Now"

I guessed that it was a typo and that it would be caught, but from this distance and at this stage of the *New Yorker's* development, there was no telling whether it was a typo or a correction. Ten years ago I would have been reasonably sure it was a typo. Today, with pigeon-checking at the pitch it had reached, I can't be so sure. You may not realize it, not being a writer and con-

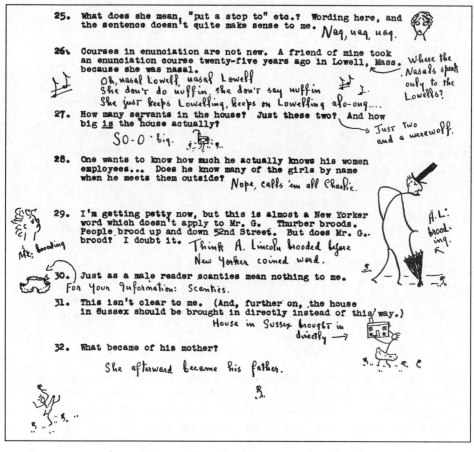

Frequent contributor Margaret Case Harriman wrote these facetious answers on a Ross query sheet.

tributor, but the impression the magazine now gives anyone turning stuff in, is that material will first be completely dismantled, then assembled again in the assembling plant. During the process, a full born squab will be reborn.

A writer loses confidence in himself. I am not as sure of myself as I used to be, and write rather timidly, staring at each word as it runs out, and wondering what is wrong with it. I don't know about editing, but my guess is that if the NYer ever reaches that degree of perfection toward which it is tending, when each word will have been taken aside and re-plated with silver, there won't be much left. I should not live 500 miles away and write about pigeons. It is too far away, and I know too much about pigeons.

> —E. B. White to Harold Ross, July 10, 1945,
>> after the word *hen* in a White Comment about pigeons
>> and squabs had been changed to *her*

The editors are so afraid of anything that is unusual, that is not expected, that they put a premium on insipidity and banality. I find, in the case of my own articles, that if I ever coin a phrase or strike off a picturesque metaphor, somebody always objects. Every first-rate writer invents and renews the language and many of the best writers have highly idiosyncratic styles, but almost no idiosyncratic writer ever gets into *The New Yorker*. Who can imagine Henry James or Bernard Shaw—or Dos Passos or Faulkner—in *The New Yorker*? The object here is as far as possible to iron all the writing out so that there will be nothing vivid or startling or personal in it. Sid Perelman is almost the sole exception, and I have never understood how he got by.

> —Edmund Wilson to Katharine White,
> November 12, 1947

I very much appreciate the system of tooth-comb checking, but have been wondering if there is a risk of destroying the author's personality, which, though it may seem faulty, *is* his personality. In fact, euphony . . . and inspiration might even escape. In India the Mohameddan has a way of leaving some slight imperfections in his work, to let out the evil eye. I feel that there is something in his philosophy. I should so much like to talk to you or Mr. Ross about it some day.

> —Rumer Godden to Katharine White, April 7, 1949

I was so goddamn bloody mad about the cutting and changing which was done in the first galley, and so discouraged by the attitude of magazine editors in general, that I have been unable to write anything since. I decided that I didn't want all the sorrow and heart boiling that editors cause, not any more any way, and I decided that I would give up whole time writing for the time being and earn my living as a bookmaker instead.

> —Roald Dahl to G. S. Lobrano, July 13, 1949

I am so glad you liked the story. I sent it in fear and trembling, remembering a previous occasion when Mr. Ross had queried a fire extinguisher as
being insufficiently accounted for, and thinking he might well ask for fuller
details about how the electricity ran along our vines.

—Sylvia Townsend Warner to G. S. Lobrano,

July 25, 1949

They really do want it, but I refuse to put in enough "he saids" and "she
saids" and "it was 4 p.m., a very hot summer, August 16, 1917. Great Village.
Nova Scotia, and my father's name was William Thomas Bishop"'s. . . . The
idea underneath it all seems to be that the *New Yorker* reader must never have
to pause to think for a single second, but be informed and reinforced com-
fortingly all the time, like newspaper writing a little.

—Elizabeth Bishop to Pearl Kazin, February 10, 1955,

about her story "In the Village"

Reaching a Wider World

New York City after the Second World War was a special place—like New
York after the First World War, only more so. Jan Morris has written an
entire book based on the premise that the city—specifically, the borough of
Manhattan—was in 1945 "entering a splendid fulfillment. This was not only
bound to be, in the postwar years, the supreme and symbolical American
city. All the signs were that it would be the supreme city of the Western
world, or even the world as a whole." Economically, the city was flush as
never before, as the pent-up demand of the war seemed to explode all at
once into a near-frenzy of spending, building, and hiring. The *New Yorker*
had a running start for this economic sprint. Between the end of 1941 and
the middle of 1945, circulation increased 32 percent, from 172,000 to
227,000—especially impressive considering that, unlike most other magazines, the *New Yorker* offered only minimal discounts on subscriptions; that
the magazine spent negligible amounts on circulation promotion (a total of
$5,000 in 1942, for example); and that during the war years, a significant
segment of the magazine's potential readership was getting it for free,
through the Pony edition. After the war, circulation shot up by close to 10
percent a year, reaching 370,000 by the end of 1952. And now, the circulation growth was accompanied by substantial gains in advertising and profits.
Total ad pages, stalled at the 2,200–2,300 level between 1938 and 1943,
jumped to 3,157 in 1946 and 3,619 in 1951.

As Morris says, New York was becoming, for the first time, a truly international city. Most dramatically, the United Nations was rising before citi-

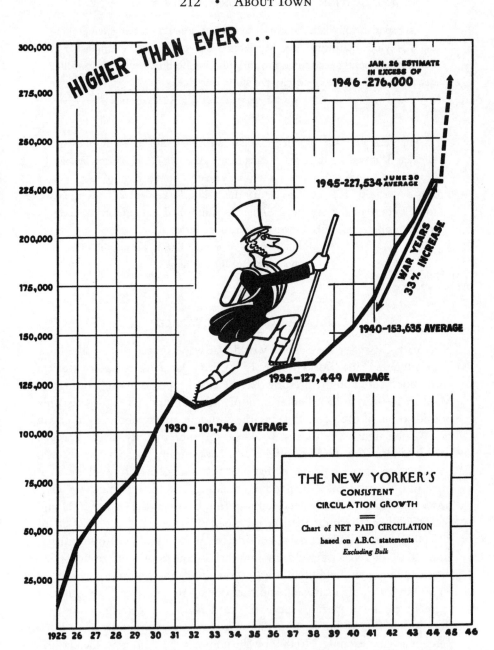

A chart from a 1946 promotional pamphlet graphically depicted the magazine's success. Circulation would continue to grow until the 1960s, when it topped out at close to 500,000.

zens' eyes on a plot of land overlooking the East River; it would open for business in 1949. Sixth Avenue was rechristened Avenue of the Americas in 1946, and two years later Idlewild (now Kennedy) International Airport opened as the city's new gateway to the world. Where the years following World War I saw a migration to New York from the rest of the United States, hundreds of intellectuals, scholars, and artists—including Albert Einstein, Thomas Mann, Aldous Huxley, Christopher Isherwood, W. H. Auden, George Balanchine, Bertolt Brecht, Igor Stravinsky, Béla Bártok, Vladimir Nabokov, Ferenc Molnár, Walter Gropius, Marcel Breuer, Hannah Arendt, Theodor Adorno, Piet Mondrian, Salvador Dalí, and Marc Chagall—came to the United States, and in most cases to New York, from the rest of the world in the years before, during, and after World War II. The arrivals gave new vigor and breadth to the country's cultural discourse, and the impetus to at least two vital institutions in the city: the New School for Social Research and the New York City Ballet.

All sorts of homegrown tremors were being felt in the arts, and the new movements were all centered in New York. Such youthful visionaries as Jackson Pollock, Robert Motherwell,* Dizzy Gillespie, Charlie Parker, Miles Davis, John Cage, Merce Cunningham, Allen Ginsberg, and Jack Kerouac were all being intensely creative within a few miles of one another. The Broadway stage, meanwhile, was experiencing a rare and happy confluence of creativity and commercialism, with the early successes of Tennessee Williams, Arthur Miller, and Rodgers and Hammerstein. A musical like *On the Town* (1944), with score by Leonard Bernstein, choreography by Jerome Robbins, and book and lyrics by the cabaret performers Betty Comden and Adolph Green, seemed to suggest exciting new possibilities for the mixing of the "high" and "low" arts; naturally, in the show, they were played out on the streets of New York. All of a sudden a flock of French restaurants opened for business in Manhattan. The fledgling medium of television, with its attendant excitement, was based in New York as well. Even the national pastime of baseball seemed to be giving the city its blessing, as the New York Yankees won pennant after pennant and, across the river, the Brooklyn Dodgers changed the very nature of the sport in 1947 by putting an African-American ballplayer, Jackie Robinson, on the field for the first time. In 1948, E. B. White wrote a long essay called "Here Is New York" for *Holiday* magazine, later published as a book, where he spoke in almost mystical terms: "The city is like poetry: it compresses all life, all races and breeds, into a small island and adds music and the accompaniment of internal engines. The island of Manhattan is without any doubt the greatest human concentrate on earth, the poem

---

New Yorker art critic Robert Coates was responsible for coining the term *abstract expressionism*.

whose magic is comprehensible to millions of permanent residents but whose full meaning will always remain illusive."

The British critic Cyril Connolly, writing about a visit to New York in November 1947 for *Horizon* magazine, felt the city was "unending delight":

> The shops, the bars, the women, the faces in the street, the excellent and innumerable restaurants, the glitter of Twenty-one, the old-world lethargy of the Lafayette, the hazy view of the East River or Central Park over tea in some apartment at the magic hour when the concrete icebergs suddenly flare up; the impressionist pictures in one house, the exotic trees or bamboo furniture in another, the chink of "old-fashioneds" with their little glass pestles, the divine glories—Egyptian, Etruscan, French—of the Metropolitan Museum, the felicitous contemporary assertion of the Museum of Modern Art, the snow, the sea-breezes, the late suppers with the Partisans, the reelings-home down the black steam-spitting canyons, the Christmas trees lit up beside the licorice ribbon of cars on Park Avenue, the Gotham Book Mart, the shabby coziness of the Village, all go to form an unforgettable picture of what a city ought to be: that is, continuously insolent and alive, a place where one can buy a book or meet a friend at any hour of the day or night, where every language is spoken and xenophobia almost unknown, where every purse and appetite is catered for, where every street and every quarter and the people who inhabit them are fulfilling their function, not slipping back into apathy, indifference, decay.

Connolly singled out the *New Yorker,* along with *Time* and *Life,* as magazines that "only just miss out being completely honorable and serious journals, in fact 'highbrow'" and as indicating "how very nearly New York has achieved the ideal of a humanist society, where the best of which an artist is capable is desired by the greatest number. Thurber's drawings, Hersey's *Hiroshima,* the essays of Edmund Wilson or Mary McCarthy, *Time's* anonymous reviews, show that occasionally the gap *is* closed."

By this time, more than two-thirds of the *New Yorker's* readers lived outside the New York metropolitan area, but even as the magazine continued to publish Manhattan theater, art, nightlife, and movie listings in Goings On About Town, it still drew its core energy from the city. And the postwar zeitgeist was invigorating. The most obvious artistic manifestation was a flowering of fiction. The following writers all published their first stories in the *New Yorker* in the years spanning the end of World War II and the death of Harold Ross, in late 1951: Jean Stafford, Peter Taylor, Elizabeth Taylor, Roald Dahl, Vladimir Nabokov, V. S. Pritchett, Rumer Godden, Rhys Davies, Frank O'Connor, Niccolo Tucci, J. D. Salinger, Eudora Welty, Jessamyn West, Nadine Gordimer, Hortense Calisher, and J. F. Powers. (Mary McCarthy and Shirley Jackson both published frequently in this period as well, but broke in a couple of years earlier.) As a result of all this momentum, the magazine became—as it would be ever after—the most sought-after literary showplace in the country. An appearance in the *New Yorker* could launch a career; Gordimer, a young South African, was signed up by Simon and Schuster on the basis of one story in the magazine. On average, more than three hundred short stories arrived hopefully in the office each week (as well as more than seven hundred Newsbreaks). In 1945, a classified ad in the *New York Times* seeking a promotion writer specified that there was *no* interest in "a frustrated *New Yorker* short story writer."

One factor contributing to this remarkable showing was the return of Katharine White in 1943. Just as Gus Lobrano pushed the magazine to a new place in the late thirties, so did Mrs. White (though now officially Lobrano's subordinate in the fiction department) in the middle and late forties. During her time away, she assiduously read the literary quarterlies and concluded that the *New Yorker* could and should print the best short fiction it could get its hands on. Her idea of the "perfect *New Yorker* writer" was Jane Austen, which gives an idea of the strengths and limitations of her taste. She did not look kindly on any manner of experimentation or abstraction (in form) or on depictions of classes lower than the upper-middle (in subject matter). The authors she responded to tended to be women and/or British, or, if American males, then ones who valued close attention to subtleties of manner, mood, and behavior. (Peter Taylor, J. F. Powers, and later, John Updike are examples.) Yet she knew her own blind spots and ceded authors to whom she was unsympathetic to other editors. She had more than enough on her plate, in any case. At one point, in 1947 and 1948, she was simultaneously courting or cultivating West, Tucci, Elizabeth Bishop, Pritchett, George Orwell, Elizabeth Hardwick, Stafford, Calisher, Elizabeth *and* Peter Taylor, and Godden.

She and William Maxwell worked wonderfully together, but there was occasional tension with Lobrano, who was more comfortable dealing with men and had an ingrained resistance to the highbrow stuff Mrs. White favored. Both editors were too well-mannered to express public irritation with each other, but White did observe, years after Lobrano's death (in 1956), "It was awkward for him that I had to reappear at that point. Ross would sometimes consult me for an opinion on a manuscript after Lobrano had sent it to him. Sometimes I would agree with Lobrano's opinion and sometimes not, and this must have been very trying for him, but it was not my fault." Their personal feelings aside, they and Maxwell, with Ross as a final watchdog making sure that every fictional emperor was clothed, made a formidable team.

At roughly the same time that Katharine White returned, Edmund Wilson came on as literary critic. Wilson was esteemed for his books *To the Fin-*

land Station, The Shock of Recognition, and *The Wound and the Bow,* but in 1942 was financially strapped and proposed to Ross that the *New Yorker* underwrite a new literary magazine "and make me editor." Nothing came of this idea, but the following year, when Clifton Fadiman stepped down as book critic, Ross offered Wilson the position (described by Bennett Cerf as "the most highly prized of its kind in the country"), telling him, "You seem to be the only man [for the job], standing alone among the possibilities like a large, isolated mountain." With flattery on that level—and a salary of $8,000 a year, plus $3,000 for living expenses—how could Wilson not accept?*

Wilson was a critic the likes of which the magazine had never seen. He believed in writing for general readers and had no truck with academic jargon—he had been a working journalist with *Vanity Fair* and the *New Republic*—but he would make no compromises for any audience in his standards or his range of allusion and reference. Unlike any previous *New Yorker* critic, with the exception of Louise Bogan and Lewis Mumford, his base assumption was that what mattered in any work under question was its artistry, not its capacity to entertain, amuse, or divert. He was particularly devastating on the polished but empty writing that had come to be called middlebrow and was presumably dear to the hearts of a great many *New Yorker* subscribers. His most notorious essay, "Who Cares Who Killed Roger Aykroyd?" published on January 20, 1945, took aim at that favorite recreation of the educated class, the detective story. Three years later he dissected a popular author with a fairly high literary reputation; the first paragraph gives a good sense of his style and method:

> It has happened to me from time to time to run into some person of taste who tells me that I ought to take Somerset Maugham seriously, yet I have never been able to convince myself that he is anything but second-rate. His swelling reputation in America, which culminated the other day in his solemn presentation to the Library of Congress of the manuscript of *Of*

---

*Before accepting the position, Wilson told Ross that his main concern was that his copy would be changed: "I should like to have it stipulated that *The New Yorker* will print what I write unless it chooses to suppress my articles or me altogether." His contract stated: "It is understood that you will read each week a proof of your book review article and shall give consideration to any questions raised by this office in the matters of style, obscurity, obscenity, fact, etc., but it is likewise agreed that *The New Yorker* will advertently make no change in your writings without your consent." Even with this stipulation, there were problems. Shortly after Wilson began, Ross wrote to Mrs. White, "There is nothing to be done about Wilson's editing that I know of. He is by far the biggest problem we ever had around here. Fights like a tiger, or holds the line like an elephant. Only course is to let him peter out, I guess."

Human Bondage, seems to me a conspicuous sign of the general decline of our standards. Thirty or thirty-five years ago the English novelists that were read in America were at least men like Wells and Bennett, who, though not quite of the top rank, were at least by vocation really writers. Mr. Maugham, I cannot help feeling, is not, in the sense of "having the métier," really a writer at all. There are real writers, like Balzac and Dreiser, who may be said to write badly. Dreiser handles words abominably, but his prose has a compelling rhythm, which is his style and which induces the emotions that give his story its poetic meaning. But Mr. Maugham, whose language is always banal, has not even an interesting rhythm.

Wilson's high standards and intellectual rigor set the model for subsequent *New Yorker* book criticism, and in the late forties, when the pace of his reviews slackened somewhat, he was spotted on various occasions by such estimable critics as Cyril Connelly, Alfred Kazin, Anthony West, Harold Laski, Lionel Trilling, and George Orwell.

The case could be made that Wilson's British counterpart was Rebecca West (Anthony's mother), and she formed a close association with the *New Yorker* at this time as well. She had contributed occasionally over the years, but a new phase began in 1945, when Ross sent her a terse cable asking her to cover the treason trial of William Joyce, who during the war had broadcast pro-German radio programs under the name Lord Haw-Haw. West's dispatch (subsequently included in her book *The Meaning of Treason*) struck a new note for the magazine's reportage: it was dense, meditative, and highly intelligent, yet grounded in the facts. You would not think of it as Ross's kind of thing, yet he was highly impressed. "Your reportorial instinct amazes me, and your thoroughness," he wrote West the next year. "It is a thing of wonder. You have exactly the right idea as to how to get such stories as you have been writing, which is to follow developments through thoroughly from start to finish and know the background and all the developments. No working reporters these days know that that is the way to cover a story. They drop around occasionally and hit the thing a couple of slap dashes, and that is that." It would be hard to imagine two individuals less alike than Ross and West, but they would form a close friendship, cemented in 1947 when she came to the United States, stayed with him in his house in Connecticut, and covered a South Carolina lynching trial for the *New Yorker* in her inimitable style.

Another factor in the new sense of the magazine as a literary institution was money. The rates the magazine had paid fiction writers had long been strikingly low, and as Ross wrote Fleischmann in a 1943 memo, "I am certain that the time has come to let the contributors share in the comparative prosperity." He initially proposed an across-the-board 10 percent increase but dropped that in favor of a scheme proposed by Lobrano: giving a bonus to writers who sold more than a set number of pieces to the magazine in a given year. Ross told Fleischmann he thought this idea was

> one of the brightest generated around this joint for some time. It has many beauties, some of which can be appreciated only by those in direct contact with the writers. The principal beauties are that it will give writers a chance to set a goal for themselves and budget themselves over a considerable period of time, that it will provide an incentive for them to work for the *New Yorker* as opposed to doing other work, and that it will assure a greater degree of continuity of interest among writers and thereby increase their output. Giving freelance writers a feeling of security is one of the greatest problems of this business, and indeed, of American letters in general.

By signing the first-reading "agreement" (Mrs. White once commented to Ross that she preferred the word *agreement,* "especially in talking to writers, rather than *contract,* which has a foreboding sound, it seems to me"), a contributor promised to give the *New Yorker* the right of first refusal on all "fiction, humor, reminiscence, and casual essays." In return, the magazine agreed, first, to pay an annual signing bonus—generally, in the 1940s, several hundred dollars—and then to pay 25 percent more than a specified minimum word rate for each accepted piece. In addition, if the writer sold six or more pieces within a twelve-month period, an additional 25 percent was added to the total payment. Finally, there was an automatic cost-of-living adjustment calibrated to the index of the U.S. Department of Labor.*

Jean Stafford was a typical new contributor in that she came to the *New Yorker,* in 1947, with an already established reputation, having published two novels and a number of short stories in literary quarterlies. As the wife (soon to be ex-wife) of the poet Robert Lowell, she was also a member in good standing of the literary establishment. She signed a first-reader agreement after Mrs. White bought the story "A Summer Day" in 1947, and she went on to bring the magazine an unaccustomed, sometimes Jamesian, psychological depth in such stories as "Children Are Bored on Sunday," "A

---

*The system was even more complicated than it seemed, if that can be believed. To begin with, each writer had a minimum rate, but depending on an individual story's merit, that rate could go up at the discretion of his or her editor. According to a *New Yorker* document from 1950, a story could be classified anywhere from AAA ("36 & 18") to D+ ("12 & 6"). The two figures after the grade reflected that, in an effort to discourage long-windedness, the magazine paid twice as much per word up to a set point in a story. Initially, it paid the higher rate for the first twelve hundred words, the lower rate for the remainder. The "bogey" was subsequently increased to fifteen hundred words, then to two thousand. In 1949 the scheme was modified so that in stories of more than four thousand words, the higher rate would be paid for the first half of the piece.

Country Love Story," and "The Echo and the Nemesis." Somewhat surprisingly, Ross was a great admirer of hers. His query sheet for one her
stories began, "This story seems to me positively terrific—moving, heart-
rending, brilliant." (He added: "I'm intimidated to a considerable degree by
my admiration for it, but I will respectfully make one suggestion on a structural point.") Stafford also became Katharine White's closest friend among
contributors and, in the late fifties, the wife of A. J. Liebling. Initially she was
paid a $100 annual bonus for signing, with a minimum rate of "18 & 9,"
meaning eighteen cents a word for the first two thousand words and nine
cents a word thereafter. "A Summer Day" totaled some sixty-seven hundred
words, which at the word rate added up to $780; her fee was rounded up to
$800, which the 25 percent first-reading agreement bonus increased to
$1,000. She was subsequently sent a cost-of-living adjustment of $200. And
she was able to sell five additional stories a year—actually, 375 days, but the
magazine was typically flexible—earning her an additional $250 for "A
Summer Day," for a total of $1,450.

For the first time, writers could make a decent amount of money from
New Yorker short stories—especially if their word rate was high and they
tended to write long. (Probably the biggest earner was Irwin Shaw, whose
rate in 1945 was 34 & 15, and who continued to knock Profiles and
Reporters at Large out of the magazine with his sprawling fiction.) But just
as important, as Ross recognized, was that the system engendered a sense of
loyalty and belonging among the magazine's fiction contributors. Much
more than it had been before, it was possible to say that fiction as well as fact
contributors were "*New Yorker* writers." A graphic recognition of this was on
the back cover of Stafford's collected short stories: a drawing of the author is
superimposed over a collage of tear sheets of her stories as printed in the
New Yorker.

Prompted by the war to direct its attention to the wider world, the *New
Yorker* did not stop in peace. Of the new group, only Salinger, Calisher,
Stafford, and McCarthy had the traditional profile of *New Yorker* contributors, the first two Manhattan natives and the others Americans from the
provinces—in Stafford's case, Colorado, and in McCarthy's, the state of
Washington—who had settled in New York City. The rest were either residents of various outposts of the British empire, émigrés in the United States
(Nabokov and Tucci), or regional American writers who paid little or no
heed to New York (Welty, Powers, West, and Peter Taylor).

(A similar, though less dramatic, opening up was taking place in factual
writing. Before the war, a "Letter" could only emanate from Paris or London; now they poured in from every continent, in the hands of a new group
of peripatetic correspondents that included Joseph Wechsberg, Alan Moorehead, Robert Shaplen, and Christopher Rand. The magazine's domestic

journalism likewise broadened its gaze away from New York, most notice-ably in Richard Rovere's Washington letter, begun at Shawn's suggestion in 1948.)

The magazine and its more exotic new voices tended to meet on some thematic or stylistic common ground and to proceed in mutually beneficial new directions. For the Irish writer Michael O'Donovan, who used the pen name Frank O'Connor, the meeting point was the first person, familiar from the early monologues of Arthur Kober and John O'Hara to all the reminiscence pieces of the thirties and forties. In 1945, O'Connor's career was at a low ebb; without his knowledge, his wife sent a short story called "News for the Church" to the *New Yorker,* which accepted it. The magazine would go on to print a total of forty-five O'Connor contributions, the last one appearing in 1967, the year after his death; his great personal and pro-fessional friendship with William Maxwell is documented in a collection of their letters to each other, *The Happiness of Getting It Down Right.* His stories would expand the *New Yorker's* fictional palette, with their complex narra-tive voice, so commanding in its modulation from humor to poignancy to irony, but they were so quickly and enthusiastically accepted because they were also colorful and charming.

The process was similar for two other important new contributors, Peter Taylor and Vladimir Nabokov, but not as easy or fast. In 1943, Maxwell wrote to Taylor, a young southern writer whose work had been appearing in the *Kenyon Review* and other literary quarterlies, saying, "Your story in the last O'Brien collection seemed head and shoulders above most of the others, and we wonder if you have any unpublished manuscripts which might work out for *The New Yorker*." Taylor, who was in the army at the time, was somewhat irked by this letter, since the very story Maxwell referred to, "The Fancy Woman," had been submitted to and rejected by the *New Yorker.* But he swallowed his pride and sent in "Supper," which was set in his native Tennessee. Maxwell rejected it, explaining, "The story belongs to a world that is essentially remote from New York City. The edi-tors have in their minds an imaginary map of Manhattan which includes, strangely, all of Connecticut and Long Island, Florida, New Jersey, Holly-wood, and wherever New Yorkers go. Since naturally a great many New Yorkers go into the army, the army is a wide open subject, and we have been hoping that you would see your way clear to do some army stories for us." In a lifetime of inspired editorial counsel, this would have to rank as one of Maxwell's less fortunate suggestions: what Dublin was to Joyce, the small, fading, and socially intricate world of the Tennessee gentry was to Taylor, and for him to attempt barracks episodes would probably have been disastrous.

Five years later, the "imaginary map" no longer held sway. In 1948, Taylor published his first book, *A Long Fourth and Other Stories,* and completed his first novel, *A Woman of Means.* His editor at Harcourt, Brace and Company, Robert Giroux, sent a portion of the latter manuscript to Katharine White, who found nothing in it that could be excerpted but asked Giroux to tell Taylor "we very, very much hope he will want to write short stories for us eventually." Within weeks Taylor sent in "Middle Age," a story set around a dinner table, in which the profound rifts between a southern doctor and his wife are revealed when their black cook lets out a dark secret about the husband. In accepting the story, which was titled "Cookie" when reprinted in book form, Mrs. White said not a word about the remoteness of the setting. She merely, and typically, noted that Ross had felt that the nature of the scandalous information about the husband was not "clean cut" enough and asked Taylor to "clarify" it. Indeed, Taylor later commented that he felt the *New Yorker* actually *wanted* "pieces concerned with regional differences," and his stories' main appeal to the magazine was that they were "attempts to represent life in the cities and towns of the upper South."

In any case, for the *New Yorker's* editors and readers, "Middle Age" represented a felicitous introduction to Taylor's unusual world, concerns, and voice. The tensions between servants and employers was a familiar theme for the magazine, with the employers invariably shown at a disadvantage; and "Middle Age" had both a brevity and a clear-cut resolution that were rather uncharacteristic for Taylor. The eight stories he sold the magazine over the next three years, including "Porte-Cochere," "Their Losses," "What You Hear from 'Em?" "Two Ladies in Retirement," and "A Wife of Nashville," were longer and less immediately accessible, and while Mrs. White and Lobrano, who shared duties as Taylor's editor, invariably pressed him to make his meaning clearer, he complied only to the point where his own sure subtlety would not be compromised. "Porte-Cochere," about the emotional gap between an old Nashville widower and his grown children, ended, in Taylor's original manuscript, with the man remembering back to the unhappiness inflicted on his childhood by his tyrant of a father. Mrs. White wrote Taylor, "Can't you add a paragraph or two of direct narrative (not memories) in order to return the reader to the progress of the story and also to explain what was on old Ben's mind in remembering the childhood episode." Taylor wrote three new paragraphs, including a final image—the old man picking up a walking stick with his father's face carved on the head, "and in the darkness, while he heard his children's voices, he stumbled about the room beating the upholstered chairs with the stick and calling the names of his children under his breath"—that left no doubt as to the story's meaning. But in his cover letter to Mrs. White he drew a kind of line in the sand: "I don't like a story that is too explicit, and I believe any more than is in the present ending would limit the story's meaning. This is the way the story was planned originally, but I was afraid the melodrama at the end would drive the point home too hard."

His next submission, originally titled "A Woman of Nashville" and later changed to "A Wife of Nashville," would have to be included in any list of the great American short stories of the century. Like "Middle Age" and "Porte-Cochere," it is about the disconnectedness between people. But where those stories treat the theme directly and "explicitly," "A Wife of Nashville," twenty-seven pages long in manuscipt, takes leisurely and ellip-tical orbits around it, finally coming to a muted conclusion, in which the title character, Helen Ruth, contemplates the unbridgeable "gulf" between people and "the loneliness from which everybody, knowingly or unknow-ingly, suffered." The nature of her understanding, and the social strictures of her world, prevent her from expressing these things directly, and the story ends as "her husband and her three sons sat staring at her, their big hands, all so alike, resting on the breakfast table, their faces stamped with identical expressions, not of wonder but of incredulity."

As in the case of S. J. Perelman fifteen years earlier, one can almost feel in the editors' responses a creaking broadening of their appreciation of the varieties of the fictional experience. In Mrs. White's initial reply to Taylor, she told him that the story in its present form "is, of course, out of bounds for us on length." However, she said, "There is a very great deal in the story that interests us greatly, a lot of particularly good writing, but what we do *not* feel sure of is your ultimate point. . . . Is the 'gulf' Helen Ruth refers to in the last paragraph merely the gulf between Negro and White or is it something far more complex such as the gulf between Helen Ruth and her husband's more elaborate world? . . . The story as a whole seems to lack focus and leave the reader puzzled."

Taylor responded generously: "Helen Ruth is, of course, speaking of the gulf between Negroes and white people, but my story is one of the gulf between a woman and her servants and a corresponding gulf between the woman and her husband. . . . Mainly I was telling the story of a woman in a society where man exploits woman and woman exploits her black servant. So far as Helen Ruth's intelligence and sensibility allowed her she came to understand her situation—their situation."

The exegesis smoothed the path to the story's acceptance. With Mrs. White in Maine for the summer, Lobrano took up the correspondence, writing, "The story seemed to me, on second reading, to be even more admirable than I had thought after the first reading," helpfully noting some ways Taylor could point up his meaning, but observing, "I am selfishly dis-couraged (since a story of this length is so extremely difficult for us to han-dle) about the possibility, or rather the desirability, of making any extensive cuts." Taylor took the suggestions in good spirit, made slight amendments, but told Lobrano he simply could not make substantial cuts, and therefore, "I think that I should withdraw the story." There is no carbon of Lobrano's response in the *New Yorker* Records, raising the possibility that Taylor's veiled threat may have sent him to the telephone. Whatever the case, he and his fellow editors ultimately decided to accept "A Wife of Nashville" in something close to its original form.* As published in the magazine on December 3, 1949, it ran to almost ten thousand words—longer than any other short story that had ever appeared in the *New Yorker*. Less than two years later, Taylor would break the record with the fourteen-thousand-word "Two Ladies in Retirement." (He held it only eight more months before Eudora Welty took possession with "The Bride of the Inisfallen," for which she was paid what she considered the "stupefying" amount of $2,760.)

With Nabokov, the period of adjustment was rougher and more protracted still. Born in St. Petersburg, Russia, in 1899, he had lived in exile since the Russian Revolution, first as a student at Cambridge University, then in Germany and France. He had developed a substantial reputation as a novelist, publishing in Russian under the name Vladimir Sirin, but after immigrating to the United States in 1940, he determined that he would henceforth write in English and as himself. He sold several fictional pieces to the *Atlantic* and, in 1942, a humorous poem called "The Refrigerator Awakes"—only the second poem he had ever written in English—to the *New Yorker*. He followed this with a half dozen others, but his true association with the magazine dated from Mrs. White's return from Maine. Edmund Wilson, who had become one of Nabokov's first and (for a time) best friends in America, wrote him early in 1944, "One of the ideas she came back with was to get you to do stories for them. She had torn out all your things in the *Atlantic*—is very anxious to meet you." In June, before Nabokov had even submitted a manuscript, she offered a first-reader agreement, with an advance of $500 against future fees. She rejected his first submission, "A Forgotten Poet," reasonably explaining that *New Yorker* readers would not recognize it "as a sort of literary hoax." But Mrs. White, and the unnamed other editors whose opinions she cited, completely failed to appreciate Nabokov's second submission, "Time and Ebb." Set in the year 2024, it is a memoir by a ninety-year-old Jewish scientist looking back on the strangeness of his childhood in America in the 1940s. It was an ingenious, and ultimately moving, way of extracting and presenting the strange magic of contemporary life, but Mrs. White had it all wrong: "These projections into the future have been done so often by would-be

---

*Ross saw it in galleys and suggested a small but critical change in the plot, to which Taylor assented.

American satirists that, by now, the reader demands something very unusual in the way of prophesy and of comment on our own age when it is presented in this particular form. One thing in your piece which we all feel hampers its effect is its mock learned style, which you use, of course, for comedy, but which sometimes, in spite of its being parody, becomes rather heavy reading."

Nabokov replied (the quotations marks punching out his irritation at being wrongheadedly patronized):

> I am a little shocked by your readers' having so completely missed the point of my story. Apart from that, I quite fail to see how it may be confused with the "projections into the future made by would-be American satirists" since there is no projection and not the faintest trace of satire in my story— either "half-exposed" or otherwise. For all I know or care the 21st century may be less "enlightened" than our time, which may or may not be "crude" etc.—but again all this has nothing whatever to do with the point of the story.
>
> I shall certainly continue to show you the things I happen to write.

Soon after this exchange, Nabokov met Katharine and E. B. White at a party at Edmund Wilson's apartment in New York. The immediate mutual sympathy felt by the highly refined and intelligent author and editor eased their subsequent professional relationship, and the *New Yorker* bought Nabokov's next submission, "Double Talk" (retitled "Conversation Piece, 1945" in Nabokov story collections). In it, the narrator, an émigré Russian writer who shares the same name and nickname of a notorious anti-Semite, is mistakenly invited to a party attended by an appalling group of apologists for Nazi Germany. Other than the intriguing doppelgänger theme, it was one of Nabokov's slighter and more conventional efforts, but that, along with the familiar cocktail-party setting, probably smoothed the path to acceptance. In any case, the pleasure Nabokov felt at the sale—and at receiving a check for $812.50, far more than he had ever been paid for a story— were tempered when he saw what the editors wanted to do with his manuscript. He wrote Wilson with the good news. "Unfortunately," he continued,

> a man called Ross started to "edit" it, and I wrote to Mrs. White telling her that I could not accept *any* of those ridiculous and exasperating alterations (odds and ends inserted in order to "link up" ideas and make them clear to the "average reader"). Nothing like it has ever happened to me in my life and I was on the point of calling the deal off when they suddenly yielded and, except for one little "bridge" which Mrs. White asked as a personal favour, the story is more or less intact. I am always quite willing to have my grammar

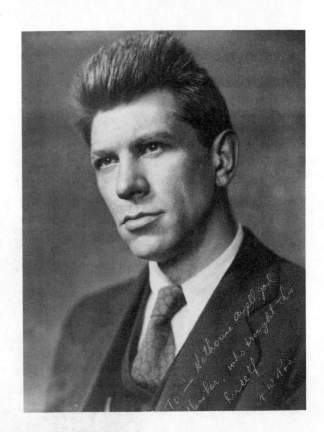

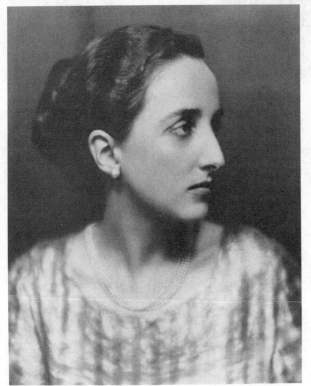

In the early years, putting out the *New Yorker* was a two-person job, and the two persons were Harold Ross and Katharine Angell (known as Katharine White after her marriage to E. B. White). Ross inscribed the above photo, taken in 1927 or thereabouts, "To Katharine Angell, God bless her, who brought this on herself."

In its first decade, the *New Yorker* was first and foremost a humor magazine. Its two reigning geniuses were E. B. White and James Thurber, shown here in 1929.

Below, another prolific comic writer, Frank Sullivan, in an inscrutable gag shot Harold Ross saved in his personal files.

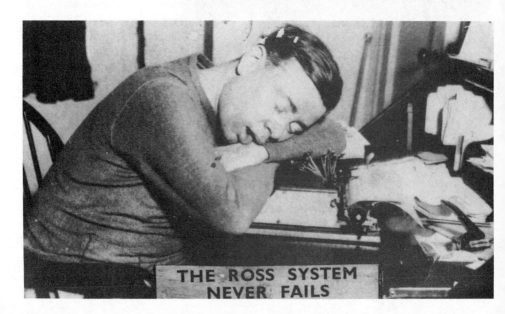

THE ROSS SYSTEM
NEVER FAILS

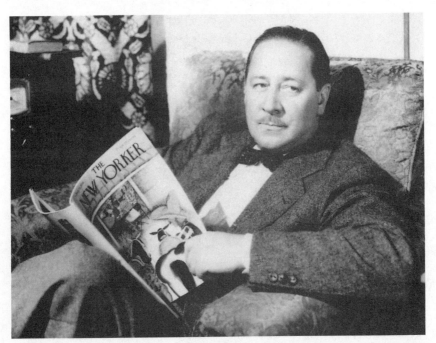

It would be hard to overstate Robert Benchley's importance to the young magazine. He was its drama critic from 1929 to 1940, he wrote the Wayward Press column (under the pen name Guy Fawkes), he contributed scores of comic essays, and he was even willing to pose for publicity photographs with the merchandise in hand.

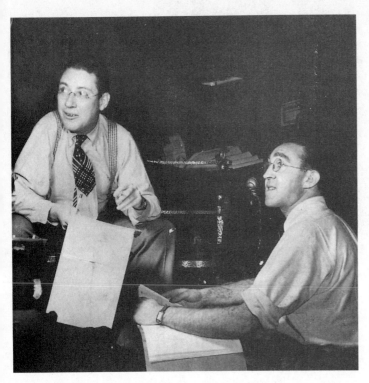

The two key members of the second wave of humorists were Ogden Nash (left) and S. J. Perelman. They are shown here during their collaboration on the 1943 musical comedy *One Touch of Venus*.

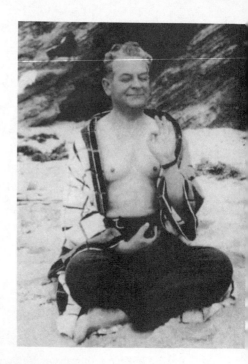

Under the supervision of Ross and art director Rea Irvin (shown posing as the Buddha, for reasons lost to history), the cartoon became the magazine's first major contribution to American culture. Peter Arno (*below*) made his mark with the pixillated Whoops Sisters, then developed the energetic line, impeccable composition, and randy old men that placed him at the head of the first rank of *New Yorker* artists.

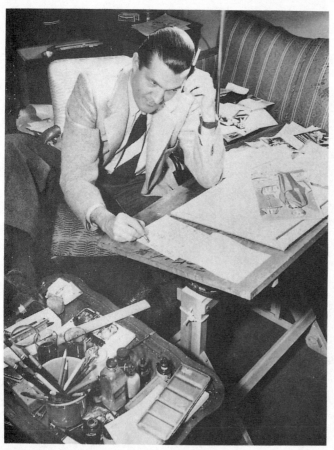

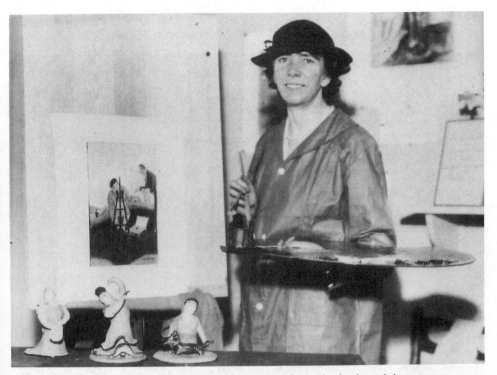

Helen Hokinson was the graphic chronicler of round suburban clubwomen; this 1934 photograph depicts the small glazed figures she sometimes used as models.

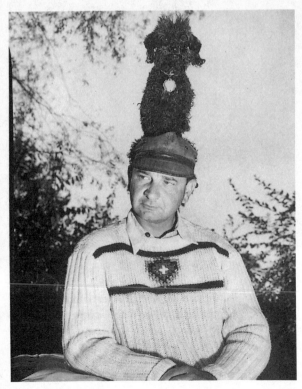

A dog sits on Charles Addams's head. Addams's attitude toward this state of affairs recalls the way the characters in his wonderful cartoons matter-of-factly confronted the uncanny and the macabre.

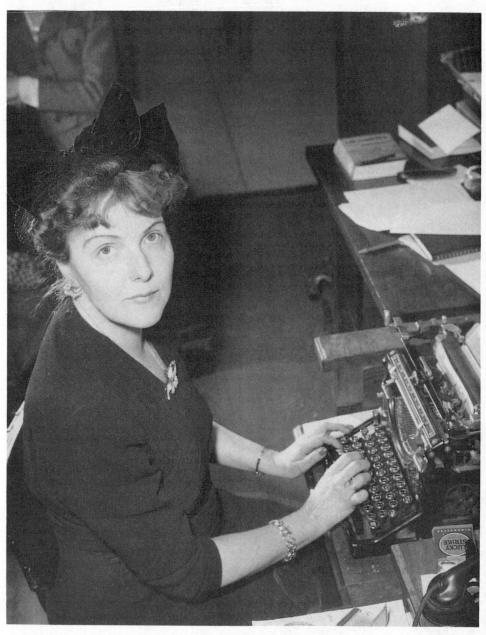

Sally Benson sold so many sharp and merciless short stories to the *New Yorker* over a twenty-five-year period that she had to publish some of them under a pen name, Esther Evarts. Benson's *New Yorker* series, Junior Miss and Meet Me in St. Louis, gave her the Hollywood connections to develop a second career as a screenwriter. Among her credits were Alfred Hitchcock's *Shadow of a Doubt* and Elvis Presley's *Viva Las Vegas*.

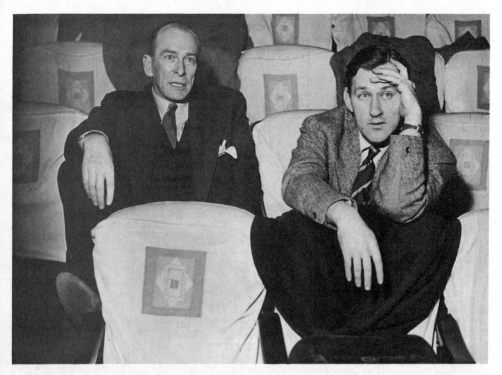

Some of the more memorable of the hundred-odd stories contributed to the magazine by John O'Hara concerned a heel of a nightclub owner known as Pal Joey. In 1940, O'Hara collaborated with Rodgers and Hart on a Broadway musical based on the series. Here, O'Hara (right) and director George Abbott conduct auditions.

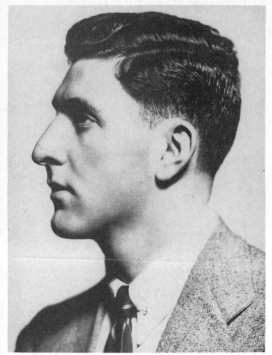

Irwin Shaw in 1936, at the age of twenty-three. He was not long out of Brooklyn College, his play *Bury the Dead* had just made a big hit on Broadway, and he was about to reinvent the *New Yorker* short story.

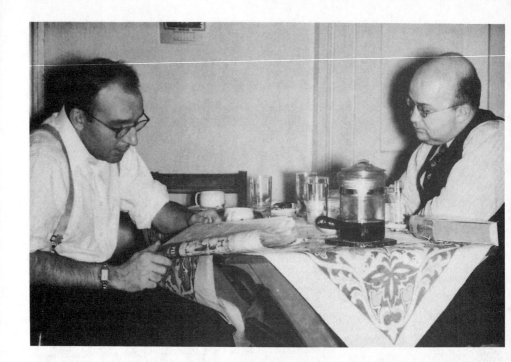

The standard-bearers of *New Yorker* journalism from the late 1930s to the early 1960s were Joseph Mitchell and A. J. Liebling. They were also each other's best friend and liked to spend time together in and out of the office. In the cozy breakfast scene, photographed by Mitchell's wife, Therese, Liebling is on the right. *(Right)* Mitchell, who came to New York from North Carolina as a young man and immediately fell in love with the city, strikes a classic reporter's pose.

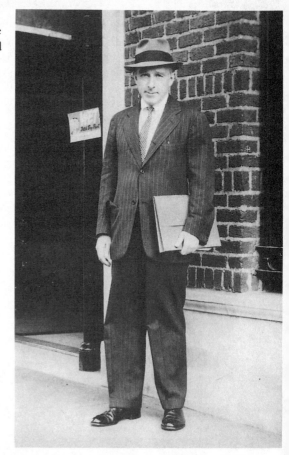

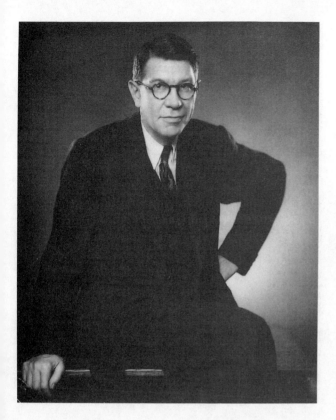

Two 1940s photographs: a formal portrait of Harold Ross and Lillian Ross's rooftop snapshot of William Shawn, who had risen from freelance reporter to managing editor, and who would become editor after Ross's death in 1951.

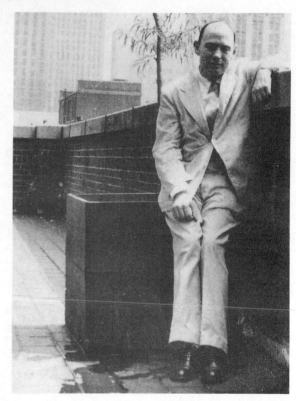

One writer who did superb work for the *New Yorker* in the 1950s was Vladimir Nabokov; substantial portions of his books *Speak, Memory* and *Pnin* were written expressly for the magazine. Another was Lillian Ross, whose 1952 series on the making of the film *The Red Badge of Courage* remains a classic of literary journalism. Referring to her ability to report dialogue, Edmund Wilson called her "the girl with the built-in tape recorder." In fact, as this snapshot indicates, her preferred tool was—and still is—a notebook. John Huston, the director of the film, kneels to the right of Ross.

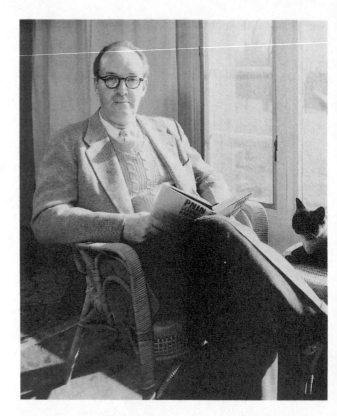

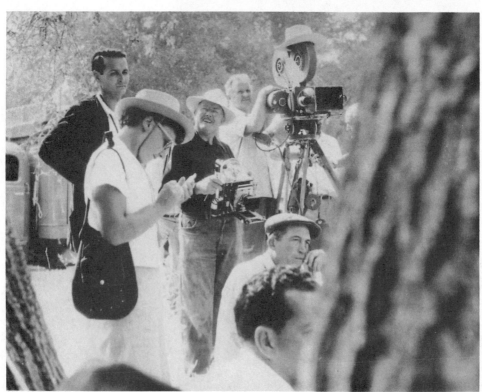

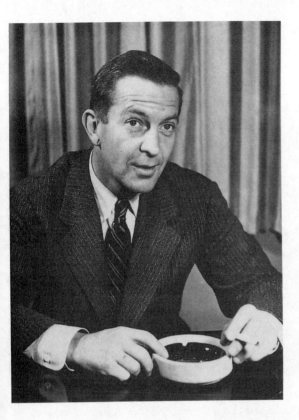

John Cheever, left, shown in 1954 at the age of forty-five, and John Updike, in 1960 at the age of twenty-eight, were profoundly different kinds of writers. But they both were named John, they both smoked, and they both, through their work in the *New Yorker*, became great artists of the short story.

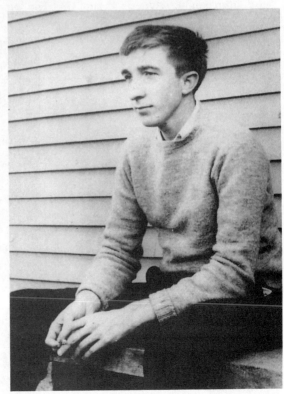

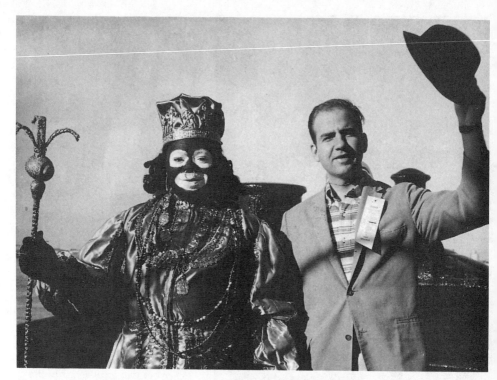

From the time he joined the *New Yorker* staff in 1963, Calvin Trillin took the United States as his beat. One of his first major articles was about the only African-American crew to march in New Orleans's Mardi Gras. The "king" of the crew is on Trillin's left.

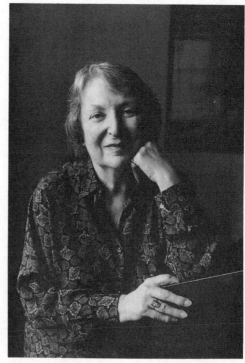

Soon after being named film critic in 1968, Pauline Kael became the best-known, best-read writer the magazine had. She had legendary battles with William Shawn over her copy. "E. B. White was Shawn's pillar of modern writing," she said. "No one was ever less like E. B. White than I was."

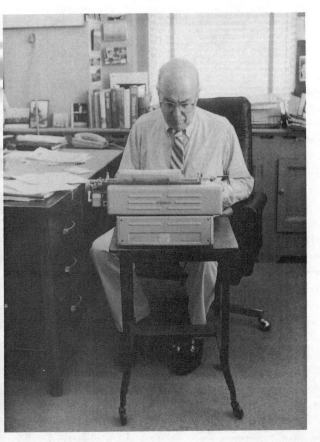

Roger Angell grew up in the *New Yorker* world of his mother, Katharine, and his stepfather, E. B. White. He sold his first short story to the magazine in the 1940s, joined the staff as a fiction editor in the 1950s, and embarked on his great baseball reportage in the 1960s. Among his discoveries as an editor were Woody Allen, Donald Barthelme, Garrison Keillor, Bobbie Ann Mason, and Ann Beattie. Angell rejected seventeen Beattie stories in a row before the magazine finally accepted "A Platonic Relationship" in 1974. *(Below)* Beattie in 1977, on the day of her move from Virginia to Massachusetts and a job teaching writing at Harvard. Her dog, Rufus, is in the driver's seat.

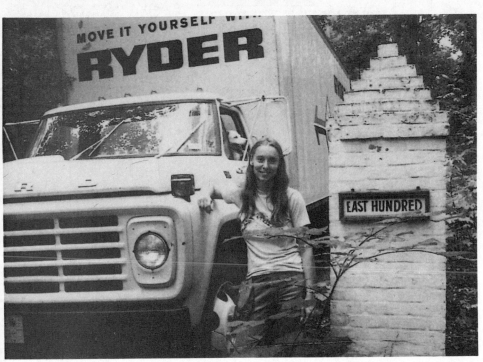

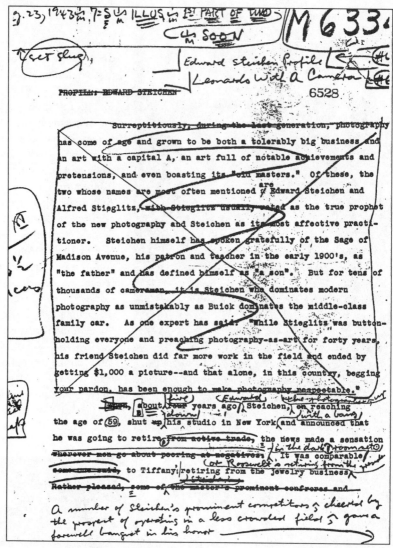

In Shawn's early years as an editor, he was a vigorous interventionist. Thus, not until the fourth manuscript page of Matthew Josephson's 1943 Profile of Edward Steichen did Shawn leave an entire line alone.

Shawn's editing style grew increasingly Socratic and Zenlike, and, as editor in chief, he would devote many hours to devising the perfect "mix" of articles, stories, and art for each issue. *(Left)* One of the pieces of paper, from the 1950s, on which he fiddled with possible lineups.

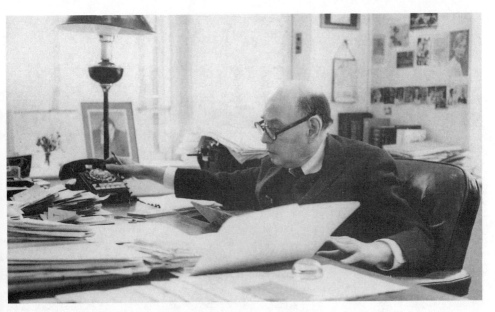

Shawn in the late seventies, photographed by the multitalented *New Yorker* contributor James Stevenson. A framed photograph of Harold Ross is visible behind Shawn's lamp.

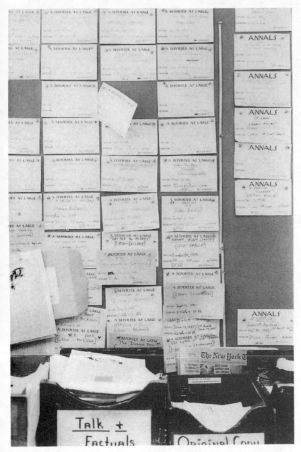

Shawn assigned and bought many more articles than the magazine could print, and authors could wait in vain a decade or more for their work to appear. *(Left)* Stevenson's photograph of a bulletin board in the makeup department showing some of the unpublished inventory.

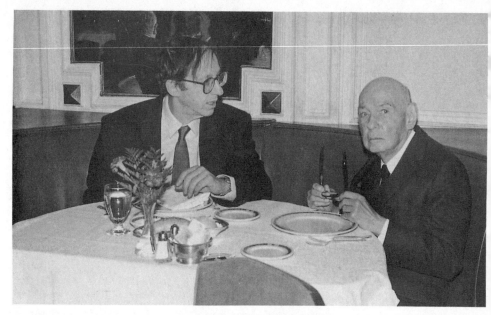

S. I. Newhouse fired Shawn in 1987 (when the editor was seventy-nine years old) and replaced him with Robert Gottlieb. Days before the change went into effect, Shawn and Gottlieb's extremely awkward lunch at the Algonquin was chronicled by the paparazzi.

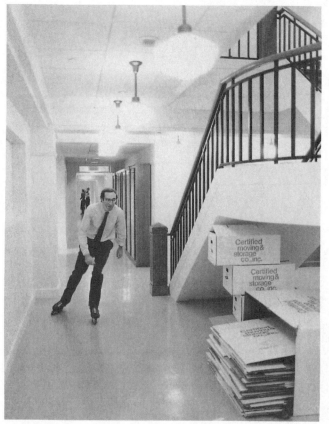

A hush prevailed in the magazine's corridors during Shawn's tenure. Gottlieb loosened things up, to the point where deputy editor Charles "Chip" McGrath could roll down the halls. The empty boxes are left over from the magazine's move to new quarters across Forty-third Street in 1991.

corrected—but have now made it quite clear to the *New Yorker* that there will be no "revising" and "editing" . . .

For the next two years, Nabokov was occupied with the completion of his novel *Bend Sinister*, the translation of nine of his Russian short stories for an English-language edition; his duties as a lecturer at Wellesley College; and his ongoing investigations as a lepidopterist. When he did finally send another story to the *New Yorker*, it was what his biographer Brian Boyd calls "one of the greatest short stories ever written, 'Signs and Symbols,' a triumph of economy and force, minute realism and shimmering mystery." On one level it is a simple and poignant story of the love of an old immigrant couple for their "incurably deranged" son; on another, a Nabokovian metatext revolving around the son's "referential mania"—an (invented) disorder in which "the patient imagines that everything happening around him is a veiled reference to his personality and existence." Mrs. White accepted it, but completely missed the point, casting it as "a parody or satire of the gloomy new school of psychiatric fiction" and suggesting adding a subtitle to make this clear to the reader, such as "After a Holiday Excursion into the Gloomy Precincts of the Modern Psychiatric Novel." Nabokov passed on this misprision to Wilson, who exploded in a letter to Mrs. White:

> If *The New Yorker* had suggested to me that the story had been written as a parody, I should have been just as angry as you say he was (I'm surprised that he has not challenged somebody to a duel). . . . Besides this, there is the whole question of *New Yorker* fiction—about which I hear more complaints than anything else in the magazine. It is appalling that Nabokov's little story, so gentle and everyday, would take on the aspect for the *New Yorker* editors of an overdone psychiatric study. (How *can* you people say it was overwritten?) It could only appear so in contrast with the pointless and inane little anecdotes that are turned out by the *New Yorker's* processing mill and that the reader forgets two minutes after he has read them—if, indeed, he has even paid attention, at the time his eye was slipping down the column, to what he was reading about.

Nabokov followed this almost immediately with another submission, "Portrait of My Uncle," the first chapter in what he had been envisioning for some time as a book of memoirs. Nabokov's past was so remote from that of *New Yorker* readers, and his treatment of it so idiosyncratic, that Lobrano, Maxwell, and Mrs. White all voted against its acceptance. However, Ross— a great devotee of family memoirs since the days of "Life with Father"— overruled them, and the *New Yorker* eventually published not only "Portrait of My Uncle" but a total of nine of the fifteen chapters of Nabokov's autobiography, called *Conclusive Evidence* when it was published as a book in 1951 and revised and renamed as *Speak, Memory* in 1966.*

"Portrait of My Uncle" represented the last time Nabokov had cause to complain seriously about the magazine's editing. In a letter to Mrs. White after the piece had been put through, he eloquently, respectfully, and persuasively staked out his position:

> I deeply appreciated your sympathetic handling of "My Uncle." It is the principle itself of editing that distresses me. I should be very grateful to you if you help me to weed out bad grammar but I do not think I would like my longish sentences clipped too close, or those drawbridges lowered which I have taken such pains to lift. In other words, I would like to discriminate between awkward construction (which is bad) and a certain special—how shall I put it—sinuosity, which is my own and which only at first glance may seem awkward or obscure. Why not have the reader re-read a sentence now and then? It won't hurt him.

Mrs. White seemed to get the point, and there were no more conflicts over the remaining eight chapters of the memoirs. Indeed, earlier troubles were magically forgotten, and within two years, Nabokov could write to her, "I always appreciate your delicate, sympathetic and careful way of dealing with my prose." The relationship was tested in 1951, when Nabokov submitted "Lance," a dense and multilayered story set far in the future, in which Nabokovian games and wordplay, allusions to medieval romances and pulp science fiction, underlay an affecting meditation on the nature of valor and of a parent's concern for a child undertaking a dangerous enterprise. It was about as far from the common perception of "the *New Yorker* story" as it was possible to get. But the magazine took it, Mrs. White writing Nabokov, "Your story is fearful, wonderful and touching. Also of course very subtle and 'difficult'—Ross, who is seriously sick, could not understand it but is taking it on the score of Lobrano's and my enthusiasm." Many *New Yorker* readers did not understand it either, and the magazine sent them an eloquent, unsigned one-paragraph précis. Mrs. White forwarded a copy

---

*Ross's continued enthusiasm for Nabokov's memoirs is documented in some of his surviving query sheets. About "Tamara," he wrote: "Think story O.K.—and quite powerful and beautiful, while I'm at it. . . . I think this piece is the one that had twenty words I'd never seen before in the first two pages. . . . I haven't looked these odd words up. They should be checked and if no warrant found for them they should be argued, I guess. In this connection, think Nobokov [*sic*] entitled to introduce a word into language if etymologically sound." And on "Garden and Parks": "Well, on leisurely reading, I found this quite a piece. I think it's the most remarkable emotional tour de force I ever read. And got humorous touches, too. Got a laugh out of the professor recognizing the Transcript by the rustle. Astonished at the vehemence of the Freud reference; probably a wholesome thing."

to Nabokov, who replied, "Please tell the author he or she has summed up the thing in a perfectly admirable way, saying exactly what I would have liked to say (but would not have been able to do so lucidly). It gave me great pleasure, great satisfaction."*

Nabokov's next, and final, prolonged association with the *New Yorker* began two years later, when he sent in "Pnin," a story about a comical but sympathetic Russian professor (and Russian émigré) at an upstate New York college. He wrote it shortly after completing *Lolita,* which he correctly foresaw would have a difficult time reaching publication (it took five years). Nabokov needed money, and he frankly planned "Pnin" as the first of a lucrative series for the *New Yorker.* He was correct here, too: the magazine had long been partial to series with continuing characters, and the Pnin stories, while far more sophisticated and complex than, say, Sally Benson's "Junior Miss," were emotionally involving and funny. The magazine published four of the eventual book's seven chapters over the next three years, with no substantive problems between editor and author. One of them needed to be trimmed, and after seeing Mrs. White's proposed cuts, Nabokov wrote her, "You have done a magnificent job. While reading your script I felt like a patient reclining under the glitter of delicate instruments. I am still under the spell of your novocaine and hastily return these pages before I start aching."†

Over ten years, Nabokov picked the *New Yorker* up and, in literary daring and true sophistication, brought it to a new place. But the association with the magazine did something for him as well. It established a name for him in the United States and, by publishing the Pnin stories, afforded him his first great public success. (The book, published in 1957, was an immediate bestseller and was nominated for the National Book Award as best novel of the year.) There was more. After reading *Conclusive Evidence,* Edmund Wilson wrote Nabokov (referring to the other great author to write in English as a second language), "The English of *CE* is at least as good as Conrad's and has

---

*Nabokov had less luck with another, even less accessible story submitted in 1951, "The Vane Sisters," in which the first letters of the words in the final paragraph spell out an important message. Nabokov was initially annoyed by Mrs. White's remark that the story was "a web" that had gotten "snarled" and "too involved," but he seemed to come around to her point of view. The story was included in his 1975 collection, *Tyrants Destroyed and Other Stories,* and Nabokov referred to the acrostic in an introductory note: "This particular trick can be tried only once in a thousand years of fiction. Whether it has come off is another question."

†"Lance" was the last short story Nabokov wrote, and none of his subsequent novels lent themselves to excerpting. But after the magazine rescinded its policy against translated works, it printed a half dozen of his Russian-language stories of the twenties and thirties.

qualities that Conrad could never have managed. I think you must have profited somewhat from the *New Yorker*'s (at times outrageously stupid) fine-tooth-combing of prose."

Late in 1955, in the midst of the Pnin series, Mrs. White announced her retirement. (She would return to the magazine the next year, after Lobrano's sudden death, and remain until 1957.) On hearing the news, Nabokov wrote her, with patent sincerity and warmth—and the selective amnesia that time and emotion can bring—"I look back on our cloudless association and it is most painful to think that it will be different from now on. Your kindness, your gentleness and understanding have always meant so much to me."

The prevalence of comparatively exotic new fiction writers had negative as well as positive significance. That is, in addition to their merits and their usefulness to the magazine, they served to take up the slack of the veteran short-story writers who, sometimes consciously and sometimes not, were struggling in the postwar years. The falloff was not dramatic. Sally Benson, Edward Newhouse, and Robert Coates continued as reliably and prolifically as before, if perhaps a bit more mechanically. Reading their stories, it was hard to avoid the sense that the traditional *New Yorker* sketch may finally have run its course. One got to the end, read the noncommittal final paragraph, and said, "Yes, but what else?"

The workhorse of the fiction stable, John O'Hara, contributed steadily through the forties, but his quality visibly dropped off: what was knowing and fresh before the war had hardened into a rather slick and easy cynicism. Busy with film work and the chores of being a famous author, he also had less patience for the *New Yorker*'s demands and bristled more than ever at the twin bugaboos of editing and rejections. In 1948, he wrote Mrs. White that he could "no longer afford to write for the *New Yorker* at the current prices" and proposed a new arrangement whereby if any story was turned down or if the editors' proposed changes were unreasonable, he would be paid "250.00 or half the amount you would have paid for the piece if bought, whichever is greater." The *New Yorker* had never paid (and would never pay) such a "kill fee" on rejected work, and Ross instructed Mrs. White to refuse the deal, commenting, "Madness would lie that way, or any way that led us into intricate special arrangements." As a peace offering, Ross sent the writer an inexpensive gold watch picked up at a Third Avenue pawnshop. Over the next year and a half, there were more skirmishes over rates. In April 1949, "shocked and very angry" over the rejection of his story "The Favor," O'Hara told Ross that the *New Yorker* "can go to hell." Four months later, Brendan Gill wrote a devastating review of O'Hara's novel *A Rage to Live*, and (with the book advancing its way up the best-seller lists) O'Hara used this as an occasion to carry through on all his threats of the past two decades and cut all ties with the magazine.*

Irwin Shaw continued to be a mainstay of the fiction pages. During the war and in the years immediately afterward, rather startlingly, he wrote *war stories*, including "Act of Faith," "The Passion of Lance Corporal Hawkins," "Gunners' Passage," "The Priest," and "Hamlets of the World," that were more heavily plotted than anything the *New Yorker* had published. They were full of action, sensitive but valiant heroes, and unexpected reversals; in two of them, the main character suffered a violent death in the last paragraph. When a Shaw story was in the *New Yorker*, it could almost be mistaken for a men's adventure magazine. Back on home territory in the late forties, Shaw seemed to falter a little bit, as if peacetime provided insufficient meat for the ripping yarns he had grown accustomed to turning out. He did, however, publish two impressive set pieces: "Mixed Doubles" (1947), which dissects a doomed marriage over the course of a tennis match, and "The Climate of Insomnia" (1949), in which the grim life prospects of a man looking out into middle age are gradually and adeptly laid out as he lies awake in the small hours of the morning.

Shaw and the others were grappling with a core problem—the difficulty, in this unsettled time, of trying to write in the *New Yorker* about the kind of men and women who read the *New Yorker*. A graphic demonstration of the dilemma was "The Mountain," written by Astrid Peters (Robert Coates's wife) and published on March 18, 1948. Like many of Peter Taylor's stories, it is about a husband and wife's inability to communicate. But Peters's familiar *haut bourgeois* setting is a ski slope, and her people are *New Yorker* people. Peter is an excellent skier and Lucy is a beginner, who struggles to make it down Pineridge and the West Slope without falling. The heart of the story, and their relationship, is her silence: she cannot express to her husband, cannot really even admit to herself, how desperately she dreads the slopes and the rope tow. It would seem a trivial matter, yet Peters seems to recognize that underneath it is a profound lack of voice. To be a part of this society at this time and in this place, one had to make some kind of settlement, each to her or his own, with the unspoken and the unacknowledged. At the end of the story, with Peter pushing off to take her on one more run, Lucy finally comes close to acknowledging her rage, but to express it would be far too much to ask:

"Goddamn you, she thought helplessly. Oh, goddamn you. But when he started, she pushed off immediately after him, doing her best to keep his swaying shoulders and the bright color of his head always in sight."

One longtime writer was attuned to such secret thoughts and tried

---

*The divorce lasted until 1960, when the magazine printed O'Hara's novella "Imagine Kissing Pete." It published some three dozen more stories before the author's death in 1970.

valiantly to give them voice. This was John Cheever, who had been a frequent contributor since 1940, writing stories in the journalistic style that flourished under Lobrano; they were accomplished but rarely memorable. Then, in 1947, came a watershed: "The Enormous Radio." The story begins with a typical pair of characters for Cheever (and the *New Yorker*): Jim and Irene Westcott, about whom Cheever tells us, "They were the parents of two young children, they had been married nine years, they lived on the twelfth floor of an apartment house near Sutton Place, they went to the theatre an average of 10.3 times a year, and they hoped someday to live in Westchester." One day their radio comes back from the repair shop. When Jim and Irene turn it on, they find that instead of the usual broadcast offerings, the machine transmits the sounds of the other apartments in their building. To Irene's shock, nearly everything she hears is venal or base: "She overheard demonstrations of indigestion, carnal love, abysmal vanity, faith, and despair." She is simultaneously repelled and fascinated by the window she has been given into her neighbors' lives, and she inevitably wonders what *her* life would sound like if it came over the radio. Jim berates her for listening so obsessively and she cries:

"Oh, don't, don't, don't. Life is too terrible, too sordid and awful. But we've never been like that, have we, darling? Have we? I mean, we've always been good and decent and loving to one another, haven't we? And we have two children, two beautiful children. Our lives aren't sordid, are they, darling? Are they?"

They are. As soon as the radio is repaired, Jim picks a fight with Irene and unpacks all the dark secrets they had devoted their lives to obscuring.

The story was accepted with enthusiasm by the *New Yorker*. Ross wrote Cheever, "I've just read 'The Enormous Radio,' having gone away for a spell and got behind, and I send my respects and admiration. That piece is worth coming back to work for. It will turn out to be a memorable one, or I am a fish. Very wonderful indeed." Three years later, Mrs. White selected it for the leadoff position in the anthology of the best *New Yorker* stories of the decade. What the editors saw in the story, one imagines, is a grim, perfectly worked-out supernatural yarn, à la television's *The Twilight Zone*. But on another level, it is a profound and stunning comment on the nature of fiction—specifically, fiction in the *New Yorker*. Cheever is acknowledging that he and his fellow contributors to the magazine have always chronicled the way some people live when other people are in the room. What the enormous radio picks up is the entire spectrum of life that the magazine denied itself, or simply denied—the secret abortion, the man beating his wife, the shouted obscenities, the smell of the apple core in the ashtray (to cite a particularly brilliant image of Cheever's), sickness, death.

But how is a writer—especially a writer who contributes to a magazine stocked with funny pictures, expensive ads, and droll comments on typographical errors—supposed to confront this other part of life? Cheever wrestled with the question over the next few years, and the answers that came to him always seemed to lead away from the realism that had been the bedrock of *New Yorker* fiction. "Torch Song" (1947) is a tour de force in which one of the characters transmogrifies in the story from an ordinary young woman from Ohio into the personification of death. "The Hartleys" (1949) begins on comfortable terrain—a story about an upper-middle-class family, published in January and comfortably set in a ski-country inn. The narrative voice has the perspective of the other guests of the inn, and though it suspects something is not quite right with the Hartleys, it cannot divine what the trouble is. Instead of an enormous radio, Cheever near the end of the story introduces a maid who "could hear Mrs. Hartley's voice, a voice so uncontrolled, so guttural and full of suffering, that she stopped and listened as if the woman's life were in danger." The story ends with a horrific event that comes so suddenly and gratuitously as to be an implicit rebuff to the nonending ending of the classic *New Yorker* story. In "The Season of Divorce" (1950), another story that starts out mildly and ends in deep despair, the veer from naturalism is subtle and comes in the form of metaphor. After a climactic loud row in another of Cheever's shabby-genteel East Side apartments, he presents, so effortlessly that we barely notice, one of the most spectacular similes in the history of fiction: "There was a loud rapping on the radiator, a signal from the people upstairs for decorum and silence—urgent and expressive, like the communications that prisoners send to one another through the plumbing in a penitentiary."

Cheever was not alone in trying to get beyond the strictures of decorum and silence. Shirley Jackson, the wife of the young Talk of the Town writer Stanley Edgar Hyman, sold the magazine several stories starting in the early forties, but suffered a far greater number of rejections, many owing to her predilection for the supernatural and the gothic. Lobrano returned one batch of stories to her agent in 1943, calling them "a pretty cryptic and loony batch. 'The Gift' seemed to be rolling along pretty well until it went into surrealism or something at the end." By 1948, the magazine was ready for a dose of surrealism. In the spring of that year Jackson, who lived with her husband in North Bennington, Vermont, wrote—in one sitting, she later recalled—an unsettling fable called "The Lottery." As the story opens, the citizens of what appears to be a present-day New England village are gathering in preparation for what we soon discern is a lottery that is a venerable local custom. But Jackson withholds—masterfully—the precise nature of the ritual until the last few paragraphs, when we grasp with horror that the villager who chose the slip of paper with the penciled black spot is to be stoned to death.

The vote to accept the story was nearly unanimous (William Maxwell being the sole dissenter), but it was so out of the *New Yorker's* usual line that Lobrano felt compelled to telephone Jackson and ask if she "cared to take any stand on the meaning of the story." She was at a loss for words, so, she later remembered, Lobrano suggested that "the story might be called an allegory which made its point by an ironic juxtaposition of ancient superstition and modern setting." Jackson assented and Lobrano said, "Good; that's what Mr. Ross thought it meant." In fact, "The Lottery"—with its New England villagers, so quaint and so ready to commit unspeakable acts—was about evil: its familiarity, its banality, and its capacity to appear at the least expected places and times.

"The Lottery" prompted more letters to the *New Yorker*—more than three hundred—than any other short story it had published. The magazine forwarded all of them to Jackson. In a lecture she gave years later, she reported that only a handful praised her or the story in any way; the rest were characterized by "bewilderment, speculation, and plain old-fashioned abuse." If the letters, she said, "could be considered to give any accurate cross section of the reading public, or the reading public of the *New Yorker*, or even the reading public of one issue of the *New Yorker*, I would stop writing now." Some of the letter writers were comical and almost touching in their bafflement over the story, such as the one who stated, "I thought it must have been a small-scale representation of the sort of thing involved in the lottery which started the functioning of the selective-service system at the start of the last war." But the abusive comments were more telling: "Tell Miss Jackson to stay out of Canada." "I expect a personal apology from the author." "I will never buy *The New Yorker* again. I resent being tricked into reading perverted stories like 'The Lottery.'" "The story was so horrible and gruesome in its effect that I could hardly see the point of your publishing it." "We would expect something like this in *Esquire*, etc., but *not* the *New Yorker*." A Minnesota reader expressed a common sense of betrayal: "Never in the world did I think I'd protest a story in the *New Yorker*, but really, gentlemen, 'The Lottery' seems to me to be in incredibly bad taste. I read it while soaking in the tub and was tempted to put my head under the water and end it all." "The Lottery" went on to become one of the most widely anthologized short stories in history. But the resistance it inspired at the time of its publication—just three years after the end of World War II, at a time when the national spirit seemed almost obsessively determined to forget the Holocaust and other horrors, a time when some citizens seemed to have no qualms about giving testimony that sent their former friends to the lions—was telling. The call was out for silence and decorum; a writer—or magazine—that wanted any level of popular success would take a strong risk by sweeping them aside.

*   *   *

Jerome David Salinger was certainly willing to take risks. A native of upper-middle-class Manhattan, he had told friends at the Valley Forge Military Academy that his ambition in life was to succeed Robert Benchley as the *New Yorker*'s drama critic. He began submitting short stories to the magazine in 1941, the year he turned twenty-two, and managed to get a rise out of first reader John Mosher, who wrote Salinger's agent, Harold Ober, about "Lunch for Three," "There is certainly something quite brisk and bright about this piece, but it hardly seems to be exactly just the right thing to us at the moment." The magazine rejected seven Salinger stories that year (the titles of some are tantalizing—"Monologue for a Watery Highball," "I Went to School with Adolf Hitler," "The Long Debut of Lois Taggett") before finally, in December, accepting "Slight Rebellion off Madison," about a New York kid named Holden Caulfield who had the prewar jitters. Unfortunately for Salinger, the Japanese then bombed Pearl Harbor, rendering the story unpublishable. It would not see print, in rewritten form, until 1946.

In the meantime, Salinger kept sending in stories, and they kept coming back, including, in 1942, another episode in the life of Holden Caulfield. The main objection in the *New Yorker* offices seemed to be that he had no sense of decorum, no recognition of when to be silent. Maxwell said of one 1942 piece that "it would have worked out better for us if Mr. Salinger had not strained so for cleverness." By the next year Maxwell was exasperated, telling Ober, "We think Mr. Salinger is a very talented young man and wish to God you could get him to write simply and naturally."

Salinger eventually got the message. Early in 1944, about to be sent overseas by the army, he wrote directly to Wolcott Gibbs, who was then filling in in the fiction department. He told Gibbs that a change had come over his writing, that he was no longer relying on his reflexive cleverness or what he referred to as "trickery." Oddly, he said he wasn't able to write a story anymore unless he had a strong affection for all the people in it. The new approach seemed to be bearing fruit, he said: the *Saturday Evening Post* had just accepted three stories from him. Salinger—barely twenty-five years old at the time—then assessed the *New Yorker* short story itself. He gave faint praise to Shaw, Cheever, Benson, and Jerome Weidman, but lamented what seemed to him the insignificant work done in the magazine by O'Hara, whom he termed a much better writer than Hemingway. He closed with a plea that the magazine "play just a little fairer with the short story" and broaden its conception of the form.

But the time still wasn't right. All his submissions were rejected in 1944, 1945 (he had a group of fifteen poems rejected that year as well), and 1946. The next year, however, saw a breakthrough. Maxwell to Ober, January 22,

1947: "We liked parts of 'The Bananafish' by J. D. Salinger very much but it seems to us to lack any discoverable story or point. If Mr. Salinger is around town, perhaps he'd like to come in and talk to me about *New Yorker* stories." The story, at this stage, was about a young man named Seymour Glass who has a conversation with a little girl on a beach in Florida, then goes back to his hotel room and shoots himself in the head with a revolver. Salinger did come in to talk to Maxwell, the result being that he added a new scene to open the story: Seymour's shallow new wife sits in their hotel suite and talks with her mother by long-distance telephone. The first rewrite was sent back, but the second one—which Salinger now was calling "A Fine Day for Bananafish"—was accepted and printed in January 1948. Its title in the magazine was "A Perfect Day for Bananafish." The week it came out, John Cheever wrote to Gus Lobrano, "I thought the Salinger piece was one hell of a story."

The magazine printed two more Salinger contributions over the next six months—"Uncle Wiggily in Connecticut" and "Just Before the War with the Eskimos." All three stories were set pieces in familiar *New Yorker* locations—the couple in a Florida resort, the old college roommates meeting in the suburban house one of them has moved to, the interchange between young members of the private-school set in a Manhattan apartment—but something about Salinger's treatment created a sensation. From Los Angeles, Arthur Kober wrote Ross, "Everybody out here talks about Salinger. My God, that guy is good. Evenings are spent, and this is on the level, discussing the guy and his work." Nineteen forty-nine would bring another classic story, "The Laughing Man," and the next year another, "For Esmé—With Love and Squalor." No question about it—Salinger *was* good. His dialogue, although a mite ostentatious (his trademark technique of italicizing just one *syl*lable of a word did not, on reflection, provide any different or additional information from unobtrusively italicizing the *entire* word), sang. And his years of apprenticeship, having stories rejected by the *New Yorker* and publishing stories in the slick magazines, had taught him to channel his spectacular narrative gifts. But Salinger burst on the scene because he was, in Maxwell's word, a "performer"—this at a time when well-made, well-behaved stories were starting to feel drab and incomplete. Especially in the first-person "The Laughing Man," "For Esmé," and *The Catcher in the Rye,* his 1951 novel narrated by his old friend Holden Caulfield, he let everything out. One felt that if it would move the story along, Salinger would have no qualms about breaking into a buck-and-wing. Underneath it all was a sometimes faint but discernible sense of desperation.*

---

*Even after his great success in the magazine, Salinger continued to experience rejections—three in 1948 and seven in 1949. After a story Salinger was particularly fond of, "A

Cheever, meanwhile, was carrying on his struggle with fiction and the world. The first evidence that he had seen his way to a new kind of understanding was "Goodbye, My Brother," which appeared in the *New Yorker* in August 1951. It is a great short story that can stand the weight of numerous readings, including the biographical (in its reflection of Cheever's complicated and ambivalent relationship with his brother), the sociological (in its tracing of the moral and financial decay of an upper-class New England family), and the stylistic (in his exquisitely subtle deployment of an unreliable narrator—a technique the *New Yorker* was traditionally leery of, because the many first-person reminiscences in its pages asked to be read straight). But Cheever thought it important enough to be first entry in his collected stories because it marked the beginning, as he wrote in his journal in the seventies, of his "break with irony and despair." It was the fictional moment when Cheever determined that despite the undeniable validity of realism— in both senses of the word—he was interested, instead, in the possibility of transcendence. The original model for the *New Yorker* short story was journalism; Cheever was moving in the direction of poetry.

The unnamed narrator's brother Lawrence, or "Tifty," is an enormous radio with two arms and legs: he gloomily walks around the Pommeroy family's summer house on an island off Massachusetts pointing out every human and architectural frailty he sees, and they are many. The family—his mother; his brother Chaddy; his sister, Diana; Chaddy's wife, Odette; the narrator and his wife, Helen—alternately ignore his outbursts and dismiss them with a hostile condescension. But one day on the beach the narrator, whose tendency to overlook the sad truths of his own life has become increasingly apparent in the story, can take it no more and tells Tifty:

> "You think that your pessimism is an advantage, but it's nothing but an unwillingness to grasp realities."
>
> "What are the realities?" he said. "Diana is a foolish and a promiscuous woman. So is Odette. Mother is an alcoholic. She'll be in a hospital in a year or two. Chaddy is dishonest. He always has been. The house is going to fall into the sea." He looked at me and added, as an afterthought, "You're a fool."
>
> "You're a gloomy son of a bitch."
>
> "Get your fat face out of mine," he said. He walked along.

The narrator picks up a root and hits Tifty in the head, with all his might. He hopes he has killed him, but he hasn't. The next morning Tifty leaves the

---

Summer Accident," was turned down, he put the genre aside for a while. He told Lobrano (to whom he would dedicate his 1953 collection, *Nine Stories*) that he had rented a small house in Westport and started work on "the novel about the prep school boy"—the book that would become *The Catcher in the Rye*.

Dear Miss Olding:

    Here, alas, is Jerry Salinger's latest
story. I'm afraid I'm incapable of expressing adequately
and convincingly our distress at having to send it back.
It has passages that are brilliant and moving and effective, but we feel that on the whole it's pretty shocking
for a magazine like ours.

    It would be wonderfully comfortable to
rest on the above paragraph, but because we have a real
interest in Jerry I have to say further that we feel the
story isn't wholly successful. Possibly the development
of the theme of this story requires more space. Actually,
we feel that we don't know the central character well
enough. We can't be quite sure whether his fight with
Stradlater was caused by his feelings for June Gallagher,
or his own inadequacy about his age (which is brought
into relief by Stradlater's handsomeness and prowess),
or a suggestion of homosexuality in Bobby. And it's perhaps our uncertainty about which of these elements is
the real one, or the predominant one, that makes it difficult to feel any real compassion for the character or to
feel (except extraneously) that the author has real compassion for him. Our feeling is that, to be quite definite and so sympathetic, Bobby would have to be developed at considerably more length than he is here.

    We are, of course, very grateful to have
had the chance to consider this story. I'm convinced
that it would have worked out for us if it had been developed as the less complicated theme which Jerry told me
about shortly after it had occurred to him, but I imagine
that that theme seemed too sparse to Jerry as the character
grew in his mind.

        Sincerely,

        G. S. Lobrano

Miss Dorothy Olding
Harold Ober Agency
40 East 49th Street
New York, N. Y.

Enc. THE BOY IN THE PEOPLE SHOOTING HAT - J.D. Salinger

GSL:tag

The J. D. Salinger story rejected here by fiction editor G. S. "Gus" Lobrano would
develop into a novel: *The Catcher in the Rye*.

house before anyone else has awakened, and the narrator imagines him on the ferry leaving the island: "while the grace of the light would make it an exertion not to throw out your arms and swear exultantly, Lawrence's eyes would trace the black sea as it fell astern . . ." The story concludes (the mythological names and imagery underlying Cheever's swerve from "the realities"):

> Oh, what can you do with a man like that? What can you do? How can you dissuade his eye in a crowd from seeking out the cheek with acne, the infirm hand; how can you teach him to respond to the inestimable greatness of the race, the harsh surface beauty of life; how can you put his finger for him on the obdurate truths before which fear and horror are powerless? The sea that morning was iridescent and dark. My wife and my sister were swimming—Diana and Helen—and I saw their uncovered heads, black and gold in the dark water. I saw them come out and I saw that they were naked, unshy, beautiful, and full of grace, and I watched the naked women walk out of the sea.

SOPHISTICATION AND ITS DISCONTENTS

As a variation of the chicken-egg controversy, which came first—the *New Yorker* or its thin, snobbish, skillfully written sketches about people without passion or money troubles?
—*New York Post,* 1946

〜〜〜

The *New Yorker* has always dealt with experience not by trying to understand it but by prescribing the attitude to be adopted toward it. This makes it possible to feel intelligent without thinking, and it is a way of making everything tolerable, for the assumption of a suitable attitude toward experience can give one the illusion of having dealt with it adequately.
—Robert Warshow, "Melancholy to the End,"
Partisan Review, 1947

〜〜〜

The *New Yorker,* an ultra-sophisticated magazine, prints many stories about the sophisticated *New Yorker* while its ads often show us sophisticated types in sophisticated homes.
—James T. Farrell, *The Fate of Writing in America,* 1947

〜〜〜

The periodical style which now characterizes the *New Yorker* excludes or dismisses various important kinds of perceptions, attitudes, and values.... When everyone begins to try to write in a style imposed from without (imposed, whether or not it is true that the editors rewrite sentences which seem inappropriate to them), then everyone sees and feels, after a time, only those sights which can be expressed in the periodical style; and in the end the readers too, see, feel, hear, and think of things in the same way. As it is common by now to say of something funny that it is just like a *New Yorker* cartoon, so we may conclude by finding all experience *New Yorkerish*.

—Delmore Schwartz, "Laugh and Lie Down,"
Partisan Review, 1950

The code which the *New Yorker* teaches its writers is evident in everything they write.... It is a code based on a fear of all emotion that cannot be expressed in the whisper of a nuance. It depends for its existence upon a view of the world as a vast cocktail party where the very best people say the most frightening things about themselves and one another in a language which the servants are not expected to understand, where the most tragic confession of personal ruin is at once diluted by the ironic titter in the speaker's voice.

—John W. Aldridge, *After the Lost Generation,* 1951

In March 1950, in the ballroom of the Ritz-Carlton Hotel, the *New Yorker* celebrated (one month late) its twenty-fifth anniversary. The round number aside, it seemed a good time to take stock, for lately an inordinate amount of attention was being paid to the magazine. In the past few years, it had been the subject of lengthy magazine articles, by former contributors Russell Maloney and Henry F. Pringle, that had focused, understandably though somewhat excessively, on Harold Ross's physical and behavioral colorfulness. Ross himself already enjoyed an improbable level of national fame stemming from a scathing St. Clair McKelway Profile of Walter Winchell in 1940; ever since, Winchell had lambasted Ross in his syndicated column on a regular basis. Ross had made the front pages for the first time in 1949, when the *New Yorker* had been crusading editorially against the broadcast of music and commercials over the public address system in Grand Central Station; in December, he testified at a hearing held by the New York State Public Service Commission called in large part because of the magazine's opposition. Ross and the *New Yorker* were the subject of not one but two Broadway plays—the short-lived *Metropole,* by his former personal secretary, William Walden, which ran for just two performances in 1949, and Wolcott Gibbs's *Season in the Sun,* which was a modest success in 1950. The following year there would be an entire gossipy book on the magazine, Dale Kramer's *Ross and The New Yorker.*

What was striking about all the representations of the magazine was how much of its complete reality each of them missed. Easiest to grab on to were the outsize lapels of Ross's eccentricities, and they were real enough, though not especially relevant to the magazine he had founded and edited ever since. There was still the same harping on the ill-defined adjective *sophisticated.* Indeed, it was *still* being reflexively attached to the magazine nearly a decade later, and when the critic Maxwell Geismar used it dismissively in a review of John Updike's first volume of short stories, William Maxwell advised the writer to pay no heed: "Sophistication, in the sense that Geismar and the English book reviewers use it, died a total death in the year 1929, and has never been seen nor heard of since, neither around here nor anywhere else."

Something new was the less than exalted place the *New Yorker* occupied in the burgeoning postwar realm of academia and literary quarterlies, of grants and scholarly conferences. Its inhabitants viewed the magazine with extreme ambivalence, reflexively denigrating it as pablum for the middle-brow masses (but probably not to the point of declining to have a story or essay of their own published in its pages). From the cultural heights, the *New Yorker* was an easy target—it appeared to be a force that alternately reflected and justified bourgeois culture, denying by exclusion any inconvenient, unpleasant, or truly subversive facets of life. By the critics' various lights its main fault was its tepidness, its smugness, or its virtual enshackling of once-promising literary artists. There was truth to this indictment as well, but, again, it was incomplete. To pick up and page through an issue of the *New Yorker* from midcentury was to consider a text of complexity to the point of self-contradiction. Advertisements that urged the consumption of high-fashion dresses, liquor, large cars, and Bermuda vacations shouted for the reader's attention, to be sure. Yet the first voice in the magazine was E. B. White's, skeptical, plain, and resistant to the core of the very enterprise of advertising. Flipping to the back pages, one could find the contributions of Lois Long, Howard Brubaker, and George T. Ryall, redolent of the Jazz Age and doing much the same thing in much the same way as they had in 1925 or 1926. But then there was John Cheever, writing fiction that, if you looked at it right, was more thrillingly experimental than what was being produced in any Greenwich Village garret. The theater critic was Wolcott Gibbs, a philistine; the book critic was Edmund Wilson, whose standards were almost impossibly high and who would learn Hebrew to write an article on the Dead Sea Scrolls. A Perry Barlow cartoon on one page would gird up the social order; a Charles Addams cartoon on the next would tear it down. A Talk of the Town piece would consider the comical sayings of a housemaid. A Joseph Mitchell piece a few dozen pages back would posit the polluted New York harbor as the objective correlative for death and madness.

Somehow, Harold Ross had created this package of paradoxes. Not intentionally, of course. But the magazine had grown from his intense dedication and his sound instincts and judgment. Over the years Ross had grown as well, to the point where he was able not only to appreciate but to take delight in a story by Jean Stafford or Vladimir Nabokov. As William Maxwell told John Updike, "He based the editorial policy of the magazine on a few simple, practical rules, and it was those that occupied his entire attention. The manias you read about were prismatic reflections of no great importance. In general the rules added up to this principle, which I don't entirely agree with but admire as an editorial objective—that it is possible to say in words what you mean, and that a writer should."

Ross would not have the opportunity to see how much farther into the new decade that principle would be able to carry the magazine. In April 1951, suffering from severe pain in his chest and a bad cough, he was examined at the Lahey Clinic in Boston and told he had pleurisy. Two months later, a follow-up examination revealed the true diagnosis: cancer of the windpipe. Ross died in December. He had just turned fifty-nine.

Back at the office, it fell, inevitably, to White to write the obituary. It was a touching tribute, and incidentally the first time Harold Ross's name had been mentioned in the magazine he had founded. White wrote:

> In a way, he was a lucky man. For a monument he has the magazine to date—one thousand three hundred and ninety-nine issues, born in the toil and pain that can be appreciated only by those who helped in the delivery room. They are his. They stand, unchangeable and open for inspection. We are, of course, not in a position to estimate the monument, even if we were in the mood to. But we are able to state one thing unequivocally: Ross set up a great target and pounded himself to pieces trying to hit it square in the middle. His dream was a simple dream; it was pure and had no frills: he wanted the magazine to be good, to be funny, and to be fair.

Across the Atlantic, Rebecca West offered her own brief obituary, in the *Evening Standard,* concluding:

> Hokusai used to sign his work, "Old Man Mad About Painting." Harold Ross was mad in many ways.

He was mad in his kindness and his generosity, his sense that he was under an obligation to get anybody who worked for him out of whatever hole they might fall into. But he was most obsessed of all about his craft. So his signature might have run, "Old Man Mad About Writing," or "Old Man Mad About the Truth."

Yet there was something so local and personal about his allegiances that a more limited form might convey more clearly what he was: and perhaps he should be written down as "Old man mad about the *New Yorker*."

CHAPTER FIVE

THE BLAND LEADING THE BLAND
1952~62

THE INFORMATION MAN

Enclosed is a check for $50 for your material on freaks. We trust this is a satisfactory settlement. You might care to know that Alva Johnston was very pleased with this, and that we hope to have some more work for you.
> —Don Wharton to William Shawn, October 10, 1933

~~~~~

We'll have Mr. Shawn, the information man, look up about the radio as soon as possible.
> —Wolcott Gibbs to Rea Irvin, April 22, 1936

~~~~~

The only real list there is of Profiles being worked on is in Shawn's head, but he can't reel it out to you. I've come upon this before; it used to concern me but I'm reconciled to it now.
> —Harold Ross to Katharine White, January 24, 1944

~~~~~

I could never have done [a Profile of playwright Ferenc Molnár] without Shawn. He is a most remarkable incubator. I feel that with his help I could write any piece—or almost any piece.
> —S. N. Behrman to Ross, June 2, 1946

~~~~~

The Liebling Wayward [Press column] is all right now. You're a
magician.
—Ross to Shawn, September 16, 1948

~~~~

I can't do anything with Shawn away, for the future is in his head.
—Ross to Kay Boyle, August 9, 1949

~~~~

I also worry about Bill Maxwell, but not so much about Shawn,
for I regard him as tougher than Harold Ross by three to one.
—James Thurber to Katharine White, May 7, 1956

~~~~

Did you know Shawn never answers any letters? After writing
him four times, I gave up. I am now told he is desperately afraid
of being quoted. What a species!
—Thurber to E. B. White, October 10, 1958

~~~~

Like most other arrivals in the early days, William Shawn was young and
footloose when he came to the *New Yorker*. A native of Chicago, where his
father, Benjamin "Jacknife Ben" Chon, owned a profitable silver, diamond,
and cutlery shop in the meatpacking district, young Bill had dropped out of
the University of Michigan; traveled to Las Vegas, New Mexico, where he
wrote short fiction and briefly worked as a reporter for the local newspaper,
the *Daily Optic*; returned to Chicago to a job writing captions and headlines
for a photo syndicate; and, on his twenty-first birthday in 1928, married the
former Cecille Lyon, another Chicago journalist. Along the way he
changed his surname, following the example of his brother Nelson, a songwriter, who called himself Shawn, thinking *Chon* sounded Chinese. (The
reasoning seems solid until one considers that *Shawn* sounds Irish and
the family was Jewish.) Bill Shawn also had musical aspirations, and in 1932
he moved to New York, hoping to establish himself as a composer. But his
future lay in words, not music. By the next year his wife was offered some
freelance fact-gathering assignments by the *New Yorker's* then managing editor, Don Wharton. She turned the work over to Shawn, who had been a
reader and admirer of the magazine since the first issue. Soon he was regularly digging up information for Talk of the Town items and longer fact
pieces, and before the year was out he was hired as a full-time Talk reporter.

It is no surprise that Shawn should have been brought on staff so quickly:
he was remarkably efficient and dogged about unearthing facts. Shawn also

proved to have considerable abilities as a writer. Both these talents are on display in a five-page, double-spaced document Shawn prepared in March 1935, when he was asked to investigate, for a possible Reporter at Large, the Hauptmann Defense Fund, formed to raise money to pay for the appeal of the man convicted for the kidnapping and killing of Charles Lindbergh's baby boy. After presenting an assortment of facts about the membership, activities, and finances of the organization, Shawn concluded with a lengthy paragraph that, in setting down an unadorned account of his own visit to the fund's offices, displayed a remarkable eye for detail and ultimately an almost startling eloquence:

> The Hauptmann Defense Fund offices are on the top floor of a 5-story, white-brick front, business building at 226 East 86 Street, which is on the south side of the street between Second and Third Avenues. The building stands between the Arthur "Room," on its west, and Kreutzer Hall, on its east. On the ground floor is a travel bureau (Deutsches Reisebüro, George Steinweg Mngr.), windows and walls covered by German travel posters. Downstairs is Martin's Rathskeller. On the second floor is the Alcazar, Dining and Dancing. On the third floor is a real estate office and a postage-stamp dealer. On the fourth floor are law offices, with "Deutsche Advokaten" on the window. On the fifth floor, separated by a short corridor in which there is a check room, are the meeting hall of the Savitar Social Club, and the Hauptmann Defense Fund. Getting up to the offices is not easy. There is one small, unsubstantial elevator, manned by an operator, who, it appears, has been given order to ward reporters and other strangers off by saying that no one is up there. Sometimes, too, there are Hauptmann workers standing around downstairs more or less on guard to keep away visitors. There is also a stairway, which might take one up, but most of the time the ground-floor door is kept locked. If, finally, you can persuade the elevator man to accept you as a passenger, you find that the door to the Hauptmann offices has no name on it. This door is also kept locked. When you knock, the door is unlocked and opened just a crack, through which you have to state your case. Reporters are not welcome. Someone says, "When we are ready to give out any information, we'll give it to the A.P., and you can get it from them." . . . Once, however, I did manage to get inside the office and have a look at the place. . . . The office is about 25 feet by 15 feet. The brick walls and the woodwork are freshly painted, yellow. A flimsy partition has been put off to make a small side-office. (The partition was put up, and the painting was done by the Hauptmann Defense people themselves, according to the elevator man—source confidential—who also said that they moved in March 1.) The entire front of the office, which faces 86 Street, is made up of three large windows, in which there are still placards announcing the mass meeting to be held at Ebling's Casino on March 5. The

entire furnishings consist of one old, oak desk, and four or five old chairs. There is a telephone: Regent 4-0060. In a corner are some "Hauptmann Defense Fund" collection boxes, some white cardboard for signs, some black paints. Seated at the desk is Mrs. Hauptmann, with a pile of newspapers, some German, before her. She is reading one of them avidly, pausing occasionally to point out some passage, and to make what seems to be a comment on its unfairness, to another woman—youngish, blonde, well-dressed—who sits working at the desk beside her. In addition to the two women, there are three men in the office. One is a big, shaggy fellow, with a heavy mop of brown hair and shell-rimmed glasses. Another, who appears to be someone in authority and may be John C. Weiss (but who says, "I'm the bouncer around here. But up to now, we haven't needed a bouncer."), is short, olive-skinned, with a pudgy face, and the kind of smile that goes with a sarcastic turn of speech. The third man is Arno C. Weber, "Mrs. Hauptmann's manager," and vice-president of the fund. He is medium-height, clean-shaven, Teutonic, trimly-dressed, well-mannered—looks about like a German hotel clerk. He tries to be polite, but answers no questions. The general atmosphere is one of chip-on-the-shoulder suspiciousness, pathetic because it conveys the feeling of their being a handful of small, stranded people pitting themselves against the world; it doesn't seem possible that they represent all that stands between Hauptmann and the chair. The offices have the bare, fly-by-night look one might expect. And there are two provocative objects. In the main office there is a new, shiny black trunk, standing unopened. And behind the partition, in the side-office, is a baby's crib.

One can only imagine what this assignment took out of Shawn. He had not yet accumulated all the phobias and eccentricities for which he would become known throughout the world of letters (the most famous being a fear of automatic elevators—and note the prominence of the elevator in his report), but he was shy and withdrawn even at twenty-seven, and certainly not one to relish confrontations with antagonistic interview subjects. Moreover, far from having a desire for fame or even recognition, he was self-effacing to a degree rarely encountered in human beings. In his fifty-four years at the New Yorker, his name would never appear in its pages. The natural place for Shawn was behind an editor's desk, and within weeks if not days after his Hauptmann labors, Ross gave him a job as "idea man," coming up with and coordinating possible subjects for Talk and longer fact pieces. Brendan Gill, who came on the staff in this period as a Talk reporter, later described his first glimpse of Shawn: "Seated at a desk heaped with newspapers and armed with scissors for cutting out likely items and a typewriter for working the items into 'Talk' suggestion form, he was as safe from the real and imaginary perils of the outside world as a monk in a cell." Shawn took to his new duties with a vengeance. In what were likely his first two days on the job, Monday and Tuesday, April 1 and 2, 1935, he typed up extensive proposals for ten separate Talk pieces, including the Mac Jac Famous School of Acrobatics, 117 W. Forty-sixth Street; the designers of Broadway's electric signs; New York's last remaining dealer in fine carriages; the pigeon farms on Manhattan rooftops; George Selkirk, who was about to replace Babe Ruth in right field for the New York Yankees; and Irving Billig, about whom Shawn wrote:

> For the past six years Billig has been exterminating rats on Riker's Island. He estimates that to date he has killed off 1,000,000 of the 5,000,000 rats on the island. Unlike most other exterminators, he specializes in rats and mice. In the Manhattan phone directory he is listed as "Irving Billig rodents." He has done some big jobs on Manhattan, especially for the city in Central Park. The current popularity of Hans Zinsser's book "Rats, Lice and History" might be used, for timeliness, as a point of departure.

This was, of course, just the kind of thing to make Ross's heart go all aflutter. Indeed, the most important factor in Shawn's immediate success at the New Yorker was his uncanny and deep grasp of its tradition and editorial requirements. Even the report on the Hauptmann Defense Fund showed that he already fully comprehended—even though it was still being formulated—the magazine's commitment to a rhetoric and even a poetry of facts. In 1936, when the fact and fiction departments were reorganized, Ross tapped Shawn and Sanderson Vanderbilt to be fact editor St. Clair McKelway's deputies. Shawn was asked to write opinion sheets on incoming articles, and here again he showed he had perfect pitch as far as the magazine's needs were concerned, as well as the ability to translate his impressions into clear and specific editorial suggestions. He wrote to Ross about a Richard Boyer Reporter at Large on the Salvation Army:

> Nothing startling, but subject matter is fresh and unexpected . . . and Boyer O.K., I think, with cutting and routine editing. Tone on the whole is all right, but here and there Boyer gets too broadly sympathetic to the Brigadier and the rest of the gang; says their voices are "oily," etc.; would be better to keep the treatment deadpan throughout, and let reader draw his own conclusions. Considerable trimming is needed in Brigadier Marshall's speech, pages 4–7; began to get tiresome toward the bottom of page 5; suggest no big cuts here but trimming through the speech. On the other hand, I'm for lopping off the entire last four pages of the piece; by the end of page 10 I had enough, and everything that followed seemed repetitious and not very interesting. The singing class is conventional stuff, not unlike descriptions of revival meetings, etc. The visitations class just didn't interest me much; some of it might be trimmed and saved, but I think piece will be stronger without it. A good and

natural ending would be the lunch, top of page 10, perhaps ending with the quote, "We'll make an officer of you yet."

But the real revelation came when he was given articles to edit himself. He was a poet with a pencil, capable of eliminating extraneous, repetitive, or discordant material with deft and vigorous strokes, and inserting just the word, phrase, or sentence to gracefully make matters clear. It is slightly embarrassing to look at a typescript heavily edited by Shawn, so completely and with such palpable vigor has he altered the author's words. It made no difference that Matthew Josephson was one of the leading popular biographers and journalists in the country; Shawn virtually disassembled his 1943 Profile of Edward Steichen, to the extent that not a single line was retained as Josephson had written it until the middle of page 4. Yet Shawn's genius was such that he was able to avoid the common editorial sin of substituting one's own sensibility and style for an author's, and his changes were always in the spirit of the piece as written. Thus there was little complaint about editing changes from Shawn's writers; they saw their work in clean galley proofs, and it generally looked to them that the language had been cleaned up a little bit, nothing more. A later *New Yorker* author, Ved Mehta, recognizing that this was almost a sleight-of-hand process, subtitled his memoir of Shawn "The Invisible Art of Editing."

The Josephson Profile was written four years after Shawn succeeded McKelway as managing editor for fact. The job involved personally supervising writers, meaning that Shawn's shyness was a hurdle. But it did not prove uncrossable, primarily because the authors could not but respond to his profound attention to, strong respect for, and unabashed flattery of their work. Contrary to appearances, Shawn was a deeply emotional man, and on occasion he expressed his sentiments to selected colleagues. From France during the war, A. J. Liebling sent in what he called a "long amorphous piece" (it would eventually be published under the title "My Dear Little Louise"). Shawn replied by cable, his preferred form of written communication:

LOUISE PIECE ARRIVED AND VERY BEAUTIFUL PERIOD CANNOT RUN
THIS WEEK BUT WILL RUN WITHIN COUPLE WEEKS PERIOD HAD ME
PRACTICALLY WEEPING PERIOD.

Such missives were much appreciated by the correspondents; Janet Flanner would fondly refer to Shawn's "odd cables with affection, appreciation & punctuation all laid out." Shawn also had a subtle, understated sense of humor—completely different from Ross's, but no less funny for that. About an earlier Profile by Matthew Josephson, of General Motors president William Knudsen, Shawn sent Josephson a memo: "A stunning piece of historical reporting. A great profile. Below a few questions." There followed 178 queries.

Touchingly, Shawn also made occasional efforts at achieving some level of jauntiness. "Have you ever thought of publishing a book of your profiles?" he asked Geoffrey Hellman in 1943. "Seems to me one is about due. If I were a writer, I'd like to write the preface; I have a lot of heavyweight notions about your style and interests, etc."

But in truth Shawn was not jaunty at all, and his intensity made some writers uncomfortable. After working with him on a few pieces, the veteran contributor Margaret Case Harriman complained to Ross that "it never used to be such a life-work, such a disheartening, endless, joyless, *boring* pain in the neck to correct proofs." Shawn was S. N. "Sam" Behrman's editor on lengthy profiles of the émigré playwright Ferenc Molnár in 1946 and art dealer Joseph Duveen in 1951. Because of the hours and hours of collaborative labor needed to get the latter into shape, Behrman complained to Katharine White, not only was he prevented from leaving for a planned vacation, "but I was unable . . . to leave this *room*. Your Mr. Shawn, you may not suspect it, is the most unassuming dictator in all history. Often one doesn't know it until very late at night!"

Three days later, Behrman sent Mrs. White another letter, because

> I thought afterward it might sound as if I were complaining. I was trying of course to be facetious, probably because, unconsciously, I felt that if I were to write seriously about Shawn I might sound maudlin. The work has, of course, been hard and exhausting over a very long period. But it has been wonderful also and chiefly because of Shawn's collaboration. He has a passion for perfection, which is so rare in this sloppy age, and what he has contributed to the pieces is, literally, more than I could possibly compute. He is one of the rarest and subtlest minds I have ever encountered.

When the Duveen pieces were collected into a book the following year, the dedication was to William Shawn. (I have been unable to make an exact count of the number of books dedicated to Shawn over the years, but my best estimate is that it is somewhere between sixty and eighty.)

As previously noted, through his direction of the *New Yorker's* coverage of World War II, Shawn truly put his stamp on the magazine for the first time. "Hiroshima," published in August 1946, was the culmination of that coverage, and shortly after it appeared, Shawn told Ross he wanted to leave his editing position and try his hand at full-time writing. Sanderson Vanderbilt assumed the managing editor job, and Shawn went off to scribble. Only a few months later, however, before Shawn had completed any work he deemed worthy of publishing, Vanderbilt badly scalded himself in an accident in his apartment, and Shawn returned to the job and the magazine, never again to leave of his own accord.

On his reinstatement, Shawn began to see what he could do with the fact department in peacetime. (He also took over the book department, assigning reviewers when Edmund Wilson was not scheduled to appear, and established it as an important institution in American letters.) S. N. Behrman's Duveen series exemplifies Shawn's most immediately apparent accomplishment—expanding, in several senses of the word, the magazine's journalism. First, he greatly broadened the sense of what was acceptable subject matter. Previously, viability had been a prerequisite for the profiled; Shawn was receptive to pieces not only on the fairly recently deceased (Duveen had died in 1939), but on an unexpected figure such as the fifteenth-century Italian poet Angelo Poliziano, profiled by Alan Moorehead in 1951. The same year, A. J. Liebling set off for Chicago to begin work on what turned out to be a sparkling three-part Profile of the city. Also in 1951, Shawn's assistant Edith Oliver brought to his attention a manuscript called *The Sea Around Us,* by a little-known nature writer named Rachel Carson. He shared her enthusiasm and purchased the rights to the book, crafting nine chapters into a three-part Profile of the sea. The series received much attention upon its publication in the magazine and helped Carson's book climb to the top of the *New York Times* best-seller list, where it remained for eighty-one weeks.

Shawn was willing, a good deal more so than Ross, to let a writer take as much space as he or she felt was necessary to do a subject justice. The Duveen Profile, which ran to six parts of roughly ten thousand words each, was the longest piece, but many others were contenders. Ross commented to Rebecca West in 1950, "Shawn was talking about running a 'short' fact piece in the next issue, to balance up the long ones we had scheduled. I asked him how long it was and he said five thousand words. It's the shortest fact piece we have in the place, and we have a lot on hand. We can use them as long as we are prosperous and the issues are big. God knows what we'll do if there's a recession. At any rate, people seem to read the stories, and not to complain about length. Although once in a while people do, violently."

A significant stylistic variation on the traditional fact piece was also effected under Shawn in the postwar years. The initiator was John Hersey, who in September 1947—thirteen months after "Hiroshima"—proposed to Shawn a three-part Profile of the financier Bernard Baruch. Two of the parts would be standard accumulations of anecdote, quotation, and fact, but the third, "A Day at Saratoga," Hersey wrote to the editor,

> would be a kind of impression of Baruch; how he looks, what he does, the things he says during an offhand day. I have some superb material for this one, and I think I could make him come pretty well to life. BUT I'd be willing to

undertake this one only if you'd allow me to stay out of the story—do it, that is, not as a Roueché visit or standard reporter piece, but as if these things were happening without my being there at all. I realize this would violate a pretty basic point of view you have, but I think I can do a piece of this kind that would be fairly convincing, and would give a far better picture of Baruch.

What Hersey was proposing would later become a common journalistic technique, commonly known as "fly on the wall," but as he recognized, it represented a significant departure from contemporary practice, especially at the *New Yorker,* where the Reporter at Large style, as most frequently undertaken by Berton Roueché, a prolific young writer who had joined the staff in 1944, had a structure reminiscent of a very leisurely detective-story: the reporter selectively narrates his efforts at finding out information, and the reader follows along. Shawn saw the virtue of this new approach and gave Hersey the green light. "A Day at Saratoga"—part one of Hersey's Baruch Profile—appeared on January 3, 1948, precisely as Hersey had envisioned it: as a kind of one-act play, with plentiful dialogue and scenic and character descriptions, about a day in the life of his subject.*

One other member of the *New Yorker* staff was prepared to take Hersey's notion and run with it. This was the youthful Lillian Ross (no relation to the editor), who in the late forties was starting to branch out from her role as Talk of the Town reporter and show a special talent for truly *listening* to the way people talk and writing it down in unvarnished form. (Edmund Wilson referred to her as "the girl with the built-in tape recorder.") Her 1948 piece "Come In, Lassie!"—about the effect of anticommunist crusades on Hollywood moviemaking—featured a priceless lunchtime dialogue among John Huston, Edward G. Robinson, Humphrey Bogart, and Lauren Bacall during the filming of *Key Largo.* The next year, her report on the Miss America pageant, "Symbol of All We Possess," had in it a number of wickedly observed exchanges, including:

> "Have you seen Nebraska? She's a definite threat," said Miss New Jersey's chaperone to Miss Arkansas's chaperone.
>
> "What's her talent?" asked Miss Arkansas's chaperone.
>
> "Dramatic recitation," said Miss N.J.'s.
>
> "Confidentially," said one chaperone to another, "confidentially, I wouldn't pick *any* of the girls I've seen to be Miss America."

---

*Hersey may not have been aware of it, but a similar approach had been taken by W. C. Heinz, a sportswriter for the *New York Sun,* in "The Day of the Fight," an article he published in *Cosmopolitan* magazine in February 1947. Heinz shadowed the prizefighter Rocky Graziano for the entire day leading up to a championship bout and completely removed himself from the account.

"Some years you get a better-looking crop than others," her companion said. "At the moment, what I've got on my mind is how I can get me a good, stiff drink, and maybe two more after it."

Near the end of the year, Ernest Hemingway, whom Lillian Ross had interviewed and befriended while writing a Profile of the American-born matador Sidney Franklin, stopped in New York for a couple of days on his way to Italy. She proposed a Profile of the author and Shawn consented, with the suggestion that she limit it to an account of his time in the city. Ross's story, "How Do You Like It Now, Gentlemen?," drew great attention when it was published on May 13, 1950, in part because in the opinion of many readers it presented Hemingway as a poseur, boor, and borderline alcoholic. Ross would always maintain that it was "a sympathetic piece" in which she "tried to give a picture of the man as he was, in his uniqueness and with his vitality and his enormous feeling of fun intact." The issue is impossible to resolve, which in itself is significant: Ross makes no editorial comments in the article, but merely (albeit selectively) presents what Hemingway had to say in three or four Manhattan set pieces, letting readers assess the man. It was, in any case, an extremely impressive performance. Thurber marveled to Harold Ross, "After all these years she has added a new dimension to the rigid Profile form, and a new spark." James M. Cain, a former jesus and now a well-known crime novelist and Hollywood scriptwriter, wrote his old boss, "I don't know who Lillian Ross is, possibly a relative for all I am aware, but would like to say the piece on Hemingway is perhaps the best piece of reporting I have seen in the magazine in a long, long time. I can't imagine a more difficult assignment, because it had to be pulled off with an objectivity that could leave no room for argument, and the way it was done has led me to reread it half a dozen times, in sheer admiration."

Ross's next assignment was a Profile of the film director John Huston, and in the summer of 1950 she traveled to Hollywood to begin her reporting. (She was eager to leave New York, she later wrote, because she was uncomfortable that her relationship with Shawn was beginning to cross the border from professional to personal. Shortly after her return—as Ross described in her 1998 memoir, *Here but Not Here: My Life with William Shawn and the New Yorker*—she did embark on a love affair with Shawn, which lasted until his death, in 1992.) Huston was then preparing to direct, for the Metro-Goldwyn-Mayer studio, a film version of Stephen Crane's *The Red Badge of Courage,* and Ross's descriptions of the preproduction, in her frequent phone conversations with Shawn, sounded so interesting that he suggested making the film itself the subject of the Profile. Ross was given complete access by Huston, and as she observed the putting together of the movie, and the complex interactions among the director and the various producers, actors, technicians, and studio personnel, she began to think that she could write about these things in a completely new way. She wrote to Shawn: "You see, if the story turns out to be what I think it is, it's really almost a book, a kind of novel-like book because of the way the characters may develop and the variety of relationships that exist among them. I don't know whether this sort of thing has ever been done before, but I don't see why I shouldn't try to do a fact piece in novel form, or maybe a novel in fact form."

Ross's series about the making of *The Red Badge of Courage* was published as a five-part Onward and Upward with the Arts in the spring of 1952 (at some ninety thousand words, it was even longer than the Duveen Profile) and later that year as a book called *Picture*. This kind of journalistic work with any number of the qualities usually associated with fiction had *never* been done before. Even more than in her previous articles, Ross showed in *Picture* an uncanny ability to observe human interaction and present it in *scenes* that were charged with drama, pathos, or comedy, and always displaying the revelation of character through language. One example among dozens is an exchange between Louis B. Mayer, the famously sentimental patriarch of Metro-Goldwyn-Mayer, who had received a special Academy Award the night before, and one of his top lieutenants, Arthur Freed. Mayer has just picked up the telephone to accept a congratulatory call.

"Thanks," he said. "I couldn't hear anything. I couldn't see anything. My eyes were blinded with tears. They're giving me a recording of the whole ceremony, so I can know what I said and what happened. So I can hear it." He hung up and turned to Freed. "*Show Boat!*" he said. "I saw *Show Boat* and the tears were in my eyes. I'm not ashamed of tears. I cried. I'll see it thirteen times. Thirteen times! Tears! Emotion!"

"It's great entertainment," Freed said. "It's show business."

Mayer stared across the top of Freed's head.

"There's a singer in the picture," he went on. "Black. He has one song. He"—Mayer jabbed a finger in Freed's direction—"got the man to come all the way from Australia to sing this one song. The way he sings, it goes straight to the heart." Suddenly, Mayer lowered his voice to a basso profundo and began a shattering rendition of "Ol' Man River." Tears came to his eyes. He stopped in the middle of a line. "It's worth more than a million dollars," he said. "Talent!" Again he jabbed a finger at Freed. "He found the singer. All the way from Australia."

"There's no business like show business, all right," Freed said.

Like a novel, too, *Picture* is animated and informed by characters. That they emerge so sharply and memorably is all the more remarkable because Ross strictly limits herself to reporting what she has seen and heard; she never presumes to say what the characters are thinking and rarely says what she thinks about them. The main figures are Huston, the charming and charismatic but undependable genius who eventually loses interest in the project (before the editing is complete, he departs for Africa to film *The African Queen*), and the man he leaves holding the bag, Gottfried Reinhardt, the producer, who is intelligent, ambitious, well-intentioned, and continually frustrated in his attempts to serve both art and commerce. The supporting players range from the chillingly buffoonish Mayer, to Reinhardt's shallow wife, to the World War II hero Audie Murphy, whom Huston has chosen to play the lead but who, it becomes obvious, lacks the presence needed to carry it off.

Ross's technique is so dazzling, her set pieces so merciless and convincing, that it comes as something of a surprise eventually to grasp a final way *Picture* resembles a work of literature—it has a tragic, or more precisely a tragicomic, arc. The underpinnings of all the great bits is the story of Reinhardt and Huston's attempt to create a film that is both true to Crane's novel and, on its own terms, a work of popular art—and how that effort is, slowly but inexorably, chipped away by the studio, until little of the original vision remains. An engrossing subplot, clearer in retrospect than it was at the time, is the sea change in the motion picture industry itself. Ross was writing just as the old studio system was enjoying its last moment of hegemony, before television and a Supreme Court ruling made Hollywood just another entertainment-industry player and indirectly ushered in a fertile era for independently produced films. (Part of Huston's problem was that he was trying to make a 1970s-style movie in 1951.) The inklings of the coming fall give added irony to the posturings of Mayer and the studio's production chief, Dore Schary.

At the end of her reporting, the one interview Ross had been unable to secure was with Nicholas Schenck, who as president of MGM was Mayer's and Schary's boss and was personally responsible for all the significant corporate decisions pertaining to *The Red Badge of Courage*. When she handed in the manuscript, she recalled in *Here but Not Here*, Shawn told her that Schenck's absence created a big hole in the story. Invoking a *Front Page* ethos that was as far from his own sensibility as it was possible to get, Shawn told Ross to go at eight o'clock the next morning to Schenck's office building and wait for him to arrive. Amazingly enough, it worked: Ross accosted the executive as he stepped out of his chauffeured car, he invited her to his office, and in Ross's finished work, the first appearance of the quiet Schenck, who had all along been manipulating the characters like so many puppets, made for a chilling ending:

> "After the picture was made, Louis didn't want to release it," he said. "Louie said that as long as he was head of the studio, the picture would never be released. He refused to release it, but I changed *that*."

Schenck puffed quickly on his cigarette. "How else was I going to teach Dore?" he said. "I supported Dore. I let him make the picture. I knew that the best way to help him was to let him make a mistake. Now he will know better. A young man has to learn by making mistakes. I don't think he'll want to make a picture like that again." Schenck picked up one of his yellow pencils and jotted something down on a memo pad. Then he buzzed for his secretary and asked her to get Mr. Schary on the telephone in Culver City. After a couple of minutes, he picked up the phone and said, "Hello, my boy. How are you doing?"

In addition to its literary and human qualities, *Picture* contained a vast amount of pure information. Far more so than any previous book or article, it described virtually everything involved in the making of a Hollywood movie, with an appropriate emphasis on what things and people cost. Thus there are frequent passages like this: "Thirty-eight days had been devoted to shooting *The Red Badge of Courage*—four more than the number allotted. Of the estimated total cost of $1,434,789, $1,362,426 had already been spent, and the latest estimated cost of the movie was $1,548,755."

Five months before those words were printed, the person who would probably have relished them most, Harold Ross, had died. Shawn took the helm and functioned as editor, just as he had done during Ross's vacations and trips to the hospital. But week after week passed without any announcement that he or anyone else would take over permanently.

In some ways Shawn appeared the inevitable choice, but it could not help representing a great change for the magazine. Ross and Shawn differed in almost every conceivable respect, which was a problem in the early years of their association. Ik Shuman, an administrative editor at the magazine, told James Thurber, "As long as I was there, he [Ross] complained to me about Shawn, and Shawn would say to me in his gentle voice that he couldn't work with Ross, but they bore with each other." It was good that they did, for their differences in temperament and sensibility paled in comparison to the two qualities they did share: a "passion for perfection" and a reverence for the written word. Ross, of course, got an intense firsthand view of his lieutenant's qualities and abilities during the war. Afterward, it was clear to all who were paying attention that he had Shawn in mind as an eventual successor. One night in 1948, Ross sat around with Thurber, H. L. Mencken, and George Jean Nathan and talked about his managing editor so incessantly that Nathan finally asked, "Who is Shawn? Who is Shawn?"

In 1945, Ross—then in the middle of one of his periodic conflicts with Fleischmann, when resignation seemed a possibility—was capable of writing to his friend and attorney Julius Baer, "The *New Yorker* will blow up like a firecracker if I leave. I am so sure of that that I wouldn't gamble five cents against it, or an hour's time." However, Lillian Ross reports Shawn saying that Ross told him many times "that he was the only person capable of being the magazine's editor." But Shawn also told her that before Harold Ross went to Boston for his last operation, he begged Shawn not to try to go on with the magazine, because, he said, "It will kill you."

It may have taken so long for Shawn to become the new editor because he was mulling over those words. On the other hand, the choice was Fleischmann's to make, and Ross had made no public designation of Shawn as chosen heir, possibly to prevent the publisher from trying to spite him by naming someone else. Finally, late in January, five weeks after Ross's death, a brief letter from Fleischmann was posted on the editorial floor: "William Shawn has accepted the position of editor of *The New Yorker,* effective today."

DEPARTMENT OF CONSERVATION

When Shawn took over as editor, he had been at the *New Yorker* for nearly twenty years and had been a senior member of the staff—overseeing the magazine's journalism and working closely with Ross—for twelve. No one expected him to make dramatic changes, and he didn't—with one exception. Within weeks of his appointment, Katharine White was asking Louise Bogan to recommend poets the magazine might solicit for contributions. Shawn, she wrote, "feels that if we use serious poetry, we ought to get the best there is and he thinks we are in a position to because of our high rates of pay. Apparently he likes more *kinds* of poetry than Ross did." Later that year, Elizabeth Bishop informed her friend Marianne Moore that Shawn, "who seems to be very nice (on the telephone is the only way I know him), is really very interested in trying to get good, better, best poems, for a change—and apparently they feel very badly about some old mistake or other and would give their eyeteeth to print a poem of yours." With Howard Moss—himself a young poet of great talent and wide-ranging taste—as poetry editor, the effort bore fruit. Within a half dozen years of Shawn's accession, a bountiful crop of poets, including Moore, John Berryman, Richard Eberhart, Donald Hall, Anthony Hecht, John Hollander, Ted Hughes, Donald Justice, Galway Kinnell, Richmond Lattimore, Philip Levine, William Meredith, W. S. Merwin, Howard Nemerov, Sylvia Plath, Alastair Reid, Adrienne Rich, Louis Simpson, W. D. Snodgrass, May Swenson, John Hall Wheelock, and James Wright, had all published their first poems in the *New Yorker,* joining such past stalwarts as Bishop, John Ciardi, Robert Graves, Theodore Roethke, Karl Shapiro, William Stafford, Richard Wilbur, and Moss himself. In a 1954 article heralding the possible beginning of a "poetic golden age" in America, Donald Hall singled out the *New*

Yorker as the popular magazine that had been most receptive to the new generation of poets.

The one other notable thing about Shawn's early years as editor was not an action but an inaction: he neither hired not promoted anyone to replace himself as chief editor for factual writing, nor did he during his entire tenure. At the time, this did not strike anyone as unusual or worthy of comment. But in retrospect, it is portentous. Shawn's feelings about power were camouflaged by his gentle manner but were deep-seated and intense. The writer Harold Brodkey, who was associated with the magazine for more than four decades starting in the mid-1950s, once described him as "combining the best qualities of Napoleon and St. Francis of Assisi." There was never any doubt that Ross was the chief executive of the operation, but for all his tantrums and rages, he delegated freely and willingly. Shawn, in his deceptively passive way, accumulated more and more power to himself, never allowing a lieutenant to have the kind of influence he himself had enjoyed with Ross. Nor, after the death of Gus Lobrano in 1956 and the retirement of Katharine White the following year, did he appoint a chief fiction editor. Under his editorship, the storied "art meeting" dwindled to a weekly evaluation of the incoming drawings between him and James Geraghty, the art editor. Geraghty frequently disagreed with Shawn, but was bemused to find that he could never engage him in battle. "When he sensed I really liked something that he didn't," Geraghty wrote in an unpublished memoir, "he would buy it, but not use it, and here, he was devious." Each time layout editor Carmine Peppe put the disputed cartoon in a dummy for the coming week's issue, Shawn would throw it out, until Peppe got the idea, and the cartoon was thereafter consigned to the inventory of unpublished material.

Geraghty finally came up with an apt description of Shawn's management style: he was a "one-man cabal." One day he shared this observation with his boss. The editor "smiled faintly."

What really changed with the accession of Shawn was the atmosphere at the *New Yorker*. Janet Flanner remarked on it in a letter to Katharine White: "Everybody knows that the give-and-take with Ross which began on his side with 'Jeezchrist' & then got down to brass tacks at once—that *burst* of communication—is gone because he had it & Shawn hasn't it to give. Something else but not that." Shawn's editorial and managerial style was marked by a certain furtiveness and intrigue. An innately secretive man, even before assuming the editorship he began to take pains to erase any public record of his actions and decisions. Rather than write letters to authors and memos to staff members—as Ross had done with a joyous and almost aggressive frequency—Shawn preferred the personal meeting, the telephone call, or if distance made written communication absolutely necessary, the cable or telegram. A writer named Hamilton Basso began occasionally relieving Edmund Wilson as book reviewer in 1945, and he wrote letter after letter to Shawn, with no reply. Finally Basso asked if the editor was even receiving the correspondence. Shawn finally wrote back: "Yes, I am here, but as I warned you, I write no letters. This is a note." Shawn wrote to S. N. Behrman the next year, "Please burn the enclosed letter if you have no immediate use for it. Or, if you don't burn letters, please tear it into an adequate number of pieces and throw it away. I am not keeping a carbon copy." Shawn would continue to habitually eliminate any paper trail. Years later, John Updike, who worked on staff as a Talk of the Town writer in the midfifties, nervously inquired of William Maxwell about the whereabouts of his own fiction and poetry manuscripts. Later, Updike apologized for having appeared alarmed: "It was just that in my tenure there I saw Shawn throw so many things in the wastebasket I became anxious."

Shawn was strongly loyal to the people who worked with him and to the *New Yorker*. But he was also inherently cautious, and in his early years as editor, he took great pains not to stick his or the magazine's neck out. This was evident in the way he dealt with the national scrutiny of individuals' political loyalties, now known as McCarthyism. The longtime contributor Walter Bernstein, blacklisted from working as a scriptwriter for the movies and television because of his leftist beliefs, hoped to make up for some of his lost income by writing for the *New Yorker*. "But the atmosphere had changed there, too," Bernstein wrote in a memoir years later. "It had become murky. Shawn was unfailingly polite, but assignments that had been habitual were not now forthcoming."

A more dramatic and ultimately disturbing case was that of Kay Boyle, who had written short stories for the magazine since 1931. In 1952 and 1953, Boyle's husband, Joseph Franckenstein, a State Department official in occupied Germany, was relieved from his duties as the result of a particularly nasty and foundationless bit of witch-hunting. He ended up as a language teacher and assistant headmaster at a girls' boarding school in Connecticut, a sad and defeated man. Boyle considered herself blacklisted by all leading American magazines and indeed had little success placing articles and stories through the decade. Until her death in 1992, Boyle would place the blame for these unhappy events on the *New Yorker*, and in particular on William Shawn.

Without question, Boyle's interpretation was an oversimplification. Yet it had some truth. Franckenstein had never been a communist or a communist sympathizer, so, in typical McCarthyist fashion, the suspicion migrated to Boyle, who, while not politically active in any organized way, had over the years signed her name to numerous petitions put out by communist-front groups and contributed small amounts of money to some of them. In addition, she had lived an unconventional personal life, giving birth to three children out of wedlock. By the spring of 1952, although she had no government post herself, she had formally been made part of the "loyalty hearing" and consequently solicited supporting letters and testimony from personal and professional associates. Boyle and her attorneys considered the *New Yorker's* endorsement the most important one, both because of the magazine's standing and because it could be presented as her employer: in 1946, Ross had accredited her as a staff correspondent, writing both fiction and journalism out of Germany. Since then she had published only one fact piece, but more than half a dozen strong short stories set in the occupied country.

Although Boyle considered Shawn's letter in support of her woefully tepid, actually it was not so bad. After stating truthfully that since it was Ross who had always been Boyle's editor, he himself had "had practically no firsthand dealings with her" nor "ever discussed politics with her," he wrote:

> Nevertheless, I have heard a good deal about Miss Boyle from Mr. Ross and others, I have read her writings, and in my few meetings with her I have formed a personal impression and everything leads me to have confidence in her loyalty to the United States and to our form of government. I believe her to be a woman not only of rare literary talent but of extraordinary character and of great spirituality. I have always taken her loyalty for granted, and I could only be astonished if it were to be questioned.

Gus Lobrano, who as fiction editor now received (and almost always rejected) Boyle's submissions, also wrote a letter, and his not only limped in four months after Shawn's but was shamefully inadequate. Astonishingly, he volunteered that he had heard Boyle "make critical comments about our government," adding lamely that he had heard General Eisenhower do so as well. Equally gratuitously, he commented that the writer, "out of an extraordinary sympathy for the human race, combined with what seems to me political naïveté, might be cozened and imposed on." Boyle's attorney at the hearings later told Boyle's biographer Joan Mellen that (in Mellen's words) he was "appalled" at the equivocal nature of the letters, and in fact Lobrano's line about her naïveté was seized on by her inquisitors.

In January 1953, after the hearings were concluded but before the board had issued its findings, a new blow came. Each year the Heidelberg Military Post asked the *New Yorker* to sign a document confirming that Boyle was an accredited correspondent. This was in the nature of a formality, since Boyle had in fact already been officially accredited for a term expiring in November 1953. But this year Shawn refused to sign. He later explained to Janet Flanner, who had testified in Boyle's behalf and was outraged by what she saw as the *New Yorker's* rejection of her friend, that he made this decision because of the language on the form: " 'Subject correspondent is a full time bona fide correspondent who will file copy on a regular schedule.' . . . I guess that's enough, Janet. She is not a bona fide correspondent at this moment, and we have no expectation whatever that she will file copy on a regular schedule." He was, he added, "constitutionally incapable" of signing a representation to the contrary.

What Shawn said could be seen as correct in a narrow sense, but he himself was being monumentally naive if he didn't realize that his decision would have a devastating effect on the hearing. Boyle wrote Shawn that it was a "grave matter" when sponsorship was withdrawn in this atmosphere, and that she was already being asked for an explanation of the *New Yorker's* abandonment of her. She had none, and the hearings proceeded on their grim course.

Shawn's letter to Flanner defending his and the magazine's actions in the Boyle case runs to three and one-half single-spaced pages—by a good margin the longest extant piece of Shawn personal correspondence, and, at least on the principle of excessive protest, proof that on some level he grasped that his actions had thrown Boyle and her husband to the wolves. Flanner, at least, was not at all convinced by his brief. "Have I been completely mistaken in the character of Bill and of the magazine too?" she asked Boyle. It was fine for E. B. White to express noble sentiments against McCarthyism in Notes and Comment, she went on. But: "When it comes to acting, proving, & bearing witness, what did the magazine DO when Kay was in trouble?"

The most devastating judgment came in a letter from Boyle to Shawn. She said, simply and unassailably, "Harold would have done it in a different way."

The Boyle affair displays, with the utmost clarity, the most notable quality of Shawn's first decade, roughly, as editor: he did not want to upset the apple cart. That meant a steadfast avoidance of controversy, or indeed, of drawing attention to the magazine in any way. The American fifties were placid and so was Shawn's *New Yorker;* it spoke in hushed and decorous tones. As Boyle had observed, Shawn was no Ross, and one more difference was that where the founding editor loudly gloated when the magazine was in a position to break news, his successor shunned the "big story" as being unseemly. Joseph Wechsberg, who set up shop in the late forties as the magazine's European correspondent, generally was drawn to topics like classical music and fine food. But in 1954 he found himself in Budapest in a moment of tumultuous political change and was almost apologetic about having to cover it. He cabled Shawn that he was relieved that the editor liked his dispatch: WAS

AFRAID YOU MIGHT CONSIDER IT QUOTE SCOOP QUOTE BECAUSE I WAS THE ONLY AMERICAN THERE.

A Letter from Vienna Wechsberg wrote the next year was scoop-free, but after it was published, Wechsberg sent Shawn a letter complaining about the magazine's "cutting out every bit of criticism of either the Austrians or the Americans in Vienna. . . . I'm not writing for the State Department or the Austrian Foreign Ministry but for the *New Yorker.*" True to his passive ways, Shawn did not respond. But Wechsberg would not let the matter drop. He cabled Shawn: YOU MUST TRUST MY JOURNALISTIC INTEGRITY AND JUDGMENT AS OBSERVER. MOST OF MY FACTS SIMPLY CANNOT BE WATERED DOWN OR ELIMINATED EVEN IF SOME ARE UNPLEASANT TRUTHS. This time Shawn cabled back, completely denying any censorship: ALL CHANGES IN YOUR PIECES HAVE BEEN MADE FOR PURELY TECHNICAL OR ESTHETIC REASONS.

The denial was not very convincing, if only because something else Shawn would avoid (in addition to scoops), with greater and greater assiduity over the years, was printing articles that criticized or mocked individuals. It was another difference between Shawn and Ross, who had taken great pleasure in commissioning, editing, and publishing scathing and sometimes devastating Profiles of, among others, Henry Luce, Frank Hague, Thomas Dewey, Walter Winchell, and the *Reader's Digest.*

The early Shawn years were a kind of conservatorship. Needless to say, there were no noticeable departures in the look of the *New Yorker.* The subtle graphic changes that did occur softened or flattened the magazine. Traditionally, fact pieces, especially Profiles, had been illustrated by caricaturists, most notably Al Frueh, but also Abe Birnbaum and Will Cotton. Shawn took over from Geraghty the assigning of illustrations for these articles, and his artists—Thomas B. Allen, Tom Funk, Burt Silverman, Bernie Fuchs—were naturalistic, muted, and designed to blend into the editorial scenery. Covers evolved under Shawn as well. The prototypical *New Yorker* cover of the Ross era was an uncaptioned cartoon in (usually bright) color, frequently by cartoonists Charles Addams, Peter Arno, Perry Barlow, Leonard Dove, Helen Hokinson, Rea Irvin, Mary Petty, Garrett Price, or Saul Steinberg, or by cover specialists Constantin Alajalov, Ludwig Bemelmans, Will Cotton, Julian DeMiskey (who signed his covers "M"), or Charles Martin ("CEM"). Shawn's covers—executed by Birnbaum, Roger Duvoisin, Ilonka Karasz, Edna Eicke, Robert Kraus, Beatrice Szanton, and especially Arthur Getz, a master of Manhattan light who, over more than five decades, contributed more *New Yorker* covers than any other artist—tended to be pictorial, sober, muted, dark-hued, and often without any human beings. In 1938, thirty-six *New Yorker* covers showed a human face with recognizable features. In 1963, the number was only eleven. (Oddly, the faces seemed to have migrated in the 1950s to the advertisements, which frequently stared readers eyeball-to-eyeball, as if challenging them to better their lives by using the recommended product.)

As for the text, few new bylines appeared in Shawn's first years. This was partly a function of demographics: so many writers had become associated with the magazine during the war that even with a new issue to put out every week, and with the issues getting fatter and fatter because of increased advertising sales, it was difficult to find a place for the work of all of them. The handful of recruits Shawn did bring in to the fact department were instructive. Almost without exception, every writer Ross hired was a former newspaper reporter. Shawn looked in different directions. The first man he brought on staff, in the spring of 1952, was Dwight Macdonald, who, though he had once been a staff writer for *Fortune* and had written Profiles for the *New Yorker,* was much more an intellectual than a journalist. Macdonald's work for the magazine in the fifties actually combined the two endeavors. Starting with a devastating, seventeen-page critique of a fifty-four volume set of the "Great Books of the Western World," put out under the auspices of the Encyclopedia Britannica (Macdonald called it a "typical expression of the religion of culture that appeals to the American academic mentality"), he made a series of caustic, invigorating, and well-researched explorations into the politics of culture in America.

The archetypal literary man was Edmund Wilson, and he did journalism for Shawn, too. Or, rather, such pieces as "The Dead Sea Scrolls" (1956) and "Apologies to the Iroquois" (1959) were blends of high-level scholarship, criticism, journalism, and advocacy such as had not been attempted before. Shawn also encouraged Mary McCarthy and S. N. Behrman, who had both previously contributed casuals, short stories, and reminiscences to the magazine, to write long (sometimes very long), literary fact pieces. In 1956 and 1959, McCarthy published Profiles of the cities of Venice and Florence, which were subsequently brought out as *Venice Observed* and *The Stones of Florence* and have become classics in the literature of travel and art. In 1960, Behrman contributed an unprecedented seven-part Profile of Max Beerbohm, the recently deceased author and caricaturist. It was roughly three times as long as "Hiroshima." McCarthy and Behrman also wrote in this period splendid childhood memoirs, later published, respectively, as *Memories of a Catholic Girlhood* and *The Worcester Account.*

Another member of Shawn's small stable was Truman Capote, who in the early forties had worked as a clerk in the *New Yorker* art department, holding up the drawings while Ross jabbed at them with his knitting needle and made suggestions for improvement. Capote was fired in 1944 after Ross got the notion (mistaken, Capote always maintained) that he had masqueraded as a *New Yorker* representative and insulted Robert Frost while the poet was giving a reading at the Breadloaf Writers Conference. Capote went on to

DOMESTIC SERVICE			WESTERN UNION		INTERNATIONAL SERVICE	

```
┌─────────────────────────┬───────┐                                    ┌──────────────────────────┐
│ DOMESTIC SERVICE        │       │   WESTERN UNION                    │ INTERNATIONAL SERVICE    │
│ Check the class of service desired. │ $ │                            │ Check the class of service desired, │
│ otherwise this message will be │   │                                │ otherwise the message will be │
│ sent as a fast telegram │ $ │       TELEGRAM        1206 (1-55)     │ sent at the full rate    │
├─────────────────────────┤       │                                    ├──────────────────────────┤
│ TELEGRAM                │       │                                    │ FULL RATE                │
│ DAY LETTER              │ E │   W. P. MARSHALL, PRESIDENT            │ LETTER TELEGRAM          │
│ NIGHT LETTER            │       │                                    │ SHORE-SHIP               │
└─────────────────────────┴───────┘                                    └──────────────────────────┘
```

NO. WDS.-CL. OF SVC.	PD. OR COLL.	CASH NO.	CHARGE TO THE ACCOUNT OF	TIME FILED

The New Yorker Magazine, Inc.

Send the following message, subject to the terms on back hereof, which are hereby agreed to

Night Cable   Via W. U. Cables   June 25, 1956

Mary McCarthy
c/o Angleton
Via Morone 8
MILAN

SECOND PROOF OF PART TWO AIRMAILED TO YOU TODAY PERIOD PLEASE CABLE WHEN RECEIVED AND AIRMAIL BACK JUST AS SOON AS POSSIBLE PERIOD YOUR SECOND PROOF PART ONE ARRIVED PERIOD THANK YOU FOR ALL THE EXPERT AND GRACEFUL FIXES PERIOD HAVE A TITLE FOR PIECE TO SUGGEST QUOTE THE REVEL OF THE WORLD UNQUOTE PERIOD IF YOU LIKE THAT ONE COMMA WOULD YOU PLEASE TRY TO WRITE BRIEF INSERT FOR BOTH PART ONE AND PART TWO WORKING IN THE BYRON QUOTATION THAT IS IN YOUR BOOK BUT NOT IN THE PIECE PERIOD THEN PLEASE CABLE INSERTS OR AT LEAST PART ONE INSERT IMMEDIATELY PERIOD EYE ALSO SUGGEST THAT YOU MIGHT CONSIDER RECASTING LAST TWO OR THREE SENTENCES OR POSSIBLY ONLY LAST SENTENCE OF PART TWO SINCE YOU DID NOT ORIGINALLY HAVE IN MIND THAT THIS WOULD BE AN ENDING PERIOD SINCE ENTIRE PIECE IS ON SUCH A HIGH PLANE OF ELOQUENCE YOU MAY WANT THE ENDING TO BE PITCHED A DEGREE HIGHER THAN IT IS NOW PERIOD HOWEVER IF YOU DO NOT FEEL THAT WAY EYE AM PERFECTLY SATISFIED WITH PRESENT ENDING PERIOD EYE MAY BE CABLING A FEW LAST MINUTE QUERIES BEFORE WE GO TO PRESS WITH PART ONE THIS WEEK PERIOD REGARDS

WILLIAM SHAWN

William Shawn did not like to be pinned down, and preferred the personal meeting or the telephone call to the letter or memo. When he had to communicate in print, his favorite vehicle was the cable. This one concerns Mary McCarthy's Profile of Venice, which was in fact published under the title "The Revel of the Earth."

have a great success with his novel *Other Voices, Other Rooms,* but he was never able to sell a short story to the *New Yorker.** Instead, he got in through the fact door. In 1955, following up on a suggestion from the composer Harold Arlen, Capote proposed to Shawn that he go to the Soviet Union to cover the tour of an American company of *Porgy and Bess.* Rather remarkably—Capote had never written a word of journalism, and the magazine never advanced substantial expense money to anyone who wasn't a staff

---

*Ross, who was totally nonplussed by Capote's mincing manner, remarked to Lobrano in 1947, "If Capote is great, I am leaving the country." But two years later, when his story "Shut a Final Door" was included in the annual O. Henry collection, Katharine White told Ross that she thought it was the best story in the book: "Yes, it is morbid perhaps, certainly neurotic, the study of a disintegrating man, but it is powerful, and not exactly a fantasy this time, and is really the only story in the volume that seems to me to carry the marks of an original writing talent. I think we are foolish to close our eyes to Capote, just because he is so objectionable a character. A lot of what he writes is pure tripe, a lot is too decadent or psychopathic for us, his novel was bad, but occasionally he crashes through with something really good. This is one of them, I think." Ross being Ross, he dispatched the editor who worked with Capote's agent to tell her to send along any Capote stories "that aren't too psychopathic."

writer or at least a longtime contributor—the editor agreed. The assent would hold a prominent place in any brief for Shawn's standing as an editor of genius. Capote's report, published as an Onward and Upward with the Arts (and later a book) called "The Muses Are Heard," was a blithe and sardonic counterpoint to Lillian Ross's tragicomic "Picture," written with a similarly unerring ear. Unlike Ross, Capote was not interested in the process by which art is produced; only at the very end of the piece's fifty thousand words do we glimpse for the first time any of the performance of the opera. Rather, he gravitates to the incongruity of his characters and setting: the mixed signals, the posturing, the unavoidable clash of cultures. As a reporter, Capote pursued a cunning, effective, and prescient strategy: he never concealed his journalistic presence, but he generally disregarded the statements his characters made "on the record," concentrating instead on the ways they revealed themselves when they assumed they weren't being observed. Genially eccentric in manner, appearance, and dress, he was the kind of person others naturally opened up to. Also helpful in getting good stuff was his casting away of all the journalist's traditional tools. He later wrote of his "talent for mentally recording lengthy conversations, an ability I had worked to achieve while researching *The Muses Are Heard,* for I devoutly believe that the taking of notes—much less the use of a *tape recorder!*—creates artifice and distorts or even destroys any naturalness that might exist between the observer and the observed, the nervous hummingbird and its would-be captor."*

Capote's own puckish presence often adds to the atmosphere of mischief, as in this passage, where he describes being at a workingman's bar in Leningrad with a new Russian acquaintance:

> Orlov ordered Russian cognac, a brackish liquid that came in large tea glasses overflowing their brim. With the blitheness of a man blowing foam off beer, he emptied a third of his glass and asked if the café "pleased" me, or did I think it "rough." I answered yes, and yes. "Rough, but not hooligan," he differentiated. "On the waterfront, yes, that is hooligan. But here is just ordinary. A workingman's place. No snobs." We had eight companions at the table and they took an interest in me, picked at me like magpies, plucked a cigarette lighter out of my hand, a scarf from around my neck, objects they passed from one to the next, glaring at them, grinning over them, and show-

*The lack of a documentary record of interviews makes fabrication a good deal easier, and Capote indulged. Nancy Ryan, an employee of the opera company who spent a lot of time with Capote on the trip and was prominently featured in *The Muses Are Heard,* told Capote's biographer that one of the main set pieces of the book, an encounter with some drunken Russians and a gallant Norwegian in the Brest Litovsk railroad station, was completely made up. "He fiddled with things," she said. "But he didn't destroy basic truth or genuine spirit at all."

ing, even the youngest, rows of rotted teeth, wrinkles for which age could not account. The man nearest was jealous and wanted all my attention. It was impossible to guess how old he was, anywhere from forty to seventy. He had an eye missing, and this circumstance enabled him to do a trick which he kept forcing me to watch. It was meant to be a parody of Christ on the Cross. Taking a swallow of beer he would stretch his arms and droop his head. In a moment a trickle of beer came crying out the gaping redness of his hollow eye socket. His friends at the table thought it was an uproarious stunt.

A year later, Shawn sent Capote to Kyoto, Japan, to do a sort of follow-up piece, about the making of a Marlon Brando film called *Sayonara*. But Capote arrived only to find that the director of the film, Joshua Logan, had read *The Muses Are Heard* and was in no mood for his own project to get the same treatment. Consequently, he had barred Capote from the set. But Brando, who knew Capote casually from New York, agreed to meet him for an interview. Capote later said that his decision to write a Profile of the actor based on the interview was a kind of literary experiment: "What is the lowest level of journalistic art, the one most difficult to turn from a sow's ear into a silk purse? The movie star 'interview,' *Silver Screen* stuff: surely nothing could be less easily elevated than that!" The Profile, published in 1957 as "The Duke in His Domain," was in fact not all that elevated. It was notable mainly for the level of painful and introspective candor Brando displayed, as he talked about watching his alcoholic mother break "like a piece of porcelain" until he "could just step right over her, her lying on the floor, and not feel a thing, not give a damn." During the interview Capote had prompted Brando's outpouring with his own confessions (he had an alcoholic mother, too); of course, he did not include any of that material in the article. Brando later said, "The little bastard spent half the night telling me all his problems. I figured the least I could do was tell him a few of mine."

Of the veteran writers, the standard-bearers, Joseph Mitchell and A. J. Liebling, continued to produce outstanding work during the fifties. Liebling, with his raucous editorial persona, would have been valuable if only for shattering the polite murmuring that otherwise prevailed in the magazine's pages. In addition to his pointed and vivid press criticism, he contributed numerous pieces about the world of boxing (collected as *The Sweet Science*) and a wonderful portrait of Earl Long, a classic lowlife subject who happened to be governor of Louisiana. (His series on an eccentric racetrack handicapper he called Colonel John Stingo was less successful, sometimes threatening to drown in its own mannerisms.)

Mitchell, who was stunningly prolific in his early years at the *New Yorker*, had slowed down visibly by this time, taking two or three years to write each piece. But the result was always worth the wait. His articles from the fifties—"The Bottom of the Harbor," "Up in the Old Hotel," "Mr. Hunter's Grave," and "The Rivermen"—were truly groundbreaking. Their leisurely and immaculate prose was familiar, as were their themes: mortality, the sea, seafood, and man's folly. But Mitchell was pioneering a new kind of literary journalism, a mix of personal revelation, rich symbolism, deep psychological portraiture, and the "graveyard humor" he had always favored, all moving with a stately rhythm in search of universal truth.

"The Bottom of the Harbor" (January 6, 1951) was exemplary. It begins with a lengthy description of how "oily, dirty, and germy" New York Harbor is, followed by an account of marine life's persistence in spite of it. Even in Brooklyn's Gowanus Canal, where "the sludge rots in warm water and from it gas-filled bubbles as big as basketballs continually surge to the surface," even there, a few fish can be found. Mitchell: "The water is dead up at the head of it—only germs can live there—but from the crook at the Sixth Street Basin on down to the mouth there are cunners and tomcods and eels. The cunners nibble on the acorn barnacles under old quays." And those old quays aren't the only human products that fortuitously support life. At the bottom of the harbor, providing shelter for fish and covered with a lush organic growth they can eat, are a hundred or more shipwrecks, as well as numerous artificial ledges made up of debris from slum-clearance projects and other urban demolitions. One of them, the "Door Knob Grounds," consists of houses that, until their demolition in 1933, were rented "to the poorest of the poor, and the tuberculosis death rate was higher in that block than in any other block in the city."

Mitchell's method is always to go from the general to the individual, and so he introduces us to an unnamed Staten Island physician in his late fifties whose father and grandfather farmed the now-condemned oyster beds, and who now, flouting the law, habitually goes out and tongs for bivalves. He takes Mitchell out on one of his expeditions, brings up an oyster, and eats it with relish. "Every time I eat harbor oysters," he says, "my childhood comes floating up from the bottom of my mind."

The bottom of the harbor, the bottom of the mind: Mitchell is interested in plumbing all kinds of depths. The piece concludes with a portrait of the Staten Island doctor's theoretical adversary, Andrew E. Zimmer, a state Conservation Department employee charged with enforcing laws relating to shellfish and finfish. One "cold, windy, spitty morning," after taking Mitchell on a patrol of the polluted skimmer-clam beds in the ocean off Rockaway Beach, Zimmer suggests warming up with a plate of oyster stew at Lundy's restaurant in Sheepshead Bay, Brooklyn. There he spies Leroy Poole, a fishing-boat captain who raises the emotional temperature of the narrative to fever level. Poole is a character out of Melville, or maybe

Kafka—"a harbor nut," Zimmer tells Mitchell as the captain finishes his oysters at the raw bar. "He's got bottom of the harbor on the brain."

When Poole comes over to join the party for some stew, this assessment proves correct. Without any prologue he relates a dream he had the previous night, a strange and terrifying dream filled with Boschean imagery:

> A great earthquake had shook the world and had upset the sea level, and New York Harbor had been drained as dry as a bathtub when the plug is pulled. I was down on the bottom, poking around, looking things over. There were hundreds of ships of all kinds lying on their sides in the mud, and among them were some wormy old wrecks that went down long years ago, and there were rusty anchors down there and dunnage and driftwood and old hawsers and tugboat bumpers and baling wire and tin cans and bottles and stranded eels and a skeleton standing waist-deep in a barrel of cement that the barrel had rotted off of. The rats had left the piers and were down on the bottom, eating the eels, and the gulls were flopping about, jerking eels away from the rats. I came across an old wooden wreck all grown over with seaweed, an old, old Dutch wreck. She had a hole in her, and I pulled the seaweed away and looked in and I saw some chests in there that had money spilling out of them, and I tried my best to crawl in. The dream was so strong that I crawled up under the headboard of the bed, trying to get my hands on the Dutch money, and I damned near scraped an ear off.

Zimmer's only response is, "Eat your stew, Roy, before it gets cold." But the dream is clearly filled with import. Poole's imagination sucks the opaque and protective coating of water from the harbor, leaving only humanity's distasteful leavings and a Darwinian struggle between noisy and distasteful creatures—rats and gulls—over a supper of eels, hardly a glorious prize.

As the two baymen talk, it emerges that Zimmer tends to look on the bright side. Not Leroy Poole. Wakefulness doesn't allow him to escape his dark vision—his perception grants him *no* protective coating on reality. He talks about the place in the harbor where a couple of dozen "drownded" bodies turn up every spring. On the subject of pollution, Zimmer allows that "they're putting in a lot of sewage-disposal plants. The water's getting cleaner every year." Poole will have none of it. Last spring's shad—Staten Island shad *and* New Jersey shad—had the worst kerosene taste ever, he says. In fact, he goes on:

> "I don't even worry about the pollution anymore. My only hope, I hope they don't pollute the harbor with something a million times worse than pollution."
>
> "Let's don't get on that subject," said Mr. Zimmer.
>
> "Sometimes I'm walking along the street," continued Mr. Poole, "and I

wonder why the people don't just stand still and throw their heads back and open their mouths and howl."

"Why?" asked Mr. Zimmer.

"I'll tell you why," said Mr. Poole. "On account of the Goddamned craziness of everything."

Mr. Poole finishes his stew and gets up to leave, and Mr. Zimmer sends him off with six words: "Take care. Take care. Take care." They are followed by the byline—JOSEPH MITCHELL. We understand that he is offering a benediction to us, as well, and we understand how much we need it.

Shawn's tack toward the writers not quite on the level of Mitchell and Liebling suggests one of the qualities he shared with Ross: a kind of cosmic patience. He essentially left them to their own devices, with the expectation that they would produce meritorious work. Michael Arlen, a young Harvard graduate (and the son and namesake of the Armenian-English author of *The Green Hat*) who began publishing casuals in the late fifties, said, "Most of journalism is a demand proposition—the supposed great editors thundering, 'Jones do this, Smith do that.' Shawn believed that the most powerful and authentic emotions are the voluntary ones. His particular kind of genius was most effective with men and women who had an innate sense of structure and a strong work ethic. In that way, it was not unlike a good progressive school."

One good pupil was Philip Hamburger, who determined, on his own, that he would attempt a Profile of the novelist John Marquand *in the style of Marquand*. The result, published in March 1952, was a nearly flawless tour de force. Frequently, Shawn's willingness not to press the issue allowed writers to follow the example of Richard Rovere, ostensibly a generalist, who one day found himself a Washington correspondent and ended up as one of the country's most influential and distinguished capitol reporters, and Daniel Lang, who was somehow drawn to writing about atomic matters and became an invaluable chronicler of the subject. And so, in the fifties, John Brooks, a young writer Ross had hired out of *Time* magazine, gravitated to the world of business and became the magazine's unofficial Wall Street correspondent. Berton Roueché, while writing a Reporter at Large about the discovery and treatment of an outbreak of rickets in the borough of Queens, had the good sense to realize that he had invented a new genre: the factual medical detective story. His subsequent narratives, meticulously written and irresistible to read, were given a new rubric in the magazine—"Annals of Medicine"; by the time of his death, in 1993, he had crafted fifty-eight of them. Shawn could take personal credit for the arrival in the magazine's pages of another distinguished new specialist. In the middle fifties, a young staff member named Whitney Balliett was working as a "collator"—the person in charge of incorporating all the changes made by the legal, fact-checking, and copyediting departments onto a single master galley proof. Balliett was an amateur drummer and a jazz enthusiast who had written some pieces on the music for the *Atlantic Monthly* and the *Saturday Review.** (His contributions to the *New Yorker* had consisted of some poems and books reviews.) One day in 1957 Shawn asked him if he wanted to do a jazz column, and Balliett agreed. He would become perhaps the single most graceful, authoritative, and sympathetic writer on the form, and he is still writing about jazz for the *New Yorker.*

In 1956, shortly after Gus Lobrano's death, Shawn hired Roger Angell—Katharine White's son and E. B. White's stepson, and a longtime contributor of short stories and humorous casuals to the magazine—as a fiction editor. Angell was a passionate and informed baseball fan, and he had observed that with the exception Liebling's boxing pieces, the *New Yorker's* sports coverage was nil. In the winter of 1962, he proposed to Shawn that he go to spring training to write about the preparations of the city's new National League baseball team, the New York Mets. Although Shawn knew so little about baseball that the concept "spring training" was unfamiliar to him, he gave Angell another one of his inspired assents, and an inspired five words of editorial direction: "Don't be sentimental or cynical." Angell avoided those pitfalls and has instead been insightful, thorough, and elegant in his nearly two score years as America's poet laureate of baseball.

Unlike Ross, Shawn would never think of effecting editorial changes through the reassigning or, much less, dismissing of contributors. A *New Yorker* column, therefore, was the equivalent of a tenured position in the academic world. In the fifties, "departmental" writers including Wolcott Gibbs on theater, John McCarten on film, Lois Long on fashion, Robert Coates on art, Lewis Mumford on architecture, and George Ryall ("Audax Minor") on the racetrack had all occupied their posts for more than a decade, and in some cases more than two. As skillful and discerning as these critics were, the reference points for all of them were an earlier time, and all to some degree gave the magazine a faintly antique air. Yet Shawn's assumption was that they would occupy their posts until retirement or death. The first of the above group to depart was Gibbs, who died unexpectedly in August 1958. Shawn's choice as a replacement was illuminating. He reached across the Atlantic to tap a man who could be argued to be the wittiest, most incisive drama critic in the language: Kenneth Tynan, then reviewing theater for the English newspaper *The Observer.*

---

*On several occasions, Balliett jammed with Shawn, who had some talent as a jazz pianist. "When I played with him, he seemed like a totally different man," Balliett recalled. "He was at peace. That was also the only time he ever called me Whitney. The rest of the time, it was always Mr. Balliett."

Tynan, then in his early thirties, had been an admirer of the *New Yorker* since he was a boy; at sixteen he had tried to produce an imitation of the magazine for provincial England. Even so, he had some trepidation about taking the post. He told a reporter, "They say the *New Yorker* is the bland leading the bland. I don't know if I'm bland enough." In truth, he was able to make the magazine a little bit spicier. Tynan remained at the *New Yorker* for only two seasons, spanning 1958–60, and during that time was unable to cover plays by Edward Albee, Samuel Beckett, Eugène Ionesco, and most of the other exciting new theatrical work in New York, since they were running off-Broadway, and he was limited to the Broadway stage. Despite these restrictions, Tynan visibly raised the level of critical prose at the magazine, as can be seen in his description of George C. Scott's performance in *The Andersonville Trial*:

> Mr. Scott is an intense performer with a voice that can achieve maximum acceleration and minimum intelligibility more swiftly than any of its Broadway competitors, and a chronic indisposition to admit that there are any nuances of volume between pp and ff. His eyes rove in a manner that recalls the German silent screen, and his profile has the steely, prehensile outline of an invariably victorious bottle opener. His very presence breathes melodrama. It does, however, breathe, and I should like to see its vitality put to less febrile uses.

SAD STATE OF HUMOR

Not long after the founding of the *New Yorker,* lamentations began to be voiced (both from within and without) that it wasn't funny anymore—or, at least, that it wasn't funny enough. And no one could deny that it didn't publish as many significant funny *writers.* The first generation—Benchley, Thurber, Sullivan, and White—were twice as numerous as the second, which consisted of Perelman and Nash, and they were followed in the 1940s by the solitary and somewhat melancholy figure of Peter De Vries. De Vries was a native of Holland, Michigan, where he grew up in a family that strictly followed the precepts of the Dutch Reformed Church. In 1943, he wrote an admiring essay in *Poetry Magazine,* for which he was an editor, called "James Thurber: The Comic Prufrock." Thurber and De Vries became friends, and the following year, under Thurber's encouragement, De Vries sent Harold Ross some Comments pieces and art ideas. Ross replied: "I have gone over them and find, to my astonishment, that they are what can readily be described, in the language of this office, as very promising. This is an unusual experience. It is rare to read anything from a new writer and find him both literate and amusing." (The same day, Ross summed De Vries up in a memo to James Geraghty: "He comes from Chicago and seems to have a sense of humor.")

With the staff ravaged by war, Ross soon offered De Vries a job as poetry editor, and he and his wife, the poet and short-story writer Katinka Loeser, came East. He immediately began publishing casuals that unmistakably came out of Thurber and Perelman but were also unmistakably De Vries. They generally centered around a bemused protagonist at the mercy, alternately, of his extravagant amorous urges, his repressive upbringing, and his uncheckable urge toward highbrow allusions and breathtaking puns. With a finely tuned sense of both language and humor, De Vries also proved helpful to the *New Yorker*'s art department, generating cartoon ideas and polishing the situations and captions of others. By 1948, he was doing so much of this that Ross assigned Howard Moss to take over poetry and arranged for De Vries to work for Geraghty three days a week (at a rate of $35 a day). De Vries continued some variant of this job until 1986, when ill health forced him to retire. (He died in 1993.) Ironically, the job led to the diminishing of and eventual halt to his *New Yorker* casuals: the financial security the part-time post gave him allowed him to devote the rest of his working week to what he really loved, writing comic novels.

But even when he was contributing steadily, De Vries was the exception proving the rule that *New Yorker* humor was in an unhappy state. In the late forties, the world was emerging from a global war that was marked not only by the customary death and rubble, but by unprecedented genocide and the use of the first nuclear weapons; being funny in the old way seemed harder than ever. In 1949, Nash wrote to Ross, "Where the hell are the young writers? Perelman, Thurber, etc. and I can't carry the ball forever; let's find a 30-year-old humorist." Ross replied:

> Yes, where are the young writers? The success, so-called, of this magazine is primarily a matter of luck. Within a year after we started we had White, Thurber, Hokinson, Arno, and within a few more years we had a lot more good people, humorists with pen, pencil, and typewriter. Now, by God, a whole generation has gone by and very few more have appeared— a couple of artists and not one (not one or two at the outside) humorous writers. I don't know whether it's the New Deal or Communist infiltration or the law of averages, or what, but I do know that if I'd known how little talent was going to develop I'd have got in some other line of work years ago.

The *New Yorker* casual limped along through the fifties. Perelman wrote with reliable brilliance, but Thurber and Sullivan were more erratic in quantity and quality. By the time the Whites finally and permanently moved back to Maine in 1957, E.B. had lost interest in humor pieces; instead, he instituted a series of longish personal essays published under the rubric "Letter from the East," in which, after two and a half decades of writing Comment, he was finally and fruitfully able to explore the possibilities of the first person singular in the *New Yorker*. He did, however, keep his perfect touch with Newsbreaks—the most consistently funny component of the magazine over the decade. One thing that helped was that there were so many of them—fifteen or twenty per issue—meaning no single entry was obliged to be a knee-slapper; the unobtrusive nine-point type took off even more pressure. Over the years, White's conception of the Newsbreak had broadened beyond the traditional skewering of typos and solecisms. It became a continuing examination of the use, misuse, and abuse of the language in written communication. There were long (more than a page sometimes) interoffice memos, form letters, quotations from legal decisions, obscure magazines, or the *Congressional Record,* each one zinged perfectly by a heading or deadpan rejoinder. The eagle-eyed readers who sent them in by the hundreds each week understood precisely what was needed and frequently unearthed remarkable finds, as in:

> HAVE A LOOK! Have you ever thought how you could break the monotony of a train or bus journey? In the Underground the other morning a charming young woman began to read AMATEUR STAGE. So, sitting opposite, I got out my copy. She looked up. She smiled. So did I. Eventually, we sat together and I gathered that she didn't think I was quite the horrid old man she had seen so often at the top of this column.—*John Bourne in the December, 1957, issue of Amateur Stage, London.*

> HAVE A LOOK! Have you ever thought how you can break the monotony of a train or bus journey? In the Underground the other morning a charming young woman began to read AMATEUR STAGE. So, sitting opposite, I got out my copy. She looked up. She smiled. So did I. Eventually, we sat together and I gathered that she didn't think I was quite the horrid old man she had seen so often at the top of this column.—*John Bourne in the February, 1958, issue of Amateur Stage, London.*

Well, you're not getting any *younger,* Bourne.

INFATUATION WITH SOUND OF OWN WORDS
DEPARTMENT(GUMMY LASH DIVISION)

[From "The Whistling Shadow," by Mabel Seeley]

. . . and her lashes were of the kind that look sticky.	—Page 31.
. . . the sticky dark lashes drooping lower.	—Page 32.

The flags of her sticky lashes might have been a bit apt to
dip in salute to covert glances from men.   —Page 41.
Tangled lashes confining her glance to her plate ...   —Page 43.
She didn't lift the lashes.   —Page 43.
... the lashes lifted at least a little ...   —Page 48.
... the half raising and lowering of the gummy lashes ...   —Page 53.
... looking downward with gaze hidden by the lashes
which were stickily adhesive.   —Page 61.
... just enough so the gummy lashes allowed a glimpse ...   —Page 63.
Dark half-moons underwrote the sticky lashes.   —Page 84.
... the dark glance from under the thickened lashes ...   —Page 97.
The lashes unsticking farther and farther in astonishment.   —Page 100.
... she'd shed all her beauty aids, including the gummy
substance ordinarily thickening her lashes.   —Page 103.
... after the first day, her lashes, when they lifted at all,
lifted gummily.   —Page 131.

The Newsbreaks had a nice internal rhythm, with the long, research-heavy items such as the above alternating with veritable poems of brevity:

MOST FASCINATING NEWS STORY OF THE WEEK

[The following item, reprinted in its entirety, is from the London Evening News]
Mr. Paremely Herrick, aged 46, of the Chase National Bank, was found dead in Paris with an arrow sticking in his side. His death, however, was due to a stroke.

SHORT SHORT STORY

[Adv. in the Washington Post]
TRAINS—Lionel O gauge, 3 sets, lots of tracks, switches, relays & accessories. Swap for pool table, go-cart, pin-ball machine.

And sometimes, the Newsbreak achieved a measure of perfection:

HOW NOT TO GET INTO THE *NEW YORKER*

We hate to do this to the *New Yorker* Magazine, but since they did it to a good friend of ours, the *NEA Journal,* we feel justified.
What the *New Yorker* did was to catch the *NEA Journal* with one of those "Shouts We Doubt Ever Got Shouted." The *New Yorker* picked up an item from the *NEA Journal* which read: "One child ... dashed into the classroom

after laying off a triangular flower bed and shouted, 'What do you think? I measured the slanting side of that triangle down there in the yard and squared it. Then I squared the other two sides and added them, and the sum was the same as the square of the slanting side.' "

Now, what we're going to do to the *New Yorker* is tell education editors how to avoid such little traps and thus deprive that doubting magazine a source of copy. Ready, editors?

The first thing to remember is that people don't shout in long and stately sentences. They shout in exclamations. Therefore, any word following the verb *shouted* should be an exclamation, such as "Halloo, whatho, gadzooks, Meingott, voilà," and so on. Having presented your exclamatory word, then simply add: "And in a more calm voice, the shouter continued . . ."

That NEA item would never have been picked up by the *New Yorker* if it had been edited as follows: "One child . . . dashed into the classroom . . . and shouted: 'Halloo and eureka!' Then, having caught his breath, the child continued in a more calm voice: 'I measured the slanting side of that triangle down there in the yard . . .' "—*Newsletter from the Educational Press Association of America.*

We wouldn't count on that.

There *were* casuals in these years, contributed by the likes of Roger Angell, Geoffrey Hellman, E. J. Kahn Jr., Gordon Cotler, Noel Perrin, Michael Arlen, Burton Bernstein, Calvin Tomkins, H. F. Ellis, Thomas Meehan, and John Sack. Many of these writers had done, were doing, or would go on to do distinguished work in other genres, and their humor pieces were clever, genial, and more or less witty, but almost without exception they were promptly forgettable.

The laments over the lack of humor continued and usually noted that in the postwar world, young writers with a comical bent were not inclined to generate and polish two-thousand-word prose gems. Instead they were working in less casual and more immediate arenas: radio, the toddling medium of television, or stand-up comedy, which in the fifties was rapidly losing its borscht-belt and rim-shot associations and starting to offer a platform for humor that was creative, intelligent, edgy, and above all personal. Thus the *New Yorker* was denied the talents of Lenny Bruce, Mike Nichols, Elaine May, and Mel Brooks, who in a previous epoch would all probably have been publishing in it. (Their contemporary and in some cases colleague Woody Allen, a true disciple of Perelman, would begin to do so in the midsixties.)

All this was true enough. But a new generation of innovative, funny, edgy writers—not comedians, but *writers*—was coming up in the fifties and early sixties, all of whom would have been delighted to be published in the *New Yorker,* and very few of whom did. The degree to which the magazine was interested in them and their work can be deduced from this selection of letters that the work of some of them prompted from *New Yorker* editors:

> There's a lot of very good writing in "Murdock, His Son, and a Man Named Flute," and in many ways it seems to us your most interesting story to date. We feel compelled to say no to it, though. . . . Somehow—and perhaps we're wrong—we find it hard to believe that a group of boys would smoke marihuana right out in the open, especially in their home neighborhood. . . . One little suggestion, though: are you writing out of your own experience? If you're not, I think it might be interesting for you to try—for a while, at least—to concentrate on people you know and emotions you share.
>
> —Donald Berwick to Joseph Heller, September 8, 1947*

> This one by Kurt Vonnegut, Jr. has some effective moments in it, certainly, but I'm sorry to say that as a whole it seems a bit too sketchy to work out for us.
>
> —Carroll Newman to Kenneth Littauer, agent,
> June 28, 1957, rejecting "The Man with No Kiddleys"

> This is a curious story. The actual events are quite well told, and the story does have form and motion. However, the man and his wife are so unattractive and behave so oddly toward each other that they seem downright unbelievable. I found it difficult to understand what the man was so sore about all the time.
>
> I suspect that the writer was trying to give his characters an ultra-sophisticated cast, and to make them needlessly complicated. We would like to see more stories by Terry Southern, but I hope that the next ones are told a little more directly.
>
> —Roger Angell to Edith Haggard, agent,
> March 5, 1958, rejecting "Janus" by Terry Southern

> Thomas Pynchon's UNDER THE ROSE just wouldn't work out for us, I'm afraid, though there were moments in it we did enjoy.
>
> —Robert Hemenway to Candida Donadio, agent, April 12, 1960

> Unhappily, the editors have decided against it, feeling that it is unpleasant and not fully convincing.
>
> —Carroll Newman to Candida Donadio, February 12, 1964,
> rejecting "The Punch" by Bruce Jay Friedman

---

*In his autobiographical 1994 novel, *Closing Time,* Heller wrote of the protagonist, "He continued writing short stories and small articles of trenchant satirical genius just right for publication in the prestigious *New Yorker* magazine; each time his pieces were rejected, and each time he applied and was turned down for an editorial post there, his respect for the magazine escalated."

It has some good touches, but for the most part the ideas are obscured by the difficult style. Or so it seemed to us.

—Carroll Newman to Martha Winston, agent, September 13, 1965,
rejecting "The Idols of the Kinder" by Stanley Elkin

Assume, for the sake of argument, that all the stories being turned down were truly unworthy. That would not account for the prevailing tone of condescension and disdain (somehow magnified through the use of the first-person plural) or explain the editors' near-total lack of receptivity to the subversive comic sensibility that was still mainly underground in the fifties, but was sometimes acknowledged with the adjective *black,* and that was on occasion admittedly "sketchy," "unattractive," "difficult," "stylized and artificial," or "not fully convincing." The stylistic mannerisms and sometimes excesses of these writers, their edginess, gloominess, and unpleasantness, was a reaction and implicit protest against the oppressively cheerful blandness that ruled the culture. This sensibility would predominate in literature and discourse in the 1960s and even make its presence felt in the *New Yorker,* through the writing of Donald Barthelme and Gilbert Rogin. But in the earlier decade, Lobrano, Mrs. White, Maxwell, Shawn, and their minions—despite the repeated cry of "Not enough humorists!"—were simply too timid and genteel to attend to what these writers had to say.

Faring better than casuals in the fifties were cartoons, where the solitary genius of the previous decade—Steinberg—was followed by two outstanding new contributors—Charles Saxon, who was a true heir to Helen Hokinson in his simultaneously caustic and sympathetic satire of suburban men and matrons, and James Stevenson, an inspired gagman. They were accompanied by a large incoming class of talented practitioners, including Dana Fradon, Lee Lorenz, Bud Handelsman, Ed Fisher, Stan Hunt, Warren Miller, Robert Weber, and Henry Martin. But this group, with the notable exception of Saxon, rarely questioned, or even took a hard look at, upper-middle-class norms. Working within the bounds of the complacent national consensus of conformity, consumption, and success, they generally offered value-neutral gags or else wrought their humor from universally accepted premises—that a wife's goal in life was to spend her husband's money, for example, that businessmen liked to chase secretaries around desks, or that the Soviets could be counted on to take credit for American innovations.

Admittedly, it would have been unrealistic to expect cartoonists to chip away at the rose-colored veneer covering American life, considering how strong and durable it was. Indeed, it blanketed the *New Yorker* itself. The magazine was read by the people who had migrated or were about to migrate to the promised land of the suburbs, who had cast their lot with the gospel of striving and success. And making the magazine enormously prof-

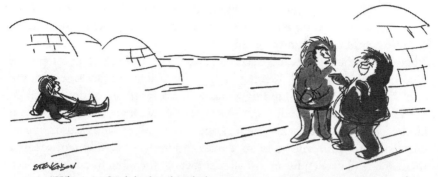

"Why is it, Oogluk, that though the years may come and the years may go, you still never fail to find it amusing when someone slips and falls on the ice?"

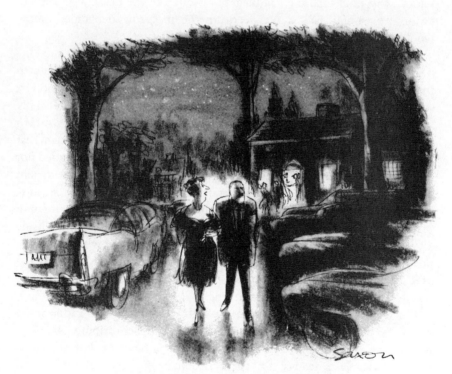

"I never realized you knew all of 'Gunga Din.'"

The two outstanding cartoonists to come to the *New Yorker* in the late 1950s were James Stevenson, an inspired gagman, and Charles Saxon, who was a worthy heir to Helen Hokinson and a novelistic chronicler of upper-middle-class suburban life.

itable—paying the shareholders' dividends, the contributors' fees, and the editors' salaries—were advertisements that incessantly spoke to the readers' desire to climb up any number of social, economic, and aesthetic ladders. The text for one 1960s full-page ad reads, "The table lighters for people who hate table lighters." Turn the page, and you find another one with the text: "There is a certain kind of woman who'd rather eat soutzoukakia in the Greek Isles than fondue in Stowe. For this woman, there is a certain kind of store: Peck & Peck." The message was deeply paradoxical: an apparent appeal to nonconformity, in a mass-produced advertisement set in a magazine read or seen by almost all members of the affluent educated class. Yet it was so natural, in the context of the *New Yorker*, that satirizing it was not an option.

To do so, the magazine would have had to call on the new generation of subversive graphic humorists, such as Jules Feiffer, Edward Gorey, Arnold Roth, David Levine, and Edward Sorel (or, at the extreme end, the "gang of idiots" who published in *Mad* magazine). But like the black humorists in prose, they simply lacked the decorum the magazine demanded. Some would make their *New Yorker* debut three decades later.

New Yorker cartoons were not unanimously innocuous. Addams, Steinberg, and George Price continued their brilliant work, which got beneath the surface of things in their varying ways. And once in a while a cartoon by someone else tried to shine some comic light on the dark facts generally obscured: that conformity could be dispiriting, that alcohol and tobacco were widely abused drugs, that many marriages were grim and harsh, that fear of different kinds was in the air. Interestingly, these cartoons tended not to be especially funny, as if stating the truth, for once, were achievement enough. A wife washing dishes in a fancy modern kitchen says to her husband, fixing a drink: "But you said you had some on the train to unwind. Just how many times do you have to unwind?" One little kid, sitting outside a gracious suburban homestead, to another: "I don't know what my father does all day. All I know is it makes him sick at his stomach." A husband and wife are watching television and the words SPECIAL BULLETIN fill the screen. The wife: "Jeffrey, hold my hand."

Once in a *great* while a cartoon was both penetrating and cathartically funny, and to these one can only, in retrospect, pay a silent tribute. Two businessmen at a bar, one in necktie and the other in bow tie, but otherwise indistinguishable. One says: "Say, this *is* a coincidence. *You've* always seemed a father image to *me*." Two women stride by a men's store window and see an evening-clothes display on a mannequin with no head. The comment: "*That's* the kind of man *I'm* going to marry." A husband and wife sit at the breakfast table, the husband reading the newspaper (a stock situation in *New Yorker* cartoons). The wife: "I didn't say anything. That was yesterday."

It was mostly through indirection that *New Yorker* cartoons could critique the status quo or give expression to the generalized discomfort, anxiety, alienation, or oppressiveness that many ostensibly successful, contented, and well-adjusted Americans felt but could not quite admit to. Such an effort would certainly help explain the reiteration—almost to the point of absurdity—of certain situations and settings in the cartoons. To be sure, these genres were popular in part simply because cartoonists recognized them as fertile fields for gags and kept harvesting them. It would certainly be difficult to ascribe a deep meaning to the endless appeal of talking-animal cartoons. According to Brendan Gill, so many of these had built up in the bank at one point that Geraghty unobtrusively filled an entire issue with them. But other motifs would seem more significant. In the entire decade of the 1940s, according to the *New Yorker's* records, twenty-five cartoons depicted shipwrecked survivors on desert islands. In the 1950s, there were one hundred four of them. Cartoons set in prisons increased from twenty-five to sixty-five. (Interviewed by *Time* magazine in 1960, James Geraghty said, "I get awfully sick of prison pictures, but they keep coming in, and they're funny.") The first cartoon with a man in robes and sandals carrying a sign saying some variant of "The World Is Coming to an End" appeared in 1955; over the next decade there would be twenty more. Over and above the gags they expressed, these cartoons would have resonated with people who felt isolated or constricted or that, some time soon, the world could very well come to an end.

FIFTIES FICTION

We are in the midst of a fiction shortage. Many of our best fiction writers, like you, are not writing short fiction now, and some few who are, are not writing very well.

> —Katherine White to Mary McCarthy, August 19, 1957

～～～

You find Mado and The Rectory "too fast, or simply too strange, or just not quite real" while I, reading some of the stories in *The N.Y.* find them too slow, or too familiar, or not quite strange enough to be real. There are these swirls and by-currents in taste, and just now in Europe we are swinging away from the probable and the well-knit. Ionesco is only the striking tip of the tail of the general cat.

Fortunately,—fortunately I hope I can always appease my craving for the improbable by recording with perfect truth my

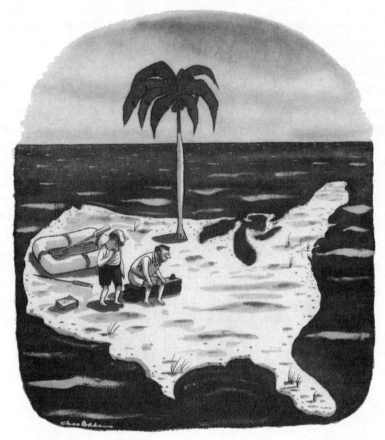

"By George, you're right! I thought there was something familiar about it."

The cartoons of the postwar period tended to be innocuous, but periodically one would tackle conformity head on, or take a mordant look at the feelings of isolation or anxiety that underlay everyday life.

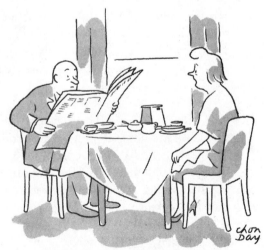

"I didn't say anything. That was yesterday."

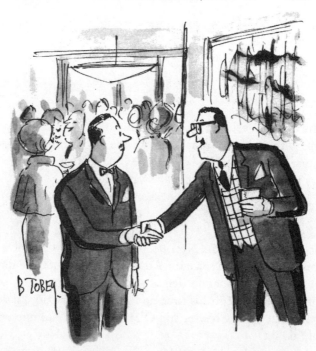

"Hi! I'm Greg Holbrook, born in L.A., now live in Stamford
with my wife and three kids, went to school at Exeter, graduated
Yale '38, did a two-year hitch in the Navy, now write copy for
McCann-Erickson, my hobbies are tennis and sailing. Who are you
and what do _you_ do?"

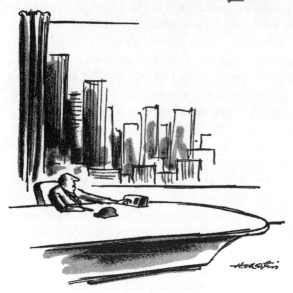

"Miss Tompkins, connect me with somebody."

own childhood (Have you observed that nobody ever had a probable childhood?).
—Sylvia Townsend Warner to William Maxwell,
July 18, 1957

~~~

None of the novel seems to stand alone so I will buckle down to stories although the form seems to me mysteriously obsolete. No one seems to make a contribution to the form anymore; and every listless story seems to take away the gains.
—John Cheever to William Maxwell, October 22, 1959

~~~

It occurs to me that the Nyer needs an American Chekhov, that is someone who can seize the American scene with the directness and very masculine delicacy and fearless entering of all doors of Chekhov, in his time and place. Easier said, for some reason, than done. Cheever and O'Hara merged into one writer might do it.
—John Updike to Maxwell, undated, probably early 1960s

~~~

The *New Yorker's* fiction of this period was similarly constricted. The body of it leaves a lingering impression of gentility bordering on blandness, with not infrequent excursions into the out-and-out dull. The genre that predominated was reminiscence, the locale Irish (followed by English, and then American southern), the authorial gender female.* No small number of first-rate works saw publication, yet notable in their absence were the vigorous, pointed, often funny, urban short stories that had traditionally distinguished the magazine; even the stereotyped "*New Yorker* story," the "tight objective sketch" without an immediately apparent point, seemed to recede. The trend accelerated with the death in 1956 of Gus Lobrano, whose taste in fiction had always run to the journalistic and sharp-edged. He was briefly replaced as head of the department by Katharine White, before she retired to Maine for good in 1957. After that there was no chief fiction editor: William Maxwell, Robert Henderson, Roger Angell, and the young editor who presently joined the magazine, Rachel MacKenzie, operated in an informal consensus system, with Shawn's ultimate approval required on any story. Years later, Maxwell remarked, "It was a peaceable kingdom under Shawn. All of us

---

*In a survey of three months' issues, chosen at random (January–March 1958), 58 percent of the twenty-four stories and reminiscences were by women.

had our own authors, and we all consulted with one another. There was great freedom. You can imagine how pleasant that was." The fiction editors, Shawn included, were readers of intelligence, sensitivity, and discernment. But overshadowing subtle differences in preference and taste was a general like-mindedness. Following the distinction made by the critic Philip Rahv, the editors were "palefaces" rather than "redskins"—constitutionally resistant, that is, to writing that pushed the boundaries of taste, decorum, or form.

Contributing to the blandness of New Yorker fiction in the period was the absence or diminished output of several longtime contributors, casualties of actuarial forces. The rates the magazine paid for fiction had steadily gone up over the years, but not nearly as much as its profits: Ross's notion that writers should never get too comfortable still held sway. So even with bonuses and cost of living adjustments, the proceeds from half a dozen short stories a year in the New Yorker were nowhere near enough to pay the mortgage, tuition, alimony, and other expenses that were but dreams in a writer's twenties but nonnegotiable obligations in his or her forties. Novels, almost always more lucrative than stories and sometimes dramatically so, beckoned, as did Hollywood. A second difficulty (for writers) was that whatever their blind spots, the New Yorker's editors did not accept subpar work from any writer. And producing high-quality short fiction over a significant span of years was not especially easy. The exception was someone like Sylvia Townsend Warner, who had a natural, inexplicable, and seemingly indistinguishable genius for the short-story form. The rule was a writer who connected with a voice, a vision, a slice of the world; exploited it all in two stories or two dozen; then either repeated him- or herself or faced the fact that the well had gone dry.

Thus the litany of distinguished absentees. O'Hara had flown the coop because of no guarantees and low rates and would not return until 1960. Nabokov, after completing the Pnin series, more or less abandoned the short form in favor of novels (Pale Fire, Ada) that did not lend themselves to excerpting. Jean Stafford found domestic happiness in her marriage to A. J. Liebling in 1959 (the match was made by Katharine White) but at that point hadn't published a story in the magazine for two years and would not for another decade. Sally Benson, for a quarter of a century an American version of Warner in her easy prolificness, had five stories in the magazine in 1955 and one in 1956. But, in the grips of alcoholism and other personal demons, she published no more for the remaining sixteen years of her life, preferring, when she was able to work, to accept the relatively easy money Hollywood offered for script-writing and -doctoring. (She had forged connections with Hollywood when Meet Me in St. Louis was adapted as a film by Vincente Minnelli, and she worked as a screenwriter through the 1960s. Her projects with sole or partial credit were eclectically impressive, including Alfred Hitchcock's Shadow of a Doubt, Anna and the King of Siam, Elvis

Presley's *Viva Las Vegas,* and *The Singing Nun,* with Debbie Reynolds.) Peter Taylor continued to contribute, but his stories of this period were not his best. Whereas his earlier work had a rich and complex tension beneath the surface placidity (as would his later, exquisite stories of the middle 1970s and after), these stories tended not to have much beyond the surface placidity. Maxwell inherited Taylor after Mrs. White's retirement, and he soon complained to her that the writer "takes so long to say anything, and what he says is so little, and then it fails to be a convincing story on top of it. I am discouraged about him."

Irwin Shaw's final *New Yorker* story appeared in 1955. The circumstances of the parting between magazine and writer who had done so much for each other are cloudy, though the magazine (especially in the absence of Lobrano) was moving ever more quickly away from the kind of sentiment and melodrama of which Shaw was a master, and the writer himself, having sampled the taste of success with his 1948 best-seller, *The Young Lions,* was concentrating his energies on the popular novels that would make him wealthy. The rift left bitter feelings on both sides. Brendan Gill told Shaw's biographer Michael Shnayerson, "Irwin never got over his rejection from the *New Yorker.* There was scarcely a time in my experience when we were speaking that it didn't come up on some level, his disappointment and enormous bitterness." The magazine, for its part, did not deign to publish even a capsule review of any novel of Shaw's between 1952 and 1971. Mrs. White, in making the selections for the 1960 anthology of the best *New Yorker* stories of the previous decade, passed over such first-rate tales as "Voyage Out, Voyage Home," "Peter Two," "Tip on a Dead Jockey," and "In the French Style" and, rather shockingly, left Shaw completely unrepresented.

Another important contributor fared better, even as he was moving into a vein as sentimental and melodramatic, in its own way, as anything Shaw ever wrote. This was J. D. Salinger. In 1951 Salinger published his first (and what would prove to be his only) novel, *The Catcher in the Rye.* Its spectacular success, and the demands of his sudden celebrity, appeared to unnerve him. Two years later, he moved, permanently, to a house on a dirt road near Cornish, New Hampshire. Also in 1953, with his collection *Nine Stories* about to be published, he asked Lobrano that the *New Yorker* not forward to him any clippings or reviews of the book; the sense that he was in the news, he said, inhibited his work. Later in 1953, he gave an interview to a local newspaper that would be his last public statement for the next three decades. Salinger's first *New Yorker* short story after *Catcher* was "Teddy," which appeared on January 31, 1953. In this long, peculiar, and in retrospect, augural work, a ten-year-old mystical prodigy holds "pretty firmly to the Vedantic theory of reincarnation." He is on a ship on his way to England and has a premonition of his death. Sure enough, in the last line, he dies in a freak accident.

Not the least strange aspect of the story was its placement in the magazine. On the way to its horrific conclusion, a reader would find cartoons by Chon Day and Dana Fradon, a picturesque spot drawing of a woman lighting a fireplace, a sixteen-panel cartoon by Alain, and ads for cruisewear (this was January, after all), for the German Monteil Beauty Balm Foundation ("The most natural of powder foundations"), for Rheingold beer, for *The Seven Year Itch,* and for *Women's Day* magazine (a two-page spread shows a photo of a man shoveling snow while his wife looked on, with the caption "She's got to go out to get *Women's Day*"). Directly under the last line of the story, with the revelation of Teddy's death, was a Newsbreak, showing a headline from an Alabama newspaper—"Accountants Hold Interesting Meeting; Money Is Speaker"—and the comment "As always." The tableau was as graphic an illustration as can be of the *New Yorker's* capacity for mixing messages. But for Salinger, "Teddy" was significant as the first step he took down the road that he would travel the rest of his career as a writer, and that would eventually terminate in a dead end. His fiction had long been animated by a Manichaean division of the world into those who were sensitive and those who were phony, the few geniuses and the great unwashed. He now began to combine this view with a newfound interest in Eastern religion and set for himself the task of explaining the elect to the rest of us. The task was quixotic and ultimately futile, given that the main criterion for Salinger's form of sainthood was a cosmic inscrutability.

For a time, Salinger's pure literary verve bundled him past the land mines he had set for himself. His next story, "Franny," appeared early in 1955. The title character, a female college student, has what seems to be a spiritual crisis, brought on by her reading of a mystical text called *The Ways of the Pilgrim,* in the middle of an Ivy League football weekend she is spending with her drippy boyfriend, Lane Coutell. Salinger's two-year layoff seemed to have invigorated his observational powers—not a gesture, a turn of phrase, a way of holding or dragging on a cigarette, escaped his notice. And completely eviscerated were Lane's academic pretensions. (He says of a Flaubert paper he has written: "But—I don't know—I think the emphasis I put on *why* he was so neurotically attracted to the *mot juste* wasn't too bad. I mean in the light of what we know today. Not just psychoanalysis and all that crap, but certainly to a certain extent.") After the story had been accepted, Gus Lobrano told Salinger that some of the editors raised the possibility that Franny's distress—she refuses to eat, perspires, and ends up fainting—may have been the result of her being pregnant. Salinger wrote back that although he couldn't be certain Franny wasn't pregnant, he didn't think so—and, in any case, he certainly didn't want any readers to think that was why she felt bad. To make sure no one got the wrong idea, he suggested (and Lobrano accepted) inserting a line of dialogue from Lane complaining that they had not had sex for over a month: "That's no good. Too goddamn long between drinks. To put it crassly." It's not clear why he thought this would rule out the pregnancy explanation. Indeed, Warren French, the author of the Twayne's American Authors book on Salinger, notes that Lane's "concern . . . about the length of time between drinks supported the interpretation that she was" pregnant. But the important point was that people, all over the country, *did* talk about "Franny" and why she had collapsed; in the history of the *New Yorker,* the story was a national cultural event on the order of "Hiroshima," "The Lottery," or "In Cold Blood."

Less than a year later, in November 1955, Salinger published a twenty-five-thousand-word story called "Raise High the Roof Beams, Carpenters." In what must have been a few feverish months of work, Salinger audaciously took two of his most memorable characters—Franny and Seymour, the unhappy husband who committed suicide in the 1948 story "A Perfect Day for Bananafish"—and made them brother and sister, two members of a large and eccentric New York Irish-Jewish family he called the Glasses. (He also recruited as a Glass one of his minor characters, Walt, the dead lover an unhappy housewife pines for in the 1948 story "Uncle Wiggily in Connecticut.") Narrated by their brother Buddy Glass, a fiction writer for whom "cleverness" is "a permanent affliction"—and from this point on, Salinger's fictional alter ego—"Raise High the Roof Beams" sets the clock back to 1942 and tells the story of Seymour's wedding, which Seymour neglected to attend because he was "indisposed by happiness." The story probably represents the high point of Salinger's career as a *New Yorker* writer—it is funny, touching, resonant, and the last point at which what would become an obsession with the holy Seymour and the rest of the Glasses is restrained by an allegiance to literary and narrative values.

His next story tipped the scales the other way, decisively. Submitted in 1957, and some fifty thousand words long, "Zooey" jumps back toward the present and takes up the story of Franny two days after her collapse. Most of it consists of tiresome, if justified, hectoring of Franny by her brother Zooey, to the effect that her breakdown, while understandable, is inconsiderate to other people, and that her disgust at the smallness, hypocrisy, and "ego" she sees everywhere around her causes her to overlook the manifestations of the holy and the beautiful that can be located in just about everyone, if you look hard enough. The *New Yorker's* fiction editors unanimously decided to reject it. According to William Maxwell, the reason was that the magazine had a policy against publishing sequels. Maxwell is a tactful and discreet man. The fact is, "Zooey" was self-indulgent, nearly endless, and ultimately silly, and he and his colleagues were certainly discerning enough to realize this. But their verdict in any case was short-lived: William Shawn reversed it, accepted the story, and took on the editing himself. When "Franny" and "Zooey" were published together as a book in 1961, Salinger's dedication was to "my editor, mentor and (heaven help him) closest friend, William Shawn, *genius domus* of *The New Yorker,* lover of the long shot, protector of the unprolific, defender of the hopelessly flamboyant, most unreasonably modest of born great artist-editors." Shawn had had books dedicated to him before, but this encomium in *Franny and Zooey*—which went through eleven hardcover printings in less than a year and dozens of paperback ones, with no end in sight—was the real beginning of what would become a widely accepted sense that this quiet man was a genius and a seer.

Salinger's next piece—"story" does not seem quite the right word—was "Seymour: An Introduction," published in 1959. It was as idiosyncratic as "Zooey" and almost as long, but, in the almost perverse aim it set for itself— Buddy Glass works himself into a series of conniption fits trying to explain just what it was that made Seymour so special—it was at least more entertaining. This time the manuscript went straight to Shawn and he accepted it and readied it for publication without consulting the fiction department. Maxwell wrote to Mrs. White in Maine, "I do feel that Salinger has to be handled specially and fast, and think that the only practical way of doing this is as I supposed Shawn did do it—by himself. Given the length of the stories, I mean, and the Zen Buddhist nature of them, and what happened with Zooey."

Salinger followed this act—six years later—with "Hapworth 16, 1924," an almost literally interminable document purporting to be a letter written home from summer camp by Seymour, age seven. The character's precociousness is so distended here as to make it impossible to suspend disbelief, and his bitter condescension toward his "inferiors" makes it impossible to extend him any sympathy, much less the veneration Salinger is presumably seeking. "Not a single day passes," Seymour remarks, "that I do not listen to the heartless indifference and stupidities passing from the counselors' lips without secretly wishing I could improve matters quite substantially by bashing a few culprits over the head with an excellent shovel or short club." Salinger continued to live and write in New Hampshire and, to some extent, involve himself in the affairs of the *New Yorker,* but after "Hapworth" he never published another word, in the magazine or anywhere else.*

For all the acclaim his stories received, and for all the undeniable virtues of most of them, Salinger was ultimately something of a literary novelty act,

---

*Salinger wisely chose not to reprint "Hapworth" in book form, and as a result many libraries' bound *New Yorker* volume containing the June 19, 1965, issue is missing pages 32 to 113, their removal effected by some fanatic devotee of the author's. In February 1997, Salinger's agent confirmed that the story would be published as a book by a small Virginia press, but publication was delayed and, as of 1999, is uncertain.

spinning out a series of variably intoxicating fantasies. It was left to John Cheever to direct his gaze at the lives *New Yorker* readers led and transform what he saw into art. It is telling that while Salinger vacated New York for remote New Hampshire, Cheever duplicated the migration of many of the magazine's readers, moving to suburban Scarborough, New York, in 1951. Luckily—and rather remarkably, in retrospect—he found in suburbia a setting as fertile and suggestive for him as the Upper East Side Manhattan apartment building had been. In the stories he set in the fictional town of Shady Hill, he regarded the cocktail parties and the commuter railroad trains, the affairs and spats and divorces, the baby-sitters and the bomb shelters, with wonder and sometimes terror, as if they were the stuff of myth. In this stylized arena he could show the many ways in which men and women had fallen, and the far less frequent occasions on which they achieved transcendence or a measure of grace.

Cheever got the details right, but his lens depicted them with a faint and uncanny distortion. In the brilliant and terrifying "The Five Forty-Eight" (April 10, 1954), the despicable protagonist, referred to only by his last name, Blake, has a one-night stand with his secretary and, the next day, does "what he felt was the only sensible thing"—fires her while she's on her lunch hour. Six months later, on his way home from work, he sees that she is stalking him. By the time he gets on his train—for Cheever, a locus as inevitable and rich as the subway had been for *New Yorker* artists and writers of the twenties—he thinks (mistakenly, it turns out) that he has eluded her.

> He bought a paper. The local was only half full when he boarded it, and he got a seat on the river side and took off his raincoat. He was a slender man with brown hair—undistinguished in every way, unless you could have divined in his pallor or his gray eyes his unpleasant tastes. He dressed—like the rest of us—as if he admitted the existence of sumptuary laws. His raincoat was the pale buff color of a mushroom. His hair was dark brown; so was his suit. Except for the few bright threads in his necktie, there was a scrupulous lack of color in his clothing that seemed protective.

(Cheever's throwaway reference to "the rest of us" is characteristic, indicating that the author—and by extension the reader—is not excepted from a certain complicity.)

"The Five Forty-Eight" is an unremittingly bleak story, but more frequently Cheever alternated sunlight and shade. In the darkly comic "O Youth and Beauty!" (August 22, 1953), Cash Bentley, forty, somehow manages to stave off the disappointments of his life with an odd ritual. At every cocktail party, at the time when his Shady Hill neighbor Trace Bearden begins to "chide" him "about his age and his thinning hair," Cash runs a hurdle course in the host's living room. "It was not exactly a race, since Cash ran it alone, but it was extraordinary to see this man of forty surmount so many obstacles so gracefully." The theme recalls Irwin Shaw's "The Eighty-Yard Run" (and anticipates John Updike's *Rabbit, Run*): the middle-aging of an ex-athlete. But starting with an ostentatiously meandering 193-word opening sentence, Cheever seems eager at every turn to defamiliarize the material and play up his writerly artifice. Through a fluke accident during one dash, Cash breaks his leg. Without the hurdles, his life is drained of meaning. He drinks even more than usual, bickers with Louise, his wife; sitting in the living room reading *Time* one night, "he noticed that the faded roses Louise had brought in from the garden smelled more of earth than of anything else. It was a putrid, compelling smell."

Two-thirds of the way through the story, Cheever suddenly and audaciously shifts to the present tense. On a summer night, in a benign version of the eavesdropping Enormous Radio, he takes us on a tour of Shady Hill, grabbing quick still lifes and snatches of conversation through the open windows of the houses. Couples watch television, a young lawyer practices his address to the jury while his wife goes on knitting, and "Mrs. Carver—Harry Farquarson's mother-in-law—glances up at the sky and asks, '*Where* did all the stars come from?' She is old and foolish, and yet she is right: Last night's stars seem to have drawn to themselves a new range of galaxies, and the night sky is not dark at all, except where there is a tear in the membrane of light. In the unsold house lots near the track a hermit thrush is singing."

But Cash feels removed from the grace and the vitality around him. He goes out, alone, to a round of cocktail parties and comes home late. "Louise was upstairs, cutting out of the current copy of *Life* those scenes of mayhem, disaster, and violent death that she felt might corrupt her children. She always did this." Cash sets up the furniture for a hurdle run, calls Louise downstairs, and hands her a starter's pistol. She has never fired one before, and when she finally gets it to work, she shoots her husband dead, in mid-hurdle. So much for *New Yorker* stories that trail off instead of ending.

In the fifties and into the early sixties, Cheever wrote his finest short stories—besides the two just mentioned, there were "The Sorrows of Gin," "The Day the Pig Fell into the Well," "The Housebreaker of Shady Hill," "The Country Husband," and many others. Indeed, no one has ever written finer. Nonetheless, it was a frustrating decade for him. For much of it he found himself unable to complete the first novel that would (he thought) finally bring him wide recognition as a major author. And, although he was certainly established as an important contributor to the *New Yorker,* his relationship with the magazine grew increasingly conflicted. As early as 1948, he was complaining in his journal about its rejection of four short stories in a brief span. "The fact that they have paid me no bonus this year and less than a living wage sets me off, frequently, on an unreasonable tangent of petulance," he continued. "This is a patriarchal relationship, and I certainly respond to the slings of regret, real or imaginary."*

Some of the slings were real indeed. In 1948, Cheever was thirty-six years old, the New Yorker was his primary means of support, and only O'Hara and Benson had contributed more short stories to it than he had. Yet this did not—and never would—give him any significant advantage over a neophyte sending in submissions to the slush pile. The New Yorker gave him no office in which to work, no retainer, no guarantee that anything he wrote would be published, nothing, in fact, beyond a check for a few hundred dollars sent out every year in exchange for his signature on the first-reading agreement. And even when stories were accepted, the wages were not high. In preparing her memoir of Cheever, Home Before Dark, his daughter, Susan, calculated the total amount he was paid by the New Yorker for the 121 stories he sold it between 1935 and 1982 and came up with a figure of less than $173,000.

It wasn't only a matter of money. Cheever felt, with some justification, that the New Yorker's editors didn't fully appreciate him. With greater frequency and greater brilliance, he was mining the element of the fantastic that he had explored in such earlier works as "The Enormous Radio" and "Torch Song," while the magazine was still committed to a literary ethos of naturalism, plausibility, and the emotional identification of reader with character. William Maxwell, who took over from Lobrano as Cheever's editor, explained to Susan Cheever: "His stories collided with the New Yorker idea of fiction. Character as a confining force got less and less strong in his work. He extricated himself from ordinary realism. . . . He tried things that we felt just weren't possible. It turned out that anything was possible."

That the relationship was "patriarchal," as Cheever had termed it in his journal, complicated matters. His own father died in 1946, and Cheever's widow, Mary, reports that he looked on Gus Lobrano, his New Yorker editor from the late thirties to the early fifties, as a surrogate. That made him reluctant to express any bitterness, much less take the route John O'Hara had traveled and leave the magazine for more lucrative markets. When William Maxwell took over as his editor, other factors came into play. Without a doubt, Cheever had deep affection and respect for Maxwell. In 1957, after he had finally completed his first novel, The Wapshot Chronicle, he wrote to the editor's wife, Emmy:

> As for the book I sometimes wonder if Bill knows how important he was. One always writes for someone and much of it was written for Bill. The

---

*In a journal entry of roughly the same time, Cheever wrote of himself and his family, "We are as poor as we ever have been. The rent is not paid, we have very little to eat, relatively little to eat: canned tongue and eggs."

advice he gave me and the advice he didn't give me was all brilliant and he wired when he read it which makes the difference between feeling alive and feeling like an old suit hanging in a closet. It all comes down to one night when I brought a story over to your house and Bill liked it. It was such a pleasant evening that I thought I would like to try something longer than a story.*

Six years later, when Cheever published a sequel, *The Wapshot Scandal,* he dedicated the book to "W.M." "The initials," he wrote Maxwell, "are meant to represent the lack between what I write for you and what I produced. If it seems better in galleys I'll add the illiam and axwell." Yet in some part of his notoriously self-contradictory being, Cheever viewed Maxwell—who was only four years older than he and, unlike Lobrano, a fellow fiction writer—as a competitor who was trying to squelch him. Years later he wrote to Allan Gurganus, a literary protégé who had just had a story published in the *New Yorker,* then had one rejected:

I should have warned you about this predictable turn of events. Once you show a trace of healthy self-esteem the *New Yorker* will yank at the rug you stand on. I was hurt the first time around; but never again. Bill, after forty years remains indecipherable. I thought I once understood him. It seemed that he was a man who mistook power for love. If you don't grow and change he baits you; if you do grow and change he baits you cruelly. I once shouted at him:"You may have invented Salinger and [Harold] Brodkey but you didn't invent me." I intended to dedicate *The Scandal* to him but he was murderous about the book and I changed the dedication to W.M. He underwent a sea-change and praised the book but the dedication remained W.M. He loves me and would love to see me dead.

Cheever had an outsized propensity for mythologizing. In 1959, he concocted for his journal a divorce from the *New Yorker,* writing, "Nearly every time I think of a story I see it set up in the magazine opposite a cartoon, and I must realize that the people who read my fiction have stopped reading the *New Yorker.* I must realize that the breach here is real and happy." In fact, five *New Yorker* contributions from 1959 are in his collected stories—more than for any other year. But a breach really did begin to form two years later. On a visit to the magazine's offices, Cheever happened to see a galley proof of his story "The Brigadier and the Golf Widow" and jumped to the (mistaken) conclusion that Maxwell intended

*Maxwell's telegram to Cheever had read: I DON'T EXPECT TO ENJOY ANYTHING AS MUCH FOR A LONG TIME. THE PLACES ARE ALL REAL, THE "HEARTY FLEETING VISION OF LIFE" IS CONSISTENT AND RECOGNIZABLY YOURS, AND THE WRITING IS BRILLIANT EVERYWHERE. I THINK IT IS GOING TO BE ENORMOUSLY SUCCESSFUL.

to make a substantive cut in the story without consulting him. If anything could have been predicted to set him off, this was it: Maxwell, the "rival" on whom his livelihood was dependent, was appropriating and altering his work (and since the *New Yorker* paid by the word, taking money out of his pocket). But in the office—as Cheever later wrote to a friend, John Weaver—he expressed no protest and agreed to the edited version. After leaving, he

> walked over to the station where I bought a copy of *Life* in which J. D. Salinger was compared to William Blake, Ludwig von Beethoven and William Shakespeare. I went into a slow burn which didn't erupt until nine that evening when I telephoned Bill who happened to be entertaining Elizabeth Bowen and Eudora Welty. "You cut that story," I yelled, "and I'll never write another story for you or anybody else. You can get that Godamned sixth-rate Salinger to write your Godamned short stories but don't expect anything more out of me."*

Cheever and the magazine patched things up, but two years later came what would turn out to be the final conflict. In August 1963, Cheever asked the magazine for an advance. Maxwell sent it to him, along with a note informing him that it brought his indebtedness up to $2,000, which was "the ceiling." Some months later, Cheever submitted "The Swimmer," a haunting short story about a suburbanite named Neddy Merrill who, at a pool party one day, realizes that a "string of swimming pools" makes "a quasi-subterranean stream" by which he could travel the eight miles to his home. A modern-day Ulysses, he endeavors to do so. "The Swimmer" has persuasively been cast as the quintessential Cheever story—an airtight and unforgettable brief arguing his vision of the world—and he knew how good it was. Having just completed *The Wapshot Scandal* and having been informed that he was to be the subject of a *Time* magazine cover story, he apparently felt emboldened to go to New York and ask Maxwell for a raise in rate. He needed the money. Two years earlier, he had bought a large and expensive house in Ossining, after ten years of renting; one of his sons was in an expensive private school and his daughter in an expensive private col-

---

*Cheever's version is useful for its psychological, not literal, truth. When asked about the incident by Ben Cheever, who edited his father's letters, Maxwell said that he merely had the second version of the story set in type "so your father could see how it would read in print.... It was a working print, for him to consider." He added: "At different times Elizabeth Bowen and Eudora Welty have been in our house in Yorktown, but never together." Cheever himself wrote an apologetic letter to Maxwell explaining his "reference or whatever" to Salinger: "I admire Salinger, of course, and I think I know where his giftedness lies and how rare it is. Another reason for my irritability is the fact that I am never content with my own work; that it never quite comes up to the world as I see it."

lege. However, the highest the magazine would go for 1964 was an annual bonus of $2,600 for signing the first-reading agreement, and a minimum word rate of eighteen cents a word for the first two thousand words and nine cents a word after that. Cheever didn't realize how low this was. As long before as 1938, Arthur Kober was getting a minimum rate of 20 & 10, and in 1945, Irwin Shaw's figure was 34 & 15. In 1964, the much younger John Updike got a bonus of $3,500, while Shirley Hazzard, younger still, got $2,000 and a minimum rate of 20 & 10.

But Cheever knew enough that, in his many retellings of the incident, he scoffed at the offer as "a key to the men's room and all the bread and cheese I could eat." Infuriated, he went to a pay phone, called a well-known literary agent named Candida Donadio (for many years he had worked without an agent), and asked if she could find him a better deal. She called back within minutes and said that the *Saturday Evening Post* was willing to pay him $24,000 a year for a first-look agreement and four stories. In his journal, Cheever assessed the situation and related his response:

> Like many men of fifty I am obliged to ask for a raise and like many men of fifty I am confronted with a blameless, monolithic and capricious organization, hobbled it seems by its own prosperity. The organizations of men, like men themselves, seem subject to deafness, nearsightedness, lameness and involuntary cruelty. We seem tragically unable to help one another; to understand one another. I am accused of improvidence and make several long speeches about how I am harassed by indebtedness. The *Post* has offered me twenty-four thousand; the *New Yorker* has offered me twenty-five hundred and I will take the latter. I'm not sure why.

The explanation that escaped Cheever lay somewhere in the territory between filial obligation, institutional and personal loyalty, and the shrewd realization that the *New Yorker* still afforded more prestige than any other magazine, prestige that could ultimately translate into commercial success. (It did so for Cheever in the 1970s, when the publication of his novel *Falconer* and his collected stories put him on a relatively equal financial footing with his Westchester neighbors for the first time.) But things were never again the same between him and the *New Yorker*. Between 1935 and 1964, he published one hundred fifteen short stories in the magazine. Between 1965 and his death in 1982, he would publish only six.

With the falling off of the older generation of short-story writers, one would think the magazine would pursue younger contributors, who, besides having fresh news to report in fresh voices, would have more modest financial needs. To an extent it did. Some notable new faces appeared in the 1950s and early sixties, including Maeve Brennan, Elizabeth Spencer,

Mavis Gallant, Harold Brodkey, Brian Friel, Frances Grey Patton, Mary Lavin, Benedict Kiely, Edna O'Brien, Shirley Hazzard, Ruth Prawer Jhabvala, and Arturo Vivante. But this talented group did nothing to reverse the prevalent climate of gentility (nor the odd overemphasis on the British Isles, especially Ireland, and the American South). The volume of their stories was subdued, the characters polite and well-bred, the ironies subtle.

As with humor, the magazine was simply not receptive to brasher and potentially more disruptive voices. Once again, a litany of rejection:

> "Round Robin" has a funny idea the editors feel but it doesn't seem to us done the right way for this magazine. We hope you'll let us see something else soon.
>
> —William Maxwell to William Gaddis, December 23, 1946

> This author is, in his way, pretty exasperating. He quite clearly has talent, but, almost as clearly, it's not quite as mature a talent as he thinks it is. Probably would be a good thing if he could, without feeling contemptible, try some simple themes. . . . "Resurrection" is perceptive in spots but more often just repellent and, on the whole, not by a long shot good enough to maintain the author's assumption that he is qualified to handle such a theme.
>
> —G. S. Lobrano to Dorothy Parker,
> Whittlesey House, 1947, rejecting "Resurrection"
> and "The Island" by William Styron

> We read with a great deal of interest John Kerouac's "Go, Go, Go," and it makes us hope that he will have other short stories to send us. This one, I'm afraid, does not seem to us possible for *The New Yorker*. The difficulty is that for such odd and, in a way perverse, subject matter, the reader has to know more than the author is able to convey in so short a space. Or so it seems to us. . . . In any case, we hope that Mr. Kerouac will try something for us that is not about this particular group of wild kids. Anything dealing with drugs, and with this peculiarly abnormal psychological material, would, we think, require absolutely masterful treatment and would have to be done, we also feel, with compassion as well as with accuracy of reporting that Mr. Kerouac does supply.
>
> —Katharine White to Robert Giroux, May 12, 1950

> I'm sorry to have to return this one, but its subject matter makes it, at best, a rather unlikely story for *The New Yorker*. We feel, however, that much of it, particularly the first part, is handled convincingly, and we'd be interested in seeing something else by Flannery O'Connor.
>
> —Carroll Newman to Elizabeth McKee, agent,
> February 28, 1952, rejecting "Running"

Unfortunately, this doesn't make our [omission *sic*] piece, but those of us who read it enjoyed it. Thanking you for thinking of us, and we hope to hear from you again.

Sincerely yours,

The New Yorker

—letter to Cynthia Ozick, March 25, 1955

This one, unhappily, strikes us as too long, and in many ways, too familiar, in spite of its lively portions.

—Robert Henderson to Darmuid Russell, agent, January 4, 1957,

rejecting "Behold the Key" by Bernard Malamud

We are very grateful to you for giving us a chance at this James Purdy novella, but it just isn't our kind of surrealism.

—Maxwell to Toni Strassman, agent, April 22, 1957,

rejecting "63: Dream Palace"

Here, I'm sorry to say, is the long Saul Bellow story. As I told you, we've decided that the length is prohibitive. It's true, of course, that we've occasionally—if rarely—published stories of comparable length, but in each case there has been a strong element of humor, whether the story itself was essentially humorous or not. We think that this is a tragic story—and a fine one—but we can't feel that, in our particular situation, we would want to devote to it the large proportion of an issue that it would require.

—Robert Henderson to Henry Volkening, agent, June 7, 1957,

rejecting "Leaving the Yellow House"

Nelson Algren, whose work we are always glad to see, is certainly in a lively mood in this one, but I'm sorry to say the piece as a whole doesn't seem right for us.

—Carroll Newman to Candida Donadio, agent,

October 2, 1961, rejecting "The Toneless Drum"

We've finally decided against this one by William Gass, I'm sorry to report. It has some fine details in it, but it's the kind of essay we don't ordinarily use, and its basic attitude toward the decay of the small town doesn't seem quite fresh enough.

—Carroll Newman to Lynn Nesbit, agent, November 21, 1963,

rejecting "In the Heart of the Heart of the Country"

And once again, this kind of exercise is not entirely fair, especially with its unsubstantiated implication that the magazine was wrong to reject these stories. Moreover, authors such as Flannery O'Connor and James Purdy engaged in the kind of dark surrealism—and someone like William Gass in the kind of linguistic experimentalism—that was simply too far removed from the *New Yorker*'s original notions of its literary purview, no matter how far these had wandered over three decades, for them to be accepted, much less welcomed, into its pages. Sometimes, as in Henderson's rejection of Saul Bellow's story, the expressions of appreciation for the submission and of regret for the rejection were clearly heartfelt. More often, however, they were condescending and patently insincere, not infrequently to the point of passive aggression (Maxwell's "isn't our kind of surrealism"). But over and above particular cases, what leaps out is the magazine's intense reluctance to stretch. Except for Bellow (who had a story published in 1952 and one in 1955) and Malamud (one in 1956), none of the writers rejected above had a single story in the *New Yorker* through the 1950s and the 1960s.

A perfect illustration of the *New Yorker*'s limitations is the case of a young writer named Philip Roth. In 1957, soon after her arrival as an editor, Rachel MacKenzie read "You Can't Tell a Man by the Song He Sings," a story Roth, then twenty-four, had published in *Commentary*. She wrote to him that she was impressed with so much—"the background, the combination of humor and seriousness"—that she wondered if he would care to submit anything to the *New Yorker*. (Coincidentally, just three months before, on his release from the army, Roth had been offered a job as a *New Yorker* fact-checker, but chose instead to accept a position teaching English composition at the University of Chicago.) Roth responded by submitting "Goodbye, Columbus," a first-person novella filled with humor, pathos, and riveting detail, about love, sex, and class among suburban New Jersey Jews. MacKenzie wrote to Roth that although the editors—"including Mr. Shawn, the editor-in-chief"—admired the work and were interested in him as a writer, it would be out of the question to print the entire novella, and no individual segment seemed to be able to stand on its own. Another problem, as MacKenzie tactfully put it, was that "taste would rule out here much of what is essential to the narrative."

Indeed, the climactic plot point, when Brenda Patimkin's mother discovers a diaphragm in her dresser drawer, was certainly outré for the *New Yorker*, which, if anything, had become even more prudish than in the Ross years. In addition to discouraging references to sex and bodily functions, Shawn had an odd list of words that made him so uncomfortable he would not allow them in the magazine: *balding*, for example, and *pimples*. W. D. Snodgrass once had a poem rejected because he declined to change or remove the word *dandruff*. The first play Kenneth Tynan reviewed had a reference to a pissoir, and he naively assumed he could mention it in his column. After hours of negotiation with Shawn, there emerged a mutually acceptable compromise: "a circular curbside construction." In the case of "Goodbye, Columbus," also in questionable taste was Roth's depiction of some of his minor characters and their nouveau riche lifestyle, which sometimes bordered on caricature. Indeed, when the novella was finally published in *Partisan Review*, Roth was accused of anti-Semitism. At the *New Yorker*, the Jewish question was a ticklish one. Shawn was a Jew, but in this he was alone among all the other significant editors, past and present, and nothing about the way he presented himself to the world (least of all his Irish-sounding name) gave any clue to his ethnicity. In their literary interests and personal style, such Jewish contributors as S. J. Perelman, S. N. Behrman, A. J. Liebling, E. J. Kahn, J. D. Salinger, Lillian Ross, Edith Oliver, and Philip Hamburger seemed as assimilated as it was possible to be, the initialed names of the first five and the Anglophilia of the first three serving as further cultural camouflage. There had once been a strong group of fiction writers who concerned themselves with Jewish milieus—Arthur Kober, Jerome Weidman, Daniel Fuchs, and Irwin Shaw—but they had all been Lobrano's authors and published little or nothing in the fifties or afterward. The bibliography John Updike concocted for his fictional Jewish novelist Henry Bech (born 1923) showed stories published in *Collier's, Story,* the *Saturday Evening Post,* and *Partisan Review,* but none in the *New Yorker.* Alfred Kazin, a casual protégé of Edmund Wilson's who strongly self-identified as a Jewish writer, began reviewing books for the *New Yorker* in 1948, but never felt "relaxed" there, in large part because of what he saw as Shawn's denial of his own heritage. "He said things about the importance of rituality and religion," Kazin recalled shortly before his death, in 1998, "but there was an unspoken attitude that it wouldn't do to be too 'Jewish.' I found him intellectually on the pretentious side." In the midfifties, somewhat to his relief, Kazin concluded he had been "dismissed" by Shawn—typically, there was no direct statement to this effect—and he wrote no more for the magazine during Shawn's regime.

So even if there were no diaphragm, the *New Yorker* would probably not have taken "Goodbye, Columbus." That is too bad, for the story was exactly what the magazine should have been printing in 1957. It was funny, it was a good read, it had characters one could care about, and—what was perhaps most important—it was about a world that had never really appeared in the magazine but was certainly of more interest and relevance to *New Yorker* readers than the inhabitants of 1920s Ireland or backwoods Alabama. As for length, if the magazine could spare one hundred thousand words for a seven-part Profile of Max Beerbohm, and fifty thousand for the fanciful and interminable "Zooey" (published in the issue dated just three days before MacKenzie's rejection letter), it could certainly afford to devote forty thousand words to Philip Roth.

MacKenzie encouraged Roth to send in more stories. He did, and six months later the magazine bought a slight back-of-the-book casual called "The Kind of Person I Am" and "Defender of the Faith," a short story the

Henderson from Newman

OUT OF SEASON   Gordimer

   Vote yes. Not an awful lot to this, really, but very neatly done, and I think
it will work all right.

Mrs. White from Henderson

   I guess ▮ yes. It's a little more ▮▮▮▮▮▮ neatly arranged than one might wish, I
feel. Fine, up to the end, and you expect some glimpse beyond the perfect ▮▮▮▮ surface
of the woman's life, but the letter is an old device, and ▮▮▮▮▮▮▮ a little disappoint-
ing. However, I'd say OK, because the characters are well done -- whole thing is well
enough done to overcome the fabrication of the end.

   Lobrano from KSW

   I feel this way and that on this story after one reading-- have no time to reread
today. It's a brittle story and the ending is contrived. Also I find it unpleasant
to have the narrator lift the pages of the letter to read the ending. I think the
last page should have been left on top and her eye almost unwittingly fall on that last
sentence. But with that fixed and with the remark that Caroline invents sounding more
natural (it should be shorter for to be natural she would have broken off reading it
sooner) I guess the story can be made passable for a C. She absolutely must place the
scene as Johannesburg early in the piece. She never seems to learn that.
Also why is she so in love with the first person short story? Well, I feel it's only
fair but it does have some good observation on women and I guess may about do.

Shawn from Lobrano

Agree yes on this for a C. Think the letter-reading by the narrator should be handled
as Mrs. White suggests. Seems to me that the invented remark is all right.

Lobrano from Shawn

Yes, liked this. An interesting collection of women. And agree with Mrs. White's
suggestion for handling letter, and agree with you that remark is all right as it is.

However, would it be worth considering turning contrived story into a natural story by
a cut (from A to B, pp 10-11) I've indicated -- if author were willing? Seems to me stor
would still have plenty of substance, and, although different, would be as truthful as
present version is. Much milder, of course.

Jan. 7, 1954

Mrs. White: Mr. Lobrano's queries on Gordimer's "Out of Season:"

[handwritten left margin: Lobrano to agree w/ every query]

1. This statement simply is not true. Whole point of story is that this isn't true, so seems unfair to reader. *[handwritten: I simply cannot agree — It's a feminine]*
   [handwritten: expression — a girlish cliché — She has everything in the world that cliché, but not actually as]

2. This "for example" seems redundant. She's been set up as the example at start of paragraph. *[handwritten margin: store too]*

3. This is practically the same as saying that the only thing she has missed in life is wanting something she can't have—which makes her sound exactly like Caroline. And, incidentally, Greta and Lottie sound a great deal alike, too. / In fact at times you feel as if you're reading about two pairs of identical twins. And the author makes each woman the representative of a category—idea is that you run across women just like them every hour on the hour. Not me. / *[handwritten margin: copy]*

4. Can a carnival daub? Maybe we'd better block this metaphor. This, in my opinion, is dreadful writing—or "writing."

5. She's a saint—purely and simply a saint.

6. Do wedding bands usually slip and slide all over the place? I never noticed. *[handwritten: Some do, on thin hands]*

7. Ummmm?

8. Odd word here. Is it allowable?

9. Not at all sure it's the disease which decrees.

10. Sixteen weeks, according to what narrator says at end of first paragraph on preceding galley. Or did they meet him when his wife wasn't around? *[handwritten: I don't think]*
    [handwritten: she's read this right]

11. All this is based on a speculative subconscious motivation. But I guess allowable?

12. I guess teeth change this way? *[handwritten: yes, they do]*

13. Seems kind of irrelevant. She's not referring to her trips but to Gideon's and those of people like him.

14. Oh now, come! Why should their faces be coarsened by sherry? She's really overdoing the contrast—doesn't have to keep on smacking us right between the eyes with it.

(Left) The "comment sheet" circulated among editors along with a short story submitted by Nadine Gordimer. (Carroll Newman was a first reader, Robert Henderson a longtime fiction editor.) *(Above)* Katharine White responded to some of Gus Lobrano's queries before they were sent on to Gordimer. The story was published in the issue of March 20, 1954.

New Yorker thought enough of to include in the end-of-the-decade fiction anthology. A well-crafted tale, full of astute observation and containing one memorable character, it is also puzzling, especially in its treatment of Jews and Jewishness. It is set on a Missouri army base in 1945. The narrator, Sergeant Nathan Marx, back in the United States after seeing combat duty in the European theater, has to deal with a manipulative private named Sheldon Grossbart (the vivid character), who wears his religion on his sleeve. One's expectation in reading the story is that Marx, who had shut down his emotions and even his sense of self as a protection against the horrors of war he had witnessed, will be prodded by his headaches with Grossbart into confronting his own feelings about himself as a Jew. But in the story as written such self-examination, if it is there at all, proceeds only on the most indirect level; it is always subservient to the vigorous plot. Just as the story is set back in time (in a year when Roth was eleven years old), so the narrator himself remains distant from any true emotional battlefield.

That remoteness, of course, was what made "Defender of the Faith" attractive to the New Yorker. "Eli, the Fanatic," which Roth included in the same submission, was a different story. The Jews in a prosperous suburb, proud and relieved at how smoothly they have fit in, are alarmed at the arrival in their town of an orthodox shul, presided over by a scruffy skull-cap-wearing teacher and attended by eighteen kids, all of them immigrants from Europe and displaced by the Holocaust. They nominate a lawyer, Eli Peck, to convince the interlopers to leave, or at least to be less ... Jewish. Eli tries to do his duty but finds the tightrope walk between tradition and assimilation increasingly impossible to perform. Like "Defender of the Faith," "Eli, the Fanatic" deals with the Jew trying to find a place in gentile America—but it does so more directly, it takes more chances, it has elements of the supernatural and the surreal, and it is a more powerful and affecting short story. MacKenzie rejected it, writing to Roth's agent, "We all agree that there are remarkable things in the story, but we feel that it keeps sliding off into caricature and farce and that in the end it falls between realism and didactic modern fable, the emotional thread breaking and the lesson taking over."

In his fiction, short and long, Roth was moving away from the proprieties of "Defender of the Faith" and toward the impolite risk-taking of "Eli, the Fanatic." The response from New Yorker editors was predictable. For the next twenty years, Roth recalled, "they turned down everything I wrote."

Since the thirties, having a short story or poem in the New Yorker had been a literary mark of honor. But the generation of writers coming of age in the fifties—Roth's generation—was the first to have grown up with the magazine, and for many of them being published there represented something more. In the postwar era, all over the country, sitting in their parents' living room or in a wooden chair at the local public library, young men and women were reading Salinger and Stafford and Shaw, and dreaming of future glory. In the literary world as well, the sense was that for a young writer to be published in the magazine was an exceedingly important milestone; a favorable placement could, by itself, actually set one off on a career. An example was Harold Brodkey, a young Harvard graduate who was "launched" (as Maxwell put it in a letter to Mrs. White) strictly on the basis of his *New Yorker* stories. Brodkey's 1958 collection, *First Love and Other Sorrows,* was dedicated (like so many others of the vintage) to William Maxwell.

Sylvia Plath, who was one year older than Roth and two years younger than Brodkey, and had grown up in a cultivated upper-middle-class home in Massachusetts, placed her literary aspirations and yearnings in the stories and poems she submitted to the *New Yorker* from the time she was a teenager. In a letter to her mother from Smith College, she referred to the magazine as one of her "unclimbed Annapurnas." When she was a collegiate guest editor of *Mademoiselle,* the interview subjects she requested were all *New Yorker* stalwarts: E. B. White, J. D. Salinger, Irwin Shaw, and Shirley Jackson. In 1956, she wrote, "I would really like to get something in *The New Yorker* before I die, I do so admire that particular, polished, rich, brilliant style." But everything she sent in kept getting sent back. Plath began to worry, she confided in her journal, that "I depend too desperately on getting my poems, my little glib poems, so neat, so small, accepted by the *New Yorker.*"

In 1956, she married the English writer Ted Hughes, who placed a poem in the magazine the following year. The year after *that,* Plath finally had her long-awaited acceptance, and the account of it in her journal conveys a combination of relief and exhilaration that was not unique to her:

> Seated at the typewriter, I saw the lovely light-blue shirt of the mailman going into the front walk of the millionairess next door, so I ran downstairs. One letter stuck up out of the mailbox, and I saw *The New Yorker* on the left corner in dark print. My eyes dazed over. I raced alternatives through my head: I had sent a stamped envelope with my last poems, so they must have lost it and returned the rejects in one of their own envelopes. Or it must be a letter for Ted about copyrights. I ripped the letter from the box. It felt shockingly thin. I tore it open right there on the steps. . . . The black thick print of Howard Moss's letter banged into my brain. I saw "MUSSEL HUNTER AT ROCK HARBOR seems to me a marvelous poem and I'm happy to say we're taking it for *The New Yorker* . . ."—at this realization of ten years of hopeful wishing waits (and subsequent rejections) I ran yipping upstairs to Ted and jumping about like a Mexican bean. It was only moments later, calming a little, that I finished the sentence ". . . as well as NOCTURNE, which we also

think extremely fine." TWO POEMS—not only that, two of my *longest*—91 and 45 lines respectively: They'll have to use front spots for both and are buying them *in spite* of having full load of summer poems and not for filler.*

If ever a writer, a magazine, and a time were made for each other, the writer was John Updike, the magazine was the *New Yorker,* and the time was the 1950s. Updike, born in a suburb of Reading, Pennsylvania, in the same year as Sylvia Plath, was a passionate *New Yorker* reader and admirer from the age of twelve, when an aunt gave his family a gift subscription for Christmas.† Indeed, the fate of the entire Updike clan became oddly tied with the magazine and its contributors. In 1945, inspired by E. B. White's essays about country living, Updike's mother, Linda (a mostly unpublished writer), bought a farm in an outlying area and moved the family there; John, an only child, was not particularly pleased by his newfound isolation. "It is one of the few authenticated cases of literature influencing life," he remarked years later. "I sought the antidote for my plight in the poison that had produced it, and devoured the work of White, of Thurber, Benchley, Perelman, Sullivan, and all those other names evocative of the urban romance that not so long ago attached to New York City, the innocent longing for sophistication that focused here."

As he grew to adulthood, Updike later said, "My sole ambition was to make the *New Yorker.*" But despite his fixation on the casual humorous essay, his real love was graphic art, and he felt his best shot at the magazine was as a cartoonist. He later recalled that he used to "pore over" the drawings as a

---

*By the time of her death by suicide in February 1963, Plath had sold nine poems to the *New Yorker.* In July 1963, the magazine published a two-page selection of her work under the title "Seven Poems." According to Plath's biographer Paul Alexander, this prominent display (with the dates, 1932–1963, after Plath's name) initiated the construction of Plath's posthumous reputation as an important poet.

†Updike later mused on the coincidence of being the same age as Plath in his poem "Upon Looking into Sylvia Plath's *Letters Home*":

> Yes, this is how it was to have been born
> in 1932—the having parents
> everyone said loved you and you had to love;
> the believing having a wonderful life began
> with being good at school; the certainty
> that words would count; the seeing Dreyer's silent *Joan*
> at the Museum of Modern Art, and being
> greatly moved; the courtship of the slicks,
> because one had to eat, one and one's spouse,
> that soulmate in Bohem-Utop-ia.
> You, dead at thirty, leaving blood-soaked poems
> for all the anthologies, and I still wheezing,
> my works overweight; and yet we feel twins.

boy, "studying the draftsmanship of Alain and Robert Day and Garrett Price and Arno and George Price of course." Updike submitted many cartoons in his high-school and college years, never successfully. But at Harvard, the *Lampoon* served for him as a sort of *New Yorker* Triple-A farm team. He published dozens of cartoons, comic poems, and humor pieces in it and was eventually elected president. In July 1953, he sent the *New Yorker* a piece of light verse called "The Lovelorn Astronomer." One of hundreds of unsolicited poems that came into the office every week, it caught the eye of Nora Sayre (veteran contributor Joel's daughter), who worked as a reader. "I like this very much," she wrote in her report, "and wondered if it were good enough to print. I think the choice of cosmic imagery works out beautifully, points out the astronomer's feeling of insignificance extremely well. The strictness of the sonnet form doesn't seem to limit this particular poet, nor his poem." Ultimately it wasn't published, but Maxwell's rejection letter to Updike was encouraging.

In 1954, less than a month after his graduation, he sent in another comic poem, "Duet, with Muffled Brake Drums." Inspired by a *New Yorker* ad reading, "50 years ago Rolls met Royce—a Meeting that made Engineering History," the poem imagines that momentous encounter (and concludes, Updike would later note, with a "triple rhyme and final hexameter . . . devices I had noticed in Dryden"). There would be no years of longing and angst for Updike, at least as far as the *New Yorker* was concerned. Katharine White wrote him personally:

> It is a great pleasure to send you your first check from the *New Yorker*, even though it is a small one, and I hope that I shall soon be sending you many others. . . . Light verse is one of our most precious ingredients and light verse writers are rare nowadays, so I hope you will keep up the good work and will bombard us with verse. Of course we are equally pleased to get humorous prose, so if you ever write what we call "casuals," in office jargon, please send them along too.

Updike replied: "Thank you very much for the kind and hopeful words. And the check didn't seem at all small to me. It seems huge, and the honor of appearing in the *New Yorker* looms titanic." But the main highway of Updike's renown would not be light verse, much less casuals, but serious fiction. He had had stories rejected by the magazine, including one about his dying grandmother that came back, as Updike remembered it, with the comment, "Look, we don't use stories of senility, but try us again." What set him in the right direction was Cheever's short story "O Youth and Beauty!" published just weeks after Maxwell's friendly rejection in 1953. Updike later said he felt "covetous dissatisfaction" with Cheever's cosmic irony; it made him think that "there must be more to say about American life than this." The story he eventually composed as a kind of tacit protest was called "Friends from Philadelphia," and the *New Yorker* accepted it shortly after it took "Duet, with Muffled Brake Drums."

Reading the story today, one is struck less by any comment offered on American life than that a twenty-two-year-old was capable of such artful and flawless craftsmanship. The story, like so many in the *New Yorker*'s early days, revolved around class distinctions. The fifteen-year-old main character's father (like Updike's) is a public-school teacher, his mother a college graduate, and they have friends who visit their small Pennsylvania town all the way from Philadelphia. But they struggle for money. By contrast, his friend Thelma's father never went to college, yet, he pointedly tells young John, he buys a new car whenever he wants. Meanwhile, John's feelings about Thelma are complicated and contradictory—he is drawn to her physically and emotionally, she represents something about his childhood and adolescence he does not want to let go of, yet he is annoyed by her accent (she calls him "Jan," to rhyme with Ann) and the way she plucks her eyebrows; with a conviction he is too self-absorbed to comprehend, he thinks she is beneath him. The mastery of the story is the subtlety and gracefulness and intricacy with which the characters' attitudes and relationships are sketched out and filled in. On each reading, new and revealing details pop out—for instance, small lies characters tell in the opening pages that are casually exposed near the end. And to tie up the package, the last sentence is what journalists call a kicker—the "snap ending" that the *New Yorker* traditionally disdained, but that in this case is so skillfully set up and deployed as to be irresistible.

However, "Friends from Philadelphia" did have something to say about America. The place name in the title is a clue: Updike's comprehensive and clear-eyed laying out and scrutiny of the circumstances of his characters' lives could only come out of a deep respect. The details that Cheever changed into metaphor and symbol, Updike paid attention to. "Friends from Philadelphia" and his next sale, "Ace in the Hole," about an ex-high-school basketball player, again in small-town Pennsylvania, who finds himself with a wife and a baby and out of a job, offered a documentary plausibility *New Yorker* fiction hadn't seen since the glory days of another native of the Keystone State, John O'Hara, in the 1930s and early forties. About a slightly later Pennsylvania story, "The Happiest I've Been," Updike was years later to reflect:

> While writing it, I had the sensation of breaking through, as if through a thin sheet of restraining glass, to material, to truth, previously locked up. [Many *New Yorker* stories] had been written in the decades preceding 1958, but none, my happy delusion was, quite in this way about quite this sort of material. Non-southern small towns and teen-agers were both, my impres-

sion was, customarily treated with condescension, or satirically, in the fiction of the Fifties; the indictments of provincial life by Sinclair Lewis and Ring Lardner were still in the air. My mission was to stand up and cry, "No, here is life, to be taken as seriously as any other kind."

"There," he concluded, "was the New Yorker reader of my imagination, pampered and urban, needing a wholesome small-town change from his then-customary diet of Westchester-adultery stories and reminiscences of Italian or Polish childhoods."

Updike had received a fellowship to study at the Ruskin School of Drawing and Fine Art in Oxford, directly following his Harvard graduation. On his way to sail, he stopped in the New Yorker offices and had lunch with Maxwell, who, with Shawn's approval, gave him to understand that a job with the magazine would be waiting for him on his return. (Maxwell's memo to Katherine White about the meeting is quoted in this book's Introduction.) But Updike was not inclined to wait. From England, he submitted and sold numerous poems and three stories ("Ace in the Hole," "Tomorrow and Tomorrow and So Forth,""Dentistry and Doubt"). He was sent and signed a first-reading agreement. ("It is rather unusual for us to offer an agreement to a contributor of such short standing as you," Katharine White wrote him, "but you have produced so much this summer and so much of it seems to be right for us that we did not think it fair to wait any longer.") He exchanged three-page letters with Mrs. White arguing the fine points of punctuation, and she developed such a fondness and admiration for him that she and her husband looked him up on a trip to England the following summer.

On his return, in August 1955, Updike took a job with the New Yorker as a Talk of the Town reporter. Characteristically, his first submission, a visit piece about a Long Island man who had invented a "rejuvenating spray," was so accomplished that Shawn immediately promoted him from "Talk reporter" to "Talk writer"—meaning that his pieces would not pass through one of the Talk rewrite men, Brendan Gill and John McCarten, but would be published as he wrote them, and that instead of a salary of $100 a week he would be paid $200 for each published story. For the next nineteen months, he proceeded "to gad about, to interview tertiary celebrities, to peek into armories, and to write accounts of my mild adventures."

Updike's arrival was fortunate, for it came as The Talk of the Town was at a creative low ebb. The venerable format of unsigned personality pieces, visit pieces, and dope pieces, punctuated by anecdotes, was certainly sturdy, but after twenty-five years it was beginning to creak a little bit. Stylistically, Talk often threatened to fall victim to preciousness and its own mannerisms, the first-person plural foremost among them. Some help had come in the form of the first-person singular. Philip Hamburger wrote dozens of Talk pieces in the persona of "Our Man Stanley," who explored the city and reported back in a charming telegraphese. In 1954, Maeve Brennan, who besides contributing short stories was on the staff of the magazine, turning out brief book and fashion notes, wrote a short vignette about an experience she had had in the supermarket. It was too short to be a casual and not funny enough to be an anecdote. Someone—presumably either Brennan or Shawn—had the idea of presenting it in The Talk of the Town as a missive from "a rather long-winded lady we hear from occasionally." The Long-Winded Lady's dispatches continued to appear until 1981, getting longer and longer-winded; they lent Talk an eloquence, a quality of observation, a connection to the city streets, a nonfacetious humor, a personality, and an ineffable sadness it had lacked.

Updike, for his part, worked within the established conventions, but stretched them. "It was perfectly obvious," recalled Brendan Gill, "that he was writing better Talk stories than anyone who had ever written them." His data compilations on Antarctica, pigeons, and (audaciously) the universe were attempts to distill a poetry of fact. More than four decades later, Whitney Balliett, a fellow Talk writer at the time, could still recite from memory the lead of the first of these: "In Antarctica, everything turns left." Updike specialized in visit pieces, he later recalled, because they "required no research and little personal encounter.... An hour of silent spying and two hours of fanciful typing from my notes would earn my month's pay." (The rest of the time, he worked on short stories, poems, and his first novel, *The Poorhouse Fair.*) One of his small but salutary innovations in this genre, picked up on by a new generation of Talk writers fifteen years later, was to ventilate the odor of hucksterism from coverage of a publicity event by including as characters in his account the publicists who had arranged it. In his favorite and most memorable visits he didn't interact with anyone. From a protected "nook" in the cocktail lounge at the Biltmore Hotel during collegiate spring vacation, he took down the pixilated snatches of overheard conversations and from them formulated a piece of absurdist theater. Another story began: "On the afternoon of the first day of spring, when the gutters were still heaped high with Monday's snow but the sky itself was swept clean, we put on our galoshes and walked up the sunny side of Fifth Avenue to Central Park. There we saw . . ." After that came a kind of epic haiku, thirty-three short paragraphs of pure description. The final twelve:

> The head of Giuseppe Maxxini staring across the white softball field, unblinking, though the sun was in its eyes.
>
> Water murmuring down walks and rocks and steps. A grown man trying to block one rivulet with snow.

Things like brown sticks nosing through a plot of cleared soil.

A tire track in a piece of mud far removed from where any automobiles could be.

Footprints around a KEEP OFF sign.

Two pigeons feeding each other.

Two showgirls, whose faces had not yet thawed the frost of their makeup, treading indignantly through the slush.

A plump old man saying "Chick, chick" and feeding peanuts to squirrels.

Many solitary men throwing snowballs at tree trunks.

Many birds calling to each other about how little the ramble had changed.

One red mitten lying lost under a poplar tree.

An airplane, very bright and distant, slowly moving through the branches of a sycamore.

This kind of thing came too easily to Updike for him to keep at it long; as he noted years later, "A man who would be an artist is obliged to keep working where he might improve." And his ego needed more nourishment than this anonymous form provided. So early in 1957, he and his young family moved to the north shore of Boston, where Updike hung out a shingle as a freelance writer. He was almost frighteningly productive. (In a letter to William Maxwell, he offered some insight into his prolificness: "It occurs to me that the world would not be significantly poorer if I stopped writing altogether. Only a bottomless capacity for envy keeps me going. That, and the pleasure of reading proofs and designing book jackets.") Besides writing a novel every other year (*The Poorhouse Fair* in 1959, *Rabbit, Run* in 1960, *The Centaur* in 1963, *Of the Farm* in 1965), he sent the *New Yorker* a steady stream of short stories and poems, occasional Talk pieces and Comments, sparkling book reviews, and one Reporter at Large, the 1960 "Hub Fans Bid Kid Adieu," about the final game of Ted Williams's career, which has become a classic of sports literature.

Everything Updike wrote was of the highest quality, but the short stories stood out. By 1966, he had filled three collections with them—*The Same Door, Pigeon Feathers,* and *The Music School*—and all but two of the entries in these books were first printed in the *New Yorker*. Generally, his most memorable stories fell into one of two categories. The first was the Pennsylvania reminiscence, such as "Friends from Philadelphia" and "The Happiest I've Been" and later "The Alligators," "Flight," and "Pigeon Feathers." These were exquisite and sometimes heartrending coming-of-age stories, later collected into a volume called *Olinger Stories,* but coming-of-age stories, for any author, will eventually be exhausted. Capable of being extended indefinitely, however, was Updike's second short-fiction genre—the refraction of his own life. An examined life unceasingly alters. His focus was the domestic sphere, and Updike's eight-year progression from "Toward Evening" to "Sunday Teasing" to "Incest" to "Walter Briggs" to "Wife-Wooing" to the harrowing 1963 "Giving Blood" is his own *Scenes from a Marriage*. The husband and wife are usually called Richard and Joan Maple, but no matter what their names and occupations, they are the same people, and as the cracks in their union appear and widen, Updike gradually removes the narrative niceties and gives us unblinking looks at the hate and love that intimately intermingle.

For the *New Yorker,* accepting "Friends from Philadelphia" was a no-brainer. But by enthusiastically publishing Updike's increasingly personal and psychologically unflinching subsequent works, the magazine, as it had so often in the past, was letting a contributor of genius subtly alter and deepen its own definition. As Maxwell, who served as his editor after Mrs. White's retirement, wrote to Updike as early as 1958, "It is a slightly different magazine because you are now published in it."

This is not to say that it was always easy for writer and magazine to adapt to each other. In 1960, Updike submitted a meditative and rather slight story that included a scene of the main character staring at his own feces in a toilet bowl. Maxwell turned the story down, writing Updike, "Shawn felt as I did about 'The Crow in the Woods'—that is, he loves it, and feels it is all right the way it is but not all right for the *New Yorker*—that is to say the 'functional' as it is called around here, delicately—and that we oughtn't to urge you to change something that is all right just because it isn't all right for us." The same year, Updike sent in "A&P," a colloquial first-person account, reminiscent of Sherwood Anderson, of a supermarket checkout kid who takes a stand on a matter of principle. The story was irresistible (and became perhaps Updike's most anthologized work), but a phrase in the opening paragraph presented a problem: "She was a chunky kid, with a good tan and a sweet broad soft-looking can . . ." Maxwell suggested replacing *can* with *butt,* to which Updike, showing rare irritation, replied:

> You must be kidding about "butt." It's really just as crude as "can." I think the real answer is "tail"—but every time I sit down to go over the proof of A & P, I choke up with the silly sacrifice of "can." Not that it's much of a sacrifice—but writing is so largely a matter of execution and detail.

(Ultimately a compromise was reached in which the young lady was described as having "a sweet broad backside." Updike restored *can* in the book version.) There would have been much more serious problems had Updike's short stories contained anything like the sexual explicitness that marked his novels from the 1960 *Rabbit, Run* on. But as close to the bone as they cut, they were not "functional," and so the *New Yorker* grew to contain them.

In a recent letter to Maxwell, Updike remarked that from the summer of 1954, when the *New Yorker* accepted "Duet, with Muffled Brake Drums" and "Friends from Philadelphia," "I have been in a writerly bliss nothing could shake." The editors knew how fortunate they were to have found Updike as well, and how little credit they or the magazine could ultimately take for his amazing career. Maxwell wrote him in 1960, "From the very beginning I have been so confident of your ability to paddle your own canoe—so positive that the day would come when you would have to go to Sweden and make a speech in white tie and tails—that I have allowed myself the fatherly feeling of pride in your career but not the equally paternal feeling of having had anything much to do with it."

URBANITY, INC.

It is easy to criticize the *New Yorker* of the fifties and early sixties for its gentility and blandness, a little harder to blame Shawn for allowing it to remain this way. Why *should* he have sought out any form of Sturm und Drang when the magazine, as it was, was so fabulously successful? The *New Yorker's* circulation grew 40 percent (331,574 to 464,119) between 1950 and 1964, while its annual advertising pages increased by an even more impressive 70 percent, to 5,959. By the midfifties, it was running more ad pages than any other general-interest magazine and was second only to *Business Week* among *all* magazines. But because of steadily rising advertising rates, total ad revenue far outpaced the page gain, jumping more than *400* percent, from $5.59 million to $24.8 million, over the same fourteen years. In a 1958 article called "Urbanity, Inc.," the *Wall Street Journal* gushed that the *New Yorker* was a "remarkably prosperous business enterprise," whose 10 percent profit margin was "probably the highest in the field."

As dramatic as the level of success was how easy it came. Circulation seemed to be a matter of unlocking the door, turning on the lights, and letting the business come. The *Journal* reported that the renewal rate among *New Yorker* subscribers was an "exceedingly high" 76 percent. The ones who didn't renew were replenished, and then some, with virtually no effort on the part of the magazine. In 1957, the magazine spent a grand total of $645.07 on soliciting new readers and, except for a modest discount for holiday gifts, offered no cut-rate subscription prices.

Who were these new readers and what drew them to the *New Yorker?* The informal survey of more than three hundred "longtime *New Yorker* readers" described in this book's Introduction suggests some answers. Seventy-five percent reported that they had started reading the magazine in graduate school, in college, or while they were kids living with their parents. The last group, who typically reported reading the cartoons first, then graduating to Newsbreaks, and finally tackling the articles and stories, tended to view a *New Yorker* subscription as something passed from one generation to the next, like a religious denomination or a set of sterling silver. Those who discovered the *New Yorker* as students described something closer to a conversion experience, generally with a teacher or another student introducing them to the gospel. A woman from Oregon recalled a college professor in the late 1930s saying, "Life is insupportable without the *New Yorker*"; another woman said she was made acquainted to the magazine in 1950, as an eighteen-year-old student at a junior college in Chicago, by an English professor "who was sympathetic to a young woman coming out of four years in a repressive Lutheran high school who wanted to know what was out there in the world beyond the Bible and Chicago." For both groups, one of the first steps in setting up a household as an adult—roughly equivalent to opening a checking account—was ordering a *New Yorker* subscription of one's own.

As for advertising, the *New Yorker* appeared to spend more time and effort turning down ads than courting them. By policy, the magazine kept liquor advertising to no more than 16 percent of the total. Raoul Fleischmann's stepson Stephen Botsford, who became president of the company in 1956, kept a rejection book of ads that the business or editorial departments deemed insufficiently tasteful to publish. He showed the *Wall Street Journal*'s reporters one that portrayed an inexpensive clothing product and said, "We can't serve these people and Brooks Brothers at the same time."* The restrictions increased. In May 1963, by official policy, the magazine barred "foundation garment advertising containing either photographs or sketches of bras, girdles, foundations, panties, waist cinches, or other garments normally worn under a slip." The next year, following the surgeon general's report on smoking, the *New Yorker* stopped accepting cigarette advertising. And some advertisers were turned away simply because there wasn't any room. After years of more and more ads, Shawn determined in the late fifties that the editorial department was not capable of producing a magazine of unlimited size, and 248 pages was set as the limit. This was regularly reached in the busy fall season, and when it was, the advertising space for the issue was officially sold out.

The magazine's popularity as an advertising forum stemmed from its base of loyal, prosperous, striving readers. According to a historian of American advertising, just by being hawked in the *New Yorker*, a product or service gained "by association a further boost up the socioeconomic scale." Some campaigns became inextricably associated with the magazine. "The man in

---

*Fleischmann's other stepson, Gardner Botsford, joined the magazine's staff in the 1940s and worked until his retirement in 1982 as a fact editor.

the Hathaway Shirt," featuring a striking male model with an eye patch, appeared exclusively in the *New Yorker* for four years, beginning in 1951, and continued in the magazine for many years thereafter. By 1956, customers were so familiar with the campaign that an individual ad could run without any copy.

Annual ad pages kept going up. They peaked in 1966 at 6,144, setting a magazine-industry record that stood until the 1990s, when it was broken by a computer publication.

Some of this enormous success was due to plain good fortune and good timing: the *New Yorker* was perfectly placed to benefit from a number of the significant postwar changes in U.S. society. From its early days, it had been pitched to the educated middle-upper or upper-middle class, and this segment dramatically increased in both numbers and visibility in the period. Between 1952 and 1967, the median income of all families jumped (in constant 1996 dollars) from $21,192 to $34,289—that is, right into the *New Yorker's* sights. Meanwhile, the number of Americans with college degrees grew from 12.1 million in 1950 to 19.9 million in 1966—the difference signifying some 8 million potential *New Yorker* readers. A more subtle phenomenon concerned gender. Nineteen-fifties America was home to more college-educated women than ever before, they were (for the most part) at home with more babies than ever before, and a significant number of them flocked to the *New Yorker*, representing as it did one of the few ways they could exercise—and in some cases advertise—their learning and culture. Internal *New Yorker* marketing surveys reveal that the magazine's readership, 53 percent male in 1949, had flip-flopped to 55 percent female in 1954. Women readers continued to outnumber men for the rest of the decade.* In the 1996 survey of longtime readers, 61 percent of the respondents were female, 39 percent male. One Iowa woman, who started reading the magazine in the 1940s as a twenty-five-year-old mother of two young children, expressed a common sentiment: "At first I thought I was reading it for the excellence of its fiction, but soon realized it was opening up a new world for me—a superior continuance of my dropped college years."

---

*The studies also revealed that women were likely to read more of the magazine than men were. The last year the magazine performed this kind of gender census was 1961, when females represented 53 percent of the readership.

CHAPTER SIX

A TIME OF TUMULT

1962~71

CARSON, BALDWIN, ARENDT

By the 1950s, the *New Yorker* represented far more to its readers than the particular words and pictures they encountered in its pages each week. It was a habit, a status symbol, a pillar of one's identity—and sometimes all of those things. Some subscribers read it cover to cover (and didn't allow themselves to crack open an issue until they had completed the previous one); others used it as coffee-table decoration. So it is difficult if not impossible to determine whether the magazine was so successful in the fifties because or in spite of its overall tepidness.

But it can conclusively be said that at a certain point, William Shawn decided that the moment had come for the *New Yorker* to make some waves. Shawn being Shawn, he made no pronouncements on the matter. But his editorial decisions constituted an unmistakable statement in themselves. Between 1962—that is, ten years after he had assumed the editorship—and 1964, the *New Yorker* published a series of articles that, in their social and political reporting and impact, are probably unmatched in the history of magazines, comprising (in chronological order) "Silent Spring" by Rachel Carson; the James Baldwin essay that would be published as the book *The Fire Next Time*; "Eichmann in Jerusalem" by Hannah Arendt; and "Annals of Law: The Gideon Case" by Anthony Lewis (published in book form as *Gideon's Trumpet*). These were only the most famous pieces. In the same two-year period, the *New Yorker* also printed "The Honoured Society," Norman Lewis's groundbreaking study of the Italian Mafia; "A Cloud of Smoke" by Thomas Whiteside, an early and influential examination of the health risks of smoking; Edith Iglauer's influential report on New York City air pollution, "Fifteen Thousand Quarts of Air"; Richard Harris's "The Real Voice," a meticulous three-part account of Senator Estes Kefauver's attempt to pass legislation regulating pharmaceutical prices; and Dwight Macdonald's fifty-page book review of *The Other America* by Michael Harrington, which single-handedly placed the book and its subject—the persistence of poverty in the United States—on the national political agenda.* In 1965, the *New Yorker* published "In Cold Blood," Truman Capote's "nonfiction novel" about a murder in Kansas—and it caused more discussion than any article since "Hiroshima."

The Carson, Baldwin, and Arendt pieces, though printed in an eight-month span between June 1962 and February 1963, had all been in the works for some time. Rachel Carson had written two brilliant pieces of natural history for the magazine, "The Sea Around Us" and "The Edge of the Sea." Late in 1957, she became interested in the issue of the deleterious effect on wildlife of DDT and other pesticides. In February 1958, she wrote a letter to E. B. White, whom she did not know but had long admired, suggesting that he cover for the *New Yorker* an upcoming trial on the issue in a Long Island federal court. White declined, but agreed with her on the perils of DDT, and forwarded her letter to Shawn with a recommendation that the *New Yorker* have someone else write about the trial. Some weeks later, Carson decided that she wanted to do the article herself and sent Shawn a proposal. He was enthusiastic about the idea and commissioned a two-part Reporter at Large, of twenty thousand to thirty thousand words. Soon afterward Shawn and Carson met in New York. She reported to her friend Dorothy Freeman, in a letter dated June 12, 1958:

> He is completely fascinated with the theme and obviously happy and excited at presenting it in the *New Yorker*. Best of all, I can (indeed he *wants* me to) present it strictly from my point of view, pulling no punches. He says, "After all there are some things one doesn't have to be objective and unbiased about—one doesn't condone murder!" Besides the importance of the theme ("We don't usually think of the *New Yorker* as changing the world, but this is one time it might") he feels that the material is just plain fascinating, and now thinks he'd like to have 50,000 words!!

One senses Shawn seeing in Carson's "indictment of what man is doing to the earth" (as she later described it to him) a chance to sound the apocalyptic alarms so they could be heard everywhere, just as he, Ross, and Hersey had done with "Hiroshima" twelve years before. However, slowed

---

*Iglauer's piece had its genesis, she later recalled, when "I stuck my head out the window and the air smelled so foul that I called Bill Shawn and said I would like to know why. He said, 'Find out if anyone is taking care of us.'"

by illness and the magnitude of her subject, Carson was not able to submit anything to Shawn until January 1962, when she delivered fifteen chapters of what had become a seventeen-chapter book. At 9 P.M. three days later, as she recounted to Freeman, "the phone rang and a mild voice said, 'This is William Shawn.'" His praise was anything but mild: " 'a brilliant achievement'—'you have made it literature'—'full of beauty and loveliness and depth of feeling.' "

Robert Gerdy, an editor in the fact department, helped Carson trim the manuscript so it could fit in three parts totaling fifty thousand words. It was published on June 16, to public reaction that, if it didn't quite reach "Hiroshima" heights, came very close. Like Hersey's piece, the meticulously reported "Silent Spring" prompted a laudatory and cautionary *New York Times* editorial. Published as a book that fall, it was a Main Selection of the Book-of-the-Month Club and was on the *New York Times* best-seller list for thirty-two weeks. More than thirty-five years after its publication, it is widely credited with giving impetus to the general sense that nature and man are inextricably entwined in a complex ecological system, to a reflexive distrust of chemicals and their side effects, and to the modern environmental movement.

James Baldwin's essay had its genesis in 1959, when the author—then thirty-five years old and a widely published essayist, critic, and novelist—approached Shawn with the notion of writing a series of articles about Africa. Shawn gave his assent and—uncharacteristically—an advance, which Baldwin used to spend several months touring the continent. Unfortunately, he found himself unable to translate his experiences into print. He had better luck with a commission he'd been given by Norman Podhoretz, the editor of the intellectual monthly *Commentary,* to write an article about Elijah Muhammad, the leader of the Nation of Islam, and his relevance to American blacks. As Baldwin worked on it, the article turned into a long autobiographical meditation about race in America, anchored by an account of his meeting with Muhammad. Realizing that he would never complete his proposed African dispatch, he sent this essay—which he decided to call "Down at the Cross"—to Shawn. His thinking was that it would absolve him of his obligation to the *New Yorker,* and after it was rejected (as he assumed it would surely be), he would send it on to Podhoretz. However, Shawn bought it (and ever afterward, Podhoretz would nurse a grudge against Baldwin and the *New Yorker*).

In two significant respects, this was a remarkable decision. For one thing, it broke with the *New Yorker* tradition, established and firmly believed in by Ross, of publishing only stories, reviews, humor pieces, and reportage and never any piece of prose whose main purpose was to express the opinion of the writer—that is, never any *essays.* Unlike Ross, Shawn thought that significant issues could and should be engaged even when there was no journalistic peg, but characteristically, he waited ten years to reverse the rule. His doing so created a problem: What should Baldwin's piece be called? One tradition Shawn did not propose to break was that every article in the magazine had to have a rubric—Profiles, Reporter at Large, Onward and Upward with the Arts, Letter from . . . , and so forth. Shawn, who had a gift for crafting extraordinary titles, gave Baldwin's piece the brilliant heading "Letter from a Region in My Mind." (Within a few years, Shawn would create a rubric for essays: "Reflections.")

The piece's second departure was its subject matter. To say that the *New Yorker* traditionally held itself at a remove from racial matters would be a significant understatement. Other than Rebecca West's 1948 Reporter at Large on a lynching trial in South Carolina, a few pointed Comments by E. B. White poking fun at discrimination, several short stories by the South African Nadine Gordimer, and a couple of recent articles by staff writer Bernard Taper (most notably "Gomillion vs. Lightfoot," about a 1961 gerrymandering controversy in Alabama), the magazine essentially ignored anything to do with race. In the early days, black people were stereotypically depicted in short stories, cartoons, and advertisements as servants, Pullman porters, and comic figures, but in the postwar period such depictions were recognized as offensive. So blacks disappeared completely. Since the magazine's overwhelmingly white readership looked to the *New Yorker* for reflections of its own life, the editorial Jim Crow was easy for them to ignore. (There were, however, an extraordinary number of cartoons about "natives." As critic Mary Corey noted in her study of the *New Yorker* in the post–World War II decade, "It is difficult to find a single issue of the magazine that did not contain at least one cartoon depicting a caveman, a cannibal, or a grass-skirted South Sea Islander up to some comic caper.") Fact pieces were slightly better, with Whitney Balliett's and Nat Hentoff's Profiles of black musicians and Joseph Mitchell's magnificent "Mr. Hunter's Grave" (1956), about one of the last surviving members of a dying African-American community in the far reaches of Staten Island. But even there, in most of the few instances where the existence of domestic people of color was recognized, one got the sense that the writer was an ornithologist studying an odd species. For example, a 1957 Christopher Rand Reporter at Large on Puerto Ricans in New York contained this sentence: "On the whole, Puerto Rican men wear less colorful clothes [than the women]; indeed, in cold weather many of them dress in Army-surplus coats, trousers, and so on, which gives them an over-all drab tone." The *New Yorker* had no black editors and no black contributors—and had not since Langston Hughes published a handful of stories and poems in the thirties and forties.

For a first step, "Letter from a Region in My Mind" was a doozy. The essay is flawed by the occasional structural non sequitur, and a lack of integration among the meditation, the autobiography, and the meeting with Elijah Muhammad, but it is an extremely powerful, eloquent, and prescient statement on the nature of race relations in America. It left in the distance the notion, generally assumed by liberals in 1962—one year before the March on Washington and two before the Voting Rights Act—that equal rights under the law and integration were dual panaceas. Baldwin referred to "the incredible, abysmal, and really cowardly obtuseness of white liberals" and scoffed at the assumption that "the solution to the Negro problem depend[s] on the speed with which Negroes accept and adopt white standards":

> It is the Negro, of course, who is presumed to have become equal—an achievement that not only proves the comforting fact that perseverance has no color but also overwhelmingly corroborates the white man's sense of his own value. Alas, this value can scarcely be corroborated in any other way; there is certainly little enough in the white man's public or private life that one should desire to imitate. White men, at the bottom of their hearts, know this. Therefore, a vast amount of the energy that goes into what we call the Negro problem is produced by the white man's profound desire not to be seen as he is, and at the same time a vast amount of the white anguish is rooted in the white man's equally profound need to be seen as he is, to be released from the tyranny of his mirror. All of us know, whether or not we are able to admit it, that mirrors can only lie, that death by drowning is all that awaits one there.

No less than "Silent Spring" had done, the piece created a sensation. The following May, for the one hundredth anniversary of the Emancipation Proclamation, *Time* magazine put Abraham Lincoln on its cover. As a follow-up the next week, to coincide with the essay's publication as a book, it selected James Baldwin. The decision makes sense in retrospect, for if the black movement of the late 1960s, with its "Black Power" and "Black Is Beautiful" slogans (both formulations Baldwin came quite close to making), had a literary progenitor, it was "Letter from a Region in My Mind."

Just three months later, another *New Yorker* fact piece caused another commotion—but this time the magazine did not come off as well. In 1960, Adolf Eichmann, who had been head of the Gestapo's Jewish section during World War II, was apprehended in Argentina by Israeli security forces and taken to Israel, where he was to be tried for his part in the Nazi extermination of Jews. The German-Jewish political philosopher Hannah Arendt, author of the influential *The Origins of Totalitarianism,* proposed to *Commentary* that she cover the trial. Podhoretz did not have the budget to cover her expenses, so on the urging of her close friend Mary McCarthy, Arendt broached the idea to Shawn. One can speculate that Shawn said yes, in part, because the situation was reminiscent of the remarkable philosophical-journalistic reports Rebecca West had written for the *New Yorker* on the trials of British traitors after World War II. A difference was that while West's prose was formidably cerebral and sometimes mannered, she had written successfully for the educated public for more than two decades. Arendt, by contrast, was a native German speaker who had never directed anything at a general rather than scholarly audience. And so it was not surprising that her report, which was published in five long parts beginning in February 1963, was dense and often difficult to read.

But some of what she had to say was quite clear. Her central notion of the "banality of evil"—that the most horrific acts tend not to be committed by demonic archfiends, but bourgeois, self-serving, dull bureaucrats such as Eichmann—was instantaneously recognized as a powerful and penetrating one and has continued to resonate in the culture in the years since. Equally clear, to some critics, was that by characterizing Eichmann and by extension other Nazis as "ordinary" men rather than as monsters; by criticizing what she saw as his overzealous prosecution by Israeli magistrates; and by alleging that fewer Jews would have been killed in the Holocaust had Jewish councils in European countries not provided the names of Jews to the Nazis, Arendt was subtly but surely shifting some small measure of the responsibility for the Holocaust from the victimizers to the victims. Controversy over "Eichmann in Jerusalem" would have erupted—and continued—irrespective of its publication in the *New Yorker,* but some detractors at the time focused on the magazine as well as the author, correctly pointing out that its first major article on the Holocaust—printed more than fifteen years after the fact—appeared to minimize the horrors that had occurred. Writing in *Commentary,* Irving Howe observed that while some critics had questioned or refuted the facts as stated by Arendt, they could not be heard in the *New Yorker* because of its refusal to sully its pages with rejoinders: "Precisely why it will not print rebuttals or running exchanges I don't know; but I imagine that the answer would be something like this: 'Polemics, arguments, that's the sort of thing little magazines do, it's incestuous, you know, what Abel said about Rosenberg's article as qualified by Hook—you know, it's all sort of grubby.'" "Sort of Jewish," one could sense Howe thinking.

A PECULIAR INSTITUTION

"Letter from a Region in My Mind," in addition to its other qualities, made it impossible any longer to ignore or justify the fact that the *New Yorker's* staff was all white. Shawn told Leo Hofeller, the man in charge of personnel matters, that he wanted to integrate it, and within the next several months

Hofeller hired two black editorial assistants: Faith Berry, a recent Barnard graduate, and Charlayne Hunter, who had been in the headlines two years before as one of the first two black students to attend the University of Georgia. A young reporter in the Atlanta bureau of *Time* magazine named Calvin Trillin had covered that story. Now, in 1963, Trillin was planning to take a leave of absence from *Time* to examine the Georgia integration story from a more leisurely perspective; he hoped to place some of what he would write in the *New Yorker*. His friend Gerald Jonas, who worked at the magazine sifting Newsbreaks and sending the best ones up to E. B. White in Maine, set up a meeting between Trillin and Hofeller.

"At one point in the interview with Leo," Trillin recalled, "he said, 'I'd like for you to talk to Mr. Shawn.' I went to see him, and we talked for a long time about the pieces I wanted to do. Eventually, he said, 'You could just come over here now and do that for your first piece.'" Trillin understood that to mean "for your first piece as a staff writer for the *New Yorker*."

"I asked, 'Don't you want to see something I've written?'

"'No, that's all right.'"

Trillin was given an office and a drawing account of $800 a month. He later concluded that Shawn's startling willingness to hire him sprang from three factors. The first was Trillin's connection and friendship with Charlayne Hunter. (Asked in her interview with Hofeller if she knew anyone at the *New Yorker*, she had apparently said, "I had dinner last night with Gerry Jonas and Calvin Trillin.") Second, Shawn had coincidentally read and admired Trillin's one and only cover story for *Time*—about Adlai Stevenson. Finally, he associated Trillin with the South, he associated the South with racial issues, and, as Trillin saw it, he had a strong desire to have race covered in the *New Yorker*.

There was a fourth factor. In the early sixties, for the first time, Shawn apparently felt secure enough in his editorship and the future of the *New Yorker* to actually do some hiring. Besides Jonas, Trillin, and Hunter (who was soon promoted to Talk reporter but shortly thereafter left for the *New York Times*), Paul Brodeur, Nat Hentoff, Ved Mehta, Susan Lardner, Renata Adler, Jane Kramer, Tony Hiss, Calvin Tomkins, Jeremy Bernstein, John McPhee, Fred Shapiro, Susan Sheehan, Michael Arlen, William Whitworth, and George Trow all came on as staff writers between 1960 and 1966.

Trillin was actually one of the few new staffers who might have been hired in the Ross days, when nearly every writer came from the newspaper world. Another was Whitworth, a talented feature writer for the *New York Herald Tribune* whose work had caught the eye of Brendan Gill. In 1965, Gill recommended him to Shawn, who initiated a series of meetings with Whitworth, where the two talked about general topics in journalism and writing. "Once," Whitworth recalled, "I told Shawn I had accepted a job with the *Times*.

"He said, 'Oh, that may not be such a good idea. Would you consider working at the *New Yorker*?'"

John McPhee, another *Time* staff writer, had read the *New Yorker* since he was a boy in Princeton, New Jersey, and, like his contemporaries John Updike and Sylvia Plath, longed to write for it. But with the exception of a light essay he published in the magazine in 1963, about playing basketball with a ragtag team in England, piece after piece, idea after idea, came back rejected. In 1964, figuring basketball was his ticket, he proposed a Profile of Princeton University phenom Bill Bradley. The editors turned it down on the grounds that they had just printed a basketball Profile. McPhee went to the back issues and determined that the piece in question had run in 1959. He put together a five-thousand-word proposal for a Bradley article, and this time the editors said they would agree to look at the finished work. McPhee turned in a seventeen-thousand-word piece, which Shawn accepted and ran in January 1965 under the title "A Sense of Where You Are." McPhee joined the staff later that year. (As with Hersey's "Survival" about Kennedy, the piece laid early groundwork for a presidential run.)

But most of Shawn's hires had little if any experience in conventional journalism: they came either straight out of college or from unlikely places. In 1960, Jeremy Bernstein was a theoretical physicist doing research at the Brookhaven National Laboratory in eastern Long Island. Having always harbored a secret urge to be a writer, and being another lifelong *New Yorker* reader, he sent the magazine an article on his past summer's experiences teaching physics to a group of Parisians on the island of Corsica. For five months he received no response. However, as he later learned, his manuscript had found its way to the desk of Shawn's deputy Edith Oliver, to whom Shawn had recently remarked that he wished he knew of a writer capable of covering the interesting new developments in the world of physics. Eventually (Bernstein recalled later),

> the phone in my office rang, and a somewhat timorous voice asked if I was Mr. Bernstein. I said I was. He said, "This is William Shawn of the *New Yorker*. Do I catch you at an opportune time?" This is the twenty-fifth year I have written for the *New Yorker*. I do not know how many such phone calls I have received from Mr. Shawn during the last quarter of a century—many of them desperately important to me, involving the acceptance or rejection of weeks, or months, of work—and in each one he has asked me if he has caught me at an opportune time. In any event, he went on to say that he had read my manuscript and that if it was "agreeable" with me he would like to publish it. I said that it was agreeable.

Bernstein's account is actually part of a by now fairly common genre—the *New Yorker* initiation tale. While they naturally differ, they do share some common attributes—the inordinately polite telephone call from Shawn, always asking if he was ringing at an "opportune" or a "convenient" time (sometimes the recipient thinks it is a hoax and hangs up); the uncomfortable first meeting with him; and often an even more uncomfortable lunch at the Algonquin Hotel across the street from the *New Yorker,* where Shawn is usually shown ordering toasted pound cake and coffee. The British writer Norman Lewis offers a memorable set piece in his memoir *The World, the World,* beginning at the point where Lewis's friend S. J. "Sid" Perelman has delivered a chapter or two of Lewis's *The Honoured Society* to Shawn.

> Shawn read my piece and must have shown excitement for Sid telephoned me to come to New York as soon as I could. I arrived three days later and Sid was there to take me to the *New Yorker* office where I found Shawn— a rubicund, smiling, almost excessively polite little man—at a desk as big as Mussolini's in a huge silent cavern of an office. To me it was astonishing that so much power should have come to rest on the shoulders of a man who was outwardly so meek. The interview took five minutes and Shawn asked me to go back to Sicily and finish the book for the *New Yorker,* mentioning what seemed an unbelievable fee for its publication in the magazine.
>
> In the summer of 1963 I returned to New York where I delivered the completed manuscript to Shawn's secretary, whose surroundings of isolation and grandeur almost matched those of her employer. Early next morning Shawn telephoned me at the Algonquin Hotel, where all *New Yorker* contributors were supposed to stay. He invited me to lunch . . . and I was subjected to a somewhat awe-inspiring phenomenon. After a short outburst of generous praise for the book, Shawn had nothing more to say. He seemed uncomfortable and after a while I became aware of the beads of perspiration rolling down his cheeks. After an agonized effort I managed to break the silence, and things slowly became easier for both of us. Later Sid Perelman said of this alarming episode, "I should have warned you. It happens to everybody. All you have to do is pitch in and keep talking."

The supreme Shawn narrative was recently offered by Ved Mehta, who most definitely was *not* the kind of writer who would have come to the magazine under Ross—he was a native of India, blind since early childhood, an Oxford graduate, and in 1959, a twenty-five-year-old graduate student in history at Harvard. In his 1998 memoir, *Remembering Mr. Shawn's New Yorker: The Invisible Art of Editing,* Mehta devotes five pages to his initial meeting with Shawn, where they discussed a piece Mehta wanted to write about a homecoming trip to India. Mehta had less of a problem than Lewis in filling the conversational void and indeed realized he was babbling—because, he reckons,

I had never before had anyone in my life listen to me at as deep a level as he was doing, with no wish to judge—with only boundless interest and curiosity. He seemed to listen with childlike wonder, his gaze so steady and penetrating that I felt he was looking straight into my soul. Most people in conversation tried to impress you, hurried you along, had their own preconceptions or agendas, or were distracted by their own worries or cares. In contrast, he seemed to absorb words as a musician absorbs music.

Mehta's piece, titled "Homecoming," was published in the *New Yorker* on May 7, 1960. Around that time, Shawn and his family—his wife, Cecille, and his sons, Wallace, sixteen, and Allen, eleven—were visiting Harvard because Wallace was interested in attending the university. They ran into Mehta, who invited them to his room for tea. In a follow-up letter, he begged that Mr. Shawn stop addressing him as "Mr. Mehta": "In India the elders never address younger people by their last name, and unless it would make you feel awkward, I would much prefer to be called Ved." Shawn in turn asked Mehta to call him Bill, but this was hardly possible for many reasons.

Soon Shawn invited Mehta to lunch at the Algonquin. Mehta's account of this event takes up nine full pages in his book, including his reaction when Shawn orders his habitual cake: "My first impulse was to blurt out, 'No, that's not all you're going to have!' I wanted to ask him if he ordinarily had a late breakfast, what time he began his work, what he did when he didn't have lunch, how late he stayed at the office." They emerged from lunch with an agreement that Mehta would write a Reporter at Large about philosophers at Oxford University. He carried this out successfully and shortly afterward asked Shawn, "Do you think I could move to the city and write for the *New Yorker*?" Shawn's reply—"Yes, of course"—was in the nature of a job offer.

But a job as a writer at the *New Yorker* was never like any other form of employment. In Mehta's case, it included Shawn's finding him an apartment in Manhattan and arranging for the magazine to pay the rent should Mehta be unable to do so. He was given an office ("a small, bare corner room on the eighteenth floor, containing only a metal desk, an old, beaten-up typewriter on a typewriter table, and a chair"), a reader/typist, and a drawing account of $700 a month. A day or so after he moved in, an elderly man who spoke of the *New Yorker* "as if it were an ancient order" came to Mehta's apartment and offered him a one-page letter for his signature. It said, Mehta recalled,

> that in the course of a year the magazine would pay me a thousand dollars for each Reporter at Large article that was accepted, would pay me an additional twenty-five percent if I wrote six or more articles, and would make a cost-of-

living adjustment "if it so wishes and in its absolute discretion." The text was silent on all my principal concerns: how long the articles had to be; when, or if, the *New Yorker* would publish those it accepted; what would happen if I couldn't write anything "acceptable"; and, in that case, how long I could have to pay back the money advanced to me. In fact, it was essentially an empty agreement: there was no mention of my having a drawing account or an office or of my writing pieces other than Reporter articles and short stories—or, for that matter, of the *New Yorker's* taking over my lease. But, having felt all along that my informal arrangements with Mr. Shawn were tokens of emotional bonds that needed no formal confirmation, I signed the agreement as eagerly as if it were my pass to an enchanted kingdom.

It's not hard to see how the kingdom might seem "enchanted" to a newcomer, or at least charmingly quirky. The *New Yorker* had always been an unusual enterprise, and over the years its peculiarities had become so pronounced one could dine out on them indefinitely. Yet they were not wholly innocuous. Indeed, while the *New Yorker* was as sound financially as any magazine had ever been, the institution had cracks, and they were deepening every year. The cornerstones of its culture were a belief in civility, a respect for privacy, a striving for clear and accurate prose, a determination to publish what one believed in, irrespective of public opinion and commercial concerns, and a sense that the *New Yorker* was something special, something other and somehow more important than just another magazine. These admirable values all had their origin in the Ross years. But under Shawn, such emotional energy was invested in each of them that they became obsessive and sometimes distorted and perverted, in the sense of being turned completely inward.

Pop and Freud —   Onward and Upward With The Arts

The decline of the ego in contemporary culture; what passivity of sensation-oriented, consumer-oriented pop culture means in psychoanalytic terms; psychedelics; how New Left is affected by same psychic impulses that produced Pop.

Sug. by and res. for Ellen Willis 4/29/68

Reserved for Willis 4/2 9/68) (Coutless...

Conventional magazines had assignments. At the *New Yorker,* a writer merely "reserved" an idea by writing a brief description and filing it in a big notebook kept by Shawn's assistant. Like many reserved stories, Ellen Willis's never saw print.

Thus Shawn didn't just hire writers—he anointed them, as if to enter a secret and particularly holy religious order. Once selected, they found they were expected to find their own path to salvation. As Mehta observes, the contract was an empty agreement that left all responsibilities on the writer's shoulders. He or she was expected to come up with all story ideas, to which Shawn offered only a kind of passive approval, with no deadline, no length requirement, no guarantee of any kind that the finished work would be published or paid for. The uncertainty wasn't necessarily a problem for the staff writers who were just out of school and could live on a shoestring, or who could depend for the bulk of their income on spouses, personal fortunes, or other jobs. Jeremy Bernstein always had theoretical physics to fall back on; Susan Sheehan was married to reporter Neil Sheehan of the *New York Times*; Nat Hentoff was a columnist with the *Village Voice*. And some of the recruits had the self-discipline and the drive to overcome the vagaries of the situation. From his home in Princeton, McPhee produced a truly awe-inspiring flow of writing of the highest quality. Trillin sensibly took it upon himself to make his position more like a real job: within a few years he devised a regular column for himself, "U.S. Letter" (later renamed "U.S. Journal"), for which he traveled around the country and produced a dispatch every three weeks.

Others were not so fortunate and found the "freedom" Shawn offered to be anything but liberating. Indeed, it is a fairly good bet that most writers with no conventional assignments, no deadlines, and no length limitation will fail to speedily produce a substantial body of work. Just before he came on staff, William Whitworth recalled, Shawn asked him, "Do you need an income?" He did, which accounted for some of the pressure he felt. On his first day of work, Shawn showed him into what had been Dwight Macdonald's office. "I said, 'What should I do?' He said, 'You'll think of something.'

"It was a struggle for me. It was so hard to write. It was a very lonely place, partly because I never felt I could talk about the stories I was working on—if I did, I had the feeling that all the energy was dissipating." Whitworth eventually escaped the loneliness by taking a job as an editor at the magazine.

"I was very fast at first," said Bernard Taper, a San Francisco native who became a staff writer in the middle fifties. "Then, as I could see an opportunity for procrastination under guise of perfection, I took longer and longer to research, longer and longer to write. I did a profile of Charles Abrams that took an especially long time. There was no single focal point. I felt it was like trying to wrap two watermelons. One day Shawn and I were looking out the window and I said, 'I started working on this profile the same day that thirty-story building started. They finished, I still haven't.' He leaned forward and said to me, 'Don't tell that to the other writers.' "

Mehta writes in his memoir that another San Franciscan, Kevin Wallace, had the office next door to his but "never said so much as a good morning to me—or, as far as I knew, to anyone else—and, no matter how early I came in or how late I left, he was there, typing away." Between 1958 and 1963, Wallace published a modest six pieces in the magazine. "After that," Mehta writes, "year after year went by to the sound of his typing but without a word from his typewriter appearing in the magazine." Needless to say, no one intruded on Wallace to inquire if anything was wrong; that would have violated the code of "civility" at the *New Yorker*. Not until 1974 did the sound of the typing cease; Wallace had finally gone back to San Francisco.

An even more dramatic case was that of Joseph Mitchell, the greatest fact writer in the magazine's history. When he was first hired, in 1938, he had insisted on being paid a straight salary because he knew he could not operate on a drawing account. The security of the salary, as well as a personal perfectionism, helped account for his diminishing output. After publishing "The Rivermen" in 1959, it took him five years to produce his next article, "Joe Gould's Secret," a two-part profile of a Greenwich Village eccentric, which is one of the masterpieces of literary journalism. Between 1964 and his death, in 1996, he came to the office regularly, he was his customary courtly self with the other members of the staff, the sounds of typing could be heard behind the closed doors of his office, he continued to receive a salary of roughly $20,000 a year, but he published nothing in the *New Yorker*. As far as it is possible to tell, no one in all that time asked him what he was working on or when he expected to finish it.

At least Mitchell had a salary. Some blocked writers dug themselves so deeply in debt, they couldn't dig their way out. The prolific A. J. Liebling never suffered from writer's block; between 1955 and his death, in 1963, he contributed a remarkable eighty-one pieces to the magazine. But his transatlantic lifestyle and family obligations were such that he almost always owed the magazine money. "The rumor in the forties," Brendan Gill recalled, "was that Liebling had run up a debt of one hundred thousand dollars. That immediately became the goal of everybody." The rumor was surely exaggerated, but the debt of Liebling—and others—periodically reached the point where Shawn would wipe the slate clean and "forgive" it, the verb indicating the paternalism inherent in the relationship. Often, when a writer was in financial difficulty for any reason, a check for a mysterious amount of money would mysteriously appear in his or her mailbox—and, of course, would never be discussed with anyone. "Shawn was like a man of God with his 'discretionary fund,'" Gill said.

In the case of St. Clair McKelway, who went on a drawing account after leaving the managing editor's position in 1939, the magazine didn't even bother to attempt to collect or forgive the debt. He *always* owed the *New Yorker* money, the amounts ranging from $7,138.76 in 1954, to $9,488.03 in

1966, to $5,357.23 in 1975. The exact figures are preserved in depositions given by *New Yorker* representatives when McKelway's creditors tried to collect what they were owed through the magazine. Aside from his profligacy, McKelway was afflicted with what seems to have been a severe case of manic-depressive disorder, marked intermittently by prolonged delusional episodes. During one period, he would come up to the eighteenth floor every day and scribble meaningless words on the walls. Of course, no one said anything to him about it. In his periods of lucidity, McKelway was a charming colleague and friend and able, remarkably, to write with lucidity and wit about his disorder. One of his most memorable *New Yorker* stories, "The Edinburgh Caper," recounts how, on a trip to Scotland in 1959, he convinced himself that he had uncovered a Russian plot to kidnap President Eisenhower, Queen Elizabeth, and the Duke of Edinburgh.

Mehta, for his part, had prodigious self-discipline and drive and was able without much difficulty to produce a sufficient amount of "acceptable" articles. If anything, he produced too much, as he commenced to tell, in extraordinary detail, the life stories of many members of his family. This suggests another flaw with the system. Into the early sixties, the *New Yorker's* rates were not notably high. The longer an article took to write, the lower they seemed, as a writer on a drawing account grew deeper and deeper in debt. The only way to catch up was to write, eventually, a really long piece: for if a one-part Profile or Reporter at Large paid a minimum of $1,000, a two-parter paid $2,000, a three-parter $3,000, and so on. Moreover, if the height of one's manuscript approached a certain number of inches, it could be published as a book, and in the sixties this became a common way for *New Yorker* fact writers to modestly bolster their incomes. This is not to say that they deliberately padded their work. The point is, writing long, with excessive attention to detail, and a literalness that sometimes approached painful levels, had become part of the editorial culture of the magazine. Shawn's view (no doubt reinforced by the need to fill all those columns and columns in all those fat issues) was that once he had determined that a writer and a subject were appropriately matched, the writer should not only be permitted but encouraged to explore the subject exhaustively. This might exhaust *readers,* but that—the understanding was—would be their problem. There is no documented instance of Shawn ever reading a draft of an article and either cutting it himself or asking the writer to do so. Indeed, he frequently requested expansion.

It was not only the articles that had gotten longer and more drawn-out— it was also the individual sentences and paragraphs. This was in part due to a natural process by which formal conventions, over time, become mannered and sometimes decadent versions of themselves. Many *New Yorker* writers over the years had expressed their "sophistication" through a deliberate long-windedness marked by the liberal use of parenthetical phrases. By the middle-Shawn era, this tendency sometimes got out of control. Thus Geoffrey Hellman, who had been associated with the magazine since 1929, began a May 7, 1960, Profile with what seemed like (but wasn't) a self-parody:

> Like a good many of his ancestors, Mr. René d'Harnoncourt, the agile, gigantic, genial, hard-working, courtly, confident, aristocratic, wildly conversational Vienna-born director and champion *installateur* of the Museum of Modern Art, who is a descendant, direct and collateral, of a cloud of Middle European noblemen who flourished as chamberlains and provosts to a cloud of Dukes of Lorraine, Counts of Luxembourg, and Hapsburg emperors, has exhibited a gift for making himself indispensable to a succession—and quite often an overlapping—of patrons.

The endless sentences—skewered in due time by Tom Wolfe as "whichy thickets"—were also partly a function of the magazine's scrupulousness in matters of fact, grammar, and style, which was established by Ross but had become exaggerated and almost fetishized under Shawn. To maintain it, he instituted a labyrinthine editorial procedure that was described with admirable precision by Ved Mehta. After a manuscript received an initial editing by Shawn or one of the other editors, Mehta writes,

> the edited manuscript was sent on to the copy desk, which was restricted to making routine corrections in spelling and punctuation. From there it traveled to the makeup department and on to the printing plant, to be set up in galleys. The galleys got at least three readings besides those of the author, the assigned editor, and Mr. Shawn. They were read by [Milton] Greenstein, who went over the piece for legal problems; by a checker, who made certain that every fact was correct; and by Eleanor Gould, who read them for grammar, sense, clarity, and consistency, and whose queries and notes on a galley were sometimes almost as long as the text. The galleys, once the editor handling the piece had dealt with the queries, were sent on to the collating department, and there all the changes were consolidated and transferred to what was known as the reader's proof. During that process, conflicts among various changes were resolved by the editor of the piece. The reader's proof then went to the makeup department and on to the printing plant to be put into pages. The page proofs were read not only by the checker, who would make any late fixes needed to keep up with current events, and by Mr. Shawn, who tried to reread everything before it ran, but also by a proofreader and an O.K.er, both of whom were seeing the piece for the first time. The new changes were consolidated on a new reader's proof and were read through again by the O.K.er to iron out any new conflicts. The checker and the editor got one last look. If there were revised pages, as there often were, the whole process was repeated.

Mehta adds that "the miracle was that the piece never lost the individual style of the writer," but that is debatable. True, except in unusual circumstances, changes were never made without the writer's consent. However, edited versions generally weren't sent to authors until they were in clean galley form, so unless they had a photographic memory for their own prose, they weren't even aware of a lot of the changes. Moreover, they were bombarded with so many *suggested* changes that only the most self-confident and rigid author would decline all, or even most of them.

And the suggested changes often had the effect of awkwardly elongating sentences. When the checkers could not give an unqualified endorsement to a statement of fact, then they or the editor would append qualifying words or phrases, or even an explanation of the exceptions to the rule or the complete circumstances. The result was ungainly prose. Similarly, the fight against vagaries of punctuation and style, and against any possible textual ambiguity, intensified. Shawn's struggle had a psychological component, as William Maxwell once noted to Sylvia Townsend Warner: "inconsistency of spelling and hyphenation does make him unhappy, even morbid." Shawn's infrequent conflicts with writers usually had to do with punctuation. Philip Hamburger recalled Shawn, while going over the proofs of a piece,

> insisting that a hyphen was grammatically required in a certain word at the end of an article. I argued forcibly that the hyphen—the mere presence of the hyphen—would destroy the sentence. "That's a ruinous hyphen," I said. I wanted two separate words, and no hyphen. I was quite worked up over the hyphen. Shawn was calm and cool. "Perhaps you had better sit outside my office and think it over," he said. From time to time he would pop his head out. "Have you changed your mind?" he asked. This continued from about ten at night until close to two-thirty the next morning. Shawn finally said, sadly, "All right. No hyphen. But you are wrong."

In his quest for perfection Shawn found a strong ally in Eleanor Gould Packard, who had come to work at the magazine in 1945 and soon afterward married fact-checker Freddie Packard. "Miss Gould" (as Shawn and the rest of the office called her even after her marriage) was officially a manuscript "okayer," or final reader, but her acuity, indeed, brilliance, in matters of syntax and logic led her to a first untitled and then official (as official as job titles ever got at the *New Yorker,* anyway) job as chief "grammarian" at the magazine. Eventually, her name became a verb, as one spoke of a manuscript being "Goulded." In a tribute read at a party celebrating her fiftieth anniversary at the *New Yorker,* in 1995, editor Hendrik Hertzberg said, "Eleanor's understanding of grammar goes deeper than stuff like making sure subjects and objects agree. It's about the *architecture* of the sentence and the paragraph. And it's about the architecture of the thought behind the sentence and the paragraph." She was unmatched at spotting indirection or nondefining phrases masquerading as defining ones, and as her influence at the magazine grew, these lapses disappeared from its pages.

Mrs. Packard could even teach E. B. White some things about the comma. In 1959, White had published a revision of a slim book called *The Elements of Style,* originally written by an old Cornell professor of his, William Strunk. As a kind of busman's holiday, Mrs. Packard went through the book and made hypothetical revisions. She and White subsequently struck up a friendly correspondence. Mrs. Packard recalled, "When he wrote to me and said that there was going to be a second edition, I felt terribly bold in telling him what I had done. But he was very sweet and said he certainly wanted to see them. And then he made most of the changes I suggested."

As the years passed, new instances were found where commas were required. In 1963, Vladimir Nabokov sent William Maxwell some of his early Russian-language stories, and Shawn decided that they were of sufficient quality for the magazine to publish translated works for the first time. After Nabokov's byline at the end of the first story was the credit "Translated from the Russian by Dimitri Nabokov, with the collaboration of the author." One might think that this was unambiguous; Shawn eventually decided that it was not, because it left open the possibility that the story could have been translated from some *other* language. And so by 1970, after a story by Isaac Bashevis Singer, we find: "Translated, from the Yiddish, by the author and Elaine Gottlieb."* For Shawn, sprinkling editorial copy with commas called to mind the way he refused ever to go through a door before his companion—an instinct that stemmed from politeness and civility but somehow had gone past the point of true thoughtfulness or even usefulness.

Some authors resisted punctuation. Upon receiving the edited galleys of his 1962 story "Novotny's Pain," Philip Roth wrote to his editor, Robert Henderson, "I did think there was an indulgence of commas, and have requested 'stet' where the suggestion has been made that a comma be added. I felt that in most instances the comma made the prose much choppier than was necessary, and was really only obeisance to an optional grammatical rule, and didn't increase sense or add to the grace of the thing one bit." The stories of Jorge Luis Borges were "translated, from the Spanish, by the author and Norman Thomas di Giovanni," and di Giovanni complained

---

*There were further, baffling variations. In a letter to E. B. White, Eleanor Gould Packard remarked, "As you may have been amused, or baffled, to observe, we run the same phrase two ways in two different parts of the magazine: in book notes, it's simply 'translated from the Spanish by Norman Thomas di Giovanni,' but in parentheses following a Borges casual it's 'Translated, from the Spanish, by Norman Thomas di Giovanni.' The former is [editor Gardner] Botsford, of course, and the latter Shawn."

to Henderson: "I think Mr. Shawn is rather heavy with his commas. This is not my first encounter with them. I read the *New Yorker* and often feel they clog perfectly good sentences. I've also run into them in Alastair Reid's translations, which I am editing. I've got a jarful of Reid's commas that I've removed and some day will ship them back to the *New Yorker*."

But other writers internalized the magazine's approach and saw their prose lose liveliness, individuality, and grace as a result. After his stint as a theater critic was over, Kenneth Tynan regularly contributed Profiles. He once wrote in his journal that receiving a set of proofs marked up with queries felt like "an artillery bombardment." After one piece appeared in print, he worried that the editing had ironed out "much that might have made it identifiably mine; also, when writing for the magazine, one automatically censors audacious phrases lest they should be demolished by the inquisitorial logicians on 43rd St." Renata Adler was a strikingly intelligent young woman who came to the staff in 1963 as a manuscript reader after receiving degrees from Bryn Mawr, Harvard, and the Sorbonne. Upon being promoted to writer, she asked to be paid simply by the piece because, as she later put it, she felt that a drawing account was potentially a "disaster. ...Debt accounted for an infinite number of endless boring pieces." Nevertheless, after three or four years, she felt that her fact pieces were getting into a rut: "I found I couldn't do one without going, 'and then and then and then.'" She escaped in 1968 by taking a job as movie critic for the *New York Times*. (She returned to the *New Yorker* after a year, but turned most of her attention to writing fiction.)

In the culture of the *New Yorker* under Shawn, a corollary to the hallmark values of civility and politeness was a respect for and encouragement of privacy. But privacy turned into secretiveness—as if he were taking the cue from his "best friend," J. D. Salinger. From his appointment as editor in 1952 until 1968 (when he spoke at length to a reporter from *Women's Wear Daily*, one of his favorite newspapers), Shawn gave no on-the-record interviews to the press. *New Yorker* staffers, taking their cue from him, would only be quoted anonymously when *Time* or *Newsweek* or the *New York Times* did their periodic takeout on the magazine. Even the arrangement of the *New Yorker* offices seemed designed to foster isolation. The tiny offices, like monks' (or prisoners') cells, were scattered over three floors, and interaction among the inhabitants was tacitly discouraged. At one point, Brendan Gill, Maeve Brennan, and William Maxwell found themselves in contiguous offices. "There was so much slipping of notes under his door, and hers, and mine," Maxwell recalled, "and so many explosions of laughter as a result of our reading them—we learned through the grapevine—Mr. Shawn decided it wasn't good for the office morale, and Maeve was moved down the hall to the other side of the building." What was Shawn afraid of? The object lesson may have been his own relationship with Lillian Ross, which continued as the decades went on and was known about, to some extent, by everyone on the staff. Yet it was never talked about, never acknowledged.

Everything, it seemed, was confidential. Philip Hamburger noted in an interview that he and other staff writers would frequently socialize, with only two taboo topics—money and their current writing projects. This only seems odd when one considers that these are most writers' favorite two subjects. In 1996, nearly six decades after he joined the magazine, Hamburger refused to discuss the nature of his financial arrangements. "I have had eccentricities in my contract for fifty-six years that I will never explain to anyone," he said. Secrecy was built into the magazine's editorial operations. When Shawn agreed that a writer would proceed on an article, no fee was ever mentioned; it was strongly understood that this would be in poor taste. Once it was completed, accepted, and set in type, the writer would receive a check for an unexplained amount of money, often bearing no relation to the minimum fee specified in the standard contract.

As the defendant in a libel suit that arose over a profile of a psychoanalyst she wrote in the 1980s, staff writer Janet Malcolm testified in a deposition about *New Yorker* practices:

"How was compensation determined?"

"By the whim of the editor."

"When you went in to see Mr. Shawn about writing this piece, did you talk money at that point?"

"No."

"You just rely on his good graces when you are all through that he will give you just compensation?"

Malcolm, recognizing a rhetorical question when she heard one, did not reply.

Everyone's situation was different. Unlike most other writers who were paid on acceptance, Renata Adler received no check until her pieces were published. (Perhaps this was a retaliation for her refusal to go on a drawing account.) "When I submitted something," she recalled, "Shawn would come down and say, 'I think it'll work.' It wouldn't occur to me to ask how much I would be paid for it, or when it would run. Sometimes my pieces weren't run till years later." More often, the writer was given to understand that he or she was favored with special terms, terms that shouldn't be discussed with the other writers. Sheila McGrath, who as editorial administrator was in charge of sending out the checks, said, "When Shawn left, almost every writer came to me and said, 'Shawn gave me a special rate.' In three separate cases, I went and checked; in every case, they were paid the standard rate, right on the button." Brendan Gill, who was on the staff during Shawn's entire editorship, flatly stated, "Every one of us thought we were

Shawn's favorite. I remember being at a dinner party with *New Yorker* people when [book critic] George Steiner said that Shawn had a private phone line in his office just to reach Steiner. Everyone was enraged."

One reason writers became so devoted to Shawn was that he seemed to *understand* what they were doing as no one else in their lives ever had. His editing (other than punctuation) had changed from the heavy-pencil style of the forties to a gnomic minimalism, often expressed in Socratic questions that suddenly made everything seem *clear*. In a memorial tribute, Calvin Trillin described the special qualities of an audience with Shawn:

> When he listened to, say, the reasons a writer thought some subject was worth a story, he sometimes shook his head in wonderment or murmured "Really!" When he responded, it was clear that he had absorbed everything said—every fact, every allusion, every nuance. Shawn was that rare bird, an inspirational listener. For thirty-five years, writers emerged from his office buoyed by the belief that at least one other human being in the world understood precisely what they were trying to get at.

"Shawn had the capacity for making you want to work harder and better than for anyone else," said Michael Arlen. "I'd turn in a column, then go up to see him. He'd nearly always start by saying some complimentary things. Then at a certain point, he'd say, 'I wonder about this part . . . I bet if you ran through this once more . . .' He would nearly always single out the one part that you weren't happy with but thought you could sneak by. You'd say, 'But I think we're about to go to press.' He'd say, 'We can wait a few more hours.' Naturally, you'd try your damnedest to get it right."

Shawn had a deep editorial idealism, remarkable in a competitive and commercial industry. Peter Matthiessen was a footloose young writer who, in the early sixties, began traveling to remote corners of the globe and submitting singular pieces of natural history and observation to the *New Yorker*. In 1967, he persuaded Shawn to send him to the Cayman Islands to write about green turtles. While there, Matthiessen had the inspiration for the novel that would eventually become *Far Tortuga*. "When I came back to New York, I met with Mr. Shawn," Matthiessen recalled. "I said, 'I'm very embarrassed, but I'm going to hold back all the best material for a novel. If you don't want the fact piece, I'll return the expenses and that will be the end of it.' Mr. Shawn wouldn't take the money. He said, 'Do what's best for the work, Mr. Matthiessen.' Tears still run out of my eyes when I tell that story."

A difficulty with this system arose when Shawn had substantial objections to a submission from a staff writer. Candor was not an option. Frequently, his sense of obligation to a writer would outweigh his editorial judgment, and the magazine would run subpar material. Other times he would buy the story but never print it. "He could not say no or anything harsh to a writer," said Gardner Botsford, an editor at the magazine from the late 1940s till 1982. "There was no manuscript he wouldn't buy. It would be set in type and put into galleys. There it would stay. Most of the writers would never ask about the story, because with Shawn you never felt you could butt in and ask a direct question. It would hurt his feelings." Nor would Shawn ever fire a writer, even those, such as Kevin Wallace and others, who produced next to nothing. Most of these, like Wallace, eventually got the message and left. Others decided to sacrifice their self-respect and productivity for this peculiar form of security. They haunted the hallways of the *New Yorker* like living ghosts.

In much of his dealings with writers, Shawn was subtly infantilizing them. Robert Coles was a noted child psychiatrist and author when he began writing for the magazine in the late sixties. Shawn told him he would be paid $1,250 per book review—but that he shouldn't tell the other writers. When he wrote a review for another magazine that technically was in violation of his contract, Shawn scolded him in such a way that Coles "felt like a child." Coles continued to write occasionally for the *New Yorker* but resisted becoming dependent on it, in part because he felt Shawn tended to play the writers off against one another. "If I weren't a teacher, a doctor, with my own independent life," he said, "this would be worse than being a little boy and fighting with my brothers—with the other writers."

Despite Shawn's shyness and deferential manner, he was unquestionably in total command at the *New Yorker*. He consolidated his power over time and never did find a second-in-command, the Shawn to his Ross. As the years went on and the magazine become fatter, Shawn took on more responsibilities for himself. "As people would die or retire," Calvin Trillin said, "Shawn would take on their jobs for himself. It once occurred to me that at a normal magazine, there had to be twenty-five or thirty people doing what this little guy did." His absolute power was most evident on the fact side, where he was the only person who could approve an idea, consult with an author as a story was being written, or buy it once it was completed. Only at that point would it be funneled to Botsford, William Knapp, Robert Gerdy, or one of the other fact editors, who, for all their talents at shaping manuscripts, served as glorified copy editors.

Shawn never had meetings with the other editors or, indeed, with anyone except for Jim Geraghty, with whom he went over the cartoons every week. The fiction department was still autonomous, but Shawn exercised his will there through personnel decisions. In 1959, he unilaterally announced to some members of the staff there that he had hired a new editor for the department, Robert Hemenway. But he did not inform Robert Henderson, whom he had previously asked to evaluate Hemenway's comment sheets. "Giving Mr. Shawn the benefit of the doubt," one editor wrote to the by then retired Katharine White, "it was thoughtless of him not to notify Mr. Henderson. I am not inclined to give him the benefit of the doubt; he did it on purpose for his own nefarious, Napoleonic reasons, and I'd like to give him a good kick in the shins."

Hendrik Hertzberg, who arrived as a Talk of the Town reporter in 1969, said, "Shawn was an absolute monarch, a dictator. There were no office politics, except in the sense that there were office politics in the Ottoman Empire."

Clearly, Shawn had extreme ambivalence about authority. "His most serious flaw was that, for private reasons, he didn't like to express power," Arlen said. "He liked to have it, but power can be misused by not expressing enough of it. At the end, he would never say, 'This is the way things are going to be.' He would vacillate between saying something like that and saying the reverse."

Shawn's shyness was honestly come by, but he used it as a tool by which he could exercise his will. He became a master of the passive-aggressive encounter. One writer liked to tell about the time when he began smoking during a conversation with Shawn. Instead of an ashtray, the editor produced a Coke bottle, leaving the writer to figure out how he was supposed to get the ashes through the small opening, much less eventually extinguish the cigarette. James Stevenson had a similar experience. As a young man in the early fifties, he had sold many cartoon gags to Geraghty. He was so good that eventually Geraghty called him up and offered him a staff job thinking up ideas. He was brought in to talk to Shawn. "He was nervous," Stevenson said. "He looked almost alarmed that you had come in. Neither one of us had anything to say. There was dead silence. Finally he offered me a cigarette box and said, 'Would you like a cigarette?' I peered into the box. There were no cigarettes in it." (Alfred Kazin also got the empty-cigarette-box treatment.)

Stevenson took the job and held it for several years. During the entire time, he says, no one on the staff except Geraghty and Shawn knew that he was working at the New Yorker. He had been sworn to secrecy.

WOLFE ATTACK

In 1965, as it celebrated its fortieth anniversary, the eccentricities of the New Yorker did not appear to be doing it significant harm. The magazine was publishing good work, holding on to its readers and attracting new ones, and selling more ads every year. Indeed, Shawn's publishing of hard-hitting political stories and recruitment of new blood were definite signs that he was trying to make the magazine more a part of, and less apart from, the contemporary world. However, its strange ways left it wide open to a blind-side journalistic hatchet job, executed by a young *Herald Tribune* reporter named Tom Wolfe.

As Wolfe later recounted, the piece originated one day when he and Clay Felker, the editor of the *Herald Tribune*'s Sunday-magazine section, *New York*, were sitting around and remarking that all the tributes to the *New Yorker* that were appearing to mark the magazine's anniversary neglected to mention one thing: that the *New Yorker* had for some years been "unbearably dull." Wolfe decided he would try "having a little fun" with the magazine and, in the style of Wolcott Gibbs's celebrated 1936 takedown of Henry Luce, write a profile of Shawn in a style that mocked the *New Yorker*'s own. But two problems immediately presented themselves. First, *New Yorker* style was so boring, he felt, that an article written entirely in it would "smother itself with sheer tedium." Second, Shawn informed Wolfe that he would not grant an interview nor answer questions in writing nor verify facts presented to him before publication, all of which made the prospect of doing any kind of profile rather daunting.

So Wolfe decided he would write what he called an "anti-parody. . . . Rather than mimicking the *New Yorker* I was going to give them a voice they couldn't stand. In the anti-parody, as I thought of it, the wilder and crazier the hyperbole, the better. It was a challenge—to use the most lurid colors imaginable to paint a room full of very proper people who had gone to sleep standing up, talking to themselves."

No one was going to fall asleep while reading Wolfe's article, that was for sure. Even the title—"Tiny Mummies! The True Story of the Ruler of 43rd Street's Land of the Walking Dead!"—with its exclamation points and *Police Gazette*–style diction, gave notice that the reader would be goosed into attentiveness at every available opportunity. The article ran in two parts and was ten thousand words long; in common with much of Wolfe's work, it was more sheer performance than parody, anti-parody, or anything else. Part I was intended to be a dissection of the culture of the magazine and got in some good shots:

> Shawn is a very quiet man. He has a soft, somewhat high voice. He seems to whisper all the time. The whole . . . *zone* around his office, a kind of horse-hair-stuffing atmosphere of old carpeting, framed *New Yorker* covers, quiet cubicles and happy-shabby, baked-apple gentility, is a *Whisper Zone*. One gets within 40 feet of it and everybody . . . is whispering, all the secretaries and everybody. The *Shawn whisper*, the whisper zone radiates out from Shawn himself. Shawn in the hallway slips along as soundlessly as humanly possible and—chooooo—he meets somebody right there in the hall. The nodding! The whispering! Shawn is 57 years old but still has a boyish face, a small, plump man, round in the cheeks. He always seems to have on about 20 layers of

clothes, about three button-up sweaters, four vests, a couple of shirts, two ties, it looks that way, a dark shapeless suit over the whole ensemble, and white cotton socks. Here he is in the hall, and he lowers his head and puts out his hand.

"Hello—Mr.—," he begins nodding, "—Taylor—how—are—you," with his head down, nodding down, down, down, down, "—it's—nice—" his head is down and he rolls his eyes up and looks out from under his own forehead "—to—see—you—" and then edges back with his hand out, his head nodding, eyes rolled up, back foot edging back, back, back, back "very—good—to—see—you—" nodding, smiling, infectious! *Good* for one! One does the same, whispering, nodding, getting the old head down, smiling, edging back, rolling the eyeballs up the precipice of the forehead. One becomes quiet, gentle, genteelly, magnificently numbly, so—

One can only imagine the fate of these paragraphs if they were fact-checked and "Goulded." The first two sentences, all right. But after that ... disaster! Indeed, as Wolfe was well aware, the passage represents everything that is antithetical to *New Yorker* style, as it had evolved. It offered not only hyperbole but *imprecise* hyperbole ("about 20 layers of clothes"); there were composite scenes instead of fact, sentence fragments, neologisms ("choooo"), and rhetorical and punctuational arm-waving that obliterated any semblance of editorial decorum. Most unacceptably of all, it mocked its subject, Shawn, on the basis of his physical appearance and personal idiosyncrasies.

But the truth of the matter was, the sheer impossibility of the *New Yorker's* ever printing this passage or anything like it was a reflection more of the magazine's failings than its virtues. It was good stuff—funny, with literary daring and flare, and, most important, based solidly on the truth.

Similarly, in the second part of the article, a piece of hopped-up literary criticism and sociological analysis, Wolfe had some clever and cutting things to say about the content and readership of the magazine. He skewered the elephantine *New Yorker* sentence as a "whichy thicket": "all those clauses, appositions, amplifications, qualifications, asides, God knows what else, hanging inside the poor old skeleton of one sentence like some kind of Spanish moss." And he blasted *New Yorker* fiction as "the laughingstock of the New York literary community for years." The magazine, he wrote, "has published an incredible streak of stories about women in curious rural-bourgeois settings. Usually the stories are *by* women, and they recall their childhoods or domestic animals they have owned." This "bourgeois-sentimental" fiction, Wolfe argued, helped make the *New Yorker* "the most successful suburban women's magazine in the country." He explained:

> Since the war, the suburbs of America's large cities have been filling up
> with educated women with large homes and solid hubbies and the taste

to ... *buy expensive things.* The *New Yorker* was the magazine—about the only general magazine—they had heard their professors mention a ... good cultural way. And now here they are out in the good green world of Larchmont, Dedham, Grosse Point, Bryn Mawr, Chevy Chase, and they find that this magazine, this cultural magazine, is speaking right to them—*their language*— cultural and everything—but *communicating*—you know?—right to a suburban woman. Those wonderful stories!

Well, first of all, the *New Yorker* is a totem for these women. Just having it in the home is, well, it is a symbol, a kind of *cachet*. But more than that, it is not like those other *cachet* magazines, like *Realites* or *London Illustrated*—people just only barely leaf through those magazines—the *New Yorker* reaches a little corner in the suburban-bourgeois woman's heart. And in this little corner are Mother, large rural-suburban homes with no mortgage, white linen valances, and Love that comes with Henry Fonda, alone, on a pure white horse. Perfect short stories! After all, a girl is not really sitting out here in Larchmont waiting for Stanley Kowalski to come by in his ribbed undershirt and rip the Peck & Peck cashmere off her mary poppins. That is not really what the suburbs are like. A girl—well, a girl wants Culture and everything, but she wants a magazine in the house that *communicates,* too, you know? And you don't have to scour your soul with Top-Dirt afterwards, either.

The problem with the article was that Wolfe did not know when—or how—to leave well enough alone. Following Shawn's lead, no one with any kind of authority or extensive experience at the magazine had been willing to talk to him, leaving him to rely on rumor, second- and thirdhand accounts, and unattributed sources. As a result—and ironically, for someone who has subsequently trumpeted himself as an indefatigable "reporter"— almost every time he attempted to state a fact about the workings of the magazine, he got it wrong. He said, incorrectly, that memos had gone around the *New Yorker* offices warning staffers not to talk to Wolfe. He said *New Yorker* contributors were never allowed to overrule editing changes on their copy; it was a traditional point of pride that they were. In attempting to show how undistinguished *New Yorker* fiction had been, he listed J. D. Salinger and Irwin Shaw as "*Esquire* writers" and Frank O'Connor as a "*Saturday Evening Post* writer." He called Roger Angell the "managing editor"; not only was Angell actually one of several fiction editors, there *was* no managing editor. Even worse, Wolfe absurdly said Shawn had picked Angell as his eventual successor. There were dozens more errors. Wolfe even made mistakes about matters that had nothing to do with the *New Yorker,* as in a long set piece in which he confused Bix Beiderbecke with Bunny Berigan as the author of a long trumpet solo in "I Can't Get Started" (the song was written four years after Beiderbecke's death) and said that Beiderbecke died "popping a vessel in his temporal fossa," when he really died of pneumonia.

Wolfe got larger points wrong, too. The "Tiny Mummies" in the title referred to his central thesis that Shawn was "the museum curator, the mummifier, the preserve-in-amber, the smiling embalmer" of Harold Ross's *New Yorker*. This had a kernel of truth but was mainly misguided: despite the surface similarities, the magazine under Shawn, circa 1965, was an immensely different enterprise than under Ross.

But even that wasn't the most infuriating thing about Wolfe's articles. The most infuriating thing was the way he took the most private of men, William Shawn, and held him up, mercilessly and awkwardly, for public inspection—and in the *Herald Tribune,* no less, which with its literary heritage and high-class panache was the New York City newspaper closest in bloodline and spirit to the *New Yorker*. Most notoriously, Wolfe trotted out an old rumor that, as a teenager, Shawn had been considered as a victim by the kidnappers Leopold and Loeb before they eventually settled on Bobby Franks. (Shawn and Franks were in fact schoolmates at a private school in Chicago.) This was supposedly offered not as truth but as an example of the way Shawn's eccentricities caused people to ceaselessly speculate and concoct stories about him. But Wolfe was being deeply disingenuous, trying to have it both ways. The three long paragraphs he devoted to the tale, with many details about Leopold, Loeb, the school, and Shawn's family, with references to "the records" in "the Cook County (Chicago) Criminal Court," implicitly urged the reader to accept this nonsense as something real.

What must have been a devastating blow for Shawn was Wolfe's treatment of the Lillian Ross situation. Wolfe never directly characterized it as a romantic liaison, but in the first part alone had three coy, winking references to Ross's relationship with Shawn, including a description of her as one of his few "intimates." Shawn had operated under the assumption that their affair would never be mentioned in the halls of the *New Yorker*—now it would be trumpeted throughout New York.

Through unknown means, Shawn got ahold of a prepublication copy of the first part of the article. If he hadn't, the episode would probably have turned out quite differently. But he did, and once he had finished reading, he sat down and wrote a letter to John Hay Whitney, the owner of the *Herald Tribune*:

> To be technical for a moment, I think that Tom Wolfe's first article on *The New Yorker* is false and libelous. But I'd rather not be technical. If you have read this piece, and if you have understood it, I cannot believe that, as a man of known integrity and responsibility, you will allow it to reach your readers. I don't know why it was decided yesterday to let the article go as far as it did toward publication; I tried to reach you all day to discuss it, and failed. The

question is now whether you will stop the distribution of that issue of *New York*. I urge you to do so, for the sake of *The New Yorker* and for the sake of the *Herald Tribune*. In fact, I am convinced that the publication of that article will hurt you more than it will hurt me, the *Herald Tribune* more than *The New Yorker*. As the editor of a publication that tries always to be truthful, accurate, fair, and decent, I know exactly what Wolfe's article is—a vicious, murderous attack on me and on the magazine I work for. It is a ruthless and reckless article; it is pure sensation-mongering. It is wholly without precedent in respectable American journalism—in one stroke, it puts the *Herald Tribune* right down in the gutter with the *Graphic,* the *Enquirer,* and *Confidential*. Yesterday I received several telephone calls from members of your own staff whom I don't know personally and whom I have never met; they had read the article and were aghast, and wanted to tell me that they were ashamed of the paper. I hope that you share their feeling of shame and that you will do something about it while there is still time. If you do not, I can only conclude—since I know that you are a decent man—that you do not understand Tom Wolfe's words. For your sake, and for mine, and, in the long run, even for the sake of Wolfe and his editor, Clay Felker (God help me for caring about them), I urge you to stop the distribution of the article.

If proof was needed that Shawn inhabited a protected world, one needn't look any further than his thinking there was any chance this letter would actually prevent the article from being published, or that it would not itself be disseminated. Wolfe, in a transparent bit of weaseling, resorted to the passive voice in his subsequent account of the affair: "copies were sent to the press sections of *Time* and *Newsweek*." Both magazines ran stories marveling at how Shawn, famous as a pillar of journalistic integrity, appeared to be asking a rival periodical to censor itself. The Thursday after publication of Wolfe's first part, the editor of the *Herald Tribune,* James Bellows, finally got around to replying to Shawn:

"We do not agree with your characterization of, or conclusions concerning Mr. Wolfe's article on the New Yorker. In our opinion, it is accurate and descriptive in all substantial respects and can certainly not be construed as a personal attack on you."

What must have struck Shawn about the letter, even more than Bellows's not italicizing the *New Yorker* or even capitalizing the *T,* even more than his odd and clearly incorrect use of "descriptive," was that he had left out the comma after "concerning."

Part II appeared in due course, and the following week the *Herald Tribune* printed sixteen letters about the articles, including vehement protests from *New Yorker* hands Richard Rovere, Muriel Spark, Ved Mehta, E. B. White, and even J. D. Salinger (who called the pieces "inaccurate and sub-collegiate and gleeful and unrelievedly poisonous"). White's letter was as simple, eloquent, humane, and devastating as one would expect from him:

> Mr. Wolfe's piece on William Shawn violated every rule of conduct I know anything about. It is sly, cruel and to a large extent undocumented, and it has, I think, shocked everyone who knows what sort of person Shawn really is. I can't imagine why you published it. The virtuosity of the writer makes it all the more contemptible, and to me, as I read it, the spectacle was of a man being dragged for no apparent reason at the end of a rope by a rider on horseback—a rider, incidentally, sitting very high in the saddle these days and very sure of his mount.
>
> The piece is not merely brutal, it sets some sort of record for journalistic delinquency, for it makes sport of a man's physical appearance and psychological problems—which is as low as you can go. If Mr. Shawn is not at ease meeting people in the hall, it should arouse, if anything, compassion, not contempt. And how can Mr. Wolfe, who does not inhabit these halls, state unequivocally that this so-called "shyness" is "deliberate"? The statement is worse than omniscient, it's false.
>
> For 40 years the New Yorker has employed parody, irony, ridicule and satire to deflate or diminish persons and institutions it deemed fair game. But I never saw it use brass knuckles, or the rope, or the police dog. The magazine is fair game for anyone, and so is its editor, because they are in the public eye, and I have no quarrel with the Tribune for taking off after the New Yorker. But your departure from the conventional weapon of satire and criticism is unsettling, it shakes the whole structure of the free press, which depends ultimately on the good temper and good report of the people. There are always a few who will pay to watch some act of particular savagery in the arena, but I would hate to depend on their patronage for the building of a good newspaper.
>
> Long before Harold Ross died, William Shawn was changing the character and scope of the New Yorker, and he is still at it. Wolfe's violent attack on him is not only below the belt, it is essentially wide of the mark, in point of fact.

That left the question of what kind of institutional response Shawn and the New Yorker would make. The first line of his letter to Whitney to the contrary, there was nothing remotely libelous about the articles, so legal action was not a possibility. Instead, Shawn permitted Gerald Jonas and Renata Adler essentially to fact-check Wolfe's articles. On her own, Adler flew to Chicago and determined that much of Wolfe's account of young Bill Shawn's involvement in the Leopold-Loeb case was erroneous or misleading. She and Jonas detailed the dozens of errors they found in a long letter to the Columbia Journalism Review. Dwight Macdonald wrote an essay for the New York Review of Books that used Adler and Jonas's research to advance his thesis that Wolfe was a practitioner of a dangerous new genre he called "parajournalism, a bastard form that has it both ways, exploiting the factual authority of journalism and the atmospheric license of fiction." He went on to compare Wolfe's technique with the "big-lie" strategy of Hitler and McCarthy: "The difference between Tom Wolfe and such types is that he doesn't tell lies, big or small, since lying is a conscious process, recognizing the distinction between what is and what it would be convenient to assume is. He seems to be honestly unaware of the distinction between fact and fabrication. You might call him a sincere demagogue."

Wolfe's articles were never replied to or even mentioned in the *New Yorker's* pages. As Irving Howe had observed in his essay about "Eichmann in Jerusalem," the magazine presented itself as being above exchanges, rebuttals, or any kind of intellectual or journalistic fray. The free-form self-consciousness that was so prevalent in the twenties and early thirties was long gone; now weeks or even months would go by without any acknowledgment in the *New Yorker* that the *New Yorker* existed. But "Tiny Mummies!" made itself felt in the magazine all the same. If there had been any possibility that Shawn would open the *New Yorker's* pages to Wolfe and the other raucous young nonfiction writers whose diverse approaches were jointly characterized as "new journalism," if there had been any possibility that Shawn would venture out from his convictions and his code of civility and agree to meet halfway the sometimes shrill, not always polite, but undeniably compelling hubbub of the world around him—those possibilities were now gone.

A postscript. Three years after his articles on the *New Yorker* came out, Wolfe was putting together his second collection of pieces, to be titled *The Pump House Gang*. While the book was still in preparation, Wolfe's publisher, Roger Straus, of Farrar, Straus & Giroux, received a call from William Shawn, who said (Straus subsequently recalled), " 'I understand you are publishing a collection of pieces by Tom Wolfe. I hope that that piece about me is not going to be in it.' I said, 'I can't tell you the answer to that.' "

Straus then phoned Wolfe, who told him, "Oh, well, you know, he feels so badly about it, and I didn't mean to make him feel so badly. That wasn't the point of it. I just thought it was an interesting article. We'll leave it out."

"Tiny Mummies!" is the only long article by Tom Wolfe that he has never included in a book.

BARTHELME, CAPOTE, KAEL

INDIAN UPRISING UPROARIOUS. PALEFACES ROUTED, SHAWN SCALPED. IN SHORT, YES.

—Roger Angell to Donald Barthelme, December 25, 1964, telegram accepting "The Indian Uprising"

Early in 1963, a young writer named Donald Barthelme—recently moved to New York from Houston, where he had successively been a newspaper reporter and the director of the Contemporary Arts Museum—sent the *New Yorker* a parody, in screenplay form, of the works of Italian movie director Michelangelo Antonioni. It found its way to the desk of Roger Angell, who accepted it with dispatch: in these years the magazine was almost desperate for clever casuals. Barthelme followed this up with a somewhat labored piece whose premise was that Lionel Bart, author of *Oliver!*, had written a musical comedy version of "The Wasteland" called *Wasteland!* Angell turned it down. Next Barthelme submitted a story called "Carl," which Angell also rejected, calling it "highly artificial and entirely unconvincing."

Then something remarkable happened. Angell bought Barthelme's next submission, "The Piano Player." To comprehend how totally it differed from anything the magazine had ever published before, one need only consider the opening paragraphs, as they appeared in the *New Yorker* of August 31, 1963:

> Outside his window five-year-old Priscilla Hess, square and squat as a mailbox (red sweater, blue lumpy corduroy pants), looked around poignantly for someone to wipe her overflowing nose. There was a butterfly locked inside that mailbox, surely; would it ever escape? Or was the quality of mailboxness stuck to her forever, like her parents, like her name? The sky was sunny and blue. A filet of green Silly Putty disappeared into fat Priscilla Hess and he turned to greet his wife who was crawling through the door on her hands and knees.
>
> "Yes?" he said. "What now?"
>
> "I'm ugly," she said, sitting back on her haunches. "Our children are ugly."
>
> "Nonsense," Brian said sharply. "They're wonderful children. Wonderful and beautiful. Other people's children are ugly, not our children. Now get up and go back out to the smokeroom. You're supposed to be curing a ham."
>
> "The ham died," she said. "I couldn't cure it. I tried everything. You don't love me any more. The penicillin was stale. I'm ugly and so are the children. It said to tell you goodbye."
>
> "*It?*"
>
> "The ham," she said. "Is one of our children named Ambrose? Somebody named Ambrose has been sending us telegrams. How many do we have now? Four? Five? Do you think they're heterosexual?" She made a *moue* and ran a hand through her artichoke hair. "The house is rusting away. Why did you want a steel house? Why did I think I wanted to live in Connecticut? I don't know."

Where to begin? The most obvious place is the egregious indirection in the first three words. As Harold Ross would have put it—*whose* windows? If that question can be tabled, one can justifiably surmise for a few sentences that this is a not unconventional story about an unhappy child. But then Priscilla eats the Silly Putty filet and "his" wife crawls through the door, and it is clear that "The Piano Player" will lack the plausibility, lucidity, and emotional identification of reader with character that the *New Yorker* had demanded of its short stories for more than thirty years. The story is funny, in a way, and there are even one or two out-and-out jokes, like the uncured ham, but its satire is immeasurably too free of identifiable references to belong to a standard *New Yorker* casual. "The Piano Player" is surreal and mystifying and dark, as if Ionesco had set to work animating the suburban characters in a Charles Saxon cartoon. A few weeks after it appeared, a young man who had sold a couple of casuals of his own to the magazine wrote to his editor, William Maxwell, "I read that story in the *New Yorker,* was it called 'The Piano Player'? And I am baffled by it. What *was* it about?"

In rapid succession, Barthelme sold more of his strange pieces to the magazine—"Marie, Marie, Hold on Tight," "A Shower of Gold," "Margins." In October, Angell commented to Barthelme's agent, Lynn Nesbit, "He certainly is one of the happiest events of the year for us." Early in 1964, informing Barthelme that the magazine would buy "A Picture History of the War," Angell remarked in an offhand way that the story would "insult" *New Yorker* readers. He wrote Barthelme the next day: "I hope you know that I have nothing but astonished admiration for that story. I meant that a lot of readers will *think* that we have insulted them, which is exactly what they deserve." Later that year, Barthelme sold the similarly assaultive "The Indian Uprising." In these two long stories Barthelme raised the stakes. They had the familiar surreal segues, the narrative vertigo, and the deadly deadpan wordplay. But with their imagery of war and torture and guerrilla forces on patrol, they also offered uncanny auguries of the street conflicts and jungle warfare that would soon insinuate themselves into the videotape loop running through the national consciousness.

A few years later, Barthelme ratcheted his method with "Snow White," a wild and sometimes maddeningly elusive variation on the fairy tale, complete with typographical experimentation and concluded by a kooky questionnaire. ("7. Do you feel that the creation of new modes of hysteria is a viable undertaking for the artist of today? Yes ( ) No ( ).") "Snow White," which occupied nearly one hundred pages in the *New Yorker's* anniversary issue in 1967, generated more mail to the magazine than any other piece in the previous ten years except "Silent Spring," "Letter from a Region in My Mind," "Eichmann in Jerusalem," and "In Cold Blood." According to an office memo, of the seventy-eight letters received, seven praised the story, forty-nine criticized it, and thirty-three expressed some combination of disapproval and bafflement. (Roger Angell put together a sort of crib sheet to send to the latter group.)

Barthelme continued to appear frequently in the *New Yorker*. By the time of his death, in 1989, he had published 129 stories or casuals (some under the pen names Lily McNeil and William White), plus thirty unsigned Notes and Comment pieces and six film reviews, contributed when Pauline Kael was on leave in 1979.

Barthelme did not come out of nowhere. One can readily spot in his work the influence of Joyce, of Beckett, of pop art (with its principle of collage and its democratic appropriation of high culture and low), of the black humor of the fifties. Indeed, he was one of a number of young American experimentalists plowing similar terrain—William Gaddis, John Hawkes, Thomas Pynchon, William Gass, Grace Paley, James Purdy, William Goyen, and others. But of these, only Purdy, Goyen, and Paley even cracked the *New Yorker* (the first two publishing a grand total of one story each, and the last not appearing until 1978). Why did Barthelme alone have such success? One reason is that he entered the magazine through the door of humor, not fiction, and even when his stories were grim or black or sad, they almost always were funny, too. The *New Yorker* casual had been moribund for some years, and Barthelme, by eschewing all preciousness and detaching his satire from any immediately identifiable object, pointed the genre in a promising, if something less than knee-slapping, new direction. He had other qualities the magazine valued. Except for "Snow White," his pieces were short. Many of them had a strong feel of Manhattan—specifically, of Greenwich Village, where Barthelme settled and lived for the rest of his life. And unlike many if not most experimentalists, Barthelme was a virtuoso stylist—he had a command of an enormous range of diction, and he took great care with every word and piece of punctuation he put down. This was a quality respected in the halls of the *New Yorker*, even when he took issue with the magazine's changes. When Barthelme received a working proof of "The Indian Uprising," he wrote to Angell about one passage: "Roger, I really feel strongly that in *this* case, this one time, we should try it without horrible commas clotting up everything and demolishing the rhythm of ugly, scrawled sentences. . . . Yes it is true that I am a miserable, shabby, bewildered, compulsive, witless and pathetic little fellow but please Roger keep them commas out of the story!!!!!!!"

Angell did indeed keep the commas out of the story, which suggests perhaps the most important reason for Barthelme's success at the *New Yorker*: he had a strong champion there. "When Don came on the scene, it was startling," Angell said. "There were these short, clear sentences. I've always had an interest in painting, and reading one of his stories was like looking at a work of art. We turned down a lot of stories over the years, but everything he did worked, in some way. His pieces had a lot to do with the times. The sixties turned out dark and strange, and his stories seemed to be about what was going on. It was somehow sustaining and comforting—you told your-

December 26, 1964

Dear Don:

First let me apologize for this long delay in writing you
about THE INDIAN UPRISING. Christmas intervened, and so did
shopping and relatives and parties and indolence. In any case,
it's a perfectly marvelous story, one of your very best, if not
the best, and I send you our congratulations and thanks,

I enclose a working proof, which is an entirely tentative
intermediate stage. You can challenge anything here, of course,
and there will be at least one more proof, with further questions,
before this thing goes into the magazine. Since this is the first
time we have tried working together via long distance, I hope you
will summon up all the patience you can with my queries and suggestions and assume, however difficult it may be, that I haven't
been casual about any of them. I have tried to make comments
about almost all of the changes in the proof, but there may be
a few changes in punctuation that I haven't gone into. I have
not made any changes in punctuation to conform to our style;
they are only to add clarity and meaning. I've explained other
matters in the margin, and I have numbered the more complicated
queries. Let's go over those.

1. I think it may be a mistake to name this character
"Joyce," since I and other readers here first believed that you
were talking about James Joyce for some highly special reason.
A story like this, let's admit it, is terribly hard on some
readers, and I don't think that they should have to struggle
with unnecessary misdirections. Can you give him another name?

2. The placing of this enigmatic Kenneth at the end of this
sentence is the kind of writer's joke, or surprise, that I wish
you would try to avoid. It has no meaning whatsoever at this
juncture, and the reader must carry his puzzlement hopelessly
along for almost a full column before you let him know that there
is a Kenneth in the story. It is such an intentional piece of
indirection that it seems self-conscious and even smart-alecky,
and I really don't think it helps your purpose that much.

3. This is a terribly hard sentence to read, but I don't

Roger Angell's letter accepting Donald Barthelme's "The Indian Uprising" was
characteristically thoughtful and detailed; what it didn't suggest was how much of a
departure the story would be for the magazine.

self that if someone was responding this way, things might not be so bad as they seemed."

According to Angell, his fellow fiction editors—William Maxwell, Rachel MacKenzie, and Robert Henderson—did not share his Barthelme enthusiasm. The colleague who did, remarkably enough, was William Shawn. Angell recalled, "Shawn was on to Barthelme before anyone else— he was beside himself with happiness over 'Snow White.' And as early as 'The Indian Uprising,' he told me that the key to Barthelme wasn't to read him like fiction, but like poetry."

In the introduction to his 1973 anthology, *The New Journalism*, Tom Wolfe argued that over the previous ten years, in the work of such writers as Gay Talese, Hunter Thompson, Jimmy Breslin, Norman Mailer, and (needless to say) himself, journalism had surpassed fiction as a forum for literary observation, creativity, and achievement. Although he charitably credited *New Yorker* writers John Hersey, Lillian Ross, and A. J. Liebling with being worthy precursors of the movement, in the anthology itself he included just one piece from the magazine: an excerpt from Truman Capote's *In Cold Blood*.

Capote's work was published as a four-part series in the fall of 1965, but it had its origin six years earlier, when the writer saw a one-column story in the *New York Times* about the brutal murder of a Kansas wheat farmer, Herbert Clutter, his wife, and two of his children. Capote, who owed the *New Yorker* a story (he had taken expense money and done the reporting for a piece on life in Russia, but had found himself unable to write it), came up with the idea of traveling to the small town where the crime had taken place and taking a long look at its effect on the community. Shawn gave his approval, and Capote set out for Kansas, accompanied by a childhood friend, Nelle Harper Lee, who would serve as a kind of research assistant. (Lee was a writer herself, having just completed her first novel, *To Kill a Mockingbird*. It would be published in 1960.)

The nature of his project dramatically changed less than a month after his arrival, when two drifters, Dick Hickock and Perry Smith, were arrested for the murders. Capote courted them in his customary manner, and they eventually spent hundreds of hours with him in intensive interviews, reliving their pasts, the crime, and their six weeks on the run. Within three months they were convicted of murder and sentenced to be hanged. But appeals delayed their execution, as well as Capote's manuscript—he felt he could not complete and submit it until there was an ultimate resolution. Hickock and Smith were finally executed in April 1965; two months later, Capote finished what was now not just an article but a book.

Capote's exhaustive interviews with Hickock and Smith, and also with Kansas law enforcement officers, gave him stunning material about events he himself had not witnessed. But how to present that material? One option was in the manner of a traditional *New Yorker* Reporter at Large—that is, as a series of interviews in which successive sources gave their "testimony." But the flatness of this approach wouldn't have come close to fulfilling Capote's literary aspirations. Instead, he chose as his stylistic model a *New Yorker* piece from twenty years earlier, John Hersey's "Hiroshima." Capote's five years of reporting had given him enough material so he could *re-create* the events of the story, as Hersey had done, and present them with the omniscience of—to use the memorable term Capote coined—a nonfiction novel. (At least one notable book had employed the technique in the interim—Cornelius Ryan's 1959 narrative of D day, *The Longest Day.*)

Shawn, of course, had edited and championed "Hiroshima" and could thus be expected to be amenable to this method. But it was not as simple as that. "Hiroshima" was about the greatest man-made disaster in human history and was intended as a warning about the nuclear peril that (Shawn believed) threatened to destroy civilization. "In Cold Blood" was about the vicious crimes of two sociopaths. What is more, Capote's work was four times longer than Hersey's and was painted on a much, much grander canvas. Where the earlier piece essentially charted the movements of a half dozen people over a matter of days, this one ranged over the continent (as Perry and Dick planned their crime, committed it, and then tried to elude the police), featured copious dialogue, and not infrequently ventured into the minds of the characters. And this presented an inevitable problem in terms of the accuracy the magazine had traditionally demanded. It wasn't that Capote was sloppy in his details; a veteran *New Yorker* fact-checker who went to Kansas to work on the piece said Capote was the most accurate author he had ever checked. But no one could guarantee the accuracy of scenes and dialogue based on the statements of sources, no matter how many hours they had been interviewed.

Shawn often edited pieces after they were set in type, and that was the case with "In Cold Blood." As he read, the explicit description of the violent murders must have greatly distressed him, but he kept this to himself. However, in penciled notations in the margins of the galleys, he did express his doubts about Capote's literary method. A particular problem was the long opening scene, set in the Clutters' house on the day on which everyone in the house would be killed. Next to one passage about the romantic travails of teenaged Nancy Clutter—"before saying goodnight, Mr. Clutter secured from her a promise to begin a gradual breaking off with Bobby"—Shawn wrote, "d/a [discuss with author]. How know? No witnesses? General problem." A few paragraphs later, he wrote, "d/a A device needed for author to account for his knowing what was said in private conversations."

There is no evidence that Shawn ever did discuss this or any other problem with the author. He may have felt that his hands were tied. As the scope of "In Cold Blood" expanded over the years, Random House agreed to bring it out as a book, and publication was set for January 1966. This was just three months after it was to appear in the *New Yorker*, meaning that there was no time for major revision. And Random House was certainly not going to postpone the book. It had already started a publicity campaign that would ultimately result in two half-hour television programs and twelve national magazine articles about Capote, including cover stories in *Newsweek* and the *Saturday Review* and an eighteen-page story in *Life*, the longest interview in its history. "In Cold Blood" ran as a four-part series in the *New Yorker* just as Capote had written it, with no changes to the first scene and no device explaining how he knew what was said in private conversations. Needless to say, the *New Yorker* did nothing to promote its publication of "In Cold Blood," and as always, nothing on the cover of the September 25 issue indicated that it contained the first installment. But Random House and Capote himself had put forth enough hype so that the four issues containing "In Cold Blood" broke the *New Yorker*'s record for newsstand sales.

Truman Capote never again wrote anything for the *New Yorker*. And the *New Yorker* never again printed an extended piece of re-created narrative. (The closest it came was C. D. B. Bryan's 1976 series, "Friendly Fire.") In the mid-1980s, over lunch at the Algonquin Hotel, Shawn told Charles McGrath, then his deputy editor, that he wished he hadn't published "In Cold Blood." He did not elaborate.

Unlike many other strong *New Yorker* voices—White, Thurber, Gibbs, Alva Johnston, Shaw, Perelman, and later Ann Beattie—Barthelme did not immediately spawn a group of imitators in the magazine's pages. The closest thing to a *New Yorker* school of Barthelme would not arrive until ten years after his debut, with the Talk pieces and casuals of George W. S. Trow, Veronica Geng, and to a lesser extent, Garrison Keillor and Ian Frazier. For the time being, his direct influence could be seen clearly in only one significant *New Yorker* writer—Michael Arlen. Arlen had been a reporter for *Life* until 1957 and subsequently contributed a number of casuals to the *New Yorker*; for several weeks, he had filled in for John McCarten as film critic. In 1966, he accepted Shawn's offer to become the magazine's television critic, a position that had been unoccupied since John Lardner's death six years earlier. Arlen started out reviewing individual programs, in a more or less conventional manner, but quickly began to see—and write about—television as one grand spectacle, alternately horrifying and absurd, with images of Vietnam, the 1968 Democratic convention, football games, the assassinations of Martin Luther King and Robert Kennedy, and *Petticoat*

Junction all running together. In a word, it was Barthelmesque. And so, frequently, was the prose Arlen used to evoke it. He called one 1968 piece "An Illustrated History of the War," an explicit reference to Barthelme's story "A Picture History of the War," and started it this way:

> Oh (I tell you, lad), the enemy kept pouring in that night, out of the hills and valleys of the central highlands, higher lowlands, lower uplands, wearing their sneakers, sandals . . . concealed sometimes in flowers, disguised as friendlies . . . bicycles streaming out of the farms and prairies, hills and valleys, all night long, all week long, all month long, past elements of the 25th Division, the 1st Air Cavalry, Frank McGee, the South Vietnamese police force, Walter Cronkite, Les Crane, the Smothers Brothers. I sat with Grigsby on the floor that afternoon and watched the shelling of Cholon, the Chinese section. "Oh, God," said Grigsby, "the element of surprise! Oh, God, observe the camerawork!" Our people brought up tanks and pistols. Grenades. Automatic weapons. Brap-brap-braaapp. Women and children ran here and there. This way, that way. Hither and yon. The loss of life was hideous to imagine, to say nothing of the disruption of public services. Our President appeared around twilight and spoke to us softly about the war. "On the other hand, there have been civilian casualties and disruption of public services" [ellipses Arlen's].

Arlen approached television as a literary humanist; in the opening words of the introduction to his first collection of essays, *Living-Room War,* "I didn't know much of anything about television when I started writing these pieces." But Shawn's general tack in this period with the magazine's critical departments was to seek out eminence and expertise. (Of course, in the mid-sixties, there *were* no experts in television.) Thus in 1966, he engaged the startlingly erudite George Steiner, a Vienna-born, Harvard-educated Cambridge don, to be a principal book reviewer. At roughly the same time, John Updike began contributing frequent book reviews and, in his insight, lucidity, and grace, proved to be as outstanding in this arena as in the short story. In 1967, when Robert Coates stepped down after a remarkable thirty years as art critic, Shawn replaced him with Harold Rosenberg, a member in good standing of the New York school of intellectuals and a bracing critic who had done more than anyone else to champion the cause of the abstract expressionist painters. That same year, John McCarten, who had taken over as theater critic when Kenneth Tynan went back to England, had health problems that prevented him from continuing in the job. Shawn moved Brendan Gill from movies to theater and chose two people to share Gill's movie-reviewing slot. One was Penelope Gilliatt, a young English woman who had been film critic for the *Observer* and was the wife (soon to be ex-wife) of playwright John Osborne.

The other was Pauline Kael, who would prove to be—in addition to

Barthelme—the *New Yorker's* other major new voice in the 1960s. Born north of San Francisco in 1919, Kael was a California bohemian in the forties and fifties, dabbling in playwrighting and experimental filmmaking and supplementing her income by working as a seamstress, cook, and textbook ghostwriter. Eventually her lifelong love of movies—a word she has always preferred to *film*—drew her to reviewing and criticism, and she began to publish in film journals and intellectual quarterlies. From 1955 until the early sixties, she managed a pair of art-film houses in Berkeley and was renowned for her eclectic programming and one-paragraph program notes. She achieved a public profile in 1965 with a collection of her essays called *I Lost It at the Movies*; Richard Schickel, in the *New York Times Book Review,* called her "the sanest, saltiest, most resourceful and least attitudinizing movie critic currently in practice in the United States."

Kael started appearing in such magazines as the *Atlantic, Holiday,* and *Life.* For several months in 1966, she was the movie critic of *McCall's*; her dismissal has traditionally been linked to her utter pan of *The Sound of Music,* which included the rhetorical question, "Wasn't there perhaps one little Von Trapp who didn't want to scream his head off, or who got nervous and threw up if he had to get out on stage?" William Shawn was paying attention. He had tracked Kael's work for some time in magazines and journals and had even, Kael remembers, attended a public forum conducted by her, Andrew Sarris, and John Simon. (Given that Kael had made her name several years before by tearing apart Sarris's "auteur" theory of filmmaking, it must have been a memorable event.) After some lunches together, Shawn offered Kael a staff writer position, with the idea that she would initially write a series of pieces on the history of movies. But she wanted to review and turned down Shawn's offer in favor of a job as the *New Republic's* critic. She had difficulty there as well. She would sometimes feel that her work was excessively edited—the magazine, as Kael recently and characteristically put it, "bitched up my copy"—and occasionally her pieces were flat-out rejected. One such was a long, reflective essay musing on the odd fact that almost the entire movie past was visible on television. She offered the piece to Shawn and he printed it, in June 1967, as an Onward and Upward with the Arts. Five months later, the *New Republic* killed Kael's six-thousand-word essay about Arthur Penn's film *Bonnie and Clyde*. Remarkably, Shawn bought it.

His decision was remarkable because while Kael's first *New Yorker* essay was conventional in subject and tone, this one decidedly was not. Penn's film about the Depression-era gangsters combined violence, comedy, action, and sex in a way that seemed oxymoronic if not unintelligible to many people accustomed to traditional Hollywood fare. Bosley Crowther, in the *New York Times,* had described *Bonnie and Clyde* as "strangely antique,

sentimental claptrap." (Gilliatt had reviewed it in the *New Yorker*, admiring-
ly and intelligently.) It is not an exaggeration to say that the opening lines
of Kael's piece, with her unmistakable mannerisms, cadences, and concerns,
ushered in a new era in American movie criticism:

> How do you make a good movie in this country without being jumped
> on? *Bonnie and Clyde* is the most excitingly American American movie since
> *The Manchurian Candidate*. The audience is alive to it. Our experience as we
> watch it has some connection with the way we reacted to movies in child-
> hood: with how we came to love them and to feel they were ours—not an art
> that we learned over the years to appreciate but simply and immediately ours.

Most amazing of all, considering Shawn's famous aversion to violence of
any kind, was that he would willingly publish what amounted to not only
a defense but an embracing of the slow-motion bloodletting in the film:

> Suddenly, in the last few years, our view of the world has gone beyond
> "good taste." Tasteful suggestions of violence would at this point be a more
> grotesque form of comedy than *Bonnie and Clyde* attempts. *Bonnie and Clyde*
> needs violence; violence is its meaning. When, during a comically botched-
> up getaway, a man is shot in the face, the image is obviously based on one
> of the most famous sequences in Eisenstein's *Potemkin*—to convey in an
> instant how someone who just happens to be in the wrong place in the
> wrong time, the irrelevant "innocent" bystander, can get it full in the face.
> And at that instant the meaning of Clyde Barrow's character changes; he's
> still a clown, but we've become the butt of the joke.

Soon afterward Kael got fed up with the *New Republic* and quit. One
night she was lying in her bed with the flu and the phone rang. It was
Shawn, offering her half a movie critic's job. Kael accepted, and her first
review—of an Italian film called *China Is Near*—appeared in the first issue of
1968.

The period of adjustment between Kael and the *New Yorker* was neither
brief nor easy. She was a completely different creature from Gill and his predecessor, McCarten, both graduates of the school of Wolcott Gibbs; their well-
bred and supercilious disdain for most films, especially those that pandered
to the popular taste, could almost always be expressed in two columns of type
or less. Kael was an almost frighteningly knowledgeable enthusiast, eager to
patrol the borders between "Trash, Art and the Movies" (in the title of a landmark essay she wrote for *Harper's* in 1969), and a literary maximalist whose
reviews went on for page after page as she circled and circled around her
subject. Shawn never tried to limit her space—and quite sensibly, since in
those fat 1960s days he had page after page to fill. On the other hand, he
continued to pay Kael on the basis of the 800–1,200-word columns Gill had

provided—a total of $600 a review. Since she was writing only half the year, this came out to a salary of a little over $15,000—not enough for Kael to support herself and her daughter. After a few years she told Shawn she needed a raise. Kael recalled, "He said, 'You mean you don't have an income?' I said, 'Since you like Gandhi, I will refuse to cash your check.' I put it on his desk. He finally said he would talk to his 'people' and arrange for me to get a retroactive increase." She was also able to supplement her income by writing long pieces in her six months off, most notably "Raising Kane," her 1970 essay about Orson Welles's *Citizen Kane,* and "On the Future of Movies," written in 1974. But even so, Kael, who retired in 1991, said the most she ever made from the *New Yorker* in a year was $75,000.

Kael's writing style was conversational (for many years she had done reviews over the radio) and emotional, marked by hyperbole, slang, and inventive euphemisms for the profanities that peppered her speech. In other words, it was not typical *New Yorker* prose. In the introduction to her collection of reviews *For Keeps,* she gives a priceless account of her run-ins with Shawn, Eleanor Gould Packard, and the magazine's copy editors during her first few years at the *New Yorker:*

> I (literally) spent more time and effort restoring what I'd written than writing it. The editors tried to turn me into just what I'd been struggling not to be: a genteel, fuddy-duddy stylist who says, 'One assumes that . . .' Sometimes almost every sentence was rearranged. The result was tame and correct; it lost the sound of spoken language. I would scramble for nine or ten hours putting back what I had written, marking the galleys carefully so they wouldn't be misread, and then I would rush to see William Shawn to get the galleys approved. Since he was the person who had instigated the finicky changes, the couple of hours I spent with him were an exhausting series of pleas and negotiations. He had given me a handshake agreement when he hired me that no word would be changed without consultation, and he stuck by his word, but I had to fight for every other contraction, every bit of slang, every description of a scene in a movie that he thought morally offensive—not my description but the scene itself. He didn't see why those things had to be mentioned, he said. . . .
>
> William Shawn and I squared off like two little pit bulls. [Kael is barely five feet tall; Shawn was a little over five foot five.] I was far from being the only writer who fought him, but it took me years to learn about the others. He told each of us that we were the only ingrates. He brought up the names of all the famous writers who, according to him, had been appreciative of the editing; it was a nightmare listening to that litany. Yet he could also be more responsive to what a writer was trying to do than anyone else I've ever encountered. The man was an enigma. On the day after my review of Mailer's *Marilyn* appeared in the Sunday *Times Book Review,* we ran into each

other in a hallway. "Why didn't you give that to us?" he asked. "What for?" I answered. "You wouldn't have printed it." "That's right," he said mournfully.

"I was hamstrung," Kael recalled. "E. B. White was Shawn's pillar of modern writing. No one was ever less like E. B. White than I was."

Kael had a hard time at first with the *New Yorker*'s readers as well as its editors. In a 1992 interview she said, "I would get letters all the time saying, 'Why don't you get a job on a magazine and learn to write?' People were more used to movies being treated in a magazine like the *New Yorker* as something a gentleman might condescend to now and then but wouldn't take very seriously. . . . I got angry responses whenever I panned anything that was liberal in intention or virtuous or European." Not only did the readers get used to her, but Kael became the *New Yorker*'s main draw. Eventually she was getting fifty letters a day from readers, some agreeing with her opinions, some disagreeing, but all wanting to talk movies with her.

Kael and Shawn came to a sort of truce as well. "They stopped bothering me, and I wasn't so argumentative," she said. This was not happenstance. The early difficulties were a result of mutual adjustment, at a time when Kael strongly needed some reining in, and the *New Yorker* strongly needed some loosening up. Eventually they met each other halfway, and the results were something to see. Kael's reviews of the early seventies—the ones collected in her books *Deeper Into Movies* and *Reeling*—represented a rare cultural moment when the vision and abilities of a single critic were perfectly matched to a new artistic movement, in this case, the groundbreaking films of Sam Peckinpah, Robert Altman, Peter Bogdanovich, Hal Ashby, William Friedkin, Francis Ford Coppola, Steven Spielberg, George Lucas, and Brian DePalma. These films were not only artistically interesting: they reflected and to some extent generated the enormous changes going on in American society. Kael had her blind spots and mannerisms—most prominently, the excessive use of the second-person singular and the first-person plural, which presumed to tell readers how they should react to a film. These would become more pronounced with the years. But she also had a way of *confronting* a film—as if she were bringing to bear everything she knew about movie history and all her intelligence and critical and literary talent—in a way that was always provocative, cogent, and entertaining and sometimes was thrilling.

Not the least of her virtues was a sharp aesthetic news sense. Reviewing Steven Spielberg's first feature, the 1974 *Sugarland Express,* she presciently remarked that Spielberg

> could be that rarity among directors, a born entertainer—perhaps a new generation's Howard Hawks. In terms of the pleasure that technical assurance gives an audience, this film is one of the most phenomenal debut films in

the history of movies. If there is such a thing as a movie sense—and I think there is (I know fruit vendors and cabdrivers who have it and some movie critics who don't)—Spielberg really has it. But he may be so full of it that he doesn't have much else. There's no sign of the emergence of a new film artist (such as Martin Scorsese) in *The Sugarland Express,* but it marks the debut of a new-style, new-generation Hollywood hand.

Kael's reviews of *M*A*S*H, McCabe and Mrs. Miller, The French Connection, Cabaret, The Godfather, Mean Streets,* and *Shampoo* all but took readers by their lapels and shouted, "This is something important, so listen." Kael's instincts were sound a remarkable percentage of the time, but when she was wrong, she tended to be *very* wrong. The classic example is her review of *Last Tango in Paris,* with its opening line, "Bernardo Bertolucci's *Last Tango in Paris* was presented for the first time on the closing night of the New York Film Festival, October 14, 1972; that date should become a landmark in movie history comparable to May 29, 1913—the night *Le Sacre du Printemps* was first performed—in music history." She concluded, "Bertolucci and Brando have altered the face of an art form."

No one could deliver a pan like Pauline Kael. In 1970, she wrote, "[Director] Lewis Gilbert's squareness about [novelist] Harold Robbins's sleaziness makes you feel you're looking at dry rot. There was not one moment in *The Adventurers* when I felt that anyone in it was trying to do a single honest thing." But it wasn't just Hollywood schlock that felt her wrath. In four memorable reviews all written in January 1972, she successively took on *A Clockwork Orange, Dirty Harry, The Cowboys* (with John Wayne), and *Straw Dogs* and made a strong case that their exploitative use of violence constituted, in various ways, cinematic fascism. It was a striking thesis, given that Kael had first made an impression in the *New Yorker* defending the violence in *Bonnie and Clyde,* but she backed up her argument by boring in on the films' manipulations with laser precision. From the *Clockwork Orange* review:

> When I pass a newsstand and see the saintly, bearded, intellectual Kubrick on the cover of *Saturday Review,* I wonder: Do people notice things like the way Kubrick cuts to the rival teen-age gang before Alex and his hoods arrive to fight them, just so we can have the pleasure of watching that gang strip the struggling girl they mean to rape? Alex's voice is on the track announcing his arrival, but Kubrick can't wait for Alex to arrive, because then he couldn't show us as much. That girl is stripped for our benefit; it's the purest exploitation.

Kael and Shawn may have negotiated a cease-fire, but they still skirmished. One confrontation came over Kael's review of the 1973 film *The Last American Hero,* which was based on a magazine article about stock-car racing by none other than Tom Wolfe. Even worse, the review contained some complimentary references to Wolfe's journalism. "Shawn was incensed," recalled Kael. "He phoned me and gave me such a reading down that a little later I passed my daughter on the street and didn't even recognize her." But the review was published as written. The next year, Kael panned *Badlands,* which was written and directed by Terrence Malick, a close friend of Wallace Shawn's. Kael recalled, "Shawn said, 'We can't print this. He's like a son to me.' I said, 'Tough shit, Bill.'" That review ran, too.

Kael continued to get a kick out of tormenting Shawn. The humorist Roy Blount Jr., a friend of Kael's, reported she once showed him proofs of her forthcoming review of the 1981 film *Reds.* Warren Beatty, she had written, played John Reed as "p____y-w_____d." "That's the way it had been set in type," Blount wrote in the *Atlantic* in 1994, "presumably because even the compositor was horrified. Shawn had adjured her to come up with some other term. She couldn't understand why. It was the right word, she insisted. 'Jesus, Pauline,' I said. 'You can't say "pussy-whipped" in the *New Yorker!*' (You couldn't then.) 'How about "uxorious"?' She rolled her eyes. Eventually she gave in to Shawn on that one, and recast the sentence, but I still feel proud of her for trying."

THE WAR AT HOME

The New Journalism, as the term came to be understood, consisted of two categories of writing, each containing two subcategories (with intermingling among all four, to be sure). The first grouping was narrative journalism. It included novelistic re-creations (such as *In Cold Blood,* John Sack's *M,* and Wolfe's *The Electric Kool-Aid Acid Test*) and works that were modeled more on a film or play, where the journalist has observed the events being described but withdraws from the narrative and presents them in the form of scenes, complete with dialogue and expository stage directions. An important model for this style was Lillian Ross's work of the fifties; notable examples in the sixties included Gay Talese's profiles of Frank Sinatra, Joe Louis, and Joe DiMaggio in *Esquire* and Joe McGinniss's book *The Selling of the President 1968.* In the second sort of New Journalism, the writer took some liberties with the time-honored journalistic code of objectivity, and with its corollary, the plain, declarative style. Sometimes this departure took the form of stylistic experimentation, excess, or playfulness, as in Wolfe's pieces for the *Herald Tribune Sunday Magazine* (which would assume an independent identity as *New York* magazine in 1968). And sometimes the reporter stepped out from the shadows, unashamedly put his or her *subjec*-tivity on display, and did what you learned not to do on the first day of Journalism 101, become a part of the story. Norman Mailer did it in *The Armies of the Night,* Joan Didion did it in her mordant essays-reports from California, such as *The White Album,* and most famously, Hunter Thompson did it in his self-styled "Gonzo journalism."

The New Journalism found expression in *Esquire, New York, Rolling Stone, Harper's* (which published *The Armies of the Night* and David Halberstam's *The Best and the Brightest*), the *Village Voice,* and even the men's magazine *True.* But to a remarkable extent it passed the *New Yorker* by. The magazine's reportage in the mid and late sixties was everything Wolfe and his school were not: serious (if not somber), more or less impersonal, and expressed in restrained and syntactically impeccable prose. To get a sense of how different the *New Yorker* was from the journalistic currents coursing through the culture, consider two descriptions of rock concerts. The first is from Wolfe's 1964 profile of Baby Jane Holzer, originally published in the *Herald Tribune.* The Rolling Stones have just taken the stage:

> The girls have Their Experience. They stand up on their seats. They begin to ululate, even between songs. The looks on their faces! Rapturous agony! There, right up there, under the sulfur lights, that is *them.* God, they're right there! Mick Jagger takes the microphone with his tabescent hands and puts his huge head against it, opens his giblet lips and begins to sing . . . with the voice of a bull Negro. Bo Diddley. You movung boo meb bee-uhtul, bah-bee, oh vona breem you' honey snurks oh crim pulzy yo' mim down, and, camping again, then turning toward the shrieking girls with his wet giblet lips dissolving . . .

Renata Adler was the *New Yorker's* main correspondent on the youth culture, covering the March on Selma in 1965, various manifestations of student radicalism, and rock music. She was about ten years younger than Wolfe, but she wrote, in a word, like a square. In a piece published in the issue of February 25, 1967, she described a concert at the Hullabaloo, on Sunset Boulevard:

> A record was cut off abruptly, the front curtain rose, a group of four whites and three Negroes was revealed, and the lead singer, dressed in a black stocking cap and brown pants and vest, leaned slightly sideways, yawned briefly, and began to sing. The group, with what seemed a kind of driving desperation, played a song called "I Flash on You." When the song was over, the audience cheered a kind of desperation cheer, as one might cheer an acquittal verdict for a defendant against whom the case looked bad.

As for the first person, *New Yorker* Reporters at Large had employed it from the days of Morris Markey through Liebling and Mitchell, through Berton Roueché, on up to John McPhee. But it was always a far more muted

I than that of the outrageous Thompson, the egoistic Mailer, or the confessional Didion. In a 1978 interview, Shawn provided a historical analysis:

> Subjective journalism, or what we call subjective reporting, is the New Journalism, which has come along in recent years and which, I think, is a debased form of journalism and a mistake. Subjective journalism never really existed in American journalism previous to the advent of the New Journalism, though forms of it were practiced in Europe. Now, subjective journalism may have had its American beginnings at the *New Yorker*, not because our writers were writing about themselves along with the ostensible subject but because writers simply employed the first person in their reporting. They often placed themselves on the scene of what they were writing about, and that's what was new. That never before existed in American journalism. But that is not New Journalism because our pieces are as objective as is genuinely possible. The I in our first person reporting is still an observer—objective and impartial.

Shawn oversimplified. True, *New Yorker* reporters would not think of putting their personalities on display (Liebling had been an exception). But in another sense the magazine's fact writing was moving decisively *away* from traditional objectivity and impartiality. The model for the *New Yorker* journalism of the sixties was "Silent Spring," which was based on rock-solid reporting but had an unmistakable political agenda. As Shawn put it in his 1968 interview with *Women's Wear Daily*, "There is no question that the magazine has come to have a greater social and political and moral awareness, and to feel a greater responsibility." The most noticeable case in point was writer Richard Harris, who contributed a string of powerful long or multipart Washington articles that were advocacy journalism, pure and simple. In 1966, he detailed how the American Medical Association sabotaged Medicare legislation, and in 1968, how the National Rifle Association sabotaged gun-control legislation. Later that year he wrote "The Turning Point" (published as a book called *The Fear of Crime*), which took the position that a crime-control bill passed by Congress "was a piece of demagoguery devised out of malevolence and enacted in hysteria." Harris followed that up in 1969 with a three-part Annals of Politics (ironically) titled "Justice," which criticized at extreme length the threats to civil liberties from the new Nixon Justice Department.

Paul Brodeur, previously a Talk and short-story writer at the magazine, contributed a long, cautionary Reporter at Large in the October 12, 1968, issue on the efforts of a researcher named Irving Selikoff to chart the perils of asbestos. It was the first of dozens of muckraking environmental exposés Brodeur would write for the magazine over the next twenty-five years. In its calmly apocalyptic conclusion, which has the feel of a 1950s science-fiction movie, Brodeur makes his way from Selikoff's office at Mt. Sinai Hospital to Midtown Manhattan and keeps noticing construction projects where asbestos is being blown into the air. In the last paragraph, he comes upon a half-completed building where some beams

> had been sprayed with asbestos insulation, which clung to them like gray frosting. Then, all at once, I saw wads of the same gray stuff falling out. . . . Some of the pieces were carried away on the wind; others that were heavier came tumbling down around me. One fell on the sidewalk at my feet. I picked it up, crumpled it between my fingers, and saw dozens of tiny fibers float away. It was the same color and texture as the material that Dr. Selikoff had shown me half an hour before. The sidewalk was covered with it, and even as I stood there more of it came showering down. A woman hurrying to make a light with a friend brushed some off the sleeve of her coat, and said, "What the devil is this stuff?" I watched her cross the avenue, and saw asbestos insulation blowing over the pavement like thistle-down across a field. The wind was southerly, and most of the asbestos was traveling north, in the direction of Mount Sinai Hospital. . . . But I was not thinking about Dr. Selikoff or the difficulties of epidemiology just then. I was thinking about the children who play in Central Park every day, and about all the other children who live in this city and breathe its air.

It was on the issue of Vietnam, of course, that the *New Yorker* became most overtly political. Robert Shaplen had been writing about Southeast Asia since the late forties, in Letters that displayed the pointed objectivity of a Flanner or a Rovere. By the midsixties they also displayed a deep skepticism about the purpose and ultimate success of the U.S. military presence. In Notes and Comment, Shaplen, Rovere, Richard Goodwin, and other writers kept returning to the apparent senselessness and futility of the war. From a December 4, 1965, Comment by Michael Arlen: "We strain our ears, but we hear no bugles, nor sounds of fifes and drums . . . we fight a ground war, but not, it would appear, in order to possess the ground." When Arlen attempted to make more definitive antiwar pronouncements, he recalled, Shawn would get "very upset." "He would say, 'This is a Comment piece. It represents the magazine. We're not ready to say that this [U.S. military involvement] is wrong. But we can say it's something to examine.'" In 1966, the magazine published a long Reflections by Goodwin, a former aide to John F. Kennedy, that argued against escalation, though it stopped short of advocating withdrawal. The same year, Susan Sheehan, in Vietnam with her husband, Neil, a *New York Times* correspondent, contributed Profiles of a Vietnamese child orphaned by the war and a captured North Vietnamese soldier that, together, showed the human costs of the conflict among the Vietnamese. A May 13, 1967, Comment by Roger Angell referred to "our belief that unrelieved bombing of a small and relatively weak country is a particularly weak and repugnant form of military coercion." In Arlen's television column, the oddly unreal and remote broadcast coverage of the war became a recurring emblem for America's hall-of-mirrors culture; he eventually traveled to Vietnam to write two memorable firsthand pieces about the network correspondents there. In 1969, veteran contributor Daniel Lang wrote "Casualties of War," a moving and horrifying story about the rape and murder of a Vietnamese girl by American soldiers.

The roommate of Shawn's son Wallace at both boarding school and Harvard—and a frequent visitor to the Shawns' apartment in New York—was a young man named Jonathan Schell. After his college graduation in 1965, Schell spent a year studying in Japan. On his way back home, more out of curiosity than anything else, he stopped in Saigon. "The correspondents there took me under their wing," Schell said. "They helped me get a press pass by pretending I was in Vietnam for the *Harvard Crimson*. Five days after I got to Vietnam, I was told, 'If you want to see something, show up at a bus stop to be taken to the airport airstrip at four-thirty A.M.'" This turned out to be one of the largest military operations of the war to that point—Operation Cedar Falls, a sweep through an enemy-dominated region west of Saigon called the Iron Triangle. Schell was permitted to go along on a forty-eight-helicopter raid of the village called Ben Suc. And so he was there as the troops landed and rounded up villagers—deciding, with more apparent madness than method, which ones were friendly and which ones were enemy sympathizers—as South Vietnamese soldiers beat up some prisoners, as women and children were relocated to a miserable nearby refugee camp, and finally as U.S. bulldozers and bombs razed and then destroyed the now-empty village.

"It was an overwhelming experience," Schell said. "This was at a point in the war when we were supposed to be winning over the hearts and minds of the Vietnamese people, and it very quickly became obvious that the entire enterprise was lacking in sense on its own terms—the idea that you would enlist people's support by burning down their village. It was the first time I had ever seen Americans engaged in such destructive activity."

Schell was in Vietnam for twelve days. On his return to New York, he went to see William Shawn and proposed writing a *New Yorker* article based on what he had witnessed. Shawn was receptive, and the result, a Reporter at Large called "The Village of Ben Suc," was published on July 15, 1967. It was a valuable and in some ways refreshing piece of writing, as Schell almost completely refrained from editorializing and confined himself to a clear account of what he had seen and heard. Shawn later described it as "a perfect piece of *New Yorker* reporting." After the article appeared, the army generated an internal response contending that the Ben Suc operation was a military success: that deep tunnels underneath the village housed Viet Cong facilities, that 285 pounds of enemy documents were recovered, and that among the prisoners were the highest political and propaganda personnel captured to that date. But Schell had not made any explicit criticisms in the piece, least of all of the strategy or effectiveness of the operation. Such disapproval as it expressed was implicit and mostly had to do with the odd way we were treating our ostensible "allies."

Schell returned to Vietnam in 1967 and wrote a much longer, two-part Reporter at Large, published in March 1968 (and reprinted as a book under the title *The Military Half*), about a bombing campaign against a coastal province in South Vietnam. A more diffuse and less effective piece than "The Village of Ben Suc," it revealed with far greater clarity Schell's disdain for what the United States had done in and to Vietnam. But his presence in the *New Yorker* offices, and his longstanding relationship with Shawn, probably had more of an impact on the magazine than his reporting pieces. "When I got back from Vietnam and started to read about the war in the newspapers, it drove me crazy," Schell said. "It had no relation to what I had seen. I had a powerful urge to make known what I had witnessed." As a result of his and Schell's long conversations about Vietnam, Shawn later said, "I became convinced that we shouldn't be there and the war was a mistake." For the issue of March 22, 1969 (coincidentally, the first *New Yorker* issue ever to have a full table of contents), Shawn decided to devote the entire Talk of the Town to a transcript of a speech by George Wald, a biology professor at Harvard; as the editor himself wrote in an introductory paragraph, "there is nothing we might print in these columns that could be more urgent." In the speech Wald called the Vietnam War "the most shameful episode in the whole of American history," accused the United States of committing "many" war crimes in it, and argued forcefully that nuclear annihilation and the population explosion were both threats to life on earth.

An antiwar editorial position was not at this point unusual. Ever since 1966, public support for the U.S. military policy in Vietnam had steadily eroded, most dramatically after the Tet Offensive in the early months of 1968. Walter Cronkite then made his famous commentary on the CBS news that we were "mired in stalemate," the percentages of the public calling themselves "hawks" and "doves" were about evenly balanced for the first time, and finally, in March 1968, Lyndon Johnson announced that he would not run for reelection. But among the establishment press, the *New Yorker's* fire-and-brimstone fervor on the issue *did* stand out. This became most apparent later in 1969, when Schell himself became the principal contributor to Notes and Comment—the first time since E. B. White's heyday that one individual had dominated the platform. But where White, an apostle of the creed of brevity, merely flitted over the surface of politics (with the exception of his world-government campaign), Schell stretched out to a thousand, fifteen hundred, and even two thousand words and dove deeply and resolutely into the issues. Schell was Emerson to White's Thoreau. He had no use for the conditional or parenthetical mode, for the measured conclusions so favored by White; he gravitated to the all-or-nothing apocalyptic pronouncement. By April 1970, he was asserting that Vietnam "has lost even the pretense of a purpose, and has become nothing more than a bloody playground for our idealism and our cruelty." The next month, after Nixon ordered the invasion of Cambodia, Richard Goodwin stepped up to the plate to pinch hit and swung for the fences with ringing condemnations in two successive weeks. As the war dragged on, it became for Schell an all-consuming symbol of the country's degradation. "Wherever we go, the war is with us," he wrote in March 1971. "Wherever we turn, the war is there. In whatever we undertake, the war intervenes. It is all around us, and it is within us."

A few weeks later came the revelation of the My Lai massacre. Schell's Comment took up three and a half pages in the magazine—more than thirty-five hundred words. It began with the declaration that "the nation's response to the massacre of hundreds of villagers at My Lai may determine whether the nation lives or dies." And it concluded by stating, "As long as the war continues, each one of us faces the choice that the nation faces: whether to repudiate the war and call for its ending or to accept it and make it—and its massacres—part of us. . . . The conviction of Lieutenant Calley seems to have shocked the country in some new way and awakened it out of a long sleep. We seem to have been given another chance—possibly our last chance—to save our souls."

But did "we" want our souls to be saved? As a result of Richard Nixon's "Vietnamization" policy, which drastically reduced U.S. casualties, antiwar sentiment in the country at large had greatly waned from its peak in 1968, to the point where in 1972 Nixon would soundly defeat a candidate who defined himself on the issue, George McGovern. Perhaps more telling, the country had by this point become sharply and irreversibly divided on the war and its corollary issues. In the universe of *New Yorker* readers, Schell's weekly ultimatums were a wedge that stretched the division until it was impossible to ignore.*

---

*A division, more or less generational in character, existed among members of the *New Yorker* staff as well, with many in the older group irritated by what they saw as Schell's stridency. In early 1974, when E. B. White published an op-ed article in the *New York Times,* William Maxwell wrote to Katharine White: "I was so happy with Andy's piece in the *Times.* I have been asking myself for months what he would have done to take the curse off the current Notes and Comment pieces, which are, God knows, intelligent, but also terribly (or so it seems to me) self-righteous. The answer is he would have described the way you make a wheelbarrow, and by so doing brought things into a proper focus."

In doing so, they exposed one of the *New Yorker's* secrets: its unprecedented success in the fifties and sixties was possible in part because a sizable proportion of its "readers" did not read the magazine (other than to glance at the cartoons and the ads and perhaps once in a while a theater or film review).They merely renewed their subscriptions, year after year, and decorated their coffee tables with its colorful covers. Among the many qualities of the *New Yorker's* writing was an eclectic innocuousness that made it on some level acceptable to these people, if not actually sympathetic, engaging, or inspiring. E. B.White crawled under this protective canopy to express his deep disdain for the institution of advertising, Edmund Wilson his unsparing aesthetic, Rachel Carson her wide-ranging critique of environmental malfeasance, John Cheever his subversive vision of the suburban class.

But as the sixties turned into the seventies, the *New Yorker* began publishing manifestos that simply could not be ignored: not only Schell's Vietnam Comments, but Harris's excoriation of the Nixon administration, and Yale law professor Charles Reich's never-ending paean to hippiedom, "The Greening of America," called "The New Generation" when Shawn excerpted it as a Reflections piece in 1970. (It came to his attention because Reich's mother ran the nursery school attended by Lillian Ross's son.) Reich charged that American society "is run for the benefit of a privileged few, lacks its proclaimed democracy and liberty, is ugly and artificial, destroys the environment and the self, and is, like the war it spawns, 'unhealthy for children and other living things.' "The incongruity between this kind of rhetoric and the advertisements sharing the *New Yorker's* pages with it—for the Princess Hotel in Bermuda, a jewel auction at Park-Bernet, a $600 porcelain ruby-throated hummingbird, and Chivas Regal, Cutty Sark, Grant's, and Teacher's Scotch whiskey—had finally reached a level too great to sustain.

And so a sizable group of long-slumbering *New Yorker* subscribers began waking up to realize, with a kind of horror, what the magazine actually contained. "Lately I have been disturbed by the caustic and, what appears to me to be biased political thoughts expressed by the writer, or writers, of the Talk of the Town," a North Carolina doctor (and forty-year *New Yorker* reader) wrote in 1970 to Peter Fleischmann (Raoul's son, who was named president of the *New Yorker* in 1968). "The editorial writer of this feature no longer confines himself to amusing and light-hearted local issues. . . . I do not deny the writer of Talk of the Town his right to a *private* opinion on anything under the sun. I *do* object to his shoving it down my throat in a one way communication in *my* magazine." The same year, a Scarsdale man sputtered, "Ever since . . . the *New Yorker* began printing distortions and misrepresentations about the Administration's position in the Indo-Chinese war and the subversive student protest, I have been searching through the magazine for a 'Letters to the Editor' column to which I could direct my objections to your totally illogical conclusions about the present situation....Why is it, I wonder, that the *New Yorker* alone among the major journals of the nation ... should provide no channel for reader response? Is it possibly because you fear the ire of those who detect the irrationality of your views?"

Also in 1970, a reader who resided on upper Fifth Avenue sent a letter to "The Editor" that seems like a parody. It was not. He wrote:

> For many years I have subscribed to the *New Yorker*. I like your covers, your cartoons and your advertisements. I rarely have time to read it fully, but your magazine is something I should greatly miss.
>
> In passing, I might say that I do not like your newer policy of mixing up Off-Broadway attractions with those on Broadway in your listings. It is difficult enough to get to the West Side to see the theatre on Broadway, but the generally uncomfortable Off-Broadway theatres offer little attraction and their productions are frequently aimed at rather avant-garde audiences. I suggest that you do not mix them up. It is confusing.
>
> This is not, however, what I am writing about. I am shocked, as is Mrs. Allen, at your editorials deriding our great President, Mr. Nixon, in the Talk of the Town in your issues of May 8 and May 15. They are most disloyal. No one likes the Vietnam war, but it has been imposed upon us by two Democratic presidents, Messrs. Kennedy and Johnson. Mr. Nixon is doing his utmost to extricate us. In attacking the Communist sanctuaries in Cambodia, he is doing his best to protect our troops in their withdrawal. I enclose an excerpt from the *Christian Science Monitor* which argues this better than I.
>
> In your May 8 issue, you made a sympathetic reference to the Black Panthers. These people are beyond the pale of human society, and we must be protected against them....
>
> All of your format, and certainly your advertisements, are designed to appeal to the better class of decent people. If you subscribe to the liberalism which has done so much harm to our country, you should at least not allow it to show so obviously.

The radicalization of the *New Yorker,* such as it was, undoubtedly lost the magazine some readers. Circulation reached an all-time high in the middle of 1969 at some 482,000; over the next year it fell by more than 5 percent—the biggest one-year drop in the history of the magazine. The numbers then began steadily creeping up, thanks in part to the magazine's first-ever half-price promotion, offered to college students and professors. By 1971, there were 78,000 campus subscribers, nearly 20 percent of the total. This itself represented a problem, at least for the short term. As the then treasurer of the magazine, J. Kennard Bosee, told author Gigi Mahon, "There was a change in the character of the readers. The numbers didn't change, but where before there were top executives of Fortune 500 companies, now they were replaced with a bunch of kids. The thrust was to a lower audience. The demographics never went up again."

The demographic erosion was only one of the New Yorker's financial problems. It also suffered from a slump the industry in general went through in the late sixties and early seventies. Magazines found themselves losing the fight for advertising dollars to television, whose advertising revenue more than doubled, from $1.5 billion to $3.5 billion, over the 1960s. The only periodicals that consistently did well were the new "special-interest" magazines, which supposedly allowed advertisers to target their customers with surgical precision; the "hot books" of the time included *Boating, Car and Driver, Flying, Golf, Popular Photography, Skiing,* and *Stereo Review.* Even the upstart *New York* magazine could attract local restaurants and retailers, with its almost entirely New York readership. By contrast, about 80 percent of the New Yorker's readers lived outside the metropolitan area. Among the *New Yorker's* fellow general-interest weeklies, the *Saturday Evening Post* went out of business in 1969, *Look* in 1971, and *Life* in 1972; all had made the fatal step of artificially and grossly inflating circulation with cut-rate offers. The overwhelming majority of the New Yorker's readers paid full fare, and the magazine was never in any danger of folding; indeed, it never stopped making money. But, given the chance to take its business elsewhere, Madison Avenue derived some enjoyment in turning the tables on the magazine that had for decades been the haughtiest market in the country. As an anonymous "media man" told the *Wall Street Journal* in 1971 (and one could almost feel the schadenfreude coming off the printed page), "The *New Yorker* rode too long on the momentum of its success." Whatever the precise causal mix, the numbers showed that between 1966 and 1971, the *New Yorker's* ad pages fell 40 percent—from 6,144 to 3,650. And over the same five years the annual net profit plummeted 66 percent, from $3.02 million to $1.03 million. The moneymaking machine had started to creak.

CHAPTER SEVEN

"LOVE IS THE ESSENTIAL WORD"

1972~87

REVIVAL

To use a cliché that had not yet been coined, the setbacks of the late sixties were a wake-up call for the *New Yorker*. Or at least for the *New Yorker* as a business enterprise—a mere drop in ad sales would never induce Shawn to change the *content*. Yet the business side did prevail upon him to make the magazine more welcoming and navigable for readers by instituting that rather earth-shattering table of contents, in 1969, and to give his blessing to a couple of other uncharacteristic firsts.* In 1970, the *New Yorker* launched—gasp!—a multimedia (newspapers, television, subway posters) advertising campaign and, the following year, hired a public relations firm to send out weekly news releases on the issue's articles. Shawn even allowed the advertising department to initiate a series of lunches in which such important contributors as Pauline Kael, Charles Saxon, and John Brooks talked informally to key Madison Avenue personnel. Perhaps most shocking, after not giving *any* press interviews for his first thirty-five years at the *New Yorker*, Shawn began acting like a veritable publicity hound, speaking to

---

*The plans for the table of contents were characteristically secretive. Daniel Menaker, then a fact-checker, said, "No one in the checking department knew about it till the actual issues came in. When I saw it, I said, 'This is terrific.' One of the other checkers said, 'But now readers will know what's in the magazine.' I asked what was wrong with that. 'Readers have no *right* to know what's in the magazine.'"

Newsweek in 1970, the *Los Angeles Times* in 1971, and *Time* in 1972. For the *New Yorker's* fiftieth anniversary, in 1975, he received in his office a succession of reporters, including Phil Casey of the *Washington Post*. After the interview the two walked to the elevator. There, wrote Casey, Shawn "asked, 'Could I shake your hand? I'm afraid my hands are cold. I was so nervous before the interview.' We told him we had been nervous, too, and that we'd had a couple of martinis to quiet all that. Shawn, who barely drinks at all, nodded approvingly. 'I should have done that,' he said."

In a move that Shawn apparently fought hard and in vain against, Peter Fleischmann and Milton Greenstein, a lawyer who served as liaison between the editorial and business departments, instituted a mandatory-retirement policy at age sixty-five, to take effect at the beginning of 1976. Writers and artists were exempted, since they were not really employees, and so was Shawn, who would turn sixty-nine that year. But editors William Maxwell, Robert Henderson, Robert MacMillan, Hobart Weekes, and Rogers Whitaker were all forced to leave. Fleischmann stepped down as president in 1975 as well, because of ill health rather than age, and named George Green, the youthful circulation director, as his successor. (Fleischmann stayed on as chairman.) Green's go-go activism and visibility in advertising and publishing circles presented a sharp contrast with his predecessors' reticence, and he shook things up even more. One early victory was convincing Shawn to permit "advertorials"—special sections with promotional text wrapped around ads.

On the circulation side, by 1971 anyone who was going to be offended by the political content had presumably jumped ship; from here on in, one could assume that people took the *New Yorker* because they actually liked to read it. And new readers came on board: between 1971 and 1981, subscriptions rose 12 percent. Advertisers now had no illusions about what they were getting into, either, and over the same decade ad pages went up 16 percent. Because of advertising and subscription rate hikes over that period, annual revenues and annual profits increased even more, the latter reaching an all-time high of $5.3 million in 1981.

The economic recovery had a creative counterpart. If the *New Yorker* in the fifties and early sixties was characterized by the dull gentility mocked by Tom Wolfe, and in the late sixties by political advocacy, in the seventies it experienced, four decades after the first one, another golden age. There are no borders with black ink between these periods, but if a date had to be assigned for the beginning of this creative renaissance, as good a choice as any would be February 1973—the month direct U.S. military involvement in Vietnam officially ended. Shawn's magazine would always retain an element of high moral seriousness, but, free from the burden of opposing the war, it was able to reclaim a part of Harold Ross's birthright that had been lost, or at least misplaced—a lightness, a capacity for wit, a subtle solicitousness to the reader. An additional burden was lifted eighteen months later, with the resignation of Richard Nixon, whose crimes and misdemeanors had continued to preoccupy Schell and Harris, and the final one on April 30, 1975, when the Vietnam War itself came at long last to an end.

Just ten weeks before, the *New Yorker* published its fiftieth anniversary issue, and the by-now-familiar table of contents announced an awesome lineup that, in a breathtaking way, spanned the decades. The magazine led off with a portfolio of drawings by Saul Steinberg, followed by a "Letter from the East" by E. B. White. There was a short story by Barthelme, a casual by Perelman, and another humor piece ("The Inquiring Demographer") written by Calvin Trillin and illustrated by Edward Koren. The poems were by Howard Moss and Richard Wilbur. Audax Minor, Mollie Panter-Downes, and Winthrop Sargeant provided a taste of earlier eras; Pauline Kael (reviewing *The Stepford Wives*), Harold Rosenberg, Arlene Croce, Andrew Porter, Michael Arlen, and John Updike (on Italo Calvino) represented the new critical heavy-hitters. Whitney Balliett had a piece about the singer Helen Humes, and the Reporter at Large was one of John McPhee's finest, the first of a three-part series later published as *The Survival of the Bark Canoe*. And you could get it all for just sixty cents.

The creative resurgence of the seventies had long roots. To begin with, the innovations of Kael and Barthelme—who themselves did fine work, perhaps their finest, in this period—prepared the magazine for other daring stylists, in the manner of a prizefighter softening up an opponent with blows to the body. A handful of other sterling contributors had also found their way in. In 1963, Gilbert Rogin, a thirty-four-year-old *Sports Illustrated* writer, decided to revive his youthful dreams of fiction and sent in to the *New Yorker* a story called "Ernest Observes." It reached the desk of Roger Angell, who accepted it, and was followed by several dozen more Rogin stories over the next fifteen years. After receiving an early story, "A Description of a Presumption," William Maxwell wrote Rogin that it "made me feel that there is no limit to how far you could go, and so I keep wanting you to go the whole way, like Chekhov and Turgeniev and Mrs. Woolf and Colette. Just your life's blood is all that's required." Maxwell's extravagant hopes were not ultimately realized. Rogin's works eventually settled into a certain sameness, as they followed the psychological, social, and sexual ups and downs (usually downs) of a rueful and obsessively reflective protagonist who, though his name changed from story to story, was identifiably a single individual, presumably a version of Rogin himself. But his ironies were so exquisite, his stories so carefully and poetically crafted, that his relatively small group of devoted readers (including Shawn) didn't really mind the repetition.* Also in fiction, the decision in the midsixties to end the prohibition against translated works meant not only the return of Vladimir Nabokov to the *New Yorker's* pages, with English versions of stories written in Russian in his youth, but the debut of two other important foreign writers, Jorge Luis Borges and Isaac Bashevis Singer, who would go on to become frequent contributors and whose very different voices and visions would rather surprisingly turn out to fit splendidly into the magazine.

Another important arrival in the midsixties was Woody Allen, a television gagwriter turned cabaret comedian who was beginning to make the transition to writing, acting in, and directing films. In 1965, *Playboy* magazine solicited a humor piece from him. Though a devotee of the works of Max Shulman and S. J. Perelman, Allen had never before attempted anything of the kind, but he was willing to try. When his piece—an epistolary chess game in which the bickering competitors lose track of the position of the pieces on the board—was finished, his fiancée, Louise Lasser, told him it was so good he should send it to the *New Yorker.* Allen recalled years later: "To me, as of everyone else of my generation, the *New Yorker* was hallowed ground. Anyhow, on a lark, I did. I was shocked when I got this phone call back saying that if I'd make a few changes, they'd print it." What Roger Angell actually asked was that Allen make the piece sound a little less like Perelman. Allen complied, and the piece was published in January 1966 as "The Gossage-Vardebedian Papers." It and the twenty-eight other pieces he published through 1980 (most of them collected in the books *Getting Even* and *Without Feathers*) were a shot in the arm for the *New Yorker* casual, precisely because, in the manner of Perelman, they were *not* casual. For decades, the typical *New Yorker* humor piece had been the more or less graceful exposition of some writer's more or less amusing and clever notion. In Allen's pieces, there was no ego, only execution. Angell always found him immediately willing to execute any requested changes, no matter how strange they seemed. "When he handed in one piece, my reaction was that it was too funny," Angell recalled. "There was a laugh on every line, and I felt it didn't give readers a chance to catch their breath. When I told that to Woody, he said under his breath, 'Hmmm. Too funny.' Then he made the changes." Allen had a gagman's discipline and sense of form, an inspired silliness, and a wonderful ear for a variety of dictions—academic prose, Jewish-

*When he began to have success with short stories, Rogin switched from a writing to an editing position at *Sports Illustrated* and in 1979 became the chief editor at the magazine. Meanwhile, his stories filled three books—*The Fencing Master* (1965), *What Happens Next?* (1971), and *Preparations for the Ascent* (1980). Soon after publication of the last, he submitted two stories to Angell, who told Rogin he was turning them down because they seemed to go over familiar ground. The criticism had a shattering effect on Rogin, and subsequently he has written no fiction.

American argot, philosophical tracts, private-eye novels, and obscure genres such as the Talmudic tale, with its accompanying commentary:

> Rabbi Zwi Chaim Yisroel, an Orthodox scholar of the Torah and a man who developed whining to an art unheard of in the West, was unanimously hailed as the wisest man of the Renaissance by his fellow-Hebrews, who totaled a sixteenth of one percent of the population. Once, while he was on his way to synagogue to celebrate the sacred Jewish holiday commemorating God's reneging on every promise, a woman stopped him and asked the following question: "Rabbi, why are we not allowed to eat pork?"
> "We're *not?*" the Rev said incredulously. "Uh-oh."
>
> This is one of the few stories in all Hassidic literature that deals with Hebrew law. The Rabbi knows he shouldn't eat pork; he doesn't care, though, because he *likes* pork. Not only does he like pork; he gets a kick out of rolling Easter eggs. In short, he cares very little about traditional Orthodoxy and regards God's covenant with Abraham as "just so much chin music." Why pork was proscribed by Hebraic law is still unclear, and some scholars believe that the Torah merely suggested not eating pork at certain restaurants.*

Making an important but little-noticed contribution to the creative advancement was The Talk of the Town. With the glory days of Thurber, and even Updike, a distant memory, the department had been precious, inconsequential, and little read in the late fifties and early sixties. With its rampant use of *we,* it was certainly the easiest target for *New Yorker* parodists. That began to change with a new generation of writers who, rather than have their reports processed through Brendan Gill's elegant typewriter, were permitted to compose Talk stories themselves. One of the first to arrive, in 1963, was the son of the Cold War icon Alger Hiss, Tony, who had been two years ahead of Wallace Shawn and Jonathan Schell at Putney and then at Harvard. Hiss was followed by a procession of Harvard class of '65 mates: not only Schell, but Jacob Brackman, George Trow, Daniel Chasan, and Hendrik Hertzberg (who did not arrive until 1969). In the following years, they would be joined by such like-minded Talk artists as Jamaica Kincaid, Ian Frazier, Mark Singer, Stanley Mieses, and later still, Bill McKibben. Lillian Ross adopted a baby in 1966 and, after publishing a tour de force Profile of Otto Preminger in the form of a screenplay that year, henceforth concentrated on Talk, becoming one of the master practitioners of the form.

---

*Allen's contributions ebbed during the late seventies and finally ended in 1980. The disappointed Angell said to him, "I hope you're not one of those writers who thinks that humor is childish." "I'm afraid I am," Allen replied.

Shawn ran Talk in his typical Zen-master way. Ideas had to be cleared through him, and when pieces were turned in, he would either accept or reject. If the former, the writer got an almost immediate phone call relaying the good news, and the piece would be published with virtually no editing. If the latter, the writer never heard another word about (or received any payment for) the piece, ever.

Each of the Talk crew had his or her own style and interests, but together they constituted a sort of literary movement. They favored offbeat subjects—or, if covering standard celebrities or publicity events, were drawn to what was happening in the corner of the frame. They had read their Barthelme and, stylistically, trafficked in a free-floating irony. The faux-naïf was a preferred mode: short and intentionally flat declarative sentences, odd lists, and "dull" details, with frequent dips into the vernacular (a favorite word was *guy*, as in one of Frazier's leads from 1974: "Randy Newman . . . was in town the other day, and we went to see him because he is a really cool guy"). The members of this school would not truly come into their respective voices until the seventies, but there were early hints of what was to come. In a piece published December 2, 1967, Trow began, "The other evening, we went to see the Sixth Annual Custom Car Show at the Coliseum. A group called Promotions, Incorporated, of 19717 East Nine Mile Road, St. Clair Shores, Michigan, puts this on, with a group called International Productions." On his way to the "really radical cars," he found himself distracted:

> For one thing, there was a Go-Go contest right in the middle of the radical area, with an announcer and a rock group from Blackwood, New Jersey. Here were girls who had won regional contests at other Custom Shows, and who were competing on a stage, two at a time, for the title of Miss U.S.A. à Go-Go. One girl in the pair we watched was named Kathy and was Miss Massachusetts Go-Go, and the other was named Yvonne and was a two-time winner from Baltimore. When the music began, they danced, and when it stopped, they stopped and caught their breath and switched places, and then the music began again. Kathy had a frantic way of dancing; Yvonne was more subdued. When the music stopped a second time, there was some applause but not much, and they went off the stage. Then a woman with a clipboard picked two others to go out. The whole thing was a little sad, and no one seemed to enjoy it very much.

Five years later, it was acceptable to take a digression, such as Trow had indulged in above, and construct an entire Talk story out of it. This is what Tony Hiss did in a piece called "Libra Birthday Party," which was, sure enough, about a birthday party for two Libras. In a deadpan tone, Hiss simply related what happened at the party. Here is one paragraph:

The older people discussed other subjects. A man in a brown velvet evening suit had a serious conversation with a woman in a Chinese embroidered silk dress about the nature of despair. They agreed that despair did not seem to be connected with specific events in their lives—what they called adolescent-type or soap-opera problems—but was something altogether more mysterious. The man said that a year or so ago he had gone through a period of feeling useless. The feeling had not been with him all the time but had just come and gone. It had lasted, altogether, a couple of weeks, perhaps a month. The woman said that, fortunately, she had spent the last few months outside the depths of despair, and that what troubled her these days was flashes of lifelessness, moments when she suddenly felt the spirit to be lacking. The man said he knew what she meant, that he sometimes felt that the flame in him—and in everything else—had flickered or gone out. He said you had to remember at those moments that you couldn't be aware of the flame flickering if you hadn't already become aware of the existence of the flame.

Helping to invigorate Talk was a new cast of eccentric characters, joining the stalwarts, the Long-Winded Lady and Our Man Stanley. The characters were generally introduced by a Homeric epithet. Tony Hiss and veteran editor Rogers Whitaker created E. M. Frimbo, "the world's greatest railroad buff"—essentially, Whitaker. Whitaker, a curmudgeon, also appeared as "our friend the curmudgeon." A motor-mouthed acquaintance of writer Susan Lardner's became "our friend Janet." Real people also put in regular appearances under their own names. Trow and Hertzberg invented a job—"discotheque editor of the *National Star*"—for a young reporter named Stanley Mieses, who eventually got a job as a Talk writer himself. Ross showcased a peripatetic friend of hers with the wonderful name Lola Finkelstein. Hiss repeatedly went back to three of his buddies: architect Henry Korman, psychologist Robert Ornstein, and comedian Henny Youngman.

The most significant of these characters was one of Trow's: "our sassy black friend Jamaica Kincaid." Kincaid was born Elaine Richardson on the island of Antigua and arrived in New York in 1966, at the age of seventeen, to be a nanny. She soon determined that child care was not her top career choice, and she took a series of jobs on the lower rungs of magazine publishing, meanwhile becoming a regular on the downtown rock-music and party circuit. A true original, she cut her hair short and dyed it blond and wore outrageous thrift-shop ensembles that would subsequently be appropriated by Woody Allen and Diane Keaton for the "Annie Hall look." To be a writer, she decided, she would need a new name—the old one represented too many of the things she wanted to get behind her. So she sat down with a group of her friends—all gay men, as she recalls—and went through a list of noms de plume, every one of which had a Caribbean island for a first name. The winner by acclamation was Jamaica Kincaid.

She met George Trow through their mutual friend Michael O'Donahue, and Trow began taking her to events and including her caustic comments in his accounts of them in Talk. In 1974, they went to a West Indian festival in Brooklyn; Kincaid took some notes and passed them on to Shawn. She later recalled, "I thought Mr. Shawn would ask George to go over what I had put down and put it into proper writing, but instead everything that I had written appeared in the magazine just as I had written it. And when I saw that, I had a shock, because I realized then what my writing would be: the thoughts in my head, the way I thought of something, expressed in words." The piece, "West Indian Weekend," led to a job as a Talk writer. Kincaid's true goal was to write fiction, and in 1978, the New Yorker published "Girl," a hectoring one-sentence monologue in the remembered voice of her mother. It and subsequent Kincaid short stories were—like the casuals and Profiles of Trow, Ian Frazier, and Mark Singer—instances of the Talk sensibility migrating into other parts of the magazine. (In 1979, Kincaid married Shawn's son Allen, a composer.)

Other parts of the magazine merged into Talk as well. Between 1972 and 1978, Donald Barthelme wrote thirteen Notes and Comment pieces. They were unsigned, of course, but evinced a characteristically antic attitude that provided some welcome leavening to Schell's earnestness. Another Talk recruit was James Stevenson, the cartoonist. He had always had a side interest in writing and in the early sixties published a short novel. "When it came out," Stevenson recalled, "Shawn said to me, 'I love the way you write,' and encouraged me to contribute pieces to the magazine. Shawn made you feel you could do anything."

Stevenson's ideas were indeed unconventional. One day he stood in the middle of Interstate 95 with the notion of writing a Talk piece about the things that came off tires on the highway. Rather than merely describe what he saw, he decided he would make drawings and include them in the piece. This made perfect sense but was radical for Talk, where illustrations had never appeared and the assumption was that crystalline prose could describe *anything*. But Shawn approved the effort, and subsequently Stevenson contributed a series of wonderful pieces, describing and showing the water tanks and other rooftop appurtenances one sees when one looks up, the various metal lids embedded in the sidewalk one sees when one looks down, the astonishing variety of shadows visible one morning on Forty-sixth Street between Fifth and Sixth Avenues, and the attitudes people struck while waiting out a furious rainstorm. "Once I found out you could write about pieces of tire," Stevenson said, "there was no stopping me."

The new Talk writers exhibited a blend of collegiality and competition.

Hiss, Trow, and Hertzberg, in a startling act of rebellion against the traditional *New Yorker* ethos of isolation, knocked down the walls between their offices to try to create more of a newsroom atmosphere. And the anonymity of Talk, far from being a problem, was viewed as a quintessential, indeed noble, attribute of the form. At the same time, Talk writers would rush to inspect each week's galleys as they were posted in the hallway, to see who had made the grade that week. Another competition revolved around who could make the most audacious variation on the traditional conventions. Kincaid did a Talk story about Milton and Rose Friedman in the form of an expense account (the building where they held a press conference, she noted, was worth $40 million); Frazier did one in outline form.

Frazier stands along Updike and Thurber in the pantheon of the finest Talk writers in the *New Yorker's* history. A native of Ohio (like Thurber), he grew up reading the *New Yorker,* and at Harvard, from which he graduated in 1973, eight years after the Schell–Hertzberg-Trow group, he wrote his senior thesis on the early years of the magazine. After graduation he went to see Robert Bingham, the editor in charge of hiring. Frazier recalled, "He told me, 'We have no writing jobs—we've got too many people from Harvard. If you want, you can have a checking job.' I said no. That was the right answer." Frazier worked for *Oui,* a *Playboy* spin-off in Chicago, for six months, then hitchhiked to New York. He called Bingham, who offered him a trial Talk piece, about a guy who photographs ice cream. "After I handed it in, Bingham called me and said, 'Shawn wants to see you.' George Trow said to me, 'That means you're hired.' I was so happy it was horrifying."

Between 1974 and 1981, Frazier published 110 Talk pieces, and the thrill never went away. "I would give my story to Shawn's secretary and she'd give it to Shawn," Frazier said. "On a good day, by the time you came back to your office the phone would be ringing. You'd pick it up and Shawn would be saying, 'That was a great piece.' It was addictive. I'd be so high I'd walk all the way home."

Frazier started publishing casuals in 1975, and probably more than any other contributor, he had a sense of the history and nobility of the form. "For a few years," he said, "I made sure to write one or two casuals a year, because I felt that if I didn't, the genre might disappear. The casual is a literary form, and by that time most people who were funny wrote show business forms." The feel of Frazier's best humor pieces reached all the way back to Robert Benchley: they latched on to different kinds of bad writing— clichéd, flat, imprecise, out-of-key writing—and somehow elevated them to an inspired, hilarious poetry. It is easy to make fun of academic prose. But to posit a really bad academic critic taking show-biz autobiographies as his subject is pure Frazier. The first paragraph (of three) from his "Niven: A Reconsideration":

Over the years, it has been the custom of literary critics to regard Niven as a lonely monument, self-created—almost as much a fiction as one of his own characters, magnificent in the uniqueness of his achievement. While I realize this is doctrine from which one of our number strays at his peril, I have always believed that such a view of the man and his work removes Niven from the historical context and neglects consideration of the author as a product of the turbulent intellectual climate of his time. One must remember that it was during Niven's age that Hope also wrote. Although Hope had produced most of his major oeuvre (including the major works, *Have Tux, Will Travel, So This Is Peace,* and his masterpiece, *I Owe Russia $1200*) a number of years before Niven wrote *The Moon's a Balloon,* he was still alive in the full noon of Niven's day, and they may even have known each other. We should remember, too, that it was about this time that McLaine produced her *Don't Fall Off the Mountain,* Arnaz his *A Book,* and Boone his *Twixt Twelve and Twenty.* And what of Davis, Jr.? His *Yes I Can,* which predates Niven's *Balloon,* has a clean, architectonic style reminiscent of Nivenian prose. Indeed, is it mere coincidence that Davis, Jr.'s work even contains some of the same characters that we find in both *Balloon* and *Bring on the Empty Horses?*

The other notable casual writer of the period was a young Minnesotan whose given name was Gary Keillor but who signed his pieces "Garrison." He went way back with the magazine—specifically, to 1956, when, as a fourteen-year-old, he came across it in the public library of his hometown of Anoka. "My people," Keillor wrote in the introduction to his first collection of humor pieces, *Happy to Be Here,*

> weren't much for literature, and they were dead set against conspicuous consumption, so a magazine in which classy paragraphs marched down the aisle between columns of diamond necklaces and French cognacs was not a magazine they welcomed into their home. I was more easily dazzled than they and to me the *New Yorker* was a fabulous sight, an immense glittering ocean liner off the coast of Minnesota, and I loved to read it. I bought copies and smuggled them home, though with a clear conscience, for what I admired was not the decor or the tone of the thing but rather the work of some writers, particularly the *New Yorker's* great infield of Thurber, Liebling, Perelman and White.
>
> They were my heroes: four older gentlemen, one blind, one fat, one delicate, and one a chicken rancher, and in my mind they took the field against the big mazumbos of American Literature, and I cheered for them.

At the University of Minnesota, Keillor edited a magazine called the *Ivory Tower,* whose opening column, "Broadsides," featured a first-person plural shamelessly lifted from The Talk of the Town's. The summer after graduation, in 1966, he hitchhiked to New York, made his way to the *New*

Yorker offices ("something of a religious experience for me"), and met with the editors Leo Hofeller and Patrick Nosher. He was given some tryout pieces for The Talk of the Town; they were turned down. Keillor retreated to Minnesota, took a job as a host of an early-morning classical-music show for the local public radio station, worked on a novel, and eventually, in his spare time, started writing humor pieces. In the summer of 1970, he sent a batch of these in to the *New Yorker,* addressed to "The Editors." One of them, a mock small-town-newspaper article about a family who has hired a prostitute as a "live-in companion" for their sixteen-year-old son, found its way to Roger Angell. As soon as Angell read the piece, which was called "Local Family Keeps Son Happy," he started walking the corridors, waving the manuscript in his hand and shouting, "This is great!" Angell's acceptance letter was a life-changing experience for Keillor: "When you are in your twenties, living in Minnesota, and have wasted a lot of time trying to write fiction, and then you get a letter from the *New Yorker* buying a story, it feels like a rescue—a ship has come and sent out a longboat and picked you up off your desert island. I sat on the front steps and read the letter three times." Keillor sold more pieces in quick succession; by November, Angell was writing him, "You have sustained such a cheerful deluge of good pieces that I keep wondering whether I have forgotten to thank you for them or even to tell you which ones we are buying."

There were a number of reasons for Keillor's success. His Midwest reference points were unfamiliar and refreshing; despite its national readership, the geographical sensibility of the magazine was still mainly limited to New York, the British Isles, and the American South. Thanks to his long reading and contemplation of the magazine, he had a deep understanding of the casual form. Of all the past *New Yorker* writers, he was most devoted to White, and the influence was unmistakable in a certain gentleness and the solemn care Keillor devoted to every word choice. (In addition, his affection for clunky prose anticipated and probably influenced Frazier's.) Also like White, Keillor, at least in his early pieces, said what he had to say with dispatch; Angell once expressed his gratitude "for such admirable brevity; I'm beginning to think you may be the only short writer in America. (Yes, I know, except for Truman Capote.)" Maybe most important, he was a natural storyteller who, amid the comedy, created breathing and sympathetic characters. Even in "Local Family Keeps Son Happy," readers got a feel for the oddly appealing Shepard family, who took action because young Robbie "had seemed restless and unhappy all last summer." In 1974, Keillor got an assignment from the *New Yorker* to write an Onward and Upward with the Arts piece about the Grand Ole Opry. The experience inspired him to start a weekly radio program in the Twin Cities called *A Prairie Home Companion*; its great success led to national broadcast in 1980 that has continued, with some interruptions, ever since. The centerpiece of the show is Keillor's monologue, "The News from Lake Wobegon," which comes through like nothing more than an ongoing Minnesota version of Thurber's *My Life and Hard Times,* served up with the meticulous empathy of E. B. White.

Cartoons flowered in the seventies, too. The era of writers providing cartoonists with gags was over, and by 1970, the magazine was showcasing a new generation of cartoonists who were creating their own worlds— Edward Koren, who established an odd, fury species who were very sensitive to one another's needs; Charles Barsotti, who came over to the *New Yorker* from the *Saturday Evening Post,* where he had been cartoon editor, and produced brilliant, minimalist line drawings, reminiscent of Otto Soglow, that featured office workers, cowboys and talking animals; William Hamilton, who acerbically chronicled the preppy upper class; and George Booth, an artistic disciple of George Price whose shabby rooms were overpopulated by deranged-looking dogs and cats. More changes came in 1973, when James Geraghty retired after nearly thirty-five years as art editor and was replaced by Lee Lorenz, an outstanding *New Yorker* cartoonist since the fifties. While he was still trying out for the job, Lorenz noticed the highly unconventional submissions of a young artist named Jack Ziegler, and in 1974, he began regularly buying them. Ziegler, who had published in the *National Lampoon,* was an absurdist gagman whose style was inspired by the comics, who reveled in pop culture, and who actually harked back to the first years of the *New Yorker,* when the odd, mannered, and brilliant creations of Ralph Barton, John Held Jr., Al Frueh, and Rea Irvin, with their arch headings and titles, had not yet been displaced by the more or less naturalistic cartoon with a single-line caption. Like Barthelme, Frazier, and Trow in prose, Ziegler in his work requested no suspension of disbelief, but rather self-consciously advertised his own artifice. Ziegler was not a revolutionary, but his cartoons were so radical in the context of the *New Yorker* that, after Lorenz had started buying them, makeup chief Carmine Peppe refused to put them into any issues and only began doing so when Shawn insisted.

Ziegler paved the way for Roz Chast, who graduated from the Rhode Island School of Design in 1977 and dropped her first stack of cartoons off at the *New Yorker* the following year. Wading through the hundreds of submissions that week, Lorenz was struck by Chast's pieces and brought them to his weekly meeting with the editor. "Shawn shared my enthusiasm," Lorenz wrote in his book *The Art of the New Yorker,* "although he asked me, 'How does she know these are cartoons?' Indeed, Roz's drawings looked more like illustrated pages torn from an eccentric's diary than traditional gag cartoons." Chast relied on the same artifice as Ziegler, but her pieces were at once less polished—in terms of draftsmanship, they appeared to be little more than stick figures—and more personal; they chronicled her mild misadventures as a child making her way in a vexing world, and as an adult staring into the refrigerator to find something to eat, and eventually raising her children. She and Ziegler were the trailblazers for a whole group of splendid and unconventional cartoonists who were in place by the end of the decade, including Arnie Levin, Robert Mankoff, Sam Gross, and Jean-Jacques Sempé.

The seventies were a good time for fact writing as well—not, for the most part, because of new writers but because some old ones had splendidly come into their own, given time to develop under Shawn's traditional strategy of editorial patience and the guidance of fact editors Robert Bingham, C. Patrick Crow, and William Whitworth. The most notable and productive were John McPhee and Calvin Trillin, worthy successors to the classic combination of Mitchell and Liebling. McPhee's early pieces—"A Sense of Where You Are," "The Headmaster," "Oranges"—showed that he was an indefatigable researcher and a graceful, scrupulous writer. He was also remarkably industrious and prolific; his avoidance of the paralysis and neurosis that afflicted many of his colleagues was due both to his temperament

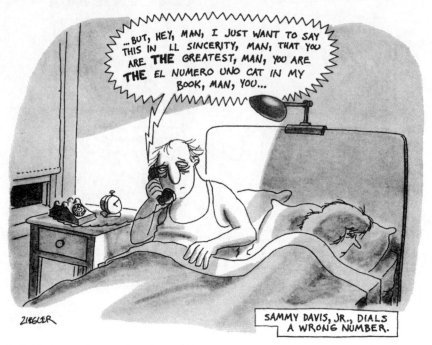

Jack Ziegler and Roz Chast looked back to the 1920s with their audacious artifice, and together helped transform the *New Yorker* cartoon.

ENTRANCE EXAM FOR THE

MILDRED SCHOOL of MEDICINE

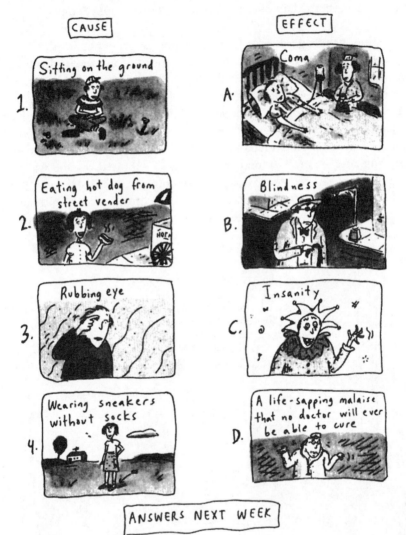

ANSWERS NEXT WEEK

R. Chast

and the fact that he worked from his home in Princeton, and only rarely ventured into the *New Yorker* offices. His singular literary qualities began to emerge slowly, initially in two pieces that played intriguingly with structure. "A Roomful of Hovings" (1967) was a profile of Metropolitan Museum of Art director Thomas Hoving in the form of a journalistic portrait gallery— eleven glimpses of Hoving, moving back and forth in time. Two years later, in "Levels of the Game," McPhee conducted a dual profile of the tennis players Arthur Ashe and Clark Graebner in the pauses between a running account of their semifinal match at Forest Hills. Meanwhile, McPhee was coming into his own special voice, which, as critic William Howarth has observed, bears a resemblance to the author himself: "Style *is* the man: wherever McPhee's prose is short, compact, brisk, and edgy, there is also a facsimile of his own basal metabolism." In "The Pine Barrens" (1967), "The Island of the Crofter and the Laird" (1969), "Travels in Georgia" (1973), and "The Survival of the Bark Canoe" (1975), McPhee gradually stepped forward as a first-person character in his stories—not a swaggering New Journalist but an subtle, ironic, self-deprecating, above all observant presence, in the manner of Joseph Mitchell. McPhee was, in any case, highly aware of working in a *New Yorker* tradition. "The Lieblings, the Alva Johnstons, the Jack Kahns, came along much earlier than I," he once told an interviewer. "In short, I feel that I've wandered into a large room that was set up before I knew the difference between a grapefruit and a softball. And since I've been inside the room, I've thrown around a few bricks. I've found my place in it, but I haven't built it."

From his first major piece, the Bill Bradley Profile, McPhee's qualities were recognized by publisher Roger Straus. His firm of Farrar, Straus and Giroux made books of everything McPhee wrote after its appearance in the *New Yorker*—the shorter articles in collections, the longer ones in volumes of their own. At this writing, Farrar, Straus has all twenty-six of McPhee's books in print, each one in both hardcover and paperback editions. At first the books sold modestly, but the notable thing is that they have made money at all, given that their contents were available in the *New Yorker* for pocket change. In any case, the books were important for the attention they garnered, which established and solidified McPhee's reputation as a master journalist in the *New Yorker* tradition. In 1976, he took on his biggest subject to date, the state of Alaska. Straus determined that finally, after thirteen tries, this was McPhee's breakout title, and he gave a major publicity push the following year to the book that resulted, *Coming Into the Country*. It worked: the book was enthusiastically reviewed on the front page of the *New York Times Book Review*, accompanied by an interview with McPhee. There were many more rave reviews, a somewhat smaller number of additional interviews. (McPhee is a notoriously private person.) The book landed on the

Times best-seller list and stayed there for twenty weeks, and McPhee became as celebrated as any *New Yorker* journalist had ever been.

Trillin was as productive as McPhee, prodded by the every-three-weeks deadline for his U.S. Journal pieces; in retrospect, this was a brilliant way of warding off two *New Yorker* curses—writer's block and the frequent experience of seeing one's pieces languish for months or years in inventory hell. Trillin was a funny man, yet his understanding of his assignment was such that his early pieces were sober journalistic dispatches. As an outlet for his comic streak, he began writing casuals about the adventures of a character named Barnett Frummer, who was constantly trying to impress his girlfriend, Rosalie Mondle, with different manifestations of midsixties trendiness: radical politics, gourmet cooking, and the like. Humor arrived in Trillin's reporting through the vehicle of food, though not the kind of food to which the adjective *gourmet* would ever be attached. In his native Kansas City and in his journalistic travels, Trillin had always sought out large quantities of superior chili, barbecue, hamburgers, and so forth—the kind of fare he would immortalize as "American Fried." In 1970, as a kind of comic relief from his serious reporting, he started to write U.S. Journal pieces about the Breaux Bridge Crawfish Festival in Louisiana, about the partisans of various Cincinnati chili parlors, about the culinary adventures of his formerly obese pizza-baron friend, Larry "Fats" Goldberg.* "I always knew I was doing one of those pieces," Trillin said, "when I found I was only carrying around one notebook. When I was writing about something serious, I had a second notebook where I kept my appointments."

Trillin's wonderful deadpan style in these pieces would be familiar to television audiences when he became a regular guest on Johnny Carson's *Tonight Show.* In person and in print, he avoided the pompousness that plagues so much food commentary by comically presenting himself as an obsessive who would resort to any means necessary to get baked farmer cheese from Ben's Dairy on the Lower East Side of New York or crisp brisket ends from Arthur Bryant's. ("It has long been acknowledged," Trillin wrote in a famous sentence, "that the single best restaurant in the world is Arthur Bryant's Barbecue at Eighteenth and Brooklyn in Kansas City.") A subtler comic touch was the mock-elevated rhetorical structure of these pieces. They proceeded in almost Ciceronian progression, punctuated with well-marked logical transitions and lush similes: when Trillin amasses the final ingredient for his perfect cream cheese and Nova Scotia on a bagel, he

---

*The only previous food writing the *New Yorker* had published with any regularity were A. J. Liebling's 1959 Onward and Upward with the Arts series, "Memoirs of a Feeder in France" (published as the book *Between Meals: An Appetite for Paris*), and the culinary essays of M. F. K. Fisher, collected in the 1969 book *With Bold Knife and Fork*.

feels "ecstatic in the way I always imagined a Manhattan real-estate specula-tor must feel ecstatic when he finally gets his hands on the last historic brownstone he needs to make up an entire block that can be torn down for a luxury high-rise"; the skill of his wife, Alice, in searching out first-rate Chinese restaurants "comes partly from confidence, I think, in the way that a professional hunter always comes out with the required water buffalo partly because he left camp assuming he would."

Trillin continued to do serious reporting and eventually developed another specialty. Once or twice a year, he would find himself traveling to an American town or city to write about the death of a person there, usu-ally as a result of murder. He eventually wrote so many of these pieces that he collected them in a book called *Killings*. Trillin was attracted to these sto-ries not because he was interested in violence in America or any other grand theme, but because, as he wrote in the introduction to the book, "a killing often seemed to present the best opportunity to write about people one at a time. . . . When someone dies suddenly shades are drawn up." Death also is a route into a community: "In these stories, the place was the context for the killing, and the killing was an opportunity to write about the place." Trillin was doing exactly the kind of thing Shawn was looking for when he assigned Truman Capote the piece that turned out to be "In Cold Blood."

A fact writer who developed in a different—though equally unpre-dictable—way from Trillin and McPhee was their approximate contempo-rary Susan Sheehan. For her first major piece after returning from Vietnam in the early seventies, she decided to attempt a Profile of a Puerto Rican welfare mother. After Shawn approved the idea, it took Sheehan three months to find an appropriate subject, a Brooklyn woman she would call Carmen Santana. For a full two years after that, Sheehan immersed herself in Carmen's life—interviewing her for hour upon hour, and simply hang-ing around the Santana apartment until she became as unobtrusive as a piece of furniture. The result was a thirty-thousand-word Profile, published in 1975 as "A Welfare Mother," that had a straightforward though startling intimacy; Sheehan never appeared in the piece as *I*, but she seemed to know everything it was possible to know about Carmen Santana. The piece repre-sented a new kind of reporting, and it could only have been done for Shawn's *New Yorker*, with its commitment to as-long-as-it-takes deadlines. As Sheehan wrote in an afterword to the book version of the Profile, "If I had a trick in my bag, it was time." Sheehan followed "A Welfare Mother" with a similar portrait, of a prisoner in a maximum-security prison, and then, in the spring of 1981, with "The Patient," a four-part Profile of a schizophrenic she called Sylvia Frumkin. This piece had taken three years in its preparation and writing and was the deepest and most exhaustive thing Sheehan had done. Brought out the following year as a book titled *Is There*

No Place on Earth for Me? it won the Pulitzer Prize for general nonfiction and is frequently assigned as a textbook in psychology and psychiatry courses in colleges and medical schools.

Much of the success of the magazine in the seventies had to do with the mix. The not noticeably political McPhee or Trillin blended nicely with the advocacy of Jonathan Schell, Richard Harris, Paul Brodeur, and such new concerned contributors as Freeman Dyson, Richard Barnet, and Barry Commoner. Two longtime staff writers, Andy Logan and Jane Kramer, were finally paired with what proved to be the perfect assignments—City Hall and Europe, respectively. Kenneth Tynan returned to the fold and between 1972 and 1979 produced a series of magnificent show-business Profiles: of Nicol Williamson, Ralph Richardson, Tom Stoppard, Johnny Carson, Mel Brooks, and Louise Brooks. In 1976, novelist C. D. B. Bryan contributed what would become a classic of reportage, "Friendly Fire." Every once in a while Shawn would dispatch Whitworth or Crow to distill the essence out of some provocative new book and shape it into a multipart series for the *New Yorker*: for example, Bruno Bettelheim's fascinating and controversial rumination on fairy tales, *The Uses of Enchantment,* and Robert Caro's biography of Robert Moses, *The Power Broker.* Meanwhile, readers could take comfort in settling into the work of the veteran contributors who had found their subject and their voice and were given all the room they needed to warm to their theme: Roger Angell on baseball, Whitney Balliett on jazz, Herbert Warren Wind (who had left the *New Yorker* in the fifties to join the new *Sports Illustrated* and finally returned) on tennis and golf, Calvin Tomkins on art, Henry Cooper on the space program, and Berton Roueché, not only in his medical detective stories but in a series he began on American places. It was hard to resist an opening line like Roueché's in a profile of a small town in Missouri: "I recently gave myself the pleasure of a leisurely stay in Hermann, Missouri (pop. 2,658), an old German town on the rolling south bank of the Missouri River, some eighty miles west of St. Louis."

Finally, the *New Yorker* offered a refreshing comparison to the prevalent journalistic culture of the seventies, in which the energy and innovations of the New Journalism were congealing into mean-spiritedness, glib hipness, and a fixation on celebrity and novelty. The *New Yorker* aggressively eschewed hype, not only in content but in form. "Most American journalism is like listening to a story your loud Uncle Harry tells you," Calvin Trillin said. "There's a headline, a subhead, call-out quotes, photo captions, all telling you what the story is about. The wonderful thing about writing for the *New Yorker* was that you could tell the story at your own pace, and maybe even surprise the reader."

Unquestionably, not a few pieces, in hewing to the magazine's editorial values, went well past the avoidance of glitz all the way to out-and-out dullness. Indeed, this could be viewed as an essential part of the *New Yorker* aesthetic. In 1973, Shawn retained a Washington reporter named Elizabeth Drew to cover the Watergate saga in diary form, and her flatly written dispatches, published weeks and sometimes months after the events they described, seemed to suck all drama out of the scandal. Some of Drew's entries were summaries of what was in the newspapers that day; one read, simply, "Spiro Agnew was out of town today." (When Richard Rovere died in 1979, Drew became the magazine's Washington correspondent, continuing until the arrival of Tina Brown in 1992.) Similarly, Ved Mehta's endless biographies of the various members of his family almost seemed to *dare* the reader to say, "This is boring!" and flip ahead to the next article.

Ian "Sandy" Frazier, an obsessive and astute observer of the magazine, felt that Shawn knew precisely what he was doing when he published this material. Frazier's silliest casual, "The Sandy Frazier Dream Team" (1977), was about a mythical all-star high-school football team, every member of which is named either Sandy Frazier or Ian "Sandy" Frazier; he wrote it, he says, for the express purpose of seeing how many times he could mention his own name in one piece (fifty, including the title, the byline, and the captions in the illustration). Shawn ran it directly adjacent to the second installment of Hannah Arendt's endless and impenetrable series "On Thinking." "It was a brilliant maneuver to have all those boring things in the background," Frazier said of the *New Yorker* generally. "The function of boredom is to strengthen authenticity. You don't think of it as being duplicitous, or as being for gain. I was delighted to be in the foreground with that in the background."

Poetry was in the background as well, as far as most readers were concerned. Yet it was an important component of the magazine's 1970s renaissance, as Howard Moss, still running the ship, published some of the best work of such notable practitioners as James Merrill, Philip Levine, L. E. Sissman, John Hollander, Robert Penn Warren, Amy Clampitt, John Ashbery, and Elizabeth Bishop. (The *New Yorker* got first crack at everything these and dozens of other poets wrote, thanks to the first-reading agreement.) To be sure, Moss's tendency was toward the decorous, cerebral, and formal, and his vision was blurry on poetry's peripheries—he had little interest in, on the one hand, the subversion and bombast of the Beats and their diverse heirs and, on the other, the experimental, the avant-garde, the obscure. But he acheived sufficient diversity to prevent a sense of sameness. By the end of the decade, there was no doubt that American poets would rather be published in the *New Yorker* than any other journal.

THE NEW YORKER SCHOOL

Early in 1972, a twenty-five-year-old graduate student in English literature at the University of Connecticut, Ann Beattie, sent a short story called "Blue Eggs" to the *New Yorker*. The first reader, Fran Kiernan, thought enough of it to pass it along to Roger Angell, and on February 18, he wrote a personal letter back to Beattie:

> These little slices and moments are often surprisingly effective, but the story itself seems to get away from you as it goes along. It seems possible that there is more form than substance here, but perhaps that is unfair. What I most admire is your wit and quickness and self-assurance. I hope you will let us see more of your work, and that you will address your future submissions directly to me.

Beattie did so, and though the answer was never yes, Angell's rejections were encouraging if only in their thoroughness. Having recognized Beattie's talent from the start, he continually pressed her to bring more direct emotion to her stories of aimless young people and sad old people (Beattie didn't seem to be interested in the middle-aged), and not to rely so much on what he saw as trendy and off-putting literary devices. Through Angell's letters to Beattie over the next twenty-two months, one can chart, even as he presses his point, a mutual accommodation: yes, she becomes more accessible and direct, but he steadily makes room in his definition of *New Yorker* fiction for Beattie's original and often discomfiting vision. Some excerpts:

> This strikes me as being merely chic—obvious despair, heartlessness in high places, lurking violence. It's all been done a thousand times, and it's just about impossible to believe any of it or to care. I think this is a pity, because there is no doubt about your abilities. I wish you would write something out of your own observations and emotions.
>
> —Angell to Beattie, August 10, 1972,
> rejecting "Sleeping Habits" and "What Are
> Your Aspirations for the Next Five Years?"

> I wish you would try a very quiet and modest story—one that relies on its own devices and is content merely to bring us to its own discoveries. But whatever you do write, please continue to send it to us.
>
> —Angell to Beattie, September 1, 1972,
> rejecting "Blowing the Whistle in 1935"

> I have the impression that you don't trust your own observations or your own writing to carry a story. What would happen if you tried a story without

any devices or stops or studied juxtapositions? I would love to see something like that from you.

—Angell to Beattie, September 28, 1972,
rejecting "Imagined Scenes" and "Marshall's Dog"

This sounds as if I wanted you to write a different kind of fiction, but I do not believe that is the case. I would prefer to see writing that is less dependent on effects and that works less visibly toward a single final emotion. I do believe this is a matter of confidence on your part. You write so well that a slightly less fevered effort may result in fiction that is clearer and more truly moving.

—Angell to Beattie, undated, 1973,
rejecting "Rat," "Victor Blue," and
"Four Stories About Lovers"

... your best story so far ... Some people who read this story found it arbitrary and irritating because of its flatness and distance.... I truly don't know what to tell you now. I think your writing is controlled and personal—that is, exactly what you want it to be.... I feel that your chances of acceptance here are not good as long as you continue in this vein.

—Angell to Beattie, undated, 1973,
rejecting "The Parking Lot"

Thank you for your letter explaining the rejection of my last story. I am at least flattered that some people at the *New Yorker* admired the story's ability to suggest "moral paralysis." Coincidentally, I was teaching *Dubliners* the same week the story was rejected.

In this story I have taken pains to do something you have said might work several times before: to write a simple story. No time shifts, characters named, backgrounds understandable, and hopefully not entirely depressing.

As you say, there are other magazines—but only a few. And with the exception of you, I wait an unreasonable amount of time to be rejected—3 & 4 months. Your courtesy has made you an easy mark.

Thank you for looking at this new one. I hope I won't put you in the position of having to think up yet another polite way to say no.

—Beattie to Angell, November 23, 1974,
submitting "A Platonic Relationship"

Oh joy ...

Yes, we are taking A PLATONIC RELATIONSHIP, and I think this is just about the best news of the year. Maybe it isn't the best news for you, but there is nothing that gives me more pleasure (well, *almost* nothing) than at last sending an enthusiastic yes to a writer who has persisted through as many rejections and rebuffs as you have. It's a fine story, I think—original, strong, and true. I have a few criticisms and reservations about it, but they are minor, really, and easily explained. I guess what I like most about the story is its sparsity. Almost everything except the essential has been done away with, leaving one with the vision of a Giacometti.

—Angell to Beattie, December 11, 1973 [ellipsis Angell's]

"A Platonic Relationship," published in early 1974, was followed over the next four years by a steady stream of memorable short stories from Beattie, including "Fancy Flights," "Wolf Dreams," "Vermont," "Downhill," "Colorado," "The Lawn Party," "Secrets and Surprises," "Shifting," and "A Vintage Thunderbird." What was initially most striking about her stories, certainly in the context of the *New Yorker*, were the characters and setting: overeducated men and women in their twenties and early thirties, drifting through unsatisfying jobs and problematic relationships in a haze of marijuana smoke. (The magazine was publishing *some* younger writers, notably Henry Bromell and Laurie Colwin, but their characters and stories seemed warm and comfortable compared to Beattie's cold-eyed glances.) It took a closer reading to see what a fine writer Beattie was. A student of Joyce, Hemingway, and Barthelme, she was interested in literature, not sociology or journalism, and her works were complex, original, and affecting.

The 1975 "Vermont" opens typically with a jumble of characters: Noel, whose wife, Susan, has just left him for John Stillerman; the narrator's husband, David; the narrator, whose name we never find out; and Beth, their five-year-old. After a few pages, we figure out who everybody is, but the characters' personalities emerge more slowly, through bits of dialogue, moments of insight, random associations, and memories. The way Beattie tells the story—in the present tense, a trademark, and in sections that range in length from a paragraph to a thousand words—adds to the sense that our understanding will have to be piece by piece and cumulative. Things change: David leaves the narrator; she begins seeing Noel; and they and Beth abruptly leave New York for an old farmhouse in Vermont. The narrator is bookish and twenty-seven; Noel is thirty-six and reads the *Wall Street Journal* and *Commentary*. She thinks she loves him but is unable to say so, in part, it seems, because she is not yet over the more graceful, competent David. This sounds dull and trite; Beattie presents it with remarkable deftness, subtlety, and wit. And her dialogue, here and in general, is smashing. Staying at Noel's sister's house in New Jersey, the narrator complains that they have to sleep in a single bed:

"What do you care?" Noel says. "You're nuts about me, right?"

He slides up against me and hugs my back.

"I don't know how people talk any more," he says. "I don't know of any of the current lingo. What experession do people use for 'nuts about'?"

"I don't know."

"I just did it again! I said 'lingo.' "

"So what? Who do you want to sound like?"

"The way I talk sounds dated—like an old person."

"Why are you always worried about being old?"

He snuggles closer. "You didn't answer before when I said you were nuts about me. That doesn't mean you don't like me, does it?"

"No."

"You're big on one-word answers."

"I'm big on going to sleep."

" 'Big on.' See? There must be some expression to replace that now."*

Immediately, Beattie was noticed. After her second story was published in the magazine, Barthelme phoned her, out of the blue; when she came to the phone, he said simply, "Who are you?" The novelist Anne Tyler (an occasional *New Yorker* contributor) wrote her a fan letter. In 1976, on the same day, Doubleday published both *Distortions,* a short-story collection mostly made up of Beattie's *New Yorker* acceptances and rejects, and a stunning novel of obsessive love very much in keeping with her short fiction, *Chilly Scenes of Winter.* The simultaneous publication raised Beattie's profile even higher, and she eventually achieved something like the status of Shaw and Salinger in decades past: her fans eagerly passed the word to each other when she was in the magazine.

Unlike the other strong short-story writers the *New Yorker* had recently been publishing—Cheever, Updike, Barthelme—Beattie spawned imitators. Those who aped her subject matter didn't get far. Angell and other editors rejected hundreds of stories about stoned young people living in group houses, justifiably reasoning that Beattie had filled the need for such characters, and then some. But something in her style and her approach to the short story generally could profitably be mined. So much *New Yorker* fiction over the past quarter century was plagued by a lack of distance from the subject. This was especially true of memoirs and autobiographical stories; only an Updike, a Rogin, or a Nabokov had the ability to turn his own experiences to art. But even the general lot of stories, too, in trying to satisfy the editors' request for emotional involvement, tended to be earnest, flat, and ultimately dull. Beattie clearly stood apart from her characters and regarded them with a potent irony—but the stories were no less involving

*Shawn appreciated Beattie's work from the start, according to Angell, but some of the youth-culture references passed him by. In "Vermont," there is a reference to a "roach" on the mantel, and later a second reference to it. In a query that must be ranked with Ross's classic "Were the Nabokovs a one-nutcracker family," Shawn wrote on the galley, "Bug did not move for five pages?" Angell responded in pencil, "Roach—short stub of marijuana cigarette."

for that. The present tense, which she used in about half of her stories, was a key. This cinematic device implied the events being described were portents, yet removed from the story the burden of stating exactly what they portended.

The approach was not as easy as it looked, and the first writer to successfully adapt it at the *New Yorker* was Mary Robison, who studied fiction writing at Johns Hopkins University with John Barth and Donald Barthelme's brother Frederick. She sent two stories to Angell early in 1977. Although he turned them down, he was extremely impressed and took pains "to congratulate you for their quality and to express my confidence in your future as a fiction writer." Sure enough, the magazine accepted her next submission, which was eventually published under the title "Sisters"—"It's a wonderful piece of work—touching and funny and absolutely original," Angell wrote—and four additional stories over the next year. Beattie had opened the door for Robison, but actually her stories—brief and spare, about blue-collar characters in middle America, and written in the past tense, with a vague sense of menace—bore more of a resemblance to Raymond Carver, whose influential collection *Will You Please Be Quiet, Please?* was published in 1976. (Carver himself would not appear in the *New Yorker* till 1981.) Robison was also significant in being the first regular fiction contributor in the magazine to come from a writing-school background.

Gradually, other members of the informal school of Beattie showed up in the *New Yorker's* pages: John Rolfe Gardiner in 1977, Marian Thurm in 1978. That year, a native Kentuckian named Bobbie Ann Mason began sending stories to Angell. She had gone to graduate school with Beattie and had once remarked that she would like to publish short stories in the *New Yorker* someday. Beattie's only advice: "You'll have to write a lot of them." She spoke the truth. Angell was complimentary and encouraging to Mason, but he rejected story after story. Although Mason had completed her Ph.D. (unlike Beattie), publishing her dissertation as a book called *Nabokov's Garden*, she was drawn in her fiction to the uneducated people of western Kentucky, caught as they were between their old ways and the homogenization of the country through K Marts, television talk shows, and popular songs. In one rejection letter, Angell proposed that what was missing in her work was "some suggestion that you, the writer, and we, the readers, should be able to draw some deeper feelings of conclusions about these people than they themselves feel. . . . The kind of insight and awareness I'm talking about is especially hard to develop in your stories because it is so easy for the reader to conclude that he is being invited to patronize these people, and that is fatal, of course." After nineteen rejections, the *New Yorker* finally took a story late in 1979—"Offerings." But Mason's breakthrough was her next acceptance, "Shiloh," the story of Leroy, a truck driver on disability, and his wife,

Norma Jean, who expresses her dissatisfaction through furious bouts of self-improvement—bodybuilding, a course in composition at the local community college. This does sound patronizing in summary, but in fact "Shiloh," which was published in October 1980, is an empathic, subtle, and precise portrait, funny and moving, of people caught in the headlights of history. It was selected for the 1981 edition of *Best American Short Stories* and, in the reckoning of one short-fiction scholar, was the most heavily anthologized American short story of the 1980s.

By the time of Mason's accession, it was beginning to be recognized that there was in fact a new *New Yorker* school of short fiction. It was sometimes disparagingly referred to as "minimalism" or "K Mart realism," and though these terms were clumsy and not applicable to all the practitioners, Beattie and her successors in the magazine—by 1981 they included Carver and Frederick Barthelme, whose haunting stories were set in the neon-lit Gulf Coast—really did belong together, however loosely. But what critics usually overlooked was that in this same period the *New Yorker* was publishing other kinds of fiction as well—first-rate, K Mart–free, unmiminal stories by such writers as Peter Taylor, William Maxwell, Philip Roth, Bernard Malamud, Alice Munro, William Trevor, Grace Paley, Mark Helprin, Laurie Colwin, Cynthia Ozick, Peter Handke, Gabriel García Márquez, Bruno Schulz, Heinrich Böll, Stanislaw Lem, and Max Frisch. (This in addition to the works of veteran contributors such as Updike, Rogin, Barthelme, Isaac Bashevis Singer, and Mavis Gallant.)

Helping to bring about this flowering was an almost complete turnover in the personnel of the fiction department on January 1, 1976, the day the mandatory retirement policy went into effect. Maxwell and Robert Henderson, who had been fiction editors since the 1930s, were gone, replaced by Daniel Menaker, Charles "Chip" McGrath, and Frances Kiernan, all youthful staffers. (The sixty-six-year-old Rachel MacKenzie had been in ill health for some time and was permitted to stay on a part-time basis. She died in 1980.) About a year later, they and Angell—the only holdover—were joined by Veronica Geng, whose 1975 parody of Pauline Kael in the *New York Review of Books* had caught Angell's and Menaker's eyes and who had gone on to write several sharp casuals for the *New Yorker*.

The new crew didn't all have the same taste in writers and stories—which itself was a refreshing development—but they did agree on the importance of variety, including welcoming the top fiction writers from around the world. This represented a subtle change from the traditional workings of the fiction department, where "*New Yorker* writers" had always had a slight edge in the decision-making, like the reigning champion in a boxing match. Now it became the exception rather than the rule for writers to make the quantity bonus (even though the number of sales required for it had been reduced from six to four), and even stalwarts such as Beattie and Barthelme began to get as many rejections as acceptances. The chief catalyst for these changes, interestingly enough, was the newest member of the staff, Geng. "She basically shook us up," Menaker said. "My understanding is that she got the job by lambasting New Yorker fiction, to Shawn and Roger. When she came on, she was the only editor I could send stories to [for comment] and not be able to more or less predict the exact reply."

For the first time in two and a half decades, the New Yorker actually solicited from fiction writers. Even more striking, many of them had repeatedly been turned down or viewed as not quite "right" for the New Yorker. The oft-rejected Bernard Malamud's "Rembrandt's Hat" was printed in 1973, thanks to the efforts of Rachel MacKenzie; in 1977, she oversaw the publication of a long adaptation from his forthcoming novel Dubin's Lives. That same year, Angell wrote a fan letter to the Austrian writer Peter Handke that resulted in the publication of the memorable long story "The Left-Handed Woman." (Angell also solicited Joseph Heller, unsuccessfully.) Just weeks after starting her job, Geng wrote to Grace Paley: "I've just come to work here, and want you to know that you have yet another admirer here, hoping you will send us a story sometime. It would be nice if we could stop feeling crazy not to have published you, by publishing you. And it would be nice to be blessed by more of your wonderful stories." It took a year and a half, but Paley eventually started selling. Geng brought Philip Roth back to the fold after more than fifteen years, convincing Shawn to publish the novella "The Ghost Writer" in 1979. (She became a close friend of Roth's and the unofficial editor of all his subsequent books.) She not only solicited William Trevor, whose previous submissions had consistently been rejected, but appreciated him, writing to him after a 1978 acceptance, "ATTRACTA is a beautiful story, and a courageous one. You seem to have written it with a classical sense of all things in their proper proportion." Geng even saw a potential contributor in the hot new comedian Steve Martin. She wrote his business representative in 1978, "We feel he might well become a writer for us—because he seems to care about writing, and because all his work seems to come straight from the unconscious and so has real originality and feeling." (Nothing came of this approach at the time, but it finally bore fruit in the mid-1990s, when Martin began frequently contributing humor pieces to the New Yorker.) McGrath, for his part, spotted a Canadian short-story writer named Alice Munro, who became a New Yorker fixture. Raymond Carver had stopped submitting stories after being rejected so many times; McGrath convinced him to start again, and shepherded some memorable Carver stories to publication beginning in 1981.

Meanwhile, the New Yorker benefited from a late flowering by two veteran contributors. Freed from the demands of editing, Maxwell wrote some of his most luminous stories, such as "Over by the River" and "The Thistles in Sweden." And Peter Taylor, whose submissions had had a tough time since the midfifties, began a group of long and remarkable stories, including "In the Miro District," "The Captain's Son," and "The Old Forest," in which memory, irony, and regret all magically mixed together in Taylor's deceptively flat prose.

In the late seventies and eighties, it was frequently remarked that a short-story renaissance was taking place in the United States. If that was the case, the *New Yorker* stood at the very center of it.

MANNING THE BARRICADES

The *New Yorker* of the mid to late 1970s was a wonderful magazine. It was wonderful in a special, irreproducible way. It had excellent and frequently surprising writing and comic art, and—almost uniquely in what was becoming a throwaway culture—it was informed by history, tradition, and integrity. It was *not* the sole embodiment of civilization and civilized values in a debased and crumbling world, which is how Shawn had come to see it. His magnification of the magazine into a movement had been in large part responsible for its triumph, but would also have to bear the brunt of the blame for its demise.

The period of twenty-two years from Tom Wolfe's 1965 "Tiny Mummies!" to Shawn's humiliating dismissal by the *New Yorker's* new owner, S. I. Newhouse, presents itself, in retrospect, as a series of crises, each one a battering ram slamming into Shawn and the *New Yorker*. At first the castle appeared invulnerable—certainly strong enough to withstand the slings and arrows of Wolfe's article, and then the complaints over the magazine's "radicalization," and then the modest downturn in ad sales and circulation. But the next crisis, which shook Shawn to the quick, was a significant dividing line in the history of the magazine—between the time when it functioned efficiently despite the eccentricities of the editor, and the time when those eccentricities began to overwhelm the institution.

In October 1976, Shawn received a letter from the Newspaper Guild of New York, naming twenty-two salaried employees who had approached the Guild to help them organize a union at the *New Yorker*. Shawn was so shocked because the letter was a bald contradiction of his sense of the magazine as people united in an almost religious mission—checkers, messengers, typists, writers, cartoonists, and everyone else. And on the whole, *New Yorker* employees *did* feel more strongly and warmly about their employer than their counterparts at *Time* or *Ladies' Home Journal*. Nevertheless, a substantial number of staffers, especially those at the lower end of the job ladder, felt with some justification that they weren't being adequately compensated and that they had no reasonable recourse for requesting raises and improved benefits. Appended to a letter sent to the staff by the organizing committee was a chart comparing some actual salaries at the *New Yorker* with minimums at other magazines represented by the Guild, and the figures were unsettling. A messenger at the *New Yorker* with three years' experience was making $125 a week; at *Time,* the minimum salary for a messenger with two years' experience was $173.50. A checker/researcher with four and a half years' experience at the *New Yorker* earned $235; at *Time* someone with three years' experience would have made a minimum of $341. And so on.

Shawn immediately called a meeting of all salaried employees—itself a startling action at a magazine where meetings were held roughly as often as press conferences. He followed it up with an equally unprecedented five-and-a-half-page, double-spaced letter to the staff that conceded, "At the moment, some salaries are lower than they should be," but pledged that they would increase. A necessarily adversarial union, Shawn went on, would unavoidably pollute the spirit of the magazine:

> I believe we have at the *New Yorker* a friendly, gentle, free, informal, democratic atmosphere. It took several decades to achieve this atmosphere, and I think it would be tragic if we lost it. It's in this atmosphere that some of the country's finest writers and comic artists have developed and flourished, and that all of us together, including every person who reads these words, have produced what may be the noblest publication that has ever existed. . . . Not long ago, a woman reader wrote to me saying that the *New Yorker* made her "proud to be a human being." Clearly, to her, and to others, the *New Yorker* is more than a magazine. At the very least, in a period in which so much of life is debased and corrupted we are trying, I believe, to do something of spiritual value. I look upon our effort with awe and gravity. The *New Yorker* is strong, but at the same time it is fragile. For everybody's sake, I hope we will do nothing to hurt it.

Despite this entreaty, the organizing committee proceeded with its plans to hold an election among staff members on the union issue. Before this took place, Shawn wrote a second letter to the staff—this one more than seven *single-spaced* pages. His opening sentence was "Much of our history has never been set down," and he then went into extraordinary detail about the financial workings of the magazine, all dedicated to the thesis that the *New Yorker* bore no resemblance to a typical business enterprise. Thanks to the enlightened ownership of the Fleischmann family, the goal had never been to maximize profits. Rather, he wrote, the guiding principle had always been that "the company *should pay everyone as much as it can afford,* stopping short only where the net profit or dividends would fall below a safe level—that is, would become so low as to threaten, directly or indirectly, the continuation of the 'business' framework within which the magazine can be published" (italics Shawn's). His strongest argument had to do with the traditional separation of church and state—editorial and advertising—at the magazine. If the organizing committee's stated wish to negotiate directly with the ownership, rather than with Shawn, was carried out, he wrote, "it may not be long before business people will be directly interfering not only with the editorial methods of the New Yorker but also with the editorial policies and, at last, the substance and character of the New Yorker."

Shawn's letter was a masterful piece of persuasion, but that was no surprise. In the words of John Bennet, then a proofreader and a member of the organizing committee, later a fact editor, and later still a candidate for editor in chief, "Shawn was the most brilliant writer on the staff." The letter, in any case, had its desired effect. The organizing committee called off the union elections and its alliance with the Newspaper Guild and arranged with Shawn that in-house committees would periodically meet with him to review staff salaries. (According to Chip McGrath, these were "a complete joke. We'd say we want this or we want that, he would get purple and say no.") But the damage had been done: no longer could Shawn sustain his idealized vision of the community of the New Yorker. He later remarked to Gardner Botsford that from the day he received the letter from the Guild, he began to "hate" his job.

What would prove to be a more intractable crisis—indeed, one that was resolved only with Shawn's dismissal—concerned the selection of the next editor of the New Yorker. Shawn was sixty-eight years old when mandatory retirement went into effect, and although he was exempted from the policy, it naturally occurred to many in and outside the New Yorker that someone would one day have to take his place. In 1972, when Leo Hofeller retired, Shawn had named Robert Bingham executive editor, with the intention of examining his suitability as an eventual editor in chief. After three years, Shawn concluded—as he would of a succession of other candidates in the years to come—that Bingham did not have the necessary attributes for the job. Shawn turned next to Jonathan Schell, with whom he had probably spent more time than any other staff member, as a result of Schell's almost weekly Comment pieces. This notion had occurred to Shawn as early as September 1975, when he gave Schell some manuscripts to edit (he had done no editing before) and had lengthy conversations with him about the special place of the New Yorker and the special duties of its editor. By February 1977, Shawn was confident enough of his choice that he went to the staff and announced that Schell would be his "deputy." Nothing was said about Schell one day becoming editor in chief, but that was the inescapable implication of the move. The overwhelming majority of the staff balked at the idea, citing Schell's lack of experience, his perceived humorlessness, and a general feeling that he was not up to the job. Within a month, Shawn called off the experiment. On March 9, he posted a three-sentence note on the bulletin board:

> To the Staff
>
> It is not my intention to make frequent appearances on the bulletin board in order to deny rumors. However, all the talk of the past couple of weeks suggests that I should provide some information. Contrary to rumor, no one has decided when I will retire, and no one has made any decision on who will succeed me.

But Shawn would not drop the Schell idea. Less than three months later, he wrote Gardner Botsford, who not only was the editor with the longest tenure but who, as Raoul Fleischmann's stepson, was perceived to have an unofficial veto power on such major decisions, that he intended to ask Schell to be "managing editor"—a position that had not really been filled since Shawn had held it under Ross. The names of other potential successors had been mentioned, Shawn wrote, but each of them had "weaknesses that would lead to disaster. I simply don't think the magazine (or the business) would survive. With Schell, on the other hand, I think it would. In my mind, he is probably our one hope—there seem to be no alternatives—and that accounts for my persistence. This is my solemn judgment." Shawn went on to offer a lengthy description of Schell's qualities:

> I know what his judgment and taste are, and I have found them faultless. He is an excellent judge of talent, and of people. As for the range of his interests, it is extraordinary. As for his character, his mind, his temperament, I think he has the qualities we have been, or should be, looking for (and I use the following words with precision): warmth and good will, truthfulness, fair-mindedness, self-forgetfulness, humor, imagination, vision, conscience, inner strength, intellectual and emotional depth. He has the ability, I believe, to lose himself in the aspirations and accomplishments of others. He has a natural simplicity, directness, lack of pretension. He is not vain.

As Botsford read those words, and as others on the staff heard Shawn express similar sentiments, they couldn't escape the feeling that the person he was describing was not Schell, but himself. Indeed, much of the opposition to Schell sprang from discomfort over the eerie way he appeared to be a younger, taller version of the editor; many had the impression that Schell (consciously or unconsciously) imitated Shawn's way of speaking and his mannerisms, up to and including the hesitant, almost inaudible way he knocked on a colleague's office door before entering. The temptation to spin psychological webs was irresistible. Most ran along these lines: Shawn had become so attached to the magazine, so constitutionally resistant to the idea of giving up control, that the only successor he would consider was a clone of himself.

What made the spectacle stranger still was the way it played out a kind of Arthurian drama. Schell was merely the most favored of an array of surrogate sons and daughters Shawn had assembled on the staff of the New Yorker, a striking number of whom—Schell, Tony Hiss, George Trow, Rick Hertzberg, and Jacob Brackman—were school- and/or classmates of his own son Wallace. As in a real family, each played a distinct role. Schell and Ved Mehta were the dutiful sons; Hiss and Trow the older brothers, cutups on the surface but loyal and reverent underneath; Renata Adler the flighty and brainy daughter; Jamaica Kincaid the one who would say the most outrageous things. Hertzberg always kept his distance. After Harvard, he got some experience under his belt before joining the magazine in 1969, then left it in 1977 to become a speechwriter for Jimmy Carter, in part because the White House paid a higher salary. (Hertzberg went on to serve as the editor of the New Republic and eventually returned to the New Yorker in 1992 to work for Tina Brown as an editor.) It was Brackman who engaged in a true filial struggle with Shawn. He had been a friend of Wally Shawn's at Harvard and after graduation went to work for Newsweek. At one point he was working on a piece about J. D. Salinger's story "Hapworth 16, 1924," published in the New Yorker in June 1965. Shawn got wind of it and phoned Brackman. "I didn't realize how strange it was," Brackman said. "I picked up the phone and a voice said, 'Mr. Brackman, this is William Shawn.' He told me, 'This is a sensitive matter.' We had a long conversation. He told me about the customs of the New Yorker. He invited me to come see him. We ended up meeting at the Algonquin once a month till Thanksgiving, when he asked me to bring along some of my writing. Then he offered me a job."

Brackman had long hair, was involved in rock music and the youth culture; one of the reasons Shawn was interested in him, he says, is that "I was plugged into whatever was brewing." He mined this territory for The Talk of the Town and at one point recommended that Shawn hire a young woman named Ellen Willis as a rock critic, which he did. But Brackman wasn't prepared to exhibit the reverence he felt Shawn demanded. "I was in some ways rebellious about customs," Brackman said. "I didn't want to be swallowed up by all that." One expression of his rebellion was to write for other magazines while on the New Yorker draw—"it was a source of tension between me and Mr. Shawn, but it was one of the things that gave me power in the struggle with him." In 1967, Brackman took an assignment from the New York Times Magazine to write an article about the phenomenon of the "put-on." It ended up being two to three times longer than the agreed-upon length. Rather than cutting it, Brackman showed the piece to Shawn, who suggested making it two to three times longer still. It ran in the *New Yorker* in June 1967 as an Onward and Upward with the Arts and was a remarkably perceptive and original look at some new patterns of behavior.

The next year, Brackman's similarly hip and trenchant *New Yorker* piece about the making of the film *The Graduate* led to an offer to become film critic at *Esquire*. *Esquire*, of course, was slick, hip, merciless—an embodiment of virtually every adjective Shawn abhorred. Brackman said, "Shawn tried to dissuade me from doing it, and when I said I was going to anyway, he said I couldn't have my office at the *New Yorker* anymore. I asked why and he said, 'I think it would be demoralizing to some of the other authors to hear your typewriter going and knowing you were writing for *Esquire*.'" Brackman continued to be a *New Yorker* "staff writer" for several years but contributed nothing more. (He subsequently wrote the screenplays for *The King of Marvin Gardens*—whose main character was loosely based on Wallace Shawn—and *Times Square* and assisted his Harvard friend Terrence Malick on *Badlands* and *Days of Heaven*. He also cowrote the lyrics of the pop song "That's the Way I've Always Heard It Should Be" with Carly Simon and has recently written lyrics with his wife, singer Mindy Jostyn.) "I had an extremely intense psychological relationship with Mr. Shawn, a seething oedipal struggle," he said. "At some points, I would cry out, 'I'm a pawn in a horrible game.' Then I'd stop and say, 'He can't be that—he's as much a saint as it is possible for a human being to be.'"

Brackman's ultimate parting from William Shawn resulted, he said, from his relationship with a woman Wallace was involved in—and such symbolically incestuous romantic entanglements were part of the general picture as well. One of Wallace's first girlfriends was an Englishwoman named Kennedy Fraser; when she came to America, William Shawn hired her as a fashion writer to replace Lois Long and in time developed an intense relationship with her. After she and Wallace parted, she had an affair with Richard Harris, a staff writer then married to a fact-checker and later a writer, Lis Harris; Richard Harris and Fraser married, then divorced. Meanwhile, Jonathan Schell met and married Kennedy Fraser's sister, and Shawn's son Allen married surrogate daughter Jamaica Kincaid.*

---

*Shawn's relationship with his son Wallace, himself a writer, appeared to be even more psychologically thorny than that with his young staffers. Since the late 1960s, Wallace had been living hand to mouth, writing intermittently produced avant-garde plays that seemed expressly designed to offend his father. They were filled with obscenity, masturbation, vomiting, violence, and simulated sex; the stage directions to one of them (according to the author of a book about Wallace Shawn's work) "mention at least eighteen orgasms." In 1980,

According to Schell's detractors, it would not be so bad if he really were a duplication of Shawn. But they felt that he was Shawn without the editorial genius, without the ability to inspire writers, without the humor—without anything, that is, except the idealism and high seriousness. Shawn took pains to counter this perception in his letter to Botsford:"Schell's sense of humor has come into question, but I can say flatly that he has humor, and appreciation of humor. He not only knows what is funny; when he wants to be, he can *be* funny. He is a laugher." The protest was not convincing, and the Schell project was again abandoned—for the time being.

In the spring of 1978, Peter Fleischmann initiated a series of conversations with Shawn, then seventy years old, on the subject of the succession. Schell, Jane Kramer, and Lillian Ross told colleagues what Shawn had told them: that Fleischmann, by exerting intolerable pressure on him to resign, was essentially "firing" him. However, like Vladimir and Estragon in *Waiting for Godot,* Shawn did not budge. The most charitable interpretation was that he took his perception of pressure and exaggerated it into a dismissal in order to rally the staff to his side. In any case, nothing at all happened until October, when Shawn sent Fleischmann a letter of resignation, to take effect after six months, at which time Gardner Botsford would succeed him. Botsford had only six more years before reaching the mandatory retirement age of sixty-five, so his would be in the nature of an interim appointment. Less than two months later, however, Shawn wrote Fleischmann a twenty-five-page letter rescinding his resignation and pleading that he be allowed to stay. He recited his accomplishments and said that it would be a "disaster" if Botsford took the helm. "I am seventy-one, but I am neither old nor tired," he wrote, and cited the accomplishments of Verdi, Picasso, Titian, Casals, Stokowski, and Balanchine when they were even older. "I am not being gently eased out," he concluded. "I am being brutally thrown out."

But Shawn had not been thrown out, brutally or otherwise: the only official action that had been taken was his own initial letter of resignation. He now decided that he wanted it torn up. Fleischmann agreed, and on December 27 Shawn posted another notice on the bulletin board:

William Shawn said of the outrageousness of Wallace's plays, "I know that he never does it to attract attention or be sensational or for commercial reasons. His intent is so pure and it all has such deep meaning for him that I would accept whatever he wrote even if it fell outside the boundaries of what I usually like or even understand." Over the years, Wallace achieved more critical and commercial success with his work, most dramatically in the 1981 film *My Dinner with Andre,* which he cowrote with Andre Gregory. By that time Wallace had embarked on an unlikely and lucrative side career as a character actor. He has appeared in such films as *Manhattan, Atlantic City, The Hotel New Hampshire, Prick Up Your Ears, The Princess Bride,* and *Clueless.*

TO THE STAFF

Peter Fleischmann has asked me to stay on in my job, and I have agreed to do that. In an atmosphere of friendship and understanding, Mr. Fleischmann and I will continue to discuss plans for the magazine's future—a subject of concern to all of us here.

With this message, all the intrigue and maneuvers of the past year and a half were erased, as if by magic. The issue of succession did not disappear, of course. One logical candidate appeared to be William Whitworth, who had great support among the staff. Typically, Whitworth was never directly told that he was under consideration, but the inference was clear. "Shawn began having lunch with me and telling me I had to be ready for 'this awful thing,' this terrible trial," Whitworth recalled. "As time went on, I began to think that this was not such a wonderful idea. The pressure would be enormous, and I also felt that his heart was still with Schell." In 1981, Mortimer Zuckerman offered Whitworth a substantial amount of money to become editor of the *Atlantic Monthly,* which Zuckerman had recently purchased. Shawn, when told of the offer, did nothing to try to convince Whitworth to stay. "Taking the *Atlantic* job was an appealing way to deal with all those problems at the *New Yorker,*" Whitworth said. So he took it.

In 1982, Shawn again floated the idea of Schell. Again, the staff sank it.

Shawn's actions throughout the succession saga were those of a leader who was isolated, mistrustful, and unwilling to accept that he would one day have to be replaced. In the midst of the events of December 1978, Roger Angell wrote a letter to his stepfather, E. B. White—who by this time had little direct involvement with the magazine but tried to keep abreast of *New Yorker* happenings from Maine—recounting some of the twists and turns in the succession saga. "As you know," Angell wrote, "[Shawn] has been unable to delegate *anything,* and he has become suspicious and over-excited and even a bit paranoid about any discussions having to do with his successor or his retirement." Angell's assessment, though harsh, was apt. Shawn increasingly began to divide the *New Yorker* staff—and the world outside—into friends and enemies (which included Angell and Botsford); he would take colleagues aside and criticize this writer, or that editor, as "ambitious" and prone to put his or her own interests ahead of the interests of the *New Yorker.* A code of secrecy, always part of the ethos at the magazine, intensified. In stressful moments, when he seemed particularly under siege, Shawn would take from the pocket of his suit a stack of supportive letters and wave them in the air, as if performing a magical incantation.

In 1983, George Green, the president of the company, devised a plan whereby certain "key" employees on both the business and editorial sides would be granted stock in the *New Yorker.* It would subsequently be charged that Green proposed it because he sensed the stock would be driven up by takeover attempts, from which he wished to profit; he has maintained that the motivation was simply to reward employees whose salaries had been below market rates for too long. In any case, he instituted the plan on the business side and journeyed from the sixteenth to the eighteenth floor to seek Shawn's approval for the editorial employees. Green did not get it. The editor rejected the proposal on the grounds that there were no "key" editors or writers at the *New Yorker*: everyone was equal. Nor would Shawn consider alternative ideas, for example, granting stock to employees on the basis of seniority. That way, such people as Howard Moss, Brendan Gill, Eleanor Gould Packard, and Roger Angell, who had worked for decades for relatively modest salaries, would have something to show for their toil. But Shawn refused to budge, and the business department ended up with all the "dirty" money.

Inevitably, the institutional eccentricities began to have deleterious effects on the content and the reputation of the magazine, manifested in what seemed like a never-ending series of embarrassments and scandals that commenced in 1979. Penelope Gilliatt had continued to share the movie critic position with Kael and had contributed short stories and Profiles as well, but, in the *New Yorker* tradition, was plagued by personal demons, including alcoholism. Also in the *New Yorker* tradition, she dealt directly and exclusively with Shawn, who would presumably act as her protector. Early in 1979, she turned in a Profile of Graham Greene, and it was assigned to a newly hired fact-checker named Peter Canby.

"When I looked at the source material she had included, it was clear that she had plagiarized whole swatches of it," recalled Canby, who concluded that Gilliatt's state was such that her lifting was not entirely conscious. "I sent word to Shawn, who could only be reached through two layers of secretaries. He told me to make up a proof flagging the troublesome sections, and include a photocopy of the source. That's what I did, drawing boxes around her passages and the corresponding passages in the originals. I didn't hear anything from him. I assumed that he was aware of the problem and it would be dealt with. But it never was, and the piece went to press with none of the plagiarism issues addressed."

The Profile was published in March 1979. Shortly afterward the author of one of the articles that had been lifted, Michael Mewshaw, complained to the press. The magazine thereupon announced that Gilliatt would take an indefinite leave of absence "for health reasons," and Mewshaw withdrew his request for an acknowledgment of the plagiarism. (Gilliatt never returned to film reviewing, although she continued to contribute short stories to the magazine until her death in 1991.) But how had the copying not been noticed? Shawn told the *New York Times* that the Profile had gone through "the usual checking procedures"—implicitly blaming Peter Canby. "But then word got out about the proof I had made," Canby said. "A messenger went and got it, and it turned out to have Shawn's marks indicating he had seen it. When that became evident, he invited me to his office. He never addressed the issue directly. But he directed my attention to a stack of letters supporting him. The two on top were from Woody Allen and Diane Keaton, who'd both been the subject of Gilliatt Profiles. That was all he said. The implication that I got was, 'Would I please be quiet about it?'"

The Greene affair had come hard on the heels of another incident that had put the *New Yorker* in an unfavorable light. John McPhee had quoted an anonymous chef he was profiling (under the name "Otto") that the celebrated restaurant Lutèce served frozen turbot. Normally, that assertion would have been fact-checked; because McPhee wanted to conceal Otto's identity from everyone, including fact-checkers, it was not. It turned out that Lutèce did not serve frozen turbot. The restaurant's proprietor, André Soltner, loudly proclaimed this fact, and the magazine was obliged to run a "Department of Amplification and Correction" to set the record straight. The McPhee affair was much less serious than the Gilliatt, but both chipped away at the *New Yorker's* reputation for irreproachable accuracy. And both affairs were exhaustively covered in the press—for the same reason Madison Avenue so gleefully thumbed its nose at the *New Yorker* a decade earlier. For half a century, the magazine had acted as though it set the standard for editorial purity. What better sport than to see it hoist with its own petard?

Five years later, in 1984, two additional incidents further tarnished the magazine's image. Interviewed for a front-page article in the *Wall Street Journal,* longtime *New Yorker* staff writer Alastair Reid acknowledged creating composite characters and actually fabricating incidents in his periodic reports from a Spanish village. When interviewed, Shawn appeared to contradict himself, simultaneously defending Reid and professing allegiance to the principle of absolute accuracy. The *New York Times* printed a front-page article whose headline could barely contain its delight: "A Writer for the *New Yorker* Says He Created Composites in Reports." There was a follow-up article on the incident and then an editorial that intoned, "The end of the world seems near now that our colleagues at the *New Yorker,* that fountainhead of unhurried fact, turn out to tolerate, even to justify fictions masquerading as facts. Quotes that weren't ever spoken, scenes that never existed, experiences that no one ever had—all are said to be permissible in journalism, provided they're composed by honest reporters to illustrate a deeper truth."

The second 1984 incident was a libel suit filed by psychiatrist Jeffrey Masson against the *New Yorker* and writer Janet Malcolm. The previous year, Malcolm had published a long Profile of Masson, who was a persistent critic of the Freudian establishment; he claimed that statements falsely attributed to him were defamatory. It took a remarkable thirteen years before the suit was finally resolved, in Malcolm and the magazine's favor. Yet during the various trials and appeals it came out that Malcolm had collapsed numerous interviews with Masson into a single scene in the article; that she had significantly changed the wording of his quotations (though not, the court ruled, the substance); and that she no longer had the audiotapes that she had claimed would provide documentation of some of the most outrageous statements.

Irrespective of any journalistic sins they may have committed, Reid and Malcolm were victims of historical circumstances. At the *New Yorker,* and in nonfiction writing in general, the lines between fact and invention had traditionally been quite blurry. In the 1940s, Joseph Mitchell had published a series of three Profiles of a man identified in the opening of the first as "a tough Scotch-Irishman I know, Mr. Hugh G. Flood, a retired housewrecking contractor, aged ninety-three." Mitchell gave no indication that Mr. Flood did not live and breathe—until the Profiles were published as a book in 1948 and he wrote in an "author's note," "Mr. Flood is not one man; combined in him are aspects of several old men who work or hang out in the Fulton Fish Market, or who did in the past." The admission, if that is what it was, did not elicit a *New York Times* editorial, or in fact any comment at all. Similarly, A. J. Liebling's three-part 1952 Profile of "Col. John R. Stingo" (a pseudonym for a horse-racing columnist named James A. Macdonald) had so large a fanciful component that the jacket of the book version, *The Honest Rainmaker,* conceded it was difficult to say "how much of the lore recounted in this engaging biography is gospel and how much is unashamedly apocryphal." Again, no one complained.

As for quotations, there was a long journalistic tradition of joining discrete quotes into lengthy monologues, seen, for example, in the work of Henry Mayhew and Frederick Law Olmsted in the nineteenth century. By the early 1930s, Morris Markey was writing *New Yorker* Reporters at Large in which untutored Manhattanites spoke at improbable length. By the midfifties, Mitchell could write a *New Yorker* piece about Gypsy con games in which no fewer than eighteen thousand of the twenty thousand words consisted of two elephantine quotations from the recently retired commanding officer of the New York Police Department's Pickpocket and Confidence Squad. A subsequent follower of this technique was Whitney Balliett, whose Profiles of jazz musicians comprised uninterrupted speeches that went on for page after page. As the magazine saw it, the only potential problem with this practice was one of craft—that is, if the quotes did not ring true. In 1948, Ross sent Shawn a memo concerning a Joel Sayre piece: "Sayre has a quote of two or three thousand words at the end of Part II that manifestly is not quote at all, but just Sayre writing. He's ostensibly quoting one of his women characters. It doesn't sound any more like a woman talking than I sound like Betty Grable." Ross followed that up with a letter to Sayre, noting, "You're vulnerable on this point, even assuming that certain allowances must be made for license in writing quotes and translation."

By the time of Reid's and Malcolm's problems, the vocation of journalism had somehow turned into a profession, with rather rigid standards. Composite characters and quote-doctoring were not among them. Another factor, in Malcolm's case, was that one can go much further with a loose-constructionist view of quotation if one has a favorable view of the speaker—as Mitchell, Liebling, and Balliett all did in the above examples, and as the *New Yorker* generally did in the benign Shawn era. Malcolm may not have libeled Masson, but she certainly looked at him askance and thereby probably disqualified herself from the traditional poetic license for quotes.

Of course, the public did not especially care about historical trends in journalistic art. What they saw was the great *New Yorker* repeatedly embarrassing itself.

Yet another 1984 embarrassment resulted from the publication and great commercial and promotional success of a novel called *Bright Lights, Big City*, by Jay McInerney. A onetime fact-checker at the *New Yorker*, McInerney had been fired for incompetence; the novel's protagonist, Alex, works in "the Department of Verification" of a magazine that is never named but is absolutely unmistakable. Joseph Mitchell, William Maxwell, Pauline Kael, and less well-known *New Yorker* figures put in appearances, in greater or lesser degrees of disguise, as does the editor in chief, whom Alex dubs "the Druid" and describes in his trademark second-person present tense:

> The Druid is elusive; one has to look very closely, and know what to look for, to see him at all. While you have never actually seen a Victorian clerk, you believe this is what one would look like. At the magazine, his temperamental reticence has been elevated to a principle. Fourth in a dynastic succession, he has run the show for twenty years. Trying to discover what he is thinking is the preoccupation of the entire staff. Nothing passes into the magazine without his enthusiastic approval and his own final edit. There is no arbitration and no explanation. It pains him that he requires a staff to assist him, but he is invariably polite. There is officially no second-in-command, because that would imply an eventual changing of the guard, and the Druid cannot imagine the magazine without himself.

In 1980, the magazine published a long Reflections by George Trow called "Within the Context of No Context." The piece was prescient, often funny, and sometimes brilliant in its diagnosis of America's cultural ennui, but it also had a great deal to say, implicitly, about the fate of the *New Yorker*. Trow charted the deterioration of the traditional mores and standards he had known while growing up as a member of the WASP upper-middle class, and their replacement by the sensation-seeking, anything-goes culture of the television age. As a result of that same process, the consensus the *New Yorker* had operated and flourished under for decades was weakened and vulnerable. The magazine had had a reasonably good decade, but the creative and commercial capital it had banked was depleted.

"Within the Context of No Context" was significant for another reason. For all its trenchant commentary, the piece also tended toward preciousness and pretentiousness—arch formulations, gnomic utterances, sleight-of-hand connections. It was an instance of the way, more and more, Shawn's practice of allowing writers complete leeway had resulted in overlong, self-indulgent, or obscure pieces. Trow's and Veronica Geng's casuals became subtle to the point of unintelligibility; the stories and Comment pieces of Harold Brodkey were similarly off-putting and obscure. Robert Gottlieb, who would take over as editor of the *New Yorker* in 1987, referred to these three as "extreme writers." In 1983, Ian Frazier wrote a Profile of Ponce Cruse Evans, author of the syndicated column "Hints from Heloise," in which he spent as much time recounting his own misadventures at a cut-rate motel in San Antonio, Texas, as describing Evans. It was audacious and funny, but in feasting on and spinning around the conventions of the Profile form, it signaled that the form had reached a moment of decadence.

The editorial malaise was felt in sundry ways. In 1979, Pauline Kael took a leave of absence from the magazine to work in Hollywood as a producer and consultant. She returned in June 1980 as the sole film critic. Several months later, in an unprecedented instance of one *New Yorker* writer attacking another, Renata Adler wrote a scathing critique of Kael in the *New York Review of Books.* The essay was hyperbolic and hurtful, yet it was true that Kael in the eighties was not on the same level as Kael in the seventies. Her reviews grew longer, her mannerisms more pronounced, and her judgments more frequently questionable. Between her return and September 1986, 114 readers sent letters complaining about Kael's writing; another fifteen were unhappy about the infrequency of her appearances. (Only thirty-two wrote to praise her.) She and Shawn had a blowup in 1985 over the nine-hour Holocaust documentary *Shoah,* which Kael pronounced "a long moan.'" "He didn't want to publish it," Kael said. "It was clear that either he would publish it or I would quit. I ended up adding one sentence. [The sentence was: 'I ask the forbearance of readers for a dissenting view of a film that is widely regarded as a masterpiece.'] The magazine got a lot of letters from Jewish groups. Shawn answered them personally, suffering on each one. He loved to suffer."

John McPhee, following his interests as he always had, found himself writing a long series of long pieces about geological phenomena; they were by necessity technical, they included few if any people, as McPhee's previous pieces always had, and they lost many readers along the way. In 1984 and 1985,

Shawn ran five lengthy Profiles by E. J. Kahn on the foodstuffs human beings around the world are dependent on—corn, potatoes, wheat, rice, and soybeans. The pieces were not uninteresting, but in the sheer number of words they brought to bear on a less than thrilling subject, they seemed to encapsulate the growing sense that the *New Yorker* had become hopelessly remote.*

Shawn was still capable of spotting talent: among the fact writers he brought to the magazine in the eighties were Bill Barich, John Lukacs, Alec Wilkinson, and Lawrence Weschler. They were very different from one another in style and sensibility, but all were in their way true to the best tradition of the magazine. Notwithstanding her legal troubles, Janet Malcolm reinvigorated the *New Yorker* tradition of essay reportage in her Masson Profile and other explorations. Mark Singer wrote a Profile of a "court buff" that, in subject and style, carried on the legacy of Liebling. In 1982, the magazine published Jonathan Schell's three-part series "The Fate of the Earth," about the prospects and dangers of nuclear war, which Shawn saw as a companion piece to "Hiroshima." According to Lillian Ross, when the first installment was about to appear, Shawn said to her, "When the magazine comes out, I fear that people are going to be running hysterically through the streets." The reaction was not quite that dramatic, but Schell's essay, published in book form soon afterward, became an important text in the disarmament debate. On the fiction side, the magazine opened its pages in the early eighties to Lorrie Moore, Cynthia Ozick, Raymond Carver, Milan Kundera (his "The Unbearable Lightness of Being" ran in 1984), Deborah Eisenberg (Wallace Shawn's girlfriend), Steven Millhauser, Susan Minot, Tama Janowitz, and Nicholson Baker, whose stream-of-consciousness meditations on the mundane were a completely original blend of Henry James, James Joyce, and James Thurber.

But now the talents of contributors new and old were unable to transcend the essential dysfunctionality of the magazine. It was simply a creepy place. A young man named John Bennet was hired in the early seventies to

---

*The piece in the early eighties that drew the greatest amount of negative attention was William F. Buckley's "Overdrive," a journal of a week in the author's life, published in two parts early in 1983. It struck some readers and reviewers (when it was published as a book) as a parody of the high-octane social life of a self-satisfied aristocrat, and it inspired the most negative letters of any New Yorker piece in history—168 of them. (Eight letters praised the article.) Ironically, as annoying and occasionally obnoxious as Buckley was, "Overdrive" had qualities sorely lacking in the general run of *New Yorker* pieces at the time—provocativeness and readability. As Curt Suplee wrote in the *Washington Post* after the articles appeared, "That incessant scrunching noise you keep hearing to the north is Wm. F. Buckley Jr. attempting to squeeze his ego between the covers of the *New Yorker*. The behemoth first half of his two-part personal journal makes Proust look positively laconic. Buckley maunders along like Macaulay on Quaaludes about his house, limo, kids and friends, gloating and quoting his snappiest ripostes . . . *And yet you can't put the damn thing down!*"

work on the copy desk and was eventually promoted to collator—a job consisting, as he put it, of "copying things from one proof to another." He had hopes of becoming an editor, and finally Shawn asked him if he "would be willing to edit after a fashion." "His" writer would be George T. Ryall, who had been writing the Race Track column since 1927. "He was in the hospital, on the edge of death, but he thought his pieces were still running in the *New Yorker,*" Bennet said. "My job was to call him on Sunday and take his copy over the telephone. He would describe fantasy races—Man of War against Secretariat. The next day I would call him and say everything went well. This went on until his death. In retrospect, it was wonderful training for becoming an editor. I learned about having a good bedside manner."

Bennet got his real opportunity in 1981, when William Whitworth left to become editor of the *Atlantic.* "Shawn asked me, 'Would you like to try your hand at something?' " Bennet recalled. "He never made someone an editor—he just gave you pieces to edit until people *thought* of you as an editor. It was important that I not move into Whitworth's office. Shawn had a policy of 'desanctifying' offices. Like almost everything else he did, it was a way of enhancing his own power. At this point, Shawn ran the magazine the way Algerian terrorist cells were organized in the battle of Algiers—no one knew who anybody else was or what anybody else was doing. He ran everything, controlled everything. One paradox about him was that even though he was so autocratic, so controlling, as far as editing itself went, he gave you absolute freedom."

For the writers, one important problem was that, with advertising down and the issues so thin, their pieces would lie in editorial limbo for months and sometimes years; no checks would emanate from Shawn, and only cryptic progress reports. It was a classic good-news/bad-news situation: you were a "staff writer" for the most prestigious magazine in the country, but no one knew it and—if you were on the draw—every week you got deeper in debt. One new fact writer, Lincoln Caplan, a specialist on legal affairs, said, "It was clear that the reckoning was coming. When I started to write for the magazine, I felt as though I'd gotten my union card just as the mills were closing. Financially, unless you had independent dough, you put yourself in jeopardy."

"By about 1980, the tradition of *New Yorker* fact-writing needed to be reinvented," said Alec Wilkinson. "But Shawn no longer had control. Things had gotten out of hand."

Shawn's standards and principles, so central to his definition of himself and the magazine, had become counterproductively rigid and sometimes appeared mystifying. For example, even though Caplan was contributing regularly, Shawn refused to let him describe himself in his books' author biographies with that notoriously vague phrase "a staff writer for the *New Yorker.*" "Shawn's view was, 'People don't understand the way we work. That

I consider you a *New Yorker* writer is the most important thing,' " Caplan said. "The wording he settled on was 'Lincoln Caplan is a frequent contributor to the *New Yorker.*' "

The magazine in this period had an elegiac air to it, for a literal reason in addition to any metaphoric ones. Since the suicide of Ralph Barton in 1931, the *New Yorker* had followed the honorable practice of noting the passing of significant contributors and employees; eventually these unsigned notices found their way to the back page, with black bars above and below. By the 1970s, actuarial realities had caught up with the magazine. In the first twenty-five years of its existence, it printed only seven such obituaries; in the next twenty-five, it printed twenty-nine (notably Thurber in 1961, Peter Arno in 1968, Raoul Fleischmann in 1969, Louise Bogan in 1970, Ogden Nash in 1971, Rea Irvin and Edmund Wilson in 1972, Robert Coates and Sam Behrman in 1973, and Lois Long in 1974). In just the ten years between 1975 and 1984, there were a remarkable thirty-two, including not only such essential figures as Otto Soglow, Hannah Arendt, Frank Sullivan, Mary Petty, Katharine White, Geoffrey Hellman, Perry Barlow, Harold Rosenberg, Janet Flanner, George Ryall, S. J. Perelman, Richard Rovere, St. Clair McKelway, Rachel MacKenzie, Kenneth Tynan, Rogers Whitaker, Daniel Lang, John Cheever, Dwight Macdonald, James Geraghty, and Joseph Wechsberg, but also hitherto anonymous editors and members of the business staff, and even Raymond (Chip) Guth, the nineteen-year-old grandson of Gus Lobrano, who had worked for the magazine one summer as a messenger and who, his obituary noted, "did his best to make himself invisible and inaudible, but he could not hide his gentleness, his tenderness, his generosity, his courage, his humor."

Those words were written by Shawn, who contributed a total of twenty-one unsigned obituaries to the magazine, having found that they were the perfect vessel for his deeply felt yet precise prose. He gave extraordinary care to these pieces. "I was in the composing room when someone brought down Shawn's obit of Hannah Arendt," John Bennet said. "I decided to stick around. Shawn called down to change a word. Twenty minutes later, he called again to change another word. He kept calling back every twenty minutes till ten at night."*

---

*In addition to Arendt's, Shawn wrote the obituaries for Howard Brubaker, Robery Gerdy, Stephen Botsford, A. J. Liebling, S. N. Behrman, Otto Soglow, Donald Malcolm, Hannah Arendt, Katharine White, Arthur J. Russell, Harold Rosenberg, Janet Flanner, Kenneth Tynan, Patricia Nosher, S. J. Perelman, St. Clair McKelway, Daniel Lang, Joseph Wechsberg, Chip Guth, Carmine Peppe, and Winthrop Sergeant; he contributed to those for Thurber and E. B. White, who died in 1985. The longest and probably the finest piece of writing Shawn ever attempted was a three-thousand-word assessment of and tribute to Ross, written to counter what he saw as the overly negative portrait of the founding editor in Brendan Gill's 1975 book, *Here at the New Yorker;* Gill, recognizing its quality, closed the book with it.

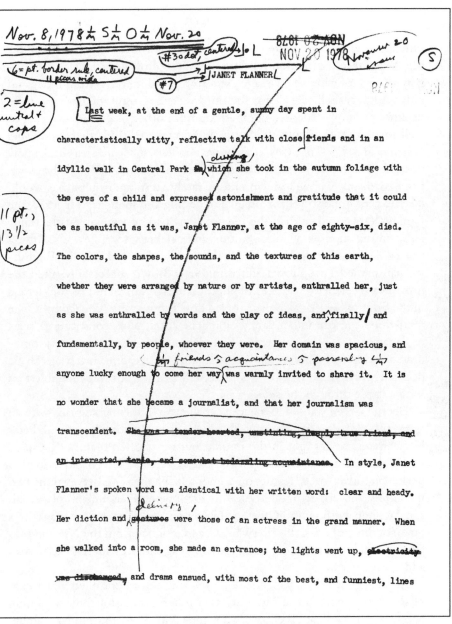

Shawn, who never had a signed piece in the *New Yorker,* became, in his autumn years, a master of the anonymous obituary. His deep feelings for Janet Flanner were partly a reflection of the fact that they had worked together for some forty-five years.

TAKEOVER

Nineteen eighty-four, with its ominous literary overtones, was difficult for the *New Yorker*. Circulation fell, and while the drop was slight, the demographics were grim: the average *New Yorker* reader was getting older and older. Ad pages fell as well, for the third year in a row. One reason for the decline was unprecedented competition from other magazines catering to well-to-do readers: all of a sudden, in addition to *New York,* there was *Travel & Leisure, Food & Wine, Gourmet, Architectural Digest, Connoisseur,* and a new upscale version of *House and Garden.* (These magazines had the advantage, from Madison Avenue's viewpoint, of rarely running articles that would take readers' minds off the main goal of getting and spending.) In 1983, the Condé Nast company had the idea of reviving the venerable title *Vanity Fair* and recasting its blend of culture and celebrity for a new era. After a few false starts, Condé Nast chief S. I. Newhouse named a young Englishwoman named Tina Brown editor in 1984. Brown successfully tilted the mix toward celebrity, with lots of photographs. In one of her editor's letters in the front of the magazine, she took a direct shot at the *New Yorker:* "Once in a while . . . I run into a flabby old cliché about what constitutes a 'serious' magazine. It's the mealymouthed idea that visual excitement is somehow at odds with intellectual content, and that reading material can be deemed worthwhile only if it is presented as a wad of impenetrable text with a staple through the side."

George Green wanted to meet the challenges of the marketplace with an aggressive courting of advertisers' business; Shawn, naturally, resisted. Peter Fleischmann was caught in the middle, but more often than not he sided with Shawn. On one occasion, Fleischmann overruled Green and refused to permit an "advertorial" feature on computers. The tension between the two men grew and was aggravated early in 1984, when Fleischmann placed his son, Stephen, with whom Green had never gotten along, on the magazine's board of directors. Shortly afterward, Green resigned from the *New Yorker* to take a position at Hearst overseeing several magazines, including *Connoisseur* and *Town & Country.*

At that point, Peter Fleischmann either owned or controlled 32 percent of the *New Yorker's* stock. The only two other major stockholders, Philip Messinger and William Reik, were unhappy with Shawn's seeming inability to find a suitable successor, and with the financial direction of the magazine; Green's departure only increased their anxiety. The magazine, as a result, became susceptible to takeover. That threat came in the form of Samuel I. Newhouse Jr., who, with his brother, Donald, owned and ran Advance Communications, a media conglomerate worth an estimated $3 billion. Advance had been started by Samuel I. Newhouse Sr., once described in the

New Yorker by A. J. Liebling as a "rag-picker of second-class newspapers" having "no political ideas, just economic convictions." Under the next generation's leadership, the company had acquired a modicum of prestige through its acquisition of the Condé Nast magazines (and the relaunch of *Vanity Fair*) and of the Random House group of book publishers. But the *New Yorker* was the most prestigious property of them all; perhaps "Si" Newhouse thought owning it would finally erase Liebling's calumny. In any case, in November 1984, he bought from Messinger and Reik, at some 40 percent above the market price, *New Yorker* stock totaling 17 percent of the outstanding shares.

There had been suitors before, including Samuel I. Newhouse Sr., William Paley of CBS, and the Nebraska investor Warren Buffett, who had held a 16 percent share of the company in the midseventies and made takeover overtures. Peter Fleischmann had cannily arranged a lunch between Shawn and Buffett, after which the investor said, "Peter, I can see there are some very difficult problems in running this organization," and got rid of his stock. Fleischmann tried the same approach with Newhouse. It backfired, extravagantly. The meeting was held in the apartment of Fleischmann's attorney Merrell Clark, and as Clark recounted to author Carol Felsenthal, Shawn explained the fragile uniqueness of the *New Yorker,* how it did not and could not operate like a profit-making institution (the magazine would send a fact-checker to London via the Concorde to check a single fact, he said). But this merely intensified the interest of Newhouse, who wanted a property as unlike a rag as possible. "Every time Shawn said something like, 'Send the Concorde to England to check a fact,'" Clark recalled, "you could see Newhouse saying, 'This is better than I thought.'"

As he reflexively did by this time, Shawn viewed the situation in terms of loyalty and betrayal. Roger Angell recalled, "During the takeover period, I would meet with Shawn almost every day. All of a sudden he grew cold. I went to see him and asked what was wrong. He said, 'Nothing.' I said, 'There must be.' He pulled out of his jacket pocket a thick wad of letters of support from staff members. He said, 'I've gotten these from all these people, but not from you.'" Angell exploded with anger at this impugning of his devotion to the magazine, and Shawn tearfully apologized.

The day after Newhouse bought his first block of shares, the *New Yorker* and Advance Publications issued a joint press release that included this sentence: "Mr. Newhouse said that there were no plans to seek control of the *New Yorker* or to influence its management." Such a plan soon emerged, however, as Newhouse convinced Fleischmann, who was in ill health, weary of the marketplace battles, and concerned about the eventual burden of estate taxes, to sell his stock for $200 a share, which added up to a payout of some $40 million. All told, Newhouse paid about $170 million in cash for the magazine.

After it had become clear that the takeover would be successful, New-house attempted to allay some of the staff's concerns in a document called "Agreement and Plan of Merger." It singled out the *New Yorker's* "tradition of complete editorial independence" and asserted, "Advance wishes to preserve this quality of *The New Yorker* through maintaining its personnel and its traditions." Recognizing the fear that the *New Yorker* would become just one more in the stable of Condé Nast magazines, the document went on to say, "Following the Merger, the business of the Company will be operated on a stand-alone basis as a separate company. All present departments ... will be maintained independently from those of Advance's magazines."

The "Agreement and Plan of Merger" didn't mention William Shawn specifically, but Newhouse was quoted in the *Washington Post* as saying, "Obviously, Mr. Shawn will continue to be editor as long as he wants to be editor."

For the issue of April 22, 1985, published just two weeks before the shareholders would vote to approve the sale in the final annual meeting of the *New Yorker* Magazine, Inc., as a public company, Shawn wrote a long piece for Notes and Comment. He had expressed some of his feelings about the *New Yorker* in his memos to the staff at the time of the union crisis, but never before had he put them down for public consumption. In a way, Shawn's manifesto was a bookend to the prospectus Harold Ross had written so many years before—the one that said the magazine would not be for the old lady in Dubuque. Shawn began by describing what he saw as the essential historical fact about the magazine: the complete independence of the editors, writers, and artists from the business side. After relating some circumstances of the impending sale to Advance Publications, he wrote:

> As we approach the beginning of a new phase, we reassert our editorial independence. We reassert it with these few formal words. We feel certain that the Newhouses will respect it as rigorously as the Fleischmanns did.
>
> But what does this editorial independence mean? What is it, actually? It is simply freedom. It frees us to say what we believe to be true, to report what we believe to be true, to write what we want to write, to draw what we want to draw—to publish what we want to publish—with no outside intervention, without fear, without constraints, in defiance of commercial pressures or any other pressures beyond those of our own conscience and sense of responsibility. It also frees us to be open to experiment and innovation, to new forms and styles, whether journalistic or literary. The freedom that the editorial office enjoys includes the freedom of every staff writer and every staff artist and every editor (and every non-staff contributor) to follow his or her own impulses, inclinations, aspirations, passionate interests. No writer or artist or editor is ever given an order. When a journalistic writer undertakes a

new project, it is always done in full agreement with the editor; the two have to bring to it the same enthusiasm. And no editing is ever imposed on a writer; every editorial suggestion is presented in the form of a question, and is settled by agreement between writer and editor. The artists are similarly free. And our editors edit only what they are willing to edit.

We edit *The New Yorker* as a magazine for readers, not as an advertising medium. We regard our readers as readers, not as consumers or as a "market." Just as advertising is an essential part of our country's life, it is an essential part of *The New Yorker's* life. But it must not be linked to the editorial content of the magazine. They belong in separate realms and the two realms must remain separate. Must remain cordially apart. In this atmosphere of freedom we have never published anything in order to sell magazines, to cause a sensation, to be controversial, to be popular or fashionable, to be "successful." We have published only what we thought had merit of one kind or another.

The business ownership of *The New Yorker* may have changed hands, but the idea of *The New Yorker*—the tradition of *The New Yorker,* the spirit of *The New Yorker* has never been owned by anyone and will never be owned by anyone. It cannot be bought or sold. It exists in the minds of writers, artists, editors and editorial assistants who have been drawn together by literary, journalistic, aesthetic and ethical principles they share, and by a shared outlook on the World. Whatever else may happen, it will endure. We need not name or define our principles or standards, for they are implicit in what we publish in our pages each week. Yet this might be the moment we say that if *The New Yorker* could be everything we want it to be, it would unfailingly combine thorough, accurate, fresh, inspired reporting with fiction that runs deep and says something that hasn't been said before; it would be funny as frequently as possible; it would contribute something of worth to the national discourse; it would cast light; it would be well-wishing and it would be humane. At an age when television screens are too often bright with nothing, we value substance. Amid chaos of images, we value coherence. We believe in the printed word. And we believe in clarity. And we believe in immaculate syntax. And in the beauty of the English language. We believe that truth can turn up in a cartoon, in one of the magazine covers, in a poem, in a short story, in an essay, in an editorial comment, in a humor piece, in a critical piece, in a reporting piece. And if any single principle transcends all the others and informs all the others it is to try and tell the truth. *The New Yorker* will continue to change, as it has changed through the years, but our basic principles and standards will remain exactly what they have been. With that knowledge, and with the assurances that we freely asked our prospective publishers to give us and that which they freely gave, we are confident that we will preserve *The New Yorker*—not merely a magazine that bears its name, but *this* magazine: *The New Yorker* itself.

* * *

Newhouse's first move was to install a publisher—Steven Florio, formerly of Condé Nast's *GQ*. George Green had been viewed in some quarters as too pushy, but compared to Florio, who was young, voluble, occasionally profane, and frequently self-aggrandizing, Green was an Oxford don. In his first year, by one estimate, Florio fired twenty advertising salespeople and executives. (So much for "maintaining its personnel.") For the first time, the magazine contained insert cards for direct-response advertisers. Two million pieces of direct-mail soliciting subscriptions were sent out, and a $2.5 million advertising campaign was unleashed. In its attempt to attract new readers, the magazine offered, again for the first time, cut-rate subscriptions and a "bill me later" option. More firsts: gatefold covers, price-code symbols on the cover of newsstand copies, and horizontal ads. In Florio's first year and a half, the *New Yorker* printed five advertorials.

A strong argument could be made that a shake-up in the *New Yorker's* business practices was long overdue. The trouble was, despite all the policy changes and expenditures, circulation, precisely 500,000 at the end of 1984, had only risen to 506,000 by the end of 1985 and 560,000 twelve months later. Even worse, ad pages continued to fall, by a substantial 15 percent in 1985 and an additional 10.5 percent in 1986. The *New Yorker* ended both years in the red—the first time that had happened since 1927.

There was an ineffable sense of weariness to the thin magazine. Two series that ran almost in succession in the spring of 1986 were lightning rods for criticism: Susan Sheehan's "A Missing Plane," an exhaustive and ultimately exhausting three-part piece about the army's attempts to identify the remains of the victims of a 1944 plane crash, and Renata Adler's eccentrically written and eccentrically argued "Annals of Law" series about libel suits brought by Ariel Sharon and William Westmoreland. Both seemed to exemplify a general feeling that the magazine was no longer put out with an eye to being solicitous of readers' needs and wants, but was rather a receptacle for large quantities of undigested data, in the first case, and for the self-indulgence of authors, in the second.

The new satiric monthly *Spy* took regular aim, including printing an accurate *New Yorker* masthead and puckishly hosting the letters-to-the-editor column that the *New Yorker* had never gotten around to starting. In 1986, Workman Press published a 265-page *New Yorker* parody called, simply, *Snooze*. In a foreword, Eustace Tilley supposedly writes that in the years after Shawn became editor, "we stayed in our increasingly dingy offices, contemplating the magazine's mission and becoming graver by the hour. The magazine acquired a pronounced political conscience, commitment to the work of a wide range of excellent—or, at least, very serious—writers, and a proclivity for exploring subjects like the antimacassar industry, yucca, or two weeks in the life of a violist at lengths that make some readers tear up their copies of our magazine into tiny strips and burn them in the wastebasket."

Critic Raymond Sokolov, in the *Wall Street Journal* in July 1986, wrote of Shawn, "He has become a laughingstock, devoting his once-distinguished, once-amusing magazine to n-part screeds on staple grains and vanished airplanes. . . . It is the only strong force for good left on the literary landscape. The rest is publicity or trend. But *The New Yorker* can still bring the general reader together with the serious writer, or could if it wanted. The worrisome thing is that the influence built up over the years is ebbing in the Shawnian twilight."

One promise Newhouse appears to have kept is not to interfere with the editorial product. A possible reason was that, at the time of the sale, he had cause to think that the succession issue was finally settled and that Shawn would be departing sooner rather than later. In November 1984, Shawn named Chip McGrath, then thirty-seven years old, and John Bennet, thirty-nine, as co-managing editors, the implication being that one would eventually be chosen as the new editor in chief; the roster of *New Yorker* writers was divided between them. Both were skilled editors with about ten years' experience at the magazine, so they knew and respected the quirks of the peculiar institution; both were widely liked and respected by the staff. The arrangement did not turn out as well as expected. "Once a week Chip and I had lunch with Shawn at the Algonquin," Bennet said. "It was a Zen-like ordeal, in which he would nervously say very little for about an hour. Then it was over till the following week." Moreover, Bennet and McGrath both found that "their" writers went over their heads to Shawn when unhappy with the editing they received. Meanwhile, Shawn had them sit in on his private conversations with writers, a process Ved Mehta describes as "excruciatingly painful." Before long the experiment was dropped.

The next candidate was a surprise. His name was Bill McKibben. In 1981, when McKibben was a senior at Harvard, his phone rang and a caller announced himself as William Shawn from the *New Yorker*. Thinking this was a prank, McKibben hung up. Some months later, Shawn called back and, this time, was allowed to stay on the line long enough to say that he had read some of McKibben's writing in the *Crimson* and was interested in talking to him about a job at the *New Yorker*. McKibben ended up as one of the magazine's most talented and prolific Talk of the Town writers; for long stretches in the early eighties he wrote most of Talk himself, and on a couple of occasions he wrote *all* of it. But no matter how much talent he had, no one at the magazine was prepared when Shawn let it be known that he felt McKibben—who had no experience as an editor—was the new successor designate. To Roger Angell, Shawn compared McKibben to "the younger Pitt"—William Pitt, who was named England's chancellor of the exchequer at the age of twenty-three and prime minister at twenty-four, in 1783. But the staff reacted even more negatively than it had to the Schell nominations, and McKibben's name was dropped.

After that, John Bennet recalled, "Shawn asked me, with guarded phrasing, 'Would you be under consideration as the sole successor?' " Bennet said yes, but after a short time Shawn came back to him and said that he was no longer the designee—that Newhouse preferred McGrath. Bennet recalled, "He told me, 'Please take my word for this. You don't really want this job. It's a horrible, horrible job, and nobody wants it.' "

This time around, McGrath had the impression that Shawn—who turned seventy-nine in 1986—was finally serious about turning over the reins. "Our conversations were much more frank and open than before," McGrath said, "though not frank and open enough." Plans were made to move McGrath's office next to Shawn's, so they could consult more easily. The problem, this time, was Newhouse. He decided for reasons he has never publicly expressed that he didn't want McGrath as editor, and indeed that no internal candidate was qualified for the job. The "Agreement and Plan of Merger" had stated: ". . . when a new editor-in-chief of *The New Yorker* is being considered, the final decision will be made by Advance, but it will consult with, and seek the advice and approval of, a group of staff members to be selected and to function in a manner then deemed to be appropriate by the senior editorial staff of *The New Yorker*." But no such group was ever formed, and Newhouse apparently sought no consultation, advice, or approval from anyone in editorial. He simply offered the job to Robert Gottlieb, editor in chief of the publishing house Alfred A. Knopf. Only after Gottlieb accepted did Newhouse inform Shawn.

One would be tempted to call the subsequent events a comedy of errors, if they were not so poignant. The following day, January 13, 1987, Newhouse distributes to the staff a memo beginning, "Recently Mr. Shawn informed me that he will retire on March 1," and announcing Gottlieb's appointment. That afternoon, more than one hundred stunned staffers gather on the eighteenth floor. They invite Mr. Shawn to address them and explain what is going on. Standing on the stairway leading to the floor above, he says, in his familiar soft and precise cadences, that he never told Newhouse he had planned to retire on March 1; he had merely mentioned that as a date by which McGrath might take over a considerable portion of his duties. After Shawn leaves, Lillian Ross suggests writing a letter to Gottlieb explaining what has happened and asking him not to accept. There is general enthusiasm for this plan, and a group of writers withdraw to draft the letter. When it is completed, it is sent through copyediting and fact-checking. Staff members get on the telephone to ask far-flung contributors if they would be willing to affix their name to the document. J. D. Salinger and Saul Steinberg agree; John Updike declines. The letter expresses "sadness and outrage" over the events of the last two days, in particular at "the appointment of an editor not heretofore affiliated with the magazine.... [I]t is our strange and powerfully held conviction that only an editor who has been a long-standing member of the staff will have a reasonable chance of assuring our continuity, cohesion, and independence." It concludes:

> We wish to assure you—and we should have done so long before this point—that none of these feelings or reservations were directed against you. Many of us know you personally and professionally, and admire your splendid record at Knopf. We also know that you are a reasonable person. With this in mind, and cognizant of your expressed deep admiration and affection for this magazine, we urge that, after consultation with our owner, Mr. Newhouse, you withdraw your acceptance of the post that has been offered to you.

There are 153 signatories. (Besides Updike, the only people who have chosen not to sign are Renata Adler, Brendan Gill, Pauline Kael, and Lee Lorenz.) The names are displayed, in a rather touching effort to emphasize their number, in a single vertical column that spans more than two pages. That evening Shawn hands the letter to Newhouse, who reportedly hollers at Shawn for permitting this insurrection, but agrees to forward a copy to Gottlieb. The next day, over an awkward lunch at the Algonquin, Gottlieb hands Shawn a response to the staff letter. On his way back to the *New Yorker*, Shawn is surprised by a photographer in the street and covers his eyes to shield himself from the flash of light. The photo of this recently humiliated seventy-nine-year-old appears on the front page of the next day's *Newsday*, with the headline "Up in Arms at the *New Yorker*." Back at the office, Shawn posts Gottlieb's reply on the bulletin board. Addressed to "the signers of yesterday's letter to me," it reads, in its entirety:

> Of course I understand the feelings you expressed in your letter, and can even sympathize with them. I also appreciate the fact that your resistance to my coming is not personal.
>
> But I do plan to take up this new job as soon as it is convenient and practical, and can only add that I'm looking forward to knowing and working with you all.

Of *course* Gottlieb planned to take the job: the notion that the letter might actually persuade him to decline it was a *folie à beaucoup*, an act of self-delusion performed by 153 people who had long spent their working lives in a protected, singular world. When word of the protest leaked to the press, the participants were roundly mocked as crybabies and worse. In *Newsweek*, Jonathan Alter called them "cultists" who "somehow believe they live in a democratic nirvana." Describing the pep rally where the idea for the letter was hatched, he wrote, "Lillian Ross might as well have been ladling Jonestown Kool-Aid."

For *New Yorker* staffers, Gottlieb's reply may have been in the nature of a ringing alarm clock, waking them up to a new world and a new reality. Interestingly, only four of them ultimately left in protest: pretenders to the throne Jonathan Schell and Bill McKibben, Lillian Ross, and fiction editor Gwyneth Cravens. According to Ross's account in her book *Here but Not Here,* Shawn was disappointed that more did not follow, but happy to be relieved of his terrible burden. Of the firing, she wrote, he "understood it, sympathized with it. For years, he had felt entrapped by his job but had not known how to free himself of it." In large part because of the general feelings of awkwardness and discomfort, Gottlieb's first day was moved up to Monday, February 16. On Shawn's final day at the *New Yorker,* he posted one last letter on the bulletin board:

Dear colleagues, dear friends:

My feelings at this perplexed moment are too strong for farewells. I will miss you terribly, but I can be grateful to have had your companionship for part of my journey through the years. Whatever our individual roles at *The New Yorker,* whether on the eighteenth, nineteenth, or twentieth floor, we have built something quite wonderful together. Love has been the controlling emotion, and love is the essential word. *The New Yorker,* as a reader once said, has been the gentlest of magazines. Perhaps it has also been the greatest, but that matters far less. What matters most is that you and I, working together, taking strength from the inspiration that our first editor, Harold Ross, gave us, have tried constantly to find and say what is true. I must speak of love once more. I love all of you, and will love you as long as I live.

The Years with Gottlieb, Brown, and Remnick

1987~99

Shortly after Robert Gottlieb assumed the editorship of the *New Yorker,* he rejected some cartoons by James Stevenson, saying (as Stevenson recalled), "These aren't for us."

"I thought to myself, 'What do you mean, "These aren't for us"?' " Stevenson said years later. " 'You're not us. *I'm* us.' " Not long afterward, Stevenson stopped contributing cartoons and text pieces to the magazine, concentrating instead on children's books.

Most other writers and staff members, however, came to terms with Gottlieb; many grew to like and admire him. He was a native Manhattanite, fifty-six years old. Unlike Ross and Shawn, he had grown up reading the *New Yorker* and dreamed of one day being its editor. He stressed to Newhouse that he had no intention of effecting any radical changes. "I told Si, 'You have to understand, I'm a conservator,' " Gottlieb said in an interview. " 'And I love the *New Yorker.* What I would do if I went there is to make it a better or stronger version of what it already is. If you want somebody to make it other than what it is, I can't do that.' And that was completely our understanding. I also said, 'If you ever change your mind, no hard feelings, but I just want you to be open and candid with me. I don't want to read about it in the newspapers.' And, completely true to the bargain, he never let me down."

The most glaring contrast with his predecessor was in matters of style. Gottlieb was almost militantly casual, wearing tennis shoes and open-necked shirts, installing coffee machines and water stations on every editorial floor. In the interest of accessibility, he took down the maze of partitions

417

that separated Shawn's office from everyone else's and did not place a secretary at the door. He was chatty, even gossipy, and startlingly liked to be called Bob. Where Shawn instinctively drew all power to himself, Gottlieb was comfortable delegating. He brought over two trusted aides from Knopf, Martha Kaplan and Adam Gopnik, and had Kaplan assume the duties of managing editor and Gopnik oversee the arts coverage (and also serve as art critic). He ceded more authority to the fact editors and elevated Chip McGrath, whose appointment he had usurped, to the new position of deputy editor.

"For the first six months, people would keep going to Chip's office and say, 'Bob just said "X" to us—what do you think he meant?'" Gottlieb recalled. "It took them six months to understand that what I meant actually was what I said."

And what he said was a world apart from Shawn's coded or halting discourse. If he didn't like a particular piece of work, he bluntly told the author. A year into Gottlieb's tenure, Mark Singer remarked to a *Washington Post* reporter that Gottlieb "takes the view that writers are children who are not to be indulged; Shawn thought they were children who ought to be indulged."

For some writers, the change was refreshing, even liberating. "I didn't emerge as a writer till Gottlieb arrived," Alec Wilkinson said. "Shawn was too intimidating. There was always this sense that you're writing for a guy who's intimate with J. D. Salinger."

True to his curatorial mission, Gottlieb's changes in the magazine itself were subtle. Although he declined to cut loose even the most unproductive writers, he had no problem with rejecting or slashing the pieces they submitted. The space he saved helped him bring in new contributors—most notably in the area of international reporting. From World War II through the sixties, the *New Yorker* had been known for the corps of correspondents it had in place throughout the world, but as these people had died or retired, Shawn had not bothered to replace them. Gottlieb recruited a distinguished new group, including Julian Barnes from England, David Remnick from Russia, Amos Elon from Israel, Raymond Bonner from Latin America, Milton Viorst from the Middle East, and others.

More generally, readers could begin to discern in the magazine a certain urbanity, a cultured knowingness. It was the beginning of a pendulum swing back to the "sophistication" of the *New Yorker*'s early years—a quality that it had moved away from long before in favor of integrity, social conscience, and comprehensiveness. A passionate devotee of the New York City Ballet, Gottlieb had a more aesthetic and less pedagogical approach to writing and to the magazine. "I am not a journalist and I don't even like journalism," he said. "On the job I learned about it and grew to appreciate it, but my entire background is cultural. It's literary, music, art, dance." He spruced up the dusty and dull Goings on About Town section, adding short essays about the cultural events of the week and snappy illustrations, some of them in color. In stories and articles, he permitted profanity and references to sex and bodily functions. Some of the notable writers who first appeared in the magazine under his editorship were Brad Leithauser, Diane Ackerman, Ethan Mordden, Sue Hubbell, Oliver Sacks, Jane and Michael Stern, Joan Didion, Susan Orlean, V. S. Naipaul, Richard Preston, Dan Hofstatder, and William Finnegan on the fact side; Richard Ford, A. S. Byatt, Julie Hecht, Michael Chabon, Salman Rushdie, Christopher Tilghman, Allegra Goodman, Martin Amis, and Haruki Murakami in fiction; and Bruce McCall in humor. This is obviously a disparate group, and some of its members—such as Preston, Sacks, Orlean, Finnegan, Goodman, Hecht, and McCall—fit into classic New Yorker molds. But many of them shared an elegance of sensibility or style, or an artiness, with which Shawn would probably not have been sympathetic. Critics of Gottlieb, who was well known for his campy collection of plastic handbags, tended to fixate on the Sterns, celebrators of American kitsch who had made their reputation writing about "Road Food"; especially derided was their New Yorker article on a convention of collectors of Scottish-terrier memorabilia.

Unexceptional changes chipped away at the general sense of New Yorker exceptionalism. In 1988, the magazine switched from its venerable brown-paper mailing wrappers to transparent plastic ones. The economics of the move were solid, but the irony was too much for the magazine that had brought "Silent Spring" into the world (and was about to publish another environmentalist jeremiad, Bill McKibben's "The End of Nature"), and the next year the paper wrappers were brought back. (They were later replaced by glued-on address labels, a regrettable development for the many subscribers who used the covers as artwork.) In 1991, the magazine packed up its offices and migrated across West Forty-third Street to number 25, its first move in more than five decades.

Editorially, Gottlieb's New Yorker was a more substantial and well-rounded product than the magazine had been under Shawn in his difficult final years. But Gottlieb's changes did nothing to improve the financial picture. To be sure, circulation, helped by heavy promotion and discounted subscription offers, increased—from 564,000 in June 1987 to 628,000 five years later. The average age of the readers stayed high, however, and when Florio sharply increased advertising rates, Madison Avenue showed its displeasure. New Yorker ad pages plummeted 15 percent in 1988, Gottlieb's first full year. By 1991, they had fallen another 10 percent, to 2,002—the lowest annual total since the magazine started keeping track, in 1938. According to an authoritative company source, the magazine's annual losses during the

Gottlieb years represented about 10 percent of revenue—more than $5 million a year.

This wasn't much in the universe of the Newhouse holdings, which, according to a *Forbes* magazine estimate, takes in more than $4 billion a year. But it was enough for Newhouse to decide, five years into Gottlieb's editorship, that the curatorial approach wasn't working. He turned, as a result, to Tina Brown, the thirty-eight-year-old Englishwoman who had made a great success with the revamped *Vanity Fair*. Gottlieb had been a natural choice—by upbringing and taste—to edit the magazine; his only sin, to those who had pleaded with him to decline the job, was being an outsider. Brown was something else again. Before coming to America, she had barely been aware of the *New Yorker*, and her *Vanity Fair*, with its fixation on celebrity, gossip, money, and power, was the diametrical opposite of Shawn's *New Yorker*. Over and above the content, she paid a great deal of attention to commercial concerns—entertaining suggestions from the advertising department, participating in parties and other events meant to promote the magazine, tying articles to movie and book releases and other events that could bring ads in. *Vanity Fair's* publisher was quoted in 1988 as saying, "She works more closely with our business side than any other editor at Condé Nast."*

Newhouse and Florio told the *New Yorker* staff about the change of editors in a meeting held in the business conference room. This in itself was a rather remarkable affront to the magazine's traditional church-state separation, but at this late date no one protested. Nor was there any great objection to the replacement of Gottlieb with Brown. The exception was Garrison Keillor, who had come on the staff under Gottlieb as a Talk of the Town writer and who, with his great radio success with *A Prairie Home Companion,* could afford to stand up for principle. He packed up his belongings and walked out the day the change was announced. "If some ditzy American editor went to London, took over the *Spectator,* and turned it into, say, *In Your Face: A Magazine of Mucus,* there would be a big uproar," he wrote in *New York Newsday.* "Here, a great American magazine falls into the clutches of a Staten Island newspaper mogul who goes out and hires a British editor who seems to know this country mainly from television and movies." Others departed in due course—Ian Frazier in protest over Brown's appointment of the comedian Roseanne as a "guest editor": Veronica Geng in protest over a perceived personal slight; George Trow in protest over the magazine's excessive coverage of the O. J. Simpson trial; Jamaica Kincaid in protest over the magazine's "vulgarity" and "coarseness"; and Bill

---

*The conspiratorially minded asserted, not unpersuasively, that Newhouse had wanted a radical change—maybe even wanted Brown as editor—all along and had only installed Gottlieb as a temporary transition to smooth the way.

Barich, Paul Brodeur, Michael Arlen, and Alec Wilkinson after it became clear to each, as Wilkinson said, quoting his friend Joseph Mitchell, "that the magazine did not 'speak to my condition.' "*

Most of the other staff members who left did not do so of their own accord. In contrast to Shawn, who was legendary for never firing anyone, and even Gottlieb, who didn't feel it was his place to wield an ax, Brown fairly rapidly severed the connection of such veterans of the Shawn era as Tony Hiss, Alex Shoumatoff, Gerald Jonas, Henry Cooper, James Lardner, Burton Bernstein, John Newhouse, Ved Mehta, Elizabeth Drew (she was replaced as Washington correspondent by Sidney Blumenthal), and a handful of writers, such as William Wertenbaker, who had for decades published little or nothing but had continued to be sustained by the *New Yorker's* quirky largesse. Others, like Whitney Balliett, found fewer and fewer of their ideas or finished stories accepted.

For years, Shawn's *New Yorker* had sustained these writers, after a fashion. But, with unintentional cruelty, the only skill it had taught them was the crafting of "long fact" stories, an expensive and extremely labor-intensive form for which there was no longer any market. Cast defenseless into a harsh economic world, they were obliged to rely on the kindness of strangers—drifting from one grant or university appointment to another, publishing an unremunerative book every few years.

Personnel policy only began the list of differences between Shawn and Brown; when you got to the end of it, you would have to conclude that they were Platonic opposites. On the most obvious level, he was an old American man and she was a young English woman. He was always called "Mr. Shawn"; she was "Tina," not only to the staff but to the media at large, which exhaustively chronicled her comings and goings. (Another difference.) She was, in short, a celebrity, and seemed delighted to be so. The magazine sent out a mailing whose selling point was the advantage of subscribing to a magazine helmed by "Tina Brown, the best magazine editor in the country."

Shawn steadfastly and irrationally refused to delegate, while Brown instituted an entire new layer of subeditors, who busily developed and assigned articles and sent them back for rewrites (virtually unheard of in the late Shawn years). He was notoriously prudish and reluctant to offend; she seemed to delight in profanity, sexual explicitness, and deliberately provocative material. Where E. J. Kahn's "Staffs of Life" series was customarily cited as emblematic of the magazine's dullness in Shawn's later years, and the

---

*Brown allowed Mitchell to keep his office and his $20,000-a-year salary and even approached him about writing an article for the magazine on a fire at the Fulton Fish Market. But Mitchell, maintaining his thirty-year silence, did not turn in any copy.

Sterns' "Wee Scots" of its feyness under Gottlieb, a lengthy list of exhibits was pointed to by the many *New Yorker* loyalists offended by Tina: the John Irving short story about a dildo; several in-your-face Art Spiegelman covers, notably the one showing a black woman and a Hasidic man locked in passionate embrace; the anniversary-issue cover with Eustace Tilley as a punk with bad skin; the two-part series that went into inordinate detail about accusations of satanic abuse; an essay in which a writer shared her obsession with being spanked; and Richard Avedon's twenty-six-page fashion spread that included a photo of a model seemingly copulating with a skeleton.

A photo! Tina's introduction of photography into the magazine was just one of many indications that while Shawn reflexively resisted change, she reveled in it. In the three months before her appointment and her first issue, she completely redesigned the magazine, and then she kept *tinkering* with it (a word as well as a concept Shawn would probably have despised). Eventually, she installed a letters-to-the-editor department, a sleek new typeface, a page of contributors' biographies, complete with pictures, a Talk of the Town section with signed contributions, regular opportunities for illustrations and portfolios in color, and a dramatically different layout for articles. Now the author was identified at the start rather than the end, and now, before you got to the piece itself, you were presented with a subheading explaining what it was all about; there was also frequently a picture caption on the opening spread offering further elucidation. This tendency to lead readers by the hand was a complete rejection of Shawn's journalistic philosophy of never pandering to readers or "selling" them a story, but rather permitting them to meet it on its own terms. Generally speaking, Tina's magazine was subject-oriented, whereas Shawn's was writer-oriented. She demanded shorter pieces and almost never published multipart stories. As a result, many more articles appeared in the magazine. In the first four issues of June of Shawn's last full year, 1986, the *New Yorker* printed just twenty pieces (not including fiction and poetry); in June of Tina's first full year, 1993, the number was thirty-six—an 80 percent increase. There were enough pieces, in fact, to support virtually any perception or argument about the *New Yorker*—that it was a good magazine, that it was a bad magazine, that it was recognizably related to the "old" *New Yorker,* that it was not.

One difference between the two, however, was indisputable and essential: Shawn aimed for timelessness and Tina aimed for timeliness. He refused to print a piece if it had a "peg" or tie-in to a current or upcoming event; she seemed unwilling to run stories *without* one. Rejecting a story proposal Daniel Menaker had once submitted, Shawn told him it was an "article"— and "the *New Yorker* does not print articles." Under Tina, it did. Whether from scoops, controversy, deliberate provocation, "hot" authors, or literary or artistic merit, her primary goal was for the *New Yorker* to be talked and written about. She and her editors would often tear up the issue two or three times in a week, to make room for a hot new story. Because of all the breaking news stories, the number of fact-checkers doubled, from eight to sixteen. She instituted a publicity department and, at a cost of about $1 million a year, arranged for weekly "hot-list" delivery of advance copies of the magazine to "opinion-makers" in New York, Washington, and Los Angeles, including every member of Congress. It worked: annual press mentions of the *New Yorker* went from about two thousand to more than seven thousand, and all across the land, debates could be heard over the merits of Tina Brown's *New Yorker.*

The old guard of *New Yorker* subscribers were of a mind about the changes, and the mind was not pleased. One representative respondent in the survey of longtime readers, a Seattle woman who had started reading the *New Yorker* in 1933 as a college student, wrote:

> Since Tina Brown became editor of the *New Yorker* the quality has been worse! She is evidently wishing to attract a different type of reader. She seems to think that no issue is complete without a picture of exposed body parts and at least four fucks. She has no sense of what the magazine used to be. I know the Brits are very amused by all types of bathroom jokes—but the readers of the *New Yorker* (and former readers) are looking for something a bit more intellectual; and dignified.

Interestingly, this woman reported that despite her distaste for the magazine, she continued to subscribe, as did nearly 90 percent of the survey respondents.

Without directly criticizing Shawn or Gottlieb, Brown often said in interviews that she wanted to go back to Ross's magazine: short and varied pieces, an irreverent, lively, and sometimes saucy feel, more equality between the text and the graphics, a sense of being a part of the social whirl, no obligation to uphold civilized values or the purity of the language. Her point was well taken, and the illustrations, in particular, by such artists as Spiegelman, Bruce McCall, Edward Gorey, Jules Feiffer, Edward Sorel, and Richard Merkin, all of whom should have been in the *New Yorker* decades before, worked splendidly. Maybe, just maybe, if she had started from scratch, she could have developed a text format that hummed as smoothly. (It could be argued that the contemporary equivalent of Ross's original *New Yorker* had already been wrought—in *Spy.*) But Shawn's *New Yorker* was too much with her—in the staff, in the fact-checking and copyediting procedures (Eleanor Gould Packard still did her Talmudic vetting, though her suggestions were often disregarded), in the Irvin type, in the department headings, in the expectations of readers. Indeed, Brown constantly pounded the *New Yorker* drumbeat, with an insistence that would probably have horrified Ross and Shawn—she brought forth special anniversary issues, many reminiscences about and photographs of *New Yorker* writers and artists of yore, and a design that reiterated and magnified the Irvin typeface almost to the point of self-parody. The magazine under her editorship displayed a great deal of care and talent, but it ended up coming off like a mixed metaphor: a collection of components that continually evoked the old *New Yorker*, but for no particular reason.

The mixed-metaphor problem troubled the economic picture as well. The *New Yorker* was competing for breaking news stories with the *New York Times*, for critics and essayists with the *New York Review of Books*, and for advertisers with *Architectural Digest* and *Vanity Fair*. The *New Yorker* suffered in the last battle because its readers were not rich or young or—as once had been the case—devoted enough to the *New Yorker* to make up for those shortcomings. True, circulation rose sharply under Brown—from 659,000 to 809,000 in her first full year, 1993, and topping off at 868,000 in 1996. But advertising sales were depressingly steady and the demographics stood still. In 1995, more than two years after her arrival, 70 percent of *New Yorker* readers were over the age of forty-five, and 49 percent were over fifty-five. The median household income was a modest $60,000.

In 1993, with enormous severance costs for old writers, high fees and contracts to new writers and high salaries to new editors, the new promotional budget, production costs associated with photography, color separation, and a much heavier paper stock, the magazine lost more than it ever had before—in *Fortune* magazine's estimation, about $30 million. Despite this dismal performance, the next year Si Newhouse promoted Steve Florio to the position of president of Condé Nast and appointed Florio's brother, Tom, as publisher of the *New Yorker*. The losses were smaller under Tom, but not much smaller: *Fortune* reckoned that in the years between 1994 and 1998, the magazine had a total deficit of $60.6 million.

One of the covenants to the 1985 "Agreement and Plan of Merger" between Advance Communications and the *New Yorker* had asserted: "Following the Merger, the business of the Company [the *New Yorker*] will be operated on a stand-alone basis as a separate company." In other words, the *New Yorker* would not become just another member of the Condé Nast stable, alongside *Vogue, GQ, Mademoiselle, Allure, Glamour*, and all the rest. Twelve years later, having spent $168 million to buy the magazine and sustained more than $150 million in additional losses, Si Newhouse announced that the *New Yorker* would join the Condé Nast magazines in a new headquarters the company was erecting on the northeast corner of Broadway and Forty-second Street. Several months later came the announcement that the *New Yorker* would no longer operate even metaphorically on a stand-alone basis, but would share business staff with the other Condé Nast titles and be offered to advertisers as part of a "combination buy." Many longtime *New Yorker* business employees were abruptly terminated, bringing modest savings that hardly seemed to justify the loss in continuity or the human cost.

In the summer of 1998 came another shocker: Tina Brown announced that she was resigning from the *New Yorker* to launch a new magazine in partnership with a movie production company. She thus became the first editor in the history of the magazine to leave the office willingly. Si Newhouse at first offered the job to Michael Kinsley, an experienced editor then at the helm of the Internet magazine *Slate,* but while Kinsley was still mulling it over, decided that the man he really wanted was thirty-nine-year-old *New Yorker* staff writer David Remnick. While a Princeton undergraduate, Remnick had studied with John McPhee, who became a mentor; he had covered the breakup of the Soviet Union as a *Washington Post* reporter and won a Pulitzer Prize for his book on the subject. Since joining the staff of the *New Yorker* in 1992, he had been almost frighteningly prolific.

The child of an educated, middle-class household in northern New Jersey, Remnick was steeped in the traditions of the *New Yorker.* The first year of his editorship showed the pendulum definitely swinging back toward gravitas. There were fewer edgy covers, celebrity profiles, and four-letter words. But true to his newspaper background, he retained Tina's enthusiasm for making news. One minor adjustment seemed to sum up the compromise feel of the early months of Remnick's tenure: he kept the contributors' page but removed the illustrations of the contributors. Such veteran *New Yorker* folk as McPhee, Alec Wilkinson, Bill Barich, and James Stevenson began drifting back. But ad pages fell even lower for 1998, and the magazine continued to bleed red ink.

With his billions of dollars of holdings, Si Newhouse could afford the luxury of a high-profile loss leader. Indeed, a Condé Nast executive said that the *New Yorker* was an economic benefit rather than a drain to the magazine group as a whole: by leading an aura of prestige, it made combination buys more attractive. But even if the magazine continued to publish indefinitely, there was no going back to what it once was.

In August 1999, the *New Yorker* moved into the Condé Nast Building. It had had three floors on West Forty-third Street, but in the new building had to squeeze into two. One of the floors was strictly editorial, but the other was shared by business and editorial employees. They got off on the same elevator stop, shared the same air and offered proof, if proof were needed, that Ross and Shawn's *New Yorker* was a thing of the rapidly receding past.

ACKNOWLEDGEMENTS

Although this is not an "authorized" book, it is the beneficiary of substantial assistance from the *New Yorker* and its staff. For encouragement, information, access, and various kindnesses, I would like to thank Tina Brown, the editor when I began writing; David Remnick, the editor when I finished; Roger Angell, who urged me on at the very start and was unfailingly helpful; Pamela McCarthy; Lee Lorenz; Christopher Shay; Eric Rayman; Rob Livingstone; and Bob Mankoff.

I requested interviews with many *New Yorker* contributors, staff members, and "family"; a few didn't answer my letters but only one turned me down (and he good-naturedly). My thanks to all those who were willing to share their memories and impressions: Renata Adler, Michael J. Arlen, Nicholson Baker, Whitney Balliett, Bill Barich, Sara Barrett, Ann Beattie, John Bennet, Walter Bernstein, Faith Berry, Gardner Botsford, Jacob Brackman, Peter Canby, Lincoln Caplan, Ben Cheever, Mary Cheever, Susan Cheever, Robert Coles, Karen Durbin, Anne Fadiman, Ian Frazier, Ann Goldstein, Robert Gottlieb, Dorothy Lobrano Guth, Donald Hall, Philip Hamburger, Hendrik Hertzberg, Dan Hofstadter, Gerald Jonas, Pauline Kael, Garrison Keillor, Mary D. Rudd Kierstead, Jamaica Kincaid, John Lukacs, Janet Malcolm, Peter Matthiessen, William Maxwell, Charles McGrath, Sheila McGrath, Bill McKibben, Ved Mehta, Daniel Menaker, Louis Menand, Stanley Mieses, Edward Newhouse, Susan Orlean, Eleanor Gould Packard, Mary Painter, Alice Quinn, Lillian Ross, Philip Roth, Dale Russakoff, Nora Sayre, Jonathan Schell, William Steig, James Stevenson, Bernard Taper, Calvin Trillin, Alice Truax, John Updike, William Whitworth, Richard Wilbur, Alec Wilkinson, Ellen Willis, James Wolcott, and Jack Ziegler. I would like to express special appreciation to Mr. Maxwell and Mr. Updike, two private men, who raised no objection to the publication of their correspondence. I will always be glad that I had the chance to talk to Brendan Gill, Emily Hahn, Alfred Kazin, and Joseph Mitchell.

Thomas Kunkel, Harold Ross's biographer, was incredibly generous in sharing information, observations, and interview transcripts. I also benefited from conversations and correspondence with other scholars, critics, biographers, and observers: Paul Alexander, Barbara Burkhardt, Matthew Bruccoli, Mary Corey, Hugh Kenner, Richard Ketchum, Eleanor Lanahan, Linda Lear, David Lehman, Andrew Levy, Marion Meade, Joan Mellen, Edward Mendelson, Brian Nerney, Janice Radway, Carl Rollyson, Ron Rosenbaum, Roger Straus, Patricia Travis, and Adam Van Doren.

As valuable as the interviews were, my most significant source was the *New Yorker* Records at the New York Public Library's Humanities and Social Sciences Library. The courtesy and professionalism of Mimi Bowling and her colleagues in the Manuscripts Division—Laura K. O'Keefe, Richard Salvato, Angelita Sierra, William Stingone, John D. Stinson, Valerie Wingfield, and Melanie Yolles—made the research there a pleasure. Other collections I consulted were the E. B. White Papers at Cornell University; the Katharine White Papers at Bryn Mawr; the Ralph Ingersoll Papers at Boston University; the William Maxwell Papers at the University of Illinois; the Janet Flanner Papers at the Library of Congress; and the James Thurber and Rebecca West Papers at Yale's Beinecke Library. The librarians at these institutions were unfailingly helpful. Susan Brynteson, the Director of Libraries at the University of Delaware, has been a great friend of this project, to the point of giving me access to her personal *New Yorker* clipping collection. Patrick Flanigan, at Booksource, LTD, found hard-to-find books.

Also at Delaware, it is my good fortune to have as colleagues Richard Davison, Steven Helmling, Dennis Jackson, McKay Jenkins, Kevin Kerrane, Thomas Leitch, Harris Ross, and Bonnie Scott; the book benefited from their insights, and I from their goodwill. George Miller, the chair of the English department as I was writing it, was consistently supportive. Richard Duggan solved numerous computer crises, and Brian Hickey, Todd Frankel, Allison Sloan, Howard Padwa, Jonathan Rifkin, Betsy Lowther, and Stephanie Smith provided valuable research assistance.

For help with photographs, I would like to thank Molly Rea, Nora Mitchell Sanborn, Calvin Trillin, Ann Beattie, Anne Hall, James Stevenson, Allene White, and the Cheever family.

I have a hard time imagining a better agent than Stuart Krichevsky or a better editor for this book than Jane Rosenman; her enthusiasm for the project and abiding interest in the *New Yorker* always sent me back to the task at hand with high spirits. Also at Scribner, I want to acknowledge the splendid and sympathetic work of designer Erich Hobbing and copy chief Jay

Schweitzer, and the efficiency and good cheer of Caroline Kim and Catherine Luttinger.

Many of the ideas in the book were nourished in conversation with my friends Bruce Beans, Marguerite Del Giudice, David Friedman, John Grossmann, Margaret Kirk, Hank Klibanoff, Ronnie Polaneczky, Bill Stempel, Robert Strauss, and Rick Valelly. Thanks, John Marchese—you give Manhattan landlords a good name. My mother-in-law, Margaret Y. Simeone, is a good egg, plain and simple. Besides helping with the research, my wife, Gigi Simeone, kept me up-to-date on the current product and listened patiently to more monologues about the *New Yorker* than anyone should be exposed to. Elizabeth Yagoda and Maria Yagoda love Charles Addams and Jack Ziegler, as they should. This book is dedicated to the memory of my mother, Harriet Yagoda, who got me started.

NOTES

In cases where no citation is given for a letter or memorandum quoted in the text, the source is the *The New Yorker* Records, Manuscripts Division, New York Public Library. In cases where no citation is given for a spoken quotation, the source is an interview with the author.

ABBREVIATIONS

Collections

Berg	The Henry W. and Albert A. Berg Collection of English and American Literature, New York Public Library
Bryn Mawr	Katharine Sergeant Angell White Papers, Bryn Mawr College Library
Cornell	E. B. White Collection, Division of Rare and Manuscript Collections, Cornell University Library
Illinois	William Maxwell Papers, University of Illinois
NYPL	*The New Yorker* Records, Manuscripts Division, New York Public Library, Astor, Lenox, and Tilden Foundations
Yale	James Thurber Papers, Beinecke Rare Book and Manuscript Library, Yale University

Individuals

Fleischmann	Raoul Fleischmann
Maxwell	William Maxwell
Ross	Harold Ross
Shawn	William Shawn
Thurber	James Thurber
White	E. B. White
KSW	Katharine S. White

INTRODUCTION

17 "If you would listen": Ross to Groucho Marx, January 23, 1929.
18 "I would like some information": John Updike to "The Editors," March 21, 1949.
18 "Just a note to tell you": Maxwell to KSW, undated, Bryn Mawr.
22 "the patronizing sniffing of critics": Irwin Shaw to G. S. Lobrano, October 1, 1943.
22 "These little slices and moments": Roger Angell to Ann Beattie, February 18, 1972.
23 "I wish you would try": Angell to Beattie, September 1, 1972.
23 "Oh, joy": Angell to Beattie, December 11, 1973.

CHAPTER ONE

25 "a big-boned westerner": Jane Grant, *Ross, the New Yorker and Me,* 7.
26 "a terrible place": ibid., 31.
26 Population gain: Cities Census Committee, *Population of the City of New York, 1890–1930,* 24; Ira Rosenwaike, *Population History of New York,* 102.
26 Arrivals in New York: Ann Douglas, *Terrible Honesty,* 15–16.
27 "had all the iridescence": F. Scott Fitzgerald, "My Lost City" (1932), in *The Crack-Up.*
27 "All over the country": "What Is America."
28 New York theaters: Hyman Howard Taubman, *The Making of the American Theatre,* 125, 155.
28 "a poem read by Edna St. Vincent Millay": Grant, *Ross, the New Yorker and Me,* 179.
30 "I never heard any literary discussion": quoted in Thomas Kunkel, *Genius in Disguise,* 77.
30 "did not find them particularly interesting": Edmund Wilson, *The Twenties,* 45.
32 "Frank asked me to play poker": Raoul Fleischmann, untitled reminiscence, NYPL, 4–5.
33 Magazine advertising increase: Theodore Peterson, *Magazines in the Twentieth Century,* 26.
33 "I started this magazine": Ross to Frank Sullivan, August 4, 1931.
34 "a dull, pompous, dated": *New Yorker,* May 30, 1931, 61.
34 "The early Twenties marked the peak": Corey Ford, *The Time of Laughter,* 2.
35 "Jokes were mostly he-and-she": White to Dale Kramer, August 25, 1950, Cornell.
35 "Our apartment was filled": Grant, *Ross, the New Yorker and Me,* 212.
36 "That we are trying to appeal": "In *Vanity Fair.*"
37 "My theory was": Ross to Margaret Case Harriman, July 12, 1949.
38 "an atmosphere as well as": John K. Hutchens, ed., *The Best in the World,* xx.
40 "The editors of the periodical": *Time,* February 25, 1925.
40 "The first issue virtually sold out": February 21, 1925.
40 "High per centage of sales": "To contributors," NYPL, no date.

CHAPTER TWO

42 "Why don't we make more of a thing": White to Ross, Ross to White, March 16, 1933.
42 "What a satisfaction to know": letter from Lucien P. Cafron, August 31, 1928.
42 "Quite a few readers find it": Fleischmann to Ross, June 26, 1936.
42 "I am violently against": Ross to Fleischmann, September 1, 1936.
43 "I would be *delighted*": Fleischmann to KSW, January 12, 1961, Bryn Mawr. Fleischmann concluded: "I haven't been an astonishingly influential man since our inception. Heaven knows I didn't have any influence over Ross, and I can't say I have any over Bill Shawn. I go good with elderly messengers."
43 Debate over table of contents: interview with Daniel Menaker.
44 1925 contributors: undated memo, NYPL. The memo lists "Evelyn Brooks White," at 112 W. 113th Street, an understandable mistake, since Elwyn Brooks White, a fairly regular contributor, signed his pieces E. B. White or sometimes simply E.B.W.
44 "Briefly, all right": Ross to Russell Lord, November 3, 1929.
44 "Alterations going on as usual": Thurber to Ross, August 15, 1947, Yale.
44 "Those early days represented a period": Robert Coates to Thurber, undated, Yale.
46 "there didn't seem to be": *New Yorker,* February 25, 1925.
46 "a gaping hole": Ford, *The Time of Laughter,* 119.
46 "would take the curse of smallness": Ross to Margaret Case Harriman, July 12, 1949.
46 Circulation, advertising figures: advertisement, *New York Post,* February 18, 1927.
47 "Observed on the elevated newsstand": *New Yorker,* November 14, 1925.
48 "Crowninshield used to say": Edmund Wilson to Thurber, May 15, 1959, Yale.
48 "Judge Wants to Know": *Judge,* February 21, 1925.
48 "far less certain than Mother Dubuque": *New Yorker,* April 17, 1926.

48 "Blackmailing them, is he?": *Judge,* February 21, 1925.
48 "We have in mind a department": undated, NYPL.
49 "I still regard newsbreaks": White to Ik Shuman, undated.
49 "because heroes aren't worshipped anymore": *New Yorker,* October 30, 1926.
49 "There is no limit to the supply": Ross to Tip Bliss, September 27, 1930. Two collections of Newsbreaks were published, *Ho-Hum* and *Another Ho-Hum.*
49 OUR PSHAW DEPARTMENT: March 19, 1927. The use of the word *ourself* was an early example of the *New Yorker* having sport with the first-person plural.
49 "Many people would rather read": *New Yorker,* April 20, 1929.
49 The Newsbreaks were in the issues of May 20, 1939, and February 3, 1940, respectively.
50 "Whether you believe": *New Yorker,* January 24, 1931. Providing precise figures, as in the dimensions of Palmer's signs, was a Talk trademark.
51 "Cloth Collector" appeared April 19, 1931.
51 "could not bear to be mentioned": Gibbs to Frank Sullivan, November 12, 1932.
52 "Ross started mag.": Cornell.
53 "What the magazine needs": KSW to Ross, August 27, 1931.
54 "Really I didn't know that": William Carlos Williams to KSW, October 12, 1930.
54 "One feels a certain quality": Grace Hazard Conkling to Katharine Angell, September 14, 1929.
55 "It is very difficult for me": Katharine Angell to Morley Callaghan, November 7, 1929.
56 "a magnificent job": [Ralph Ingersol] "The *New Yorker.*"
56 "the semi-official organ of sophistication": quoted in Joshua Taylor, *America as Art,* 197.
56 *Vanity Fair* article: Alexander King, "The Sad Case of the Humorous Magazines."
56 "For some strange reason": *New Yorker,* April 15, 1933.
56 "The word is now so slipshod": Dixon Wecter, "A Brief History of Sophistication."
57 "Your first advice": Ross to Hugh Wiley, September 9, 1925.
58 The Herman W. Alpert poem appeared July 17, 1926.
58 "out of town subscribers": Mildred Ungar to Ross, July 19, 1926.
58 1930 percentage: "Rebuke from Dubuque," in-house pamphlet, 1940.
59 1945 percentage: "The National Weekly of the Leadership Market," in-house pamphlet, 1946.
59 New York population figures: Cities Census Committee, *Population of the City of New York, 1890–1930.* Rosenwaike, *Population History of New York,* 190. Nineteen twenty is a convenient cutoff point for this discussion because severe restrictions on immigration started the following year, ending the era of the "urban frontier."
60 "to speculators and traders": "The Vanishing of New York's Social Citadels."
60 Form letter: August 21, 1925.
60 "The fact is that none": Ross to Fleischmann, November 2, 1927.
60 "Oddly enough": White to Walter Blair, February 1, 1964, Cornell.
63 "more familiar art ideas": Katharine Angell to Ross, October 23, 1929.
64 "two half-shot, bellowing old bats": Philip Wylie to Thurber, January 3, 1958, Yale.
65 "Everybody talks of the *New Yorker*'s art": Ross to Hugh Wiley, October 15, 1925.
65 "The one thing Ross had demanded": Wylie to Thurber, January 3, 1958, Yale.
68 "At first the magazine was": KSW note, 1973, Bryn Mawr.
68 "For years and years, before": Ross to Alice Harvey, undated.
69 "Coming upon her first, quiet": Lee Lorenz, *The Art of the New Yorker,* 26.
69 "present an idea or predicament": Thomas Craven, *Cartoon Cavalcade,* 103.
70 "I didn't think it was": Ross to George W. Stark, June 5, 1931.
71 "We are growing wary of": Katharine Angell to Mary Graham Bonner, July 30, 1928.
71 "This isn't it yet": Ross to John O'Hara, March 23, 1928.
71 "Really it will be": O'Hara to Ross, April 7, 1928.
72 The O'Hara sketch was published May 17, 1930.

72 "those dreadful little potboilers": O'Hara to Maxwell, December 26, 1961, quoted in Matthew Bruccoli, *The O'Hara Concern*.
73 E. B. White's obituary of Ross appeared December 15, 1951.
75 "I don't try to scare anyone": Ross to Brendan Gill, May 16, 1941.
76 "Constant Reader, in the early days": Ross to White, October 1938.
76 "It was entirely novel to": Morris Markey, *That's New York!*
76 "He wants anecdotal and incidental stuff": quoted in Brenda Wineapple, *Genêt*, 97.
76 "precisely accurate, highly personal": Janet Flanner, *Paris Was Yesterday*, xix–xx.
78 "We have read with much": Katharine Angell to Morley Callaghan, October 23, 1928.
78 "We were more delighted than": Katharine Angell to Morley Callaghan, November 7, 1928.
79 "I regard Mrs. White as": Ross to Fleischmann, December 11, 1933.
79 "I always felt that the": Edmund Wilson to Thurber, undated, Yale.
79 "Ross, though something of a genius": White, "The Art of the Essay I."
80 "I burned with a low steady fever": White, *Here Is New York*, 31–32.
80 "was attracted to the newborn magazine": in White, *Letters of E. B. White*, 72.
80 White's Comment on advertising was published July 11, 1936.
81 "I had never heard such": quoted in Thurber, *The Years with Ross*, 94.
84 "the gag lines showed": Lorenz, *The Art of the New Yorker*, 49.
84 "struck the shining note": Thurber, *Credos and Curios*, 138.
84 Ingersoll on White and Ross: Harrison Kinney, *James Thurber*, 366.
84 "Would he want to do": Ross to KSW, undated, 1943, Bryn Mawr.
84 "Sometimes in writing of myself": White to Stanley White, January 1929, in *Letters of E. B. White*, 85.
84 "The things that matter": White to Frank Sullivan, December 17, 1951, Cornell.
85 The Notes and Comment appeared January 8, 1926.
86 "From our seat overlooking": *New Yorker*, March 5, 1927.
86 "The answer is Yes": *New Yorker*, December 5, 1931.
87 "I was lounging on a sofa": in Kinney, *James Thurber*, 313.
88 White's obituary of Thurber appeared November 11, 1961.
89 "The precision and clarity of": Kinney, *James Thurber*, 389.
89 "It was I who invented": Ingersoll to Thurber, August 1, 1959, Ralph Ingersoll Papers, Boston University.
90 The Pringle and Thurber manuscripts for the Talk item are in the NYPL.
90 A selection of Thurber's best Talk originals is included in his 1948 collection, *The Beast in Me and Other Animals*.
91 "Who and Whom" was published January 5, 1929.
93 "It came back with a note": in Kinney, *James Thurber*, 420.

CHAPTER THREE

96 Circulation figures: "The New Yorker Magazine, Inc. Subscription and Single Copy Sales (ABC) & Prices." Figures represent averages for the preceding six months. Incidentally, a subscription cost five dollars a year until 1942, when it went up a dollar; single copies cost fifteen cents until 1947, when they went up a nickel.
96 "Without premiums, short term offers": advertisement, *New York Post,* February 18, 1927.
97 Advertising pages: "Rebuque from Dubuque or Where, Indeed, Are the Limits of New York?" self-published promotional pamphlet, 1940.
97 Advertising figures and liquor-advertising information: Fleischmann to Ross, December 31, 1941; "NOTES REGARDING F-R PUBLISHING," undated document, NYPL.
98 "I have lived all my life": White to Charles Morton, May 6, 1963, *Letters of E. B. White*.
98 "It is not benighted capitalistic hoggishness": Fleischmann to Ross, December 31, 1941.
99 "Well, I am as bitter": Ross to H. R. Spaulding, March 12, 1930, Ralph Ingersoll Papers, Boston University.

99   "I am forced to acknowledge": Ross to Ralph Barton, April 6, 1928.
99   "Mr. Ross, Mr. Shawn and I": Ik Shuman to Fleischmann, November 19, 1940.
99   "the filthy excretions of the body": Ross to KSW, July 31, 1946.
99   Elmer Davis letter: Davis to Ross, September 24, 1926.
100   "Cut our throats if you will": Ross to Rea Irvin, October 13, 1930.
100   "We are a little in": Frank Crowninshield to Ross: April 18, 1933.
101   "The use of daring words": Ross to Crowninshield, April 20, 1933.
101   "the members of the advertising staff": Ross to Fleischmann, April 17, 1926.
102   White letter: White to Mr. Jones, January 30, 1976, Cornell.
103   Length limitations: "As to our length requirements, we haven't any, really. We try to run this magazine without rules and with an open mind. It is, however, difficult for us to handle pieces over 1,800 or 2,000 words, although sometimes we do it. . . . From 1,000 to 2,000 words is always easy to handle and is, I presume, our most ideal length." Ross to Elmer Rice, November 14, 1930.
103   "In my judgment 'Profiles' ": Joseph Pulitzer Jr. to Ross, July 13, 1926.
103   "I think it is a mistake": Lawrence Winship to Ross, November 15, 1930.
103   "It seems to me that": KSW to Ross, June 19, 1941.
104   "I favor your immediately doing": Ross to Frank Sullivan, October 2, 1935.
104   Ross's comment on Clarence Day: Frank Sullivan to Thurber, October 5, 1957, Yale.
107   The obituary of Carmine Peppe appeared June 10, 1985.
107   "Woollcott had mannerisms in writing": White to Wayne Chatterton, October 1971, Cornell. When fact writer Joseph Mitchell arrived in 1938, he felt the magazine's prose was still under Woollcott's influence. "I called it sophisticated winsomeness," Mitchell said in a 1995 interview with the author. "I couldn't stand it."
107   Auden on Louise Bogan: Bogan to William Shawn, December 9, 1941, in Elizabeth Frank, *Louise Bogan.*
108   "To the best of my knowledge": Clifton Fadiman, *Reading I've Liked,* xxxviii.
108   Fadiman's account of his hiring: interview with Anne Fadiman.
108   Fadiman's reviews of *Absalom, Absalom!, The Hamlet,* and *Of Mice and Men* appeared, respectively, October 31, 1936, April 6, 1940, and February 27, 1937.
108   "The chief quality of *New Yorker*": Dwight Macdonald, "Laugh and Lie Down."
108   Benchley's review of *Paradise Lost* appeared in the *New Yorker,* December 21, 1935.
109   "That any group of citizens can": *New Yorker,* December 7, 1929.
109   "During the first three days": *New Yorker,* March 25, 1933.
110   "As a boy, I never dreamed": Ross to Don Marquis, March 5, 1930.
111   "How to Pass Time in a Bread Line" was published in the *New Yorker,* December 6, 1930, and "It's About Time Department," October 17, 1931.
111   White's Comment on the New Deal's critics was published December 23, 1933.
113   Mrs. White's memos on S. J. Perelman and Wolcott Gibbs's reply were all sent March 27, 1932.
114   The staff editors' memos are undated; Ross's letter to Perelman was sent February 14, 1933.
114   "It was just a matter of time": in S. J. Perelman, *Strictly from Hunger,* 16–17.
121   "only two first-class character artists": Ross to Perry Barlow, May 1, 1941.
126   The figures on family income and family size come from the U.S. Census Bureau.
129   The quote from *City Editor* can be found on page 34. Walker's own fact-checking was deficient, as he referred to the Reporter at Large department as "The Roving Reporter."
130   Walker listed his *New Yorker* hires in a letter to Thurber, August 23, 1957, Yale.
130   "I have never been sure": in Brendan Gill, *Here at the New Yorker,* 391–92.
131   Here is an example of what one of Ross's queries looked like when the dope piece based on it saw print, on February 1, 1936:

    You probably know that typists always warm up with "Now is the time
    for all good men to come to the aid of their country." A man told us one day

that similar tests are used in trying out telephones, telegraph wires, etc., citing a couple of interesting examples, and we sent one of our detail workers to get further facts. The Bell Laboratories test the volume of a new telephone with "Joe took Father's shoe bench out" and "She was waiting at my lawn." Lots of vowels, you see. For testing articulation, words with lots of consonants are used, because unless an instrument can transmit consonants properly—especially "s," the hardest of all—it's no good. The Bell Company uses for this "Sister Susy sewing silk shirts for Southern soldiers" and "Some settlers suggest settling Southern settlements in succession," which is a honey. A tester keeps phoning these sentences over and over to another tester in another room. Some of these gentlemen have been doing it for years, but none of them has ever gone crazy.

Mr. John Mills, who's been with the Bell people for twenty-three years, told us that decades ago they used to use "Mary had a little lamb" and "Mary, Mary, quite contrary." After that, there was a vogue for "One, two, three, four, five," but that got tiresome. In 1915, a man named Heising used to run through the list of Presidents, from Washington to Wilson. He never made a slip. Nobody remembers who invented the shoe-bench and the waiting-lady lines. Nobody cares who thought up the Sister Susy and the Southern-settlement lines.

The cable companies use: "Freshest eggs at bottom market prices" and "She is his sister." The first sentence consists mainly of dashes, the second of dots. Another line is used by the telegraph companies in the morning to test out any instrument that has lain idle all night: namely, our old friend "Now is the time," etc.

Both Western Union and the Phone Company use teletypewriters extensively. You know: a letter struck on a typewriter in a New York office is electrically reproduced on a machine in some other city. The Phone Company tests with "The quick brown fox jumped over the lazy dog's back" and Western Union sends "William Jax quickly taught five dozen Republicans." In studying teletypewriting, typists practice on finger-breakers like these: "Widow whizz whip; pique 2010X; make zigzag up Ave." and "Julia, vivid coquette, why go Zanzibar if fog awes Max?" and "Quick, Jim, put fez away; find jovial squaw by aquarium." For radio telephony, the A.T.&T. sends "The barking dog's bark is worse than its bite." If the circuit isn't working properly, the words will be "clipped" and the sentence will sound like "The arking og's ark is worse than its ite." There is also a telephoto test for pictures sent out by wire. One of the first telephotos transmitted by the Telephone Company was Coolidge's inauguration, and a picture of the east side of the Capitol in Washington, taken when the stand was being arranged, is always sent out as a test before the transmission of any picture. It contains 350,000 tiny little squares called "details," an average number for a picture, and is therefore a good standard test.

The exhaustive nature of the dope was typical, as was the intermittently arch way in which it was presented.

131 Mitchell described his insistence on a salary in an interview with the author.
131 "The respect for science": Jean-Paul Sartre, quoted in *New York Times Magazine*, February 2, 1947.
133 "The *Saturday Evening Post* and": Ross to Clifton Fadiman, June 9, 1938. Also common in other magazines in the twenties were autobiographical sketches by celebrities, invariably penned by ghostwriters.
133 "We want the main biographical facts": Katharine Angell to Ernest Gruening, January 4, 1929.

133 "sometimes it is not even necessary": Ross to W. W. Walker, March 12, 1928.
134 "Gosh, Duchess, you don't realize": John K. Winkler to Katharine Angell, November 20, 1928.
134 Bergman-Johnston anecdote: Bergman to Thurber, undated, Yale.
134 "technique of defining character": A. J. Liebling, "Ross—The Impresario," in *The Most of A. J. Liebling,* 319.
134 "The perfect *New Yorker* Profile": in *Princeton Tiger,* February 14, 1951.
135 The Zanuck Profile appeared November 10, 1934. What elevates the passage to a high level of comedy, it seems clear, is the *second* use of the verb *sock.*
136 "are going to get too much": Don Marquis to Ross, February 15, 1930.
136 "You're right in saying we've": Ross to KSW, August 25, 1943.
136 McKelway's piece on arson was published January 18, 1936.
137 "We've got to have more journalism": McKelway remembered this in a letter to Thurber, April 2, 1958, Yale.
137 "In those days, two magazines": Yagoda interview. According to Mitchell, the reporters even had disdain for Thurber and White, whom Liebling called "the sons of the prophet." "I couldn't stand the quality in the Talk section—that precious use of *we,*" Mitchell said.
138 "The only job on the": Janet Flanner to KSW, October 19, 1938, Bryn Mawr.
138 The Frank Hague Profile appeared February 12, 1938. In 1945, McCarten took over the film critic's job and held it for more than a decade, also doing some work as a Talk rewrite man. Journalism's loss was not criticism's gain: McCarten was a thoroughly undistinguished reviewer.
140 Stories "reserved" for Liebling: Don Wharton to Liebling, July 6, 1933.
140 "Everybody here seems to": St. Clair McKelway to Liebling, January 16, 1935.
140 "His problem was one of tone": Raymond Sokolov, *Wayward Reporter,* 106.
140 "a million-word book": Liebling, "Ross—The Impresario."
140 "Everybody agreed it was": McKelway to Thurber, April 2, 1958, Yale.
141 "Liebling is the big success": Ross to Ik Shuman, June 1, 1939.
141 "I knew very little": Liebling, *The Road Back from Paris,* 18.
141 "The Jollity Building" was published in the *New Yorker,* April 26–May 10, 1941.
142 Fadiman reviewed *My Ears Are Bent* on January 22, 1938.
142 "We would argue endlessly": Mitchell interview with Thomas Kunkel.
143 "Mr. Addams is a special problem": Ross to Hawley Truax, September 11, 1946.
144 "The conventional way of reporters": interview with Kunkel.
146 "For God's sake, can those": quoted in Roy Hoopes, *Cain,* 214.
147 "Okay, kill the old ending": the story O'Hara was referring to was published on April 29, 1939, under the title "The Ideal Man."
148 "the great flood of casuals": this letter can be found in Bryn Mawr.
149 "We have great hopes for Cheever": the story Maxwell was rejecting was called "The Simple Life."
150 Shaw-Mosher correspondence: the story in question was "Second Mortgage," which Shaw would eventually sell to the *New Republic.*
150 "There's something I don't want": the ellipses are in the original.
150 "In the typical *New Yorker* story": in *Writers at Work: The Paris Review Interviews, Seventh Series.*
151 "What this book should be": KSW to Ross, Ik Shuman, November 7, 1939.
152 Handbooks on short fiction: Andrew Levy, *The Culture and Commerce of the American Short Story,* 38.
152 "The short story is by": Gilbert Seldes, "The Best Butter."
152 "Overindulgence in the short story": Walter Dyer, quoted in Levy, *The Culture and Commerce of the American Short Story.*
153 "She writes a brilliant letter": F. Scott Fitzgerald to Dr. Jonathan Slocum, March 22, 1934, quoted in the *New York Times Magazine,* December 1, 1996.

153 "tight, objective sketches": Stanley Edgar Hyman, "The Urban New Yorker."
154 "through the back door": interview with author.
154 "Three of us here": KSW to Maxim Lieber, April 24, 1936.
154 "creamy sob stories from the *New Yorker*": Alfred Kazin, "Books and Things."
155 "He'd say, 'Goddammit, Cheever' ": Scott Donaldson, ed., *Conversations with John Cheever,* 74. Joseph Mitchell, increasingly obsessed with mortality and doom, remembered that Ross once told him, "You're a pretty gloomy man, but then I'm no goddamned ray of sunshine myself."
155 "The only thing I have": Ross to Christopher LaFarge, September 9, 1941.
155 "If it is chiefly a": Mark Schorer to Maxwell, February 29, 1939.
155 "an intense awareness of human loneliness": Frank O'Connor, *The Lonely Voice,* 19.
155 "The *New Yorker* publishes": Lionel Trilling, "*New Yorker* Fiction." In a memo to Ross about the review, Mrs. White protested, "Apropos his statement that *New Yorker* fiction writers are fundamentally cruel, one could generalize as much on their loving kindness if one took some of the stories he failed to mention. Parker is cruel in the way he says, so is O'Hara, and probably Weidman, and Benson in some moods, but most of the others love the people they write about." Ross replied, "You can take a book like that and make any point you want to make. Perhaps the public is more hard-boiled, at least literally, than it might be but, if so, I don't think this is our responsibility. We print what the public likes. Times have changed since O. Henry."
156 "fastest writers I know": Thurber to Malcolm Cowley, March 11, 1954, quoted in Kinney, *James Thurber,* 966.
157 "Little Woman" was published January 8, 1938.
158 "Ella and the Chinee" was published January 23, 1932.
159 E. B. White on "The Short Life of Emily": quoted in Frank, *Louise Bogan,* 213.
159 "The day a casual from you arrives": KSW to Louise Bogan, 1931.
162 "We would gasp at how": quoted in Michael Shnayerson, *Irwin Shaw,* 92.
163 "In almost everything I wrote": Irwin Shaw, "The Art of Fiction IV."
165 The advertisements appeared in the *New Yorker* of July 15, 1940.
165 "Practicing American Christians feel bitterly": *New Yorker,* March 7, 1936.

Chapter Four

169 "in Germany . . . a helpless minority": *New Yorker,* December 31, 1938.
169 "Gibbs is, of course, skeptical": Ross to White, 1941, Cornell.
169 "I have been strongly suspicious": Ross to White, June 24, 1941.
170 "CAN YOU CABLE US UP": St. Clair McKelway to Mollie Panter-Downes, September 1, 1939.
171 "IN FUTURE OKAY DISCUSS POLITICS": McKelway to Panter-Downes, September 19, 1939.
171 "I changed his mind": KSW to Elizabeth Frank, June 14, 1975, quoted in Linda Davis, *Onward and Upward,* 112.
172 "is effective as a change": KSW to Ross, undated memo, Bryn Mawr.
173 Wallace Stevens anecdote: interview with Richard Wilbur.
173 "Yes, but not all of it": James Geraghty, unpublished memoir.
174 "The *New Yorker* is a worse": *Letters of E. B. White,* 250.
174 "If the war had started": Ross to White, December 1942.
174 "If you want to help out": *New Yorker,* January 2, 1943.
175 "Liebling adapted the Reporter-at-Large": Sokolov, *Wayward Reporter,* 152.
175 "Perhaps what was needed was": Phillip Knightley, *The First Casualty,* 323.
179 Steinberg's arrival: James Geraghty to James Cummings, August 18, 1977. In his unpublished memoir, Geraghty wrote of Steinberg's first submissions, "I remember those drawings to this day, line for line. Ross and the other editors didn't seem to feel what I sensed in those first drawings. For the only time in all my years at the *New Yorker* I had something in hand that seemed important enough to fight for."

179 "This theatre of war being": Saul Steinberg to Ross, October 12, 1943.
180 "a group of short and tall fellows": Steinberg to Geraghty, April 27, 1944.
180 "I don't know what our": quoted in Wineapple, Genêt, 180.
180 "a historical moment in journalism": Flanner to Natalia Denesi Murray, January 21, 1945, quoted in Flanner and Murray, Darlinghissima: Letters to a Friend, 44.
180 "one of the most satisfying": Ross to Flanner, March 27, 1945.
181 Amount of New Yorker war coverage: Raoul Fleischmann to Stephen Sheridan, Area Essential Activities Committee, February 10, 1944. Some people felt the magazine had too much war stuff. The writer Samuel H. Adams had voiced this complaint to Ross, who replied: "One big psychological factor is that the government never gave us any break at all, considering us useless in all its rulings on paper supply, essentiality, etc., and out of subconscious perversity we may have swung more toward war than we ordinarily would have. But the big thing is that practically the whole staff went to war one way or another, those that weren't in the Army insisting on being correspondents. We more or less have to take what we get from writers, for in the long run we depend on more or less the same bunch of them. Most of the regulars write war stuff. . . . But the hell with it. We've got a lot of prestige out of our war stories and we've done a pretty good job on it, and it's only a few of you older birds that complain." Ross to Adams, August 21, 1944.
181 Ratio of service to civilian readers: White, Notes and Comment, December 28, 1946.
182 "It is my conviction": Ross to Stephen T. Early, March 14, 1944.
182 "Shawn is now highly eligible": Ross to White, undated letter.
182 "The army looked me over": Shawn to E. J. Kahn, February 23, 1943.
183 "really deserves all the credit": Ross to Robert Sherwood, February 19, 1947.
183 John Lardner story: Ring Lardner Jr., The Lardners, 311.
183 "regarded by some as heir-apparent": "Talk of the Town."
183 "hardest-working and most self-sacrificing man": Ross to Rebecca West, August 12, 1947.
184 Hersey visit with John F. Kennedy: Herbert Parmet, Jack, 117.
185 Shawn's dislike of the word killing: Shawn to Hobart Weekes, 1943.
186 "obsessed, as any serious writer": John Hersey, Here to Stay, vii.
186 "STILL THINK IT WOULD BE": Hersey to Shawn, March 22, 1946.
186 "EYE WAS ABOUT TO CABLE": Shawn to Hersey, March 22, 1946.
186 Background on "Hiroshima": Michael J. Yavenditti, "John Hersey and the American Conscience: The Reception of 'Hiroshima' "; Frederick S. Voss, Reporting the War: The Journalistic Coverage of World War II, 208.
187 "Hersey had, in typical New Yorker": Newsweek, September 9, 1946. In its September 9 issue, Time also ran an article about "Hiroshima" and suggested another reason Ross may have agreed to the proposal of "able, shy co-managing editor Bill Shawn": the regular departments "were in the summer doldrums" and copy was in short supply.
187 "It is a pity you never": Maxwell to John Updike, June 15, 1960.
188 "A diamond is found": in Donaldson, Conversations with John Cheever, 105.
188 "A very fine piece beyond": Harold Ross query sheet, August 6, 1946.
191 "Dr. Fujii sat down cross-legged": reading a reference to this event in the second section of Hersey's initial draft, Ross spotted an inconsistency: "First part this sentence says whole building in river, second part said 'most of.' I'd push the whole damned thing in and have done. Part I had it all in river."
192 "We think the story is": The letter was simply signed "The New Yorker," but its diffidence and emphasis on Hersey's factual scoops unmistakably marks it as Ross's work: "We think there are some new things in the story, or more or less new things, such as, for instance, the figures on the casualties . . . ; the curious fact that nobody Mr. Hersey talked to in Hiroshima remembered having heard any sound when the bomb exploded; the effects of the explosion at various given distances from the center; how the Japanese scientists determined the exact center of the explosion, and their calculations on its force and the heat it generated."

192 Reaction to "Hiroshima":Yavenditti, "John Hersey and the American Conscience." A random sample of 339 letters, telegrams, and postcards to the *New Yorker* found favorable comments outweighing negative ones by a ten-to-one margin. Joseph Luft and W. M. Wheeler, "Reaction to John Hersey's 'Hiroshima.' "

193 "We find it hard to conceive": quoted in Charles Poore, " 'The Most Spectacular Explosion in the Time of Man.' "

193 "I don't think I've ever": Ross to Irwin Shaw, September 19, 1946.

194 "Your new world line of comments": Ross to White, October 1944.

194 "Nuclear energy and foreign policy": *New Yorker,* August 18, 1945.

195 "the profusion of ancient themes": Daniel Lang, *Hiroshima to the Moon.*

196 "All around him heads nodded": *New Yorker,* April 3, 1948.

196 White referred to "a political purge" on February 26, 1949, and to "American political prisoners" on August 6, 1949.

196 "a contributor would describe some": Mary Corey, *The World through a Monocle,* 49.

196 "Come In, Lassie!" was published February 21, 1948.

197 The *Plain Talk* references to Liebling and the *New Yorker* appeared in the issues of October and November 1949 and are quoted in Herbert Mitgang, *Dangerous Dossiers,* 133.

197 "careless journalist of the *New Yorker* set": quoted in Natalie Robins, *Alien Ink,* 154–55.

197 "incapable of having partisan politics": Ross to John O'Hara, September 24, 1947.

197 "conservative with an isolationist bent": Kunkel, *Genius in Disguise,* 402.

197 "Nobody was going to tell":Walter Bernstein, *Inside Out,* 20–21. Bernstein never did the story because the State Department, for unspecified reasons, delayed approving his passport until the trial was over.

197 The E. J. Kahn anecdote is in Kunkel, *Genius in Disguise,* 404.

198 Richard Rovere segregation story: Richard Rovere, *Arrivals and Departures,* 68–70.

198 "wore no beard, spoke with": quoted in Corey, *The World through a Monocle,* 75.

198 "permit my views to embarrass": Boyer to Ross, November 14, 1949.

198 "you *can't* be fired": Ross to Boyer, November 18, 1949.

198 "When Boyer wrote (for the *Daily Worker)*":White to (name deleted), November 20, 1949, Bryn Mawr.

200 "the foundation of a very good piece": KSW to Anthony Gibbs, May 8, 1931.

200 "I am still a little nervous":Anthony Gibbs to KSW, September 23, 1931.

201 "Oh these good editors!": Lewis Mumford to Babette Deutsch, June 2, 1931, quoted in Mumford, *My Works and Days.*

201 "I am frequently regarded as ignorant": Ross to John O'Hara, September 34, 1947.

202 "The *New Yorker* is madly hospitable": Kenneth Tynan to Terence Kilmartin, December 12, 1958, quoted in Tynan, *Letters.*

202 Edna St.Vincent Millay Profile: KSW to Nancy Milford, October 5, 1973, Bryn Mawr. The Profile was published February 12, 1927, and the letter from the poet's mother on April 23.

203 "Add Fact Checking to your list": Ross to Ralph Ingersoll, September 30, 1930.

203 "Once, in a spirit of sacrilege": *New Yorker,* April 26, 1941.

203 "What with our making fun": Ross to Fleischmann, March 21, 1927.

204 "This pretty darned good story": Ross query sheet, June 20, 1949. Nine days later, commenting on Elizabeth Taylor's "The Beginning of a Story," he complained, "These British authors don't understand about pegging, apparently . . ."

204 "There is something repellent": John Updike to Maxwell, February 17, 1958.

204 "sometimes seemed to be editing":Thurber, *The Years with Ross,* 96.

204 Gibbs's qualifiers: Donald E. Houghton, "*The New Yorker:* Exponent of a Cosmopolitan Elite," 95.

205 "which may be, in part": Kay Boyle to Ross, September 27, 1948. Ross was not as vigilant about eliminating *little* from *titles.* Between 1925 and 1940, the titles of forty *New Yorker* pieces or poems began with "Little," "A Little," or "The Little"; between 1940 and 1955, the number was thirty.

205 "The curse of our formula editing": James Thurber to Ross, October 7, 1949, Yale.
206 Nabokov and the nutcracker: Nabokov changed the reference to "a nutcracker carelessly passed." He quoted Ross's query in the introduction to his memoir *Speak, Memory*, which included "Lantern Slides" and nine other chapters originally published in the *New Yorker*.
206 Ross's commas: Grant, *Ross, the New Yorker and Me*, 239.
206 "The serial comma is important": Ross to Fleischmann, April 1, 1946.
207 "When I read, the other day": W. L. Copithorne, "Flower, Fruit, and Fan," *New Yorker*, March 20, 1948. Note that there would have been eight commas if Copithorne had not chosen to use parentheses.
207 "Commas in the *New Yorker*": White, "The Art of the Essay I."
207 Sally Benson anecdote: Russell Maloney, "Tilley the Toiler."
208 "If Mr. Ross wants the house": Louise Bogan, *What the Woman Lived*, 74.
211 "entering a splendid fulfillment": Jan Morris, *Manhattan '45*, 7.
211 Promotion spending: Ik Shuman to Ross, September 27, 1943.
213 "The city is like poetry": White, *Here Is New York*, 21–22.
214 "The shops, the bars, the women": Cyril Connolly, *Ideas and Places*, 176.
215 Gordimer: George Plimpton, ed., *Writers at Work*, Sixth Series, 252.
215 Short-story submissions: Mason to Ross, June 15, 1948.
215 "frustrated *New Yorker* short story writer": quoted in *New Yorker* Newsbreak, August 4, 1945.
215 Katharine White on Jane Austen: KSW to Edmund Wilson, June 21, 1944.
215 "It was awkward for him": KSW, Notes on *Here at the New Yorker*, Bryn Mawr.
216 Wilson's proposal to Ross: Edmund Wilson to Ross, April 22, 1942.
216 "the most highly prized": *Saturday Review*, October 23, 1943.
216 "You seem to be the only man": Ross to Edmund Wilson, October 14, 1943.
216 "It has happened to me": *New Yorker*, June 8, 1948.
216 "I should like to have": Wilson to Ross, October 17, 1943.
216 "It is understood that you": *New Yorker* to Wilson, October 28, 1943.
216 "There is nothing to be": Ross to KSW, 1943.
217 "Your reportorial instinct amazes me": Ross to Rebecca West, February 11, 1946, Rebecca West Papers, Beinecke Rare Books and Manuscript Library, Yale University.
217 "I am certain that the": Ross to Fleischmann, April 21, 1943.
218 "one of the brightest generated": Ross to Fleischmann, May 18, 1943.
218 "especially in talking to writers": KSW to Ross, February 6, 1950.
218 Fine points of first-reading agreement: Hawley Truax to Ross, February 10, 1949.
219 "This story seems to me": Ross query sheet, January 10, 1949.
219 Stafford's financial arrangment: KSW to Marian Ives, December 12, 1947; KSW to Jean Stafford, December 20, 1948.
220 "Your story in the last": Maxwell to Peter Taylor, January 27, 1943.
220 Taylor was somewhat irked: Herbert T. McAlexander, ed., *Conversations with Peter Taylor*, 73.
220 "The story belongs to a world": Maxwell to Taylor, April 30, 1943.
221 "we very, very much hope": KSW to Robert Giroux, July 2, 1948.
221 Acceptance of "Cookie": KSW to Taylor, August 4, 1948.
221 "pieces concerned with regional differences": McAlexander, ed., *Conversations with Peter Taylor*, 15.
221 "Can't you add a paragraph": KSW to Taylor, October 21, 1948.
221 "I don't like a story": Taylor to KSW, October 24, 1948.
222 "is, of course, out of bounds": KSW to Taylor, June 20, 1949.
222 "Helen Ruth is, of course": Taylor to KSW, July 5, 1949.
222 "The story seemed to me": Lobrano to Taylor, July 14, 1949.
223 "I think that I should withdraw": Taylor to Lobrano, July 21, 1949.
223 Welty's fee: Michael Kreyling, ed., *Author and Agent*, 156.
223 "One of the ideas she": Edmund Wilson to Vladimir Nabokov, January 15, 1944, in Simon Karlinsky, ed., *The Nabokov-Wilson Letters*, 125.

223 Rejection of "A Forgotten Poet": KSW to Nabokov, June 14, 1944.

223 "These projections into the future": KSW to Nabokov, September 25, 1944.

224 "I am a little shocked": Nabokov to KSW, September 28, 1944. As he almost always did, Nabokov included an ink drawing of a butterfly at the bottom of the letter. Two weeks later, he wrote to Wilson about the change (using French, as he usually did for sensitive matters), "The *New Yorker* had the gall to send me back my story, accompanied by a letter filled with a farrago of nonsense. Being in a bad mood that day, I told Mrs. White off rather rudely." Nabokov to Wilson, October 11, 1944, in Karlinsky, ed., *The Nabokov-Wilson Letters*, 143–45, translation by Simon Karlinsky. The story was published in the *Atlantic Monthly* in January 1945.

224 "Unfortunately, a man called Ross": Nabokov to Wilson, June 17, 1945, in Karlinsky, ed., *The Nabokov-Wilson Letters*, 154. The "bridge" Nabokov referred to concerned two sentences in the story that originally read: "Then—last month, to be precise—there came a telephone call. In a hard and glittering voice, she said she was Mrs. Sybil Hall . . ." Correctly arguing that "a telephone call isn't a 'she,'" Mrs. White wanted the second sentence to begin, "In a hard and glittering voice, a woman said she was . . ." When the story was collected in book form, Nabokov retained the change.

225 "one of the greatest short stories": Brian Boyd, *Vladimir Nabokov*, 117.

225 "a parody or satire of the gloomy": KSW to Nabokov, July 10, 1947.

225 "If *The New Yorker* had": Wilson to KSW, November 12, 1947.

226 "I deeply appreciated your sympathetic": Nabokov to KSW, November 10, 1947.

226 "I always appreciate your delicate": Nabokov to KSW, March 4, 1949.

226 "Your story is fearful, wonderful": KSW to Nabokov, November 14, 1951. Harold Ross would die less than a month later.

226 Ross queries sheets are dated September 20, 1949, and April 24, 1949, respectively.

227 "Please tell the author": Nabokov to KSW, March 10, 1952, quoted in Boyd, *Vladimir Nabokov*, 210. As someone who had received dozens of letters from Katharine White, Nabokov surely realized that this note—which is reproduced on pages 209–10 of Boyd's book—was her work, but since she had not acknowledged it, perhaps he felt a veiled expression of appreciation was more appropriate than a direct one.

227 "You have done a magnificent job": Nabokov to KSW, September 25, 1955.

227 "The English of *CE*": Wilson to Nabokov, March 26, 1951, in Karlinsky, ed., *The Nabokov-Wilson Letters*, 261.

228 "I look back on our": Nabokov to KSW, November 24, 1955.

228 "no longer afford to write": John O'Hara to KSW, February 3, 1948.

228 "Madness would lie that way": Ross to KSW, February 9, 1948.

228 "shocked and very angry": O'Hara to Ross, stamped April 6, 1949, Matthew Bruccoli Collection.

230 "The Enormous Radio" was published May 17, 1947.

230 "I've just read 'The Enormous Radio' ": Ross to John Cheever, April 3, 1947.

231 "a pretty cryptic and loony batch": Lobrano to Frances Pindyck, November 22, 1943. In that year alone, the magazine rejected about a dozen stories by Jackson. "The Gift" was eventually bought and published by *Charm*, a women's magazine.

232 Lobrano felt compelled to telephone Jackson: Thurber, *The Years with Ross*, 263.

232 "bewilderment, speculation, and plain old-fashioned abuse": Shirley Jackson, "Biography of a Story," in *Come Along with Me*, 213–14, 220–22.

233 "There is certainly something quite": John Mosher to Harold Ober, February 14, 1941.

233 "it would have worked out": Maxwell to Ober, February 26, 1942.

233 "We think Mr. Salinger is": Maxwell to Ober, n.d.

233 He told Gibbs that a: J. D. Salinger to G. S. Gibbs, January 20, 1944.

234 "I thought the Salinger piece": John Cheever to Lobrano, n.d.

234 "Everybody out here talks about": Kober to Ross, June 15, 1948.

235 "break with irony and despair": Cheever, *The Journals of John Cheever*, 340.

235 He told Lobrano: Salinger to Lobrano, October 12, 1949.

237 "As a variation of the": quoted in *New Yorker* Newsbreak, January 18, 1947.
237 The *New Yorker,* an ultra-sophisticated": quoted in *New Yorker* Newsbreak, September 6, 1947.
239 "Sophistication, in the sense that": Maxwell to John Updike, May 7, 1958.
240 "He based the editorial policy": ibid.
240 "Hokusai used to sign his work": *Evening Standard,* December 7, 1951.

CHAPTER FIVE

245 "The Hauptmann Defense Fund offices": undated typescript, NYPL. Ultimately, no article on the Hauptmann Defense Fund was published.
246 "Seated at a desk heaped": Gill, *Here at the New Yorker,* 150.
247 "For the past six years": Shawn, idea sheet, April 1, 1935.
247 "Nothing startling, but subject matter": Shawn to Ross, October 25, 1939.
248 "long amorphous piece": A. J. Liebling to Shawn, August 9, 1944; Shawn to Liebling, August 11, 1944.
248 "odd cables with affection, appreciation": Flanner to KSW, 1952, Bryn Mawr.
248 "A stunning piece of historical reporting": Shawn to Matthew Josephson, February 19, 1941.
249 "Have you ever thought of publishing": Shawn to Geoffrey Hellman, February 19, 1943.
249 "it never used to be": Margaret Case Harriman to Ross, 1941.
249 "but I was unable": S. N. Behrman to KSW, October 9, 1951.
240 "I thought afterward it might": Behrman to KSW, October 12, 1951.
250 "Shawn was talking about running": Ross to Rebecca West, March 21, 1950.
250 "would be a kind of impression": John Hersey to Shawn, September 2, 1947.
251 "the girl with the built-in": Wilson to Thurber, undated, Yale.
251 "Come In, Lassie!" was published February 21, 1948, and "Symbol of All We Possess" on October 22, 1949.
252 "a sympathetic piece": Lillian Ross, *Reporting,* 189.
252 "After all these years she": Thurber to Ross, May 16, 1950.
252 "I don't know who Lillian": James M. Cain to Ross, May 28, 1950.
253 "You see, if the story": Ross to Shawn, August 12, 1950.
255 "As long as I was there": Ik Shuman to Thurber, September 22, 1957, Yale.
255 One night in 1948: Thurber, *The Years with Ross,* 304.
255 "The *New Yorker* will blow up": Ross to Julius Baer, November 12, 1945.
256 However, Lillian Ross reports: Lillian Ross, *Here but Not Here,* 100.
256 "feels that if we use serious poetry": KSW to Bogan, February 18, 1952.
256 "who seems to be very nice": Bishop to Marianne Moore, August 24, 1952, in Elizabeth Bishop, *One Art.*
256 Donald Hall singled out the *New Yorker.* Donald Hall, "The New Poetry."
256 "combining the best qualities": quoted by Brendan Gill in *Here at the New Yorker,* x. This comparison has also been attributed to several other people.
257 "Everybody knows that the give-and-take": Flanner to KSW, 1952, Bryn Mawr.
258 "Yes, I am here": Shawn to Hamilton Basso, March 12, 1946.
258 "Please burn the enclosed letter": Shawn to Behrman, August 22, 1947.
258 "It was just that in": Updike to Maxwell, October 18, 1957.
258 "But the atmosphere had changed": Bernstein, *Inside Out,* 155
259 "had practically no first-hand": Shawn to Department of State, June 11, 1952, quoted in Robins, *Alien Ink,* 203–4.
259 "make critical comments about our government": Lobrano, "To Whom It May Concern," October 3, 1952, quoted in Joan Mellen, *Kay Boyle,* 343.
259 he was "appalled": ibid., 345.
260 " 'Subject correspondent is a full' ": Shawn to Flanner, April 24, 1953, Janet Flanner Papers, Library of Congress.

260 Boyle wrote Shawn that it was a "grave matter": Boyle to Shawn, March 21, 1953, quoted in Mellen, *Kay Boyle,* 363.

260 "Have I been completely mistaken": Flanner to Boyle, February 3, 1953, ibid., 362.

260 "Harold would have done it": Boyle to Shawn, February 1, 1953, ibid.

260 WAS AFRAID YOU MIGHT CONSIDER: Joseph Wechsberg to Shawn, November 19, 1954.

261 YOU MUST TRUST MY JOURNALISTIC: Wechsberg to Shawn, December 27, 1955.

261 ALL CHANGES IN YOUR PIECES: Shawn to Wechsberg, December 28, 1955.

263 "If Capote is great": Ross to Lobrano, April 3, 1947.

263 "Yes, it is morbid perhaps": KSW to Ross, 1949.

263 "that aren't too psychopathic: Ross to Lobrano, July 27, 1949.

264 "Orlov ordered Russian cognac": Capote, "The Muses Are Heard," in *The Dogs Bark,* 262–63.

264 "He fiddled with things": Gerald Clarke, *Capote,* 294

265 "What is the lowest level": Capote, *The Dogs Bark,* xviii.

265 "The little bastard spent half": Clarke, *Capote,* 302.

270 "They say the *New Yorker*": Kathleen Tynan, *The Life of Kenneth Tynan,* 203.

270 "Mr. Scott is an intense performer": *New Yorker,* January 9, 1960.

270 "I have gone over them": Ross to Peter De Vries, June 8, 1944.

271 "Where the hell are the": Ogden Nash to Ross, November 5, 1949.

271 "Yes, where are the young writers?": Ross to Nash, November 14, 1949.

272 The Newsbreaks quoted were printed, respectively, in the issues of March 1, 1958, 95; January 1, 1958, 84; March 8, 1958, 37; November 30, 1963, 112; and February 22, 1958, 59.

275 "He continued writing short stories": Joseph Heller, *Closing Time,* 159.

282 "It occurs to me that": Illinois.

282 "It was a peaceable kingdom": quoted in Robert Dahlin, "William Maxwell."

284 "takes so long to say anything": Maxwell to KSW, undated, Bryn Mawr.

284 "Irwin never got over his rejection": quoted in Shnayerson, *Irwin Shaw,* 238.

284 Salinger's request not to forward reviews: Salinger to Lobrano, April 1, 1953.

285 Salinger's letter: Salinger to Lobrano, December 20, 1954.

285 "concern . . . about the length of": Warren French, *J. D. Salinger,* 139.

286 Rejection of "Zooey": Maxwell to author.

287 "I do feel that Salinger": Maxwell to KSW, undated, Bryn Mawr.

289 "The fact that they have": *Journals of John Cheever,* 15.

290 "His stories collided with the": Susan Cheever, *Home Before Dark,* 148.

290 "As for the book I": Cheever to Emmy Maxwell, April 5, 1957, Berg.

290 "We are as poor as": *Journals of John Cheever,* 14.

291 "The initials are meant to represent": Cheever to Maxwell, August 28, 1963, Berg.

291 "I should have warned you": Cheever to Allan Gurganus, *Letters of John Cheever,* 314–15.

291 "Nearly every time I think": *Journals of John Cheever,* 121.

291 I DON'T EXPECT TO ENJOY: Maxwell to Cheever, 1965.

292 "walked over to the station": Cheever to Weaver, December 5, 1961, in *Letters of John Cheever,* 232.

292 Cheever's indebtedness: Maxwell to John Cheever, July 15, 1963.

292 *New Yorker's* offer: agreement dated December 10, 1963, *New Yorker* Records.

292 "so your father could see": ibid., 233.

292 "I admire Salinger, of course": ibid.

293 "a key to the men's room": Susan Cheever, *Home Before Dark,* 150.

293 "Like many men of fifty": *Journals of John Cheever,* 189. After the confrontation, Cheever was characteristically conciliatory, writing to Maxwell, "I'm very glad you liked the piece. After leaving you I felt I had been drunken and disorderly in pricing it and I know how complicated these arrangements can be." Undated, Berg.

296 "the background, the combination of": Rachel MacKenzie to Philip Roth, November 20, 1957.

296 Rejection of "Goodbye, Columbus": MacKenzie to Roth, May 7, 1958.
300 "We all agree that there": MacKenzie to Candida Donadio, November 11, 1958. "Eli, the Fanatic" was published in *Commentary.*
300 "they turned down everything": Roth to author, November 14, 1998. Roth was forgetting about "Novotny's Pain," an interesting, Kafkaesque story about a man (not Jewish, apparently) who wakes up one morning with a mysterious pain in his back and is never able to get rid of it. The *New Yorker* published it in 1962.
301 "unclimbed Annapurnas": Sylvia Plath to Aurelia Plath, April 25, 1953, in Plath, *Letters Home,* 109.
301 Interview requests: Sylvia Plath to Aurelia Plath, May 13, 1953, ibid., 114. None of the interviews panned out, but Plath did have a moment of special satisfaction at *Mademoiselle,* as she wrote to her mother on June 8: "Also writing and typing rejections, signed with my own name! Sent one to a man on the *New Yorker* staff today with a perverse sense of poetic justice." In Plath, *Letters Home,* 116.
301 "I would really like to": Sylvia Plath to Aurelia Plath, January 17, 1956, ibid., 207.
301 "I depend too desperately": Plath, *The Journals of Sylvia Plath,* 99.
301 "Seated at the typewriter, I": ibid., 242.
302 "It is one of the": John Updike, *Picked-Up Pieces,* 435.
302 "My sole ambition was to": Jane Howard, "Can a Nice Novelist Finish First?" *Life,* November 4, 1961; reprinted in James Plath, ed., *Conversations with John Updike,* 12.
302 "Yes, this is how it": John Updike, *Collected Poems, 1953–1993,* 252.
303 "studying the draftsmanship of Alain": Updike to Maxwell, August 5 (no year), Illinois.
303 "triple rhyme and final hexameter": Updike, *Collected Poems 1953–1993,* 369.
303 "It is a great pleasure": KSW to Updike, July 17, 1954.
303 "Look, we don't use stories": Updike to author, July 1, 1996.
303 "covetous dissatisfaction": John Updike, *Odd Jobs,* 115.
303 "there must be more to say": Updike to author, November 23, 1998.
304 "While writing it, I had": Updike, *Odd Jobs,* 134.
305 "It is rather unusual for": KSW to Updike, September 15, 1954.
305 "to gad about": John Updike, *Assorted Prose,* vii.
306 "required no research": John Updike, *Talk from the Fifties,* x.
306 "On the afternoon of the": Updike, *Assorted Prose,* 51–53.
307 "A man who would be": Updike, *Talk from the Fifties,* xii.
307 "It occurs to me that": Updike to Maxwell, March 6 (no year), Illinois.
308 "It is a slightly different magazine": Maxwell to Updike, May 7, 1958.
308 "Shawn felt as I did": Maxwell to Updike, September 6, 1960. "The Crow in the Woods" was published in the *Transatlantic Review.*
308 "You must be kidding about 'butt'": Updike to Maxwell, September 8, 1960.
309 "I have been in a": Updike to Maxwell, May 19 (no year), Illinois.
309 "From the very beginning I": Maxwell to Updike, July 6, 1960.
309 *Wall Street Journal* article: Bart, P. B., and J. H. Rutledge, "Urbanity, Inc."
310 "foundation garment advertising": quoted in Jim O'Hara, "*New Yorker,* at 40, Prospers, Also Retains Character as Choosy Medium."
310 "by association a further boost": Stephen Fox, *The Mirror Makers,* 231. Fox also discusses the Hathaway shirt campaign.
311 this segment dramatically increased: U.S. Census Bureau figures.
311 Internal *New Yorker* marketing surveys reveal: Mary Corey, *The World through a Monocle,* 435.

CHAPTER SIX

313 The account of the genesis of "Silent Spring" was in large part taken from Linda Lear, *Rachel Carson.*

314 "He is completely fascinated": Carson to Dorothy Freeman, in Martha Freeman, ed., *Always, Rachel*, 257.

314 "indictment of what man is doing": Carson to Shawn, July 20, 1961, quoted in Lear, *Rachel Carson*, 395.

314 "I stuck my head out": Edith Iglauer, *The Strangers Next Door*, 63.

315 "the phone rang and a": Carson to Freeman, January 23, 1962, in Freeman, ed., *Always, Rachel*, 394.

315 The account of the genesis and publication of "Letter from a Region in My Mind" is based on that in James Campbell, *Talking at the Gates*, which in turn was based on interviews with William Shawn and Norman Podhoretz.

316 "It is difficult to find": Corey, *The World through a Monocle*, 177.

317 "the incredible, abysmal, and really cowardly": James Baldwin, "Down at the Cross," in James Baldwin, *Collected Essays*, 320.

317 "the solution to the Negro problem": Baldwin, *Collected Essays*, 340–41.

318 "Precisely why it will not": Irving Howe, " 'The New Yorker' and Hannah Arendt."

320 The description of Jeremy Bernstein's recruitment is based on his essay "Breaking in at the *New Yorker*."

321 "Shawn read my piece": Norman Lewis, *The World, the World*, 208–9.

322 "I had never before had": Ved Mehta, *Remembering Mr. Shawn's New Yorker*, 13

322 "In India the elders never": Mehta to Shawn, May 3, 1960.

322 "My first impulse was to": Mehta, *Remembering Mr. Shawn's New Yorker*, 71.

322 "that in the course of": Mehta, ibid., 94.

327 "the edited manuscript was sent": Mehta, ibid., 133–34.

328 "inconsistency of spelling and hyphenation": Maxwell to Sylvia Townsend Warner, October 14, 1957.

328 "insisting that a hyphen was": Philip Hamburger, *Curious World*, xv.

329 "I did think there was": Philip Roth to Robert Henderson, April 7, 1962.

329 "As you may have been": Eleanor Packard Gould to White, October 18, 1971, Cornell.

330 "I think Mr. Shawn is rather": Norman Thomas di Giovanni, May 6, 1968. The poet W. S. Merwin once deleted a large quantity of commas from a proof and sent it back to poetry editor Howard Moss with the note: "Please give the extra commas to Jose Garcia Villa if you can find him." September 30, 1961.

330 "an artillery bombardment": quoted in Tynan, *Life of Kenneth Tynan*, 484.

330 "There was so much slipping": William Maxwell, "Introduction," in Maeve Brennan, *The Springs of Affection*, 5.

338 "To be technical for a moment": Shawn to Whitney, April 9, 1965.

341 "The difference between Tom Wolfe": Dwight Macdonald, "Parajournalism II: Wolfe and *The New Yorker*."

343 "I read that story in the *New Yorker*": C. D. B. Bryan to Maxwell, September 29, 1963.

343 "He is certainly one of": Angell to Lynn Nesbit, October 13, 1963.

343 "I hope you know that": Angell to Donald Barthelme, February 25, 1964.

343 Reaction to "Snow White": Leo Hofeller to Karen Durbin, January 23, 1968.

344 "Roger, I really feel strongly": Barthelme to Angell, undated, 1965.

347 Capote's accuracy: Clarke, *Capote*, 351.

348 record for newsstand sales: "The Country Below the Surface."

349 "I didn't know much of": Michael Arlen, *The Living-Room War*, vii.

353 "I would get letters all": Will Brantley, ed., *Conversations with Pauline Kael*, 156.

355 "That's the way it had": Roy Blount Jr., "Lustily Vigilant."

356 "The girls have Their Experience": Tom Wolfe, *The Kandy-Kolored Tangerine-Flaked Streamline Baby*, 208. Ellipses Wolfe's.

357 "Subjective journalism, or what we": quoted in Brian James Nerney, "Katharine White, *New Yorker* Editor."

357 "There is no question that": Richard Cohen, "Shawn's Letter from 43d Street."

359 "a perfect piece of *NewYorker*": quoted in Ben H. Bagdikian, *The Media Monopoly*, 108.
359 The army's internal response: William M. Hammond, *Reporting Vietnam*, 84–85.
360 "I became convinced that we": quoted in Bagdikian, *Media Monopoly*, 108.
360 Public opinion after the Tet Offensive: Daniel C. Hallin, *The "Uncensored War,"* 170.
361 The Schell Comment pieces quoted appeared on April 18, 1970 and March 12, 1971.
361 "I was so happy with": Maxwell to KSW, January 21, 1974, Bryn Mawr.
363 "There was a change in": quoted in Gigi Mahon, *The Last Days of the New Yorker*, 81.
364 The figures for television advertising revenues come from David Abrahamson, *Magazine-Made America*, 23. Abrahamson also provides information on the boom in special-interest magazines.
364 "The *New Yorker* rode too": *Wall Street Journal*, March 24, 1971.

CHAPTER SEVEN

367 "made me feel there is": Maxwell to Gilbert Rogin, June 7, 1965.
368 "To me, as of everyone": "Woody Allen, "The Art of Humor I."
369 "Rabbi Zwi Chaim Yisroel": Woody Allen, *Getting Even*, 54–55.
371 "The older people discussed other": *New Yorker*, October 21, 1972.
372 "I thought Mr. Shawn would": "Remembering Mr. Shawn," *New Yorker*, December 28, 1992–January 4, 1993.
374 "Over the years, it has": Ian Frazier, *Dating Your Mom*, 31–32.
374 "My people weren't much for": Garrison Keillor, *Happy to Be Here*, x–xi.
375 "When you are in your": Keillor to author, E-mail message.
375 "You have sustained such a": Angell to Keillor, November 30, 1970.
375 "for such admirable brevity": Angell to Keillor, August 31, 1970.
376 Carmine Peppe's resistance to Jack Ziegler: interview with Lee Lorenz.
376 "Shawn shared my enthusiasm": Lorenz, *The Art of the New Yorker*, 131.
379 "Style *is* the man": William Howarth, introduction to *The John McPhee Reader*, xi.
379 "The Lieblings, the Alva Johnstons": Stephen Singular, "Talk with John McPhee."
381 The quotations from Trillin's food articles can be found in Calvin Trillin, *American Fried*, 38, 90–91, 171.
381 "a killing often seems to": Calvin Trillin, *Killings*, xii, xiv, xviii.
381 "If I had a trick": Susan Sheehan, *A Welfare Mother*, 108.
382 "I recently gave myself the": *New Yorker*, February 28, 1977.
387 Shawn's "roach" query: interview with Ann Beattie.
388 "to congratulate you for their": Angell to Mary Robison, January 18, 1977.
388 "It's a wonderful piece of": Angell to Robison, May 3, 1977.
388 "You'll have to write a": interview with Ann Beattie.
388 "some suggestion that you, the writer": Angell to Mason, June 26, 1979.
389 Heavy anthologizing of "Shiloh": Levy, *The Culture and Commerce of the American Short Story*, 108.
390 "I've just come to work": Veronica Geng to Grace Paley, January 31, 1977.
390 "We feel he might well": Geng to Gary Kenton, June 5, 1978.
392 Salary figures: organizing committee to staff, October 27, 1976.
392 "At the moment, some salaries": Shawn to staff, October 12, 1976.
392 "Much of our history has": Shawn to staff, November 11, 1976.
393 Shawn on hating his job: Gardner Botsford, "The Priest-King of Nemi," unpublished typescript, 26.
394 "It is not my intention": ibid., 9.
394 "weaknesses that would lead to disaster": ibid., 10–12.
396 "mention at least eighteen orgasms": W. D. King, *Writing Wrongs*, 82. The play was *A Thought in Three Parts*, written in 1975 and given a workshop production at Joseph Papp's Public Theater in New York the following year.
397 "Schell's sense of humor has": Botsford, "Priest-King of Nemi," 26.

397 Schell's, Kramer's, and Ross's statements to colleagues: ibid., 22–23; Mehta, *Remembering Mr. Shawn's NewYorker,* 331–32.

397 "I am seventy-one": quoted in Mahon, *The Last Days of the NewYorker,* 108–9.

397 "I know that he never": quoted in Lucinda Franks, "The Shawns—A Fascinating Father-and-Son Riddle."

398 "Peter Fleischmann has asked me": quoted in Botsford, "Priest-King of Nemi," 37.

398 "As you know": Angell to White, December 20, 1978, Cornell.

400 "The end of the world": *NewYork Times,* June 20, 1984.

401 "Sayre has a quote of": Ross to Shawn, August 10, 1948.

402 "You're vulnerable on this point": Ross to Joel Sayre, August 11, 1948.

402 "The Druid is elusive": Jay McInerney, *Bright Lights, Big City,* 25–26.

403 Readers' letters about Pauline Kael: O. Peters to Shawn, September 29, 1986.

404 "When the magazine comes out": Ross, *Here but Not Here,* 160.

404 Reaction to "Overdrive": ibid.

404 "That incessant scrunching noise you": quoted in William F. Buckley, *Overdrive,* xiv.

406 "did his best to make himself": *NewYorker,* May 28, 1984.

408 "Once in a while . . . I": quoted in Mahon, *The Last Days of the NewYorker,* 145.

409 "rag-picker of second-class newspapers": quoted in Mehta, *Remembering Mr. Shawn's NewYorker,* 352.

409 "Peter, I can see there": quoted in Thomas Maier, *Newhouse,* 274.

409 "Every time Shawn said something": quoted in Carol Felsenthal, *Citizen Newhouse,* 259.

409 "Mr. Newhouse said that there were": quoted in Maier, *Newhouse,* 274.

413 "He has become a laughingstock": quoted in Mahon, *The Last Days of the New Yorker,* 322.

415 "cultists" who "somehow believe they live": Jonathan Alter, "The Squawk of the Town."

416 "understood it, sympathized with it": Ross, *Here but Not Here,* 218.

416 "My feelings at this perplexed": By pointedly referring to the "eighteenth, nineteenth, or twentieth floor," Shawn was excluding the business side of the magazine from his tribute.

EPILOGUE

418 "takes the view that writers": quoted in *Washington Post,* January 26, 1988.

420 "She works more closely with": quoted in Maier, *Newhouse,* 255.

420 "If some ditzy American editor": quoted in Felsenthal, *Citizen Newhouse,* 363.

420 Jamaica Kincaid on Tina Brown's *NewYorker:* ibid., 365.

423 Number of press mentions of the *NewYorker:* interview with Robert Silverstone.

424 Statistics on *New Yorker's* readers in 1995: "Who Reads the *New Yorker,*" promotional booklet, 1996.

424 Losses between 1994 and 1998: Nocera, Joseph, and Peter Elkind, "The Buzz Factory."

BIBLIOGRAPHY
OF WORKS CITED

Abrahamson, David. *Magazine-Made America: The Cultural Transformation of the Postwar Periodical.* Cresskill, N.J.: Hampton Press, 1996.

Adler, Renata, and Gerald Jonas. "The Letter." *Columbia Journalism Review,* winter 1966.

Allen, Woody. *Getting Even.* New York: Random House, 1971.

———. "The Art of Humor I." *The Paris Review,* fall 1995.

Alter, Jonathan. "The Squawk of the Town." *Newsweek,* January 26, 1987.

"Americana." *The American Mercury,* April 1925.

Arlen, Michael J. *Living-Room War.* New York: Viking, 1969.

Bagdikian, Ben H. *The Media Monopoly.* Fourth edition. Boston: Beacon, 1992.

Baldwin, James. *Collected Essays.* New York: Library of America, 1998.

Bart, P. B., and J. H. Rutledge. "Urbanity, Inc: How the New Yorker Wins Business Success Despite Air of Disdain." *Wall Street Journal,* June 30, 1958.

Bernstein, Jeremy. "Breaking In at the New Yorker." *The American Scholar,* winter 1987.

Bernstein, Walter. *Inside Out: A Memoir of the Blacklist.* New York: Alfred A. Knopf, 1996.

Bishop, Elizabeth. *One Art: Letters.* Selected and edited by Robert Giroux. New York: Farrar, Straus, Giroux, 1994.

Blount, Roy. "Lustily Vigilant." *The Atlantic,* December 1994.

Bogan, Louise. *What the Woman Lived: Selected Letters of Louise Bogan, 1920–1970.* Edited by Ruth Limmer. New York: Harcourt Brace Jovanovich, 1973.

Boyd, Brian. *Vladimir Nabokov: The American Years.* Princeton: Princeton University Press, 1991.

Brantley, Will, ed. *Conversations with Pauline Kael.* Jackson: University Press of Mississippi, 1996.

Brennan, Maeve. *The Springs of Affection: Stories of Dublin.* Boston: Houghton Mifflin, 1998.

Bruccoli, Matthew J. *The O'Hara Concern: A Biography of John O'Hara.* New York, Random House, 1975.

Buckley, William F. *Overdrive: A Personal Documentary.* Boston: Little, Brown, 1984.

Campbell, James. *Talking at the Gates: A Life of James Baldwin.* New York, Viking, 1992.

Capote, Truman. *The Dogs Bark: Public People and Private Places.* New York: Random House, 1973.

Cheever, John. *The Letters of John Cheever.* Edited by Benjamin Cheever. New York: Simon & Schuster, 1989.

———. *The Journals of John Cheever.* Edited by Robert Gottlieb. New York: Alfred A. Knopf, 1991.

Cheever, Susan. *Home Before Dark*. Boston: Houghton Mifflin, 1984.

Cities Census Committee. *Population of the City of New York, 1890–1930*. New York: Cities Census Committee, 1932.

Clarke, Gerald. *Capote: A Biography*. New York: Simon & Schuster, 1988.

Cohen, Richard. "Shawn's Letter from 43d Street: 'We Are Not as Aloof as We Once Were.'" *Women's Wear Daily*, July 1, 1968.

Connolly, Cyril. *Ideas and Places*. New York: Harper & Row, 1953.

Corey, Mary F. *The World Through a Monocle: The New Yorker at Midcentury*. Cambridge: Harvard University Press, 1999.

"The Country Below the Surface." *Time*, January 21, 1966.

Craven, Thomas. *Cartoon Cavalcade*. New York: Simon & Schuster, 1943.

Dahlin, Robert. "William Maxwell." *Publishers Weekly*, December 10, 1979.

Davis, Linda. *Onward and Upward: A Biography of Katharine S. White*. New York: Harper & Row, 1987.

Donaldson, Scott, ed. *Conversations with John Cheever*. Jackson: University Press of Mississippi, 1987.

———. *John Cheever: A Biography*. New York: Random House, 1988.

Douglas, Ann. *Terrible Honesty: Mongrel Manhattan in the 1920s*. New York: Farrar, Straus, Giroux, 1995.

Elledge, Scott. *E. B. White: A Biography*. New York: W. W. Norton, 1984.

Fadiman, Clifton. *Reading I've Liked*. New York: Simon & Schuster, 1945.

Felsenthal, Carol. *Citizen Newhouse: Portrait of a Media Merchant*. New York: Seven Stories Press, 1998.

Fitzgerald, F. Scott. *The Crack-Up*. Edited by Edmund Wilson. New York: New Directions, 1945.

Flanner, Janet. *Paris Was Yesterday, 1925–1939*. New York: Viking, 1972

Flanner, Janet, and Natalia D. Murray. *Darlinghissima: Letters to a Friend*. New York: Random House, 1985.

Ford, Corey. *The Time of Laughter*. Boston: Little, Brown, 1967.

Fox, Stephen R. *The Mirror Makers: A History of American Advertising and Its Creators*. New York: William Morrow, 1984.

Frank, Elizabeth. *Louise Bogan: A Portrait*. New York: Alfred A. Knopf, 1985.

Franks, Lucinda. "The Shawns—A Fascinating Father-and-Son Riddle." *New York Times*, Agust 5, 1980.

Frazier, Ian. *Dating Your Mom*. New York: Farrar, Straus, Giroux, 1986.

Freeman, Martha, ed. *Always, Rachel: The Letters of Rachel Carson and Dorothy Freeman, 1952–1964*. Boston: Beacon, 1995.

French, Warren. *J. D. Salinger*. New York: Twayne, 1963.

Gill, Brendan. *Here at the New Yorker*. New York: Random House, 1975.

Gingold, Alfred, and John Buskin. *Snooze: The Best of Our Magazine*. New York: Workman, 1986.

Grant, Jane. *Ross, the New Yorker and Me*. New York: Reynal, 1968.

Hall, Donald. "The New Poetry." *New World Writing 7*, April 1954.

Hallin, Daniel. *The "Uncensored War": The Media and Vietnam*. New York: Oxford University Press, 1986.

Hamburger, Philip. *Curious World: A New Yorker at Large*. San Francisco: North Point Press, 1987.

Hammond, William M. *Reporting Vietnam: Media and Military at War*. Lawrence: University Press of Kansas, 1998.

Harris, Richard. *The Fear of Crime*. New York: Praeger, 1969.

Heller, Joseph. *Closing Time*. New York: Simon & Schuster, 1994.

Hersey, John R. *Here to Stay*. New York: Alfred A. Knopf, 1963.

Hoopes, Roy. *Cain*. New York: Holt, Rinehart and Winston, 1982.

Houghton, Donald E. "*The New Yorker*: Exponent of a Cosmopolitan Elite." Ph.D. dissertation, University of Minnesota, 1955.

Howe, Irving. "'The New Yorker' and Hannah Arendt." *Commentary,* October 1963.

Hull, Helen. "The Literary Drug Traffic." *The Dial,* September 6, 1919.

Hutchens, John K., ed. *The Best in the World: A Selection of News and Feature Stories, Editorials, Humor, Poems, and Reviews from 1921 to 1928.* New York: Viking, 1973.

Hyman, Stanley Edgar. "The Urban New Yorker." *The New Republic,* July 20, 1942.

Iglauer, Edith. *The Strangers Next Door.* Madeira Park, B.C.: Harbour Publishing, 1991.

"In Vanity Fair." *Vanity Fair,* May 1914.

[Ingersoll, Ralph]. "The New Yorker." *Fortune,* August 1934.

Jackson, Shirley. *Come Along with Me: Part of a Novel, Sixteen Stories, and Three Lectures.* New York: Viking, 1968.

Jong, Erica. *Fear of Flying.* New York: Holt, Rinehart and Winston, 1973.

Kael, Pauline. *For Keeps.* New York: Dutton, 1994.

Karlinsky, Simon, ed. *The Nabokov-Wilson Letters: Correspondence Between Vladimir Nabokov and Edmund Wilson, 1940–1971.* New York: Harper & Row, 1979.

Kazin, Alfred. "Books and Things." *New York Herald Tribune,* August 28, 1939.

Keillor, Garrison. *Happy to Be Here.* New York: Atheneum, 1982.

King, Alexander. "The Sad Case of the Humorous Magazines." *Vanity Fair,* December 1933.

King, W. D. *Writing Wrongs: The Work of Wallace Shawn.* Philadelphia: Temple University Press, 1997.

Kinney, Harrison. *James Thurber: His Life and Times.* New York: Henry Holt, 1997.

Knightley, Phillip. *The First Casualty: From the Crimea to Vietnam: The War Correspondent as Hero, Propagandist, and Myth Maker.* New York: Harcourt Brace Jovanovich, 1975.

Kreyling, Michael, ed. *Author and Agent: Eudora Welty and Diarmuid Russell.* New York: Farrar, Straus, Giroux, 1992.

Kunkel, Thomas. *Genius in Disguise: Harold Ross of The New Yorker.* New York: Random House, 1995.

Lang, Daniel. *Hiroshima to the Moon: Chronicles of Life in the Atomic Age.* New York: Simon & Schuster, 1959.

Lardner, Ring Jr. *The Lardners: My Family Remembered.* New York: Harper & Row, 1976.

Lear, Linda. *Rachel Carson: Witness for Nature.* New York: Henry Holt, 1998.

Levy, Andrew. *The Culture and Commerce of the American Short Story.* New York: Cambridge University Press, 1993.

Lewis, Norman. *The World, The World.* New York: Henry Holt, 1997.

Liebling, A. J. *The Most of A. J. Liebling.* New York: Simon & Schuster, 1963.

———. *The Wayward Pressman.* Westport, Conn.: Greenwood, 1981.

———. *The Road Back from Paris.* New York: Modern Library, 1997.

Lorenz, Lee. *The Art of the New Yorker.* New York: Alfred A. Knopf, 1995.

Luft, Joseph, and W. M. Wheeler. "Reaction to John Hersey's 'Hiroshima.'" *Journal of Social Psychology* XXVIII, August 1948.

Macdonald, Dwight. "Laugh and Lie Down." *Partisan Review,* December 1937.

———. "Parajournalism II: Wolfe and the New Yorker." *New York Review of Books,* February 3, 1966.

Maier, Thomas. *Newhouse: All the Glitter, Power, and Glory of America's Richest Publishing Empire and the Secretive Man Behind It.* New York: St. Martin's, 1994.

Mahon, Gigi. *The Last Days of the New Yorker.* New York: McGraw-Hill, 1988.

Maloney, Russell. "Tilley the Toiler." *Saturday Review,* August 3, 1947.

Markey, Morris. *That's New York!* New York: Macy-Masius, 1927.

McAlexander, Hubert T., ed. *Conversations with Peter Taylor.* Jackson: University Press of Mississippi, 1987.

McInerney, Jay. *Bright Lights, Big City.* New York: Vintage, 1984.

McPhee, John. *The John McPhee Reader.* Edited by William Howarth. New York: Farrar, Straus, Giroux, 1976.

Mehta, Ved. *Remembering Mr. Shawn's New Yorker: The Invisible Art of Editing.* New York: Overlook Press, 1998.

Mellen, Joan. *Kay Boyle: Author of Herself.* New York: Farrar, Straus, Giroux, 1994.

Mitchell, Joseph. *Up in the Old Hotel.* New York: Random House, 1993.

Mitgang, Herbert. *Dangerous Dossiers: Exposing the Secret War Against America's Authors.* New York: Donald I. Fine, 1996.

Morris, Jan. *Manhattan '45.* New York: Oxford University Press, 1987.

Mumford, Lewis. *My Works and Days: A Personal Chronicle.* New York: Harcourt Brace Jovanovich, 1979.

Nabokov, Vladimir. *Speak, Memory.* New York: Putnam, 1966.

Nerney, Brian. "Katharine White, *New Yorker* Editor: Her Influence on the *New Yorker* and on American Literature." Ph.D. dissertation, University of Minnesota, 1982.

Nocera, Joseph, and Peter Elkind. "The Buzz Factory." *Fortune,* July 20, 1998.

O'Connor, Frank. *The Lonely Voice.* Cleveland: World Publishing, 1963.

O'Hara, Jim. "*New Yorker* at 40, Prospers, Also Retains Character as a Choosy Medium." *Advertising Age,* February 15, 1965.

Parmet, Herbert. *Jack: The Struggles of John F. Kennedy.* New York: Dial, 1980.

Perelman, S. J. *Strictly from Hunger.* New York: Random House, 1937.

Peterson, Theodore. *Magazines in the Twentieth Century.* Champaign: University of Illinois Press, 1964.

Plath, James, ed. *Conversations with John Updike.* Jackson: University Press of Mississippi, 1994.

Plath, Sylvia. *Letters Home: Correspondence, 1950–1963.* Edited by Aurelia Schober. New York: Harper & Row, 1975.

———. *The Journals of Sylvia Plath.* Edited by Ted Hughes and Frances Monson McCullough. New York: Dial, 1982.

Plimpton, George, ed. *Writers at Work: The Paris Review Interviews.* Sixth Series. New York: Viking, 1984.

———, ed. *Writers at Work: The Paris Review Interviews.* Seventh Series. New York: Viking, 1986.

Poore, Charles. "The Most Spectacular Explosion in the Time of Man." *New York Times Book Review,* November 10, 1946.

Review of *The New Yorker Book of War Pieces. The New Republic,* January 18, 1948.

Robins, Natalie. *Alien Ink: The FBI's War on Intellectual Freedom.* New York: William Morrow, 1992.

Rosenwaike, Ira. *Population History of New York.* Syracuse: Syracuse University Press, 1972.

Ross, Lillian. *Reporting.* New York: Simon & Schuster, 1969.

———. *Here but Not Here: A Love Story.* New York: Random House, 1998.

Rovere, Richard. *Arrivals and Departures: A Journalist's Memoirs.* New York: Macmillan, 1976.

Schickel, Richard. Review of *I Lost It at the Movies,* by Pauline Kael. *New York Times Book Review,* March 11, 1965.

Seasons at the New Yorker: Six Decades of Cover Art. East Hartford, Conn.: United Technologies Corp., 1984.

Schell, Jonathan. *The Military Half: An Account of Destruction in Quang Ngai and Quang Tin.* New York: Alfred A. Knopf, 1968.

Seldes, Gilbert. "The Best Butter." *The Dial,* April 1922.

Shaw, Irwin. "The Art of Fiction IV." *The Paris Review,* winter 1953.

Sheean, Vincent. Review of *The New Yorker Book of War Pieces. The New York Herald Tribune,* November 23, 1947.

Sheehan, Susan. *A Welfare Mother.* Boston: Houghton Mifflin, 1976.

Shnayerson, Michael. *Irwin Shaw: A Biography.* New York: Putnam, 1989.

Singular, Stephen. "Talk with John McPhee." *New York Times Book Review,* November 27, 1977.

Sokolov, Raymond. *Wayward Reporter: The Life of A. J. Liebling.* New York: Harper & Row, 1980.

Steinman, Michael, ed. *The Happiness of Getting It Down Right: Letters of Frank O'Connor and William Maxwell, 1945–1966.* New York: Alfred A. Knopf, 1996.

"Talk of the Town." *Newsweek,* September 9, 1946.

Taubman, Hyman Howard. *The Making of the American Theatre.* New York: Coward McCann, 1965.

Taylor, Joshua. *America as Art.* Washington, D.C.: Smithsonian Institution Press, 1976.

Thurber, James. *The Beast in Me and Other Animals.* New York: Harcourt, Brace, 1948.

———. *The Years with Ross.* Boston: Little, Brown, 1959.

———. *Credos and Curios.* New York: Harper & Row, 1962.

Trillin, Calvin. *American Fried: Adventures of a Happy Eater.* Garden City, N.Y.: Doubleday, 1974.

———. *Killings.* New York: Ticknor and Fields, 1984.

Trilling, Lionel. "'New Yorker' Fiction." *The Nation,* April 11, 1942.

Tynan, Kathleen. *The Life of Kenneth Tynan.* New York: William Morrow, 1987.

Tynan, Kenneth. *Letters.* Edited by Kathleen Tynan. New York: Random House, 1998.

Updike, John. *Assorted Prose.* New York: Alfred A. Knopf, 1965.

———. *Picked-Up Pieces.* New York: Alfred A. Knopf, 1975.

———. *Talk from the Fifties.* Northridge, Calif.: Lord John Press, 1979.

———. *Odd Jobs: Essays and Criticism.* New York: Alfred A. Knopf, 1991.

———. *Collected Poems, 1953–1993.* New York: Alfred A. Knopf, 1993.

"The Vanishing of New York's Social Circles." *Vanity Fair,* October 1925.

Voss, Frederick S. *Reporting the War: The Journalistic Coverage of World War II.* Washington: Smithsonian Institution Press, 1994.

"The Vanishing of New York's Social Citadels." *Vanity Fair,* October 1925.

Walker, Stanley. *City Editor.* New York: F. A. Stokes, 1934.

Wecter, Dixon. "A Brief History of Sophistication." *Southwest Review,* April 20, 1935.

"What Is America?" *The Nation,* June 26, 1929.

White, E. B. *Here Is New York.* New York: Harper & Row, 1949.

———. "The Art of the Essay I." *Paris Review,* fall 1969.

———. *Letters of E. B. White.* Edited by Dorothy Lobrano Guth. New York: Harper & Row, 1976.

Wilson, Edmond. *The Twenties: From Notebooks and Diaries of the Period.* Edited by Leon Edel. New York: Farrar, Straus, Giroux, 1975.

Wineapple, Brenda. *Genêt: A Biography of Janet Flanner.* New York: Ticknor and Fields, 1989.

Wolfe, Tom. "Tiny Mummies! The True Story of the Ruler of 43d Street's Land of the Walking Dead!" *New York Herald Tribune,* April 11, 1965.

———. "Lost in the Whichy Thicket: The New Yorker—II," *New York Herald Tribune,* April 18, 1965.

———. *The Kandy-Kolored Tangerine-Flaked Streamline Baby.* New York: Noonday Press, 1966.

———. "The New Journalism: A la Recherche des Whichy Thickets." *New York,* February 21, 1972.

Yavenditti, Michael J. "John Hersey and the American Conscience: The Reception of 'Hiroshima.'" *Pacific Historical Review,* February 1974.

INDEX

455

Interborough Rapid Transit, 62
"In the Charming City" (Callaghan), 54–55
"In the Heart of the Heart of the Coun-
    try" (Gass), 295
"In the Village" (Bishop), 211
Into the Valley (Hersey), 184
"intramural" references, 51*n*
Ionesco, Eugène, 270, 279, 343
Iron Curtain, 193
Iron Triangle, 359
Irvin, Rea, 13, 39–40, 65–68, 69, 93, 100,
    119, 171, 243
Irving, John, 422
Irvin type, 13, 40, 423, 424
"Island, The" (Styron), 294
"Island of Dr. Finkle, The" (Perelman),
    113–14
Island of Dr. Moreau, The (Wells), 113–14
isolationism, 169, 197
Is Sex Necessary? (Thurber and White),
    92–93
Is There No Place on Earth for Me? (Sheehan),
    381–82
"It Must Be Milk" (Nash), 115
It's About Time Department, 111
Ivory Tower, 374

Jackson, Shirley, 231–32, 286
James, Henry, 91, 210, 404
"Janus" (Southern), 275
jazz, 269, 382, 401
"jesus," 44, 45, 53, 77, 88, 130, 134, 137
Jews, 59, 60, 61, 64, 65, 67, 161*n,* 164–66,
    168–69, 170, 195, 233, 296–97, 300,
    317–18, 368–69, 403
"Joe Gould's Secret" (Mitchell), 325
"Joe Is Home Now" (Hersey), 184
Johnson, Jack, 90
Johnson, Lyndon B., 360
Johnston, Alva, 103*n,* 133, 134–35, 136,
    141, 243
"Jollity Building, The" (Liebling), 141–42
Jonas, Gerald, 319, 340
Jong, Erica, 15–16
Josephson, Matthew, 248–49
Joyce, James, 154, 220, 344, 386, 404
Joyce, William, 217
Judge, 34, 35, 37, 39, 48, 54, 68, 113, 126,
    152, 172
"Junior Miss" series (Benson), 105, 156,
    227
"Just Before the War with the Eskimos"
    (Salinger), 234
"Justice" (Harris), 357

Kael, Pauline, 76, 344, 349–55, 367, 389,
    399, 402, 403, 415
Kahn, E. J., Jr., 174, 182*n,* 197, 403–4, 421
Kaplan, Martha, 418
Katzenjammer Kids, The, 70
Kaufman, George S., 30, 32
Kazin, Alfred, 154, 297, 334
Kazin, Pearl, 211
Keaton, Diane, 371, 400
Keep Your Head Down (Bernstein), 177*n*
Kefauver, Estes, 314
Keillor, Garrison, 24, 348, 374–76, 420
Kennedy, John F., 184
Kenyon Review, 220
Kerouac, Jack, 294
Key Largo, 251
Kiernan, Frances, 384, 389
"kill fee," 228–29
Killings (Trillin), 381
Kincaid, Jamaica, 371–72, 373, 395, 396,
    420
"Kind of Person I Am, The" (Roth), 297
Kinkead, Eugene, 119
Kinney, Harrison, 84, 87
Kinsley, Michael, 425
Kitchen, Karl, 47
"K Mart realism," 389
Knapp, William, 333
Knightly, Phillip, 175, 181
Knudsen, William, 248–49
Kober, Arthur, 65, 71, 105, 164, 220, 234,
    293
Koren, Edward, 367, 376
Korman, Henry, 371
Kramer, Dale, 239
Kramer, Jane, 382
Kubrick, Stanley, 354
Kundera, Milan, 404
Kunkel, Thomas, 23, 72, 201

Ladies' Home Journal, 391
"Lady Olga" (Mitchell), 143, 145
La Farge, Christopher, 105, 155
"Lance" (Nabokov), 226
Lang, Daniel, 179, 195, 196, 268, 359
"Lantern Slides" (Nabokov), 205–6
Lardner, David, 137, 175, 179, 181, 205
Lardner, John, 175–76, 187, 348
Lardner, Ring, 32, 34, 70–71, 108, 109, 154,
    305
Lardner, Susan, 371
Lasser, Louise, 368
Last American Hero, The, 354–55
Last Tango in Paris, 354

CREDITS AND PERMISSIONS

PHOTO INSERT CREDITS (FOLLOWING PAGE 224)

ABOUT THE AUTHOR

Ben Yagoda was born in New York in 1954. He is a graduate of Yale University and received a master's degree from the University of Pennsylvania. He is the author of *Will Rogers: A Biography* and the coeditor (with Kevin Kerrane) of *The Art of Fact: A Historical Anthology of Literary Journalism*. He has worked as an editor on *The New Leader, New Jersey Monthly,* and *Philadelphia Magazine,* and was the movie critic for the *Philadelphia Daily News.* As a freelance writer, he has published in *The New York Times Magazine, Esquire, American Heritage, GQ, Rolling Stone, The New Republic, The New York Times Book Review,* and many other periodicals. He is currently associate professor of English and a member of the journalism program at the University of Delaware. He lives in Swarthmore, Pennsylvania, with his wife and two daughters.